The Northern Bahamas Guide

From Grand Bahama and the Abacos
South to Cat Island

by

Stephen J. Pavlidis

Seaworthy PUBLICATIONS

Cocoa Beach, Florida

The Northern Bahamas

By Stephen J. Pavlidis

Copyright © 2013, 2012 Stephen J. Pavlidis
ISBN 978-1-892399-28-1
3.1/12.22.12

Published in the USA by:
Seaworthy Publications, Inc.
2023 N. Atlantic Ave., Unit #226
Cocoa Beach, Florida 32931
Phone 310-610-3634
Fax 321-400-1006
email orders@seaworthy.com
www.seaworthy.com - Your Bahamas and Caribbean Cruising Advisory

CAUTION: Sketch charts are not to scale and are not to be used for navigational purposes. They are intended as supplements for NOAA, DMA, or British Admiralty charts and no warranties are either expressed or implied as to the usability or the information contained herein. The Author and Publisher take no responsibility for their misuse.

A publication like this is actually the result of a blending of many people's knowledge and experiences. I would like to take this opportunity to thank the following for their help in this effort: Andy and Star on the S/V *Moria*, for their help with the dive sites, Capt. Lee Bakewell on the S/V *Escape Cay* for his help with programming; A1 Broadshad of Spanish Wells; Gene Ballou on the S/V *Harrison*; BASRA Nassau, Chris Lloyd, Ken Waton, and Courtney Curtis; Steven Clareridge; Mike and Suzi Cope of the S/V *Awakening*; Craig and Paige on the S/V *Carribean Soul*; Roger and Beth Day on the S/V *42*; John DeCarion of the S/V *Packadreams*; Doug and LouAnn on the Schooner *Whisper*; Dan Doyle, skipper of the R/V *Sea Dragon* for once again making his vast knowledge of these waters available to all; Anne and Norm Dupont of M/V *Carpe Diem*; Flapper 1%er, Milwaukee *Outlaw*; the folks at the *Forfar Field Station*; Tom Gill on the S/V *Windrider*; Rev. David Goodrum on the S/V *Ephesians*; Captain Paul Harding of *Seaplane Safaris* in Nassau; Morgan and Caroline Jackson of the S/V *Catalyst*; Manny and Ora Mae Lacour at *Hawks Nest Resort And Marina*; Nicola Leslie; Louis and the staff at the *Nassau Land And Surveys Department* for their help and for putting up with me in those long hours of research at their office; John McKie, *Sunseeker*, for sharing his vast knowledge, what little John has forgotten about these islands is more than many of us will ever know about them; Nicolas Popov of *Island Expeditions*; Bob Rader (NU4P) and Anita Martinec (WZ4U); Captain Tom Shepherd, Treasure Island, Florida; Skeet LaChance and the Abaco and Grand Bahama chapters of the *Scurvy Few Motorcycle Club;* Surfer 1%er Chicago Outlaw, retired National President of the *Outlaws M.C*; Linda Turner, WD4OCl, and her late husband Ron, KA4FNP, S/V *Moonshadow*, for their help, inspiration, and friendship over the years; Hugh Verkerk of the S/V *Trekker*; Ed Wagner of the M/V *Gambier*; Carolyn Wardle for her help with the section on ham radio and weather broadcasts, and let's not forget her tireless efforts on the *Bahamas Weather Net* which benefits all mariners plying these waters; Yon on the S/V *Asapwal*; and last but not least Gene Zace of the S/V *Joshua*. If there is anybody that I have neglected to mention here, rest assured that it is an oversight and I sincerely apologize.

A very special thanks goes out to Captain Paul Harding of *Safari Seaplanes* for his aerial photographs and to Bob Gascoine of *Wavey Line Charts* for his help. Cover Design by Ken Quant, *Broad Reach Marketing & Design*, Milwaukee, Wisconsin.

Library of Congress Cataloging-in-Publication Data

Pavlidis, Stephen J.
  The northern Bahamas guide : from Grand Bahama and the Abacos
south to Cat Island / by Stephen J. Pavlidis.
    p. cm.
  Rev. ed. of: The Abaco guide. c2002.
  Includes bibliographical references and index.
  ISBN-13: 978-1-892399-28-1 (pbk. : alk. paper)
  ISBN-10: 1-892399-28-8 (pbk. : alk. paper) 1. Boats and boating--
Bahamas--Grand Bahama--Guidebooks. 2. Boats and boating--
Bahamas--Abaco--Guidebooks. 3. Boats and boating--Bahamas--Cat
Island--Guidebooks. 4. Pilot guides--Bahamas--Grand Bahama. 5. Pilot
guides--Bahamas--Abaco. 6. Pilot guides--Bahamas--Cat Island. 7.
Nautical charts--Bahamas. I. Pavlidis, Stephen J. Abaco guide. II. Title.
  GV776.24.A2P378 2009
  797.109729'6--dc22

                        2008050780

You can go online to download the latest updates for this guide at http://seaworthy.com

INTRODUCTION

Well, once again it's time for a new edition. Reviewing the islands and waters of the Northern and Southern Bahamas over the last few years I found that many places have changed. New marinas have opened, new businesses have sprung up, Internet access is now regarded as a necessity by some cruisers (myself included), and I've sounded the waters of more areas to offer you even more anchorages to enjoy, especially in the Bight of Acklins, which I promised in the last edition of *On and Off The Beaten Path*.

The Bahamas seem to be getting smaller, new fast ferries connect most of the islands on a regular basis carrying people, cars, and cargo over long distances in a short period of time. Fast ferries now service Nassau, Sandy Point (Abaco), Spanish Wells, George Town (Exuma), Andros, and Grand Bahama, with one ferry plying the waters between Freeport and Ft. Lauderdale. A new fast ferry service connecting Nassau to Ft. Lauderdale is scheduled to be up and running by the time this guide is published.

In many places, such as Eleuthera, many older establishments have closed, such as *Club Med* in Governor's Harbour. In other places construction is forging ahead an extremely fast pace. A huge new development is under construction at the northern end of Bimini that when it gets up and running promises to be a huge draw, though one must wonder how much the local economy will be affected by this almost self-sufficient complex.

The Internet has made its presence felt in the cruising community; more and more people need to stay in touch and for that reason cyber cafés are springing up throughout the islands and many marinas and stores offer Internet service for their customers. Almost every major settlement has someplace that offers to connect you to the Internet to access your email or what have you.

One of the things you will likely notice if you've already used this work, are the colorized charts in this edition as well as some new aerial photos courtesy of Captain Paul Harding of *Seaplane Safaris* in Nassau. I've also included some short stories concerning the history of these cays; tales of the pirates that inhabited these waters long ago, and stories of some of the people who inhabit these waters today.

For the most part, the routes to be found within this publication are nothing new. They have been around in different forms for years, generously given to us by Linton Rigg, Harry Etheridge, and Harry Kline. A few of these routes and anchorages have not been presented before in any publication. For instance, the routes through the reef west of Man of War Cay in the Jumentos are the same routes the Bahamians have been using for years and years, nothing new, except that now you have access to this local knowledge. What is new is that you can now enter an area and have a detailed, and geographically correct chart that was unavailable even a few years ago. I hope you enjoy this book and its charts. There is no greater compliment than cruisers telling me they used my work and that it enabled them to have a safer journey and to enjoy the area they visited. Enjoy your cruise, few things in life are as rewarding.

Stephen J. Pavlidis

Table of Contents

The Basics

Anchoring

Just as important as getting your vessel moving and keeping her heading along your chosen courseline quickly and efficiently is the fine art of keeping your vessel from moving. Many of the anchorages in this book are swept by swift tidal currents, sometimes up to 3 knots, and to avoid bumping into your neighbor in the middle of the night or putting your vessel on the rocks or beach, two anchors, such as in a Bahamian Moor, are required.

Anchor choice is basically a personal preference. Some skippers prefer *CQRs*, while others swear by a *Bruce* or a *Danforth*. Of the "Big Three," you will find that a *Danforth* holds as well or better than a *CQR* or *Bruce* in sandy bottoms while the *CQR* or *Bruce* is preferred when anchoring in rocky bottoms. Whatever your choice of anchor, you must deploy your anchor correctly and with sufficient scope to hold you when the tide changes, if a front approaches, or if a squall should blow through at 2:00 a.m. (which seems to be the time they choose to blow through). Your anchor should have a length of chain (at least 15') shackled to your anchor to keep your rode from chafing against coral or rocks and to create a catenary curve that helps absorb shock loads while lowering the angle of pull on your anchor. Too high an angle may cause your anchor to pull up and out of the bottom. Some cruisers prefer all chain rodes with a nylon snubber to absorb the shock loads. This is an excellent arrangement but a windlass may be needed unless you prefer the workout involved with hauling in the chain and anchor every time you move.

In many of the leeward anchorages in The Bahamas you will find that you can lie quite comfortably to only one anchor. When setting your anchor do not just drop it and let your rode run out, piling itself on top of your anchor. Lower your anchor to the bottom and deploy the rode as you fall back with the current or wind until you have at least a 5:1 scope out, 7:1 is preferable but not always possible. When calculating the amount of scope required, be sure to allow for high tide as well as the height of your anchor roller or fairlead above the water. Without being precise, you can figure on a 2½'-3' tidal rise in The Bahamas although occasionally you may find a 4½' rise, and in general a little more rise during a full moon and a little

less with no moon (remember that the soundings in this guide are at *MLW, Mean Low Water*, this means that it is possible to have a lower tide with less depth that what is shown). When you have secured your rode, back down with the engine at about ½ throttle to set the anchor. If you have not succeeded in securing your anchor, try again. To check the set it is best to dive on your anchors or at the very least, look at their set through a glass bottom bucket from your dinghy. You may find that you will have to set them by hand, especially in rocky areas.

If there are other boats in the anchorage when you arrive and they are riding to two anchors, or if you are in an area beset by tidal currents, it is best to set two anchors in a Bahamian Moor. Although one anchor may be fine if you have the swinging room, when the tide changes it may pull out and fail to reset. These anchorages are often very crowded and while you may swing wide on your one anchor and not find yourself endangered by the rocks or beach, you and your neighbor may go bump in the night because his two anchors have kept him in one spot. If unsure the best thing to do is follow the lead of those boats that are there before you. Conversely, if you arrive at an anchorage and everyone is on one anchor and you choose to set two, do so outside the swing radius of the other boats. If you are riding on one anchor and find that you are lying to the wind but that the swell is rolling you, position another anchor at an angle off the stern so as to align your bow into the swell making for a more comfortable night. Another option is to rig a bridle which allows your vessel to lie to the swells and not the wind.

To set a *Bahamian Moor* you must first decide where you wish for your vessel to settle. You will lay out two anchors, one up-current and one down-current of that spot which will keep you swinging in a small circle. Head into the current to where you will drop your first anchor and set it properly. Let out as much scope as you can, setting your anchor on the way by snubbing it, until you are at the spot where you are to drop your down-current anchor. If the wind has pushed you to one side or the other of the tidal stream, you will have to power up to the position where you will set your second anchor. Lower your second anchor and pull your vessel back up current on your first rode, paying out the rode for the second anchor and snubbing it as you maneuver back up current to your chosen spot. You may want to dive on your anchors to check their set. Keeping your rodes tight will keep you swinging in a tighter circle. Check your anchor rodes daily as they will twist together and make it extremely difficult to undo them in an emergency.

In some tight anchorages you will be unable to set your anchors 180° apart. An alternative is to set them 90° apart in a "Y" configuration perpendicular to the wind. A skipper with a large swing radius in very tight quarters is apt to find out what his neighbors think of his anchoring technique as soon as the wind shifts. Responsible anchoring cannot be over-stressed.

Always set an anchor light. Some cruisers feel this is unimportant in some of the more isolated anchorages. What they probably do not understand is that many locals run these islands at all hours of the night, even on moonless nights, and an anchor light protects your vessel as well as theirs. There are no "designated anchorages" in The Bahamas.

It is important to note that the lee-side anchorages, especially those in the outer islands (Inagua, Plana, etc.), can get rolly at times (yes, you will learn a new dance, "The Out Island Roll"). The Atlantic Ocean surge seeks out any way it can to round the tips of these islands to cause you seemingly no end of discomfort and here is not much you can do about it except possibly use a second anchor or bridle arrangement to keep your bow or stern into the swell. If using a bridle, set up your line on the opposite side that you wish to turn your vessel. For instance, if you need to turn your bow to port to face the incoming swells and make for a calmer ride, run your bridle line from a winch to a block on your starboard quarter and then forward outside your shrouds to your anchor line. Either tie it to your rode or, if you use all chain, attach it to the shackle where your nylon snubber (be sure to use a long one, at least 10'-20' if you are setting up for a bridle arrangement) hooks to your chain. After your anchor is set, simply crank in your bridle line bringing your bow to port and off the wind.

Anchorages on the eastern shores of the Bahamian out-islands are all daytime anchorages only due to the prevailing winds and should be used only in settled or westerly weather.

Never anchor in coral, even with your dinghy anchor. An anchor can do a great deal of damage to a very fragile ecosystem that will take years to recover if it is to recover at all.

In the Summer you may wish to anchor a good distance from shore to keep away from the relentless biting insects. Cays with a lot of vegetation or mangroves will have a higher concentration of biting insects.

Proper anchoring etiquette should by practiced at all times. For instance, if the anchorage is wide and roomy and only one boat is at anchor, do not anchor right on top of them, give your neighbor a little breathing room and some solitude. You would probably appreciate the same consideration should the situation be reversed. All too often cruisers exhibit a herding instinct where they seek the comfort of other nearby cruisers, anchoring much too close at times. Many boaters, after a long, hard day in rough seas or bad weather, anxiously await the peace and tranquility of a calm anchorage. The last thing they want is noise and wake. If you have a dog aboard that loves to bark, be considerate of your neighbors who do not wish to hear him. They do have that right. Jet skis can be a lot of fun, but only when you are astride one. Many cruisers have little tolerance for the incessant buzzing back and forth of high speed jet skis. It is a good show of manners to slowly leave the anchorage where you can have your high speed fun and games and not disturb anyone. The same can be said of water skiing which is prohibited within 200' of the shoreline in The Bahamas unless the skier is approaching or leaving the shore at a speed of 3 knots or less. If at all possible, try not to run your generators at sunset or after dark. At sunset, many cruisers are sitting in their cockpits enjoying cocktails and watching the sun go down and do not want a generator disturbing their soft conversations. Courtesy shown is usually courtesy returned.

Clothing

If you are heading to The Bahamas, especially the more southerly out-islands you will enter a tropical climate where the theme for clothing is light. You will most likely live in shorts and T-shirts (if that much). Long pants and sturdy, comfortable shoes are preferred when hiking for protection from the bush and the rugged terrain. Long sleeved shirts (or old cotton pajamas) and wide brimmed hats are important in keeping the sun off you. Polarized sunglasses (helpful for piloting) and suntan lotion (suntan oil tends to leave a long lasting greasy smear all over everything) should be included in your gear. In winter months it is advisable to bring something warm to wear, especially in the evenings. Long pants and sweaters are usually adequate and a light jacket would be a good idea as some frontal passages will occasionally drop the temperature to 60° F.

It is important that men and women dress appropriately when entering settlements. Skimpy bathing suits for men as well as women are excellent for the beach or boat but in town they are not apropos. Men should wear shirts in town as some local inhabitants are quick to remind you to cover up. Remember, you are a visitor here and that entails a certain responsibility.

Currency

The legally acceptable currency of The Bahamas is the Bahamian dollar whose value is on par with the American dollar. American money is readily acceptable throughout the islands at all stores, marinas, and hotels. Bahamian coins come in 1¢, 5¢, 10¢, and 25¢ denomination while Bahamian paper money comes in $.50, $1, $3, (yes, a three dollar bill), $5, $10, $20, $50, and $100 denominations.

Customs and Immigration

Bahamian Ports of Entry
ABACO: Green Turtle Cay, Marsh Harbour, Spanish Cay

ANDROS: Congo Town, Fresh Creek (*Lighthouse Marina*), Mangrove Cay, Morgan's Bluff

BERRY ISLANDS: Chub Cay (*Chub Cay Marina*), Great Harbour Cay (*Great Harbour Cay Marina*)

NORTH BIMINI: Alice Town (*any marina*)

SOUTH BIMINI: *Bimini Sands Marina*

CAT CAY: *Cat Cay Marina*

CAT ISLAND: Smith's Bay, New Bight, Airport

ELEUTHERA: Governor's Harbour, Harbour Island, Rock Sound, Spanish Wells, Powell Point

EXUMA: George Town

GRAND BAHAMA: Freeport Harbour, Port Lucaya (*Port Lucaya Marina, Lucayan Marina Village, Xanadu Marina,* West End (*marina*)

INAGUA: Matthew Town

LONG ISLAND: Stella Maris

NEW PROVIDENCE: Nassau (*any marina*), *Lyford Cay Marina*

MAYAGUANA: Abraham's Bay (the office is at the *Batelco* tower)

RAGGED ISLAND: Duncan Town

SAN SALVADOR: Cockburn Town (*Riding Rock Marina*)

All vessels entering Bahamian waters must clear in with *Customs* and *Immigration* officials at the nearest port of entry listed above. Failure to report within 24 hours may subject you to a penalty and make you liable for confiscation and forfeiture of your vessel. When approaching your selected port of entry be sure to fly your yellow "Q" flag. Tie up to a dock or marina and await the officials if directed. In places like Bimini (where the dockmasters will usually have the necessary forms for you) or Green Turtle Cay, only the captain of the vessel may go ashore to arrange clearance and no other shore contact is permitted until pratique is granted. In some places, such as Nassau, *Customs* will actually come aboard your vessel. Some of the marinas that you use may levy a charge for using their dock, Cat Cay and Chub Cay in particular. If any marina does not charge you, good manners suggest that you at least make a fuel purchase. Most southbound vessels usually clear in long before reaching the outer islands while those northbound skippers have a choice of ports of entry.

The *Customs* and *Immigration* fee structure has changed considerably over the last decade and it has caused a tremendous amount of contention in various segments of the cruising community. Regardless, cruisers still come to The Bahamas, and likely will, at least until Cuba opens up I'd wager. The cruising permit fee is $150 for vessels to 30' in length, and $300 for vessels over 30', and is valid for one year (tenders over 18' are charged an additional $150). This fee allows the owner to keep the vessel in Bahamian waters for up to one year without paying duty, and also covers the cost of *Immigration* charges for up to 4 people. Also included are all transportation and overtime charges as well as a one-year fishing permit for up to six reels. This fee allows you to also leave The Bahamas within 90 days of your first clearance and return without having to pay the duty a second time (this may change by the time this edition has been published). It is sometimes possible to get an extension for this permit for $500, but it is at the option of the *Customs* officer on duty. If you wish to leave your boat permanently in The Bahamas you will have to pay a 27% duty on vessels under 30' and 6% on vessels from 30-100'. A $15 departure tax is included for those of your crew who choose to fly home but they'll need a copy of your cruising permit when flying out so they won't have to pay the $15 departure tax a second time.

U.S. citizens need a passport, but visas are not required for visitors from the U.S., Canada, and persons from any British Commonwealth country. If you are flying in and returning by way of a boat in transit you need some proof that you are able to leave the country. It is suggested that you purchase a round trip ticket and leave the return reservation open. When you return aboard your boat you may then cash in your unused ticket or use it for a future flight. Check with the airline when buying your ticket as to their policy in this matter.

If yours is a pleasure vessel with no dutiable cargo, the captain will fill out a *Maritime Declaration of Health, Inwards Report* for pleasure vessels, and a crew list. Do not mistakenly call your crew "passengers" or it may be interpreted that you are running a charter. An *International Marine Declaration of Health* in duplicate will be accepted in lieu of a *Bill of Health* from vessels arriving in The Bahamas. Smallpox vaccination certificates and cholera inoculation certificates are required only if the vessel is arriving directly from an infected area.

Each crewmember will fill out and sign an *Immigration* form. You will be asked to answer several tourism related questions. You can ask for and receive a stay of up to eight months however some Immigration Officials will only give three or four months for reasons that are clear only to them. This is an inconsistency that one sees every now and then as you talk to different cruisers and find out about their clearing-in adventure. An *Immigration* official in Nassau explained that it is up to the individual officer to determine how long a stay to permit. If you have guests flying in they also must have a return trip ticket and proof of citizenship.

The captain will be issued a *Cruising Permit* (*Transire*) for the vessel that is valid for up to 12 months. This permit must be presented to any *Customs* official or other proper officer (if requested) while in The Bahamas. If you wish to keep your vessel in Bahamian waters for longer than one year without paying import duties, special arrangements must be made with *Customs* (see above). Spare parts for installation aboard your vessel are duty free. If the parts are imported as cargo they are subject to a 6% duty. Bicycles and motorcycles (including scooters), are required to be licensed at the yacht's port of entry. If they are to be brought ashore they may be subject to a *Customs* duty or a bond in the form of a cash deposit.

If you have pets on board they must have an import permit. An application for the permit may be requested by writing to the *Director of the Department of Agriculture*, P.O. Box N-3704, Nassau, Bahamas (242-325-7502, fax # 242-325-3960). Return the completed application with a $10.00 fee in the form of a *Postal Money Order* or *International Money Order* payable to the *Public Treasury*. This will hasten the process of obtaining your permit although you should allow three to four weeks processing time. Rabies certificates are required of all animals over three months old and must be more than 10 days but less than 9 months old and should be presented when you clear *Customs* and *Immigration*. If you wish your permit to be faxed to you, include a fax number and an extra $5 in the money order.

Non-residents of The Bahamas entering aboard a foreign vessel are not required to obtain permits nor pay duties on firearms during their visit to the islands. This exemption is for three months following the arrival of the vessel at a designated port of entry. After three months a certificate must be obtained from the *Commissioner of Police*. All firearms must be kept safe from theft under lock and key and be declared on your cruising permit with an accurate count of all ammunition. Firearms may not be used in Bahamian waters nor taken ashore. Hunters should contact the *Department of Agriculture and Fisheries* in Nassau for information on hunting in The Bahamas.

Completely forbidden are tear gas pens, military arms such as artillery, flame-throwers, machine guns, and automatic weapons. Exempt are toy guns, dummy firearms, flare guns, and spear guns designed for underwater use.

In the Summer of 2009, the Government of The Bahamas passed an amendment to the *Tariff Act* reinstating the Duty Free exemption for printed matter and original artwork. The amendment also reinstates the original exemption for printed matter and original artwork. All Bahamian Customs Officers have been informed of this change, but if you should happen to come across an official who insists on charging duty on these items, you can call Bahamas Entry Checking in Nassau, 242-302-3509, for assistance.

American flag vessels are not required to obtain clearance when departing U.S. ports. If you are clearing back into the United States you must, upon entry, call the *U.S. Customs Service* to clear in. You are required to go to a nearby telephone immediately upon arrival and dock nearby. You can dial 1-800-432-1216, 1-800-458-4239, or 1-800-451-0393 to get a *Customs* officer on the line to arrange clearance. If the line is busy, call back later.

Each resident of the United States, including minors, may take home duty-free purchases up to $800 U.S. if they have been outside the U.S. for more than 48 hours and have not taken this exemption in 30 days. This includes up to 2 liters of liquor per person over 21 provided that one liter is manufactured in The Bahamas or a member of the *Caribbean Basin Initiative* (*CBI*). A family may pool their exemptions. Articles of up to $1000 in excess of the duty-free $800 allowance are assessed at a flat rate of 10%. For example, a family of four may bring back up to $3200 worth of duty-free goods. If they were to bring back $7200 worth of goods, they would have to pay a duty of $400 on the $4000 above the duty-free allowance. This flat rate may only be used once every 30 days. If the returning U.S. resident is not entitled to the duty-free allowance because of the 30 day or 48 hour restrictions, they may still bring back $25 worth of personal or household items. This exemption may not be pooled. Antiques are admitted to the U.S. duty-free if they are over 100 years old. The Bahamian store selling the antique should provide you with a form indicating the value and certifying the age of the object. Importation of fruits, plants, meats, poultry, and diary products is generally prohibited. More than

$10,000 in U.S. or foreign coin, currency, traveler's checks, money orders, and negotiable instruments or investment securities in bearer form must be reported to Customs. Importation of Bahamian tortoise or turtle shell goods is prohibited. Many medicines purchased over the counter in The Bahamas such as *222*, a codeine-aspirin-caffeine compound, are not allowed entry. Although you can buy Cuban cigars in Nassau, enjoy them on your cruise and do not attempt to bring them back into the U.S. The *U.S. Customs Service* frowns on Americans spending money on Cuban products. Hopefully that will change in time.

Any number of gifts may be sent to the U.S. from The Bahamas and the recipient will pay no duty provided that the gift is worth U.S. $50 or less. If the value is over U.S. $50, duty and tax is charged on the full value. The following regulations must be complied with. Only $50 worth of gifts may be received by the U.S. addressee in one day. The value of the gifts must be clearly written on the package as well as the words "Unsolicited Gift." No alcoholic beverages or tobacco may be sent. Perfume with value of more than $5 may not be sent. Persons in the U.S. are not allowed to send money to The Bahamas for gifts to be shipped to them duty-free, the gifts must be unsolicited. Persons may not mail a gift addressed to themselves. For more information, contact the *U.S. Customs Service* before you leave or call them in Nassau at 242-327-7126.

Canadian residents may take advantage of three categories of duty-free exemption. If you have been out of Canada for 24 hours, you may make a verbal declaration to claim a CDN$20 duty-free allowance any number of times per year. This exemption does not include alcohol or tobacco. If you have been out of the country for 48 hours, any number of times per year, a written declaration must be made and you may claim a CDN$100 allowance. This allowance can include up to 200 cigarettes, 50 cigars, or 2 lbs. of tobacco, and 1.1 liters of alcohol per person. If you have been out of Canada for over 7 days, you may make a written declaration and claim a CDN$300 exemption including the above mentioned amounts of tobacco and alcohol. After a trip abroad for 48 hours or more you are entitled to a special 20% tax rate on goods valued up to CDN$300 over and above the CDN$100 and CDN$300 personal exemption. For importation of tobacco the claimant must be 16 years of age.

Unsolicited gifts may be sent to Canada duty-free as long as they are valued under CDN$400 and do not contain alcoholic beverages, tobacco products, or advertising matter. If the value is above CDN$400 the recipient must pay regular duty and tax on the excess amount.

The Defence Force

The *Royal Bahamas Defence Force* officially came into existence on March 31, 1980. Their duties include defending The Bahamas, stopping drug smuggling, illegal immigration, poaching, and to provide assistance to mariners whenever and wherever they can. They have a fleet of 26 coastal and inshore patrol craft along with 2 aircraft.

I have been associated with a number of *Defence Force* personnel through my efforts at Exuma Park and I have developed a healthy respect for these men and women. Every officer and seaman that I have met has been highly intelligent, articulate, dedicated, and very professional in regards to their duties. These are not the thugs and hoodlums that so many cruisers have come to fear over the last few years. As late as 1991, horror stories were coming out of Nassau concerning improprieties during routine boardings. The *Defence Force* has taken corrective steps and reports of trouble caused by boarding parties are almost non-existent now. What complaints I have heard I have found to have two sides, and quite often cruisers take the boaters side instinctively while giving no thought to the other side of the coin. There is no reason to dread the gray boats as they approach. The *Defence Force* has a very difficult job to do and it often becomes necessary for them to board private pleasure vessels in routine searches. The boarding party will do everything they can to be polite and professional, however, due to the violent nature of the criminals they seek, standard procedure is to be armed. Unfortunately, in the process of protecting themselves, they inadvertently intimidate cruisers. Please do not be alarmed if a crewman bearing an automatic weapon stays in your cockpit while the officer conducts a search below decks in your presence.

If you are boarded you will be asked to sign a statement saying that the search was carried out politely and in the presence of the owner or skipper. I have been boarded and found the boarding officer and crew to courteous and professional. It is not unusual for the *Defence Force* to enter an anchorage and board all the vessels anchored there. Normally they will not board a vessel that is unoccupied, preferring to keep an eye out for your return.

Defence Force Vessel

Photo Courtesy of Anne DuPont

Cruisers often ask why single me out, why search my boat? What are they looking for? Besides the obvious problem with drugs, The Bahamas has problems with people smuggling illegal weapons and ammunition into the country. With bullets selling for $5 and more a piece on the street in Nassau a boater could fatten his or her cruising kitty very easily. You must keep accurate records on all your weapons and ammunition and make sure you record them on your cruising permit when you check in.

The *Defence Force* also must defend the richness of the marine fisheries in The Bahamas. It is not unknown for a boat to cross over from the states without a permit and fill up its freezers with Bahamian caught fish, conch, and lobster. In 1997, a boat from south Florida was boarded upon its return to Florida and the owners and crew arrested and charged under the *Lacy Act*. The *Defence Force*, if they board your vessel, will probably want to see your fishing permit and ask you whether you have any fish aboard. For most cruisers this does not pose a problem. If, however, you have 100 dolphin aboard, you will find yourself in a world of well deserved trouble. You might have a better understanding of what the *Defence Force* goes through if you learn about the four *Defence Force Marines* who died a decade ago when Cuban MIGs sank their boat after the rest of the crew boarded Cuban fishing boats illegally operating in Bahamian waters along the southern edge of the *Great Bahama Bank*. Theirs is a serious business.

Dinghy Safety

Most cruisers spend a considerable amount of time in their dinghies exploring the waters and islands in the vicinity of their anchorage. It is not unknown for a dinghy engine to fail or a skipper to run out of gas miles away from the mother vessel. For this reason I urge boaters to carry some simple survival gear in their dinghies. First, I would recommend a handheld VHF radio for obvious reasons. If there are any other boats around this may be your best chance for getting some assistance. A good anchor and plenty of line are also high on the list. I do not mean one of those small three pound anchors with thirty feet of line that is only used on the beach to keep your dinghy from drifting to Cuba. It may pay to sacrifice the onboard room and use a substantial anchor with a couple of feet of chain and at least 100' of line. Just as you would go oversize on your mother vessel do the same with your

dinghy. If you are being blown away from land a good anchor and plenty of line gives you a good chance of staying put where someone may find you. Next, a dinghy should have a supply of flares. Local boaters often carry a large coffee can with a rag soaked in oil lying in the bottom. If they get in trouble lighting the rag will produce an abundant amount of smoke that can be seen from a quite a distance. A dinghy should be equipped with survival water, a bottle or some small packages manufactured by a company called *DATREX*. It would be a good idea to throw in a few *MRE*'s. These are the modern, tastier version of *K-Rations* that our armed forces survived on for years. Each *MRE* also contains vital survival components such as matches and toilet paper. Another handy item that does not take up much room is a foil survival blanket. They really work and take up as much space as a couple of packs of cigarettes.

Please don't laugh at these suggestions. I have seen people forced to spend a night or two in a dinghy and these few items would have made their experience much more pleasant if not entirely unnecessary. I have run out of gas and used flares to attract some local attention even though one of my boat mates was ready to dive in and swim for the nearest island to fetch some help. Now, I never leave in my dinghy without my little survival bag stashed away in the dink. It doesn't take much effort to prepare a small bag for your dinghy and it will be worth its weight in gold should you need it.

One final word, if you find the need to skirt a large sandbank lying to leeward of a cay remember that even though the sandbanks stretch out quite a way to the west, there is usually a channel of slightly deeper water nearer the shoreline of the cays.

Diving

From shallow water reef dives to deep-water wall drop-offs, the diving in The Bahamas is as good as it gets anywhere and much better than most places. You don't need scuba equipment to enjoy the undersea delights that are available; many reefs lie in less than 30' and are easily accessible to those with snorkels, dinghies, and curiosity. Although the waters in The Bahamas are crystal clear and the obstructions plainly visible in the ambient light, divers must take proper precautions when diving in areas of current. Experienced divers are well aware of this but it must be stated for novices and snorkelers. Tidal fluctuations can produce strong currents, which must be taken into account when diving. Waves breaking over the and around inshore reefs can create strong surges, which can push or pull you into some very sharp coral. For safety's sake, only experienced divers should penetrate wrecks and caves.

Ferries in Abaco

In the area of the *Hub of Abaco*, the waters between Great Guana Cay, Marsh Harbour, and Hope Town, you will find a mode of transportation that is quite unique in The Bahamas...the ferry. These little pastel colored vessels move a lot of people safely and for what a very economical fare.

Abaco Island Transportation offers ferries from Great Guana Cay to Marsh Harbour at 0800, 1500, and 1700, with return trips running at 0900, 1600, and 1800.

The G*reen Turtle Ferry* runs from Green Turtle to Treasure Cay at 0800, 1330, and 1500, and returns at 1030, 1430, and 1615. The ferry also offers special charter runs from Green Turtle Cay to Treasure Cay at 0915, 1115, and 1215, with return trips running at 0945 and 1445.

Albury's Ferry Service is probably the busiest ferry in the Hub with daily ferries from Marsh Harbour to Man-O-War Cay at 1030 and 1600 daily, and trips from Man-O-War to Marsh Harbour at 0800 and 1330. *Albury's* also leaves Hope Town for Marsh Harbour at 0800, 1130, 1330, and 1600, and returns at 1030, 1215, and 1600 daily. On Mondays, Wednesdays, and Fridays *Albury's* has a special ferry that leaves Man-O-War Cay for Marsh Harbour at 1130 and returns at 1215. On all weekdays, except holidays, *Albury's* runs from Marsh Harbour's *Union Jack Dock* to Scotland and Guana Cays at 0730, 1100, and 1530, with return trips arriving in Marsh Harbour at 0900, 1215, and 1645. *Albury's Ferry Service* requests advance notice for passengers wishing to go to Scotland Cay.

Fishing

Fishing in The Bahamas is hard to beat. Trolling in the *Gulf Stream*, the *Atlantic Ocean*, *Exuma Sound*, or *Crooked Island Passage* you are likely to hook a dolphin, wahoo, or tuna, all excellent eating. Trolling on the banks you will usually catch a barracuda although it is possible to bring up a snapper, jack, or grouper. Bonefish can be found in the tidal flats scattered throughout the islands. Chris Lloyd of *BASRA* in Nassau offers this little ditty to those who are unsure what color lure to use for trolling offshore. Chris says:

Red and black-Wahoo attack.
Yellow and green-Dolphin fishing machine.

Chris works Monday through Friday and *BASRA* HQ in Nassau Harbour and is quite an authority on fishing Bahamian waters. If you have any questions stop in and ask Chris. He loves visitors and is a wealth of fishing and diving information. Chris reminds us that the cooler months are ripe for wahoo while dolphin are more abundant from March through May.

The back of your fishing permit will have a brief but incomplete description of the fishing regulations in The Bahamas. Only six lines are permitted in the water at one time unless you have paid for a commercial permit (very expensive). SCUBA is illegal for the taking of marine life and an air compressor such as a *Third Lung* or similar type of apparatus, must have a permit issued by the *Minister of Agriculture*. Spearguns are illegal for fishing in The Bahamas and are illegal to have aboard. You may only use a Hawaiian sling or pole spear for spearfishing. It is illegal to use bleach, firearms, or explosives for fishing. Spearfishing is illegal within one mile of New Providence and within 200 yards of any family island (defined as any cay with a residence). The capture of bonefish by net is illegal as is their purchase or sale. Conch, with a daily limit of 10 per person, may not be taken if they do not have a well formed, flared lip. Possession of a hawksbill turtle is prohibited. The minimum size for a green turtle is 24" and for a loggerhead, 30". The bag limit for kingfish, dolphin, and wahoo is a maximum combination of 6 fish per person aboard.

Crawfish, the spiny lobster that is such a treat as well as being a large part of the economy for local fishermen, has a closed season from April 1-August 1. The minimum limits are a carapace length of 3 3/8" and a 6" tail length. It is illegal to posses a berried (egg laying) female or to remove the eggs from a female. As of 2004, the Government of The Bahamas has declared that the month of January is a closed season for Nassau Grouper.

This has a serious effect on the economy of the local fisherman who remain very vocal in protest. The future of this ban is uncertain, it may be lifted or it may be expanded. Ask when you clear.

Lobster fisherman, Abaco   Photo Courtesy of Nicolas Popov

In the out-islands there are far fewer jobs than there are people looking for jobs. The people here must eke out a living the best way they can. Remember that when you are fishing. Please catch just enough to eat and maybe put some away for tomorrow. So often cruisers come through this area with huge freezers just waiting to be filled to the brim to help their owners offset vacation costs. If you over-fish an area you may be taking food out of the mouths of children. To help protect the livelihood of the people of The Bahamas, some of richer fishing spots will not be mentioned in this guide.

Although you can no longer take conch, FYI, conch can usually be found on the bottom in beds of sea grass or soft corals where they prefer to feed. They are usually in areas with a swift current such as in the cuts between cays. The conch that you don't plan to eat right away can be left in a dive bag hanging in the water or may be put on a stringer. Punch or drill a small hole in the lip of the conch shell and string four or five together and set them on the bottom, they won't go far. After you clean the conch, save the tough orange colored skin and put it in your freezer for later, it is an excellent fish bait and a small piece of it should be placed on all lures to give them an attractive aroma to fish.

The reefs in The Bahamas can provide you with a plentiful supply of fish such as grouper, snapper, hogfish, turbots (trigger fish), and grunts. How many you can get is dependent on your skill with the spear. Groupers are especially wary and prefer holes hide in which to hide.

Crawfish is the principal delicacy that most cruisers search so hard for and which are getting increasingly difficult to find. They prefer to hide during the day under ledges, and rocks, and in holes where the only visible sign of them will be a pair of antennae resembling some sort of sea fan jutting out from their hiding spot. If you are fortunate enough to spear a few, and they are large enough, do not overlook the succulent meat in the base of the antennae and in the legs. So many cruisers ignore these pieces and just take the tail. Watch a Bahamian as they prepare a lobster, very little goes to waste.

Garbage

When I first began cruising I had this naive idea that all cruisers lived in a certain symbiosis with nature. My bubble finally burst with the bitter realization that many cruisers were infinitely worse than common litterbugs. So often they have the attitude of "out of sight, out of mind." I sometimes wonder if they believe in supernatural beings, hoping that if they dump their trash somewhere imaginary garbage fairies will come along and take care of the disposal problems for them. One cruiser leaves a few bags of garbage in some secluded (or not so secluded) spot and the next cruiser says "My, what a good spot for a garbage dump. Ethel, bring the garbage, I've found the dump!" This is why you often go ashore on otherwise deserted islands and find bags and piles of bags of garbage. Nothing is worse than entering paradise only to discover some lazy, ignorant, slob of a cruiser (no, I have not been too harsh on this type of person, I can still think of plenty of other adjectives without having to consult a thesaurus) has dumped his bags of garbage in the bushes. Please do not add to this problem. Remember, your garbage attracts all kinds of foul creatures such as rats (and other careless cruisers).

Nobody likes storing bags of smelly garbage aboard but if you cannot find a settlement nearby to take your garbage for free, you will have to make an allowance in your budget to pay for the local garbage disposal service. If you are nowhere near a garbage facility you should stow your trash aboard separated into three groups for easier disposal. First cans and bottles (wash them first to remove any smells while being stored), then into another container stow the organic stuff such as food scraps, rinds, and eggshells, and finally paper and plastic trash. Your food scraps, you can store them in a large coffee can with a lid, should be thrown overboard daily on an outgoing tide. The paper and plastic should be burned completely when necessary and the ashes buried deep and not on the beach. Cans and bottles should be punctured or broken and dumped overboard in very deep water at least a few miles offshore. Cut off both ends of the cans and break the bottles overboard as you sink them. If you cannot implement a garbage disposal policy aboard your vessel, stay home, don't come to these beautiful islands. Do not abuse what we all use.

GPS

Navigators of today have it made! No longer do you need to keep a running DR log or take a sun sight, all we need do now is take a quick glance at the screen of that marvelous navigator-in-a-box, the GPS, the main source of navigational data on nearly all vessels. Anyone with a hundred dollars can now become an instant navigator and let's face it, the GPS is here to stay, it is the standard for navigation today and for the foreseeable future as well.

The waypoints listed in this guide are for general usage only. I do not intend for you to follow a string of waypoints to an anchorage. Instead, I will bring you to the general area where you can pilot your way in the rest of the way. Do not attempt to maneuver your vessel from waypoint to waypoint without a constant lookout. It seems that everybody is using waypoints of some form or another, whether they are mine or a competitor's, never forget that somebody may be running a reciprocal course using the same waypoints as you. Always keep a sharp lookout. I have experienced this firsthand and the vessel approaching me had nobody in the cockpit on watch! Not a smart way to cruise!

The GPS is truly a marvel, but I have yet to find one that will locate and steer around a coral head or sandbar. Any skipper who attempts to navigate a tricky channel such as *The Devil's Backbone* in Eleuthera, the inside passage at Andros, or the entrance to George Town, Exuma, at Conch Cay by using waypoints deserves whatever ill fortune befalls them. Use these waypoints only as a guideline.

GPS datum used in all areas of the Northern Bahamas is WGS 84.

A Tale of Marsh Harbour
Celestial Navigation and
Charlie Murphy

I wonder how many cruisers have said, "I don't know celestial navigation, but once I get out there, I'll teach myself to navigate by the stars." Certainly I'm not the only one that has flown this banner. I'd be willing to bet that for every cruiser that did teach themselves celestial in this manner, there's probably a dozen that did not, and whose sextants are sitting quietly in some very visible locker or on a shelf so people can see it and think, "My, the owner of this vessel must know celestial, there sits an expensive sextant in a beautiful wooden case." I did the same thing, I confess. I had a beautiful Plath sextant in an equally beautiful hardwood case, the price of which was more than my first car, a 1966 GTO.

When I first started cruising, I purchased a sextant and several books on celestial navigation and like so many others, I mistakenly thought I could teach myself while underway. At this time there was no GPS and LORAN was iffy the further you ventured from Florida and practically useless past Nassau. I could not make heads nor tails of celestial though I loved having a sextant to play with and enjoyed pulling it out and looking like I knew what I was doing. I had the tools, the books, but no practical experience, in short, I needed professional help.

At that time I was primarily cruising in the islands of The Bahamas where most of the islands are within eyesight of each other, much as the islands from Puerto Rico to Anegada, or from St. Martin to Grenada for the most part...as soon as you leave one island astern, another looms ahead on the horizon.

When a skipper leaves the deep waters of the Atlantic Ocean and embarks upon a voyage on the shallow banks of The Bahamas, they leave behind them the normal deep-water navigational methods that they used to get themselves to The Bahamas in the first place. In its place they begin to learn the art of eyeball navigation.

For the most part, the waters of The Bahamas are crystal clear; there is no runoff from the islands to cloud the waters, no muddy rivers emptying onto the banks. It's not unusual to see every aspect of the bottom in 60' of water on a calm day. Some folks are quite unnerved by this. They think nothing of puttering along on the ICW in 10' of murky, black water, but all of a sudden that same 10' in The Bahamas reveals rocks and heads that, although deep and posing no hazard to navigation, make the normally reserved skipper slow down and wildly dodge objects far below his keel. Time and miles soon teach the nervous navigator the differences between water color and the corresponding depth, and between the ripples on the surface and the hidden danger lying just under the surface that you can't see because of the sun's glare. Before too long the neophyte eyeball navigators are testing the limits of their newfound abilities, seeing just how far they can go in that pale green water before bumping, how close to the beach they can anchor, how far up inside the little cove they can tuck. The next thing you know some of them are moving around on full moon nights when the sandbars and heads show up as clearly as they do in the daytime.

When I first came to The Bahamas I had little or no deep-water skills to leave behind, but unlike most people, I was able to adjust very quickly to eyeball navigation. I was fortunate in that everything just looked right to me. The learning curve was almost vertical as I immediately found exactly in what shade of water my 5' draft would run aground. Soon, the delicate hues between 4' and 6' deep stood out like black and white and I realized I would not be happy until I could discern the subtle difference between 4' 11" and 5' 1" of water. After almost three decades I'm still trying to hone my skills as the bottom of my keel stays free of lasting growth. And those of you who are bound for these waters will learn to appreciate polarized sunglasses and come to hate cloudy days when the sun plays hide and seek with you, as also do the rocks and sandbanks. My only real problems in navigating were in learning the deep-water methods that I had neglected in getting to The Bahamas.

Celestial navigation requires the ability to count and a little basic geometry. Every sextant sight reduction is essentially solving a right triangle. The formulas for solving problems such as bearings and distances off, cross track error, vectors, course over ground, were taught to me in one form or another back in high school. However, when I began navigating my own vessel from point A to point B, my 10th grade geometry class took on an entirely new meaning.

While struggling through nine months of Mrs. Barbara Carter's geometry class I felt that there was no way on God's green Earth that I would ever need to know this stuff to help me get through life. It was actually on God's blue earth, the sea, where I found myself needing the wisdom Mrs. Carter attempted to impart to me lo those many years ago. For instance, in crossing the Gulf Stream from South Florida to The Bahamas, the navigator must solve a triangle, to be more specific, a plane oblique triangle. It is a vector problem in which you know only one angle and the length of two sides. It's fairly simply to do with just a pencil, a ruler, and a pair of dividers or a drafting compass. Trying to figure it out mathematically however is a "whole 'nother can of worms." Sines, cosines, sine law. Gawd help me Mrs. Carter. If I had known then what I know now, I would not have forgotten now what I learned then.

Many years later, my celestial navigation mentor, Charlie Murphy of Marsh Harbour, Abaco, re-introduced me to the world of geometric equations. Charlie and Barbara would have got along famously if they had ever met. They both had keen intellectual minds, a good insight into the psychology of people who are trying to learn something, and me for a student. Charlie was able to take the basic geometric foundation that was laid by Mrs. Carter and build a strong framework of celestial ability upon it. Ahh, Charlie. If all the nuns, priests, and lay teachers that I had over the years could have had just a smidgen of your charisma I might have savored my school years more, I might not have missed so much school, I might have even done my homework more often. Well, maybe not the homework.

Charlie Murphy, the long time Commodore of the *Royal Marsh Harbour Yacht Club*, used to teach celestial navigation classes in Marsh Harbour for next to nothing; the cost was only $10 for a two-week hands-on course, which included a huge notebook of forms and miscellaneous information. Charlie's only rule was that you had to leave his blankety-blank beer alone. Charlie Murphy just plain enjoyed sharing his knowledge with us pseudo-navigators (some of whom did not know which end of a sextant to look into even though we all had one on board) and turning out confident, competent navigators, most of whom, if the truth be known, would never again take a sight. He tempered his celestial course with a great deal of common sense and spiced it with some knowledge he picked up during his stint as an artillery spotter in the Canadian Army. He taught us how a one-eyed, one-handed man could estimate angles.

Try this as an experiment. Using either hand, make a fist and hold it out at arms length. Unfold and spread out the thumb and little finger and sight down your arm. For general purposes, the span of distance between the tip of your thumb and the tip of your little finger held out at arm's length is approximately 20°. If you make a fist, the span between the knuckle on your first finger and your pinky is approximately 5° while the span between the knuckle of your first finger and the middle finger is about 2°. If you measure the distance between *Polaris* and the horizon with this method you will be very close to your actual latitude. In fact, with this method, along with a chronometer and a means of *measuring* precise high noon (perhaps a sextant?) to acquire longitude, you can navigate anywhere on the planet.

Charlie led us in classroom studies, actual shots onboard one of our boats while underway, walks on the beach to measure the vertical angle of the Hope Town Lighthouse, and then he sent us home to try our skills at dusk with star sights. One night I was shooting a star that I thought I had identified correctly. I reduced the sight, plotted it, and was patting myself on the back when its LOP intersected in a nice small triangle with my previous shots of *Polaris* and *Vega*. It was only after this that I noticed my star had moved, and not in the direction it was supposed to have, and I realized that my star was actually a masthead light.

In the 15 years since taking Charlie's course, I have taken maybe, oh, a couple of dozen shots. I have not crossed oceans and therefore had no real need for celestial but I thank my navigational stars that I had the good fortune to meet Charlie Murphy. The coming of the GPS age was long awaited by mariners and it has indeed has made accurate and safe navigation possible with the touch of a button. I for one love it. Unfortunately we have lost something

in the process. Today any skipper with a hundred dollars can purchase a GPS and become an instant navigator who can expertly recite his cross track error, course over ground, speed over ground, bearing and distance to the next waypoint, and GMT in an instant. But just ask this navigational wizard how to advance an LOP, or find *Dubhe* in the night sky, or derive latitude from *Polaris*. With the exception of naval officers and some professional mariners, celestial navigation is fast becoming a forgotten art, much as learning Morse code is to fledgling ham radio operators. But like Morse code, celestial navigation should be mandatory, especially for all skippers transiting large bodies of water. If the box fails, and it will, celestial will get you home

Celestial navigation, for some unknown reason, creates a learning block in even the most intelligent skippers. Overcoming this block is often times more difficult than ingesting the knowledge that is offered. Physically taking a sight on a moving boat is relatively easy to master. Practice, practice, practice, and you'll soon instinctively know when you've taken a good sight. The rest is simple math. All the unknowns are in a couple of books that will set you back a few dollars.

Keeping your head straight while actually working the math one step at a time is the hardest part and where most navigators will make an error. You have to double-check every step and you cannot forget a thing. Celestial is a little like doing math homework four or five times a day except that your grade is extremely important and vitally connected to your health and well being. Failure is not acceptable and you must do your homework.

There is no excuse for venturing upon the open ocean without knowing celestial and any skipper with only a GPS or three and no means of taking celestial sights is, pardon me if I offend anybody, a fool. It's like driving cross-country in a car with no spare tire.

Fortunately celestial navigation is not really needed in The Bahamas, or for that matter in the chain of islands in the eastern Caribbean from The Bahamas to Venezuela; distances are short between the islands and eyeball navigation just about covers it all, especially with GPS. Even on the longer runs, just a compass course and a little knowledge of the currents will get you within sight of your landfall, but it's still nice to know you can do it if you have to.

The only problem would be if you got caught in bad weather, or if Murphy's Law came into effect and you wound up drifting who knows where.

Charlie Murphy has moved back to Canada from Marsh Harbour and he is sorely missed; not only by me, but by the *Royal Marsh Harbour Yacht Club* where he anchored the club for so many years But there are quite a few celestial navigation courses around and learning celestial is no more difficult than a little high school geometry and we all know how easy high school geometry was don't we Mrs. Carter? Now if I could just find a use for that calculus course...

Ham Radio

The following is a listing of ham nets you may wish to participate in during your Bahamas cruise.

Net Name	Time ET	Freq. KHz
Bah. Am. Radio Society	0830 Sundays	3,696
Bah. Wx Net	0720	3,696 or 7,096
Caribbean Net	1100-1200 UTC	7,420*
Computer Net	0900 Fridays	7,268
CW Net - slow	0630 M,W,F	7,128
CW Net - fast	0630 T, T, S, S	7,128
Hurricane Net	As needed	14,325; 14,275; 14175
Intercontinental	1100 UTC	14,300, 14216*
Maritime Mobile	After Intercon.	14,300, 14216*
Waterway Net	0745	7,268

*This frequency changes often

Amateur radio operators will need a Bahamian reciprocal license, C6A, to operate in the waters of The Bahamas. To obtain one you must write at least 2 months before you will leave for the islands (give yourself plenty of time to go through the red tape) and actually need your license. Send a copy of your valid General class or better license along with a copy of the photo page of your passport and a money order for $25.00 to: *Public Utilities Commission, Radio Licensing*, P. O. Box N4860, Nassau, N.P., Bahamas.

Holidays

The following public holidays are observed in The Bahamas:

New Year's Day-January 1
Good Friday
Easter Sunday
Easter Monday
Whit Monday-six weeks after Easter
Labour Day-first Friday in June
Independence Day-July 10
Emancipation Day-first Monday in August
Discovery Day-October 12
Christmas Day-December 25
Boxing Day-December 26

Holidays that fall on Sunday are always observed on Monday. Holidays that fall on Saturday are also usually observed on Monday. Bahamians are very religious people so expect stores and services to be closed on Sundays as well as on Holidays. Some businesses may be open all day on Saturday but may close for a half day on Wednesdays. A must see is the *Junkanoo* parade that begins about 4:00 a.m. on Boxing Day and New Years Day in Nassau and Freeport.

Hurricane Holes

THERE IS NO SUCH THING AS A HURRICANE HOLE! There is no anchorage so secure that it cannot be decimated by a strong hurricane and a high storm surge. There are no guarantees; there is no Fort Knox to hide in when a named windstorm threatens. Now, with that out of the way we can discuss how to protect yourself in those special places that offer the best hurricane protection. Let's begin our discussion with what constitutes protection and pass along a few hints as to how to secure yourself as well as get along with your neighbors.

First, make sure your fuel is topped off and you have enough food and water for an extended period. Also, make sure you have enough cash to see you through as phone lines may be down for a while which would prohibit credit card usage. Once you tanks, lockers, and wallet are topped off, you can head for protection. Some skippers prefer to head to sea when a hurricane threatens. Some will take off at a ninety-degree angle from the hurricane's forecast path, usually heading south to Venezuela. I cannot advise you as to what course to take, but I for one, unless absolutely necessary, will not gamble with racing a storm that is unpredictable (no matter what the forecasters claim).

For protection, most of us would prefer a narrow creek that winds deep into the mangroves where we will be as snug as the proverbial bug-in-a-rug. These creeks are rare, and to be assured of space you must get there early. When a storm threatens, you can bet that everybody will soon be aware of it and the early birds will settle in the best places. Sure, those early birds might have to spend a night or two in the hot, buggy mangroves, but isn't that better than coming in too late and finding the best spots taken and your choices for protection down to anchoring in the middle of a pond with a bit of fetch and no mangroves to offer protection? Hint number one...get to safety early and secure your vessel.

So how do you secure your vessel? Easy! First, find a likely looking spot where you'll be safest from the oncoming winds. Try to figure out by the forecast path of the storm where the wind will be coming from as the storm passes and plan accordingly (remember that the winds blow counterclockwise around the center in the northern hemisphere). If your chosen spot is in a creek that is fine. Set out bow and stern anchors and tie off your vessel to the mangroves on each side with as many lines as you can, including lines off the bow and stern to assist the anchors. Use plenty of chafe gear (I like old fire-hose, leather, and towels) as the lines lead off your boat and rig your lines so that they don't work back and forth on the mangroves as well. If chain can be used to surround the mangroves that will help. If other boats wish to proceed further up the creek past your position, remove your lines from one side of your boat to allow them to pass. Courtesy amongst endangered vessels will add to the safety factor of all involved.

If your only choice is to head into the mangroves bow or stern first, always go in bow first; if you place your stern into the mangroves serious rudder damage could result. I prefer to go bow-in as far as I can, until my boat settles her keel in the mud (trying to keep the bow just out of contact with the mangroves), tie off well, and set out at least two stern anchors. If other boats will be tying off into the mangroves in the same manner on each side of you, courtesy dictates each skipper assist the other in the setting of anchors (so that they don't snag on each other) and the securing

of lines in the mangroves (and don't forget to put out fenders).

If you must anchor in the open, away from any mangroves, place your anchors to give you 360° protection. The greatest danger to your vessel will likely be the other boats around you, and in the Caribbean there's going to be a better than average chance that you'll be sharing your hole with several unattended boats, often times charter boats that are not secured in the best of manners. A good lookout is necessary for these added dangers.

Once secure, your next step is to strip everything off your boat and stow it below. Sails, bimini top, dodger, awnings, rail-mounted grill, wind-generators, solar panels, jerry cans, and anything small and loose that can become a dangerous object should it fly away at a hundred plus miles an hour. And, don't forget to secure your dinghy as well! Keep a mask and snorkel handy in the cockpit, you might need it to stand watch. Also, keep a sharp knife close at hand; you never know when you might need it. Pack all your important papers in a handy waterproof container, and in the most severe of circumstances, use duct tape to secure your passport, wallet, and/or purse to your body. Plan ahead as you secure your vessel so that you will not have to go on deck if you don't absolutely have to, it is most difficult to move about in 100-knot winds.

If you are going to be cruising in The Bahamas from June through November, hurricane season, you should always keep a lookout for a safe hurricane hole. In the northern and central Bahamas you're never too far away from some sort of refuge, some holes are better than others but like the old adage advises: Any port in a storm. With that in mind let me offer a few of the places I consider hurricane holes. Bear in mind that if you ask ten different skippers what they look for in a hurricane hole you're likely to get ten different answers. Some of these holes may not meet your requirements. I offer them only for your consideration when seeking safety for your vessel. The final decision is yours and yours alone. For the best information concerning hurricane holes always check with the locals. They'll know the best spots.

Abaco

The best protection in the Abacos lies in places like Treasure Cay where you can anchor in the narrow creeks surrounding the marina complex. There is a man-made canal complex called Leisure Lee lying just south of Treasure Cay on Great Abaco. Here you will find excellent protection from seas in 8' but you will have to tie off to the trees along the shore as the entire complex is dredged and the holding is not good. Green Turtle Cay offers White Sound and Black Sound. I much prefer White Sound though there is a bit more fetch for seas to build up. Black Sound, though smaller, has a grassy bottom and a few concrete mooring blocks scattered about. At Man Of War Cay you can choose either anchorage. Just to the south on Elbow Cay, Hope Town Harbour boasts very good protection. If you arrive early enough and your draft is shallow enough you may be able to work you way up the creek for better protection. There is an old hurricane chain stretched across the harbour that you may be able to secure your vessel to. Ask any local where to find the chain.

Just a few miles away lies Marsh Harbour with that wonderful sand/mud bottom that anchors so love (but the harbour is open to the west for a fetch of over a mile). For small shallow draft (3') monohull vessels there is a small creek on the eastern side of the harbour just to the east of the Conch Inn Marina. Get there early. Farther south you might consider Little Harbour though it is open to the north with a 3' bar across the mouth. Between Marsh Harbour and Little Harbour lies Snake Cay which has excellent protection in its mangrove lined creeks. To the north, you can try Hurricane Hole on the SE end of Allan's Pensacola Cay. Excellent protection can be found in 6'-8' of water but the bar at the entrance will only allow about 4'-6' at high water, depending on the tidal height that particular day. Small shallow draft vessels can work themselves well up into the creeks at Double Breasted Cay if unable to get to better protection to the south.

Andros

An excellent spot for vessels drawing less than 4' is in the small pocket at Stafford Creek that lies north of the bridge. Enter only at high tide. If you draw over 6' and are in Andros when a hurricane threatens you would be better off to get to New Providence or someplace in the Exumas, although I know several boaters that weathered *Hurricane Michelle* at the dock in Fresh Creek (the eye of that hurricane passed directly over Fresh Creek and winds were in excess of 100 mph).

The Berry Islands

There are only three places to consider in the Berry Islands and two of them were hit hard by powerful *Hurricane Andrew*. *Chub Cay Marina* is a possibility if you didn't mind a slip or perhaps tying off between pilings. The marina was devastated by Andrew and quite a few boats destroyed. Something to remember when it's decision making time. Another possibility would be to work your way into Little Harbour. There is a winding channel into the inner anchorage where you can tuck into a narrow channel just north of the Darville's dock in 7'-11' of water with mangroves to the east and a shallow bar and a small cay to the west. Little Harbour is open to the north but there is a large shallow bank with 1'-3' over it just north of the mangroves. By far the best place to be in a hurricane is in Bullock's Harbour at *Great Harbour Cay Marina*. Check with the dockmaster prior to arrival to make sure there is room at the marina as the holding in the harbour is poor.

Bimini

The best protection in the Biminis is up the creeks of South Bimini by way of Nixon's Harbour. Seven feet can get in over the bar at high tide where you'll find plenty of secure water inside. On the west side of South Bimini lies the entrance to the Port Royal canals. Five feet can make it over the bar with spots of 7'-10' inside. Be sure to tie up in vacant areas between houses. On the north side of South Bimini is another entrance to some small canals with a 4' bar at the entrance from the harbour at North Bimini. Take into consideration that these canals have plenty of wrecks lining the shores along with old rotten pilings jutting up here and there. The surrounding land is very low and the canals may become untenable in a high storm surge. From Bimini Harbour you can follow the deep-water channel, 5' at MLW, northward to *Bimini Bay Resort* where you can find protection in a deep mangrove lined creek. There is only room for two or three boats here at best. As with any hurricane hole, get there early.

Cat Island

Unless you have a small, shallow draft vessel and can get up Orange Creek or Bennett's Creek along the western shore of Cat Island, your only choice may be Hawksnest Creek on the southwestern tip of Cat Island. Six feet can enter here at MLW and work its way up the creek. Bennett's Harbour offers good protection but it is small and open to the north.

Crooked/Acklins

The only protection here will be found in the maze of creeks between French Wells and Turtle Sound for boats with drafts of 3' or less, or by going through The Going Through towards the *Bight of Acklins*. Here you will find a maze of shallow creeks leading to numerous small mangrove lined holes, perfect little hidey-holes for the shallow draft cruiser (up to 4' or less draft) seeking shelter.

Eleuthera

There are a few holes in Eleuthera but they all suffered considerable damage from *Hurricane Andrew*. Royal Island offers excellent protection and good holding, but during *Hurricane Andrew* the fleet washed up on one shore only to be washed up on the other shore after the eye passed. Hatchet Bay is often considered a prime hurricane hole but it too has a history of damage as the hulls along the shore will testify. At Spanish Wells you will find Muddy Hole lying off the creek between Russell Island and St. George's Cay. Muddy Hole is the local hurricane hole and 4' can enter here at MLW if you get there early. Every boat (and there are a lot of them) at Spanish Wells will be heading there also.

Some skippers like *Cape Eleuthera Marina* at Powell Point but I wouldn't use it as shelter unless I had no other choice. The dogleg marina channel is open to the west and large seas easily work their way into the basin rocking and rolling everybody. The huge concrete breakwater at the bend in the dogleg has suffered considerable damage and offers testimony to the power of the seas that enter the marina.

Just south of Powell Point lies No Name Harbour, Un-Named Harbour on some charts. Seven feet can enter here at MLW and 6' can work farther up the small coves that branch off and offer fair protection. You might consider tying your lines to the trees and setting your anchors ashore here, the holding is not that great being as this is a dredged harbour.

The Exumas

The Exumas Cays are home to some of the best hurricane holes in The Bahamas. From the north you should consider the inner pond at Norman's Cay. The pond offers excellent protection and good holding although there is a mile long north-south fetch that could make things rough at best. Shroud Cay has some excellent creeks with a reputation as good hurricane holes. Dr. Evans Cottman rode out a fierce hurricane here as documented in his book *Out Island Doctor*. Compass Cay has a snug little cove for protection with moorings, a marina, and creeks for shallow draft vessels. Farther south at Sampson Cay you may be able to tie up in the marina on the eastern side of the complex in the shallow and well-protected basin. I have known people to anchor between the Majors just north of Staniel Cay for hurricane shelter though I personally would try to find someplace a little more protected. At the north end of Great Guana Cay lies a small, shallow creek that gives fair to good protection for one or two small vessels drawing less that 5'. Cave Cay is an excellent hurricane hole with room for four boats in 6' at MLW. Many experienced captains like the pond at Rudder Cut Cay as a refuge but I see the eastern shore as being very low. I believe a strong hurricane with a large storm surge and high tide might make this anchorage a death trap.

The George Town area is home to what may be the finest holes in The Bahamas. Holes #0, #2, and #3 at Stocking Island are excellent hurricane holes in every sense offering protection from wind and wave. The only problem here is that these holes will be crowded and Hole #3 is usually full of stored boats with absentee owners. The inner cove at Red Shanks offers good protection if you can get in close to the mangroves. Another possibility is inside the western arm of Crab Cay.

Grand Bahama

If you're in the area of Grand Bahama Island you might consider tying up at *Old Bahama Bay Marina* at West End. Although the marina offers excellent protection a direct hit by a major hurricane would likely do considerable damage to this complex. From the north of Grand Bahama you can consider entering Hawksbill Creek though it only has 2' over the bar at its entrance with 5'-6' inside at MLW. The *Grand Lucayan Waterway* offers very good protection. You can tie up anywhere deep within its concrete lined canals (which could be a problem in a blow) but you cannot pass under the *Casuarina Bridge* unless your height is less than 27' at high water. The canal has a fairly uniform depth of 5' throughout although the northern entrance has shoaled to around 3'-4½' at MLW. Another option would be to tie up at *Lucayan Marina* or in the small coves surrounding the complex that offer some very good protection.

New Providence

Here, in the capitol of The Bahamas, Nassau

Harbour has fair to good holding along with a long east-west fetch. There are two hurricane chains crossing the harbour whose approximate locations are shown on the chart for Nassau. If you fortunate enough to know someone in Coral Harbour you may be able to use their dock to escape the seas. On the southwestern shore of Rose Island is the entrance to a very good hurricane hole shown as Salt Pond on charts. It is a circular harbour with a small island in the center. The channel is easily 50'-60' wide and 7'-9' deep. Anchor and tie off between the shore and the island. Get there early as everyone in Nassau and the northern Exumas will have the same idea.

Long Island

If I had to find a place to hide from a hurricane while visiting Long Island my first choice would be in the canals that wind behind the marina at Stella Maris. Some skippers have suggested Joe's Sound but I find the land to the west too low and a tidal surge like the one in *Hurricane Lili* (9'-14') would make this anchorage untenable. Another consideration is in the mangrove tidal creeks in the Dollar Harbour area but the best protection is hard to get into unless you have a draft of less than 4'.

The Jumentos and Ragged Island

There are only two possibilities here and both are in the vicinity of Ragged Island. A boat with a draft of less than 5' can work its way up the mangrove lined channel to anchor in the harbor at Duncan Town. Here you will find 4'-6' at high water with mangroves and cliffs surrounding you. This would be a fantastic hurricane hole if it were just a couple of feet deeper. The people of Duncan Town are in the process of having their channel re-dredged, perhaps they will do something with the harbour area also. Just south of Ragged Island is a small hole called Boat Harbour that some Ragged Islanders use as a hurricane hole. There is 9' inside but there is a winding channel with a 3' bar at the entrance. Ask any Ragged Islander for directions, they'll be happy to help.

The Southern Bahamas

If you are cruising the southern Bahamas from Crooked-Acklins to Mayaguana or Inagua you will not find a truly safe hole. Although I have heard about a large sailboat riding out *Hurricane Klaus* lying between Samana and Propeller Cay I would not attempt to test my luck. I would either head north to better protection at George Town or continue on to The Turks and Caicos for protection at Sellar's Pond

or up the canals at Discovery Bay lying northeast of Five Cays, at Leeward Going Through, or up *North Creek* at Grand Turk. If I had enough time I would try to make Luperon in the Dominican Republic, which is as good a hole as any in the Caribbean.

Internet in The Bahamas

It's not too difficult to access the Internet while cruising in The Bahamas. *Wifi* is becoming more and more available with great coverage in The Bahamas, especially in the Abacos. Cyber cafés are springing up everywhere and many marinas and stores throughout the islands now offer Internet access, check *Appendix C* for a listing (probably incomplete for by the time this is published several more cyber cafés will have been born and one or two of the old ones closed).

Batelco, The *Bahamas Telecommunications Company*, offers a *BaTel/Net* account for those who wish to surf the web. It is a monthly plan whereby you take your computer into the *Batelco* office in Nassau to activate your account and then you may access the Internet from any *Batelco* office or phone jack in The Bahamas. For more information call *Batelco* at 242-394-7638, or toll free from inside The Bahamas at 242-300-2638.

In the Abacos, cruisers will find that *Wi-Fi* Internet access is now available in parts of Treasure Cay, Marsh Harbour, Green Turtle Cay, Elbow Cay (Hope Town and the outer anchorage), Tilloo and Lubbers Quarters, Baker's Bay and the Settlement on Great Guana Cay, the southeastern end of Man O' War Cay, and at the southeastern end of Manjack Cay, in general you'll receive a signal from Green Turtle Cay to Tilloo Cay depending on your receiving card and antenna.

If you would like to sign up for *Wi-Fi* access, *The Coconut Telegraph* and *OII* can set you up with wireless internet access, or you can contact www. accounts@abacoinet.com. If you need any hardware to set up your *Wi-Fi* system on your boat, you can contact *Out Island Inter-Net* (*OII;* 367-3006) *Coconut Telegraphs* (365-8836), both companies are located in Marsh Harbour. For more information about the current status of *Wi-Fi* reception and service plans in the Abacos you can visit the following websites: www. abacowifi.org, www.awsltd.net, and www.abacoinet. com.

Junkanoo

The culture of The Bahamas, its heart and soul, the eyes through which it sees and is seen, is Junkanoo, with its spirit, music, dancing, singing, costumes and color. Standing along Bay Street in Nassau in the early hours of Boxing Day or New Years Day, one cannot help getting caught up in the frenzy that is Junkanoo. Junkanoo must be experienced on the street, where the clamor of the bells, whistles, and goombay drums approaching in the distance creates an electric feeling in the crowd who sway and jostle with the building excitement. The source of all this energy is the participants, organized groups and "scrap gangs", throbbing forward to the rhythm of the music. Groups vie in a heated competition for awards for best music, costumes, and dance.

Junkanoo was introduced to the American colonies by slaves from Africa's western coast. From there it quickly spread to Jamaica and The Bahamas. Its exact origins are unknown and the numerous derivations of the name *John Canoe* further complicate the matter. The West African name *Jananin Canno* was derived from a combination of the Quojas tribe's *Canno*, a supreme being, and *Janani*, who were the dead who became spirits and were seen as patrons or defenders of the tribe. The Jamaican John Canoe, a slave who insisted on his people having the right to their celebration, was known in eastern North Carolina as *John Kuner*, *John Kooner*, *John Canoe*, *Who-Who's*, and *Joncooner*. A West African trait often attributed to the origin of Junkanoo was an Ashanti figure known as *Jankomo*. *Jankomo* was famed for his dance where he took two steps forward and one step back, a form of Junkanoo dancing prevalent in today's festival. Some researchers theorized that the name is a corruption of the French *gens innconnus* which, roughly translated, means unknown people or masked people.

Junkanoo developed as a celebration during the pre-emancipation days when slaves were allowed a special Christmas holiday. Not wanting to waste any of their holiday, they took to beginning their celebration well before dawn. It is said that the wild costumes, masks, and makeup were used by the slaves as a way to disguise themselves while exacting revenge upon their masters and settling grudges with fellow slaves. During the late 1800's, Junkanoo began taking on added dimensions and significance for Bahamian people. It became a vehicle for political expression and a catalyst for social change. The *Street Nuisance Act* of 1899 was aimed directly at Junkanoo attempting to reduce the amount of noise and length of celebration of the event in the hopes that Junkanoo would extinguish itself. Junkanoo continued, albeit a little quieter. During the economic depression of the early 1900's, Junkanoo was characterized by rival masked and costumed gangs from the various districts of New Providence. Money was scarce and the costumes changed from cloth to papier-mâché and became more frightening and grotesque.

Junkanoo Reveler   Photo Courtesy of Alicia Bonnet

World War I saw the suspension of Junkanoo when the white inhabitants of Nassau felt the celebrations were unsuitable considering the wartime conditions and Junkanoo was banned from Bay Street until well after the war. It moved to the "over the hill" section of Nassau where it grew and prospered. The prosperous bootlegging period of the 1920's in The Bahamas was reflected in more flamboyant costumes and headdresses. Junkanoo moved back to Bay Street in 1923 when its potential for increasing tourism revenue became apparent. It was at this time that Junkanoo became a competition with prizes being awarded.

Junkanoo was again banned from Bay Street in 1942 when riots broke out due to labor unrest. Junkanoo still thrived on various parts of New Providence and was back on Bay Street by 1947.

Junkanoo today is basically the same with some minor changes. It is no longer considered a social taboo to participate in Junkanoo and more and more women are parading in this once male dominated event. Junkanoo is a national event on the edge of becoming an international festival.

The heart of Junkanoo is the music which has changed little over the last 50 years. A typical Junkanoo band consists of lead drums, second or bass drums (goombay), cowbells, clappers, bugles, trumpets, horns, conch shells, and whistles. A few obscure instruments, such as the fife, are no longer used. The drum is the core of the music. Drums are made every year from goat or sheep skin and represent a sacrifice, the spilling of blood to make a drum. Drummers often place a flame inside the drum or heat it up over a fire, this is called "bringing it up" and helps produce various drum tones. The combined effect of the music, the bells and drums and horns, all fueled by the emotion of the participants, is overwhelming

The costumes create a tremendous visual effect and are painstakingly manufactured by hand. The costumes are brightly colored and usually represent some theme. There are no weight restrictions on costumes and one single piece may weigh over 200 pounds. Competition among the various groups is fierce and members are very secretive about their upcoming productions.

Mailboats

You do not have to own a yacht to see The Bahamas, you can go almost anywhere within the island chain by mailboat. One need only approach the dockmaster on Potter's Cay for schedules and costs. Shipping times are announced three times daily on ZNS radio in Nassau. The mailboats are subsidized by the Bahamian government for carrying the mail, but they also take on freight and passengers. It is an inexpensive and rewarding way to see the out-islands. If you book passage you will gain a different view of the Bahamian people as travel by mailboat is a cultural experience as well as being a mode of transportation. People on the outer islands would find life hard indeed if not for the mailboats, they are the lifeline of the Bahamian out-islands and the arrival of the mailboat is somewhat of a celebration. Costs range from $30.00 for a trip to Little Farmer's Cay to slightly higher for George Town or Inagua.

Some mailboats include food in the fare. For more information on schedules and fares, visit the office on Potter's Cay.

And while we're on the subject of Mailboats, let me clarify something. I've heard people say that if you can't find the way you wish to go, follow a Mailboat. This is fine for deepwater passages, but you must remember that Mailboat captains know these waters and they accept the fact that they must frequently pay the price for error, which does happen no matter how well somebody knows the waters. To be more succinct, the Mailboats carry spare props, do you?

Medical Emergencies

Most of the out-islands of the Northern and Central Bahamas have small clinics in their major settlements so you may not be very far from some sort of medical help.

In the Northern Bahamas, you'll find that Grand Bahama has several hospitals; *Rand Memorial Hospital*, (242-352-6735), *Sunrise Medical Center* (242-373-3333), *Port Lucaya Medical Center* (242-373-1711), and the *Lucayan Medical Center East* (242-352-7400), and *West* (242-352-7288). If you need dental work done, try the *Dental Centre* at 242-352-4552. At Eight Mile Rock is the *ABC Health-World Holistic Clinic* (242-352-2222). If you need the services of a vet while visiting Grand Bahama you can call Dr. Bater or Dr. Rich at 242-352-6521, or try Dr. Hanna at 242-352-9511. If you need an ambulance on Grand Bahama call 242-352-2689.

In Marsh Harbour, Abaco, the local doctors, Dr. Lundy and Dr. Boyce, have excellent clinics and provide great health care service. The *Agape Family Dental Centre*, 367-4355, is a few blocks south of the traffic light. If you need to fill a prescription head for the *Chemist Shoppe* or *Lowe's Pharmacy*. If you need pet supplies, for dogs, cats, or even parrots, check out *Pets R Us* just off Don Mackay Blvd. or visit *Pets R People Too* near *Solomon's*.

On Great Abaco, the very professional *Trauma One* ambulance team has been providing emergency service to Abaco residents since September of 1995. *Trauma One* could use any donations you would care to offer. Donations may be sent to *Trauma One*, P.O. Box AB 20594, Marsh Harbour, Abaco, Bahamas. All contributions are recorded and appreciated. If you need a dentist while at Treasure Cay, Abaco, call Dr. Spencer at 242-365-8615.

In the Central Bahamas, there are two hospitals in Nassau, *Princess Margaret Hospital* on Shirley Street and *Doctor's Hospital* on the corner of Shirley Street and Collins Ave. On Lyford Cay, also on the island of New Providence, is the *Lyford Cay Hospital and Bahamas Heart Institute*. Near the airport is a new *Doctor's Hospital* that only recently opened.

If more medical assistance is needed the patient will be flown into Nassau, usually to *Princess Margaret Hospital*. *National Air Ambulance* out of Ft. Lauderdale, Florida (305-359-9900 or 800-327-3710), can transport patients from The Bahamas to the United States. If you join *DAN*, the *Divers Alert Network*, for a small yearly fee, you are covered under their *Assist America Plan*. This program offers emergency evacuation for any accident or injury, diving related or not, to the nearest facility that can provide you with adequate care.

After you have been stabilized to the satisfaction of the attending physician and the *Assist America* doctor, *Assist America* will arrange your transportation back to the United States, under medical supervision if necessary. Bear in mind that this is a reimbursement policy, make sure you are clear on this matter before joining.

The *Bahamas Air-Sea Rescue Association*, BASRA, has stations in Nassau, Elbow Cay in Abaco, Black Point, and George Town in the Exumas, Salt Pond in Long Island, and at Landrail Point on Crooked Island. All *BASRA* stations monitor VHF ch.16, while *BASRA* Nassau monitors 2182 KHz and 4125 KHz on marine single sideband from 9:00 a.m.-5:00 p.m. Monday through Saturday. *BASRA*, Nassau, can be reached by phone at 242-322-3877. Bear in mind that the *BASRA* stations in the out-islands may not monitor the VHF 24-hours a day.

If you need an emergency contact while in the Abacos, your friends can email cruisers@cocotels. net and it will be broadcast on the VHF *Cruiser's Net* in the Hub Of Abaco.

Phoning Home

If you are expecting speedy phone connections you will find that the telephone service in The Bahamas to be quite frustrating. Although there is a *Marine Operator* in Nassau monitoring VHF ch. 27, there are no marine operators in the out-islands and public phones are few and far between. In 2006, The *Bahamas Telecommunication Company*, *BTC*, some still call it Batelco, introduced *GSM* cell service to Abaco. This has resulted in greater coverage for US based GSM cell phones such as *Cingular* or *Verizon* (although the rates are upwards of $1.50 per minute). Cruisers may also establish an account with *BTC* which gives them a *BTC SIM* card to install in their US *GSM* phone, which allows user to access the Bahamian phone system directly instead of paying higher roaming charges.

Most cays with settlements will have a *BTC* office where you may place a phone call. If you call the States, try to get an *AT&T USA Direct* line (1-800-872-2881); the quality and rates are much better. Most prepaid calling cards are blocked from usage except for *Batelco* cards and U.S. 800 numbers generally do not work from The Bahamas. Calling cards and direct access numbers that work from The Bahamas are: *AT&T*-800-872-2881, *MCI*-800-888-8000, *Sprint*-800-389-2111, and *Working Assets* 800-999-9000. If you are calling The Bahamas the area code for all islands is 242.

Provisioning

If you are on a tight budget, it would be best for you to stock up on provisions in the United States prior to your Bahamas cruise. Take enough for the length of your cruise and then some. The cheapest place after the U.S. for provisioning is Puerto Plata (or Santiago, both are easily reached by car or bus from Luperon) in the Dominican Republic. With few exceptions, prices in The Bahamas are considerably higher than American prices. Beer and cigarette prices will seem outrageous with cigarette prices some 2-3 times higher than in the States. The local Bahamian beer, *Kalik* (named after the sound that cow bells make when clanged together), is very good and more reasonably priced than foreign beers. Try the *Kalik Gold Label*, it is more full-bodied and a little stronger. Rum, as one would think, can be very inexpensive while American whiskies and certain Scotches are very high. Staples such as rice, beans, flour, and sugar are just slightly higher than U.S. prices. Vegetables can be quite reasonable in season. The vegetable market on Potter's Cay in Nassau is a good spot to pick up a large box of mixed vegetables for around $15.00 in season. Meats, soft drinks, and milk all are considerably higher than in America. As you shop the various markets throughout The Bahamas you will find some delightful items that are not sold in the U.S., foreign butter and meats for example. The shopping experience will give you the opportunity to purchase and enjoy some new treats. Of course, the prices on fresh fish, conch, and lobster are all open to bargaining with the local fishermen.

Good drinking water is available throughout the islands from some of the cisterns and wells on various cays. Well water will have a higher salt content than cistern water, which is rainwater. Always check with the owners before you remove any water. Most stores sell bottled water and you can buy reverse osmosiswater in quite a few places.

I have found prices on Long Island, particularly at Salt Pond and southward to Mangrove Bush, to be equivalent to and sometimes better than prices in George Town, Exuma. Prices in Provo, Turks and Caicos, are equivalent to Nassau prices and sometimes better with some prices near stateside levels.

If you plan to dine out while in the islands, you will find the prices to be higher than stateside prices. It is common for dining establishments in The Bahamas to include a 15% gratuity in the check.

Tides and Currents

The islands of The Bahamas are affected by the west setting *North Equatorial Current* on both their eastern and western extremities. After entering the Caribbean the *North Equatorial Current* splits into two branches, the northern branch flowing northeast of The Bahamas off Abaco, Eleuthera, Cat Island, and Long Island as the Antilles Current with an average velocity of approximately ½ knot. To a lesser extent the *Antilles Current* also flows through the *Old Bahama Channel* along the northern coast of Cuba and through the islands of The Bahamas themselves. The more southern branch of the *North Equatorial Current* makes its way around the Caribbean and the Gulf of Mexico and enters the *Straits of Florida* as the *Gulf Stream* with an average velocity of approximately 2.5 knots in a northward direction (for more information see the chapter *Crossing the Gulf Stream*). Once north of The Bahamas the stronger *Gulf Stream* merges with the weaker *Antilles Current* and bears off north and

northeastward across the North Atlantic. The *Sailing Directions for the Caribbean Sea* (DMA# SDPUB147) advises that the eastern entrance to the *Northwest Providence Channel* has a northwest setting current of approximately 2-3 knots which may reverse to a southeast set after strong northwest to north winds. Within the *Northeast* and *Northwest Providence Channels* themselves the current is nominal although after strong northerly winds the set may be easterly with a velocity of approximately 1 knot.

Where the shallow banks drop off to deeper ocean waters in such areas as the Abacos, the Berry Islands, the Biminis, the Exumas, and the Jumentos, tidal currents flow in and out the passes and cuts sometimes reaching 2-4 knots in strength and even more in a few of the more narrow passes. Some cuts may be impassable in adverse wind conditions or in heavy swells that may exist with or without any wind. Even in moderate conditions, onshore winds against an outgoing tide can create very rough conditions.

As a rule of thumb you can estimate the tidal rise and fall to be about 2½'-3' at most times. Where the banks drop off to the deeper waters of the Atlantic Ocean, the *Straits of Florida*, the *Tongue of the Ocean*, or *Exuma Sound* for instance, the tides ebb and flow in and out the passes and cuts with ferocity in places, sometimes reaching 2-4 knots in strength and even more in a few of the more narrow passes. All tides in The Bahamas are based on the tides in Nassau, which have a mean rise of 2.6'. Tides immediately after the first and last quarter of the moon, rise approximately ½' less, while tides after new and full moons rise approximately ½' more.

During Spring tides, when the moon is nearest the Earth, the range is increased by another ½'. Cruising through The Bahamas during Spring full moon tides will give you some of the lowest lows and highest highs. It is quite easy to run aground at this time on some of the banks routes. Boats with drafts of 5' have reportedly run aground in what is normally a 6' depth at low water during this time. To receive tidal information while in The Bahamas see the section entitled *Weather* later in this chapter.

When attempting to predict the state of tide at any time other than at slack tide, you can use the *Rule of Twelfths* for a generally reliable accuracy. To do this take the amount of tidal fluctuation and divide it into twelfths. For example, if high tide in Nassau is expected to be 3.0' and the low water datum is 0.0', the tidal fluctuation is 3', and each twelfth is 0.25' or 3". To predict the state of tide at different times you can use the *Rule of Twelfths* in the following table. The table is merely to demonstrate a point and uses an imaginary charted high tide of 3'. Always consult your chart tables or listen for tide information broadcasts and calculate accordingly.

Time of Low Water	Tide Datum - 0 Feet
1 hr after low, add 1/12	¼' above datum-3"
2 hr after low, add 3/12	¾' above datum-9"
3 hr after low, add 6/12	1½' above datum-18"
4 hr after low, add 9/12	2¼' above datum-27"
5 hr after low, add 11/12	2¾" above datum-33"
6 hr after low, add 12/12	High Water-3'*

*Caution: assumes a 3' tidal fluctuation.

Chart tables give the times and heights of high and low water but not the time of the turning of the tide or slack water. Usually there is little difference between the times of high and low water and the beginning of ebb or flood currents, but in narrow channels, landlocked harbors, or on tidal creeks and rivers, the time of slack water may vary by several hours. In some places you will find that it is not unusual for the currents to continue their direction of flow long after charted predictions say they should change. Strong winds can play havoc on the navigator attempting to predict slack water.

The current may often appear in places as a swift flowing river and care must be taken whenever crossing a stretch of strong current to avoid being swept out to sea or onto a bank or rocks. Some of the currents may flow from 2.5 to over 4 knots in places and in anchorages with tidal flow two anchors are a must. Some cuts may be impassable in adverse wind conditions or in heavy swells that may exist with or without any wind. Even in moderate conditions, onshore winds against an outgoing tide can create very rough conditions.

Towboat US

Although life-threatening emergencies are usually handled by *BASRA,* The *Bahamas Air/Sea Rescue Association,* minor breakdowns and boats needing a tow are now handled by *Towboat US. Towboat US* has two franchises in The Bahamas; one at West End,

Grand Bahama, and one based at *Rainbow Rentals* in Marsh Harbour (operated by Wayde Collins). Their website is www.towboatbahamas.com.

VHF

The regulations pertaining to the proper use of VHF in The Bahamas are basically identical to those in the United States. The *Public Utilities Commission* now handles all licensing for VHF, SSB, and amateur radios. In The Bahamas, channel 16 is the designated channel for hailing and distress. Please shift all traffic to a working channel when you have made contact with your party. The *Public Utilities Commission* requests that all vessels in Bahamian waters use ch. 68 as a hailing frequency and then switch to a working channel after contact is made. This works fine in most places, except in Nassau where so many fishermen use ch. 68 that people often revert back to ch. 16 because they don't care to listen to the fishermen all day.

People throughout The Bahamas use the VHF as a telephone. Almost every household has a VHF radio while few can afford the luxury of a cellular phone. You will often hear businesses announcing their latest deals, or the local restaurant describing the delights of their upcoming seafood night and inviting you for a meal in exchange for a small amount of cash. Technically this is illegal and improper by American as well as Bahamian laws. Bear in mind that this is a way of life in the Bahamian Out Islands and that you are a visitor here and only temporary.

There are a few cruisers who bring with them into this paradise the very things that many of us are here to escape. Some of these people insist on playing radio vigilante, sitting by the VHF anxiously awaiting an opportunity to spring into action and place the restrictions of the dreaded "proper radio etiquette" that have been placed on them, upon someone else. If you are one of the Radio Police, please relax. You are doing nothing but making an unpleasant situation intolerable and increasing your blood pressure in the process. This is just the way it is on ch.16 and 68 in The Bahamas and you had best learn to live with it. There is absolutely nothing that you, the Bahamian government, or the *Public Utilities Commission* can do to change things. Besides, you will find few other cruisers that will agree with you. If you don't wish to hear the ads or traffic, simply turn your radio off.

When you are using your VHF assume that at least a half-dozen of your neighbors will follow your conversation to another channel. If you have a "secret" channel it will not take too long to find you. It is a fact of life that everybody listens to everybody else.

In Marsh Harbour, Abaco, you can hail a taxi on VHF ch. 06 simply by calling for "any taxi," or any particular taxi if you know their number, such as "Taxi 13." Please, never use VHF ch. 06 as a working channel, it is unofficially reserved for taxi usage. Please be sure to reserve the following channels in the Abacos: ch. 70 is for digital selective calling, ch. 65 is for *Dolphin Research* (more on this in a moment), ch. 71 is used for the fishing tournaments which usually occur from Feb.-July, ch. 72 is used as the working channel for *Hope Town Fire Rescue*, ch. 78 is used during the *Abaco Regatta* (usually late June/early July), and ch. 80 is used by *Marsh Harbour Emergency Services.*

BASRA and the medical clinic on Treasure Cay stand by on VHF chs. 20 and 83 with a powerful rig that covers most of the surrounding waters. Many of the residents of Treasure Cay also monitor VHF ch. 66 while some of the folks on Guana Cay stand by on VHF ch. 08.

Cruiser's within VHF range of Marsh Harbour can participate in the morning Cruiser's Net on VHF ch. 68 at 0815. This is a well-organized and very helpful net that will likely become a part of your morning ritual while cruising in the Hub of Abaco. Here you will get weather forecasts as well as reports on conditions at Whale Cay Passage, North Man-O-War Cut, Tilloo Cut, and North Bar Channel. You can also listen to messages from arriving and departing cruisers as well as commercial announcements covering everything from Cruiser's emails to the latest happy hour offerings.

If you need an emergency contact while in the Abacos, your friends can email cruisers@cocotels.net and it will be broadcast on the VHF *Cruiser's Net.*

Just before the *Cruiser's Net* the *Royal Marsh Harbour Yacht Club* meets on VHF ch. 78 from 0800-0814. The *RMHYC* has over 800 members and meets monthly, the 2nd Tuesday of every month, at *Boat Harbour Marina* ($5 for all you can drink and hors d'oeuvres). The fee is $120 for new members

to join as well as $30 annual dues. You can visit their website at www.rmhcy.com or contact the Commodore at rmhyc@juno.com.

There is an active dolphin research program in the Abacos, The *Bahamas Marine Mammal Survey*, and they urge any boater spotting marine mammals, and that includes manatees, to please call "Dolphin Research" on VHF ch. 65. You will need to give them a position report of the sighting, the number of animals sighted, and especially any identifying marks such as nicks on their fins or scars on their bodies. Please reserve VHF ch. 65 for this purpose.

In the Northern Abacos, *Fox Town Texaco* and the *Tangelo Hotel* have volunteered to broadcast the weather and announce waiting emails each morning on the VHF. There will be an announcement on VHF ch. 68 between 0700 and 0800 with a message to switch to a working channel. The exact time depends on the workload at *Fox Town Texaco.*

Weather

The weather throughout The Bahamas is sub-tropical with a rainy season from June through October, coinciding with hurricane season. In the winter, temperatures in the Out Islands rarely fall below 60°F and generally are above 75°F in the daytime. During the summer months the lows are around 75°-78°F while the highs seldom rise above 90°F. Seawater temperatures normally vary between 74°F in February and 84°F in August.

Humidity is fairly high all year long, especially during the summer months, but there is usually a breeze to lessen the effect. In the summer, winds tend to be light, 10 knots or less from the southeast with more calms, especially at night. In the winter, the prevailing winds tend to be more easterly or north of east and stronger. It is not unusual to get a week of strong winds, 20 knots or better, during the winter months as fronts move through. These fronts tend to move through with regularity during the winter months and become more infrequent as spring approaches. The wind will usually be in the southeast or south before a front and will often be very light to calm. As the front approaches with its telltale bank of dark clouds on the western and northwestern horizon (sometimes there may not be an associated bank of clouds), the winds will steadily pick up and move into the southwest, west, and northwest as the front approaches. Strongest winds are usually from the west and northwest and this is the direction from which the squalls usually arrive. After the front passes the winds will move into the north and northeast for a day or two before finally settling back into an east/southeast pattern until the next front. Winds just after a front tend to be strong and the temperature a little cooler. A front passing off the southeast Florida coast will usually be in Nassau in about 12-24 hours and from there it may arrive in the Exumas within 12-36 hours and points south a little later.

In the summer the weather pattern is typically scattered showers with the occasional line squall. Although the main concern during June through November is hurricanes, The Bahamas are more often visited by a tropical wave with its strong winds and drenching rains. Tropical waves, sometimes called easterly waves, are low-pressure systems that can strengthen and turn into a tropical depression or hurricane. Cruisers visiting The Bahamas during hurricane season are advised to monitor weather broadcasts closely and take timely, appropriate action (also see previous section on Hurricane Holes).

Staying in touch with weather broadcasts presents little problem in The Bahamas. From Nassau you can receive the local Bahamian radio station *ZNS I* at 1540 KHz (with weather at 0735 and 0755), which broadcasts simultaneously on FM at 107.1 MHz. *ZNS II* on 1240 KHz and *ZNS III* at 810 KHz can usually be picked up in the northern Exumas. *WGBS* also from Miami at 710 KHz has weather four times an hour 24 hours a day. In the New Providence you will be able to pick up *BASRA* Coral Harbour giving the weather and tides at 0715 every morning. *BASRA* will place a call on VHF ch.16 and then move to ch. 72 for weather information. Skippers can contact the *Nassau Marine Operator* on VHF ch. 27 and ask for the latest weather report from the *Nassau Meteorological Office*. In Abaco, you can pick up the weather broadcasts of Silbert Mills on *Radio Abaco*, FM 93.5, at 0700, and again between 1800-1830 during the evening news. Vessels planning a *Gulf Stream* crossing can hail *Blue Dolphin* on VHF ch. 73 at 0730 for the latest on the *Stream*.

If you have ham radio capabilities you can pick up The *Bahamas Weather Net* every morning at 0720 on 3.696 MHz, lower sideband. Carolyn Wardle, C6AGG, whose husband Nick is Ranger in Nassau, begins with the local weather forecast and tides from the *Nassau Met. Office*. Next, hams from all over The Bahamas check in with their local conditions which Carolyn later forwards to the *Nassau Met. Office* to assist in their forecasting. If you are interested in the approach of a front you can listen in and hear what conditions hams in the path of the front have experienced. All licensed amateur radio operators with current Bahamian reciprocals are invited to participate. The local conditions in the weather reports follow a specific order so listen in and give your conditions in the order indicated. If requested, Carolyn will send you some information on the types of clouds and their descriptions along with a log sheet. Be sure to thank Carolyn for her tireless efforts that benefit all mariners, not only those with ham licenses. Thanks Carolyn.

At 0745 on 7.268 MHz you can pick up the *Waterway Net*. Organized and maintained by the *Waterway Radio and Cruising Club*, this dedicated band of amateur radio operators begin the net with a synopsis of the weather for South Florida and then proceed to weather for The Bahamas (with tides), the southwest north Atlantic, the Caribbean Sea, and the Gulf Of Mexico.

If you have marine SSB capabilities you can pick up *BASRA's* weather broadcasts every morning at 0700 on 4003 KHz, upper sideband. Later in the day you can pick up the guru of weather forecasters, Herb Hilgenberg, *Southbound II*, from Canada. Herb operates from his home in Canada and you can find Herb on 12.359 MHz, upper sideband, at 2000 Zulu daily.

The *United States Coast Guard* in Portsmouth, Virginia weather broadcasts can be received on your SSB on 4428.7 KHz (ch. 409), 6506.4 KHz (ch. 601), 8765.4 (ch. 816), 13113.2 KHz (ch. 1205), and 17307.3 (ch. 1625). Times are 0600, 0800, 1400, and 2200.

All cruisers suffered a loss when David Jones passed away in November of 2003. But the *Caribbean Weather Center* continues to provide all the same services that David provided with Chris Parker at the microphone from his sailboat *Bel Ami*. Chris' weather nets are conducted 6 days a week, Monday through Saturday, but also Sundays when Tropical or other severe weather threatens. Chris' summer schedule, April to October, begins on 4.045 MHz at 0630 AST/EDT; then Chris moves to 8.137 MHz at 0700 AST/

EDT; Chris is back on 4.045 MHz at 0800 AST/EDT; then Chris moves to 8.104 MHz at 0830 AST/EDT; Chris moves up to 12.350 MHz at 0915 AST/EDT; and finishes up at 6.221 MHz at 0930 AST/EDT. When severe weather or tropical weather systems threaten Chris will also transmit in the evenings, usually on 8.104 MHz at 2000 AST/EDT and Chris will usually announce this on the morning net.

Chris' winter schedule, November to March, begins at 0700 AST/0600 EST on 8.137 MHz; Chris then moves to 4.045 MHz at 0730 AST/0630 EST; Chris can then be found on 8.104 MHz at 0830 AST/0730 EST; Chris them moves up to 12.350 MHz at 0930 AST/0830 EST; Chris then finishes on 6.221 MHz at 1000 AST/0900 EST. Quite often during the winter months Chris may be late in getting to the 12 meg frequency. When severe weather or tropical weather systems threaten Chris will also transmit in the evenings, usually on 8.104 MHz at 1900 AST/1800 EST and Chris will usually announce this on the morning net. Chris begins the net with a 24-48 hour wind and sea summary followed by a synoptic analysis and tropical conditions during hurricane season. After this, Chris repeats the weather for those needing fills and finally he takes check-ins reporting local conditions from sponsoring vessels (vessels who have paid an annual fee for this service). Those who seek more information about weather, weather patterns, and the forecasting of weather, should pick up a copy of Chris Parker's excellent publication: *Coastal And Offshore Weather, The Essential Handbook*. You can pick up a copy of Chris Parker's book at his web site: http://www.mwxc.com.

One of my favorite forecasters is a ham operator named George Cline, KP2G. George can be found on the *Caribbean Maritime Mobile Net* located at 7.241 MHz, lower sideband at 0715 AST, 15 minutes into the net. George gives an overview of the current Caribbean weather beginning in Trinidad and working his way up the chain to Puerto Rico. At 0730 AST, George moves to 7.086, lower sideband for further Caribbean weather information and questions and answers. The same weather information is then transmitted in a weatherfax format. George returns to the airwaves at 1630 AST, 15 on the afternoon cocktail net at 7.086 lower sideband.

For Bahamian weather information on the Internet, visit www.bahamasweather.org, the website of The *Bahamas Department of Meteorology* featuring

forecasts, tide tables, and satellite images. You can access the *National* Hurricane Center at www.nhc.noaa.gov, and the NOAA weather site at www.nws.noaa.gov. The Hydrometeorological Prediction Center offers a broad overview of weather patterns at www.hpc.ncep.noaa.gov/. For Nassau-based radar coverage of Abaco visit www.bahamasweather.org/radar/local/loop. When using this site make sure that the time stamp on the image is current; this website is notorious for using out-dated images.

Using the Charts

For the soundings on the charts I use my dinghy (*Afterglow*) with a computer-based hydrographic system consisting of an off-the-shelf GPS and sonar combination that gives a GPS waypoint and depth every two seconds including the time of each observation. The software used records and stores this information in an onboard computer. When I begin to chart an area, I first put *Afterglow's* bow on a well-marked, prominent point of land and take GPS lat/lons for a period of at least ten minutes. I use the average of all these positions to check against the lat/lon shown on the topos that I use to create the charts. I also use cross bearings to help set up control points for my own reference. At this point I begin to take soundings.

My next objective is to chart the inshore reefs. Then I'll plot all visible hazards to navigation. These positions are recorded by hand on my field notes as well as being recorded electronically. I rely primarily on my on-site notes for the actual construction of the charts. The soundings taken by the system are later entered by hand but it is the field notes that help me create the basis for the chart graphics. Next I will run the one-fathom line as well as the ten-fathom line and chart these. Here is where the system does most of the work. Finally, I will crisscross the entire area in a grid pattern and hopefully catch hazards that are at first glance unseen. It is not unusual to spend days sounding an area of only a couple of square miles.

Due to the speed of *Afterglow*, each identical lat/long may have as many as ten or twenty separate soundings. Then, with the help of *NOAA* tide tables, the computer gives me accurate depths to one decimal place for each separate lat/long pair acquired on the data run. A macro purges all but the lowest depths for each lat/long position (to two decimal places). At this point the actual plotting is begun including one fathom and ten fathom lines. The charts themselves are still constructed from outline tracings of topographic maps and the lat/long lines are placed in accordance with these maps. The soundings taken are shown in feet at MLW, *Mean Low Water*, the average low tide. Since MLW is an average, cruisers must be aware that there are times that there will be less water than shown, particularly on Spring low tides, during the full moon and new moon.

These charts are as accurate as I can make them and I believe them to be superior to any others. However, it is not possible to plot every individual rock or coral head so piloting by eye is still essential. On many of the routes in my guides you must be able to pick out the blue, deeper water as it snakes between sandbanks, rocky bars, and coral heads. Learn to trust your eyes. Remember that on the banks, sandbars and channels can shift over time so that what was once a channel may now be a sandbar. Never approach a cut or sandbar with the sun in your eyes, it should be above and behind you. Sunglasses with polarized lenses can be a big help in combating the glare of the sun on the water. With good visibility the sandbars and heads stand out and are clearly defined. As you gain experience you may even learn to read the subtle differences in the water surface as it flows over underwater obstructions. Yes, I could have included lovely color photographs of the different water colors and label them accordingly lulling you into thinking that you know the depth of the water by looking at the photos, but I chose not to. The only true way to gain the ability to read the water is to get out there and do it. Explore. Keep one eye on your depth sounder and one on the water around you. Soon you'll be an expert.

All courses shown are magnetic. All waypoints for entrances to cuts and for detouring around shoal areas are only to be used in a general sense. They are meant to get you into the general area, you must pilot your way through the cut or around the shoal yourself. You will have to keep a good lookout; GPS will not do that for you. <u>The best aids to navigation when near these shoals and cuts are sharp eyesight and good light</u>. The charts will show both deep draft vessel routes as well as some shallow draft vessel routes. Deep draft vessel routes will accommodate a draft of 6' minimum and often more with the assistance of the tide. Shallow draft vessel routes are for dinghies and small outboard powered boats with drafts of less than 3'. Shallow draft monohulls and multihulls very often use these same routes.

Not being a perfect world, I expect errors to occur. I would deeply appreciate any input and corrections that you may notice as you travel these waters. Please send your suggestions to Stephen J. Pavlidis, C/O Seaworthy Publications, 2023 N. Atlantic Ave., Unit #226, Cocoa Beach, Florida, 32931, or email me at stevepavlidis@hotmail.com.

List of Charts

**The prudent navigator will not rely solely on any
single aid to navigation, particularly on floating aids.**

CAUTION:
*The Approach and Index charts are designed strictly for orientation, they are not to be used for
navigational purposes. All charts are to be used in conjunction with the text.
All soundings are in feet at Mean Low Water. All courses are magnetic.
Projection is transverse Mercator. Datum used is WGS84.*

*Differences in latitude and longitude may exist between these charts and other charts of the area;
therefore the transfer of positions from one chart to another should be done by
bearings and distances from common features.*

The author and publisher take no responsibility for errors, omissions, or the misuse of these charts. No warranties are either expressed or implied as to the usability of the information contained herein.

Note: Some *NOAA* and *DMA* charts do not show some of the reefs and heads charted in this guide. Always keep a good lookout when piloting in these waters.

Chart #	Description	Page #
AB-BI-10	Sandy Point	74
AB-BI-11	Castaway Cay (Gorda Cay)	74
AB-BI-12	Channel Cay to Mores Island	76
AB-BI-13	Mores Island	76
	The Abacos	
AB-1	Walker's Cay to Carters Cays	81
AB-2	Great Sale Cay	81
AB-3	Walker's Cay	84
AB-4	Grand cays	84
AB-5	Double Breasted Cays	87
AB-6	Strangers Cays	87
AB-7	Carters Cays	90
AB-8	Carters Cays to Spanish Cay	90
AB-9	Fox Town	92
AB-10	The Fish Cays	92
AB-11	Moraine Cay	94
AB-12	Umbrella Cay, Allan's-Pensacola Cay	96
AB-13	The Hog Cays	96
AB-14	Crab Cay Anchorage	98
AB-15	Spanish Cay to Green Turtle Cay	98
AB-16	Spanish Cay	100
AB-17	Coopers Town to Powell Cay	100
AB-18	Manjack Cay, Crab Cay	103
AB-19	Green Turtle Cay	104
AB-19A	Green Turtle Cay, Black Sound	106
AB-19B	Green Turtle Cay, White Sound	106
AB-20	No Name Cay to Marsh Harbour	109
AB-21	Whale Cay Passage, Don't Rock Passage	110
AB-21A	Treasure Cay Marina	112
AB-22	Great Guana Cay	114
AB-22A	Great Guana Cay Harbour	115
AB-23	Scotland Cay	118
AB-24	Leisure Lee	119
AB-25	Marsh Harbour	120
AB-26	The Hub of Abaco	121
AB-27	Matt Lowe's Cay to Marsh Harbour	130
AB-28	Man-O-War Cay, Man-O-War Channels	133
AB-28A	Man-O-War Harbour	134
AB-29	Hope Town Harbour	136
AB-30	Lubbers Quarters Channel	139

Chart #	Description	Page #
AB-31	Cormorant Cay to Pelican Point	142
AB-32	Tilloo Pond	141
AB-33	Snake Cay	142
AB-34	Pelican Point to Little Harbour	145
AB-35	Little Harbour	145
AB-36	Cherokee Sound	148
AB-36A	Schooner Bay Marina	151
	The Biminis	
BI-1	Great Isaac	154
BI-2	Northern Biminis	155
BI-3	North Bimini, Harbour Entrance	156
BI-3A	Channel to Bimini Bay	159
BI-4	North Bimini, Paradise Point	161
BI-5	South Bimini, Nixon's Harbour	161
BI-6	Turtle Rocks to Gun Cay	162
BI-7	Gun Cay, North Cat Cay	165
BI-8	South Cat Cay	165
BI-9	Ocean Cay	167
BI-10	South Riding Rock	167
	The Berry Islands	
BR-1	Little Stirrup Cay, Great Stirrup Cay	174
BR-2	Great Harbour Cay, Bullock's Harbour	177
BR-2A	Great Harbour Cay Marina	177
BR-3	Haines Cay, Anderson Cay	178
BR-4	Haines Cay to Money Cay	180
BR-5	The Soldier Cays to Hoffman's Cay	180
BR-6	Hoffman's Cay, Devil's Cay	181
BR-7	Little Harbour Cay, Alder Cay, Frozen Cay	183
BR-8	Bond's Cay	187
BR-9	Whale Cay	188
BR-10	Sandy Cay, Cockroach Cay	190
BR-11	The Fish Cays	190
BR-12	Bird Cay	192
BR-13	Chub Cay	192
BR-14	Northwest Channel Light to Chub Cay	194
	Andros	
AN-1	Northwest Channel Light to Morgan's Bluff	201
AN-2	Morgan's Bluff to Conch Bay	203
AN-3	Mastic Point to Saddleback Cays	206
AN-4	Stafford Creek, Blanket Sound	208

Chart #	Description	Page #
AN-5	Staniard Creek	210
AN-6	Lightborn Bank	213
AN-7	Fresh Creek	214
AN-7A	Fresh Creek Basin	216
AN-8	Fresh Creek to Plum Cays	219
AN-9	Plum Cays to Mastic Cay	219
AN-10	Mastic Cay to Kits Cay	220
AN-11	Kits Cay to Man O' War	220
AN-12	North Bight	222
AN-13	Middle Bight	222
AN-14	South Bight	224
AN-15	Kemps Bay	226
AN-16	Green Cay	228
	New Providence	
NP-1	Nassau Harbour, Western Entrance	234
NP-2	Nassau Harbour	237
NP-3	Potters Cay to Burnside Point	237
NP-4	Nassau Harbour, Eastern Entrance	239
NP-5	Silver Cay	244
NP-6	Silver Cay to Gambier	246
NP-7	Gambier to Clifton Bluff, Lyford Cay	246
NP-7A	Lyford Cay Marina	247
NP-8	Coral Harbour	248
NP-9	Southern Shore	248
NP-10	East End Point to Malcolm Creek	250
NP-11	Chub Rock to Porgee Rocks, Rose Island	253
NP-12	Rose Island to Current Island	254
NP-13	Fleeming Channel to Current Island	254
	Eleuthera	
EL-1	East End Point	270
EL-2	Davis Harbour	270
EL-3	Powell Point, Davis Channel	272
EL-4	Rock Sound, Davis Channel	275
EL-5	Tarpum Bay	277
EL-6	Ten Bay to Creek Bay	277
EL-7	South Palmetto Point, Pineapple Cays	278
EL-8	Governor's Harbour	280
EL-9	Pelican Cay, Holmes Bay	282
EL-10	James Cistern	282
EL-11	Rainbow Bay	282

Chart #	Description	Page #
EL-12	Hatchet Bay	284
EL-13	Hatchet Bay Pond	284
EL-14	Gregory Town to Muttonfish Point	286
EL-15	Muttonfish Point to the Glass Window	288
EL-16	Rotten Bay, The Bogues	288
EL-17	Current Island	290
EL-18	Current Cut	290
EL-19	Royal Island to Spanish Wells	292
EL-20	Royal Island	293
EL-21	Egg Island, Egg Island Cut	293
EL-22	The Devil's Backbone	300
EL-23	Harbour Island	304
	Cat Island	
CT-1	Hawks Nest Creek	310
CT-2	Hawks Nest Creek to Whale Creek	311
CT-3	Whale Creek to Fernandez Bay	312
CT-4	Fernandez Bay, Smith's Bay	314
CT-5	Smith's Bay to Gaitor's	316
CT-6	Bennett's Harbour	316
CT-6A	Bennett's Harbour	319
CT-7	Arthur's Town, Orange Creek	320
CT-8	Half Moon Cay (Little San Salvador)	323

Legend

▨	water depth less than 1 fathom	☐	water depth over 10 fathoms
▧	water depth between 1 fathom and 10 fathoms		
— – –	large vessel route-6' draft	⚲	light
— - -	shallow vessel route	⚓	anchorage
+	rock or coral head	⊕	GPS waypoint
++++	reef	◉	tower
═══	road	⟘	wreck–above hw
m	mooring	⊂┼┼⊃	wreck-submerged
dm	dinghy mooring	☐	building

Index of Charts

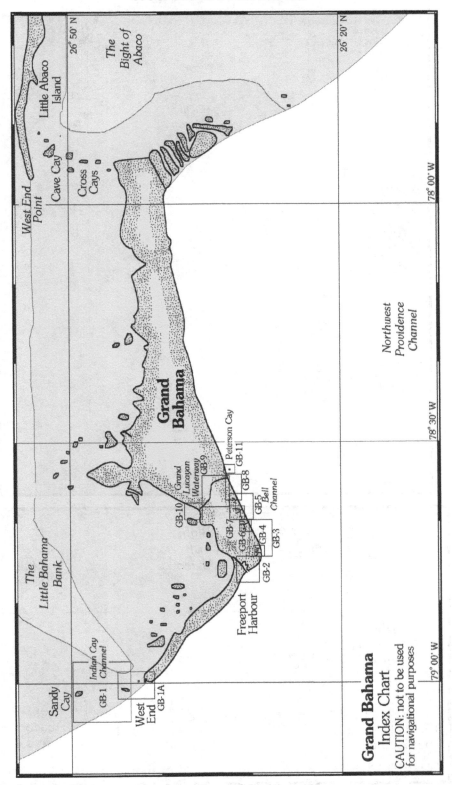

Grand Bahama
Index Chart
CAUTION: not to be used
for navigational purposes

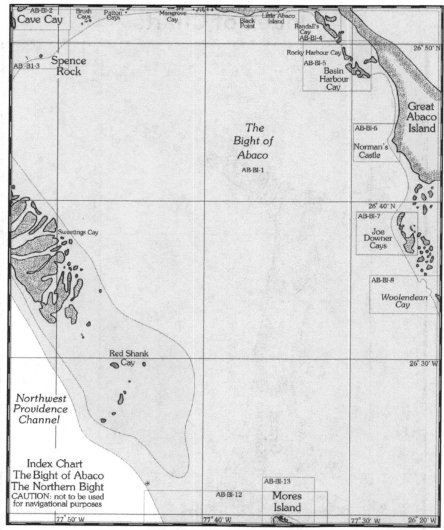

Cave Cay
AB-BI-2
Brush Cays
Patton Cays
Mangrove Cay
Black Point
Little Abaco Island
Randall's Cay
AB-BI-4

AB-BI-3
Spence Rock

Rocky Harbour Cay
AB-BI-5
Basin Harbour Cay

Great Abaco Island

The Bight of Abaco
AB-BI-1

AB-BI-6
Norman's Castle

26° 50' N

26° 40' N
AB-BI-7
Joe Downer Cays

Sweetings Cay

AB-BI-8
Woolendean Cay

Red Shank Cay

26° 30' W

Northwest Providence Channel

AB-BI-13
AB-BI-12
Mores Island

Index Chart
The Bight of Abaco
The Northern Bight
CAUTION: not to be used
for navigational purposes

77° 50' W
77° 40' W
77° 30' W
26° 20' N

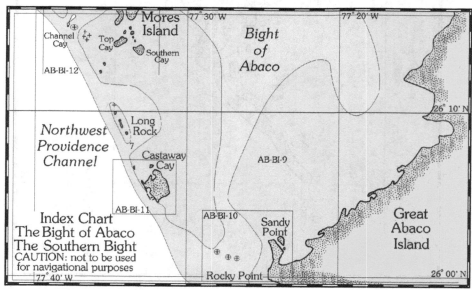

Mores Island
77° 30' W
77° 20' W

Channel Cay
Top Cay
Southern Cay
AB-BI-12

Bight of Abaco

26° 10' N

Long Rock
Castaway Cay
AB-BI-11
AB-BI-9

Northwest Providence Channel

AB-BI-10
Sandy Point

Index Chart
The Bight of Abaco
The Southern Bight
CAUTION: not to be used
for navigational purposes

Great Abaco Island

77° 40' W
Rocky Point
26° 00' N

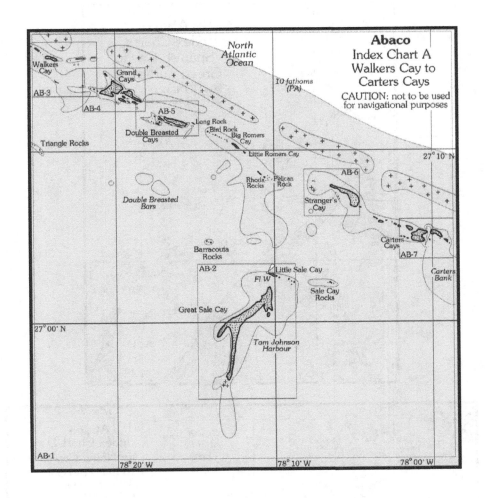

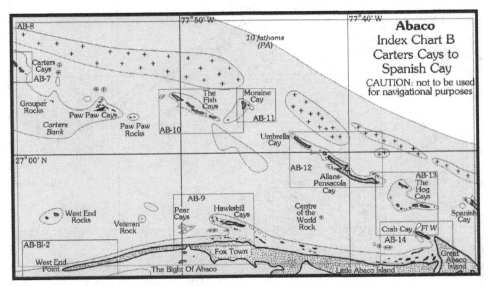

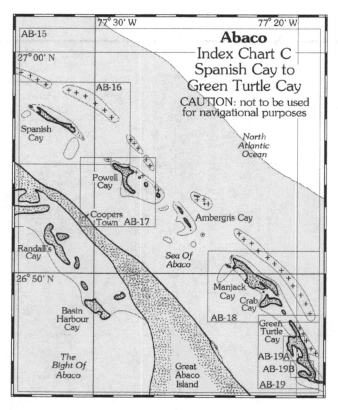

Abaco
Index Chart C
Spanish Cay to
Green Turtle Cay
CAUTION: not to be used
for navigational purposes

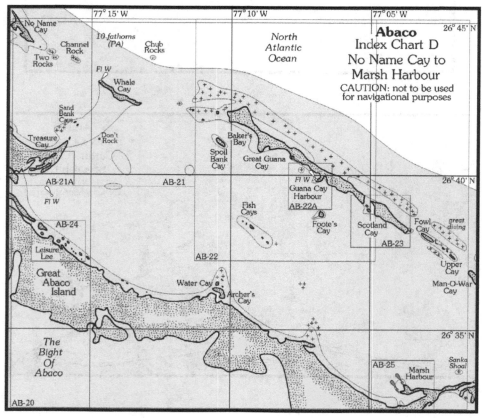

Abaco
Index Chart D
No Name Cay to
Marsh Harbour
CAUTION: not to be used
for navigational purposes

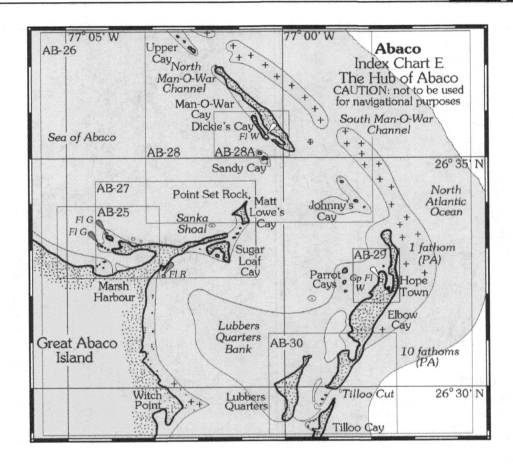

Abaco
Index Chart E
The Hub of Abaco
CAUTION: not to be used
for navigational purposes

77° 05' W
77° 00' W
AB-26
Upper Cay
North Man-O-War Channel
Man-O-War Cay
Dickie's Cay
Fl W
South Man-O-War Channel
Sea of Abaco
AB-28
AB-28A
26° 35' N
Sandy Cay
Point Set Rock
AB-27
AB-25
Matt Lowe's Cay
Johnny's Cay
North Atlantic Ocean
Fl G
Sanka Shoal
Fl G
Sugar Loaf Cay
AB-29
1 fathom (PA)
Parrot Cays
Gp Fl W
Hope Town
Fl R
Marsh Harbour
Elbow Cay
Great Abaco Island
Lubbers Quarters Bank
AB-30
10 fathoms (PA)
Witch Point
Lubbers Quarters
Tilloo Cut
26° 30' N
Tilloo Cay

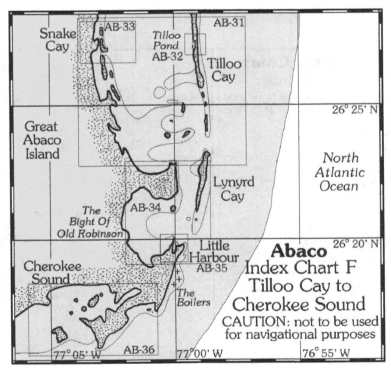

Snake Cay
AB-33
AB-31
Tilloo Pond
AB-32
Tilloo Cay
26° 25' N
Great Abaco Island
North Atlantic Ocean
Lynyrd Cay
The Bight Of Old Robinson
AB-34
Little Harbour
26° 20' N
Cherokee Sound
AB-35
Abaco
Index Chart F
Tilloo Cay to
Cherokee Sound
CAUTION: not to be used
for navigational purposes
The Boilers
77° 05' W
AB-36
77° 00' W
76° 55' W

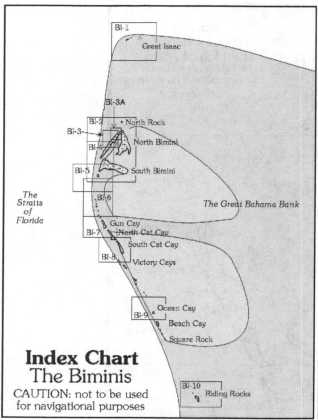

Index Chart
The Biminis
CAUTION: not to be used
for navigational purposes

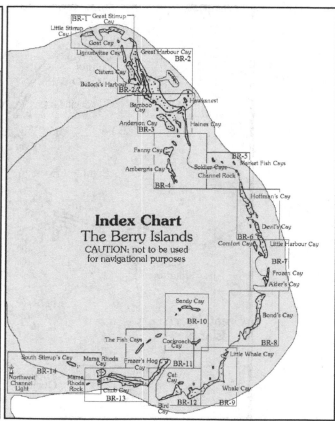

Index Chart
The Berry Islands
CAUTION: not to be used
for navigational purposes

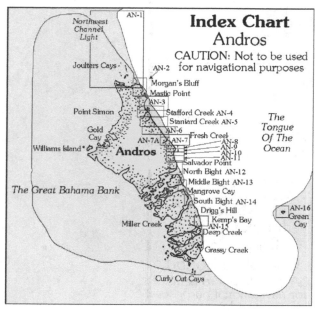

Index Chart
Andros
CAUTION: Not to be used
for navigational purposes

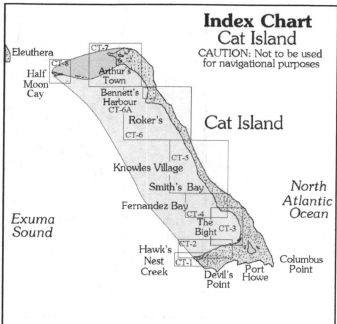

Index Chart
Cat Island
CAUTION: Not to be used
for navigational purposes

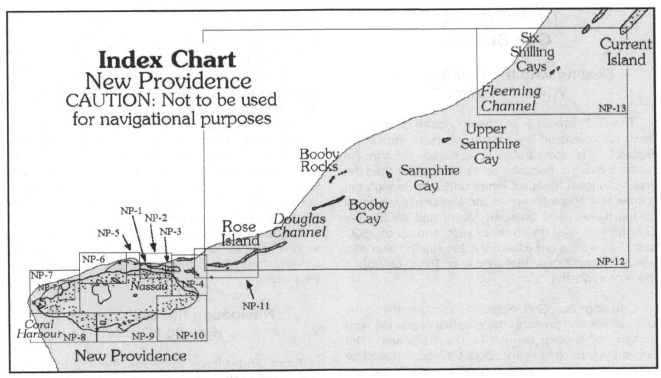

Index Chart
New Providence
CAUTION: Not to be used
for navigational purposes

Six Shilling Cays

Current Island

Fleeming Channel

NP-13

Upper Samphire Cay

Booby Rocks

Samphire Cay

Booby Cay

NP-12

Rose Island

Douglas Channel

NP-1 NP-2

NP-5 NP-3

NP-6

NP-7

NP-4

Nassau

NP-11

Coral Harbour

NP-8 NP-9 NP-10

New Providence

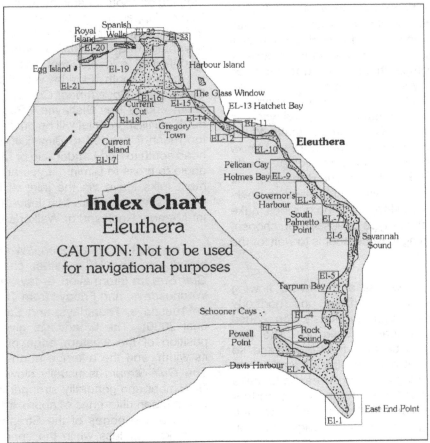

Index Chart
Eleuthera
CAUTION: Not to be used
for navigational purposes

Royal Island

Spanish Wells

El-22

El-23

El-20

Egg Island

El-19

Harbour Island

El-21

The Glass Window

El-16

El-15

EL-13 Hatchett Bay

Current Cut

El-18

El-14

El-11

Gregory Town

El-12

Eleuthera

El-10

Current Island

Pelican Cay

El-17

Holmes Bay El-9

Governor's Harbour El-8

South Palmetto Point El-7

El-6

Savannah Sound

El-5

Tarpum Bay

Schooner Cays

EL-4

El-3

Rock Sound

Powell Point

Davis Harbour El-2

East End Point

El-1

Crossing The Gulf Stream

Dealing with the Gulf Stream... When do I Cross?

The *Gulf Stream* is a powerful ocean current that flows northward off the eastern shore of the United States. It is comparable to a mighty river in the ocean moving a thousand times more water than the widest, longest, deepest rivers on Earth through the narrow bottleneck known as the *Straits of Florida*. At its narrowest point between Miami and Bimini, the *Gulf Stream* may be 45 miles wide and up to 2500' deep. Its waters are a beautiful deep indigo blue with a warm temperature that averages 76° even during the winter months.

Crossing the *Gulf Stream* provokes the most uneasiness and presents the greatest challenge, and danger, for anyone headed to The Bahamas. Not only do you have to worry about the seas created by opposing wind and current, bear in mind that if you break down the *Gulf Stream* will move you northward away from your present position at 2-4 knots. However, for a well-equipped and crewed vessel, the inherent dangers in the crossing can be lessened immensely by doing only one simple thing...waiting for weather. I'm not going to tell you what type of vessel to take on your adventure and how to equip her. There are many naval architects and maritime experts who can do a far better job than I. Only you can testify to the seaworthiness of your vessel. Make sure you know her well, that she is sound, that she is equipped with current charts of both Florida and The Bahamas, and carries up to date safety devices. I have seen boats as small as 15' plywood sloops with no engines make the crossing, so whatever type of vessel you choose, the most important thing to remember is to wait for the right weather window.

Since the *Gulf Stream* is a northward flowing current, an opposing wind (from any northerly direction northwest through northeast) can cause some truly dangerous seas to build up. The *Gulf Stream* is no place to be in a frontal passage so unless you absolutely have to go, stay put and wait on the weather. I can't imagine a single reason to make a skipper want to cross the *Gulf Stream* in a norther although I've known many that have and a few who thrive on the challenge and enjoy the bragging rights.

But most veteran skippers will wait until the seas are down and the wind is somewhere between east and south at less than 15 knots. An east or southeast wind of 15 knots or more can build up quite a chop that will have to be bucked for the entire trip. Winds from south to west would be quite favorable for sailing vessels but they are rare and can be the forerunners of a frontal passage during the months from October through May. When the wind seems right for you, and you have given the *Gulf Stream* enough time to settle down if it has been boisterous, it may be time to go. Personally I prefer to look out upon the water from a high vantage point before I leave. If I see what appears to be camel humps on the horizon I will postpone my departure for a while no matter what the wind is forecast to be. When you do get a weather window don't delay, take advantage of it and enjoy your cruise.

Navigating the Gulf Stream... How do I Cross

From Fort Pierce to Miami there are several jumping off spots for sailors heading to The Bahamas. Some skippers prefer to leave from Angelfish Creek at Key Largo or Marathon to make the most of the advantage that the *Gulf Stream* has to offer. That is definitely a good idea, but most boats choose to depart south Florida via Hillsboro Inlet, Port Everglades, *Government Cut*, or Cape Florida at the south end of Key Biscayne. Passages from points north of Hillsboro Inlet will be bucking the *Gulf Stream* too much if headed to Bimini; it would be better to head south to Fort Lauderdale or Miami to get a better angle to cross to Bimini. If you are headed to Abaco most folks leave via the inlet at Lake Worth. I've known some skippers that leave Fort Pierce bound for Memory Rock and/or Walker's Cay.

The south Florida *National Weather Service* radio broadcasts on VHF weather ch. 1 give the latest *Gulf Stream* information 6 days a week; Mondays, Wednesdays, and Fridays from 1600 until 2000, and on Tuesdays, Thursdays, and Saturdays from 0400 until 2000. The broadcasts give the approximate position of the western edge of the *Gulf Stream*, its width, and the average northward flow in knots. The *Gulf Stream* is usually slower in October and November and generally stronger in July and August with a mean difference of approximately ½ knot. The speed at the edges of the Stream may be as little as ½ knot or less while the speed at the axis, the "hump", may be as high as 4 knots or more. For the most part, strong northerly winds will slow the *Gulf Stream* while strong southerly winds will increase its speed. Normally you can figure on an average drift of approximately 2.5 knots setting in a direction of 010°.

Crossing the *Gulf Stream* poses a nifty navigational problem in vectors. Due to the northward flow of the *Gulf Stream* a certain amount of compensatory southerly heading must be employed. For example, steering the rhumb line course from Fort Lauderdale to Bimini in a sailboat making 5-6 knots will cause you to make landfall somewhere in the vicinity of *Great Isaac Light* in normal conditions. By applying a certain amount of southerly heading to offset the strength of the *Gulf Stream* your vessel will travel the shortest, straightest path to Bimini.

The navigational problem is a classic one of finding the course to steer to make good an intended track given the set and drift of the current and your vessel's speed. For solving you will need a plotting sheet or a current chart of the area, a pencil, a compass, and parallel rules. As in the diagram, plot point *A* as your position on the western edge of the *Gulf Stream* on your plotting sheet or chart. Next, pencil in line *AB* of an indefinite length on the bearing that is your direct course to Bimini. Next plot vector *AC*, representing the *Gulf Stream* current in the direction of the set of the *Gulf Stream*, approximately 010°, for a distance equivalent to the estimated drift in one hour, (be sure to listen to the *NOAA* weather broadcasts for the latest information, see above paragraph). Next take your compass with the center on *C*, and swing an arc of radius equal to your vessel's speed, if you will be making 6 knots set it for 6 nautical miles. This will intersect line *AB* at point *B*. The line *CB* will be your course to steer allowing for the set and drift of the *Gulf Stream*. Use your parallel rules to measure the angle. The length of line *AB* in *nautical* miles, will be your speed of advance towards Bimini. In other words, you might be making 6 knots through the water but you may only be making 5.1 knots towards Bimini thanks to the *Gulf Stream*. Never forget that there are built in inaccuracies in figuring your course. Wind and wave conditions, your own ability to maintain a consistent speed, and the strength of the *Gulf Stream* itself all combine to give slight errors to even the best calculations but you should be "in the neighborhood" so to speak. For example, a vessel leaving Port Everglades would find its course to Bimini to be 121°.

After solving the vector problem the skipper might find that he must now steer 143° to reach Bimini on the shortest and straightest route.

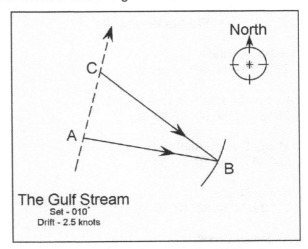

The Gulf Stream
Set - 010°
Drift - 2.5 knots

Even if you have a GPS aboard you must still solve the vector problem for your course. If you allow the GPS to steer to your waypoint and correct for the current you will be constantly changing course and covering more miles in a highly inefficient manner that is sometimes called a "dog curve".

If you have ever seen a dog trying to swim across a river you will understand how inefficient this type of course is. A dog will always keep his nose pointed to his destination even as the river's current pushes him downstream. If a dog is heading east towards a certain tree and the current is pushing him south he will keep his nose pointed at that tree even as he gets pushed downstream and finally has to swim north-northeast to his destination. If the pup had simply swam more northeast to begin with or moved upstream before crossing he would have a had a far easier passage.

A final word on crossing the *Gulf Stream*. This narrow passage is very busy and getting busier every year. Keep a sharp lookout for other vessels and take the proper precautions to avoid collisions well ahead of time. If you don't know the "Rules of the Road", learn them.

Courses from South Florida across the Gulf Stream

Florida Waypoints

Hillsboro Inlet:
26° 15.19' N, 80° 04.55' W

Ft. Lauderdale/Port Everglades:
26° 05.57' N, 80° 05.40' W

Miami-Government Cut:
25° 45.70' N, 80° 05.80' W

Cape Florida:
25° 38.74' N, 80° 07.70' W

Angelfish Creek:
25° 19.35' N, 80° 12.60' W

From Florida	To West End, GB
Jupiter Inlet	110° – 60 nm
Lake Worth Inlet	099° – 56 nm
Hillsboro Inlet	070° – 65 nm
Port Everglades	065° – 69 nm
From Florida	**To North Bimini**
Hillsboro Inlet	133° - 53.0 nm
Port Everglades	124° - 48.3 nm
Government Cut (R2)	093° - 42.8 nm
Cape Florida	090° - 44.5 nm
Angelfish Creek	069° - 53.9 nm
From Florida	**To Gun Cay**
Hillsboro Inlet	139° - 58.3 nm
Port Everglades	131° - 52.7 nm
Government Cut (R2)	109° - 44.5 nm
Cape Florida	100° - 45.0 nm
Angelfish Creek	077° - 51.6 nm

I will not endeavor to give the reader the proper courses to steer because all boats travel at different speeds through the water and make more or less leeway than other boats. However I will give you the bearings and distances to and from different locations and the reader may plot his or her own course using the vector method. In other words, I will not do your homework for you as it won't hurt you to do it yourself, and besides, many skippers have forgotten how to plot a course across a current. The following table will give you bearings and distances from south Florida to the Biminis. All courses are magnetic and corrections for the set and drift of the *Gulf Stream* must be applied to these bearings to arrive at your course to steer. Both my publisher and myself take no responsibility for the misuse of the following courses.

Making Landfall

As you leave south Florida in your wake you will find yourself alone on a big ocean. You will be traveling approximately 46-50 plus miles depending on your departure point and most of those miles (25-40) will be out of sight of land and any type of navigational aids. First timers will likely have feelings of apprehension. Don't panic! Even veteran skippers have those same feelings, it is quite natural when leaving port. You might be fortunate and find other cruisers going the same way and most don't mind the company. It usually increases the safety margin a little for all involved.

If you are heading for Memory Rock you will be aiming for a small rock that is barely visible until you get within a few miles of it. And if you are bound for Bimini or Gun Cay you will be heading for a small set of islands that you probably won't see until you get within 7-10 miles from their shores depending on your height of eye. This is no problem for GPS, but those who don't have a *boxed navigator* can still use other sources for directions. First, the high-rise buildings along the south Florida coast will stay within view for at least 10-15 miles from shore depending on their height and your own height of eye. Remember, if you have trouble or get lost you can always turn towards the west (that's where the sun sets) and sooner or later you will find Florida. Important: make sure your compass is correct and learn to trust it.

Those skippers heading for West End, Freeport, or Lucaya, will have an easier landfall. Lucaya sits on the southern shore of Grand Bahama well out of the path of the *Gulf Stream* while West End lies of the northwestern tip of Grand Bahama at the eastern edge of the *Gulf Stream*. If you can sight Grand Bahama, it will be a simple matter to pilot to either West End, Freeport, or Lucaya.

Grand Bahama

Ports of Entry: Freeport, Lucaya, West End
Diesel Repairs: Freeport, Lucaya
Fuel: West End, Lucaya
Haul-Out: Freeport
Outboard Repairs: Freeport, Lucaya
Propane: Freeport, West End, Lucaya
Provisions: Freeport, West End, Lucaya
Important Lights:
    Barracuda Shoal: Fl W ev 4 sec
    Sweetings Cay: Fl W ev 5 sec
    Grand Lucayan Waterway Sea Buoy: Fl W
    Bell Channel Sea Buoy: Fl W ev 2 sec
    Freeport Lighthouse: Fl (3) WR ev 15 sec
    Pinder Point Light: Gp. Fl (3) WR ev 5 sec
    Riding Point Tower: Fl R (airwarning top) Fixed
    Settlement Pt. (West End): Fl W ev 4 sec
    Indian Cay: Fl W ev 6 sec

The fourth largest island in the Bahamian archipelago, Grand Bahama, lies just 55 miles off the coast of Southeastern Florida. The island itself has been settled since pre-Columbian times, several remnants of Lucayan inhabitation have been found on Grand Bahama. Today the island boasts the second largest city in The Bahamas, Freeport/Lucaya, and it is only on Grand Bahama that you will find such a wide variety of Bahamian lifestyles.

In the more cosmopolitan areas of Freeport and Lucaya you will find excellent marinas, casinos, first rate hotels, championship golf courses, tennis courts (over 50), national parks, international shopping, and miles and miles of beautiful beaches and the associated water sports that go with them. But the Freeport/Lucaya area is not all there is to Grand Bahama. Once past the confines of Freeport and Lucaya, you'll discover Bahamians living as their out-island cousins do; fishing, conching, and living off the bounty of the sea. From the smuggling history of West End to the *Conch Cracking Contest* of East End, this island is much more than just the show that is Freeport and Lucaya.

The shores of Grand Bahama offer mariners good protection as well as shoreside and offshore activities. The northern shores of Grand Bahama are shallow, a bonefisherman's delight. Off the southern shore of Grand Bahama lies a wonderful reef for snorkeling or SCUBA enthusiasts. West End, at the northwestern end of the island, is routinely used by cruisers as the "door" to the Abacos and is usually the first stop on an Abaco cruise, so we will begin our tour of Grand Bahama there.

West End

Memory Rock - 2¼ nm south of:
26° 54.75' N, 79° 05.75' W

Indian Cay Channel - E entrance to channel:
26° 46.37' N, 78° 57.15' W

Barracuda Shoal: ¼ nm S of:
26° 45.65' N, 78° 58.30' W

Indian Cay Channel - NW of piling #3:
26° 44.75' N, 78° 59.20' W

Indian Cay Channel - ¼ nm SW of western entrance to channel:
26° 42.80' N, 79° 00.60' W

West End - ½ nm W of entrance channel:
26° 42.23' N, 79° 00.15' W

Mangrove Cay - ½ nm NW of:
26° 55.50' N, 78° 37.50' W

Navigational Information

A waypoint at 26° 42.23' N, 79° 00.15'W, will place you approximately ½ mile west of the entrance channel leading into the marina as shown on Chart GB-1A. From this position head straight in between the well-marked jetties and follow the channel around toward the fuel dock and slips. You'll pass the fuel dock and *Customs* office on your starboard side and you can take a slip on the eastern side of the marina or if you need to clear *Customs* and *Immigration* you may tie up along the seawall on the western side of the marina, please be sure to check with *Old Bahama Bay Marina* first on VHF ch. 16. Please note that as construction continues here these directions may change somewhat.

You can anchor temporarily in settled weather in *Cross Bay* but a wind shift could put you on the beach as it has done many other boats in the past. The seabed in *Cross Bay* has a lot of small rocks and coral heads scattered about and is notoriously poor holding though there are sand spots that will grab well. A better anchorage, though quite current ridden and almost as poor as far as holding goes, lies north

Grand Bahama
Sandy Cay to
Indian Cay,
Indian Cay Channel
Chart GB-1
Soundings in feet at MLW

The Little Bahama Bank

Caution: sandbores and many intricate, shallow channels lie just north of Sandy Cay

Sandy Cay

Barracuda Shoal
Fl W ev 4 sec

26° 46.37' N
78° 57.15' W

To Mangrove Cay
067°, 22 nm

26° 45.65' N
78° 58.30' W

Wood Cay

26° 44.75' N
78° 59.20' W
piling (missing)

1 fathom

47

32

10 fathoms (PA)

22

breaks

Caution: All pilings were missing in 2008

piling

Fl W ev 6 sec, 40', 8M
Indian Cay Rock

piling

26° 42.80' N
79° 00.60' W

Indian Cay

Grand Bahama
West End,
Marina Entrance
Chart GB-1A
Soundings in feet at MLW

Indian Cay
dries
dries

26° 42.50' N

strong current

poor holding

Fl G 3

19

13

Fl R 11

26° 42.23' N
79° 00.15' W

West End Point

fuel

Customs

marina

26° 42.00' N

poor holding

Cross Bay

Grand Bahama

and northeast of the northern jetty lining the entrance to the marina. You can tuck in as far as your draft allows but be prepared to ride to the current and not necessarily the wind. If a frontal passage threatens, by all means, get a slip in the marina! If you'd like a ride into Freeport, there is a daily shuttle bus to Freeport from the marina that leaves at 0900 and returns at 1530; the cost is $5.

What You Will Find Ashore

Old Bahama Bay Marina has diesel, fuel, rooms for rent, water, showers, telephones, laundry, internet access, two restaurants (one for fine dining and one for casual), a boutique and ship's store with a few charts and other sundry goods (no real marine hardware or supplies as of this writing), a car rental service in the lobby, a *Tiki Hut* snack shack on the beach, and a wonderful heated pool with a waterfall for guests of the hotel and marina.

If your vessel draws less than 3½', you can, with the help of the tide, work your way around the eastern shore of West End Point towards the settlement of West End. From the anchorage north of *OBB*, work your way around the north side of the marked piling and follow the poorly defined and even poorer marked *Goodwill Channel* (some of the local fishermen tell me that the channel will be marked soon, but if it's like everything else in the islands it will take it's own sweet time to come about). When you take the piling to starboard, basically you'll be paralleling the shore through here for a little over two miles until you come to the *Harbour Hotel Marina and Restaurant*. Because of the depth of the entrance channel, the marina is primarily used by local fishing boats. The marina has a Laundromat on premises (there's also one in town). The marina is a *Texaco Star Port*, and the *Harbour Hotel* is one of the best eating spots in West End (breakfast, lunch, and dinner) with a free glass of wine with each dinner.

In West End itself you can find groceries at *Angler's*, *J&M Grocery*, *Neely's*, and at the *Seaside Bakery*. For dining a must stop is *Yvonne's Café* for true Bahamian fare, or you can visit *Ralph's Restaurant and Bar*, *The Star Restaurant and Pub*, or *Bayside Dairy and Snacks*. Despite West End's history of liquor smuggling, today the only liquor stores are *Butler and Sands* and the *T&T Liquor Store*. There is a government clinic downtown and a *Batelco* office next to the Police station. If you need propane you can make arrangements through *Old Bahama Bay Marina* to have your tanks taken to Freeport and filled. If you need a car rental or taxi, call *Seaside Bakery*.

West End has a colorful and rich history as a base for smugglers during the rum running years of Prohibition. During the years from 1920-1934, huge tin warehouses lined the shoreline and housed nothing but liquor. Bootleggers would stop here, either by boat or plane, load their wares, and then set off across the Gulf Stream to America and eager, waiting hands full of money. But it was not an easy life; there were many shootouts with the U. S. Coast Guard and many bootleggers lost their lives. For those that survived, the rewards were rich indeed. West End was a boomtown with all the trappings. Bars, money strewn about carelessly, easy party girls from Nassau, and when it was all over, the Bay Street Boys took their profits back to Nassau and left West End little more than a ghost town.

After the Prohibition years, West End's history is a tale of feast and famine periods. A huge crawfish canning factory built during WWII gave a boost to the local economy until the owner was suspected of collaborating with the Nazis. Then in the late 1940's, a developer attempted to make West End a resort phenomenon, but that plan failed when the pound was devalued and the operation went bankrupt. In 1958, the *Jack Tar Village Resort* opened and was quite a success before it folded in the late 1980s. Today *Old Bahama Bay* is trying again to bring a cash flow into the West End area and so far they are doing that just fine. Their plans are coming together on time and the future looks bright for West End, that's why everybody's walking around with sunglasses on.

For those cruisers bound for Abaco via Indian Cay Channel or by passing north of Sandy Cay, we will study those routes in the section entitled *The Northern Abacos; Routes from West End, Grand Bahama*.

There are several small towns between West End and Freeport and since these are primarily visited by road, we will discuss them in the section entitled *Grand Bahama by Car* section.

Freeport/Lucaya

Freeport Harbour - 1 nm SSW of jetties:
26° 30.10' N, 78° 47.05' W

We will start our tour of the southern shore of Grand Bahama at *Freeport Harbour*. Freeport is the second most popular tourist destination in The Bahamas, second only to Nassau but with a faster pace and a more cosmopolitan atmosphere than the old-world sophistication of The Bahamas' capital city. Freeport and Lucaya, although separate, are often referred to as one entity, as in Freeport/Lucaya, and many people will tell you that they visited Freeport when it is most likely that they actually spent most of their time in Lucaya. It's a difficult situation and I often have trouble separating the two. Both were at one time Freeport, then the community subsequently split with Lucaya becoming primarily tourism oriented. Freeport has been called by other names as well over the years; *Magic City*, for the way it was carved out of the bush in 1955 and grew to be a metropolis in one decade. Freeport has also been labeled the *Singapore of the Atlantic* for its vibrant, free-market, industrialized economy. And finally, it has also been known as the *Queen of Clean*, known for its impeccable streets.

Freeport owes its existence to Wallace Groves; you might remember him from Little Whale Cay in the Berry Islands. Groves had a dream of a city that would be an industrial and commercial giant. That dream became reality on August 4, 1955, with the signing of the *Hawksbill Creek Agreement*. That agreement gave the newly formed *Grand Bahama Port Authority* full autonomy over a large region of what was formerly Crown land with streets and bridges becoming *Port Authority* property. Under the agreement there can be no real estate or personal property taxes at least until 2015, in addition to the absence of income, sales, capital gains and death duties that the entire country enjoys. Moreover, the Port Authority, which governs the zone, can issue licenses that allow the license holder to import one car and the materials and furnishings for one house, duty-free.

Many tend to joke that the date of this agreement made Freeport a Leo, the king of the beasts. The city planners soon realized that all work and no play might not be as beneficial to their coffers as a fat slice of the tourism pie would be. With that in mind, they struck a deal for a pair of first-class casinos and Lucaya was

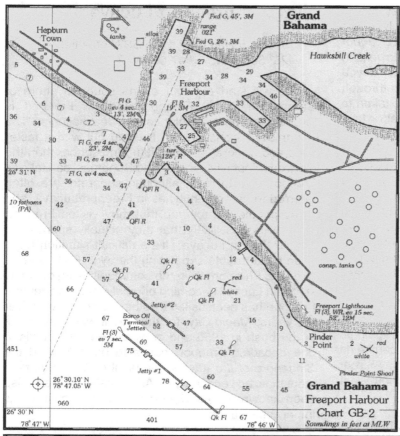

born. That which was little more than bush less than a half-century ago, today Freeport/Lucaya is a virtual fantasy vacationland.

Today, Freeport is a significant economic force in The Bahamas. Freeport Harbour has a unique and valuable position as it straddles the major trade routes between the Eastern and Gulf coasts of the United States, as well as Mexico, Panama, the Caribbean, South America and the trade lanes to Europe, the Middle East, Asia, and Australia. A recent multi-million dollar harbor project has made Freeport one of the world's foremost transshipment terminals. *Hutchison Port Holdings*, a subsidiary of *Hutchison Whampoa* of Hong Kong and the world's largest port operator, purchased 50% of the *Freeport Harbour Company* and began a $130+ million construction project. Recently completed, the port now has the ability to handle the largest container ships afloat which will make Freeport the transshipment hub of the Western Hemisphere. *HPH*

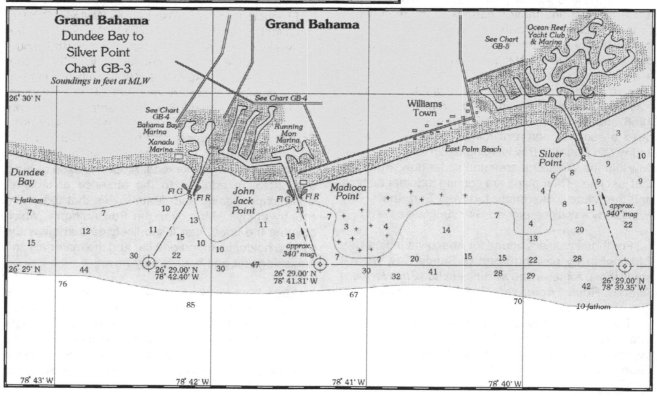

combined 2,500 acres of airport land, nearby industrial acreage, and 1,630 acres of harbor (including 56 acres of container port), into a 5,000-acre complex that includes a comprehensive air/sea business park, with new passenger terminals/facilities at the airport and secure storage areas at the container port. In addition, *HPH* plans a $150 million development of 1,600 four-star resort rooms in a huge complex comprising 50 acres of hotels (connected by walkways and plazas), waterfalls, fountains, landscaping, and exquisite beachfront.

Navigational Information

As you can see, Freeport Harbour, Chart GB-2, is a busy commercial port (and it will just get busier) with no yacht facilities save *Bradford Yacht and Ship* a short distance up Hawksbill Creek. A waypoint at 26° 30.10' N, 78° 47.05' W, will place you approximately one nautical mile southwest of the entrance channel to Freeport Harbour. From this position take up a course of approximately 021° magnetic and you will soon see the lighted (G) range inside the harbor. You can clear *Customs* and *Immigration* at Freeport Harbour, but you must call *Harbour Control* first on VHF ch.16 for berthing directions.

Probably the only reason a recreational yacht would have for entering Freeport Harbour would be to make its way to *Bradford Yacht and Ship*. If you work your way up dredged Hawksbill Creek you will quickly come to *Bradford Yacht and Ship*, the only full service yard on Grand Bahama. *Bradford* services a variety of different sized vessels and has a 150-ton travel lift, a prop shop, a full machine shop as well as fiberglass, carpentry, fiberglass, welding/fabricating, and paint shops with specialists in each one. You can reach *Bradford Yacht and Ship* by VHF on ch. 16, or by phone at 242-352-7711 or by fax at 242-352-7695.

There are several marinas where boaters can stay in the Freeport/Lucaya area and we will discuss them as we would approach them, from west to east.

Xanadu Channel to Silver Cove

Xanadu Channel - ½ nm SW of entrance:
26° 29.00' N, 78° 42.40' W

Madioca Point - ½ nm SE of entrance channel:
26° 29.00' N, 78° 41.31' W

Along the southern shore of Grand Bahama is a long and shallow barrier reef. Though there are quite a few shallow spots between *Xanadu Channel* and *Bell Channel* (mostly close in to shore), the really shallow areas begin west of *Bell Channel* so use extreme caution and keep a good lookout. It would be prudent to stay one mile off along this shoreline.

Navigational Information

Beginning just a few miles east of *Freeport Harbour* are several channels leading to marinas and private developments. The first of these is *Xanadu Channel* named after the famed *Xanadu Hotel*. As shown on Chart GB-3, a waypoint at 26° 29.00' N, 78° 42.40' W will place you approximately ½ mile southwest of the entrance to the channel between two marked jetties. The flashing red and green lights may not work, so bear that in mind if attempting to enter at night. From this position head towards the channel mouth between the jetties trying to remain parallel to the lay of the channel. If you stray a bit don't fret, it's fairly deep on either side of the channel with no hazards. Once inside the channel continue between the jetties as shown on Chart GB-4 and the marina and hotel will open up to your port side very soon.

What You Will Find Ashore

Xanadu Marina boasts 77 slips and can accommodate vessels up to 100' in length with 8' drafts. They offer fuel, ice, water, showers, cable TV, full electric and telephone hookups, a marine store and tackle shop (*Paradise Marine Supplies*), a pharmacy, and a restaurant. Room service is available to boats and a liquor store is nearby. The dive shop, *Xanadu Undersea Adventures,* has been taking divers to the most impressive and beautiful reefs of Grand Bahama for the past 6 years. Their professional and multi-lingual staff has more than 20 years of experience guiding and teaching all levels of divers.

If you continue past *Xanadu Marina*, and take a turn to port at the next cove, you will come to the small but friendly, *Bahama Bay Marina*. This marina offers about twenty slips with a least depth of 7' and has full electric hookups but little else except friendliness and a quiet place to tie up.

Navigational Information

Less than a mile to the east of the *Xanadu Channel* is the channel leading into *Sunrise Marina*. As shown on Chart GB-3, a waypoint at 26° 29.00' N, 78° 41.31' W will place you approximately ½ mile

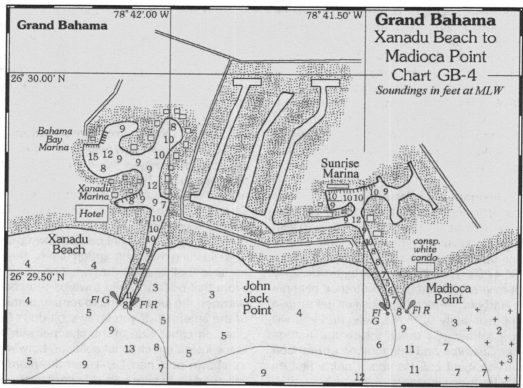

Grand Bahama
Xanadu Beach to
Madioca Point
Chart GB-4
Soundings in feet at MLW

Grand Bahama

78° 42'.00 W
78° 41.50' W
26° 30.00' N

Bahama Bay Marina

Sunrise Marina

Xanadu Marina

Hotel

Xanadu Beach

consp. white condo.

26° 29.50' N

Fl G   Fl R

John Jack Point

Fl G   Fl R

Madioca Point

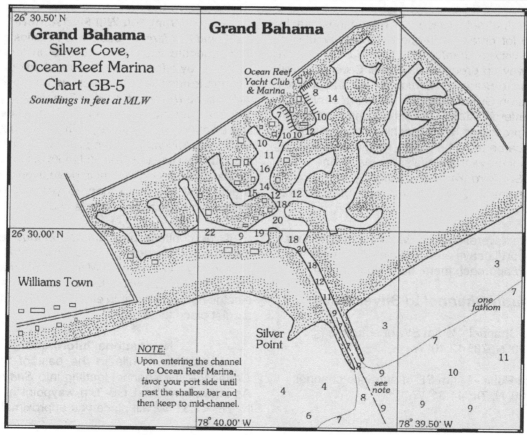

26° 30.50' N

Grand Bahama
Silver Cove,
Ocean Reef Marina
Chart GB-5
Soundings in feet at MLW

Grand Bahama

Ocean Reef Yacht Club & Marina

26° 30.00' N

Williams Town

NOTE:
Upon entering the channel
to Ocean Reef Marina,
favor your port side until
past the shallow bar and
then keep to mid-channel.

Silver Point

one fathom

see note

78° 40.00' W
78° 39.50' W

southeast of the jetties at the entrance to the channel. From this position take up a course of approximately 340° to enter the channel mouth between the two jetties. The course here is not as important as staying parallel to the lay of the channel inside the jetties as shown on the blowup on Chart GB-4. After you enter the channel you'll pass over a shallow spot with a depth of 5' at MLW so if you draw more, plan on using the tide to enter. The flashing red and green lights on the jetties may or may not be working so bear that in mind if you are attempting to enter at night. Once inside and past the shallow spot, forge ahead past the canal that works off to the west and the marina will open up in front of you. Also here is Knowles Marine, a great haul-out yard.

Silver Cove

Silver Cove - ¾ nm SE of entrance channel:
26° 29.00' N, 78° 39.35' W

Silver Cove is the name of the man-made canal network that lies approximately 2 miles east of *Xanadu Channel* and approximately 1½ miles west of *Bell Channel*. Silver Cove is home to the *Ocean Reef Yacht Club and Marina* as well as a large private development.

Navigational Information

A waypoint at 26° 29.00' N, 78° 39.35' W will place you approximately ¾ nautical miles southeast of Silver Point and the jetties as shown on Chart GB-3. Steer approximately 340° to enter the channel. The course here is not as important as staying parallel to the lay of the channel inside the jetties as shown on the blowup on Chart GB-5. The shallower water lies to the west of the channel and to a minor degree just south and east of the eastern jetty tip as shown on the chart. As you enter the jetties keep to your port side a bit, as there is a small bar along the eastern jetty just inside the channel. You will have 7' at MLW around this bar and once past the end of the jetties the canal becomes very deep, 18'-20' in most places. To find the *Ocean Reef Yacht Club and Marina* keep in the center channel as it winds around past two curves. The marina and office will open up on your left; you can't miss it. There's even a floating dinghy dock for your convenience. If you are having any problems finding your way inside or to the marina, contact *Ocean Reef Marina* on VHF ch. 16. The *Ocean Reef Yacht Club* has 52 slips and can accommodate vessels to 80' with a 6' draft though some slips are a bit deeper. They have the usual electricity, water and ice, as well as a bait and tackle shop.

Bell Channel

Bell Channel - 1 nm SE of entrance channel:
26° 29.95' N, 78° 37.70' W

Bell Channel and Bell Channel Bay are by far the most popular stop on Grand Bahama for boaters of all types. Two excellent marinas with full amenities, excellent shopping, and even anchoring room can be found right here.

Navigational Information

A waypoint at 26° 29.95' N, 78° 37.30' W will place you approximately ¾ mile southeast of the jetties and the entrance to *Bell Channel* and just a bit northeast of the *Bell Channel Sea Buoy* (Fl W ev 2 sec). As shown on Chart GB-6, if approaching from offshore keep a good lookout for the unmarked buoys to the west of this waypoint; they are for cruise ship use and constitute a hazard to the small boater. At night a flashing amber light marks their field but the individual buoys (7) are not lit. From this waypoint take up a course of approximately 340° towards the entrance between two flashing red and green markers and the lit jetties. Try not to stray to the east here as there is a shallow reef in that direction as shown on the chart. Watch out for small boat traffic and the ever-present tourist parasailing above. If you need a pilot, *Lucayan Marina Village* offers one at no charge; call them on VHF ch. 16.

What You Will Find Ashore

Once inside *Bell Channel Bay* (as shown on Chart GB-7), if you turn to port you will find the spacious and upscale *Port Lucaya Marina*, a first class marina and a Port of Entry. The staff here pampers the visiting boater as well as those yachts that are left here on a long-term basis. This is a great spot to leave your boat if you need to fly back home for whatever reason. Capt. Chester and his crew will perform weekly or daily bilge checks, wash-downs, engine starting, as well as security patrols. The marina boasts 160 slips, twenty of which can handle boats of over 100' in length (to a maximum of 175'). The docks have first rate power, phone, and satellite TV hookups while the fuel dock sells gas and triple filtered diesel with a high-speed fuel pump (open from 0700-0000). A pump-out facility is also available.

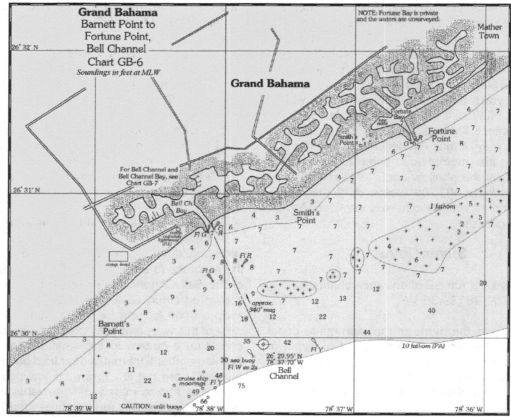

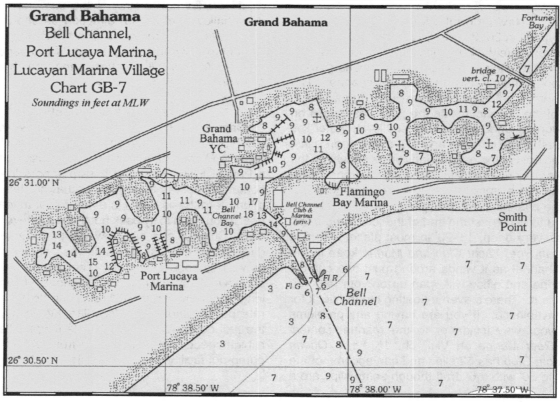

The marina offers courtesy transportation to the local grocery store and airport. Their concierge service can help you find a reliable doctor or mechanic, and even assist you in arranging air transportation. The newest amenity at Port Lucaya is their *Yacht Club* with its comfortable outdoor dining terrace. Visiting yachtsmen are given a complimentary membership in the *Yacht Club* while staying at the marina which allows them to dine on excellent cooked to order seafood dishes and sample their extensive wine list and assorted whiskies at the *Yacht Club* bar. The *Yacht Club* is open from 5:00pm to 1:00am nightly and you might wish to catch a movie at their *Mini-Cinema* or simply enjoy the *Piano Bar*. The marina itself sits across the street from a casino and fronts the *Port Lucayan Marketplace* where you can browse some 85-odd shops including restaurants, a straw market, water-sports rental facilities, a dive shop, or stay at the *Port Lucayan Resort Hotel*. If all this shopping and nightlife tires you, just walk across the street and enjoy the beach. Ask at the marina office for their evening and weekend cultural activities for children as well as adults. *Port Lucaya Marina* will hold your mail for your arrival; please address it to you, on your boat, c/o *Port Lucaya Marina*, PO Box F-43233, Freeport, Grand Bahama, Bahamas.

If, upon entering *Bell Channel*, you keep to starboard, you will immediately come to another first class marina, the *Grand Bahama YC and Lucayan Marina Village* complex, a private residential community with a private marina that offers the best in transient dockage and service. *Lucayan Marina Village*, newly rebuilt in 1995, is an official Port of Entry and can accommodate vessels up to 150'. The marina staff can find you a mechanic or a fishing guide if you so desire. The docks have first rate power, phone, and satellite TV hookups, and the fuel dock will fill you up with the highest quality diesel or gasoline. The *Pelican Bay Hotel* offers first-class accommodations with a complimentary water taxi service to the *Port Lucaya Marketplace*. For something a little more casual, try the *Pool Bar* (yes, right by the pool!) for breakfast, lunch, or dinner, and check out their afternoon munchie specials. The marina will also hold your mail for your arrival; address it to you, aboard your vessel, c/o *Lucayan Marina Village*, PO Box F-42654, Freeport, Grand Bahama, Bahamas. If you need propane you can leave you tank with the guard by the gate and get it back the next day.

If you wish to anchor here, work your way into some of the coves to the east of the marinas and pick a spot. Now that you're all secure in your berth or at anchor, let's see what's available to see and do in Lucaya. There is so much to experience in the Freeport/Lucaya area that I will only touch upon a few of the more popular sites, for a complete listing of activities, pick up any of the free booklets or small newspapers at any marina, hotel, or store in the area.

Probably the number one stop in Lucaya is the *International Bazaar* and probably the most remembered landmark is the huge oriental arch at its entrance. The *International Bazaar* is one of the oldest shopping areas in Freeport, and it truly lives up to its name. The 10 acre complex has over 80 stores that are built in the architectural style of the countries they represent. Upon entering the *Bazaar* you will notice that it has been divided into sections each representing different parts of the world such as the Mideast section, French section, Oriental section, Scandinavian and the South American section. In each of the international sections you will find shopping and dining from that region of the world.

Another one of the most popular stops is the *Garden of the Groves*, regarded as one of the most beautiful retreats in the Caribbean, opened in 1973. It is named for the one-time owners, Mr. and Mrs. Wallace Groves. In 1996, the *Garden* was taken over by Dr. Bern Levine, owner of Miami's *Parrot Jungle*. Levine implemented a five-year plan that is transforming the *Garden of the Groves* into a full-theme animal park with an amphitheater for special events, a playground for kids, and a picnic area. Levine has already added a children's petting zoo with colorful macaws and cockatoos, a potbellied pig, and pygmy goats. The retreat also has several footpaths that wind their way past cascading waterfalls, several duck-ponds, the aptly named Fern Gully, and majestic statues all set amid ornamental and native Bahamian flora.

The 100-acre *Rand Nature Center* lies just outside downtown Freeport, and is a marvelous stop for nature-minded folks. The *Rand Nature Center* is a protected Park under the jurisdiction of The Bahamas National Trust and is home to West Indian flamingos, the same kind that inhabit much wilder Inagua in the southern Bahamas. Here you can walk a beautiful 2000' long nature trail past the Flamingo Pond and its lush tropical setting complete with lily pads, reeds,

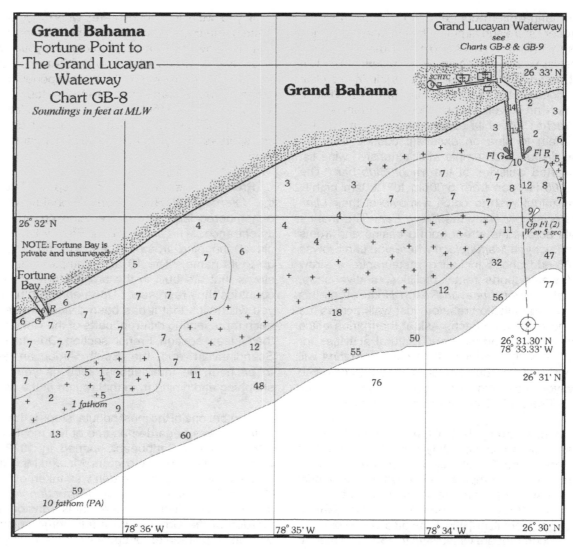

Grand Bahama
Fortune Point to
The Grand Lucayan
Waterway
Chart GB-8
Soundings in feet at MLW

Grand Bahama

Grand Lucayan Waterway
see
Charts GB-8 & GB-9

26° 33' N

SCHYC

Fl G   Fl R

26° 32' N

NOTE: Fortune Bay is
private and unsurveyed.

Fortune
Bay

Gp Fl (2)
W ev 5 sec

26° 31.30' N
78° 33.33' W

26° 31' N

1 fathom

59
10 fathom (PA)

78° 36' W   78° 35' W   78° 34' W   26° 30' N

Port Lucaya Marketplace

Photo Courtesy of Nicola Leslie

wild native birds, and local and imported flora (130 local types including 20 types of wild orchids). There is also a replica of an ancient Lucayan village and a museum that documents Grand Bahama's history. The guided tours are a must. You'll learn a ton of information about the local flora and fauna, such as how certain plants are used in bush medicine and the strange courting rituals of the wild birds you'll see.

The Hydroflora Gardens are a unique showcase of flora and fauna with the centerpiece being the *Timothy Gibson Musical Cave*. The cave is actually a sunken garden named after the author of the Bahamian national anthem and even has a musical backdrop courtesy of hidden speakers. In the center of the cave is a fish pond with a huge turtle shell. A sign informs the reader that the former inhabitant of the shell traveled some 4,000 miles before being found in The Bahamas at Sandy Cay in 1974. The previous owner had been originally tagged in the Galapagos in 1971, and is thought to have traveled through the Panama Canal.

Those who love the sea will probably also want to check out *UNEXSO*, the *Underwater Explorer Society*, at Port Lucaya. *UNEXSO* has been described by *Skin Diver* magazine as the most sophisticated and best equipped diving facility in The Bahamas. Here is the opportunity for a once in a lifetime experience of swimming with dolphins. The *UNEXSO Dolphin Experience* is a place where visitors can swim with wild dolphins that are free to come and go as they please. The *Experience* was designed to study how dolphins and humans interact. Due to its immense popularity, it is necessary to make reservations at least several weeks ahead of time.

Many folks come to Grand Bahama for the casino action. As of this writing Grand Bahama has only one casino, the elegant *Bahamas Princess Casino*. Here you'll find non-stop action including slots, roulette, craps, baccarat, blackjack, spacious lounges, and cabaret shows. The *Lucayan Beach Resort* is scheduled to premier early in 2000 with its renovated hotel and casino.

As I mentioned before, Grand Bahama has been noted for its golf courses. Two fine courses await you on the grounds of The Bahamas Princess: Dick Wilson's "Emerald" and Joe Lee's "Ruby" championship courses will excite you. There's also the demanding *Lucaya Golf & Country Club* championship course nearby and the *Fortune Hills Golf & Country Club*. When the *Lucayan Beach Resort* reopens, the golf course that was formerly known as the *Bahama Reef* will reopen with it. The course has been redesigned by Arnold Palmer.

The world's first semi-submersible is now available in Freeport – "a submarine experience at a fraction of the price" is how it's advertised. This unique craft allows you to relax in an air-conditioned viewing area suspended beneath the vessel, then submerge 5' below the surface where you can stay dry and gaze at colorful coral reefs teaming with marine life that a diver hand feeds.

If you need groceries, you'll find them at *Winn Dixie*, *Food World*, *Grand Union* and at the *World Food Market*. For hardware try *Lucayan Hardware* next to *Winn Dixie* or *World of Products* on the Queen's Highway. If you need propane, consult with your dockmaster, or take your tank to *Freeport Oil* on the Queen's Highway near the harbour.

The Grand Lucayan Waterway

Dover Sound - 1½ nm NW of entrance:
26° 38.40' N, 78° 39.70' W
GLWW - ¾ SSE of jetties at S entrance:
26° 31.30' N, 78° 33.33' W

Just to the east of *Bell Channel* lies the entrance to the *Fortune Cove* private canal complex. There are no facilities here, only homes and private docks. The entrance is gained by paralleling the shore inside the reef. From *Bell Channel* simply parallel the shore outside of the one fathom line until you can line up the entrance *to Fortune Bay*. You will have 7' through here at MLW but keep a sharp eye out.

A little less than three miles east *of Fortune Cove* lies the *Grand Lucayan Waterway*, a manmade canal that effectively splits Grand Bahama in two and offers some of the best residential opportunities on the island; you will see some of the finest homes on Grand Bahama lining these banks. For the most part, the entire system is concrete walled with many small coves leading off the main canal.

Navigational Information
If you need shelter the *Grand Lucayan Waterway* offers excellent protection from seas for vessels with drafts of over 7', but of course, if you draw that much you can only enter the waterway from the south. As shown on Chart GB-8, a waypoint at 26° 31.30' N, 78° 33.33' W will place you approximately one mile south of the entrance to the *GLWW* between two lit jetties. From the waypoint head north, keeping the sea buoy to starboard, and enter between the jetties to continue up the canal in good water

If you are seeking shelter a nice cove lies on the north side of the first canal that branches off to port (to the west as shown on Chart GB-9) as you head northward. Although the bottom was dredged when this area was built decades ago, the holding is very good in a sand/mud bottom and almost every little cove along the waterway offers a good anchorage in even the worst frontal passage. If you plan to anchor off the *Grand Lucayan Waterway*, remember;

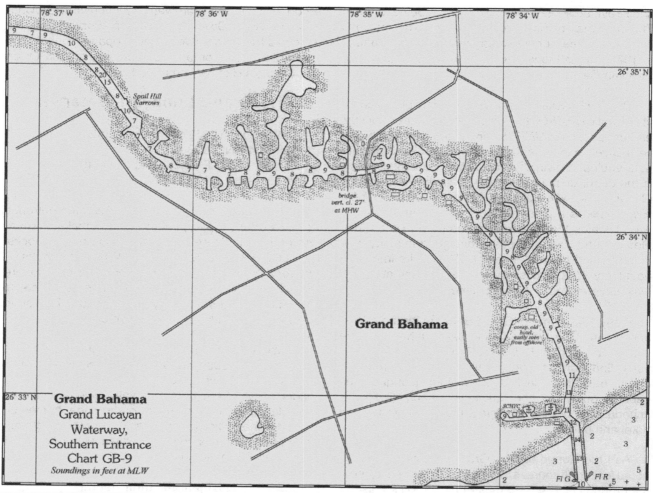

Grand Bahama

Grand Bahama
Grand Lucayan
Waterway,
Southern Entrance
Chart GB-9
Soundings in feet at MLW

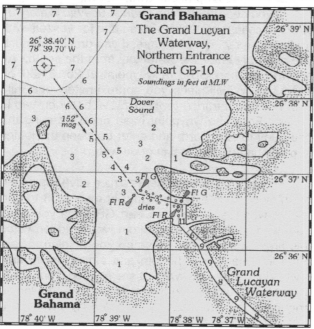

Grand Bahama
The Grand Lucyan
Waterway,
Northern Entrance
Chart GB-10
Soundings in feet at MLW

since the lots all are privately owned, never tie up to someone's dock without permission.

A few miles up the waterway is the *Casuarina Bridge*, a fixed bridge with a 27' vertical clearance at high water. This is the controlling height for the waterway and bars sailboats and tall powerboats from utilizing the shortcut through to the *Little Bahama Bank*.

If you're approaching the *Grand Lucayan Waterway* from the north, from Mangrove Cay, you must first clear the point of a sandbank that lies south/southwest of Mangrove Cay and is marked by a lit, though not working, piling and light (FL W). A heading of 200º from Mangrove Cay for ten miles will take you to this position. From here, head to a waypoint at 26º 38.40' N, 78º 39.70' W, which sits in 7' of water in *Dover Sound* as shown on Chart GB-10. From this point take up an approximate course of 152º to the first set of lit markers that will lead you in to the *Grand Lucayan Waterway* proper via a dredged channel. The water shallows to 3' here at MLW and the tide must be used if you draw more (note that the tide here is 2 hours behind the tide at Freeport or Lucaya). Once between the two markers, split the rest of the pilings and you will come to a lit pair at the end of the channel at the entrance to the GLWW. Turn to starboard keeping the two single pilings to starboard. The depths in the Waterway itself run from 6'-12' and there is a bit of current that you will really notice at the *Casuarina Bridge* and at the conspicuous *Spoil Bank Narrows* where the waterway narrows in width.

Peterson Cay

Peterson Cay – ½ nm SE of:
26° 32.60' N, 78° 30.65' W

Tiny Peterson Cay lies some two miles east of the southern entrance to the *Grand Lucayan Waterway*. The cay is protected by *The Bahamas National Trust* and the anchorage here should be considered a day anchorage only, or a night anchorage if one can expect only settled weather (if the wind should pipe up and/or shift during the night, you may not be able to find your way out).

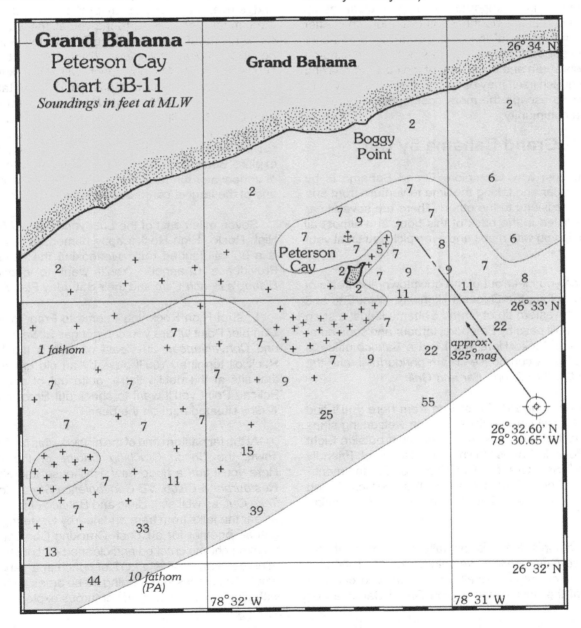

Grand Bahama
Peterson Cay
Chart GB-11
Soundings in feet at MLW

Grand Bahama

Peterson Cay is rarely used by cruisers, it is however, very popular with the local boating crowd as well as some commercial operations that like to stop and serve their customers lunch on the small beach. Be prepared to share the cay during daylight hours, especially on weekends and holidays.

Navigational Information

As shown on Chart GB-11, a waypoint at 26° 32.60' N, 78° 30.65' W, will place you approximately ½ mile southeast of the entrance to the anchorage in the lee of Peterson Cay. From this position take up a course of approximately 325°. The course is not that important, what is important is that you clear the tip of the reef that lies northeast off Peterson Cay. After you round the tip of the reef, turn to port to anchor where your draft allows. There's good snorkeling on the reefs south and southwest of the cay and relaxing on the beach itself may be all you really need if you're seeking to escape the more cosmopolitan Freeport/Lucaya community.

Grand Bahama by Car

The best way to explore Grand Bahama is by renting a car and taking the time to venture from one end of the island to the other. There are several car rentals listed in the back of this book and almost all will equip you with maps and even pick you up at your marina.

Once you clear out of the downtown and traffic of Freeport along the Queen's Highway, West End and the northwestern tip of Grand Bahama is just a short jaunt. You'll pass by Freeport Harbour and soon enter Eight Mile Rock. Here you'll find a *Batelco* office, a *Winn Dixie*, a combo ice cream parlour/deli, and the *Above the Rim Sports Bar and Grill*.

Heading towards West End from here you'll find several small communities, all with welcoming signs that boast of each town's virtues. Just outside Eight Mile Rock is Jones Town, "The Home of Friendly People," Sea Grape, "The Home of Contentment," Holmes Rock, "The Home of Togetherness," and Deadman's Reef, "The Home of the Enchanting Reef."

Deadman's Reef is actually the home of the *Paradise Cove Resort*, well hidden off the road and only marked by one small sign. Here you can find some of the best snorkeling on Grand Bahama just

50 yards offshore, while 200 yards inland is the Duck Pond where you'll see a variety of native bird life such as herons, wild ducks, and egrets.

Just before you reach West End, "The Home of Hospitality," you'll pass through Bootle Bay where you can grab a bite to eat at *Bernie's Place,* or you can venture further to Smith's Point and eat at *Mama Flo's.* We've already discussed what is in store for you in West End, so now let's turn our attention to the road east of Lucaya.

Heading east from Lucaya you'll first cross the bridge over the *Grand Lucayan Waterway*, and from then on tall pines will surround you all the way to the eastern end of the island. Your first stop will likely be at the *Lucayan National Park* whose 40 acres showcases a 1,000 foot beach with a backdrop of high sand dunes. A truly fine adventure is to take the tour of the *Lucayan National Park* where you set off from Gold Rock Creek in kayaks through a canopy of mangrove roots to a wooden boardwalk. Here you'll set off on foot and discover a beautiful beach and explore Ben's Cave. The cave has a vast network of underwater tunnel systems that lead to the ocean, one of the largest charted systems in the world.

Seven miles east of the *Lucayan National Park* is High Rock. High Rock's aptly named highest point is a 30' tall jagged rock overlooking the Northwest Providence Channel. You'll want to check out *Bishop's Beach Club* and their Saturday Fish Fry.

East of High Rock you'll come to Free Town and Gambier Point where you can get gas at *Smith's Gas and Convenience*. Just east of here is the Riding Rock oil terminal. You'll pass by an old cruise ship that sits at the docks there, quite out of place. At Pelican Point you'll want to check out *Breezer's Bar & Grill* situated right on the beach.

At the far eastern end of the highway lies McClean's Town, the *Conch Cracking Capital of the World.* Here you'll find a huge new fish house, the *Sunrise Restaurant & Disco, VB Convenience Store, Zelma's Take Out*, as well as a clinic and *Batelco* office. Once a year the folks from here and nearby Sweetings Cay gather together for a Conch Cracking Contest. The reigning champ cracked and cleaned 42 conch in two minutes. Now that is a LOT of conch in a very short time! The creeks surrounding these areas are dotted with blue holes awaiting adventurous explorers.

Deep Water Cay and the *Deep Water Cay Club* lie just west of McClean's Town and are one of the premier bonefishing destinations on Grand Bahama, with access to over 250 square miles of bonefishing flats. The club was established in 1958 by Gilbert Drake, a gentleman sportsman and avid fisherman, who created this sanctuary for folks that shared his passion for the elusive bonefish. Club tradition has everyone (up to 22 guests) dining together in celebration of the day's adventures and triumphs in an intimate and relaxed atmosphere. The club also has a marina with two slips that will accommodate boats with drafts of less than 5'. Call the club on VHF ch. 16 for the intricate entry instructions or a pilot. The club also has a website at http://www.deepwatercay.com.

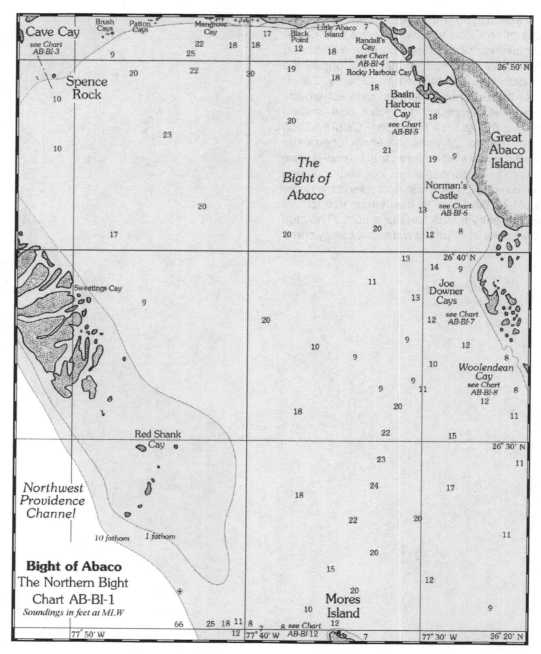

The Northern Bight
Chart AB-BI-1
Soundings in feet at MLW

The Bight of Abaco

Fuel: Mores Island
Propane: None
Haul-Out: None
Diesel Repairs: None
Outboard Repairs: None
Major Lights:
    Rock Point (Sandy Point): Fl W ev 6 sec
    Channel Cay (Mores Island): Fl W ev 2.5 sec

The Bight of Abaco is so rarely visited by cruising yachts and that's a shame. In good weather it's a fantastic cruising ground with several lee-shore anchorages and two cays that offer protection from the shifting winds of a frontal passage (even more safe havens if yours is a shallow draft vessel, say 3' or less).

The shorelines of the cays in the Bight tend to be a bit rocky, with less sandy beaches than on the Abaco cays that line the *Sea of Abaco* while tall pines grace the western shoreline of Great Abaco in so many places. To the west of Great Abaco and in close to her shoreline there are several areas of shallow water where bonefish abound and anchoring is impossible for all but the shallowest draft vessels. You'll see few other boats on your cruise through here, but some folks enjoy that, and the boats you do see are escaping the masses the same as you. You'll notice a never ending supply of local fishermen from Abaco out for a day's sport, and here and there a bonefishing boat silently poles along through the shallows in search of their elusive, skittish prey.

As you travel the western shore of Abaco you can still stay in touch by VHF with your friends at Green Turtle Cay, Manjack Cay, Powell Cay, Spanish Cay, Coopers Town, Treasure Cay, and sometimes even Marsh Harbour. You'll only be a few miles west of them although you're a long way away by boat.

Although many of the boats that cruise here enter the Bight from the south, we'll explore the *Bight of Abaco* from the north. As I've shown you in the first edition of this guide, I'm going to present you with a great route into the *Bight of Abaco* from the north for boats with drafts over 6'. So let's begin our *Bight of Abaco* cruise with West End Point and the "Northwest Passage" and work our way southward along the western shore of Great Abaco to Sandy Point. Here we'll turn our bow northward and visit Castaway Cay and Mores Island.

West End Point and The Northwest Passage

Northwest Passage - N waypoint:
26° 53.90' N, 77° 58.15' W

Northwest Passage - S waypoint:
26° 52.83' N, 77° 58.15' W

Whether northbound or southbound in the Bight, until now the biggest obstacle to a *Bight of Abaco* cruise has been negotiating the *West End Bar* just off West End Point at the western tip of Little Abaco Island. By the way, please do not confuse West End Point on Little Abaco with West End, Grand Bahama. Most skippers who contemplate a Bight of Abaco cruise are aware of the route around the tip of West End Point that only carries 3' at MLW. This has been a huge deterrent for many cruisers with a 6' draft.

There is no reason that a vessel of 6' (and with the help of the tide 6½' and more) cannot enjoy the *Bight of Abaco*. The passage around West End Point is no longer the controlling depth for a *Bight of Abaco* cruise, the shallows north of Spence Rock now hold that honor, but we will deal with that route in just a moment.

West End Bar is a long shallow area made up of rocks, corals, and sand that stretches west/southwest from West End Point. In dealing with the *West End Bar* some publications suggest passing the eight miles to the west of West End Point to avoid them while other publications suggest only 4½ miles to clear the same area. As I mentioned, there is a viable alternative to this madness, a sort of "Northwest Passage" if you will, that carries 6'-7' in most places at MLW with only a small spot that shows 5½'.

The amazing thing about this route is that it lies only ¾ mile west of West End Point and saves cruisers time and fuel if headed to the east from the *West End Bar* or if headed into the *Bight of Abaco* from Fox Town, Great Sale Cay, or points east and north. I am shocked that nobody has shown this passage before; I came by it quite by accident. I was sounding the route close-in around West End Point and I looked to the west and saw that the rocky brown bar eventually ended. I headed west in my 16' boat and found plenty of water. Before long *IV Play* had made this passage some thirty times as we ventured into the *Bight of Abaco* at will to explore and sound the areas. Now, nearly everybody shows it on their charts, and one guide writer calls it by the same name, uses the same waypoints, and gives no credit for its discovery or its discoverer...a lack of professional ethics if you ask me, but what do I know? I just find the routes and report them.

If approaching from Fox Town, Great Sale Cay, Mangrove Cay, or anywhere in the northern Abacos, head for a waypoint at 26° 53.90' N, 77° 58.15' W as shown on Chart AB-BI-2. This will put you in deep water just north of the *West End Bar*. From this position the "Northwest Passage" is a breeze if you have a GPS. Simply head dead south, straight down 77° 58.15' W, until you're in deeper water. This route takes 5½' at MLW and will take over 7' with a good high tide. Note that the tides here are 3-4 hours later than Nassau tides so plan accordingly, less or more according to wind and sea conditions. For instance, strong southerly winds will produce a longer ebb

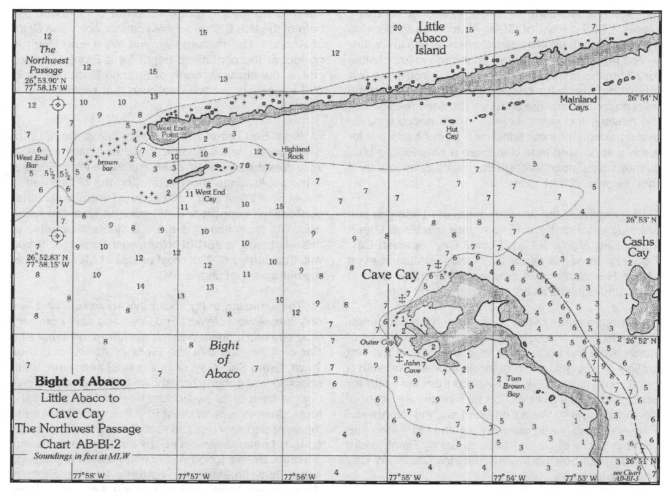

Bight of Abaco
Little Abaco to
Cave Cay
The Northwest Passage
Chart AB-BI-2
Soundings in feet at MLW

while strong northerly winds will produce a longer flood tide. As you run down your longitude you will enter depths of 7', then 6', then a small area where the depth is 5½' before getting progressively deeper. Once you're back in water of 7' and more you can head east towards Cave Cay or shelter from northerly winds behind Little Abaco Island. If you are leaving Cave Cay and heading north, make for a waypoint at 26° 52.83' N, 77° 58.15' W, as shown on Chart AB-BI-2. From here, run northward up your longitude, until over the bar where you can take up a course for Great Sale Cay, points north and east, or head along the shore of Little Abaco eastward to Fox Town.

The shallow passage close in around West End Point is still usable by boats with drafts of less than five feet. It is far easier to follow it from the south, northward around West End Point, than it is to pick it up heading southward. If heading northward from the Bight of Abaco pass between the West End Cays and Highland Rock in 7'-12' of water as shown on Chart AB-BI-2 and follow the deeper, darker water around to the west passing between Little Abaco and the West End Cays. Whether heading north or south through here, as you round West End Point about 50-100 yards off, you'll want to keep between the brown bar to port and the rocks to the east just off West End Point, and be careful…there's a lot of current here. Some local fishermen have buoyed this channel but don't expect the markers to be there and don't trust them if they are there. These buoys are made to guide small, shallow draft powerboats through here, not a 5' draft sail or power cruiser. Better to go ¾ mile to the west and use the "Northwest Passage."

Skippers seeking shelter from northerly winds can duck in behind Little Abaco Island wherever their draft allows, but be prepared to move when the wind moves into the east.

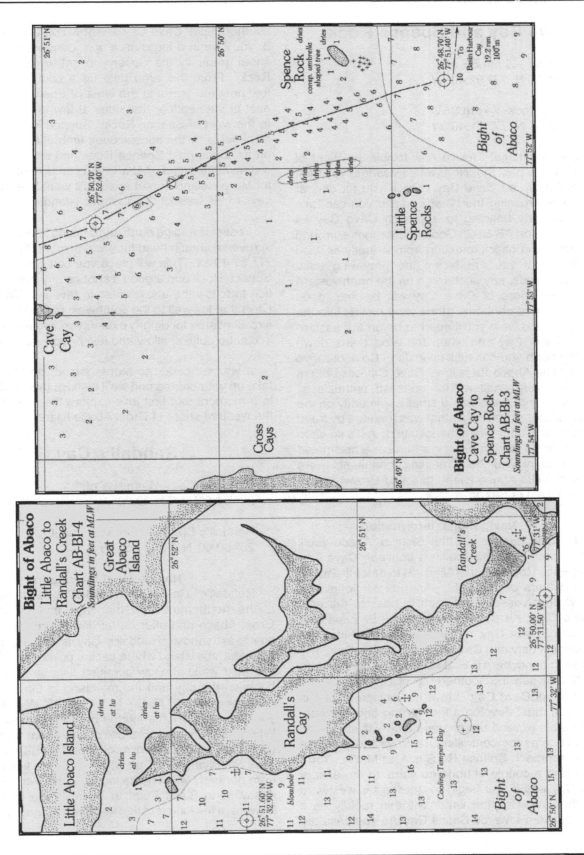

Bight of Abaco
Cave Cay to
Spence Rock
Chart AB-BI-3
Soundings in feet at MLW

Bight of Abaco
Little Abaco to
Randall's Creek
Chart AB-BI-4
Soundings in feet at MLW

Cave Cay and Spence Rock

Cave Cay - ½ nm SE of:
26° 50.70' N, 77° 52.40' W

Spence Rock - ½ nm SSW of:
26° 48.70' N, 77° 51.40' W

Congratulations! You're now inside the Bight of Abaco! Once past the "Northwest Passage" your first stop will likely be Cave Cay. Once you hit deeper water after crossing the *West End Bar* you can take up an easterly heading to approach Cave Cay as shown on Chart AB-BI-2. Good anchorages surround this island and offer protection from virtually all wind directions. If you are facing the prevailing east/southeast winds, any anchorage on the northwestern or western shore of Cave Cay will be fine, good holding in sand abounds. If the wind moves into the southwest and west you'll need to be on the eastern side of Cave Cay and when the wind bears down from the north you can tuck up in John Cove or move behind Little Abaco for a lee. Cave Cay also offers some excellent shallows for bonefish enthusiasts. Many years ago there was a small community on the eastern shore of Cave Cay that was founded by freed slaves shortly after their emancipation. As is so often the case in Bahamian history, a hurricane decimated the settlement and the remaining inhabitants were moved to Little Abaco Island to found Crown Haven lying just west of Fox Town.

Navigational Information
If heading deeper into the Bight of Abaco you'll need to pass over the shallows between Cave Cay and Spence Rock (Chart #AB-BI-3) to enter the much deeper waters of the Bight. And unless yours is a shallow draft vessel you'll want to pass to the east of Cave Cay. As shown on Chart AB-BI-2, pass to the east of Cave Cay, rounding the northeastern tip and passing between Cave Cay and Cashs Cay. The controlling depth here is 6' at MLW with a deeper area of 7'-9' between the southern tip of Cashs Cay and the "knee" of Cave Cay. I give no waypoints for this route; you must develop a feel for the deeper water and be able to read the channel (you will also need a rising tide as the controlling depth for this passage as you approach Spence Rock is 4' at MLW). You'll be passing a couple of hundred yards to the east of Cave Cay and if you begin to get too far westward towards Cave Cay the water will thin rapidly as it does eastward towards Cashs Cay. As you pass the

southern tip of Cave Cay as shown on Chart #AB-BI-3, you'll be in a large area of 7' deep water that will shoal gradually the closer you get towards Spence Rock. From this area take up a course to pass a few hundred yards to the west of Spence Rock and east of the sandbar that dries at low to mid-tide well to the west of Spence Rock. Spence Rock is easily identifiable by the conspicuous umbrella shaped tree on it. Once past Spence Rock and into the deeper waters of the *Bight of Abaco* you can take up a course for Mores Island or perhaps you'll want to explore the cays to the west of Great Abaco Island.

Vessels heading north and wishing to run this route in reverse should head for a waypoint at 26° 48.70' N, 77° 51.40' W. This will place you south/southwest of Spence Rock and a good a spot as any to wait on the tide to follow the above route in reverse. The Cross Cays that lay well to the southwest of Cave Cay is an excellent area for dinghy exploration, the waters close in can be quite shallow and few people go there.

If you're headed to Mores Island, go ahead and take up your course and we'll discuss that destination in a moment, but first let's explore the cays lying off the western shore of Great Abaco Island.

Randall's Cay

Randall's Cay - ¼ nm NW of:
26° 51.60' N, 77° 32.90' W

Randall's Creek - ¼ nm W of mouth:
26° 50.00' N, 77° 31.50' W

Navigational Information
Randall's Cay, Charts AB-BI-1 and AB-BI-4, is the northernmost of the cays that lie west of Great Abaco and offers a fair lee in prevailing east/southeast winds. Randall's Cay is actually quite a beautiful little island where cactus covered bluffs face the west while shallow bonefish flats lie to the east between the cay and the mainland of Great Abaco. A waypoint at 26° 51.60' N, 77° 32.90' W, will place you just west of the northernmost lee anchorage. When approaching Randall's Cay from the west (Spence Rock), as shown on Chart #AB-BI-1, you'll pass tiny Mangrove Cay where you can find shelter from northerly winds in its lee or maneuver your way eastward to Black Point to lie in its lee in 10'-12'. Beware of the long reef that lies east of Mangrove Cay.

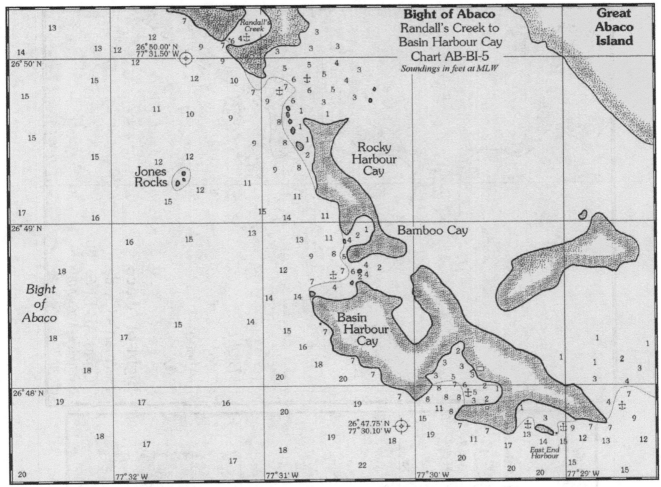

As you approach Randall's Cay, a good landmark is the Batelco tower in Cooperstown. As shown on Chart AB-BI-4, one can anchor off the northwest tip in prevailing winds. About midway down the western shore is Cooling Temper Bay where, in a small bight between some off-lying rocks and Randall's Cay, you'll find good protection from north through east winds.

A shallow draft vessel of 4' or less can work it's way up into Randall's Creek at the south end of Randall's Cay for protection from a frontal passage, but this anchorage has a lot of current and a rocky/marl bottom in many places. If seeking shelter from a front, you would be better off two miles further south at Basin Harbour Cay. A waypoint at 26° 50.00' N, 77° 31.50' W, will place you approximately ¼ mile west of the mouth of Randall's Creek.

Just south of Randall's Cay, as shown on Chart AB-BI-5, is Rocky Harbour Cay and Bamboo Cay. Once separate, they are now joined and the creek that separated them is now just a shallow basin that will allow only the shallowest draft vessels inside.

There is a wonderful anchorage just north of Rocky Harbour Cay as shown on Chart AB-BI-5. It lies in a small bight and shallows out the further east and northeast you steer. This is even a good spot in winds from northeast to southeast as the waters to the east are very shallow and little chop builds up. If you head east/northeast in your dinghy you'll come to a small landing that will lead you to Coopers Town.

A shallow creek divides Bamboo Cay from Basin Harbour Cay and offers good protection from frontal passages, but only for shallow draft vessels. Take care setting your anchor as the bottom is rocky in here.

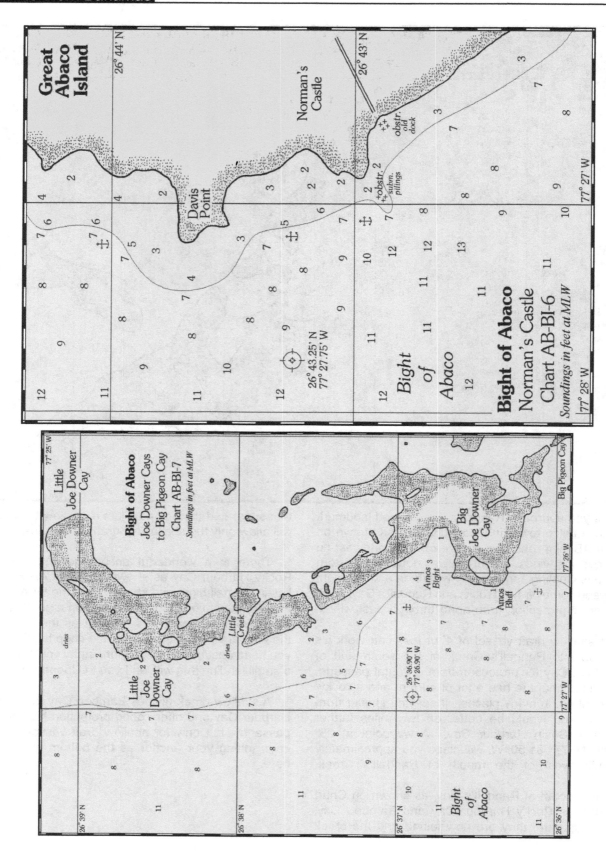

Great Abaco Island

26° 44' N

26° 43' N

Davis Point

Norman's Castle

obstr.
old dock

obstr. 2

subm. pilings

77° 27' W

77° 28' W

Bight of Abaco
Norman's Castle
Chart AB-BI-6
Soundings in feet at MLW

Bight of Abaco

26° 43.25' N
77° 27.75' W

Bight of Abaco
Joe Downer Cays
to Big Pigeon Cay
Chart AB-BI-7
Soundings in feet at MLW

77° 25' W

Little Joe Downer Cay

Little Joe Downer Cay

dries

dries

Little Creek

Big Joe Downer Cay

Amos Bight

Amos Bluff

Big Pigeon Cay

77° 26' W

77° 27' W

26° 39' N

26° 38' N

26° 37' N

26° 36' N

26° 36.90' N
77° 26.90' W

Bight of Abaco

Basin Harbour Cay

Basin Harbour Cay - ¼ nm SW of entrance:
26° 47.75' N, 77° 30.10' W

Basin Harbour Cay, besides being one of the prettiest cays in the *Bight of Abaco*, offers some of the best protection in all weather conditions. If you wish to make one place your base of operations for your Bight of Abaco explorations, Basin Harbour Cay should be the spot. The shoreline is lovely, high rocky bluffs covered in cactus lead to an opening with an excellent anchorage that is only open to the southwest.

Navigational Information

If approaching Basin Harbour Cay from the north, a fair anchorage can be found in the bight between its northwestern tip and the mouth of the creek that separates Basin Harbour Cay and Bamboo Cay as shown on Chart AB-BI-5. Some charts inaccurately portray this anchorage as having much more water than what I show, but don't expect to tuck in very close; it is indeed as shallow as I have marked.

For all around protection it is best to head for the center of Basin Harbour Cay and it's wonderful anchorage. A waypoint at 26° 47.75' N, 77° 30.10' W will place you approximately ¼ mile southwest of the entrance to this anchorage and a bit over 19 nautical miles east/southeast from Spence Rock. From this position enter the harbor and anchor where your draft allows. You will find that the harbour rapidly shallows to a fairly uniform 5' or so and gradually shallows as you approach the shore. There is a house on the eastern shore of the harbour that is often used and another, smaller house on the southern shore of the harbour. The anchorage itself is open to the southwest and west so if southwest winds are forecast it is best to anchor in the southwestern corner of the anchorage for the best protection. After the winds moves into the west it would be better to move to the northern side of the anchorage where the water is a little deeper. In strong southeasterly through southwesterly winds, this anchorage develops a surge as swells work their way into the harbour around the southern tip of the harbour mouth. This surge is not dangerous, only uncomfortable; a bridle arrangement that allows you to pivot your bow into the swell will take care of the problem and give you a pleasant night's sleep. As the wind swings into the southwest your bow will automatically come more into the wind and sea easing

the motion. The bottom in this harbour is marly and the holding here is tricky at times, make sure your anchor is set well.

Another possible anchorage is either east or west of the unnamed rock in East End Harbour (also shown on Chart AB-BI-5). This entire harbour was once deep but has now filled in between the unnamed rock and the shore of Basin Harbour Cay. If you anchor to the west of the unnamed rock, you will find shelter from west through northeast, almost east, winds, while if you anchor to the east of the rock you will have shelter from northwest to northeast winds.

Another anchorage that will give you shelter from west winds is off the eastern tip of Basin Harbour Cay. Round the eastern tip and venture in as far as your draft allows. This is not a good anchorage in winds from southeast through south and a bit choppy in winds from northeast through east.

Norman's Castle

Norman's Castle - ¾ nm W of:
26° 43.25' N, 77° 27.75' W

Norman's Castle lies a bit over five nautical miles south/southeast of Basin Harbour Cay with deep water all the way (12'-15'). Norman's Castle is an old logging transshipment settlement which provides a nice lee anchorage with plenty of opportunities for land exploration. The settlement was built just prior to 1920 and by 1925 the community was a certified boomtown with its own doctor, 250 company built houses, and a railroad. From a production highpoint of over twelve million board feet of lumber in 1925, there was a steady decline over the next two decades as Norman's Castle passed into history.

Navigational Information

Approaching from the north your landfall will be the conspicuous hill and bluff at Davis Point (shown on Chart AB-BI-6). You can anchor north or south of Davis Point in 6'-7' of water in prevailing wind conditions. The anchorage north of Davis Point gives better protection from southeast winds while the anchorage south of Davis Point gives better protection from northeast winds.

A waypoint at 26° 43.25' N, 77° 27.75' W will place you approximately ¾ mile west of the point and ruins of Norman's Castle and equally as far southwest of

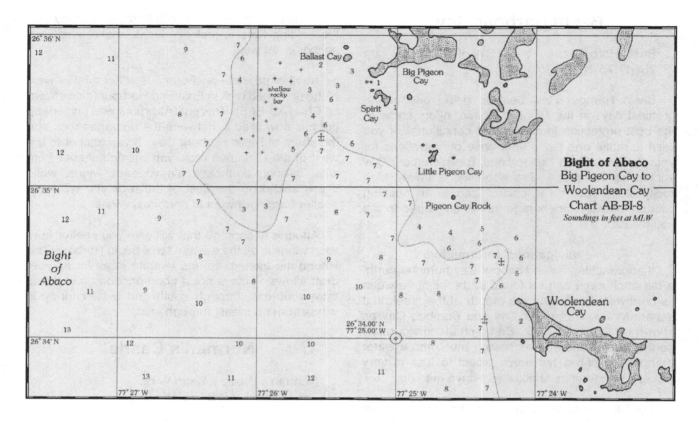

Bight of Abaco
Big Pigeon Cay to
Woolendean Cay
Chart AB-BI-8
Soundings in feet at MLW

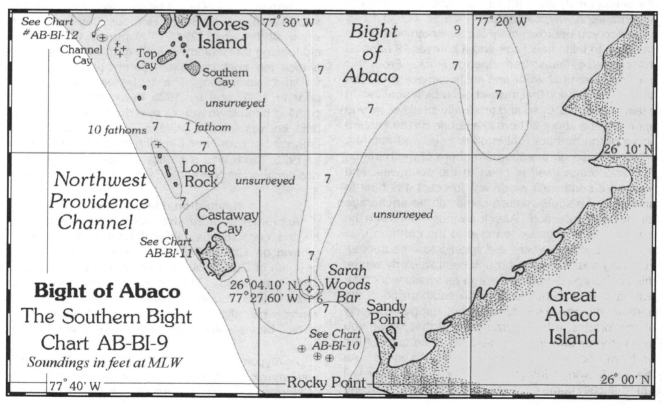

Bight of Abaco
The Southern Bight
Chart AB-BI-9
Soundings in feet at MLW

Davis Point. Don't venture too close in to shore as shown on the chart, there are numerous submerged hazards such as concrete and steel pilings. There is an old dock and some ruins at the end of the road just south of the point. You might get lucky and see some folks that have driven here from the Great Abaco Highway and it might be possible to hitch a ride into Treasure Cay or Marsh Harbour from here.

The Joe Downer Cays

Big Joe Downer Cay - ¾ nm W of anchorage:
26° 36.90' N, 77° 26.90' W

Woolendean Cay - ¾ nm W of:
26° 34.00' N, 77° 25.00' W

About three miles south of Norman's Castle lies a small string of cays known as the Joe Downer Cays as shown on Charts AB-BI-7 and AB-BI-8. At the northern end of the chain lies Little Joe Downer Cay where a hard bar stretches north/northwest. The cay has several small beaches that invite dinghy exploration. At the southern end of the cay, in Little Creek, is a small pool of deep water but only small shallow draft vessels can work their way in as the shallows to the west of the creek dry in places at low water.

Navigational Information
Just south of Little Joe Downer Cay lies Big Joe Downer Cay, sometimes shown as South Joe Downer Cay, where the best anchorage is in Amos Bight. A waypoint at 26° 36.90' N, 77° 26.90' W places you ¾ mile west of Amos Bight and the anchorage area. Amos Bight is good for winds from northeast to southeast with good holding in sand. Here you'll find several more beaches just waiting for you to land and explore.

South of Big Joe Downer Cay lies a rocky bar that extends south/southwest as shown on Chart AB-BI-8. The southern end of this bar is sometimes marked with a stake or small buoy but these are not likely to be there, and if they are, give them a wide berth, the bar is easily seen. Skippers can work their way inside the bar to the northeast where you can tuck up behind it for shelter from westerly winds. This shallow (1'-2') bar offers a good lee with little sea working its way over it. It's actually pretty amazing how much this bar breaks the seas! From this position you can head over to anchor in the lee of Big Pigeon Cay and Pigeon Cay Rock or in the small bight north of Woolendean Cay. From here a channel heads to

Great Abaco Island that many fishermen use. The channel used to take 6' at MLW but today has filled in to about half that.

Another good lee anchorage is off the beach on the northwestern edge of Woolendean Cay. On the beach you'll see some small fishermen's shacks that are still used. The small cays stretch southward for about ten miles from Woolendean Cay, but they only offer fair lee protection at best. Mastic Point lies farther south and offers a good lee anchorage in sand but you must anchor over ½ mile off as closer in the bottom is extremely rocky.

Sandy Point

Sarah Wood Bars:
26° 04.10' N, 77° 27.60' W

Sandy Point - ¼ nm W of anchorage:
26° 01.10' N, 77° 24.70' W

Rocky Point - 1½ nm W of Rocky Point:
25° 59.60' N, 77° 25.80' W

Sandy Point lies at the southwestern tip of Great Abaco Island and is a favorite stopover for cruisers bound north or south through the Bight of Abaco as well as those bound east and west using the *Northwest* or *Northeast Providence Channels*.

Navigational Information
If you are approaching Sandy Point from the north you must negotiate rocky *Sarah Woods Bar*. From inside the Bight of Abaco make your way to a waypoint at 26° 04.10' N, 77° 27.60' W as shown on Chart AB-BI-9. Use caution to avoid the shallows lying east of Mores Island and Castaway Cay and the shallow areas lying west of Great Abaco Island. From here you can head approximately 150° to pass south and west of the *Sarah Woods Bar*. A flooding tide will tend to push you northeastward onto the bar, which is easily seen and just as easily skirted.

If approaching Sandy Point from the south, from the Northwest or *Northeast Providence Channel*, you must clear the vast shoals that lie southwest of Rocky Point as shown on Chart AB-BI-10. Head for a waypoint at 25° 59.60' N, 77° 25.80' W which will place you in deep water well to the southwest of the southwestern tip of the shoals. From this position head north/northeast towards Sandy Point keeping

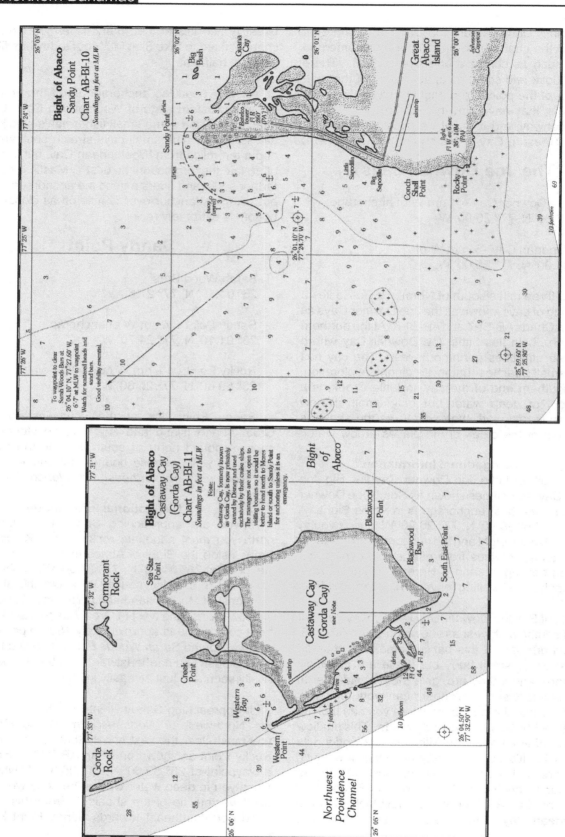

clear of the shallows lying west of the mainland. Watch out for a few small patch reefs to the west of this route also.

A waypoint at 26° 01.10' N, 77° 24.70' W will place you just off the community in a bight between shallow water to the north and south as shown on Chart AB-BI-10. If a front threatens, and if your draft is 5' or less, you can work your way northward around the point to anchor to the east of Sandy Point in a narrow, but deep channel. The route is fairly easy to see, you'll notice the deeper water curving eastward around the northern tip, picking up the beginning of the route is the tricky part. At the time of this writing a small buoy marked the shallowest area, but like all privately maintained navigational aids in The Bahamas, it cannot be trusted to be there. If you're good at eyeball navigation you'll be able to pick out the channel as the water is very, very shallow on either side of it, 1' in places. The best time to attempt this passage is on a rising tide, just before high so that if you run aground, you'll have a bit of high tide still to come to help you float off. From the previously mentioned anchorage, head almost due north and try to pick out the channel as it curves around to the east. If you need a pilot, simply place a call on VHF ch. 16 for *Pete and Gay's Guest House*. Pete Dean runs a fine inn with excellent accommodations where the focus is on bonefishing.

What You Will Find Ashore

Sandy Point is a delightful, picturesque community of colorful houses set amid a stand of coconut palms. Besides *Pete and Gay's Guest House* you'll have *Oeisha's Resort* a bit closer to the airstrip. Ask about their Sunday barbecues at the beach. You can find water at the government dock and trash receptacles also. *Lightbourne Marine* is just up from the government dock and has its own dredged channel to Capt. Ernest Dean's dock where you will find fuel, water, and electricity. You can jerry jug gas from *Thompson's Esso* just up from the town dock.

For dining you can chose from *Pete and Gay's, Nancy's Seaside Inn, Oeisha's, Big J's*, and *Marion's Takeaway*. The *E&E Department Store and Florence's Grocery* can handle all your pantry needs. There is a shuttle bus, the *Islander Express*, that goes to Marsh Harbour Monday-Saturday. It's possible to get your propane filled by using this convenient service. Phone and fax service is available at the local *Batelco* office and there is a medical clinic in town that opens from 0900-1300 on weekdays.

Castaway Cay
(Gorda Cay)

Castaway Cay (Gorda Cay) - ½ nm WSW: 26° 04.50' N, 77° 32.90' W

Castaway Cay, once called Gorda Cay, lies about nine miles northwest of Sandy Point on the edge of the bank bordering the *Northwest Providence Channel* and can be seen from Sandy Point. The cay is home to a major Disney cruise ship stopover and visits ashore are by invitation only. The best way to access Castaway Cay is via the *Northwest Providence Channel* as shown on Chart AB-BI-9. It is possible to head to Castaway Cay from Sandy Point by skirting the Sarah Woods Bars, but that area is filled with heads, small patch reefs, and shallow bars which must all be negotiated with good light and visibility.

The inner harbour at Castaway Cay can be used by yachts in emergencies, but visiting yachtsmen are not encouraged to visit the cay, this is strictly for the paying guests.

Navigational Information

A waypoint at 26° 04.50' N, 77° 32.90' W will place you approximately ½ mile southwest of the newly dredged harbor and cruise ship docks. It is still possible to work your way up between the small off-lying cay and the new breakwater, but only in emergency situations. If yours is an emergency situation try calling the cay first on VHF ch. 16. You can also anchor south of the cruise ship dock in northerly to easterly winds and north of the cay in Western Bay.

Tales of Gorda Cay

Not too long ago, when Castaway Cay was still Gorda Cay, the island was the hub of smuggling operations in the Abacos between 1979 and 1983. The island's operations went through four phases each.

Frank Barber first bought Gorda Cay in 1979, and hired a Bahamian, Barry Thompson, as caretaker. Thompson, who had just finished doing three years and eight months in prison, hired on for $500 a week. When Thompson realized that the cay was being used as a smuggling operation he demanded more money which he finally received after several arguments and threats.

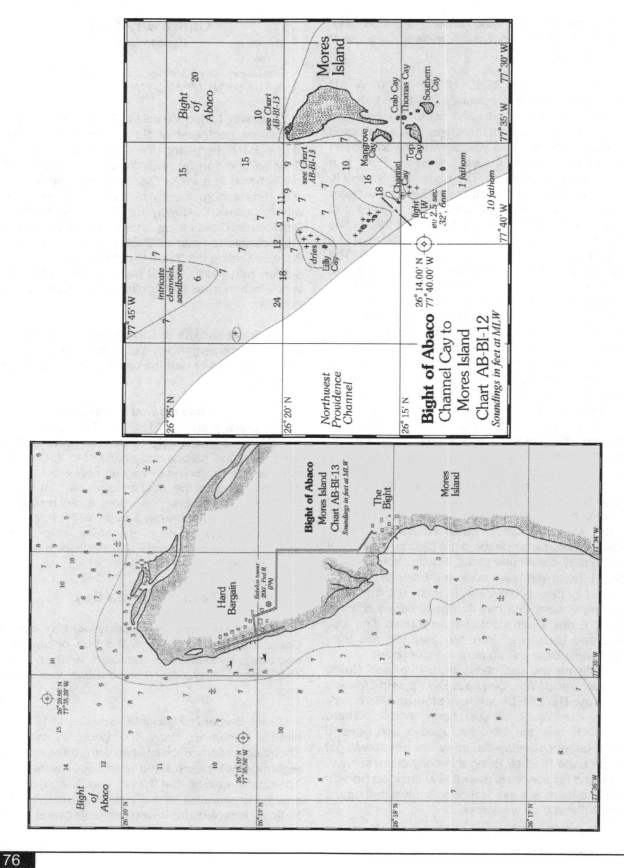

Bight of Abaco
Channel Cay to
Mores Island
Chart AB-BI-12
Soundings in feet at MLW

26° 14.00' N
77° 40.00' W

Bight
of
Abaco

Mores
Island

Crab Cay
Thomas Cay
Southern
Cay
Mangrove
Cay
Top
Cay
Channel
Cay

see Chart
AB-BI-13

see Chart
AB-BI-13

light
Fl W
ev 2.5 sec
32', 6nm

1 fathom

10 fathom

intricate
channels,
sandbores

Lilly Cay
dries

Northwest
Providence
Channel

77° 45' W
77° 40' W
77° 35' W
77° 30' W

26° 25' N
26° 20' N
26° 15' N

Bight of Abaco
Mores Island
Chart AB-BI-13
Soundings in feet at MLW

Bight
of
Abaco

Hard
Bargain

Batelco tower
200' Fxd R
(PA)

The
Bight

Mores
Island

26° 20.55' N
77° 35.20' W

26° 19.10' N
77° 35.50' W

77° 36' W
77° 35' W
77° 34' W

26° 20' N
26° 19' N
26° 18' N
26° 17' N

Barber's security was lax on Gorda Cay and in October of his first year on the cay two young men from Sandy Point stumbled onto the airstrip and Barry Thompson brought them to Barber at gunpoint. Barber wanted to kill them on the spot but changed his mind and told Thompson to take them instead to Gorda Rock, a tiny uninhabited scrub covered rock, and maroon them.

Security was no better when on March 10, 1980, five masked men armed with automatic weapons arrived on Gorda Cay and took Barry Thompson hostage. The next day Barber and several of his associates arrived and were also held at gunpoint. The gunmen went about looting and eventually left the island but were later arrested and charged with kidnapping. During routine questioning after their arrest, they informed police of Barber's smuggling activities on Gorda Cay. When questioned by Police about these allegations Barber said that the people of Sandy Point had been using Gorda Cay for years as a smugglers base but that since he arrived all smuggling activity had ceased and he intended to keep it that way. Barber and his men then established a security system using armed guards and dogs to keep intruders off the cay but which did nothing but create animosity with the population of nearby Sandy Point.

When Frank Barber boasted of cleaning up Gorda Cay the *DEA* did not believe him and their *Operation Grouper* focused on the drug smuggling activities alleged to be going on at Gorda Cay. Prime Minister Sir Lynden Pindling contended that the *DEA* operation was illegal and was executed without the knowledge and cooperation of the Bahamian government. The Bahamas insisted that the *DEA* even helped set up Barber's operation on Gorda Cay to catch smugglers and that they actually caught some of their own people. The Government of The Bahamas insisted that when Frank Barber was caught, he was offered a chance to help the *DEA* nab more suspects in return for reducing his charges to a minor offense. Barber allegedly agreed and the *DEA* netted some 90 persons in the U.S. and Bahamas in connection with Barber's activities on Gorda Cay. The Bahamian government insisted that Jeffery Scharlatt, whom the *DEA* called an "investor in Gorda Cay" and who was sentenced to five years and fined $15,000, was actually a former *DEA* agent. Perhaps I should explain something at this point. During those years, many law enforcement agencies took to running "sting" operations to lure

smugglers and would-be smugglers. Unfortunately, they often snared members of other law enforcement agencies involved with other investigations. For security reasons data was not passed between agencies; so often the left hand of the law did not know what the right hand of the law was doing. There are several tales of cops busting cops during this period.

Barber had been arrested in the spring of 1982, and later that year sold the island to Abner Pinder, a fisherman from Spanish Wells. Garcia began his operations on the Cay just after Barber's arrest and continued until the end of 1982. Pinder also started operations in October of 1982 overlapping Garcia by a few months during which time Garcia paid Pinder for the use of his island. Actually, on the first night of Pinder's new ownership, Barry Thompson and some of his associates, all armed with automatic weapons, confronted Pinder. They told Pinder that they worked for Garcia and that if Pinder did not allow them to use the cay, Thompson would make sure that Pinder would never be able to make use of it. Pinder agreed and Garcia eventually paid Pinder $1,000 per kilo of coke and $20 per pound of pot that he moved through Gorda Cay. By this time Garcia had virtually retired from the drug smuggling business for a quieter life in sunny South Florida. In a meeting with Garcia in Miami where he had gone to pick up a payment, Pinder told Garcia that he did not trust Barry Thompson and wanted him off the cay. Word of this filtered down to Thompson who once again confronted Pinder at gunpoint, stealing a large quantity of marijuana and a boat from him. In January of 1983, through Garcia's intervention, Pinder settled his differences with Thompson. By mutual agreement, Pinder left the workings of Gorda Cay to Thompson and Garcia guaranteed Pinder would continue to receive his payments. Although Pinder received no further payments from either Garcia or Thompson, he did receive $120,000 from two Cuban Americans for using his cay. The Cubans should have paid him more but they complained that Barry Thompson had stolen part of their shipment.

Disillusioned, Abner Pinder agreed to sell Gorda Cay to Barry Thompson for three million dollars. Thompson gave him a down payment of $400,000 and a subsequent payment of $300,000 and then, true to form, the payments stopped. Thompson continued to run drugs through Gorda Cay until September of 1983 when a permanent police presence was established on the island and the illegal activities came to an end. That same year Pinder claimed to have given up involvement with drugs of any kind and estimated that he cleared over a million dollars from Gorda Cay.

And while we're discussing the wealth passing through this area, let me remind you that there have been several wrecks of Spanish treasure ships in the waters between Mores Island, Gorda Cay, and Sandy Point. In 1719, between Gorda Cay and Sandy Point, the *San Pedro* sank with over half-a-million in gold and silver aboard. In 1595, a Spanish treasure vessel sank off Mores Island and in 1717, the *El Capitan* sank off Southern Cay with over $2 million in treasure aboard.

Mores Island

Mores Island - ½ nm NW of:
26° 20.55' N, 77° 35.20' W

Mores Island - ½ nm W of anchorage:
26° 19.10' N, 77° 35.50' W

Channel Cay - 2 nm SW of channel:
26° 14.00' N, 77° 40.00' W

Mores Island lies northwest of Castaway Cay and southeast of the shallow banks area that is the southeastern tail of Grand Bahama. There are two small settlements on Mores Island, Hard Bargain and The Bight, both of which were established by freed slaves. Landfall can be fairly easy as the 200' Batelco tower (Fxd R at night) at Hard Bargain can be seen for miles.

Navigational Information

If you are approaching Mores Island from the northern *Bight of Abaco*, from Spence Rock to Norman's Castle or even Woolendean Cay, head for a waypoint at 26° 20.55' N, 77° 35.20' W (as shown on Chart AB-BI-13) which will place you about ¾ mile northwest of the northern tip of Mores Island. From here simply head south keeping at least a quarter mile offshore to reach Hard Bargain.

If approaching Mores Island from the deep water of the *Northwest Providence Channel* you can head to a waypoint at 26° 14.00' N, 77° 40.00' W, which will place you approximately two miles southwest of Channel Cay and the entrance channel to Mores Island as shown on Chart AB-BI-12. From this position head northeast passing Channel Cay to starboard (north

of the cay). Tiny Channel Cay is easily picked out by its conspicuous 32' tall light (flashing white every 2½ seconds). You can pass south of Channel Cay, but this is not recommended as there are submerged rocks in that area that are a hazard to navigation. Never attempt to enter by Channel Cay at night; it would be prudent to heave to offshore and wait for daylight. As you pass Channel Cay keep heading in a general northeasterly direction heading for the northern tip of Mores Island and the Batelco tower at Hard Bargain some five miles away.

As you approach the lee anchorages at Mores Island as shown on Chart AB-BI-13, you can head for a waypoint at 26° 19.10' N, 77° 35.50' which lies about ½ mile west of Hard Bargain. In prevailing wind directions, northeast to southeast, the anchorages along the western shore of Mores Island are great... tuck up as close as your draft allows but watch out for a few submerged and easily seen wrecks just off the main street at Hard Bargain. You'll find few conveniences in Hard Bargain, there are a couple of small stores and tiny gas station right on the shoreline where you can pick up some gasoline or diesel.

Off the northeast shore of Mores Island you can gain shelter from winds from southwest to northwest. Round the northern point of Mores Island staying about ¼ mile off and proceed around the northern and northeastern tip in 6'-9' of water. Anchor wherever your draft allows. The deeper water, 6'-7', lies about 200 yards or so offshore and as far south as the beach that sits under the conspicuous casuarinas about ¾ mile southeast of the northern tip of the island. As you round the northern point of Mores Island you will come upon two small creeks, the first is far too shallow for anything of any real draft, perhaps a *Gemini* catamaran but that's about all. The second creek that you come to as you head eastward around the northern tip is quite a bit deeper, 5'-7' at MLW in spots, of course there are a few places where it's 2'-3' in spots also but this is a good spot to ride out a front if you're caught in one while in the area. The bar at the mouth of the creek will take drafts of less than 5' at high tide, and 5' on a very high tide. This is one of those places you're going to check out with the dinghy first. Needless to say good visibility is needed here. The entrance channel is straightforward, steer for the middle of the opening parallel with the lie of the creek itself and squiggle around any shallow spots that you come upon. Once over the bar, about 3'-4' at MLW, you will be in 5'-6' at MLW. You can venture farther up the creek but the channel shifts around some shallow, grassy bars of about 2' at MLW. Five feet can be carried all the way to the end of the creek and you can even pass between the small mangrove islets and the large cay to the northeast but that channel will end in a 2' grassy bar as shown on the chart. It should go without saying that you'll need two anchors set in a Bahamian moor here as there is a lot of tidal current. The creek is open to the northwest but even a strong northwest wind send very little sea into the creek, the bar breaks most of it.

Tiny Black Rock, lying just northwest of Mores Island, was a focal point for smugglers back in the late 70's and early 80's. The government of The Bahamas claims that their officers found a cache of marijuana on the cay that, if stacked 6' high, would stretch for two miles.

If I am headed out into the *Northwest Providence Channel* and Grand Bahama from Mores Island, I will head west from the northern tip of the island to pass north of the shallows lying northeast of Lilly Cay as shown on Chart #AB-BI-12. Keep an eye peeled for shallow bars and heads on this route, but rest assured it is a safe shortcut to the deep water if you have good light and maintain a lookout.

To the northwest of Mores Island lies the tail of Grand Bahama Island where you'll find numerous cays separated by narrow channels, some deep, some shallow. You'll find a couple of lee anchorages here and several places to explore such as Burrow's Cay, Water Cay, and Red Shank Cay. You'll need good visibility to maneuver around the heads and shallow bars that abound hereabouts but it will be worth it if you just want to get off the beaten path.

The Abacos
The Northern Abacos

Ports of Entry: West End
Fuel: West End, Grand Cays, Fox Town
Haul-Out: None
Diesel Repairs: West End
Outboard Repairs: West End
Propane: West End
Provisions: West End, Grand Cays, Fox Town
Important Lights:
Memory Rock: Fl W ev 3 sec
Barracuda Shoal: Fl W ev 4 sec
Indian Cay Rock: Fl W ev 6 sec
Little Sale Cay: Fl W ev 3 sec
Carter's Cay: Fxd R (airwarning)
Crab Cay (Anglefish Point): Fl W ev 5 sec

Routes from West End, Grand Bahama

Memory Rock - 2¼ nm south of:
26° 54.75' N, 79° 05.75' W

Indian Cay Channel - E entrance to channel:
26° 46.37' N, 78° 57.15' W

Barracuda Shoal: ¼ nm S of:
26° 45.65' N, 78° 58.30' W

Indian Cay Channel - NW of piling #3:
26° 44.75' N, 78° 59.20' W

Indian Cay Channel - ¼ nm SW of western entrance to channel:
26° 42.80' N, 79° 00.60' W

West End - ½ nm W of entrance channel:
26° 42.23' N, 79° 00.15' W

Mangrove Cay - ½ nm NW of:
26° 55.50' N, 78° 37.50' W

As I mentioned in the section on Grand Bahama, West End is often used as the "door" to the Abacos; more Abaco-bound cruisers stop here to clear in than any other Port of Entry. From West End, Grand Bahama there are two places where you can enter the *Little Bahama Bank* for your trip to the Abacos, *Indian Cay Channel*, or the route that lies north of Sandy

Cay; your draft will likely decide for you which one you choose. There is another route via Memory Rock, but that is primarily used by vessels that ordinarily bypass West End, Grand Bahama.

Navigational Information

If you intend to use *Indian Cay Channel* as shown on Chart GB-1, head to a waypoint at 26° 42.80' N, 79° 00.60' W. This position lies approximately ½ mile north/northwest of West End, Grand Bahama and just a bit west of Indian Cay, about ½ mile southwest of the entrance to *Indian Cay Channel*. *Indian Cay Channel* can be a pain during a really low tide and there are a few spots that show only 4½' at MLW. This route is not recommended for vessels with drafts of more than 6'-6½' and only a rising, almost high tide.

From the waypoint, take *Indian Cay Light* (Fl W ev 6 sec, 40', 8M) and the piling to the west of the cay to starboard and proceed northeastward towards the next piling. These pilings were missing as of 2008 and their future is uncertain. These pilings may or may not be replaced, let us hope the powers-that-be in The Bahamas decide to replace them and make our navigation of this channel easier. The third piling (as shown on Chart GB-1) is also missing, but you can head for a waypoint at 26° 44.75' N, 78° 59.20' W which will place you just a bit northwest of the missing piling. From this waypoint you can continue to a waypoint south of *Barracuda Shoal* at 26° 45.65' N, 78° 58.30' W. A light that flashes white every four seconds and should be considered unreliable, marks the southern edge of *Barracuda Shoal*. From the *Barracuda Shoal* waypoint head to your next waypoint at 26° 46.37' N, 78° 57.15' W where you'll find deep water all the way to Mangrove Cay or Great Sale Cay.

If you're heading across the banks and wish to exit the banks via *Indian Cay Channel*, make your way to the waypoint at 26° 46.37' N, 78° 57.15' W and then follow the above directions in reverse. If you're unsure about using the *Indian Cay Channel*, or if your draft is simply too deep, you can always enter the banks a few miles north of Sandy Cay. From West End, Grand Bahama, head northwestward, paralleling the edge of the bank as it curves in that general direction. Try to stay in 10 fathoms or so of water as the edge of the bank has numerous shallow banks and rocks along through here (Never attempt any entrance onto the bank hereabouts at night.). When you reach latitude 26° 52.50 N, you can turn east and head onto the banks. Use extreme caution here at all times. If

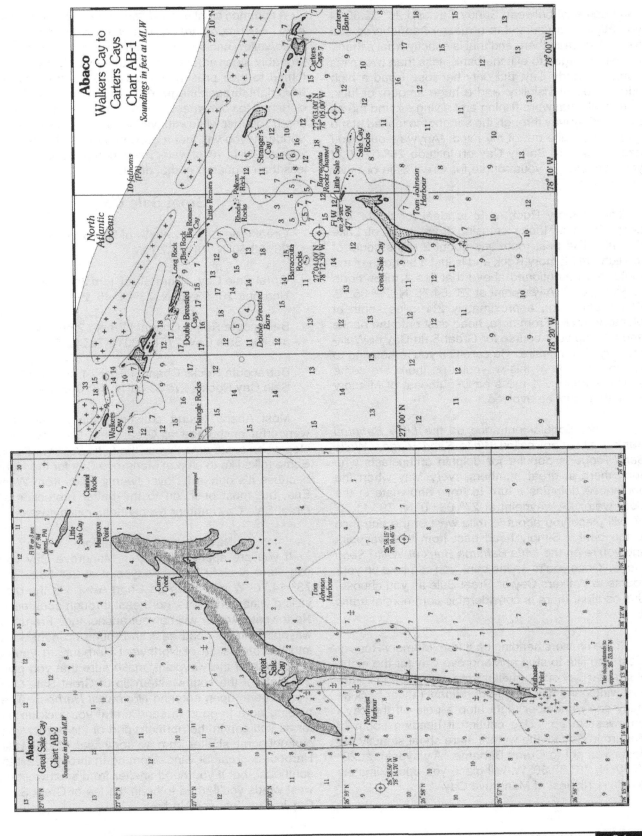

Abaco
Walkers Cay to
Carters Cays
Chart AB-1
Soundings in feet at MLW

North Atlantic Ocean

10 fathoms [PA]

Abaco
Great Sale Cay
Chart AB-2
Soundings in feet at MLW

you head east between Sandy Cay and 26° 52.50' N you might find yourself in a maze of sandbores and rocks, I've been there and that is exactly what's there. I once managed to exit the banks less than two miles north of Sandy Cay, but only because I had a high tide, excellent visibility, and a huge amount of luck. The locals that were fishing and diving around me as I worked my way through the sandbores looked at me as if I was quite out of my mind. Anyway, once you pass abeam of Sandy Cay on latitude 26° 52.50 N you can take up your course for Great Sale or other destinations.

The Memory Rock route is ideal for boats with deep drafts or those crossing from north of Lake Worth. The best route lies about 2 miles south of the light on Memory Rock and is just a bit north of the route that I mentioned above that lies 4 miles north of Sandy Cay. A waypoint at 26° 54.75' N, 79° 05.75' W will place you approximately 2¼ miles south of Memory Rock. From here, head east onto the banks and take up your course for Great Sale Cay or Walkers Cay, if you desire. Be careful if you're heading to Walkers Cay from this waypoint as there are some shallows about 2½ miles east/southeast of Memory Rock that must be avoided.

Another popular entrance on the *Little Bahama Bank* is at a spot called *White Sand Ridge*. *White Sand Ridge* is popular for dolphin enthusiasts who flock there in great numbers every May when the bottlenose dolphins return to frolic and mate in the clear water. A waypoint at 27° 08.00' N, 79° 11.00' W, will place you about ½ mile west of the entrance to the bank. Simply head east from this waypoint and you're on the *Little Bahama Bank* at *White Sand Ridge*. Once you're on the bank you can take up your course to Walkers Cay or Great Sale as you choose. Use caution, there is considerable commercial traffic here.

Some cruisers heading east from Memory Rock or West End like to stop at Mangrove Cay for the night. Mangrove Cay offers shelter from east through southeast winds and has a non-operational (as far back as many can remember) light atop a pole off the cay's northwestern tip. Use caution if heading south of Mangrove Cay as the waters there shoal steadily the closer you get to Grand Bahama. A waypoint at 26° 55.50' N, 78° 37.50' W, will place you approximately ½ mile northwest of Mangrove Cay.

A common sight on the *Little Bahama Bank* is *a fish mud*. *Fish muds* are large areas that appear sandy white/yellow and seem to be shoal water. At first you'll probably steer around them, but as you grow accustomed to their presence you'll build up the nerve to pass right through them. You'll find your hands tightly clenched to your wheel or tiller, your eyes fast on your depth sounder while your vessel slowly inches ahead. Suddenly you will feel a growing sense of relief that you are still in 16' of water even though it appears like less than a quarter of that depth.

Great Sale Cay

Great Sale Cay - ¼ nm W of NW Harbour: 26° 58.50' N, 78° 14.70' W

Great Sale Cay - 1 nm SE of Tom Johnson Harbour: 26° 58.15' N, 78° 10.45' W

Barracouta Rocks Channel West - 2 nm NW of Little Sale Cay: 27° 04.00'N, 78° 12.50' W

Barracouta Rocks Channel East - 1 nm NE of Sale Cay Rocks: 27° 03.00' N, 78° 05.00' W

Most Abaco bound cruisers usually make the wonderful anchorage at Great Sale Cay their first stop when eastbound across the *Little Bahama Bank*. Some folks like to stop at Mangrove Cay for the night because it's only a bit over twenty miles from West End, but most push on to the better protection at Great Sale Cay another twenty or so miles eastward.

Navigational Information

If you are approaching from Mangrove Cay you can steer straight for the waypoint at 26° 58.50' N, 78° 14.70' W as shown on Chart AB-2. In the prevailing wind conditions, northeast through southeast, Northwest Harbour will be your anchorage. From the waypoint simply head east and round up northward into the protection of Northwest Harbour. If you're a bit north of the waypoint, make sure that you give the reefs of the southwestern tip of Great Sale Cay a wide berth upon entering *Northwest Harbour*. The holding here is good in sand and if you tuck up as far as you can in the northern part of the harbor you can get some shelter from westerly seas. Northwest Harbour is great for winds from north through east to southeast, but if you need shelter from southwest or west winds you'll need to be in the lee of Great Sale Cay in Tom Johnson Harbour.

If you are approaching *Tom Johnson Harbour* from the east, from Fox Town or Allan's-Pensacola, head for a waypoint at 26° 58.15' N, 78° 10.45' W. This will put you in deep water just southeast of *Tom Johnson Harbour and* south of the shallow bank as shown on the chart. From here work your way westward as far as your draft allows. A note on approaching *Tom Johnson Harbour*, using caution when heading west from Allan's-Pensacola Cay, you'll want to avoid the large shoal south of Moraine Cay. If you're bound westward from Fox Town, make sure you clear Veteran Rock and West End Rocks. These hazards are shown on Chart AB-8.

If you wish to enter *Tom Johnson Harbour* from the western side of Great Sale Cay you have two options. The long way or the short way, your draft will likely decide for you which route you'll take. The long way is to head north around Great Sale Cay and Little Sale Cay and then turn eastward in the *Barracouta Rocks Channel* to pass the large shoal area to port passing between the Channel Cays and the Sale Cay Rocks (see Chart AB-1). Once past Sale Cay Rocks you'll head south to finally round back westward into *Tom Johnson Harbour*. This route is good for deeper draft vessels, 7' or more. The short route is to head south of Great Sale Cay. Vessels with drafts of 6' or less can cross right over the shoal that extends south of Great Sale Cay. From *Northwest Harbour* clear the shallows off the southern tip of Great Sale Cay and you will come to an area where the shoal is between 4'-6' at MLW (as shown on the chart) where you can cross with the tide. Once over the shallows head north/northeast to *Tom Johnson Harbour*. In settled weather a nice anchorage is off the northwestern shore of Great Sale Cay where you can tuck in fairly close to shore.

Vessels heading north from *Northwest Harbour* around the northern tip of Great Sale Cay via the *Barracouta Rocks Channel* (as shown on Chart AB-1), can head to a waypoint at 27° 04.00' N, 78° 12.50' W, which places you northwest of Great Sale Cay at the western end of *Barracouta Rocks Channel* 2 miles northwest of Little Sale Cay. From this position you can head to the eastern waypoint for the channel passing north of Great Sale Cay. A waypoint at 27° 03.00' N, 78° 05.00' W, will place you at the eastern end of *Barracouta Rocks Channel* about 1 mile northeast of Sale Cay Rocks. Vessels heading north from points south of here can head to this waypoint to transit the *Barracouta Rocks Channel*.

Snorkelers and divers will want to investigate the blue hole located in the shoal area south of Great Sale Cay.

Walker's Cay

Walkers Cay - ½ nm N of entrance W of Seal Cay:
27° 16.20' N, 78° 21.55' W

Walker's Cay - beginning of staked route:
27° 14.00' N, 78° 24.20' W

Navigational Information

Walkers Cay is the northernmost inhabited island in the entire Bahamas archipelago and is most noted for its fishing (tuna, dolphin, marlin, kingfish and more) and diving opportunities and is a favorite stop for boaters leaving Ft. Pierce and St. Lucie Inlets in Florida. If you're coming from offshore, an easy entrance is by approaching the waypoint at 27° 16.20' N, 78° 21.55' W, which places you approximately ½ mile north/northwest of Seal Cay as shown on Chart AB-3. Do not simply plug in this waypoint and head straight for it. You must use caution to avoid the large reef system that lies just north/northwest of Walkers Cay that is partially shown on Chart AB-1. From this waypoint you have two choices for entrance. The easiest lies just a bit west of south from the waypoint as you pass between Tom Browns Cay and Seal Cay. Once clear of Tom Browns Cay you can head westward paralleling the shoreline of Tom Browns Cay as shown on Chart AB-3. Pass Gully Rocks and head for the marked entrance to the marina in 7'-9'. Watch out for a couple of shallow patches south of Tom Browns Cay as shown on the chart. The second route, 9' at MLW, takes you from the Waypoint as you pass between Gully Rocks and the submerged rocks that lie west of Walkers Cay. Once past Gully Rocks just parallel the shoreline of Walkers in good water until the entrance opens up.

There is an abandoned drilling rig lying approximately 2 nautical miles southwest of Walker's Cay. The coordinates are: 27° 14.067' N, 78° 25.514' W. The rig is easily seen and avoided in daylight, keep an eye out for it if you're traversing this area.

Vessels approaching Walker's Cay from Grand Cays or Double Breasted Cays should pass south of the Grand Cays as shown on Chart AB-4. Keep the small string of rocks that end with Burying Piece

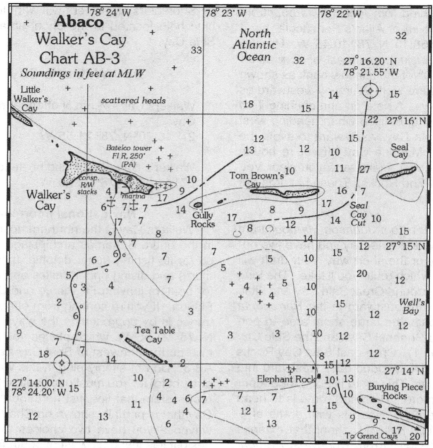

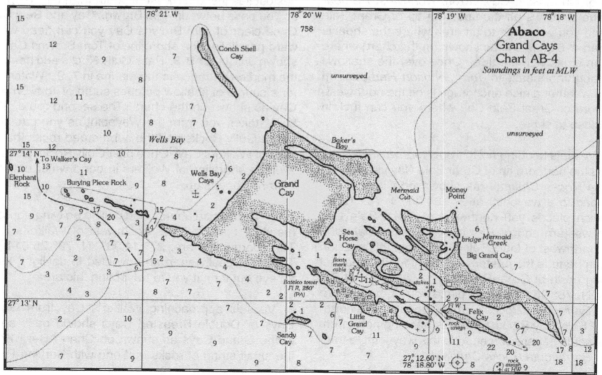

Rock to starboard, passing between them and the easily seen shoal to port. Once clear of Burying Piece Rock, turn to starboard and head northward between Burying Piece Rock and Elephant Rock as shown on Charts AB-3 and AB-4. Head towards the eastern tip of Tom Browns Cay and when you are clear of the shoal area to your west, turn to port and pass between it and Tom Browns Cay and head straight for Walkers and the marina entrance.

There is one more option for entrance to Walkers Cay from the bank, and that is the marked channel as shown on Chart AB-3. From *White Sand Ridge*, Memory Rock, West End, Mangrove Cay, or even Great Sale Cay, you can make for a waypoint at 27° 14.00' N, 78° 24.20' W, which places you approximately ¼ mile south/southwest of the entrance to the marked channel leading to the old *Walkers Cay Marina*.

The primary hazard on this route is the Triangle Rocks as partially shown on Chart AB-1. You must use caution when approaching this crescent shaped string of small rocks. Also, do not attempt to pass from Burying Piece Rock to the above waypoint using a route passing south of Tea Table Cay. The area there has shoaled considerable and there is a stretch where the depth is about 2' at MLW.

From the waypoint you'll see a string of marked pilings leading off across the very visible bank marking a difficult-to-see channel that carries about 5' at MLW. Pass between the first two pilings, they will be marked red and green (red, right, returning), and will have small arrows that point to which side to take pass them on. You'll actually split the first and last pair, and unless they've added some new pilings since this writing, the rest can be taken to starboard when approaching Walkers from the south. Once past the last pair, head straight for the marina entrance.

What You Will Find Ashore

In its heyday, Walker's Cay was a hotspot for offshore fishing. Today, the marina lies abandoned and partially in ruin from several hurricanes. The marina property has been for sale for over three years with no buyers yet in sight. The future of Walker's Cay is uncertain at this point in time. Cruisers are advised to clear *Customs* and *Immigration* at another *Port of Entry*. This once thriving fishing Mecca, which employed many of the local residents, is now but a memory.

Grand Cays

Grand Cays - ¼ nm S of entrance channel: 27° 12.60' N, 78° 18.80' W

The Grand Cays are a wonderful destination; a lot of things to do ashore, as well as a protected anchorage in case a front should approach. There is a sizable population on these cays, most of whom work at Walkers Cay or fish for a living. Trivia lovers might wish to know that the Grand Cays were one of former President Nixon's favorite haunts.

Navigational Information

There are several ways to access the Grand Cays. From Walkers Cay or offshore of Walkers, head to the waypoint north of Seal Cay as described in the last section on Walkers Cay. From the waypoint pass between Tom Browns Cay and Seal Cay (see Chart AB-3) and continue southward to pass between Elephant Rock and Burying Piece Rock. Once clear of Burying Piece Rock turn to port and parallel the shoreline of the Grand Cays as shown on Chart AB-4. Vessels in this area can also take advantage of a very nice anchorage off the western shore of Grand Cay in Wells Bay as shown on Chart AB-4. As you'll see on the chart there is a deep-water passage between Grand Cay and the first small rock to its west. This cut is a shortcut to the route along the southern shore of Grand Cay, but is only mentioned for those skippers who are experienced in piloting such passageways since there is a lot of current there.

As you parallel the southern shore of the Grand Cays you will pass south of Sandy Cay and head for a waypoint at 27° 12.60' N, 78° 18.80' W. At this point you will be approximately ½ mile south of the entrance channel to the protected anchorage off Little Grand Cay as shown on Chart AB-4. From the waypoint head north and then northwestward as you pass south of Felix Cay and the light on its western tip. The channel here carries about 6' at MLW and winds its way west/northwest to the anchorage area off Little Grand Cay. The deepest water is just as you enter and it shallows the further in you go to the west and north. This is a nice anchorage in all conditions short of a hurricane, but make sure your anchor is set well, the bottom tends to be marl in places.

If approaching from Double Breasted Cays follow the long string of cays that lie northwest of the Double Breasted Cays as shown on Chart AB-5. Head for the waypoint and as you approach the Grand Cays you'll see some more small rocks, some awash, that you need to keep to starboard. Enter the channel as described above. If approaching from Great Sale Cay you can steer for the waypoint mentioned above but you must make sure you avoid the *Double Breasted Bars* as shown on Chart AB-1.

What You Will Find Ashore

On shore you'll find nice walkways to carry you around the small island. *Rosie's Place* offers dockage (15 slips), but use caution, the bottom is only 5' or so in spots here at MLW. At *Rosie's* you can get water, ice, bait, fuel, and rooms at the *Island Bay Motel*. The restaurant serves up good food and cold drinks as well. *Rosie's* answers to *Love Train* on VHF ch. 68. In town you'll have your choice of several small stores for groceries, but don't expect a large assortment. Try *Ida Cooper's Bakery and Dry Goods* and *Ena's Bakery* for fresh baked breads. There is also a small *Batelco* office and a new clinic in town. If you wish to dine out you can of course eat at *Rosie's* or you can try *The Hilltop Bar and Restaurant*, the *Runway 87 Snack Bar,* or the *New Palms Restaurant and Bar.*

Double Breasted Cays

Double Breasted Cays - ½ nm S of:
27° 10.85' N, 78° 16.40' W

The uninhabited Double Breasted Cays are arguably the most beautiful cays in the Abacos; they certainly are one of my favorite spots. This area offers a great beach, good snorkeling and diving, conch, fishing and a well-protected, tricky to access anchorage that is excellent for riding out those tough winter fronts.

Navigational Information

A waypoint at 27° 10.85' N, 78° 16.40' W will place you approximately ½ mile south of the cays as shown on Chart AB-5. If you're approaching Double Breasted Cays from Great Sale Cay as shown on Chart AB-1, you can set your course directly for this waypoint once you clear the anchorage at Great Sale Cay. The only dangers on this route are Barracouta Rocks and the *Double Breasted Bars*, but these usually lie well to the west of the courseline from Great Sale Cay to Double Breasted Cay. This does not mean that you should not keep a lookout, the tide may push you off your course so keep an alert watch at all times.

If you are approaching Double Breasted Cays from Grand Cays, simply keep west of the long string of rocks (see Chart AB-5) that lie northwest of the Double Breasted Cays toward the Grand Cays. From the waypoint at Double Breasted Cays, as shown on Chart AB-5, you have several options for anchoring. In north to northeast winds you can anchor directly off the southern shore of the Double Breasted Cays in 9'-15' of water at MLW. The holding is good, but it is not the place to be in winds from east through south to northwest. Another note, cruisers anchoring here will have to endure the passing wakes from the sportfishing boats returning to Walkers Cay that pass through here at speed.

A much quieter anchorage lies to the west and south of beautiful Sandy Cay. From the waypoint head northward towards the southern shore of Double Breasted Cay and turn to port to pass close along the Double Breasted Cay shore between Double Breasted Cay and the aptly named Sand Cay. There are a couple of 6' spots through here, so use the tide a bit if your draft is more than that. Parallel the Double Breasted shoreline and once past the northwestern tip of the cay turn to port to make your way into the visible deeper water that lies west and south of Sand Cay. Anchor wherever your draft allows. The most serene spot is south of Sand Cay between Sand Cay and the unnamed cay south of Sand Cay. There is a lot of current here so two anchors in a Bahamian moor is a must. This is a good anchorage for a front as the shallows break almost all the seas that can find their way in. Sand Cay is a great spot for swimming and lazing, but cruisers will have to share it with the sportfishing boats from Walker's Cay at times.

Double Breasted Cays is noted for shark sightings; usually seen in the waters between the cays, they can also be seen off Sand Cay at times, not always, but sometimes. I've seen a lot of fishermen clean their catch right off the back of their boats at the beach on Sand Cay. This practice should cease as it does nothing but attract large predators. I urge you not to clean your catch here, do it before arriving or after you leave, this is a very popular spot and children use these waters!

My favorite anchorage lies in the creek between the cays at Double Breasted Cay. Buggy when there's no wind, this anchorage offers great holding and an excellent place to ride out even the fiercest frontal passages. You must be careful when entering

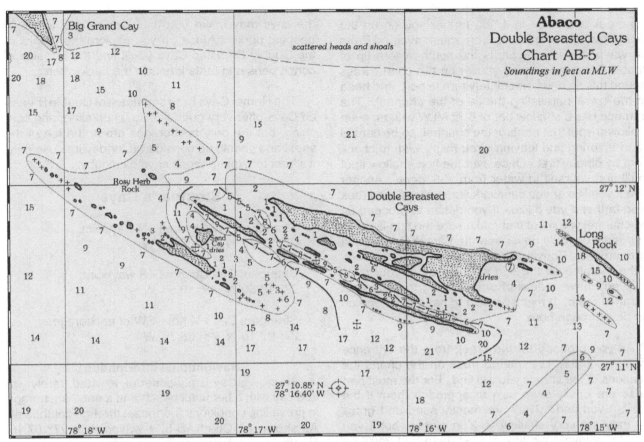

Abaco
Double Breasted Cays
Chart AB-5
Soundings in feet at MLW

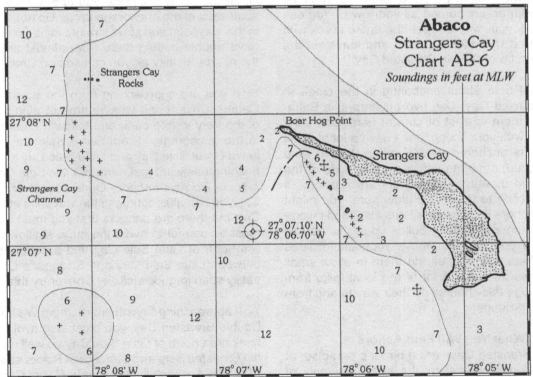

Abaco
Strangers Cay
Chart AB-6
Soundings in feet at MLW

this creek and once in it, the farther you go up the creek, the more hazards you must avoid. From the waypoint, steer towards the southeastern tip of Double Breasted Cay as shown on the chart. Pass around this tip and immediately turn to port, and head up the creek paralleling the lie of the channel. The entrance has a shallow bar of 6' at MLW with an even shallower spot just north of the channel, so be careful when entering and leaving. You might wish to check it out by dinghy first. Once over the first shallow spot you'll find yourself in water from 7'-9' deep. Anchor here if you like or you can work your way up the creek even farther if you'd like. If you desire to proceed up the channel you must first make sure the sun is not in your eyes or you'll never see the bars that you must steer around. Conversely, you cannot leave too early in the morning as the sun will also be in your eyes and you'll have a devil of a time trying to trace your entrance route. It might be best to have someone on the bow through here.

As you proceed up the creek from the entrance you'll notice that I've tried to mark on the charts the locations of the shoals you will find. For the most part these are easily seen as you approach them if the sun is overhead. They are mostly sand and grass but they are very shallow, 1'-2' in places, but if you dare to, weave your way around them and you'll be rewarded with an anchorage all your own. You can actually work your way through the entire creek with the tide, but it's far safer to enter and leave via the southeastern tip of Double Breasted Cay.

One final note about anchoring in the creek at Double Breasted Cay: Use two anchors in a Bahamian moor, there is a lot of current here, and don't be careless with your scope, don't have a lot of slack in it. If you're anchored NW/SE and a SW/NE wind should pipe up, it might push you to the side of the channel even though your anchors are holding. If you're expecting to ride out a blow here, you might consider anchors in those directions also (don't worry about seas though, nothing builds up in this narrow channel). If you have to weave your anchor lines here and there in the creek, rig them to allow small boats to pass through. A lot of the local folks from Grand Cay use this channel on their way to and from their fishing grounds.

What You Will Find Ashore
Double Breasted Cays are a birder's paradise; at night the sounds created by the avian residents of the cays may make you think you're in a jungle in deepest darkest Africa. If you explore the creeks of the Double Breasted Cays you'll find the remains of conch pens and turtle kraals in the backwaters.

The Romer Cays lying southeast of Double Breasted Cays offer very good fishing, snorkeling, and conching, but the only anchorages are in the lee of the shoal and should be considered for daytime use only. It's best to explore these cays by dinghy.

Stranger's Cays

Strangers Cay Channel - N waypoint:
27° 12.33' N, 78° 09.80' W

Strangers Cay Channel - S waypoint:
27° 10.50' N, 78° 10.50' W

Strangers Cay - ½ nm SSW of anchorage:
27° 07.10' N, 78° 06.70' W

Navigational Information
Strangers Cay is a wonderful, isolated, rarely visited cay with a beautiful beach and a good anchorage in prevailing conditions (northeast through southeast). As shown on Chart AB-6, a waypoint at 27° 07.10' N, 78° 06.70' W will place you approximately ½ mile southwest of the anchorage area. Do not simply plug in this waypoint and steer straight for it, you'll certainly have trouble getting there from almost anywhere in the nearby vicinity as you can see on Chart AB-1.

If you are approaching from the southeast, from Carters Cays, head west/northwest along the edge of the very visible bank and follow it around right up to the anchorage. From Great Sale Cay you must leave Great Sale Cay and Little Sale Cay to starboard heading eastward just north of Little Sale Cay in *Barracouta Rocks Channel*. Once abeam of Little Sale Cay you can alter course to the waypoint at Strangers Cay, but there are dangers that you must avoid. You must be careful to avoid the huge shallow bank that lies north of Little Sale Cay and a couple of shoals between Little Sale Cay and Stranger's Cay, all are easily seen in good visibility...never try this at night.

If approaching from the north, from Walkers Cay or Double Breasted Cay, you must also avoid the large bank area north of Little Sale Cay as well as the *Double Breasted Bars* and Barracouta Rocks as shown on Chart AB-1. Once in *Barracouta Rocks Channel* and clear of the large shoal area north of Little Sale Cay alter course to Strangers Cay and keep an eye out for the smaller shoals that I mentioned are on this route.

From the waypoint at Strangers Cay as shown on Chart AB-6, head roughly north/northeast towards a point a bit east of Boar Hog Point. The anchorage lies between Strangers Cay and the reef that lies northwest of the small offlying cays southwest of Strangers Cay. As you approach the northern tip of Strangers Cay keep an eye out for the reef to starboard. Round this reef in 6'-7' at MLW and proceed southeastward and anchor where your draft allows (4'-6' at MLW); please note that the water shallows the closer you get to the small offlying cays.

Strangers Cay Channel, as shown on Chart AB-1, is a wide and deep passage between the reefs and an excellent passage onto and off of the banks. Approaching from the ocean, a waypoint at 27° 12.33' N, 78° 09.80' W will place you approximately ¼ mile north of the channel. From this waypoint, steer just west of south, approximately 190°-200°. The course is not as important here as using your eyes and staying between the reefs. *Strangers Cay Channel* is almost a mile wide and from 18'-30' deep and the reefs are easily seen in good light.

Never attempt this cut or any cut at night using just waypoints, that is asking for disaster! Once inside the reef steer approximately 155°-160° until the tiny Strangers Cay Rocks come into view (see Chart AB-6). Once again, the course is not as important as avoiding the reefs to the north and the large shoal area the borders the Romers Cays. Take Strangers Cay Rocks to port and turn southward avoiding the reef south of Strangers Cay Rocks and the shoals between these rocks and *Barracouta Rocks Channel*.

Vessels wishing to exit the banks via *Strangers Cay Channel* should make their way to the area between the outer reefs and the shoal area that borders the Romers Cays. If you're leaving the anchorage at Strangers Cay, head generally west/southwest following the edge of the bank that lies west of Strangers Cay. Once past the reefs south of Strangers Cay Rocks, head for a waypoint at 27° 10.50' N, 78° 10.50' W, but use caution and avoid the Romers Cays shoal area. From the waypoint head just east of north, approximately 10°-20°, passing between the reefs in Strangers Cay Channel. As I mentioned earlier, the course is not that important as staying between the

reefs here. If you find you must head 000° then by all means do just that, anything to stay between the reefs. I cannot repeat this enough...TRUST YOUR EYES AND YOUR DEPTH SOUNDER!

Carters Cays

Carters Cay Bank - route across bank from east, ¼ nm E of start:
27° 04.25' N, 77° 58.75' W

Carters Cays - 1 nm SSW of Gully Cay:
27° 03.80' N, 78° 01.15' W

The Carters Cays, though a bit tricky to access, offer a good anchorage in the event of a frontal passage as well as a small hurricane hole. You'll find that although Big Carters Cay is inhabited there are no real amenities ashore. Entry to the anchorages must be made with the tide and I'll show you a new one that is far easier than the traditional approach which has shallowed over the years. So let's begin.

Navigational Information

As shown on Chart AB-7, a waypoint at 27° 03.80' N, 78° 01.15' W, will place you about a mile southwest of Gully Cay in water from 7'-9' in depth. From here, the closer you get to the Carters Cays the shallower the water becomes. If you're approaching from Great Sale Cay, once you clear Little Sale Cay in *Barracouta Rocks Channel* you can head directly for the waypoint at Carters Cays.

If you are approaching from the southeast, from Angelfish Point, Fox Town, or perhaps Allan's-Pensacola, you must avoid the large sandbank south of Moraine Cay and the *Carters Bank* as you approach the waypoint (as shown on Chart AB-8). We'll discuss the route north of the *Carters Bank* in a few minutes.

From the waypoint southwest of Carters Cays you have two options to access the anchorages. The traditional route is to put the diamond shaped range on Gully Cay on your bow and approach it on a course of approximately 40°. When you're only about 50' off Gully Cay turn to port, roughly to the northwest, and cross over a shallow bar into the conspicuous deeper water.

This route used to work fine, but over the last few years this area has filled in and the controlling depth now is about 2'-2½' at MLW here. As you approach Gully Cay you'll notice lots of long

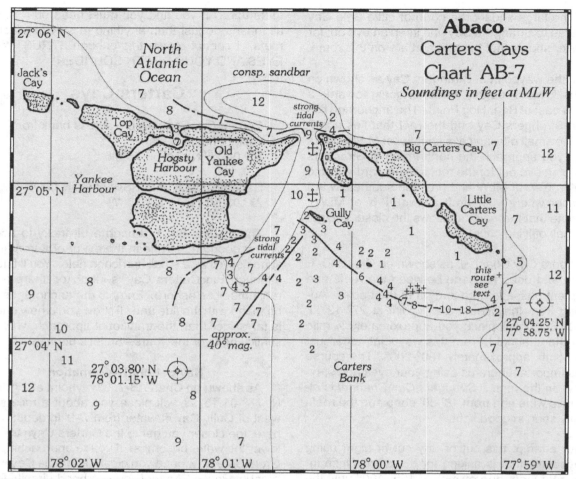

Abaco
Carters Cays
Chart AB-7
Soundings in feet at MLW

27° 06' N

North
Atlantic
Ocean

consp. sandbar

Jack's
Cay

7

12

8

strong
tidal
currents

2

7

7

9

4

Top
Cay

3

7

Old
Yankee
Cay

Hogsty
Harbour

Yankee
Harbour

27° 05' N

10

9

1

Big Carters Cay

7

12

Little
Carters
Cay

11

1

1

2

Gully
Cay

7

3

1

1

1

7

5

strong
tidal
currents

2

3

3

4

this
route
see
text

12

8

8

3

3

4 4

2

3

2 2 2

4

4 4 1

6

4 4

7

4 4

4

7

2

27° 04.25' N
77° 58.75' W

9

7

4 3

7 7

2

3

4 4

7-8-7-10-18

10

8

7 7

2

27° 04' N

11

27° 03.80' N
78° 01.15' W

9

8

2

Carters
Bank

7

7

12

9

7

approx.
40° mag.

78° 02' W

78° 01' W

78° 00' W

77° 59' W

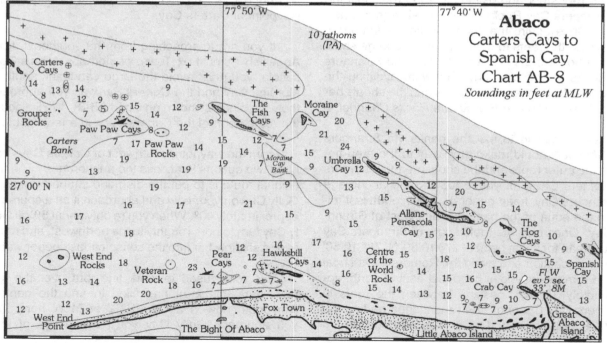

77° 50' W

77° 40' W

Abaco
Carters Cays to
Spanish Cay
Chart AB-8
Soundings in feet at MLW

10 fathoms
(PA)

Carters
Cays

14

13

14

8

12

9

The
Fish
Cays

9

Moraine
Cay

20

Grouper
Rocks

7

15

14

12

Paw Paw Cays

8

12

9

15

12

7

21

24

Carters
Bank

17

Paw Paw
Rocks

14

14

Moraine
Cay
Bank

15

Umbrella
Cay

9

12

9

19

13

19

19

Cay

9

27° 00' N

19

9

13

15

12

20

16

17

21

15

9

15

14

16

17

18

15

Allans-
Pensacola
Cay

8

The
Hog
Cays

10

9

12

West End
Rocks

18

Pear
Cays

12

Hawksbill
Cays

16

Centre
of the
World
Rock

15

15

12

18

15

15

15

Spanish
Cay

16

13

14

Veteran
Rock

23

16

7

7

8

16

14

13

12

Crab Cay

FL W
ev 5 sec
33', 8M

15

20

20

18

7

7

9

10

7

13

12

13

West End
Point

The Bight Of Abaco

Fox Town

Little Abaco Island

Great
Abaco
Island

marks in the bottom where people have drug keels and damaged props. This is no longer a boater friendly route for deeper draft vessels (over 4'). I use a different approach. From the waypoint you'll notice the deeper blue water that lies southwest of Gully Cay and you should be able to discern the shallow bank that lies between you and that deeper water as shown on Chart AB-7. When used with the tide, this route saves a lot of wear and tear on your boat as well as your nerves. You can also cross the same bar at the extreme southwestern tip of the deeper water.

Whichever route you take, once you're in the deeper water you can anchor north of Gully Cay between Gully Cay and Big Carters Cay. This spot is a bit out of the strong currents here and is a favorite. The other spot is near the northwestern tip of Big Carters Cay just off the houses. Use a Bahamian Moor here!

Now let's discuss the route north of the *Carters Bank*. This route is primarily for those who wish to access this anchorage when approaching from *Moraine Cay Channel* or the Fish Cays. If approaching from *Moraine Cay Channel*, pass between the outer reef and Moraine Cay passing north of the Fish Cays heading for the Carters Cays as shown on Chart AB-8. When approaching from the Fish Cays pass north of the Paw Paw Cays and watch out for some scattered heads along through here. Head to a waypoint at 27° 04.25' N, 77° 58.75' W, which will place you southeast of Little Carters Cay and just north of the *Carters Cay Bank* as shown on Chart AB-7. The next part of this route is very tricky and demands that you have the ability to read the water (at least) and nerves of steel (it helps). Only run this route on a rising tide!

From the waypoint look to the west and you'll see a very shallow bank with a patch of deeper water to the west of it. As you leave the deeper water at the waypoint you'll be heading for a small slot where two shallow banks come together, this will lead you to the deeper water. (CAUTION: The configuration of these two shallow banks may change by the time this guide is published, check it first with your dinghy if in doubt.) Cross over the shallows into the deeper water and proceed westward aiming for a point just a bit north of west at the far end of the deeper water where you'll see some submerged rocks. You'll want to keep these rocks to starboard as you head north of west as shown on Chart AB-7. Just as you pass abeam of the rocks you'll want to adjust your course

towards Gully Cay taking Gully Cay and the lone rock halfway to Gully Cay to starboard. You'll have 4' and a bit more through here at MLW but it will shoal to 3' MLW at Gully Cay. Pass close to Gully Cay and cross the bar into the deeper water.

A vessel can also pass to the north of Big Carters Cay giving it a wide berth. Pass westward around the conspicuous curving sandbank that lies north of the anchorage between Big Carters Cay and Yankee Cay. Take the western arc of the sandbank on your port side and then head eastward, paralleling the shoreline of Old Yankee Cay to enter the harbor as shown on Chart AB-7. You can also cross over the southeastern end of the curving sandbank just north of Big Carters Cay with the tide; it's almost 4' at MLW through here.

Between Top Cay and Old Yankee Cay is the entrance to Hogsty Harbour, sometimes called *Safety Harbour*, the local hurricane hole. The entrance is straightforward from the north over a 3' bar at MLW. Inside you'll find room for two good sized boats in water 7'-10' deep.

Fox Town

Fox Town - ½ nm NW of Hawksbill Cays:
26° 57.00' N, 77° 48.80' W

What a great anchorage awaits you at Fox Town. Though there really aren't any beaches to speak of, you can avail yourself of some fine dining in town as well as fuel. The anchorages between Fox Town and the Hawksbill Cays are wonderful in prevailing winds, but no place to be in the event of a frontal passage when the winds blow from the southwest to northwest. Explorers will want to check out *The Crossing* west of Crown Haven. Here is a man-made cut that was designed to be a shortcut to the *Bight of Abaco*, but in reality is a small break in the land with a heck of a lot of current. About three miles west of Fox Town, and northwest of the Pear Cays, is a very visible sunken barge, ideal for snorkeling, and the Hawksbill Cays offer excellent dinghy exploration opportunities as well. You can also ask around town for a guide to *Saunder's Hole*, a wonderful blue hole lying just south of Little Abaco and southwest of Moses Cay.

Navigational Information
There are several ways to access the anchorage at Fox Town. If you are approaching from West End

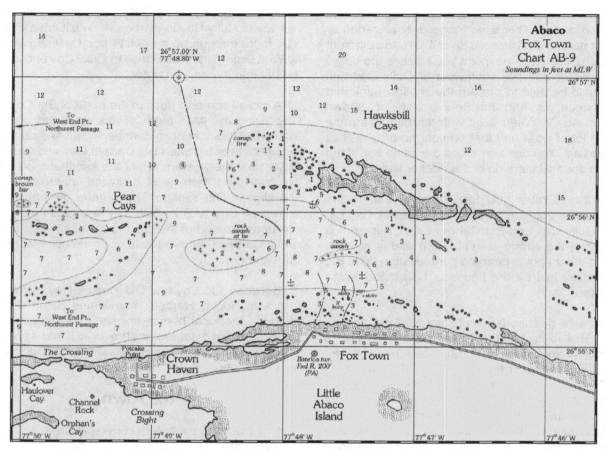

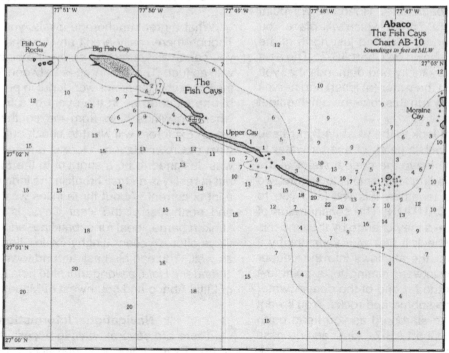

Point on Little Abaco as shown on Chart AB-8, you can simply parallel the shoreline of Little Abaco, staying about ¼ mile or more offshore to avoid the shallows and small rocks that line the shore. As you approach Fox Town you can pass between the Pear Cays and *The Crossing* as shown on Charts AB-8 and AB-9.

If you're approaching from Great Sale Cay, you can head either north of south of Great Sale Cay, and when in deeper water (once you've cleared the bar south of Great Sale Cay or once you've cleared Sale Cay Rocks to the north), you can make a beeline for the waypoint at 26° 57.00 N, 77° 48.80' W as shown on Chart AB-9. Your only hazards on this route are the West End Rocks and the shoal north of Veteran Rock as shown on Chart AB-8.

If you are approaching from Angelfish Point you can head directly to the waypoint keeping an eye out for tiny Centre of the World Rock. From the anchorage at Crab Cay you can also parallel the shoreline of Little Abaco westward, but if you choose this route you must keep an eye out for the reefs shown on Chart AB-8.

From the waypoint the entrance to the anchorages is not difficult. Pass to the west of the Hawksbill Cays, giving them a wide berth as the shallows stretch a bit more westward than shown on some other charts of the area. The northwestern-most of the Hawksbill Cays is a small rock that is easily spotted, it has a very conspicuous tire sitting atop a piling. As you pass south of the string of cays leading westward from the Hawksbill Cays you'll want to bring your bow around a bit more to port to avoid the huge shoal area that dries at low water (as shown on Chart AB-9). From here you can anchor to the south of the largest of the Hawksbill Cays, which offers great protection in north through east winds. Or if you prefer you can work your way closer to town to anchor just outside the string of rocks that lay north of Fox Town and mark the edge of the deeper water; this spot is good in winds from east through south.

Fox Town Shell has been rebuilt since Hurricane Floyd and is fully operational once again and the directions into the dock remain the same. Getting the big boats into the dock at *Fox Town Shell* takes some doing as there's only 3' -4' here at MLW. The best advice I can give is to call ashore on VHF for instructions or to request a pilot while still outside the string of four small cays, unless you are content to jerry jug your fuel in your dinghy. The routes I show on Chart AB-9, although somewhat marked (privately maintained mind you), may seem quite intimidating to someone unused to piloting in shallow water, if in doubt ask for a pilot. *Fox Town Shell* sits right on the edge of the water and offers fuel, water, ice, groceries, and carries 5½-7' at high water. The entrance here is not too difficult; leave the four conspicuous cays to starboard when entering the channel to the dock, keeping the easternmost rock close to starboard. From here simply head straight for the *Fox Town Shell* dock. Just south of *Fox Town Shell* is *Boom Boom*, a very friendly and busy local bar just next to *Juicy's Sports Bar & Grill*. There is also a payphone by *Fox Town Shell* and a *Community Clinic* on the *Bootle Highway* by the *Police/Post Office* building. If you plan to stay overnight in Fox Town, you can get a room at the *Tangelo Hotel* or *Mimi's Guest Cottages*.

To the west of Fox Town is the tiny community of Crown Haven. Crown Haven, little more than a good walk west of Fox Town, offers a telephone, the *Black Room Bar and Restaurant*, and *E&J's Ice Cream Parlour and Video Tape Rental*. If you're hungry and have forgotten to call ahead for a meal, simply stop by and see Bookie Butler at the *Chili Bar Restaurant*, he's pretty handy in emergencies. Crown Haven, has an interesting past; many of the residents remember when they lived on nearby Cave Cay in the Bight of Abaco. A hurricane in the 1930's destroyed their homes and the Government moved them to the island of Little Abaco at the end of the road and today we have Crown Haven – a haven courtesy of the Crown.

The Fish Cays

The Fish Cays - ½ nm SW of:
27° 01.90' N, 77° 50.20' W

The Fish Cays, as shown on Chart AB-10, is a small sting of low-lying cays that offer a pair of decent anchorages, though no place to ride out a frontal passage. Located just west of popular Moraine Cay, you'll find some nice snorkeling and diving on the reefs just to the north of these cays as well as in between the cays themselves. Don't confuse these Fish Cays with the Fish Cays that lie south of Great Guana Cay between Guana and the mainland of Great Abaco.

Lower Cay offers a great lee in south through west winds. I ducked in behind this cay once when it was blowing about twenty from the southwest and found a great, flat, anchorage. Though the island is low and I still had the wind, the water was flat calm as I tucked in close.

Navigational Information

If you are at Fox Town, you can head generally west of north to arrive at the Fish Cays as shown on Chart AB-8. A waypoint at 27° 01.90' N, 77° 50.20' W will place you approximately ½ mile southwest of the Fish Cays in 15' of water. If you're approaching the Fish Cays from Great Sale Cay or Carters Cays, you must first clear the southern tip of *Carters Cay Bank* before working your way towards the Fish Cays as shown on Chart AB-8.

A good stop on this route is at the Paw Paw Cays to dive on the wrecks there. You can pass between the Paw Paw Cays and in 8' though other charts and publications do not show this. In east through southeast winds, pass north of the Paw Paw Rocks to anchor in their lee off their western shore. Watch out for a couple of scattered heads and shoals on this route. If you are approaching the Fish Cays from Carters Cays and you have crossed or passed Carters Cay Bank to the north, simply head straight for the Fish Cays as shown on Chart AB-8 keeping a sharp eye out for the shoals and heads along this route.

If you are at Moraine Cay and want to access the Fish Cays, leave the anchorage at Moraine and head southwest keeping the very visible shallow sand bank to starboard as shown on Chart AB-10. Once you clear the offlying rock and its surrounding reefs, you can pass between it and Lower Cay to anchor in the lee of Lower Cay. If you want to head to the anchorage between Upper Cay and Fish Cay, pass south of the lay of the Fish Cays (watch out for the shallow bank to the south of Lower Cay) and then follow their lie. Make sure to give a wide berth to the large shoal that lies west of Upper Fish Cay. In prevailing wind conditions you can anchor in the bight of the southwestern tip of Big Fish Cay or, by playing the tide, you can work your way into the anchorage between Fish Cay and Upper Cay. This is a deep anchorage, 8' and more in places, but there is a lot of current here so two anchors are a must. The anchorage is a good spot in winds from north through east to southwest.

Moraine Cay

Moraine Cay Channel - N waypoint:
27° 05.00' N, 77° 14.00' W

Moraine Cay - ½ nm S of anchorage:
27° 01.80' N, 77° 46.25' W

A surveyor described Moraine Cay in the 1920's as "...the most attractive cay in the (Abaco) range. It would suit a person who desires to be monarch of all he surveys." The island was once farmed for sisal but today its primary attraction is its anchorage and its reefs and flats.

Navigational Information

As shown on Chart AB-11, a waypoint at 27° 01.80' N, 77° 46.25' W, will place you approximately ½ mile south of the anchorage. The entrance to the small anchorage is straightforward and the small bight is open to the southeast through south to west. Moraine Cay is good in winds from northwest through north to east but it can get lumpy in southeasterlies. There is a lovely beach by the anchorage and the island itself is criss-crossed with trails to ease exploring.

If you're approaching Moraine Cay from Allan's-Pensacola or Angel Fish Point it is virtually a straight shot as shown on Chart AB-8 with the only hazards being the shallows off Umbrella Cay. If you're approaching from Fox Town you'll need to avoid the large shoal area lying south of Moraine Cay, also shown on Chart AB-8. If you're approaching Moraine Cay from the Fish Cays you just need to follow the southern edge of the very visible bank around to the anchorage as shown on Charts AB-8 and AB-10.

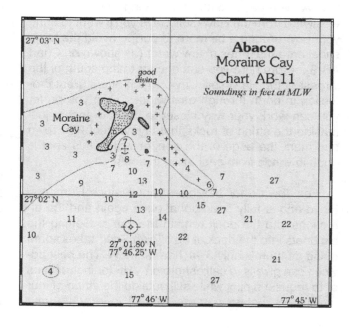

Just to the north/northeast of Moraine Cay is *Moraine Cay Channel* (Chart AB-8), wide and deep it is an excellent spot to head out into the ocean if you so desire. If you're approaching *Moraine Cay Channel* from the ocean, you can make your way to a waypoint at 27° 05.00' N, 77° 14.00' W. From this waypoint simply put Moraine Cay on your bow and head towards it, turning southeastward to avoid the reefs that lie to the northeast of Moraine Cay of course.

Allan's-Pensacola Cay

Allan's-Pensacola Cay - ½ nm WSW of:
26° 59.20' N, 77° 42.20' W

Allan's-Pensacola Cay is a bit of a paradox. On the northwestern end is a fair harbor with notoriously poor holding, while on the eastern end is one of the best hurricane holes in this section of the Abacos. Once two cays, Allan's Cay and Pensacola Cay, they were united during a hurricane in the not too distant past and remain as one today. Onshore there are the remains of a missile tracking station and along the northern shore are several areas where cruisers have hung up flotsam and jetsam and decorated a nice little niche in the shoreline.

Navigational Information

A waypoint at 26° 59.20' N, 77° 42.20' W will place you approximately ¾ mile west/southwest of the entrance to the harbour on the northwestern shore of Allan's-Pensacola Cay as shown on Chart AB-12. If you're approaching from Great Sale Cay, actually *Barracouta Rocks Channel*, you must be sure to avoid the shallow sandbank lying south of Moraine Cay as shown on Chart AB-8. From Fox Town, once you clear the Hawksbill Cays you have a straight shot to the harbor at Allan's-Pensacola. If you're approaching from the south, from Spanish Cay or other spots in the *Sea of Abaco* south of Angel Fish Point, make sure you clear the shoals at the Hog Cays (passing between the Hog Cays and Angelfish Point) before turning towards Allan's-Pensacola.

From the waypoint outside the harbor at Allan's-Pensacola you can head a bit north of east and pass north of the submerged rocks lying northwest of Allan's Cay Rocks. Once past the submerged rocks, turn to starboard and anchor where your draft allows. The water thins gradually the further in you go, and the holding is poor at times. You must make sure

your anchor is set well here. I was anchored here one night and we had a succession of three very violent squalls pass through between 0200-0500 with 40+ knot westerly winds. Six out of 15 boats wound up on the beach and I myself wound up 100' short of the beach after a dragging trawler fouled my starboard anchor. For some reason every time I anchor at Allan's-Pensacola Cay we have bad weather from the west. So if you see me anchored at Allan's-Pensacola you'd better check your anchors, it's a sure sign of bad weather!

In southwesterly and westerly winds I have anchored off the northern shore of Allan's-Pensacola and the water was flat calm. But bear in mind that westerly winds usually mean a shift to the north, especially in the winter months, and the northern side of Allan's-Pensacola is no place to be when that happens. There are two ways that you can access these anchorages as shown on Chart AB-12.

First, you can head east around the eastern tip of Allan's-Pensacola and the Murray Cays and then double back to the west once you clear the Murray Cays and the Money Cays. The Money Cays are called that because a squatter named Murray is said to have found a treasure trove there. Your other option is to round the northwestern tip of Umbrella Cay and parallel the lie of Umbrella Cay, Guineaman's Cay, and Allan's-Pensacola Cay staying ½ mile offshore until you find the spot that you like.

At the eastern end of Allan's-Pensacola Cay is the aptly named Hurricane Hole. As shown on Chart AB-12, the entrance is between two spits of land with your course favoring the southern spit. Don't stray north here as the water shallows quickly and the bottom is rocky. It's best to sound this route by dinghy first. This route will take 5' at high water and the shallowest spot is just inside the end of the southern spit with about 3' at MLW. From here the water gets progressively deeper, 7'-9' in spots in the narrow creek that leads back to the small, shallow pond. The creek is lined with mangroves on both sides and if a hurricane threatened, I would choose to tie up in the creek just before it leads into the pond.

The Hog Cays

The Hog Cays lie just to the southeast of Allan's-Pensacola Cay. Hog Cay is private and visits ashore must be by invitation only. There is an

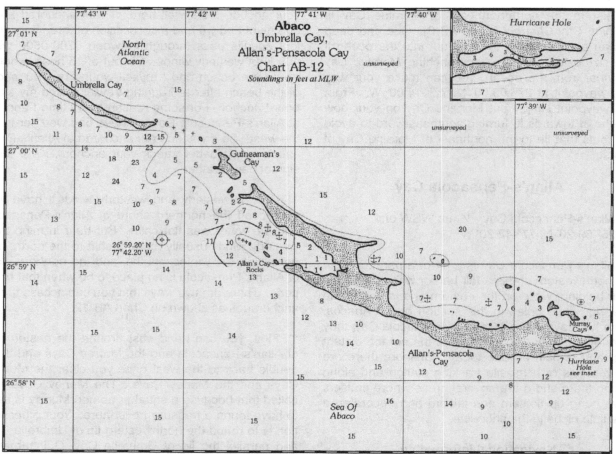

Abaco
Umbrella Cay,
Allan's-Pensacola Cay
Chart AB-12
Soundings in feet at MLW

Hurricane Hole

North Atlantic Ocean

Umbrella Cay

Guineaman's Cay

Allan's Cay Rocks

Allan's-Pensacola Cay

Murray Cays

Hurricane Hole
see inset

Sea Of Abaco

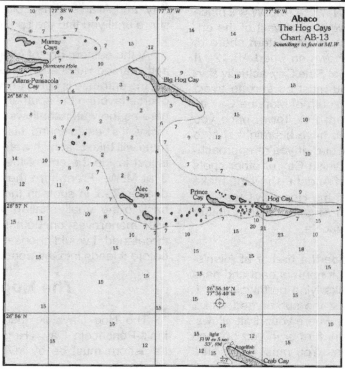

Abaco
The Hog Cays
Chart AB-13
Soundings in feet at MLW

Murray Cays

Hurricane Hole

Allans-Pensacola Cay

Big Hog Cay

Alec Cays

Prince Cay

Hog Cay

light
Fl W ev 5 sec
33', 8M
Angelfish Point

Crab Cay

entrance to a small cove on the north side of Hog Cay that is never used. I only mention it in that it might be a place to duck into in the event of a hurricane. The entrance takes 5' with 6' and more inside at MLW.

Crab Cay and Angelfish Point

Crab Cay - ¼ nm N of Angelfish Point:
26° 56.10' N, 77° 36.40' W

Angelfish Point lies at the northern end of Crab Cay, the small island that itself lies off the northern-most tip of Great Abaco Island. A 33' tall light that flashes white every 5 seconds marks the point. The anchorage in the lee of Crab Cay and Great Abaco Island is great in winds from north through east to south with good holding in sand mixed in with a few rocks.

Navigational Information
Getting here is easy. A waypoint at 26° 56.10' N, 77° 36.40' W places you approximately ½ mile north of Angelfish Point as shown on Chart AB-8. If you're approaching from Moraine Cay, Allan's-Pensacola, Spanish Cay, or if you're heading north along the Great Abaco shoreline you can head directly for this waypoint. If you're approaching from Great Sale Cay or Fox Town, you can head more for the northern point of Crab Cay as you get within a mile or so. If you're paralleling the shoreline from Fox Town to Crab Cay, or in reverse, from Crab Cay to Fox Town, beware of the reefs a mile and more west of Crab Cay as shown on Chart AB-8.

Crab Cay is bounded to the southwest by a large shallow bar and vessels wishing to access the anchorage have two options here. You can either go all the way around the bar to the southwest or pass close in along the Crab Cay shore and parallel it southeast-ward into the main anchorage area. There is a shallow bar with 6' over it at MLW just southeast of the light, but you'll have 7' or more the rest of the way along this route. You can anchor in the lee of Great Abaco in 6'-8' of water just off the small beach.

The small but very rocky beach is not worth exploring, but there are miles of shallow waterways that are worth exploring. You can even work your way back to where the locals keep their boats by the *Bootle Highway Bridge* that connects Little Abaco Island with Great Abaco Island. Shallow draft vessels can even work their way up in here for excellent all-around protection (with lots of current and bugs).

There is a little known shortcut between Crab Cay and Great Abaco Island, but it is only for skippers with an adventurous spirit, a high tide, and a vessel that draws less than 6'. Before I tell you about this one, I'm going to insist that you sound this passage first by dinghy, going in and out several times to familiarize yourself with it before you try it with your seagoing home. A good suggestion would be to set up a visual range for yourself. I use the small cay directly south of the cut and the small rock that lies east of Hog Cay directly north of the cut. I'll put the southern cay on my stern and the northern rock on my bow to get myself lined up with where the deeper water is. The hazards are a rocky bar that lies southeast of Crab Cay that dries a bit at low water and a few rocks lying northwest of Great Abaco Island. You must pass between the two in a narrow channel that is closer to the Great Abaco Island shoreline.

As I said, try this with your dink first and if you don't feel comfortable, don't attempt this shortcut...it's not that far around Crab Cay anyway. I only mention this route because it's fun to surprise people when they see you enter or leave by it. One time I was heading to this anchorage in company with another boat that was well ahead of me. He thought he had me beat until he rounded Angelfish Point and saw me setting my anchor.

The Central Abacos

Ports of Entry: Spanish Cay, Green Turtle Cay
Fuel: Spanish Cay, Cooper's Town, Green Turtle Cay, Great Guana Cay, Treasure Cay
Haul-Out: Green Turtle Cay
Diesel Repairs: Green Turtle Cay
Outboard Repairs: Green Turtle Cay
Propane: Green Turtle Cay
Provisions: Spanish Cay, Cooper's Town, Green Turtle Cay, Great Guana Cay, Treasure Cay
Important Lights:
   Whale Cay: Fl W ev 5sec
   Treasure Cay (entrance): Fl W
   Guana Cay: Fl W

Spanish Cay

South Spanish Cay Channel - outer waypoint:
26° 56.55' N, 77° 28.85' W

Spanish Cay - ½ nm WSW of marina:
26° 56.10' N, 77° 32.10' W

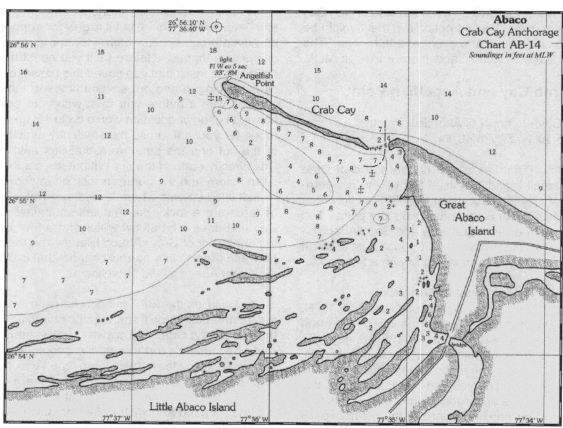

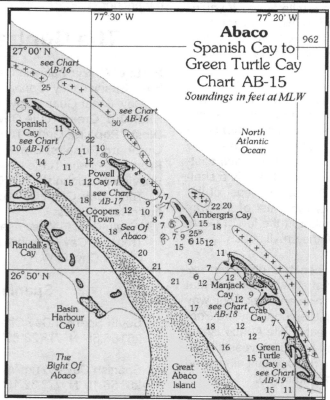

South Spanish Cay Channel - inner waypoint:
26° 56.00' N, 77° 29.50' W

Over the past few years Spanish Cay has come into its own as a major destination in the Abacos. The new marina is one of the finest in the islands, the airstrip has reopened, and Spanish Cay has become a *Port of Entry* for The Bahamas as well as an extremely popular haven for cruisers.

Navigational Information

If you're approaching Spanish Cay from the north or west on the *Little Bahama Bank* (as shown on Chart AB-8), you'll need to pass between Crab Cay (Angelfish Point) and the Hog Cays as you approach Spanish Cay. You can pass south of the small shoal that lies off the northwestern tip of Spanish Cay to make a direct approach to a waypoint at 26° 56.10' N, 77° 32.10' W, which will place you approximately ½ mile west/southwest of the entrance to *Spanish Cay Marina*. From the waypoint head in towards the marina entrance as shown on the chart; the entrance is marked by a red and green marker on the outer pilings (red, right returning here).

If you're approaching from Powell Cay or Coopers Town you need to avoid the large shoal that lies just south of the southeastern tip of Spanish Cay as shown on Chart AB-15. You can pass between the shoal and Goat Cay as shown on Chart AB-16. Watch out for the conspicuous brown reef that lies northwest of Powell Cay and that is shown on Charts AB-16 and AB-17.

Cruisers can enter or leave the *Little Bahama Bank* via *North Spanish Cay Channel* and *South Spanish Cay Channel* as shown on Chart AB-16. The southern channel is a bit wider so let's discuss it first. Leaving the marina at Spanish Cay, parallel the shoreline southeastward passing between the conspicuous shoal to the south and Goat Cay as shown on the chart. Once clear of the small rocks that lie southeast of Goat Cay, turn and head for a waypoint at 26° 56.00' N, 77° 29.50' W, which will place you approximately ¼ mile inside *South Spanish Cay Channel*. There will be reefs off both sides of your vessel but you have a wide and deep cut here, 25' and more at MLW in places. Head through the cut on a northeastward course or head to the outer waypoint at 26° 56.55' N, 77° 28.85' W. The course here is not as important as staying between the reefs! If approaching from the North Atlantic Ocean, make

your way to the outer waypoint at 26° 56.55' N, 77° 28.85' W. From here you can head southwest or make your way to the inner waypoint at 26° 56.00' N, 77° 29.50' W. Whatever way you choose to enter, just keep your eyes open, and trust them.

North Spanish Cay Channel is narrower than the southern channel, but can be safely transited by the prudent skipper. From the marina at Spanish Cay, work your way northwestward around the northern tip of Spanish Cay, passing between Spanish Cay and the shoal off its northwestern tip in 8'-10' at MLW as shown on Chart AB-16. Round past Squashes Cay and head for the inner waypoint at 26° 57.90' N, 77° 32.70' W, which will place you approximately ¼ mile southwest of *North Spanish Cay Channel*. From here the reefs on both sides of the channel should be visible; you'll want to stay between them. Head for the outer waypoint at 26° 58.40' N, 77° 31.90' W keeping an eye out for the reefs. Once again, trust your eyes and depthsounder, not a chart when entering any cut in any island group. If you're approaching *North Spanish Cay Channel* from the deep waters of the *North Atlantic Ocean*, head for the outer waypoint at 26° 58.40' N, 77° 31.90' W and follow the above route in reverse.

There is a small, but well-protected anchorage at the northwestern end of Spanish Cay, but the entrance is shallow and tricky and the holding is poor. To enter the anchorage, round Squashes Cay as shown on Chart AB-16 and then pass over the shallow bar 3' at MLW, favoring the eastern shoreline. Inside you'll find 6'-8' over a grassy bottom. Occasionally someone will place a small stake or piece of PVC pipe to mark the starboard side of the channel so use caution when entering.

What You Will Find Ashore

Spanish Cay Marina, rebuilt after *Hurricane Floyd*, has 81 slips and can accommodate vessels to 200' LOA, with drafts to 8.5'. All slips have full electric and water, and the marina offers showers, a laundry, RO water, a fresh water pool and spa, a marina store, golf cart rentals, condos, and hotel suites. You can also dine at the *Point House Restaurant* or enjoy your favorite beverage at the *Wrecker's Bar*, both of whom monitor VHF ch. 16. *Spanish Cay Marina* is a *Port of Entry* with *Customs* and *Immigration* available 7 days, a week; if you need to clear-in give the marina a hail on the VHF and they will notify *Customs* and *Immigration* for you.

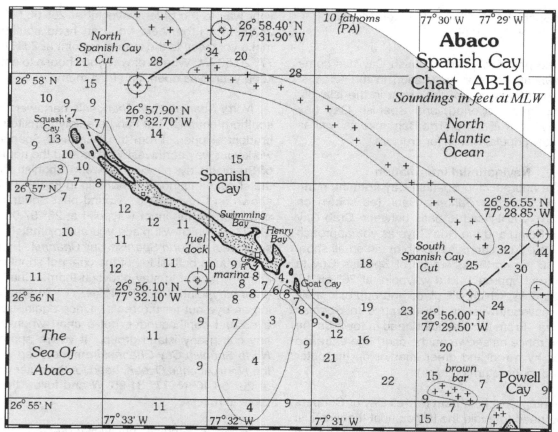

Abaco
Spanish Cay
Chart AB-16
Soundings in feet at MLW

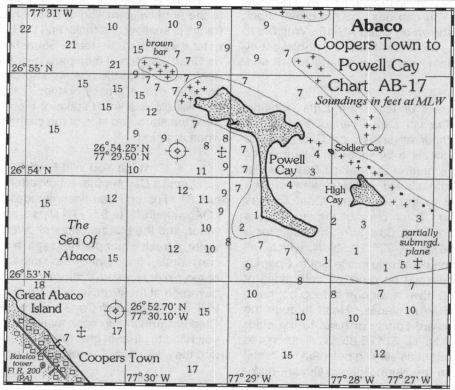

Abaco
Coopers Town to
Powell Cay
Chart AB-17
Soundings in feet at MLW

A Tale of Spanish Cay

Spanish Cay may have once played a part in a drama that began in Washington D.C., at the headquarters of the *Federal Bureau of Investigation*.

For many years Spanish Cay was owned by Texas oil mogul Clint Murchison who built an airstrip on the deserted cay and imported over 1,000 palm trees. Murchison was a personal friend of *FBI* Director J. Edgar Hoover and several alleged "Mafiosos" such as Santos Trafficante, Carlos Marcello, and Sam Giancana, the trio that many believe were behind JFK's assassination. Murchison owned the *Del Charro* hotel in La Jolla, California, near the *Del Mar Racetrack*, and Hoover often stayed months at a time with Clint, always picking up the tab.

Jimmy G.C. Corcoran, a former *Bureau of Investigation* (the *Bureau* did not acquire the term *Federal* until 1935 when it became the *FBI*) agent and close associate of J. Edgar Hoover, left the *Bureau* just after World War I. Over the next three decades Corcoran grew to become a very powerful figure in Washington political circles. Working as a lobbyist during World War II Corcoran attempted to collect a huge $75,000 fee, illegal at that time, and he received word that Hoover was going to "set him up." An enraged Corcoran confronted the Director, called him every type of SOB he could think of, and reminded him of the "favor" he had once done for him. Hoover, a closet homosexual, had been arrested in the late 1920's in New Orleans on sex charges involving a young man. Corcoran, who had by then left the Bureau and had several powerful contacts in Louisiana, stepped in and prevented Hoover's prosecution and the career ending scandal it would have produced. Hoover relented; Corcoran got his money and was not arrested. Several years later, in 1956, Corcoran died in a mysterious plane crash off Murchison's Spanish Cay.

Powell Cay

Powell Cay - ½ nm W of anchorage:
26° 54.25' N, 77° 29 .50' W

Powell Cay has a great anchorage in the prevailing northeast through southeast winds, and it also has the advantage that if you need supplies you can shoot right across the Sea of Abaco to Coopers Town for fuel, food, or even a taxi to the airport at Marsh Harbour. There's great diving on the oceanside reefs, nice beaches, plenty of land to trek around upon, great views from the hill, a marina nearby (at Spanish Cay), and even a submerged plane to explore when you've done everything else.

Navigational Information

As shown on Chart AB-17, a waypoint at 26° 54.25 N, 77° 29.50' W, will place you approximately ¼ mile west of the main anchorage area. But don't simply plug in this waypoint and hit "Go To." If you're at Coopers Town, that would be fine, it's a straight shot, but if you're approaching from any other direction care must be taken.

If you're approaching from the north, from Spanish Cay or Angelfish Point, you must avoid the large shallow area that lies south of Spanish Cay as shown on Chart AB-15. Most simply head south of it before altering course to Powell Cay. If you're leaving the marina at Spanish Cay bound for Powell Cay, you can pass between the shoal and Goat Cay as shown on Chart AB-16. If you're taking this route keep an eye out for the conspicuous brown reef that lies just northwest of Powell Cay as shown on Chart AB-17.

If you're approaching Powell Cay from the south, from Manjack or Green Turtle, simply parallel the shoreline of Great Abaco, deep water runs almost right up to the land, and head northwestward. Once you pass abeam of the southern tip of Powell Cay turn to starboard and head northward into the anchorage.

Coopers Town

Coopers Town - ½ nm NE of:
26° 52.70' N, 77° 30.10' W

Coopers Town is the northernmost settlement on the island of Great Abaco. Coopers Town was originally settled in the 1870's by the Cooper family from Grand Bahama and the Bootle family from Green Turtle Cay. Although Coopers Town had no natural harbor, their intention was to create a transshipment point for the growing and exporting of produce. Today, many of Coopers Town 900 residents now work down the road at Treasure Cay and the town's principal claim to fame these days is that it is the home district of the former Prime Minister of The Bahamas, the Right Honorable Hubert Ingraham.

Navigational Information
A waypoint at 26° 52.70' N, 77° 30.10' W, will place you approximately ½ mile off Coopers Town in the *Sea of Abaco* as shown on Chart AB-17. Access is easy here; if you are approaching from the north, from Angelfish Point, or from the south, from Green Turtle Cay, all you need to do is parallel the shoreline of Great Abaco to arrive at Coopers Town. Don't fret the depths here, if you stay ¼ mile or more off Great Abaco you'll have 12'-20' of water (at MLW) the entire way. A mile or more north of Coopers Town is a small indentation in the Abaco shoreline that offers protection in south through west/northwest winds. The entrance is straightforward and will carry 3' at MLW with more inside.

At the waypoint off Coopers Town you can turn in and pull up to the *Coopers Town Shell* dock (call ahead on VHF ch. 16) or you can anchor if conditions allow. This is a good lee anchorage in southwest to westerly conditions! *Coopers Town Shell* offers diesel, gasoline, water, and ice.

What You Will Find Ashore
Ashore, Coopers Town has a large community clinic, a *Batelco* office, an office of *Scotia Bank*, and a large new government office building. Just across the street from *Coopers Town Shell* (which may or may not be open by now) is a nice grocery store while just to the south is a small bar and restaurant perched above the water on Coopers Town's beautiful new post-*Hurricane Floyd* seawall. About ¼ mile south of the *Shell* dock is *Richie's Restaurant*, a good spot to grab a bite to eat. On the *Bootle Highway* at the southern edge of town is *M&M's Restaurant and Guest House* on the western side of the road. Visitors may wish to check out the *Albert Bootle Museum* where you'll learn about the early settlers, the Bootles and Coopers, as well as sponging, sisal, and lumber.

Several years ago, a man in Coopers Town believed he had struck oil in his yard. Digging down 100', his bit brought up a dark substance that he believed to be oil. The owner, proclaiming that the oil led straight to the *Persian Gulf*, declared that God had led him to dig there and that the oil would be used to benefit the people and the government of The Bahamas. Unfortunately for The Bahamas, a Texas oil company took rock and water samples and announced that there was no presence of oil at the site. It is not known if the digger will keep trying in his quest.

Manjack Cay

Manjack Cay - ¾ nm SW of anchorages:
26° 48.80' N, 77° 22.80' W

Manjack Cay, sometimes shown as Nunjack Cay on older charts, is home to a half-dozen lovely beaches and secluded coves, great hiking trails, and some interesting ocean-side reefs as well as a couple of wrecks for underwater explorers to investigate. The cay is popular with locals as well as cruisers as you can tell when you visit the "Manjack Hilton," a small collection of picnic tables that visitors have constructed.

Navigational Information
The primary anchorage is found in the bight between Manjack Cay, Rat Cay, and Crab Cay. A waypoint at 26° 48.80' N, 77° 22.80 W will place you approximately ½ mile west/southwest of this anchorage area. If you're approaching from Green Turtle Cay you can simply parallel the shoreline of Green Turtle Cay northward keeping the conspicuous shallow area between Crab Cay, Crab Rock, and Green Turtle Cay to starboard (see Chart AB-18). Once past Crab Cay turn to starboard and anchor wherever your draft allows.

If you're approaching from the north you must avoid the large shoal area that lies south of the northwestern tip of Manjack Cay. You can either pass south of this shoal or, if you're feeling adventurous, you can pass over it with the tide in 4' at MLW as shown on Chart AB-18. Approach the northwestern tip of Manjack Cay and Manjack Rocks keeping an eye out for the conspicuous brown bar as shown on the chart. Your course will parallel the shoreline of Manjack Rocks and Manjack Cay over the shoal area in 4' at MLW as shown on the chart.

There is a great anchorage in a small cove off the northwestern tip of Manjack Cay as shown on Chart AB-18. If approaching from the north you can round Manjack Rocks and head straight into the small cove, but if you wish to access this anchorage from the main anchorage you must once again avoid the large shoal that lies south of the northwestern tip of Manjack Cay. As previously mentioned, you may also choose to cross the shoal with the tide if your draft allows. From the main anchorage head northwestward paralleling the shoreline of Manjack Cay past *Coconut Tree Bay*, which is a nice little anchorage itself in north/north-

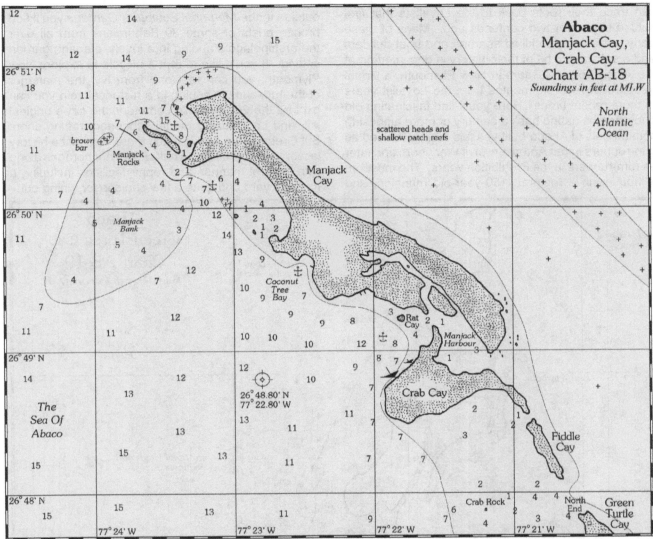

Abaco
Manjack Cay,
Crab Cay
Chart AB-18
Soundings in feet at MLW

east through east winds. As you proceed towards the northwestern tip of Manjack Cay you'll pass several small rocks where you can also anchor just off their northwestern side as shown on the chart. Continuing northwestward you'll take Manjack Rocks to starboard (as shown on Chart AB-18) and cross over the bar with 4' at MLW. Once past Manjack Rocks, and clear of the brown bar that lies west of them, you can turn to the north to round Manjack Rocks and enter the small cove with 6'-15' at MLW. This anchorage is good in east through southwest winds, but it can get a bit rolly at times with strong northeast-east winds.

What You Will Find Ashore

Those cruisers who wish to explore the cays they anchor off, will have an excellent opportunity to do just that at Manjack Cay. On Manjack Beach there is a large dock where you can land your dink and find a nature walk. Tiny Fiddle Cay is a popular spot with local boaters and the surrounding waters offer good shelling and the offshore reefs offer numerous diving opportunities.

Green Turtle Cay

Green Turtle Cay - ½ nm W of New Plymouth:
26° 45.70' N, 77° 20.35' W

New Plymouth, with its pastel painted houses, picket fences, and stone walls may remind you more of a quaint New England fishing village than a Bahamian Out Island. Most of the 500 or so residents of New Plymouth, the settlement perched on the southern end of mile-long Green Turtle Cay, can trace their roots back to the Loyalists that first settled here over two centuries ago. Many of these early settlers were skilled seaman and boat builders and a substantial bit of their history is documented at the *Albert Lowe Museum* in New Plymouth, a virtual treasure trove of momentos from the Loyalist years to more recent times. Here you'll find fascinating old photographs dating back a century or more alongside ship models of Abaco-built vessels that were used as gun-runners in the American Civil War years and later as rum-runners in the Prohibition years. The museum is housed in a restored 150-year-old mansion, and

outside in the *Memorial Sculpture Gardens* you'll find bronze busts of some 30 Bahamians from all over the archipelago standing in a lovely, elegant, garden setting. If you'd like to rent a bicycle to explore New Plymouth, you can rent one from Ivy, the manager of the museum. Keeping in a historical vein you can explore the 200-year-old cemetery, the cay's original jail, and an amazing model schooner crafting shop. But Green Turtle Cay is much more than just a history lesson. Here you'll find a half-dozen anchorages along with several marinas and repair facilities including a haul out yard and quite a few choices for dining out.

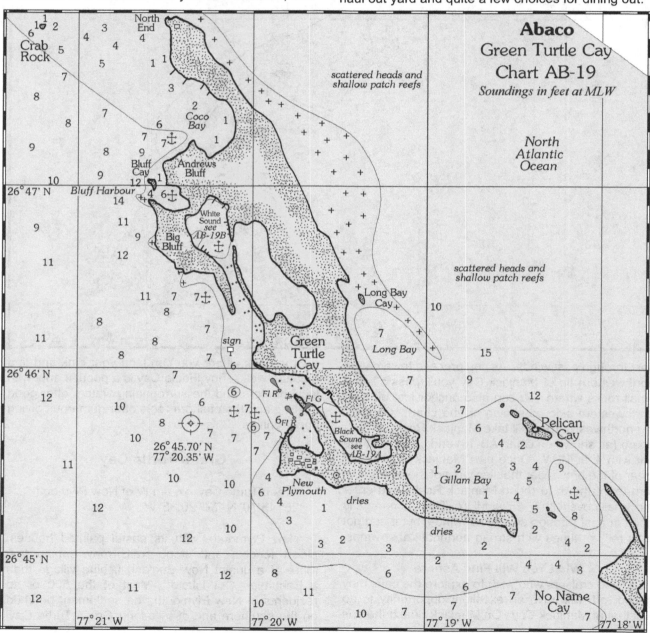

Navigational Information

Green Turtle is a "must" stop on nearly everyone's tour of the Abacos and access is fairly easy. As shown on Chart AB-19, a waypoint at 26° 45.70 N, 77° 20.35' W will place you about a half-mile west of the town of New Plymouth and the popular lee anchorage lying west of town (as also shown on Chart AB-19A). This anchorage is good in winds from northeast through east and almost to southeast. I've found iffy holding in places here so make sure your anchor is set before you leave your boat. If you need to clear in, you'll have to tie up to the large government dock on the western side of New Plymouth.

As shown on the chart, shallow draft vessels can also access Settlement Harbour and the town dock from this anchorage. I don't recommend this, but I show it because it's the best dinghy route into town. From the anchorage, pass between the outer pair of red and green markers (*Fl R* and *Fl G*) and continue on passing between the markers as you approach the large town dock.

If you're approaching Green Turtle Cay from the north you'll have few hazards as the *Sea of Abaco* is deep between Green Turtle and Great Abaco Island. The only real hazards from Coopers Town southward is a small shoal area southwest of Ambergris Cay and the large shoal south of the northern end of Manjack Cay as shown on Chart AB-15. If you're approaching from Manjack Cay you can simply follow the edge of the shallow bank lying between Crab Cay and Green Turtle Cay and then parallel the shoreline of Green Turtle Cay (as shown on Charts AB-15, AB-18, and AB-19).

If you're approaching Green Turtle Cay from the south, from *Don't Rock Passage*, you'll need to avoid the large shoal area that lies south and southwest of Green Turtle Cay (see Chart AB-19) which blocks your courseline from the Sand Bank Cays. If you're approaching from *Whale Cay Passage* you'll need to keep Channel Rock, Two Rocks, No Name Cay, and the shoal south of Green Turtle Cay to your starboard side as shown on Charts AB-21, AB-20, and AB-19. The hazards here are very visible and you can see the large shoal area well with good visibility. If in doubt, or if you just prefer deeper water, simply head more over to the Great Abaco Island side of the *Sea of Abaco* until you come abeam of the southern tip of Green Turtle Cay and can work your way east/northeast towards the anchorage and waypoint.

There are three more lee anchorages along the western shore of Green Turtle Cay. Just north of the anchorage off the settlement and north of the entrance to *White Sound* sits a nice lee anchorage as shown on Charts AB-19 and AB-19B. You can actually anchor anywhere along the shore here from Joyless Point northward, but if you tuck up as far north and east as you can you'll pick up some shelter from north winds as well as northeast through southeast winds. The *Bluff House* fuel dock lies to the west of this anchorage; you'll need to keep an eye out for the submerged rocks south of the fuel dock as shown on the chart.

A very protected anchorage lies in tiny Bluff Harbour as shown on Charts AB-19 and AB-19B. The entrance lies south of Bluff Cay between Bluff Cay and the mainland of Green Turtle Cay. The entrance bar has almost 4' over it at MLW and you'll find 6'-7' and more in a small pocket inside. Watch out for the submerged rocks off the point to the south of the entrance channel. As protected as this anchorage appears, it is no place to be in strong west to northwest winds. A bit further north cruisers can anchor in a small bight just to the west of shallow Coco Bay as shown on Chart AB-19. This spot is good in winds from north of east through southeast and almost south.

Besides the above mentioned lee anchorages, there are two excellent well-protected anchorages, one in *White Sound* and one in *Black Sound;* both offer all-around protection and could be considered as shelter in the event of a hurricane. The entrance to *Black Sound* lies just north of the town of New Plymouth as shown on Chart 19-A. To enter *Black Sound* from the lee anchorage west of New Plymouth you must pass between the outer red (FL R) and green markers that lie between the mainland to the north and the point of land to the south (as shown on Chart AB-19A). Split the rest of the markers as you pass over the shallowest spot (4' at MLW) and continue past the large *Abaco Yacht Services* yard on your port side and the *Other Shore Club* dock on your starboard side. When you're back in deeper water anchor wherever your draft allows. The bottom is quite grassy here so make sure your anchor is set well.

The entrance to *White Sound*, as shown on Chart AB-19B, lies a bit north of the entrance to *Black Sound* (as shown on Chart AB-19), between the two

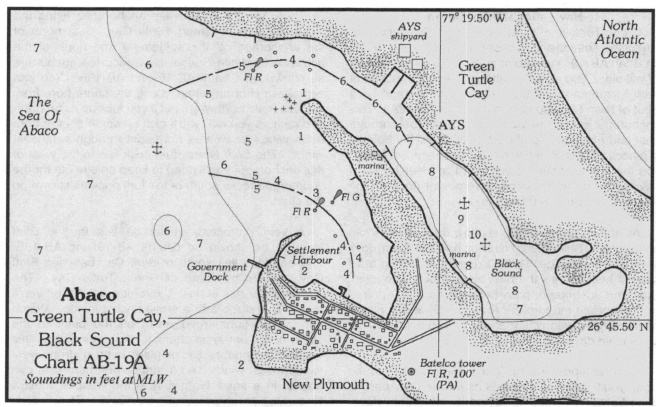

The Sea Of Abaco

AYS shipyard

77° 19.50' W

North Atlantic Ocean

Green Turtle Cay

7

6

5

Fl R

4

6

6

AYS

1

5

1

6

6

7

8

marina

6

5

5

4

3

Fl G

Fl R

9

10

8

Black Sound

7

6

7

Settlement Harbour

4

4

2

4

8

8

Government Dock

Abaco
Green Turtle Cay,
Black Sound
Chart AB-19A
Soundings in feet at MLW

7

26° 45.50' N

4

2

4

Batelco tower
Fl R, 100'
(PA)

6

4

New Plymouth

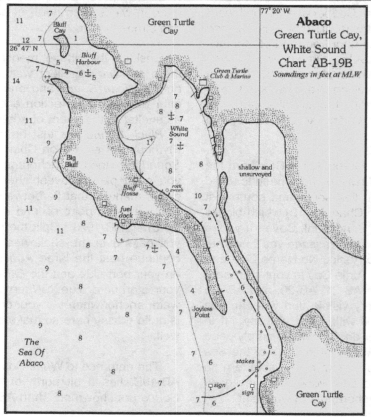

77° 20' W

11

7

Bluff Cay

Green Turtle Cay

Abaco
Green Turtle Cay,
White Sound
Chart AB-19B
Soundings in feet at MLW

12

1

26° 47' N

5

Bluff Harbour

7

4

6

5

Green Turtle Club & Marina

14

7

7

8

8

7

11

White Sound

7

9

7

8

10

Big Bluff

1

7

shallow and unsurveyed

9

Bluff House

8

rock awash

10

11

fuel dock

8

7

9

8

7

7

4

9

7

4

8

Joyless Point

9

7

stakes

8

The Sea Of Abaco

8

sign

sign

7

6

Green Turtle Cay

conspicuous signs, one of which sits well out into the water. The entrance is via a long, narrow (dredged to 30' wide), shallow (4½'-5'), but well-marked channel where you'll need the help of the tide. To enter you will need to pass south of the outer sign, north of the inner sign (obviously!), and split the outer green and red buoys. You'll split a couple of pairs of markers here, and then as the channel curves to the north you'll want to favor the eastern side of the channel, hugging the stakes as you proceed northward into *White Sound*.

White Sound is a good anchorage in all conditions, but you must avoid the shallow bar that works out from the western shore; there's a rock awash at the eastern tip of this shoal (see Chart AB-19B). There are moorings available in both *White Sound* and *Black Sound*.

What You Will Find Ashore

Now let's discuss the facilities found in *Black Sound* and *White Sound*. *Black Sound* has excellent facilities for the visiting boater, a good marina and a full-service haul-out yard. As you enter *Black Sound* you'll first pass the large *Abaco Yacht Services* (AYS) on the northern side of the channel. This huge yard has been providing marine services and storage to Abaco boaters and yachtsmen for over twenty years; the owners are 7th generation Abaconians. Their 40-ton lift can handle boats up to 65', a 6½' draft, with a 21' beam. You can also arrange with *AYS* for dry storage for vessels up to that same size. *AYS* can haul your boat, pressure clean the bottom, and paint it with *TBT* anti-fouling paint. They also offer cleaning and waxing of hulls, factory trained *Yamaha* mechanics, welding, fiberglass work, and repairs of struts, props, and cutlass bearings. You'll also find showers, a laundry, ice, and water at their docks.

Directly across (almost) from *AYS* sits the *Other Shore Club and Marina*, a very friendly marina with 15 slips (full electric) as well as diesel, gasoline, water, ice, showers, and a short walk to town. Here too is *Pineapple's Restaurant* serving lunch and dinner daily. A bit further in you'll find *Black Sound Marina* on the southwestern shore of *Black Sound*. This marina offers 15 slips accommodating boats up to 140' with drafts of up to 7' at MLW. The newly constructed docks boast 30-50amp electricity, water, ice, a Laundromat, showers, and a barbecue/picnic area. "Downtown" is only a five-minute walk, but if you don't feel like walking you can rent a golf cart at the marina.

Also in *Black Sound*, *Roberts Marine*, a *Johnson* dealer, offers outboard and diesel repairs, boat rentals, batteries, ice, and the usual assortment of quality marine supplies. A bit further in you'll find *Roberts Cottages and Dock* offering secure, private dockage for boats up to 65' with either short or long-term storage available. The docks are equipped with full electric, 30-50 amp and 110V/220V. *Roberts Cottages* monitors VHF ch. 16. The *Leeward Yacht Club and Marina* lies on the eastern shore of *Black Sound* is private with few spaces available.

Not to be outdone by its southern neighbor, *White Sound* also offers the finest in Abaco amenities for the visiting boater. As you approach the end of the entrance channel as it opens up into White Sound you'll find *Dolphin Marine* on the western shore. *Dolphin Marine* is an *OMC* dealer and they monitor VHF ch.16. Their factory-trained mechanics and fully stocked parts department can help you solve any outboard problems you might be having. They are dealers for *Carolina Skiff* and *Boston Whaler* and a line of inflatables as well.

On the western shore of *White Sound* sits the *Bluff House Club Hotel & Marina*. *Bluff House* can accommodate boats drawing up to 7' although part of the marina has only 4' at MLW. Their docks have full electric hookups, water, ice, showers, a laundry, the *Bluff House Boutique* and a restaurant and bar on location. The *Bluff House* fuel dock sits on the western shore of Green Turtle Cay as shown on Charts AB-19 and AB-19B. The *Bluff House Restaurant* serves lunch from 1130 and seats for dinner at 1930 with reservations a must. Dockage can be applied to your dinner or bar bill and allows use of all the facilities at the Bluff House.

At the northern end of *White Sound* resides the *Green Turtle Club and Marina*, proud owners of a four-star rating from *Fielding's Travel Guide* in 1992. The marina can accommodate vessels with a beam of up to 25' and a draft of 5'-7'. They offer 35 slips with full electric hookups and satellite TV, fuel, water, ice, showers, a laundry, marine supplies, a grocery/liquor store, the *Green Turtle Club Boutique* and an excellent restaurant on site. Try breakfast or lunch on the patio of the restaurant and then enjoy dinner in their *Queen Anne* style dining room (reservations before 1700 are a must; your dockage can be applied to your dinner or bar bill). The *Green Turtle Club* also hosts live music on Monday and Saturday nights.

The *Green Turtle Club* has a unique history. Originally an old wooden boathouse, it was converted into a yacht club style pub and became the cornerstone for today's *Green Turtle Club*. Even in its infancy the *Green Turtle Club,* under the leadership of its owner Allen Charlesworth, gained an international reputation THE spot to escape from the daily rigors and trappings of civilization. Mr. Charlesworth passed away in 1989, but his family has continued to maintain the timeless charm of the tradition-filled *Green Turtle Club.* Today the Club is proud of its newest addition, the *Green Turtle Club Divers* operation. The dive shop offers Scuba and snorkel trips as well as island tours to other Abaco Cays. *GTC Divers* is a complete PADI and NAUI affiliated dive shop with sales, rentals, and air fills. But this isn't the only dive shop around; you can also visit *Brendal's Dive Shop* on Green Turtle Cay. Brendal is the dean of the Green Turtle Cay diving operations, he's been doing this for over 20 years. Brendal offers *SCUBA* certification, daily snorkel, *SCUBA*, and glass bottom reef trips, wreck and cavern dives, stingray and grouper feedings, and he has a full-service retail store. Give Brendal a shout on VHF ch. 16.

Now that we've covered White Sound and *Black Sound*, let's check out what's in store for you in New Plymouth. If you're coming into the town dock in Settlement Harbour by dinghy you'll find several stores on the waterfront or just around the corner from it. There's *Robert's Hardware, New Plymouth Hardware, Sid's Grocery Store, Lowe's Food Store, The Island's Restaurant and Grill* (breakfast, lunch, and dinner; they monitor ch. 16), *Curry's Food and Liquor Store, B & M Seafood, Laura's Kitchen,* and the *McIntosh Restaurant and Bakery.* At the popular *Wrecking Tree Bakery and Restaurant* you can order breakfast, lunch, and dinner; they specialize in seafood (and they also monitor VHF ch. 16). *Curry's* and *Sid's* can fill your propane tanks for you and you can bring your laptop to *Sid's* to hook up to the Internet. Next to Curry's is the *Sunlight Medical Clinic,* open Tuesdays and Thursdays from 1000-1400.

In the center of town you'll find the *New Plymouth Club and Inn* where you can have breakfast, lunch, and dinner daily or partake in their Sunday Brunch. The inn is a restored colonial inn, an intimate place with a beautiful garden, pool, and restaurant that offers candlelight dinners. *Plymouth Rock Liquors and Café* is open Mondays-Thursdays from 0900-1800 and Friday and Saturdays from 0900-2100.

The store proudly stocks over 50 different brands of rum and they will deliver! Next door, the *Ocean Blue Gallery* offers Bahamian inspired artwork with over 50 artists represented. *Barclay's Bank* is open on Tuesdays and Thursdays from 1000-1300.

Two places you must not miss are *Mike's Bar,* on the southern side of New Plymouth, and the world famous *Miss Emily's Blue Bee Bar.* If you're an aficionado of quality alcoholic concoctions, you will bask in the history that surrounds you at *Miss Emily's Blue Bee Bar,* the birth place of the *Goombay Smash,* that world famous rum punch that is today served throughout the Caribbean basin. *The Rooster's Nest,* near the school, hosts live music on Friday and Saturday nights.

South of Green Turtle Cay lies No Name Cay whose beaches are popular with cruisers as well as Green Turtle-ites (yes I know, that probably isn't a word, but it could be…couldn't it?). There is a large, deep (7'-10') pocket of water between No Name Cay and Green Turtle Cay that is a pleasant anchorage, especially in southeast winds. The entrance is gained by crossing the shallow bar (2'-4' at MLW in places) between No Name Cay and "The Bumps," the southern tip of Green Turtle that until recent history was only a sandbar. Check out the route with your dinghy first as the deeper water here changes from time to time. Shell collectors will want to investigate the shallow waters of "The Bumps."

Whale Cay Passage, Don't Rock Passage

Whale Cay Passage - outer N waypoint:
26° 43.70' N, 77° 14.10' W

Whale Cay Passage - outer S waypoint:
26° 42.90' N, 77° 12.60' W

Whale Cay Passage - inner N waypoint:
26° 42.80' N, 77° 15.60' W

Whale Cay Passage, although far from difficult in good weather, is always a major concern for Abaco cruisers. The problem with *Whale Cay Passage* occurs when seas build up and make the cuts north and south of Whale Cay downright dangerous. You don't need strong winds for a rage to occur here, a storm far to the north can generate sufficient seas to close *Whale Cay Passage.* Do not try *Whale Cay*

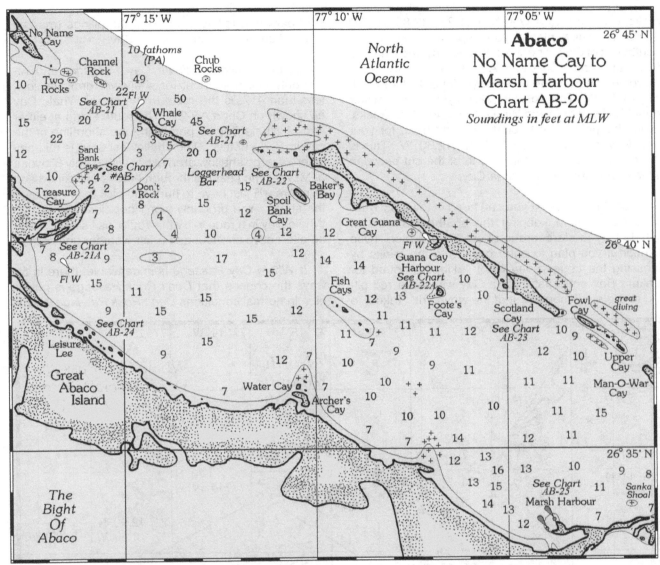

Abaco
No Name Cay to Marsh Harbour
Chart AB-20
Soundings in feet at MLW

Passage in a rage, it is not a playground; *Whale Cay Passage* has a history of wrecks and has earned every bit of its nasty reputation. For daily information on the conditions in *Whale Cay Passage*, listen in to the *Cruisers Net* every morning on the VHF.

Whale Cay Passage really doesn't require waypoints, it is so very easily run simply by eyeball navigation, but for those folks that need a waypoint I'll offer a few for your use in a moment, first let me tell you how to do the *Whale Cay Passage* by eye. If you're approaching from the north, as you head out into deeper water in the cut between Whale Cay and Channel Rock you can turn to starboard to parallel the shore of Whale Cay staying at least ¼ mile off the island. On the other hand, don't go so far out

into the *North Atlantic Ocean* that the Chub Rocks become a hazard to navigation. When you approach the cut between Whale Cay and Great Guana Cay you can take the southeastern tip of Whale Cay to starboard to head for *Treasure Cay Marina*, or follow the marked pilings that will lead you into Bakers Bay on Great Guana Cay as shown on Chart AB-21. Take care if you plan to cross the *Loggerhead Bar*, seas can pile up on that shallow area and make for a very rough ride. Northbound cruisers can follow the above directions in reverse. Now for those of you that feel a bit better with a waypoint to head for, let's see what we can do about that.

Navigational Information
If you're approaching this route from the north,

make your way to a waypoint at 26° 42.80' N, 77° 15.60' W, which places you approximately ¾ mile southwest of the cut between Whale Cay and Channel Rock as shown on Chart AB-21. From this inner waypoint, head to the outer waypoint at 26° 43.70 N, 77° 14.10' W. This position places you in deep water about halfway between Whale Cay and Chub Rocks. From this point, turn to starboard and head for your next waypoint at 26° 42.90' N, 77° 12.60' W. This is the outer waypoint that lies north of the cut between Whale Cay and Great Guana Cay.

From this waypoint you can head in towards *Treasure Cay Marina* keeping the southeastern tip of Whale Cay to starboard in about 20' of water. (Use caution if you plan to enter back onto the banks by crossing the *Loggerhead Bar.*) Skippers bound for Bakers Bay on Great Guana Cay will see a red piling to the south/southeast of the waypoint. Take it to

starboard and follow the rest of the pilings (marked red and green) right into Bakers Bay.

An alternative to *Whale Cay Passage*, and really only just a shortcut for shallower draft vessels, less than 4½', is the route in the lee of Whale Cay as shown on Chart AB-21. The route starts at either end of Whale Cay by paralleling the shoreline of the cay in 5'-7' at MLW. The shallowest area is mid-cay where a large shallow area exists with barely 3' over it at MLW. The channel through here is undefined and skippers will just have to hunt and pick their way over the shoal. You probably won't get close enough to Whale Cay in a rage to try this route, as I said, it's only an alternative shortcut and a fair weather one at that.

If *Whale Cay Passage* is impassable, there is always the chance that *Don't Rock Passage* is possible. In normal conditions *Don't Rock Passage* is sim-

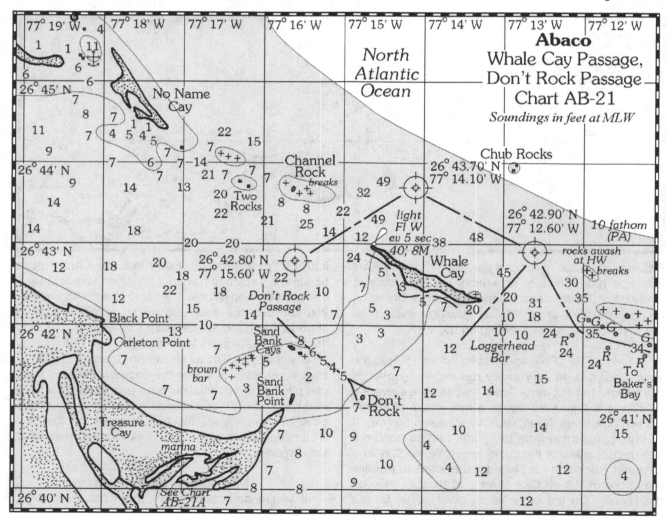

ply a shortcut across the *Sand Bank*, the shoal that lies between Whale Cay and Treasure Cay as shown on Chart AB-21. The controlling depth for *Don't Rock Passage* as of the time of this publication was 4' at MLW so a 6' draft is passable at most high tides. The depths here may change, and usually do every so often, so use care when traversing the bank here. When a rage is occurring at *Whale Cay Passage*, some swells will work their way through to *Don't Rock Passage*, so if it looks rough at *Don't Rock Passage*, don't try it! Bear in mind that this passage changes every year and after every major storm (some will tell you that it changes after each front as well), so use caution as these directions may change over time.

Southbound cruisers should make their way to a position just north of the Sand Bank Cays as shown on Chart AB-21. From this position, take the Sand Bank Cays to starboard as you head for Don't Rock (once called Don't Ye May Rock). You'll have 6'-8' just north of the Sand Bank Cays, but the depths will shallow to about 4' (at MLW) or so halfway between the Sand Bank Cays and Don't Rock. Stay on your courseline for Don't Rock and when the water starts getting deeper you can actually pass north or south of Don't Rock. Once past Don't Rock you can alter course to *Treasure Cay Marina*, Baker's Bay, or even Marsh Harbour (watch out for the shallow bank just southeast of Don't Rock on this route).

Northbound cruisers should make for a position just off Don't Rock as shown on Chart AB-21. Though you can pass either south or north of Don't Rock, I prefer to start the *Don't Rock Passage* from the northern side of Don't Rock; it gives me a better view of my courseline past the Sand Bank Cays. So, as you pass just to the northern side of Don't Rock, you'll want to keep the Sand Bank Cays on your port side, aiming for a spot about 50-100 yards north of the northernmost of the cays. The rest is as described above, but in reverse. Once past the Sand Bank Cays you'll be in deeper water and can take up a course for Green Turtle or other points north.

Treasure Cay

Treasure Cay - ¼ nm SE of entrance channel: 26° 39.53' N, 77° 17.00' W

Treasure Cay, although not really a "cay" in the traditional sense of the word, it's more of a peninsula, has an absolutely first-rate upscale marina, moorings

for rent, one of the prettiest beaches in The Bahamas, and several small canals where you could hide in the event of a hurricane.

Navigational Information
As shown on Chart AB-21, the entrance to *Treasure Cay Marina* lies along the southern shore of Treasure Cay just south of *Whale Cay Passage* and west of Great Guana Cay. As shown on the enlarged Chart AB-21A, a Waypoint at 26° 39.53' N, 77° 17.00' W, will place you approximately ¼ mile southeast of the entrance channel to the Treasure Cay complex. Use caution when approaching this position as just south of the waypoint stands a light (Fl W) that marks the entrance as shown on Chart AB-20.

From the waypoint you will see a string of stakes leading past a small spoil island with a few trees on it. The entrance channel is to the west of this small spoil island as shown on the chart. Enter between the two rows of stakes, one to port and one to starboard, and follow them as they curve around to the northeast where you'll parallel the shoreline past the fuel dock and into the marina and canal area. Just before the marina you'll see some moorings to starboard, pick one up and call the marina on VHF. There is a fee for anchoring here.

If you're approaching Treasure Cay from Baker's Bay or Great Guana Cay Harbour (as shown on Chart AB-20), your course needs to avoid the small shoals lying east of the entrance to the marina as shown on the chart. If you're approaching from Man-O-War Cay you must detour around the Fish Cays as you make your way to the waypoint.

If you are approaching from Marsh Harbour you can simply follow the shoreline as shown on Chart AB-20, but you must make certain that you give a wide berth to Water Cay and the point just southeast of it as submerged rocks stretch out a bit into the *Sea of Abaco*.

What You Will Find Ashore
Treasure Cay Marina offers 150 slips with a minimum depth of 7' at MLW with full electric hookups (20/50/100 amp), free *Wifi*, water, ice, showers, repairs, wet and dry storage, and luxury accommodations at the new $30 million *Bahamas Beach Club*. If you walk across the road from the marina you'll find the beautiful curving Treasure Cay Beach, absolutely superb! If the beach doesn't keep your full attention,

you can always try a round of golf on the Dick Wilson designed course at the *Treasure Cay Golf Club*. You also find other amenities such as tennis courts, boat rentals, and facilities for fishing and Scuba diving. If you have guests flying in or leaving, Treasure Cay has its own airport.

One of the best ways to tour the Treasure Cay area is by golf cart and you can pick one up at *Cash's*

Resort Carts or *Blue Marlin Golf Cart Rentals*. If you prefer, you can rent an automobile from *McKenzie's Car Rentals*, *Triple J Car Rentals*, *Cornish Car Rentals*, and *R&A Rentals and Tours* (they monitor VHF ch. 16). You can even get your teeth cleaned or repaired at the *Treasure Cay Dental Clinic* (365-8625/8425, in U.S. 800-224-6703). If you need someone to do your laundry, check out *Annie's Laundry*.

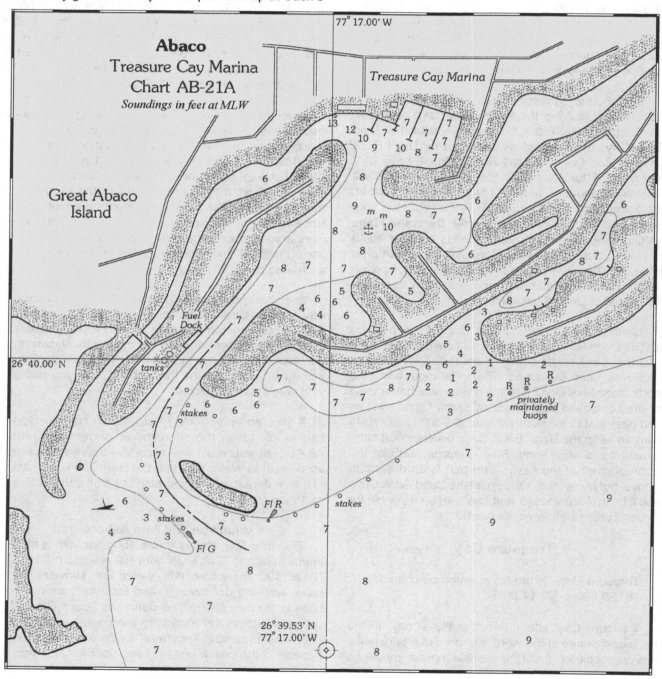

If you have shopping to do you can visit the *Treasure Cay Mini Mart* located at the *Treasure Cay Shopping Centre* where you'll find fresh meats, frozen foods, dairy products, fresh produce, and all sorts of staples. In the same shopping center you'll also find *Bill's Upholstery and Canvas Shop*, *Bristol Wine and Spirits*, a *Batelco* office, and a police station. The best spots to eat here are the *Sand Bar* at the *Banyon Beach Club*, *The Spinnaker Restaurant*, the *Tipsy Seagull Bar*, *Hudson's Delight*, *Touch of Class*, and *Café Florence*. The *Island Boil Restaurant and Sports Lounge* offers true Bahamian cuisine specializing in souse, fish, and lobster. There's also *Lee's Diner*, a fairly new restaurant located in Madera Park at *Parker Plaza*, they're open from 0730 till late serving breakfast, lunch, and dinner. The *Flour House Bakery* in Marsh Harbour will deliver fresh bread for you to *Lee's Diner* so be sure to ask about it. The most popular places around are probably *Café Florence*, the *Coco Bar*, *The Spinnaker Restaurant* and *The Tipsy Seagull Bar*. *The Spinnaker*, and *The Tipsy Seagull* were both damaged by the remnants of *Hurricane Mitch* in November of 1998, but they should both be up and running again by the time you read this. You must not miss a visit to the fashionable *Spinnaker Restaurant* or the livelier *Tipsy Seagull Bar*, especially if you need a place to unwind.

Just north of Treasure Cay on the mainland is a blasted entrance into a small lake called *Jackson Hole*. Some have suggested it as a possible hurricane hole, but it is quite rough in northerly winds and seas. I haven't sounded the lake yet as the entrance was just opened. There is an entrance from the *Bootle Highway* as you head down the road to *Treasure Cay Marina*. Look for two stone pillars, about 3' tall, which mark either side of a narrow road that leads to *Jackson Hole*.

Great Guana Cay

Whale Cay Passage - outer S waypoint:
26° 42.90' N, 77° 12.60' W

Whale Cay Passage - inner N waypoint:
26° 42.80' N, 77° 15.60' W

Great Guana Cay Harbour - ¼ nm S of:
26° 39.50' N, 77° 06.90' W

Great Guana Cay has long been known for having one of the longest and most beautiful beaches in the entire Bahamas. Couple that with some great diving on the offshore reefs and easy access from any of several anchorages and you'll probably come to appreciate Great Guana Cay as one of your favorite stops in the Abaco chain.

Ashore at *Bakers Bay,* probably the most popular of the Guana Cay anchorages, are the remains of the old cruise ship depot, now long deserted and a haven for cruisers that like to poke around that sort of place. Some of the docks are deep enough to allow you to tie up if you need to do some work on your vessel. Don't forget to look for the new *Baker's Bay Marina* to open sometime in 2009 (see Chart AB-22). And if you do not want to take your boat to Great Guana Cay, you can always hop on a ferry.

Navigational Information
Bakers Bay lies at the southern terminus of the *Whale Cay Passage* at the northwestern end of Great Guana Cay. A lovely curving sand beach offers good protection from north/northeast through southeast winds but does allow a little swell to work in sometimes causing a bit of a roll.

If you're approaching from the north, from *Whale Cay Passage*, head for the waypoint at 26° 42.90' N, 77° 12.60' W (keep an eye out for the rocks awash about ¾ mile east of this position). This waypoint is approximately ½ mile northwest of the well-marked entrance channel leading into the old cruise ship mooring basin at Bakers Bay as shown on Charts AB-21 and AB-22. From the waypoint you will see a red marker to the southeast; take it to starboard and turn to enter the marked channel, red markers to starboard and green markers to port. There are the remains of an old range west of Spoil Bank Cay that leads you southeastward towards this marked channel, but the range is hardly needed here. As you head generally south of east down the marked channel (see Chart AB-22) you will pass south of some small rocks and between Gumelemi Cay and Spoil Bank Cay (created when this basin was dredged for cruise ships in the late 1980's, and now a great spot for shelling). As you pass to the east of Spoil Bank Cay you will be in the old mooring basin, you'll see the old mooring buoys, and you can weave your way between the buoys and the pilings to the east of the basin to head into the anchorage at Bakers Bay.

Though most of the depths in Bakers Bay are 7'-8', there are a few scattered 6' spots, small sandy

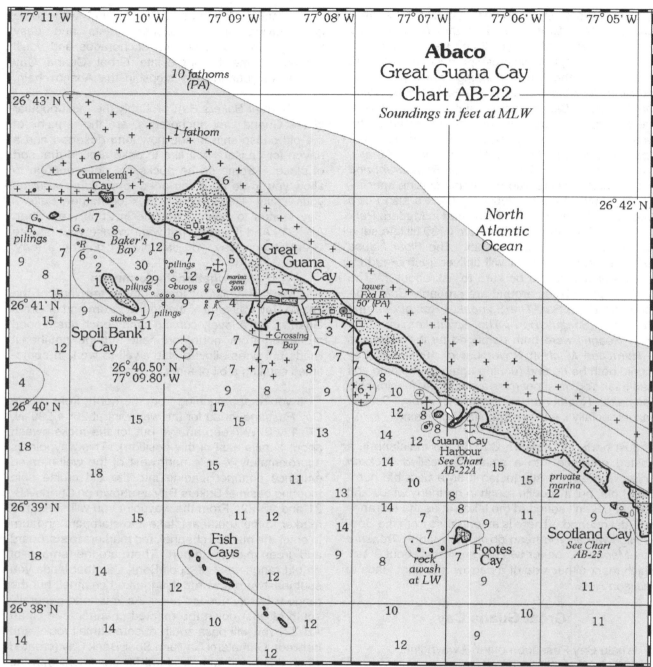

Abaco
Great Guana Cay
Chart AB-22
Soundings in feet at MLW

North Atlantic Ocean

10 *fathoms*
(PA)

1 *fathom*

Gumelemi Cay

Baker's Bay

Great Guana Cay

marina opens 2008

tower Fxd R 50' (PA)

Spoil Bank Cay

26° 40.50' N
77° 09.80' W

+ Crossing Bay

Guana Cay Harbour
See Chart AB-22A

private marina

Fish Cays

Footes Cay

rock awash at LW

Scotland Cay
See Chart AB-23

humps here and there. If you don't wish to make use of the old cruise ship channel, you can pass to the west of Spoil Bank Cay and round its southern tip to anchor in Bakers Bay.

If you are approaching Bakers Bay from the south, from Marsh Harbour, you can head for a waypoint at 26° 40.50' N, 77° 09.80' W. This position lies approximately ¾ mile south of Bakers Bay as shown on Chart AB-22. Use caution here, keep a sharp eye out for

obstructions; don't just plug in the waypoint at Marsh Harbour and head straight for it, you must avoid the Fish Cays and Foots Cay as shown on Charts AB-20 and AB-22. If you're approaching Bakers Bay from Guana Cay Harbour, keep an eye out for a pair of rocky areas, one only 6' deep at MLW, the other not much better at 7' at MLW; both are shown on Chart AB-22. Southeast of Bakers Bay lies Crossing Bay as shown on Chart AB-22.

North
Atlantic
Ocean

8

10

11 *stake* 9

Blue Water
Grill
Fishers
Bay

Great
Guana
Cay

Nippers

26° 40.00' N

9 Delia's
Cay

8 6

11

11

6

8

11

14 10

2

1

*light
Fl W
30', 5M*

6

4

Fishers
Bay

7

10 12

2

7

3

8 *Texaco*

5

Settlement
Harbour

marina

11

12

Minus
Bight

11

14

15

Abaco
Great Guana Cay
Harbour
Chart AB-22A
Soundings in feet at MLW

26° 39.50' N
77° 06.90' W

13

14

13

26° 39.50' N

77° 07.50' W

77° 07.00' W

77° 06.50' W

Nipper's Bar, Great Guana Cay

Photo Courtesy of Nicola Leslie

There are two other nice harbors along the southern shore of Great Guana Cay. As shown on Chart AB-22A, a waypoint at 26° 39.50' N, 77° 06.90' W will place you approximately ¼ mile south of Great Guana Cay Harbour and about ½ mile southeast of the anchorage at Delia's Cay. From the waypoint you can head west and round the small, unnamed rock lying southwest of Delia's Cay to enter the Fishers Bay anchorage north of Delia's Cay. You can also pass between Delia's Cay and this rock in 7' at MLW as a shortcut. Keep and eye out for the submerged rocks that stretch towards Delia's Cay from the small rock, you'll see the deeper, hazard free water. If in doubt, it only takes a couple of minutes to go around the rock, don't take a chance in bad visibility. When anchoring north of Delia's Cay you must keep an eye out for the shallow rocky bar that is sometimes marked with a stake. This anchorage is good in winds from north/northeast through east to southeast and almost south if you can tuck in far enough.

If you wish to enter Guana Cay Harbour (sometimes shown on charts as Settlement Harbour) from the waypoint, simply head north/northeast into the cove and anchor where your draft allows a shown on Chart AB-22A. Once you manage to get your anchor to set in the grassy bottom, this spot is good in winds from west through north to southeast. At the southeastern end of the harbor, protected by a jetty, is *Orchid Bay Marina*, a *Texaco Star Port*. The marina offers 66 slips (up to a 7½' draft) with full electric, a pool, 24-hour weather service, and *Wifi*.

What You Will Find Ashore

Ashore you'll find the *Guana Beach Boutique*, the *Guana Harbour Grocery*, and *My Two Sons Liquor Store*. If you're looking for a place for lunch you can slide over to the *Sand Dollar Café* Monday through Saturday from 1000-1400. One of the more interesting stops is *Milo's Art Gallery/Gift Shop*; you MUST meet Milo. Milo's shop offers unique native crafts, gifts, and clothing and the bright yellow shop itself is an old Loyalist cottage. Nearby you'll want to stop under the Fig Tree to take a load off your feet and chat with whomever is present and enjoy the view. Also nearby are *Guana Hardware*, the *Bikini Hut*, and *Tom's T-shirts* where you can indulge in Great Guana Cay information while smoking a Cuban cigar and browsing through all the shirts and hats that are for sale. On the ocean side is the new *Dolphin Beach Resort* with a good restaurant and 20 cottages for rent. On the eastern shore of Fisher's Bay is *Grabber's Bar and Grill*, the old *Guana Harbour Club*, offers the original *Guana Grabber* and even has a pool and rooms for rent for those who've had too many *Grabbers* and don't want to try to get back to their boat (or miss the ferry). And if you need transportation on Guana, try *Donna's Golf Cart Rentals* at 242-365-5195. Nearby is *Docksider's Seafood and Steak House* with their own dinghy dock (they monitor VHF ch. 16).

The most popular spot on Great Guana Cay is *Nipper's Beach Bar*. *Nipper's* is set upon a sand dune overlooking the beautiful North Atlantic Ocean, an absolutely spectacular view. *Nipper's* host a fantastic *Sunday Pig Roast* right on the beach that is not to be missed. Nipper's will pick you up on the docks in a golf cart, and if you wish to come over from Marsh Harbour you can catch a ferry for only $15 for a round trip. The place is rapidly becoming the party spot in Abaco and the ambiance is definitely "pirate." The bar has a pirate wind vane and the new pool has a pirate's face painted on the bottom with painted fish surrounding it. The solar heated 4' deep pool is divided into two levels by a waterfall with a pirate's cannon standing sentinel. *Nipper's* has added a new deck next to the bar and sun-weary party animals can enjoy the shade provided by beach umbrellas while lounging around the pool in chairs and hammocks.

What Do You Do With A Drunken Sailor?
(A Tale of Great Guana Cay)

My first time in Nassau harbor I made the mistake of anchoring off *Club Med*, the long pink building along the north side of the channel on Paradise Island. Normally this would not have been too unbearable but this particular night was *Karaoke Night* at the *Club Med* bar. If there is one thing our old beleaguered and troubled world did not need (next to PWCs in a quiet anchorage) it is *Karaoke*. Who discovered and unleashed this wretched, foul-smelling curse upon us? I personally am not fond of beautiful, noble, stirring melodies and questionable standards being used to showcase a vacuum of talent by slightly to fully-inebriated pseudo-entertainers, most of whom couldn't carry a tune if it had a handle and instructions. Yes, yes, I know...it's all in the name of fun. Needless to say, I immediately raised anchor and moved across the harbor. After resetting my CQR three more times I finally moved east of the *Paradise Island Bridge* to find a little peace and quiet. I really had to compliment *Club Med* on their tremendous sound system that puts out decibels of bad taste at a level just shy of Gabriel's horn (today, Club Med is no longer on Paradise Island, be that for the better or worse, but the memories remain of that pink building).

Ah, but such is the miracle of alcohol consumption. It brings out the inner man (or woman as the case may be) who immediately becomes the Hyde to our Jekyll. The weak become strong, the old young, the timid brazen, and those who lack any sort of natural talent insufferable in their attempts to display just the opposite, albeit for their own pleasure and not ours so who the hell cares what we think anyway?

Now hold on there Pardner, as the old TV cowboys would say. Don't take this the wrong way. This is not a Carrie Nation attack on one of the few pursuits of freedom that we are still allowed. I enjoy a sundowner as much as the next person and have more than paid my dues getting bottle emptying, falling down, knee walking, room spinning, toilet hugging drunk. I have been five exits past Margaritaville and countless sheets to the wind in "no class dives" where nobody cares where you puke (as long as it's not on them), to "high class establishments" where all the other drunks look down their noses at you as you barf all over the turkey buffet causing a stream of patrons to rush to the head to stick perfumed or cologned fingers well down their incredibly cultured throats. Proof that an overindulgence of distilled or fermented beverages can make a normally intelligent human being into an unthinking hazard to themselves and others. Such is the story of Gus.

Gus, which may or may not be his name, is a South African cruising sailor whose acquaintance I first made while on a repair layover in Jacksonville, Florida. Later that same year I saw Gus at Green Turtle Cay and in Marsh Harbour, Abaco, and witnessed his Hyde's misdeeds. Gus is normally a very fair and conscientious person, the sort of person who believes in righting wrongs, but his inner man unfortunately believes in wronging rights.

At that time there was a concession on the northern end of Great Guana Cay in the Abacos that featured a dolphin exhibition. Dolphins, as we all know, are highly intelligent creatures and most sailors look forward to their appearance alongside their vessels, delighting in their frolicking and cavorting with us as we share the miles. We feel a certain kinship with these pelagic roamers, and who among us can look in their eyes and deny their intelligence? I personally feel about dolphins the way I feel about birds. They are beautiful creatures to behold but not in captivity. Birds can only be birds when they are free to fly, that is their nature. Dolphins can only be dolphins when they are free to roam the open waters. I do not care to witness the antics of either one in captivity; it is saddening to my soul. Gus felt this same way as did some of his friends. After numerous concoctions of one sort or another I retreated to the sanity of my own boat as Gus and his fellow conspirators gathered in secret and a plan was hatched. "Free the Dolphins" became the mantra for these self-styled activists, these bottle-nosed freedom fighters.

The next day around noon, as I dropped anchor in Marsh Harbour, I noticed a commotion over by the town dock. There were two dolphins in the water and about 15 people gathered around taking pictures. By the time I hopped in the dinghy and cruised over, a couple of people were already in the water swimming with the gentle creatures. One of the dolphins was very friendly and could be petted, the other was a little standoffish, yet he knew what a camera was and gleefully posed for pictures. People were feeding them pieces of bread and even slices of watermelon. I never knew dolphins ate watermelon. These were obviously very well trained and, it seemed, very hungry dolphins.

Someone mentioned that the dolphins from Great Guana Cay escaped the night before and another person said that this pair had followed his trawler from Baker's Bay to Marsh Harbour earlier that morning. A cruiser got in touch with the dolphin's trainers on Great Guana Cay, and relayed the message back to everyone gathered to give the dolphins plenty of attention and to keep them occupied until they could get to Marsh Harbour within the hour.

A little over three hours later the trainers had the dolphins safely loaded aboard their boat and thanked everyone who helped out. It seems that this pair of dolphins was raised in captivity and had never been in the wild. They had been hand fed for over 12 years by their trainers, and did not know how to fend for themselves much less protect themselves from sharks. They would have starved to death very quickly had it not been for their fans in Marsh Harbour. When asked how they escaped the trainers had no answers, it seemed as if someone had released them. Imagine that Mr. Hyde.

I talked to Gus later that day and related to him all that had transpired in Marsh Harbour. He shrugged his shoulders and for the first time I found Gus with little to say. In the painfully sobering hours of the morning after, while Gus' Jekyll paid for Hyde's amusement, the only consolation his aching mind found was in the realization that another wrong had been righted, justice was served, and the world was now a better place in which to live. Even when Gus came to realize what the consequences could have been from the *Great Great Guana Cay Raid* he still insisted it was right and muttered something about a damn good idea, high ideals, courageous hearts, and excellent execution. I agreed on the latter parts and then added poor planning due to a lack of intelligence. We both decided it was time for a drink.

Scotland Cay

Navigational Information

Scotland Cay, once called Cotland Cay, lies just southeast of Great Guana Cay as shown on Chart AB-23. Scotland Cay is private and visits ashore must be by invitation only. Although you can anchor anywhere in the lee of Scotland Cay in winds from northeast through east, the best spot is off the northwestern tip south of Cane's Cay or even in the lee of Cane's Cay south of Jobe's Cay. There are some deeper pockets of water that offer good shelter between Jobe's Cay and Scotland Cay, but access to them is limited as you must cross a 2' bar (MLW) to avail yourself of their protection. If you're shallow enough to get in there you'll need two anchors, there's quite a bit or current here. There's good snorkeling in the cut between Scotland Cay and Great Guana Cay. The two small marinas shown on the chart are private.

Southeast of Scotland Cay, as shown on Chart AB-20, lies the Fowl Cay Preserve, protected by *The Bahamas National Trust*. You'll find excellent reef diving on the reefs off Fowl Cay, but nothing can be taken. You can anchor in the lee of Fowl Cay or Upper Cay in settled weather and investigate the reefs full of holes and tunnels at your leisure, either snorkeling or by Scuba. Watch out for tidal currents here north and south of the reefs and especially at the mid-reef break.

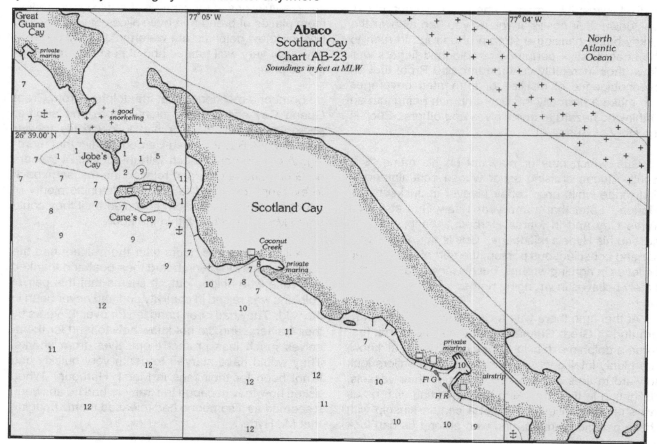

Leisure Lee

Leisure Lee - ¼ nm NE of entrance:
26° 37.90" N, 77° 15.20' W

Navigational Information

Leisure Lee is a small canal community just south of Treasure Cay that is a wonderful hurricane hole, certainly one of my first choices for protection. As shown on Chart AB-24, a waypoint at 26° 37.90' N, 77° 15.20' W, will place you approximately ¼ mile northeast of the entrance channel into Leisure Lee. A range that sits northwest of the conspicuous condos marks the entrance channel to Leisure Lee. The range consists of a white "X" in front and a white rectangle behind it.

As you enter keep the rock with the small tree on it to port and head in on the range. As you approach the point of land northwest of the condos give it a wide berth if you can; there are submerged rocks just off the point. Round this tip of land to port and you can enter the canal complex. Quite a few of the lots have not been sold and there are plenty of places to secure your vessel in the event of a hurricane. You will probably have to set your anchors ashore as the bottom has been dredged and the holding is not very good. Please don't tie up your vessel so as to block homeowners here and don't tie up to their docks.

There is small and seldom used anchorage north of Leisure Lee at *Hill's Creek*. The entrance is between Hills' Cay and Lower Hill Cay and will barely take a 5' draft at high water. Inside is a small area of deeper water in which to anchor. I strongly urge you to check out this route by dinghy first before entering. Look for bonefish on the flats here.

The Hub of Abaco

Ports of Entry: Marsh Harbour
Fuel: Marsh Harbour, Man O' War Cay, Elbow Cay

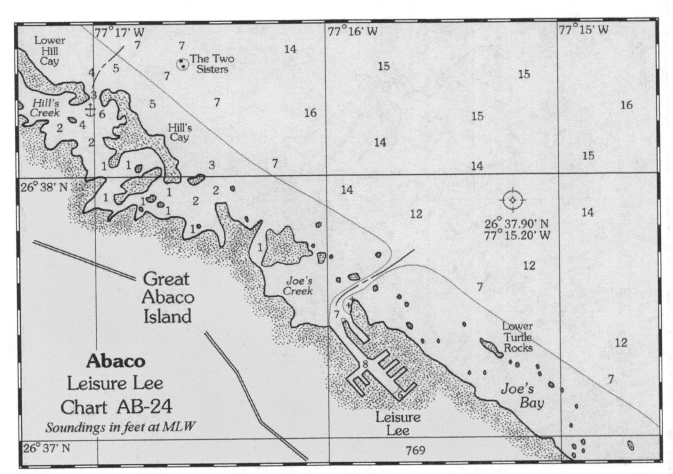

Abaco
Leisure Lee
Chart AB-24
Soundings in feet at MLW

Haul-Out: Marsh Harbour, Man O' War Cay

Diesel Repairs: Marsh Harbour, Man O' War Cay, Elbow Cay

Outboard Repairs: Marsh Harbour, Man O' War Cay, Elbow Cay

Propane: Marsh Harbour, Man O' War Cay, Elbow Cay

Provisions: Marsh Harbour, Man O' War Cay, Elbow Cay

Important Lights:
  Man-O-War Cay: Fl W
  Marsh Harbour: Fl G ev 4 sec

Marsh Harbour: Fl G
North Parrot Cay: Fl R
White Sound: Fl W
Elbow Cay Lighthouse: Gp. Fl W (5) ev 15 sec

Marsh Harbour

Marsh Harbour - ¼ nm NW of Outer Point Cay: 26° 33.60' N, 77° 04.40' W

Boat Harbour Marina - ¼ nm SE of entrance: 26° 32.50' N, 77° 02.50' W

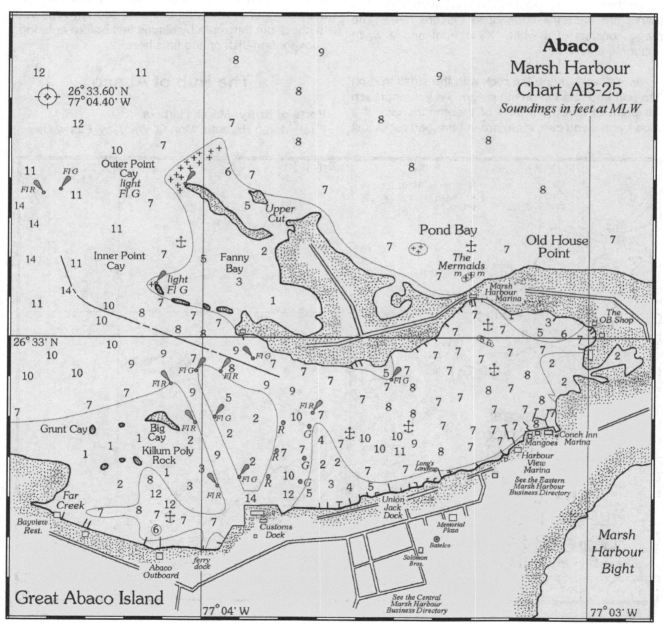

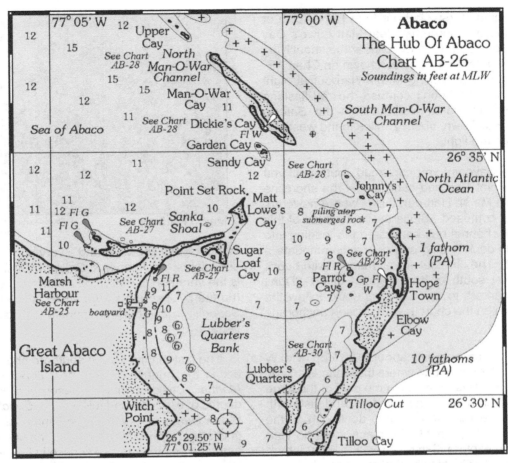

Abaco
The Hub Of Abaco
Chart AB-26
Soundings in feet at MLW

Marsh Harbour Boatyard - ¼ nm E of entrance:
26° 31.85' N, 77° 02.80' W

Well, this is it, the Mecca of Abaco cruising, the hub of the Hub of Abaco, the George Town of the Northern Bahamas. Whatever moniker you hang on it, you will most likely stay a while in Marsh Harbour and make it your base of operations while in the area...and why not? Its got everything you need or want. There are more marinas here than in the entire Exuma chain. There's very little that you cannot find when shopping...*UPS* delivers here...there's usually a happy hour special somewhere every night of the week....the international airport is perfect for guests that wish to visit you, or if you just wish to visit home once in a while...the holding is superb...the protection is excellent save for a small fetch from the west...and, you'll have the camaraderie of numerous other cruising boats...I'm running out of things to say! You'll have to go there and decide for yourself the reasons that keep you there; I guarantee you won't regret it.

Navigational Information

As shown on Chart AB-25, the entrance to Marsh Harbour is fairly easy, although with the construction of the marked channel leading to the *Customs* docks, newcomers are often confused, following the marked channel to the turning basin off the dock instead of entering the harbor proper. As shown on the chart, a waypoint at 26° 33.60' N, 77° 04.40' W, will place you approximately ¼ mile northwest of the shallow reef off Outer Point Cay. If you're approaching from Great Guana Cay you'll need to avoid the Fish Cays and Footes Cay as shown on Chart AB-20, and if you're approaching from Treasure Cay or Leisure Lee you can parallel the shoreline of Great Abaco Island giving Water Cay and the reefs off the point southeast of Water Cay a wide berth as shown on Chart AB-20. Once clear of the reefs here you can put Inner Point Cay on your bow and head straight for it actually passing south of the waypoint.

If you are approaching form Man-O-War Cay you can head for the waypoint once you clear Garden Cay and Sandy Cay as shown on Chart AB-26. If you are approaching Marsh Harbour from Hope Town or the Bight of Abaco you must clear Matt Lowe's Cay before heading southwesterly to clear the shoal lying northwest of Outer Point Cay as shown on Chart AB-26. If you are approaching Marsh Harbour at night (not recommended), don't confuse the red-flashing *Batelco* tower in Marsh Harbour with the *Batelco* tower in Dundas Town, about 2 miles to the west and shows a fixed red light.

From the waypoint you can head south until you clear Inner Point Cay and can parallel the shoreline eastward into Marsh Harbour, this is where newcomers often get confused. Since the last edition of this guide a new channel has been dredged leading into the *Customs* dock (which can now accommodate a 400' vessel). The channel is well marked with buoys beginning just south of the waypoint given. Don't follow the markers to the *Customs* dock; follow the course shown on the chart to your chosen anchorage or marina.

Most of the harbor is only about 7'-8' deep at MLW but there is a deeper trough where the water is 10'-14' deep in places. This area lies to the east of the large shoal lying north of the *Customs* dock and just north of the *Union Jack Dock*, the large dock with all the dinghies tied to it, probably the place you'll tie your dinghy as you explore Marsh Harbour. I must inform you of some of the local folks that may to try help you tie up your dinghy, and watch it for you while you're gone. They'll also hand you down your bags or boxes of supplies after you climb into your dink. They may also remind you of services rendered if you fail to tip them. They mean well, they're only trying to make a few bucks. I cannot advise you to pay them or not, that choice is yours, but the services rendered can be helpful.

As you set your anchor take a look and check out your neighbor's ground tackle arrangements. If they are all lying to two anchors, that's a good hint that you should as well. If they're laying to only one, and the holding is so good here that one is often all you need, then you should consider a similar arrangement. This decision also depends on your estimated length of stay and the upcoming weather forecasts.

Just a bit east of the *Union Jack Dock* you'll come to *Harbour View Marina* offering fuel, water, ice, and 36 slips with depths ranging from 5' to over 6' at MLW. All slips have full electric and the marina has a nice

Marsh Harbour   Photo Courtesy of Paul Harding
Seaplane Safaris

laundry, good showers, and a very popular restaurant and nightspot, *Snappa's Grill and Chill*. Next door is the very popular *Mangoe's Marina and Restaurant* (no fuel). Just across the street is the very popular *Sapodilly's*, another very popular nightspot and restaurant.

The last marina on the southern shore of the harbor is the huge and extremely popular *Conch Inn Marina*. Besides offering diesel, gas, 80 slips with depths of 9' (MLW) and full electric, *Conch Inn Marina* is now owned by *The Moorings* and houses their fleet of charter boats as well. You can have your mail sent here and use their phone service in the office for your Internet connection. The hotel offers air-conditioned rooms if you wish to get away from the water for a night or if you have guests arriving. The marina's restaurant, *Curly Tails*, offers truly innovative island cuisine serving breakfast, lunch, and dinner. Just across the street from the *Conch Inn* is *Sharkey's Pizza* with pizza, subs, homemade ice cream, and pies (they'll deliver to your slip). Right next door is *Barefoot Gifts* where you can pick up all types of resort-wear, gifts, and island-made jewelry and music.

On the northern shore of Marsh Harbour you'll find the *Marsh Harbour Marina*. With 57 slips and dockside depths of 7' at MLW, the marina also offers fuel, water, ice, showers, a laundry, and a great restaurant and bar, the *Jib Room*. The *Jib Room* has daily happy hours from 1700-1900 and great BBQs on Wednesdays and Sundays.

There is one more marina in the Marsh Harbour area, large and upscale *Abaco Beach Resort* and *Boat Harbour Marina*, and it must be accessed from Marsh Harbour Bight as shown on Chart AB-27.

At the eastern end of Marsh Harbour, just south of the old *Sunsail* docks, is the shallow entrance to a small creek. This creek is good for drafts of less than 4' at high water only and is an excellent hurricane hole for small, up to 40', shallow-draft vessels. If you need this protection better plan on getting there very, very early or the charter boats may beat you to it.

What You Will Find Ashore

There are so many businesses in the Marsh Harbour area, from marine services to bars, restaurants, grocery stores, and boutiques that I cannot tell you of them all, but I will discuss the most important, those that will appeal most to the visiting cruiser. For more information as to their locations, take a look at the *Central* and *Eastern Marsh Harbour Business Directory* maps.

As far as getting around town, walking will get you to most places, if you're not up for that you can hail a taxi on VHF ch. 16, ch. 06 (hail *Any Taxi* or if you already have a favorite, hail them by their taxi number), or stop by the *Conch Inn* or *Union Jack Dock*, there is usually a taxi waiting for a fare at these locales.

To begin with, if you need medical help you'll find it 24/7 in Marsh Harbour. The local doctors, Dr. Lundy and Dr. Boyce, have excellent clinics and provide great health care service. The *Agape Family Dental Centre*, 367-4355, is a few blocks south of the traffic light. If you need to fill a prescription head for the *Chemist Shoppe* or *Lowe's Pharmacy*.

If you need pet supplies, for dogs, cats, or even parrots, check out *Pets R Us* just off Don Mackay Blvd. or visit *Pets R People Too* near *Solomon's*.

On Great Abaco you'll find the very professional *Trauma One* ambulance team providing emergency service to Abaco residents and visitors for no fee; they are supported entirely by contributions. *Trauma One* had been operating since September of 1995 and your help is needed. Donations may be sent to *Trauma One*, P.O. Box AB 20594, Marsh Harbour. All contributions are recorded and acknowledged.

If you need electronic, marine, outboard engine and related repairs, Marsh Harbour has more of these facilities than any other city in The Bahamas except Freeport and Nassau. At the northern end of Marsh Harbour, east of *Marsh Harbour Marina*, sits the *Outboard Shop*, Marsh Harbour's OMC dealer. They can

be reached on ch. 16, (*Outboard Shop*) or by phone at 367-2703. *Abaco Outboard* is the local *Yamaha* dealer and their dock is west of *Admiral's Yacht Haven* in Dundas Town. You can reach them on ch. 16 (*Abaco Outboard*) or by phone at 367-2452. *Abaco Outboard* can haul small boats up to 30' and 8 tons.

Just across the street from *Abaco Outboard* is a new prop shop, *Abaco Marina Props* (242-367-4276). *Abaco Marine Props* also does sandblasting, stainless steel and aluminum welding, and some fabrication. If you need a *Suzuki* dealer, try *B & D Marine, Ltd.* at the traffic light in Marsh Harbour. *B & D* offers fine marine products, dive gear, Petit paints, *Suzuki* parts and service, *Standard Horizon* VHF radios, and fishing supplies. They can be reached on ch. 16 or by phone at 367-2622. *National Marine*, the local *Mercury/Mariner* dealer, is located next to *Bristol Liquors* just east of the traffic light and just up from *Port of Call Marina* and the *Union Jack Dock*.

For diesel work try *Asterix*. They can be reached on ch. 16 (*Asterix*) or by phone at 367-3166. *Pinder's Marine and Auto* also specializes in diesel repairs and can be reached by phone at 367-2274. Another option is *Sea Services* at *Boat Harbour*. Their phone number is 367-6805. *Marsh Harbour Boatyard* in Calcutta also has a very good diesel mechanic. If you need electrical work contact Andrew at *Andrew's Marine Electric*, 242-367-2163, or hail Andrew on VHF ch. 16 (*Andrew's Electric*).

If you require the services or goods of a hardware store try *Abaco Hardware* (367-2170), where you can also pick up some marine supplies as well as hardware, lumber, and power tools. If you need propane you can pick it up at *Corner Hardware* one block east of the traffic light. *Standard Hardware* sits two blocks east of the same light while *True Value Hardware* sits up from the light about one block toward the airport. There's also a *Western Auto* store on *Don Mackay Blvd.* If you need a coin laundry try the *Classic Coin Wash*, just off *Don Mackay Blvd.* next to *Kool Scoops Ice Cream Parlour*. Just across the street from *Standard Hardware* is the huge *Bristol Liquors* store and *National Marine*.

If you need to do some banking while in Marsh Harbour, you have several to choose from and they are all open Monday –Thursday from 9:30am to 3:00pm and Fridays from 9:30am to 5:00pm. *Barclay's Bank* and the *Commonwealth Bank* can be found at the

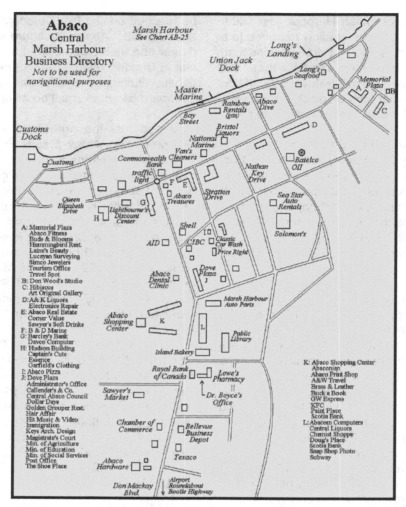

Abaco
Central
Marsh Harbour
Business Directory
*Not to be used for
navigational purposes*

A: Memorial Plaza
  Abaco Fitness
  Buds & Blooms
  Hummingbird Rest.
  Laine's Beauty
  Lucayan Surveying
  Simco Jewelers
  Tourism Office
  Travel Spot
B: Don Wood's Studio
C: Hibiscus
  Art Original Gallery
D: A&K Liquors
  Electronics Repair
E: Abaco Real Estate
  Corner Value
  Sawyer's Soft Drinks
F: B & D Marine
G: Barclay's Bank
  Davco Computer
H: Hudson Building
  Captain's Cuts
  Essence
  Garfield's Clothing
I: Abaco Pizza
J: Dove Plaza
  Administrator's Office
  Callender's & Co.
  Central Abaco Council
  Dollar Days
  Golden Grouper Rest.
  Hair Affair
  Hit Music & Video
  Immigration
  Keys Arch. Design
  Magistrate's Court
  Min. of Agriculture
  Min. of Education
  Min. of Social Services
  Post Office
  The Shoe Place

K: Abaco Shopping Center
  Abaconian
  Abaco Print Shop
  A&W Travel
  Brass & Leather
  Buck a Book
  GW Express
  KFC
  Paint Place
  Scotia Bank
L: Abacom Computers
  Central Liquors
  Chemist Shoppe
  Doug's Place
  Scotia Bank
  Snap Shop Photo
  Subway

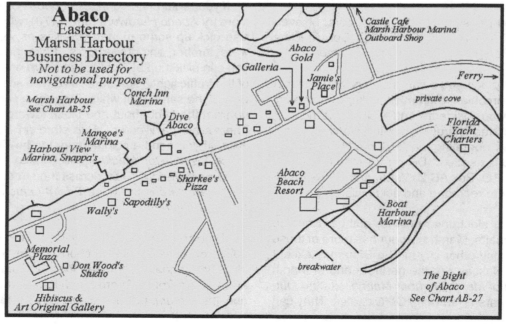

Abaco
Eastern
Marsh Harbour
Business Directory
*Not to be used for
navigational purposes*

light while *CIBC* is one block south of the light and next to the *Shell* station. And while we're speaking of the *Shell* station, let me remind you that *Abaco Pizza* is behind the *Shell* station about 2 blocks from the *Batelco* tower, also, next door to *Shell* is *Marsh Harbour Auto Parts*.

If you need office products and the like try *Abaco Office Products*, formerly *The Loyalist Shoppe*, and now next to the *Texaco* station on *Don Mackay Blvd*. *Abaco Office Products* sells magazines, books, newspapers, gifts, and office supplies. The newest addition in office supplies is the *Bellevue Business Depot* in the *B & L Plaza*. The *Bellevue Business Depot* is modeled after the U.S. chain that we know as *Office Depot*. They offer faxes, copies, computer supplies, printer supplies, and office machines. If you need computer repairs or supplies see the folks at *Oii.Net*, they're located in the turquoise building at the base of the *Batelco* tower.

For groceries you have several very good choices. South and east of the *Union Jack Dock* is *Solomon's* where you can buy bulk at wholesale prices. Nearby is *Abaco Wholesale*, which was heavily damaged by *Hurricane Floyd* but now rebuilt and enlarged to serve you better, here too you can buy bulk at very good prices. *Abaco Wholesale* offers full galley stocking with free delivery to marinas or the *Union Jack Dock*. *Abaco Market* is located in the *Abaco Shopping Center* and carries groceries, meats, canned goods, and fresh produce. Just west of the traffic light on *Queen Elizabeth Drive* is the new *Captain's Cuts* meat market where if you make a $20 purchase you can get it delivered to your marina for you. In *Memorial Plaza*, a small strip mall lying a block or so south of *Port of Call Marina*, is home to a small store, *Wilson's Quik Trip* offering fresh meat and produce and several other stores as shown in the *Central Marsh Harbour Business Directory*. To the south and east of the *Shell* station is *Price Right*, a very good place to shop as well. In the *Flamingo Place Shopping Center* is *Price Busters* offering household goods, OTC medicines, health and beauty aids, and housewares." *Sawyer's Market* lies to the west of *Don Mackay Blvd*. as shown on the Central Marsh Harbour Business Directory map.

Memorial Plaza is also home to the *Hummingbird Restaurant*; a good place to eat. Behind *Memorial Plaza* is one of my favorite's, *Hibiscus*, a very popular spot with local folks and a great lunch buffet. The *Art Original Gallery* offers fine locally made basketry and jewelry made by local artist Marlee Mason. Don Wood is a local artist whose house/studio is just across from *Memorial Plaza*, while next to the plaza is an electronics repair shop and *A&K Liquors*, which lies on the road toward the traffic light.

Chelsea's Choice drinking water and ice, will deliver water, water coolers, and bottle pumps. *Abaco Ice, Ltd.* sells ten pound block and cubed ice and will deliver with a ten bag minimum. *Sawyer's Soft Drinks* located near the traffic light sells bulk quantities of soft drinks.

Heading south on *Don Mackay Blvd*. towards the airport and the roundabout you'll pass *Island Bakery*, a *Subway*, *Beacon Books*, *Computer Creations* (a computer repair shop), a veterinary clinic (242-367-3551; the *Community Animal Hospital* can be reached at 242-367-3647), and *The Bellevue Business Depot* office supply center next to the *Texaco* station. Just before the roundabout you'll find the *17 Plaza* with its 5-screen movie house. Just before the roundabout is *Abaco Gas*, a propane refill station.

If you wish to dine out for a change, Marsh Harbour has more choices than you could sample in a couple of week. Surrounding the harbour you can of course sample the offerings at the *Pizza Hut*, *Mangoes*, *Sapodilly's*, *Wally's*, the *Tiki Hut*, *Bistro Mezzomare*, the *Jib Room*, and *Sharkey's Pizza*. At the extreme southwestern end of the harbour you'll definitely want to try the *Bayview Restaurant* right on the waterfront in Dundas Town, west of *Abaco Outboard*. They have an excellent Sunday Champagne Brunch.

The Castle Café sits high on the hill overlooking Marsh Harbour and serves lunch daily on the terrace of the old house. *The Castle Café* was once the home of Dr. Evans Cottman (*Out Island Doctor*).

One of the best spots to dine out in the Marsh Harbour area is, without a doubt, *Mother Merle's Fishnet* in Dundas Town. The *Fishnet* is a down–home, family-style restaurant that opened in 1968 and has been going strong ever since. Mother Merle Swain is the proprietor and chef, and will serve you one of the finest meals you will ever eat in The Bahamas.

Downtown you'll find the *Golden Grouper Restaurant* in the *Dove Plaza* and *Kool Scoops Ice Cream Parlour* behind the *NAPA* near the traffic light. The *Ranch Sports Bar and Lounge* on D*on Mackay Blvd*.

has a pool table, darts, and satellite TV. Just outside Marsh Harbour is *Kipco's Place*. Kipco is a tall Bahamian Rastafarian whose little bar and restaurant sits amidst a mass of wrecked cars and other items of salvage, as well as a 4 hole golf course! Kipco loves to talk and his eloquent style and flowing commentaries on anything you wish to discuss is entertaining to say the least. *Nettie's Museum Restaurant* offers fantastic sunset views from their decks 18 miles south of the airport.

Heading east from *Port of Call Marina* you'll pass *Harbour View Marina* and the popular *Snappa's* restaurant. Next door is *Mangoe's Marina* with their restaurant of the same name. Across the street you'll find *Wally's* and *Sapodilly's*, both highly popular establishments that are a MUST visit when in *Marsh Harbour*. Almost across the street from the *Conch Inn* is *Sharkey's Pizza*, one of my favorite stops. East of *Conch Inn* are numerous shops including the *Galleria*, *Abaco Gold*, and a local dining favorite, *Jamie's Place*, the *Lofty Fig Villas*, and the *Sandollar Shop*.

Regatta Time in Abaco

By far, the biggest party in Abaco is held during late June/early July...*it's Regatta Time in Abaco*! The first *Abaco Regatta* was held September 1, 1976 with 4 workboats and 10 cruising boats participating. After a couple of years of hosting the event in early September, the organizers realized that few cruising boats were actually in Abaco in the middle of hurricane season and in 1978 the event was moved back to a late June-early July time frame.

Thirty boats participated in the *Regatta* that year, and many of them then moved on to Green Turtle for what was considered to be the second regatta. From Green Turtle, the fleet moved just a bit to Treasure Cay for what was called the third regatta. The number of participants began to grow as word of the event spread throughout the southeastern United States. A major change was taking place, the end of Bahamian work-boat participation. Traditionally those crews were paid to participate and unless there was compensation they would not show up. This was not the case with the cruisers whose only motto was "Will sail for fun and beer."

In the early 1980's, the three-race format was the norm and the schedule was set for the next decade. The *Regatta* kicks off in Marsh Harbour, then the fleet moves to Treasure Cay, and finished up at Green Turtle Cay. By now participation was nearing 150 boats and climbing.

A unique sideline event to watch was the annual dinghy tow from Marsh Harbour to Treasure Cay. The race to Treasure Cay is usually a spinnaker run and since it was not fair to have sailors tow their dinghies during the race a dinghy tow was organized. It often took as long to arrange and tow the dinghies to Treasure Cay that the racing fleet was already at Treasure Cay waiting to enter the marina. What may have been the largest dinghy tow in the event's history, some 80 dinghies, were hauled by singer David Crosby's schooner, *Mayan*.

The bronze "lost-wax" castings of Little Harbour artist Pete Johnston (see the section on *Little Harbour*) that were given as trophies soon approached cult status. Racers soon found themselves competing not only for the line honors, but for Pete's castings, too. In the 1990's the regatta picked up sponsorship from *Mount Gay Rum* and *Beck's Beer*. Pretty soon the *Mount Gay* hats became almost as sought after as Pete's castings.

Soon the racing became more and more competitive, and the cruising boats found themselves vying for honors against true racing boats. The powers that be came up with an idea, a "Mother Tub Class." This allowed the cruisers to still compete and have a chance at the awards. Over the years the MTC became the largest fleet in the race, and it is still based on the principle of "FUN," or if you prefer, "PARTY!" *Regatta Time in Abaco* spans two grand holidays, Independence Days for both the United States (July 4th) and The Bahamas (July 10th), which certainly helped the party spirit.

In 1991, the organizers reversed the schedule of the races and dropped the Treasure Cay race entirely. The regatta then started with the Green Turtle race, moved on to Guana Cay, and then to Marsh Harbour. The dates and schedules changed, but the racing and parties remained the same. *Regatta Time in Abaco* is still rolling along, is still the number one summer attraction in Abaco, and it's still attracting sailors from far and wide. If you can plan to be in Abaco during regatta, by all means do so, don't miss it! How could you go home from your Abaco cruise, with all those wonderful memories, and not have a single one of *Regatta Time in Abaco*?

The Wild Horses of Abaco

If you' are an animal lover, particularly a horse lover, you'll probably want to try to catch a glimpse of the wild horses of Abaco while you're in the Marsh Harbour area. Nobody is really sure of their origin, some say they were left behind by the Conquistadors and probably settled in Abaco in the late 1500's to the early 1600's. Still others say they are descendents of the horses that the Loyalists brought with them. However they came to be here, their herd once numbered in the hundreds and they lived contentedly in the pine barrens of Great Abaco.

The opening of the *Queen's Highway* in the 1960's brought an increase in the number of hunters into their habitat and the wild horses were almost eradicated, some captured to work on other islands, some killed for no reason at all. In the mid-1960's, a local girl took two of the wild horses and broke them to the point that people could ride them. A little girl mounted one of the horses and kicked it and the horse did what it was taught to do, and that was run. The young girl was dragged behind and died from her injuries. Friends of the family took it upon themselves to destroy all the horses for this one unfortunate accident and killed over 200, leaving only three alive. Finally, the three horses were found, a stallion and two mares, and they became the core of the current herd on Abaco. They were sheltered and cared for and as soon as the herd built up to a dozen, they were released into the wilds of Abaco again. By 1994, the wild horses of Abaco numbered 30, not a lot, but certainly much better numbers than two decades earlier.

In 1992, an American, Mimi Rehor, visited the area and took up their cause. She discovered that in 1996-1997 the herd was decreasing again. One mare died while giving birth and the foal was killed when only ten days old. Corpses of horses once again began appearing and the herd shrank to an alarming 16 rather quickly. Nobody is really sure what killed the horses, some say wild dogs, some say traps, some say humans. In all of 1998, only one wild horse was born...this is not the way to build a herd.

In 1998, representatives of the *U.S. Humane Society Equine Protection Division* and the *Pegasus Foundation* visited Abaco to see these magnificent creatures. The experts concluded that the horses are indeed of the Spanish Barb Type with only five lumbar vertebrae, all other domestic horses have six. Pending DNA testing, the researchers announced that they are potentially unique in that they have not been tampered with by man for several hundred years and are genetically very close to the first horses imported into the New World. Some of the horses have been linked to the Narragansett Pacer, a breed developed in the U.S. during the Revolutionary War years and who were exported all over the Caribbean. These are most likely the horses that the Loyalists would have had with them.

Whatever their origins, the wild horses of Abaco have been called a national treasure that needs to be preserved. Today the wild horses are down to 15 in number, 8 stallions and 7 mares, but there is good news, they are now on 160 fenced acres in the middle of a special reserve of some 3,800 acres and should show improvement. Mimi, who lives aboard her sailboat *Alnilam* can be faxed at the local *Batelco* office at 242-367-4756. Mimi gives tours of the paddock and the horses and usually there's a notice of an upcoming tour on the daily VHF *Cruiser's Net*. If you wish to contact Mimi to set up you your own tour, hail her sailboat on VHF, fax her, or email her through her wild horses of Abaco website, www.arkwild.com. You can also support the horses by visiting Mimi's *Buck a Book* trailer by the *KFC* in the *Abaco Shopping Center* in Marsh Harbour (see the *Central Marsh Harbour Business Directory* map) where all books are one dollar (donations of books and or money are appreciated) and all the money raised goes to the wild horses fund.

Great Abaco by Car

If you wished to drive around Abaco in years past you had to put up with hellish roads that ate tires, shocks, and mufflers for breakfast. Until about the mid-1950's there was no highway to carry motorists from one end of Abaco to the other. There were only logging roads, cut out of the scrub brush so timber could be hauled to waiting ships. Today, the roads from south to north are newly paved, fairly smooth, and almost pothole free. They are a delight to cruise on at almost any speed, and one of the best ways to see the island of Great Abaco. Formerly called the Great Abaco Highway, the road is now known as the *Scherlin Bootle Highway*, or just the *Bootle Highway*.

Let's begin our tour of Great Abaco by heading south on *Don Mackay Blvd.* to the roundabout where we'll pick up the *Sherlin Bootle Highway*. Once on the *Bootle Highway* we'll head south (go straight at the roundabout) for Cherokee Sound, Little Harbour, Sandy Point, and Hole in the Wall. Please note, for navigational information to the settlements on Great Abaco, see their relevant section in this chapter. For your information, Sandy Point lies approximately 49 miles south of the airport roundabout at Marsh Harbour via the *Bootle Highway*.

Beginning at the roundabout at the *Marsh Harbour Airport on Don Mackay Blvd.* and heading south you will quickly come to the *Abaco Big Bird Poultry Farm*. Here the owners raise all of Abaco's chickens, some 30,000 a month. This company has become so popular and successful that they are now able to ship many of their charges to Freeport, Nassau, and Eleuthera. A little further on you will come to the turn-off to Snake Cay, the old lumber port for the *Owens-Illinois Company* that was still active into the 1960's. The creek at Snake Cay is an excellent hurricane hole.

A bit further south on the main highway is the well-marked turn-off to Cherokee Sound, and Little Harbour. Eight miles down this winding but well paved road is the turnoff to Little Harbour where you can drive right up to *Pete's Pub* for a cold one while you explore the gallery. Check out the small "blue hole" on the side of the road on your way in. Forget the turnoff to Little Harbour and in three miles you'll approach Cherokee Sound. Take a left at the small *BEC* generator building and drive up and over the hill to the parking lot to leave your car. It's best to park here and explore on foot as the roads in Cherokee are narrow and little more than wide sidewalks in places, but if you take the time to investigate, you will find that you have entered a marvelous little settlement. Cherokee Sound was once a thriving boat building and fishing community, and its population welcomes visitors.

South of the Cherokee Sound turn-off is the road to Casuarina Point, a small residential community that was once the residential area for the executives of the *Owens-Illinois Company*. On the road leading in you'll find the *Different of Abaco* bonefishing resort with its bar and restaurant. Owner Nettie Symonette's forty-plus years of experience has enabled her to open a unique hotel/eco-tourist resort/bonefishing club along Abaco's eastern shore. Here you'll stroll the preserved grounds alongside a friendly donkey, chickens, ducks, geese, rock iguanas, and even pink flamingos. Ms. Symonette once had a dream of nesting flamingos on Abaco, and with that in mind, several years ago she brought 15 flamingos to her resort, but several died right away and most of the survivors were scattered during a hurricane. Some survivors are said to be doing well in the marls north of Casuarina Point. The two remaining birds are still there, in full plumage and looking great as they slowly make their way through the water, feeding, preening and watching the people who stop to admire them. Last year Ms. Symonette imported nineteen young West Indian Pink Flamingos from Inagua in the hopes that they will be the beginning of a breeding colony. Good luck Ms. Symonette.

A few miles further south on the *Great Abaco Highway* is the road that leads to *Bahamas Palm Shores*, a small residential community with a beautiful beach. About 11 miles south of Bahamas Palm Shores is the town of Crossing Rocks, a small community located on the eastern shore of Great Abaco island where you'll find a small restaurant and bar right on the highway.

Once back out on the *Bootle Highway* the next stop is Sandy Point. About 7 miles south of Crossing Rocks is the Sandy Point/Hole in the Wall junction. If you wish to visit Hole in the Wall, a truly rough trip whose 15 miles requires at least an hour or more each way as well as a high-clearance vehicle, take a left here (southeast) to get to the lighthouse. Keep an eye out for the rare Bahamian parrot on this route, you're in the vicinity of the *Abaco National Park*, a 20,000-acre site encompassing the nesting area and habitat of the Abaco Parrot.

If you continue on to Sandy Point (another 6 miles) you will find *Pete and Gay's Guest House* right next to the town dock at the end of the highway. If you're looking for a good spot to spend the night in Sandy Point, they have eight rooms that are usually booked by serious bonefishermen. Nearby are the *Seaside Inn Restaurant and Bar* and *Oeisha's Resort* for your dining pleasure.

Okay, now we've been south of Marsh Harbour all the way to Sandy Point, and you're probably wondering what's to the north of Marsh Harbour. Well, we're heading there right now. From the roundabout head north on the *Bootle Highway* (take a right at the roundabout) and your first stop will probably be Treasure Cay. On the way north you'll pass a small stretch where you can view the beautiful waters of the Bight of Abaco on the western side of the *Bootle Highway*. Heading north you'll be driving down a well-paved highway between two pine forests and you might think you are in south Georgia instead of The Bahamas.

At the turn to the right that leads to Treasure Cay you'll find *Coconuts Restaurant and Bar* (open only for dinner) on the western side of the intersection while across the street, on the eastern side of the *Bootle Highway*, is *Kulas Grocery*. As you head east towards Treasure Cay you'll pass the Treasure Cay Golf Course and as you approach the marina you'll find the signs that direct you to...(they monitor VHF ch. 16). Heading north again on the *Bootle Highway* you'll pass *McKenzie's Car Rentals* and a *Shell* station. Just past the *Shell* station is a dirt road to the left that takes you to the wild horse preserve (lying two miles down the road). Just before you arrive at the airport you'll find *Johnny's Airport Bar & Grill* and a small gift shop. A half-mile north is a *Texaco* station and a small mini-mart.

A few miles or so north of Treasure Cay is the small community of Blackwood with a small auto parts store on the eastern side of the *Bootle Highway*. Just past Blackwood is *Fire Road* with its small fishing harbor and an *Esso* station on the right as you head north. There's also a small hardware store here.

Coopers Town is the next settlement if you're heading north and it is covered in its own section. Leaving Coopers Town you'll cross a small bridge and find yourself on the island of Little Abaco heading west now instead of north. The first stop is Cedar Harbour where you'll find a *Batelco* office, a small jetty with a fuel pump, a small store, and *Netty's Restaurant*. Five miles west is Wood Cay with a small *Esso* station and an auto repair shop. If you'd like to spend the night here the *Tangelo Hotel* offers fine accommodations as well as good food at a fair price.

A few miles or so north of Treasure Cay is the small community of Blackwood where you'll find the *Poinciana Restaurant and Bar*. Just past Blackwood is Fire Road where you can dine at *Lankin's Restaurant* or *Pizza World*. *Murray's Service Station* has better prices on cases of sodas than you'll find in Marsh Harbour (as of this writing). Fire Wood is almost a suburb of Coopers Town, the next stop to the north.

Coopers Town is well known to boaters...it has a *Shell Fuel Dock* and navigational information for the area will be found elsewhere in this chapter. Cooper's Town has a large *Community Clinic*, a *Shell* station, a *Batelco* office, and a *Government Office* building. You can dine at *The Place Bakery and Souse House*, *Gelina's Pizza* (free delivery if you're at the dock), *M & M's*, the *Conch Crawl*, and at the *Same Ol Talk of the Town*. There are also two small grocery stores in Coopers Town. Visitors might wish to check out the *Albert Bootle Museum* where you can learn a little about the early settlers, the Bootles and the Coopers, as well as sponging, sisal, and lumber.

Leaving Coopers Town you'll cross a small bridge and find yourself heading west on the island of Little Abaco. The first stop is Cedar Harbour whose only amenity is a small *Batelco* office. *Wood Cay* lies 5 miles west, an excellent spot for lunch or to stay overnight. The *Tangelo Hotel* offers very nice accommodations and great food at a good price. The community also has an *Esso* gas station and a mechanic at *Chuck's Auto Service*. The next community is Mount Hope where you can treat yourself at *Trippers Ice Cream Shoppe* or grab a meal at the *BJ Restaurant and Bar*. Try the *V & M Grocery Store* if you need to pick up a few supplies for the road.

The next stop is Fox Town, which is very accessible by big boat. Fox Town is in the middle of a bit of a construction boom - they are building a huge new *Community Clinic*. There is a *Shell* station on the water's edge next to the *Valley Bar and Restaurant*. Nearby is the *Texaco Star Port* dock where you can fuel up and purchase oil if needed. If you plan to stay overnight, check out *Mimi's Guest Cottages*.

The next stop Crown Haven, is the end of the road. Crown Haven, little more than a good walk west of Fox Town, offers a phone, the *Black Room Bar and Restaurant*, and *E&J's Ice Cream Parlour and Video Tape Rental*. If you're hungry and have forgotten to call ahead for a meal, simply stop by and see Bookie Butler at the *Chili Bar Restaurant*, he's pretty handy in emergencies. Crown Haven, like so many communities in The Bahamas, has an interesting past. Many of the residents remember when they lived on nearby Cave Cay in the Bight of Abaco. A hurricane in the 1930's destroyed their homes and the Government moved them to the island of Little Abaco, at the end of the road and today we have Crown Haven; a haven courtesy of the Crown.

Matt Lowe's Cay to Marsh Harbour

Boat Harbour Marina - ¼ nm SE of entrance:
26° 32.50' N, 77° 02.50' W

The area between Matt Lowe's Cay and Marsh Harbour offers a fairly nice anchorage, first rate snorkeling, some private dockage, and a shortcut to *Marsh Harbour Bight* for vessels that draw less than 5'. Snorkelers will marvel over the beauty and ease of access at the *Mermaids*, a small protected reef in Pond Bay as shown on Chart AB-25. This is a must stop when in the Hub of Abaco, especially if you're anchored at Marsh Harbour. Guests of *Marsh Harbour Marina* can visit this reef simply by crossing the road from the marina to the small beach and then swimming out to the reef. But if you're anchored out, or if you're the guest at another marina, the best way to visit the *Mermaids* is by dinghy. There is a small

mooring where you may tie up your dink to while you investigate the undersea life. Please do not anchor your dinghy on the reef.

Navigational Information

There is a nice anchorage just inside the small cove on the southwestern shore of Matt Lowe's Cay as shown on Chart AB-27 (as of this writing there was a lot of construction in progress on Matt Lowe's Cay including a jetty so keep your eyes open for new development here). You can anchor here in 6'-8' at MLW over a nice sandy bottom where you'll find shelter from northeast through southerly winds.

There is a bit of small boat traffic coming and going through the cut south of Matt Lowe's Cay, and the ferries use the small channel that lies between Sugar Loaf Cay and the Eastern Shore of Great Abaco Island. If you're transiting the waters between Matt Lowe's Cay and Marsh Harbour, be sure to keep

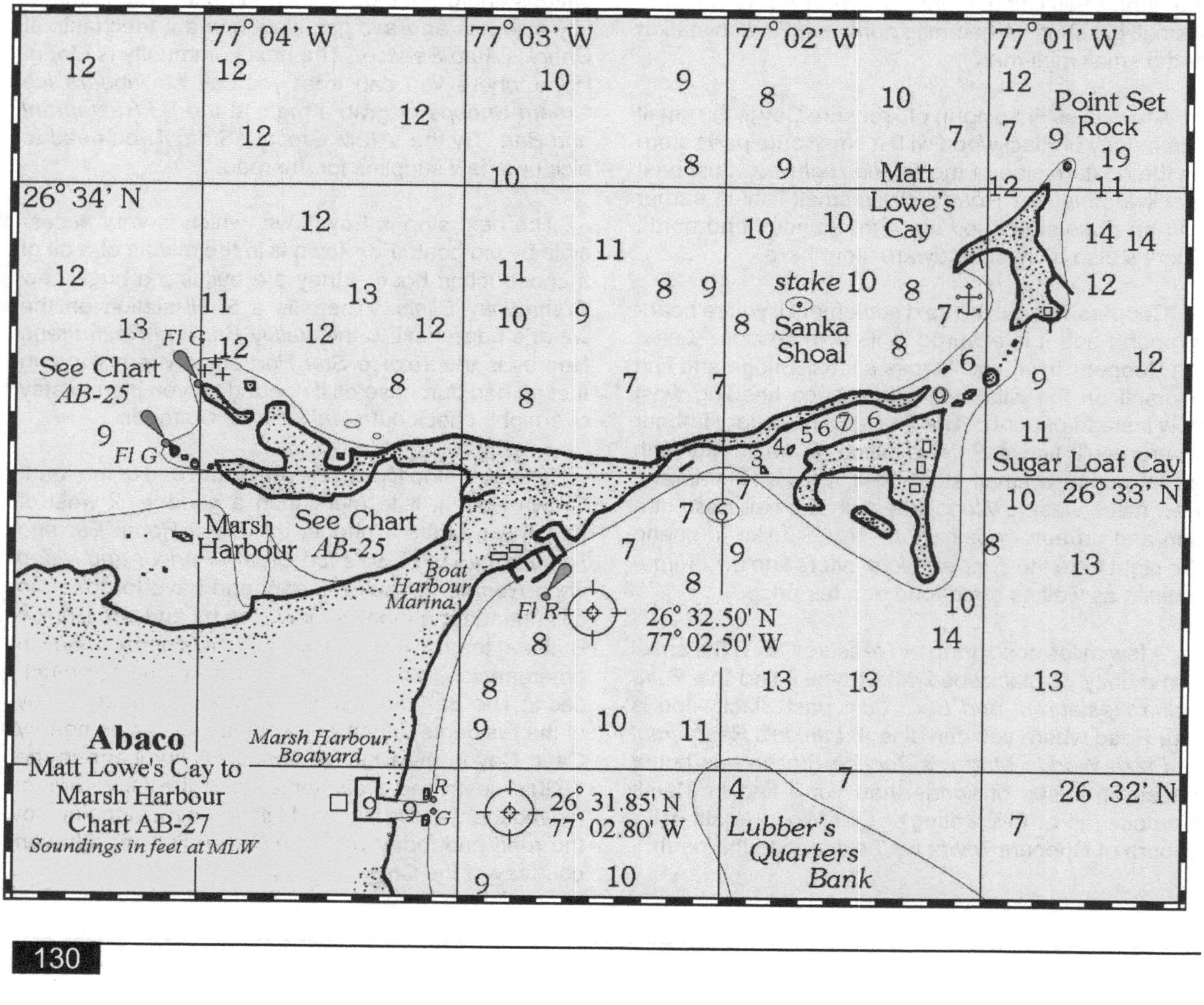

Abaco
Matt Lowe's Cay to
Marsh Harbour
Chart AB-27
Soundings in feet at MLW

an eye out for the well marked (a conspicuous stake) *Sanka Shoal* as shown on Charts AB-26 and AB-27.

As I mentioned earlier, there is a shortcut between Sugar Loaf Cay (once called Hall's Point) and Great Abaco that the ferries use on a regular basis. Vessels with drafts of less than 5' can also use this passage, but it helps if the skipper can read the water a bit and has a high tide on his side. If you're attempting to use this passage as a shortcut into the Bight of Abaco, make your way around *Sanka Shoal* and pass northeast of the small rock that lies just off the eastern tip of Great Abaco. The channel lies between this rock and the string of rocks that stretch between Matt Lowe's Cay and Sugar Loaf Cay. The entrance carries 6' at MLW and should be easy to make out. If in doubt, anchor and watch the ferries as they come through here or check the route with your dinghy first. As you pass to the north of Sugar Loaf Cay you'll see several nice houses and private docks and the water depths will vary from 6'-9' and more in places. As you approach the southwestern tip of Sugar Loaf Cay you'll see two small rocks lying to the southwest of Sugar Loaf Cay. Take these two rocks to port and you'll pass over a shallow area that barely carries 3' at *MLW*. Don't stray too far either way here as the water will just get shallower. As soon as you're over the shoal you can make your way to *Boat Harbour Marina* or wherever else you choose.

If you prefer the safer and deeper long way around into Marsh Harbour Bight this route will be far less of a test on your nerves and a simple bit of eyeball navigation. From Marsh Harbour take Point Set Rock to starboard as shown on Charts AB-26 and AB-27. Point Set Rock is hard to miss; it's the small rock just off the northern tip of Matt Lowe's Cay that has a conspicuous white shack upon it. Keep at least 100 yards off the rock and never anchor in its vicinity. Once past Point Set Rock you can simply follow the shoreline past Sugar Loaf Cay and onward to the waypoint for *Boat Harbour Marina*.

Located along the western edge of *Marsh Harbour Bight*, *Boat Harbour Marina* is the largest and most upscale of Abaco's marinas. As shown on Chart AB-27, a waypoint at 26° 32.50' N, 77° 02.50' W, will place you approximately ¼ mile southeast of the entrance to the marina. There is a large piling with a light (Fl R) that will lie between the waypoint and the marina entrance. Enter the wide opening passing between the two jetties into the marina proper. *Boat Harbour*

Marina offers 198 slips and can accommodate large vessels with a draft of 9' and a beam of up to 33'. The marina boasts full electric hookups, satellite TV, water, ice, showers, laundry, a restaurant, a swim-up bar (*The Sand Bar*), and several shops. Repairs can also be arranged and guests can stay at the lush *Great Abaco Beach Hotel*, also on site.

Private *Carambola Cottage* is located on the southwestern tip of Sugar Loaf Cay at Parrot Point, approximately one mile east of the entrance to *Boat Harbour Marina*. While the cottage is just one of many fine places for rent throughout the Abacos, cruisers will be interested in the private dockage at the 54' by 70' L-shaped dock. Dockage includes fresh water and 30-amp or 50-amp electricity in a very protected little harbor. Dockage is free for cottage guests.

About a mile south of *Boat Harbour Marina* is the *Marsh Harbour Boatyard*, a large haulout facility located in the area known as Calcutta. As shown on Chart AB-27, a waypoint at 26° 31.85' N, 77° 02.80' W, places you approximately ¼ mile east of the marked entrance channel to the boatyard. From the waypoint head west between the red and green markers to enter the haulout basin (9' at MLW). *Marsh Harbour Boatyard* has an 85-ton lift that can handle boats with a beam of up to 24½'. The yard can handle all your fiberglass repairs, wooden boat repairs, pressure cleaning (but no sandblasting), and hull painting, even *Awlgrip*. The yard carries a good basic selection of marine supplies and parts and their mechanic can help you with all your diesel repair needs (*MHBY* is a *Yanmar* dealer). You can even work on your boat, but you'll have to purchase your supplies from the yard, standard for *DIY* yards. On site is *CJ Welding* who can handle all your welding and fabrication needs. The boatyard offers limited dry storage for large boats and much more room for smaller boats and runabouts. You can reach *MHBY* on VHF ch. 16, or by phone at 242-367-4011, or by email at mhby@abaco.net.com.

Vessels heading southward, towards Witch Point, *North Bar Channel*, Lynyard Cay, or Little Harbour, can follow the shoreline of Great Abaco Island staying between it and Lubbers Quarters Bank as shown on Chart AB-26. Stay outside the small string of rocks lying off Great Abaco and you'll have 7'-10' all the way. If you favor Lubbers Quarters Bank you find several areas where the water shallows to 6' at MLW in spots. Once past Witch Point you can take up your course for Snake Cay, Tilloo Pond, or Til*loo Bank* as you wish. Northbound cruisers can head for a waypoint at 26° 29.50' N, 77° 01.25' W, which will place you approximately ¼ mile east of the shallows off Witch Point. From here follow the above directions in reverse to head to *Marsh Harbour Boatyard*, *Boat Harbour Marina*, and the *Hub of Abaco*.

Man-O-War Cay

North Man-O-War Channel - outer waypoint:
26° 38.00' N, 77° 01.30' W

North Man-O-War Channel - inner waypoint:
26° 37.00' N, 77° 01.90' W

South Man-O-War Channel - outer waypoint:
26° 36.10' N, 76° 58.65' W

South Man-O-War Channel - inner waypoint:
26° 35.60' N, 76° 59.10' W

Man-O-War Cay - 200 yards S of entrance:
26° 35.30' N, 77° 00.22' W

Man-O-War Cay is the traditional boat-building center of the Abacos, in fact of the entire Bahamas. As you probably know by now, Loyalists settled in the islands of The Bahamas in the 1780's. Those that settled farther south, in Exuma, tended to be farmers, but those that settled in Abaco tended to be merchants and boat builders and these traditions have endured to this day. There are no descendants of Loyalists in the Exumas today, but they can still be found in Abaco. Almost all the residents of Man-O-War Cay can trace their roots back to Nellie Archer and Ben Albury. Nellie Archer used to visit Man-O-War Cay to farm a plot of land that her family owned there. On hot days she and her family would visit the beach for a break from the heat. One particular day they heard voices coming from the beach and when they investigated, Nellie found several survivors from a wreck being led ashore by 16 year old Ben Albury. True love being what it is…the rest is history.

Navigational Information

Man-O-War Cay offers excellent all-around protections, a quality marina, a nice lee side anchorage, and two passages through the reef into the ocean. As shown on Chart AB-26, the cay lies north of Point Set Rock, northwest of Elbow Cay, and northeast of Marsh Harbour…within an hour or two

sail from each of those places. As shown on Charts AB-28 and AB-28A you can anchor in the lee at the northern end of Dickie's Cay or n the lee of Man-O-War Cay just north of Dickie's Cay. Vessels wishing to enter the harbors at Man-O-War Cay should make for a waypoint at 26° 35.30' N, 77° 00.22' W, which will place you approximately 250 yards south of the entrance channel. It is imperative that you don't just plug in this waypoint and hit "GO TO," especially if you're approaching from Marsh Harbour. The waypoint lies between the entrance channel and the offlying Garden Cay and Sandy Cay. From the waypoint enter the channel midway between the two points of land as shown on Chart AB-28A. The point of land to port is actually the southern tip of Dickie's Cay and is marked by a white flashing light. If you're heading into the *Eastern Harbour*, once you split the first pair of markers, you can turn to starboard and keep the next marker to port as you avoid the shoal area off the northern shore of the harbor and head into *Eastern Harbour* proper. *Eastern Harbour* is primarily used for vessel storage and there are a lot of moorings here.

If you intend to enter *North Harbour*, enter the main channel as described above and instead of turning to starboard to head into *Eastern Harbour*, bear more to port splitting the next pair of markers and following the channel into *North Harbour*. You'll find that *North Harbour* is usually crowded and the best idea is to pick up a mooring or get a slip at *Man-O-War Marina* (the moorings are $10 per night as of this writing-contact the marina on VHF ch. 16 for more information).

The northern entrance to the harbor is shallow and should be avoided by all but the shallowest draft vessels and small outboards.

Man-O-War Marina, well known for its service and hospitality offers the visiting yachtsman all of the comforts of home in a very protected harbor setting. The marina can accommodate yachts to 115' with drafts of up to 8'. The marina's 60 slips have full electric hookups and cable TV as well as showers, a laundry, a fuel dock, and they can handle cosmetic, mechanical, and even refrigeration repairs. The marina is home to the *Pavilion Restaurant* featuring barbecue nights on Fridays and Saturdays. The marina also sends and receives e-mail for cruisers. The marina dive shop rents and fills *SCUBA* tanks and has a great selection of beach and casual wear.

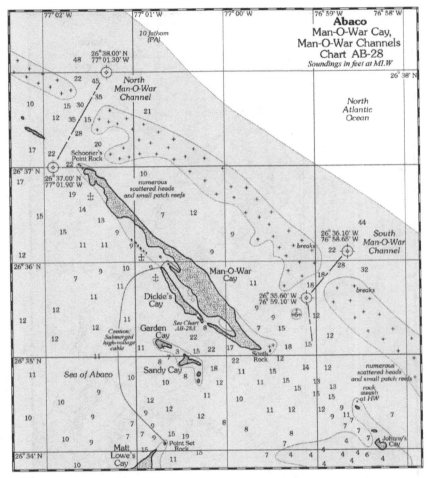

Northwest of *Man-O-War Marina* lie two of the best boat yards in The Bahamas...*Edwin's Boat Yard 1* at the northwestern end of the harbour next to *Albury's Sail Shop*, and *Edwin's Boat Yard 2* which is located closer to the center of the waterfront. It is my firm belief that this is the best place to take your vessel for repair in The Bahamas. The prices are right, the service is the best, and the only problem is the wait; everybody seems to be lining up for this quality service. Just northwest of *Edwin's 2* is *Albury Brothers Boat Building*, makers of high quality fiberglass outboard boats.

As I mentioned earlier, there are two cuts to the ocean at Man-O-War Cay. The best by far is the *North Man-O-War Channel* as shown on Chart AB-28. This is the preferred channel by veteran Abaco boaters as it is wide, deep, and because it will be open when most others are closed. If approaching from the sea, head for a waypoint at 26° 38.00' N, 77° 01.30' W, which will place you about ¼ mile north/northeast of the channel. Head generally south/southwest to a Waypoint at 26°

37.00' N, 77° 01.90' W, your courseline bringing you approximately halfway between Schooner's Point Rock off the northern tip of Man-O-War Cay and Fish Hawk Cay. Once clear of Schooner's Point Rock you can parallel the shoreline of Man-O-War Cay southeastward towards the entrance to the harbors. If outbound via *North Man-O-War Channel*, simply use the waypoints mentioned and follow the course in reverse. The channel is wide here and you'll likely see the seas breaking on the reefs on either side.

South Man-O-War Channel is narrower and a bit more complicated, I much prefer *North Man-O-War Channel* and highly recommend it over its southern counterpart. If approaching from the ocean, head for a waypoint at 26° 36.10' N, 76° 58.65' W, which will place you approximately ¼ mile north of the entrance to this channel as shown on Chart AB-28. Use caution when approaching this waypoint; to the southeast of this waypoint lies a vast area of shallow reefs stretching for over a mile off the northern shore of Elbow Cay. From the outer waypoint head in

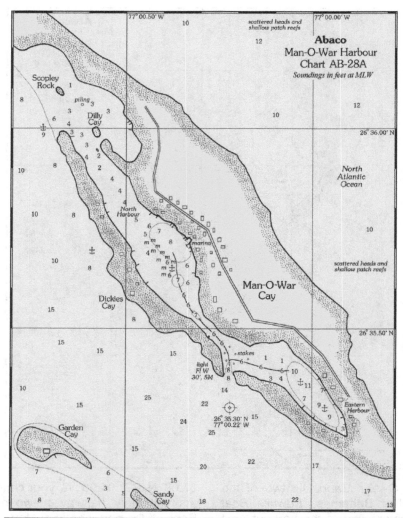

Man-O-War Cay & South Man-O-War Channel

Photo Courtesy of
Paul Harding, Seaplane Safaris

towards the inner waypoint at 26° 35.60' N, 76° 59.10' W, keeping between the obvious reefs on both sides. Once at the inner waypoint you must avoid a rocky patch with only 6' over it at MLW that lies between the inner waypoint and South Rock as shown on the chart. Detour around this rocky patch and South Rock and pass between Sandy Cay and Man-O-War Cay to head for the harbour entrance channel. If you seek to head outbound via the South Man-O-War Channel, you must work your way to the inner waypoint by avoiding South Rock and the rocky patch north/northeast of it. Follow the above directions in reverse and watch out for the reefs off Elbow Cay!

What You Will Find Ashore

There are two fine grocery stores on Man-O-War Cay. *Albury's Grocery Store* is right on the harbor while the *Man-O-War Grocery* sits behind *Man-O-War Marina*. Both will deliver your order to the dock. Across the street from *Man-O-War Grocery* is *Albury's Bakery* where you can pick up fresh baked goods daily. There is a branch of *CIBC* bank in town that's open only on Thursdays from 1000-1400. You can get your propane tanks filled at *Man-O-War Gas*.

If you're in search of good dining try the *Hibiscus Café*, *Island Treats*, *Sheila's Deli*, or *Ena's Place*. *Sheila's* is on the waterfront while *Ena's* sits on the road southeast of the settlement. At *Ena's* you can eat in on the porch or take it with you. *Ena's* is open for lunch every day and every night for ice cream; Wednesday and Saturdays are dinner nights (other nights by reservation only).

Man-O-War Hardware carries marine supplies and can handle all your hardware needs; they can deliver to Hope Town, Green Turtle, and even Little Harbour. *Joe's Studio and Emporium* is a must-visit. Here Joe Albury crafts fine wooden gifts and art objects such as beautiful half-hull models along with chairs, books, T-shirts, and jewelry. *Mary's Corner Store* also sells T-shirts, books, gifts, postcards, jackets, and bags.

One of the must stops here is *Albury's Sail Shop*, a misleading name as you will come to find out. They no longer build or repair sails here; their primary business is the construction of fine canvas bags, hats, and purses. If you need sail repair, look up Jay Manni at *Edwin's Boat Yard*, he might be able to help you.

Southeast of Man-O-War Cay lies Johnny's Cay. You can anchor in the lee of Johnny's Cay and enjoy the fishing and diving opportunities on the reefs that lie about a mile or so off the cay. With the help of the tide you can cross the shoal area south of Johnny's Cay if you're bound for Hope Town, controlling depth is 3'-4' here at MLW and it is sometimes marked by a stake to the south of Johnny's Cay.

Elbow Cay

Hope Town Harbour - ¼ nm W of entrance:
26° 32.65' N, 76° 58.10' W

White Sound, Elbow Cay - ¼ nm WNW of:
26° 31.10' N, 76° 59.00' W

Most cruisers who visit Elbow Cay come for one reason...Hope Town. Hope Town is another one of those Abaco locales that if you haven't been there, well, you just haven't been to Abaco. Well marked by its candy-striped lighthouse, Hope Town is so popular among the boating community that some folks make it the focus of their Abaco cruise. Hope Town is an excellent hurricane hole and there are several marinas where you can tie up, or if you prefer, you can take one of the many well-maintained moorings in the harbour (and with the popularity of moorings in Hope Town harbour, anchoring is getting harder to do, I suggest a mooring).

Hope Town

Navigational Information

The entrance to Hope Town is fairly shallow and should be done on a high tide if you draw over 4'. From Point Set Rock you can head north of the Parrot Cays (the northernmost cay is marked by a flashing red light) for a waypoint at 26° 32.65' N, 76° 58.10' W, which will place you approximately ½ mile west of the entrance channel to the harbor as shown on Chart AB-29.

From the waypoint head eastward as if to pass north of Eagle Rock. Use caution in this area as it's pretty shallow...deeper draft vessels can proceed towards the conspicuous quarry on the western shore of Mouth of Harbour Cay before turning northeast towards the entrance channel to avoid some 5' at MLW spots. This part of the Elbow Cay shoreline is also a popular anchorage and a good spot from which to dinghy over to Parrot Cay where you'll find *Island Marine*, an *OMC* dealer.

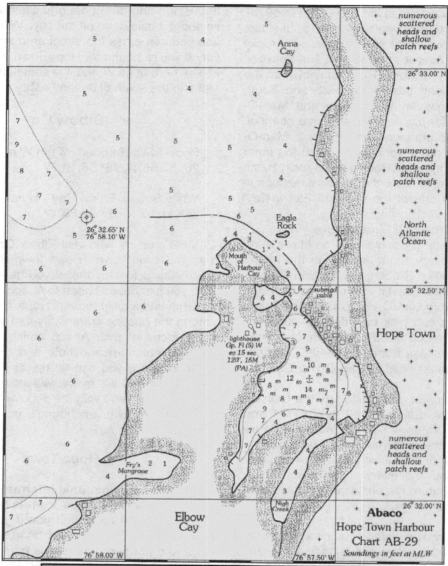

numerous scattered heads and shallow patch reefs

Anna Cay

26° 33.00' N

numerous scattered heads and shallow patch reefs

North Atlantic Ocean

Eagle Rock

26° 32.65' N
76° 58.10' W

Mouth of Harbour Cay

submgd cable

26° 32.50' N

Hope Town

lighthouse
Gp. Fl (5) W
ev 15 sec
120', 15M
(PA)

numerous scattered heads and shallow patch reefs

Fry's Mangrove

Nigh Creek

26° 32.00' N

Abaco
Hope Town Harbour
Chart AB-29
Soundings in feet at MLW

Elbow Cay

76° 58.00' W

76° 57.50' W

Hope Town

Hope Town, Elbow Cay   Photo Courtesy of Paul Harding, Seaplane Safaris

As you approach the channel between Eagle Rock and Mouth of Harbour Cay, take a look down the channel towards the shoreline of Elbow Cay where you'll see a concrete road leading away from the water's edge. Steer your vessel as if to head straight down this road (148° mag.) and you'll spot a range on shore consisting of two white poles with red reflectors. Favor the Eagle Rock side of this channel; there may or may not be some privately maintained markers here to show you the channel. When Hope Town harbor opens up to starboard, turn and enter the harbor mouth staying approximately mid-channel. Before you actually enter Hope Town harbour you'll see a small cove to starboard, this is used primarily for storage of vessels and haul outs at *Lighthouse Marina*.

As you enter the harbor proper you can head for one of the marinas, pick up a mooring, or anchor where your draft allows. The community of Hope Town requests that visiting yachtsmen leave a channel approximately 200' wide along each shore of Hope Town harbour. I suggest that you pick up a mooring, as the harbour is almost always full. Call *Lucky Strike,*, *Capt. Jacks*, or *Abaco Bahama Charters* on VHF ch. 16 for a mooring ($10 per night as of this writing). All of the marinas in Hope Town also monitor VHF ch. 16.

Directly to starboard upon entering the harbor is *Lighthouse Marina* offering 6 slips with full electric hookups, water, ice, showers, a laundry, fuel, and 7' at MLW. *Lighthouse Marina* also offers wet and dry storage, a well stocked marine supply store, and a selection of fishing tackle and bait. A restaurant/bar is on site and groceries can be picked up in town. *Lighthouse Marina* can help you with *Yamaha* outboard repairs, they're a *Yamaha* dealer (they also have a 20-ton lift). If you need *OMC* help, *Sea Horse Marine* is the local dealer (they monitor VHF ch. 16).

Just past *Lighthouse Marina* is *Hope Town Marina* (formerely *Club Soleil*), with 16 slips, 7½' at MLW, full electric hookups, fuel, water, ice, showers, fishing tackle and bait. Minor repairs and cosmetics can be handled here. *HTM* has an excellent restaurant featuring Bahamian and European cuisine. *HTM* can also handle e-mail for cruisers and can help you with *Nissan* outboard repairs.

Just past *Hope Town Marina* are the docks of *Hope Town Hideaways*. Primarily featuring vacation

homes and waterfront property, the marina offers 12 slips with full electric, a fresh-water pool, provisions, and a restaurant.

What You Will Find Ashore

There are several places for moored or anchored cruisers to gain shore access in Hope Town. The large government dock sits in the southeastern end of the harbor at the northern end of *Nigh Creek*. If you tie up here please don't block the Ferry access. By the way, cruisers can find some excellent hurricane protection up the creeks at the southern end of Hope Town harbor. You can tie your dinghy up at the *Harbour View Grocery* dock where you can stock up on groceries, sundries, meats, veggies, and even get your propane filled. *Harbour View* is open Monday-Friday from 0800-1300 and then from 1400-1800. Saturdays they're open from 0800 until 1900.

One of the more popular waterfront hangouts is the *Harbour's Edge Restaurant* that opens daily at 1000. Here you can dine while gazing at your lovely yacht, can shoot some pool, rent a bike, buys some ice, or catch the latest news or weather on satellite TV. Saturday night is pizza night with live music; Sunday's there's live music too.

Every bit as popular is *Capt. Jack's* right on the water's edge. You can get breakfast, lunch, or dinner here in an extremely casual atmosphere. The specialties are Bahamian dishes and you can watch satellite TV and listen to live music on Wednesday and Friday nights.

There is so much to see and do in Hope Town, the first place to start might be with *Island Cart Rentals*, they'll deliver right to your marina and they monitor VHF ch. 16. In town you can shop at *Vernon's Grocery and Upper Crust Baker*, where if you can't find what you want at *Harbour View*, you'll probably locate it here. You must sample their fresh baked pies and breads. I remember sitting in the harbour one morning when an announcement came over VHF ch. 16 saying that fresh bread was available at *Vernon's*. All of sudden a mass of dinghies made their way to shore in a mad rush to share in the tasty treats that made the bakery famous.

Also in town you'll find the *Abaco Ocean Club*, the *Bike Shop*, a *CIBC* bank that is open Wednesdays from 1000-1400, the *Water's Edge Studio*, the *Island Gallery*, and high on the hill is the *Hope Town Harbour*

Lodge with its excellent restaurant. The restaurant serves breakfast and lunch daily except Sundays. The *Reef Bar and Grill* at the *Lodge* serves lunch Monday-Saturday from 1130-1430, with a happy hour from 1600-1700 Monday-Saturday. You can also satisfy your appetite by visiting *Munchies, Hollywood Temptations*, and *Rudy's Place* just outside of town.

A wonderful spot to spend an hour or three is at the *Wyannie Malone Historical Museum*. Here you'll learn the secrets of Hope Town's history dating back to Lucayan times. The museum was founded in 1785, and is maintained by the community.

One thing that you MUST DO while in Hope Town is climb to the top of the lighthouse. Many, many years ago the folks of Elbow Cay made their living off the salvaging of wrecked vessels that came to grief on the reefs of Elbow Cay. A popular tale recounts the time that a minister was preaching to his congregation when he spied a ship on the reef. His flock had their back to the sea and could not see this windfall. The minister asked everybody to bow their heads for a few minutes of silent retrospection and prayer. After a few minutes of this silence, some of the members started raising their heads and they noticed that the preacher was nowhere to be seen, until he was spotted in his boat heading to the wreckage. The next day the congregation turned the altar around so that they had the view of the sea, not the preacher.

When the lighthouse was scheduled to be built in 1864, Abaconians who lived off salvaging protested but to no avail. Today, the candy-striped landmark still stands as sentinel for Abaco, but it has been a long uphill battle to keep its distinct and historical flavor. This symbol of Bahamian maritime heritage is one of the last three oil-burning, hand-wound lighthouses in the world. The lighthouse keeper must climb the 101 steps to the top every two hours to hand crank the weights that operate the beacon.

The light mechanism sits in mercury and its five bulls-eye lenses focus its kerosene fueled light once every 15 seconds. Faced with modernization, the community of Hope Town pulled together and managed to preserve the lighthouse in its original state. This involved a huge fund raising effort as well as immense difficulties in finding much needed out-dated parts. Help came from some of the oddest places...a group of professional bridge painters agreed to repaint the lighthouse in exchange for room and board. Today, the lighthouse gleams in her new paint!

White Sound

White Sound - ¼ nm WNE of entrance:
26° 31.10' N, 76° 59.00' W

Navigational Information

Lovely White Sound lies about a mile north of the southern end of Elbow Cay and Tilloo Cut. Here you'll find a dredged entrance channel, the *Abaco Inn*, the *Sea Spray Resort Villas and Marina*, and a fair sized residential community. The entrance is fairly straightforward as shown on Chart AB-30. A waypoint at 26° 31.10' N, 76° 59.00' W, will place you approximately ¼ mile west/northwest of the entrance channel to White Sound. If you're approaching from Hope Town, simply parallel the shoreline of Elbow Cay southward passing between the Parrot Cays and Elbow Cay (see Chart AB-26). If you're heading for this waypoint from Point Set Rock you'll pass west of the Parrot Cays, and you'll have to avoid the small rock that lies southwest of this group as shown on Chart AB-26. Once abeam of that small rock you'll pass over a shallow area (5' at MLW) before getting back into deeper water at the waypoint (7').

East of the waypoint you'll see a turning mark indicating the beginning of the dredged channel (6' at MLW) into White Sound as shown on Chart AB-30. The entrance channel lies south of the light shown on the chart, and a range at the *Abaco Inn* (two red disks-lit red at night) will lead you in on a bearing of 123°M. There really isn't any room to anchor here, you can't anchor in the channel and the rest of White Sound is too shallow, but the *Abaco Inn* offers complimentary dockage for guests of their restaurant and bar. Dockage here is Med-style, drop a hook and back in to tie up stern to. Cruisers wishing to anchor and enjoy White Sound by dinghy can anchor south of the entrance as shown on Chart AB-30 in prevailing east/southeast winds.

If a slip is more to your liking, you can take the dredged channel south in White Sound to the *Sea Spray Resort Villas and Marina* located at the extreme southern end of White Sound. The well-marked channel turns sharply southward (as shown on the chart) and as you approach the marina you will pass to the west of a jetty that protects the marina.

What You Will Find Ashore

Sea Spray Resort Villas and Marina boasts 24 slips with full electric, water, ice, showers, and a laundry on site. They can handle boats with a maximum beam of 22' and the docks carry 6' at MLW. *Sea Spray* monitors VHF ch. 16 and is a *Texaco Star Port*. Guests can dine at the *Boat House Restaurant* (breakfast, lunch, and dinner) or have a beverage at the *Garbonzo Bar* before or after taking a dip in their fresh water pool. For a real treat, try some of their fresh baked goods.

If you need groceries, visit *Sweeting's Grocery Store*. *Sweeting's* offers meat, beverages, ice, and fresh fruits and vegetables.

The *Abaco Inn* sits on a dune with views of both White Sound and the *North Atlantic Ocean*. Their restaurant offers elegant gourmet Bahamian and American cuisine in a casual setting. In Hope Town, contact the *Abaco Inn* for a pick up at the *Govt. Dock*.

Lubbers Quarters to Tilloo Cut

Tilloo Cut - ¼ nm W of:
26° 29.80' N, 76° 58.55' W

Witch Point - ½ nm ESE of Witch Point Shoal:
26° 29.50' N, 77° 01.25' W

Cormorant Cay - ¼ nm SE of anchorage:
26° 27.45' N, 77° 02.75' W

Remote but accessible Lubbers Quarters lies just to the west of *Tilloo Cut* as shown on Charts AB-26 and AB-30. The principal draw is *Cracker P's Bar and Grill*, on the eastern side of the Cay. Here you can dine on fresh grilled foods while enjoying a great view.

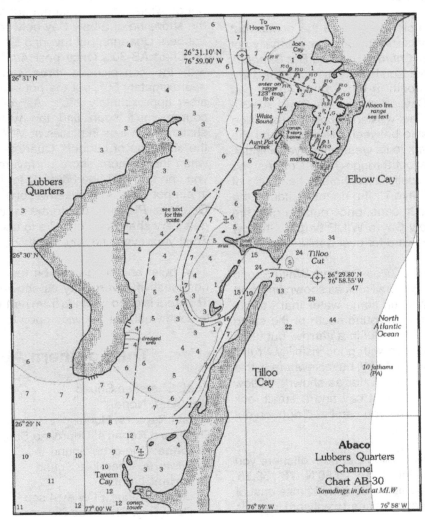

The best way to access Lubbers Quarters by boat is to anchor in White Sound or at Tahiti Beach and dinghy over and tie up at *Cracker P's*. You can anchor to the east of *Cracker P's* in 4'-6' but only in westerly winds.

Navigational Information

If you're approaching *Tilloo Cut* from the north, from White Sound, once out of White Sound turn south paralleling the shoreline of Elbow Cay between Elbow Cay and Lubbers Quarters, but favoring Elbow Cay as shown on Chart AB-30. Once past *Aunt Pat's Creek* and the conspicuous three story house (once owned by Burl Ives), put the house on your stern and steer approximately 230°. Continue on this course for about ¼ mile and you'll see Bakers Rock and Tahiti Beach at the extreme southwestern tip of Elbow Cay as shown on the chart. Head in towards Tahiti Beach and anchor where your draft allows.

Tilloo Cut is a viable passage to the ocean, but usually only local boats use it. Cruisers normally opt for *North Man-O-War Channel* or *North Bar Channel*, which lies a bit further south. If you're approaching *Tilloo Cut* from the south in the *Sea of Abaco* you can round Tavern Cay as shown on Chart AB-30, and head in along the western shoreline of Tilloo Cay. You'll be passing between Tilloo Cay and the conspicuous sandbank to its west where you'll find 7' and more all the way out through *Tilloo Cut*. As you approach *Tilloo Cut* itself, favor the southern side of the cut where you'll have 7'; the northern side of the cut is shallow. By all means, once outside give the northern end of Elbow Cay a WIDE berth. Shallow reefs here stretch seaward for over a mile.

If you're approaching *Tilloo Cut* from White Sound or Tahiti Beach, clear Bakers Rock as shown on Chart AB-30 where you'll pick up some water that's about 7' at MLW. Your aim is to round south of the string of cays lying west of *Tilloo Cut* in a narrow, but deep channel that is easily seen with good visibility. You'll cross a spot with only 6' at MLW, but elsewhere in this channel you'll have deeper water as shown. Follow the channel between the last cay and a small rock as shown on the chart and you can head right on out *Tilloo Cut*.

If you're approaching *Tilloo Cut* from offshore you can head for a waypoint at 26° 29.80'N, 76° 58.55' W, which will place you approximately ¼ mile east of *Tilloo Cut*. From the waypoint head westward towards

the cut favoring the northern tip of Tilloo Cay, rounding it about 50 yards off. Watch out for the shallow area on the northern side of *Tilloo Cut*.

Skippers wishing to head southward from White Sound or Tahiti Beach, between Lubbers Quarters and *Tilloo Cut* may find that this short passage is the most challenging of their Abaco cruise. The waters between Lubbers Quarters and *Tilloo Cut* have shallowed a bit over the last few years and you must have a high tide to transit this area. When heading south, I much prefer to follow the channel between Great Abaco and Lubbers Quarters Bank as shown on Chart AB-26. It's a lot easier and less stressful... but if you insist on passing east of Lubbers Quarters here's how. (I don't recommend this route if you draw over 5'.)

If you're heading south from White Sound, once out of White Sound head generally south paralleling the shoreline of Elbow Cay between Elbow Cay and Lubbers Quarters, but favoring Elbow Cay as shown on Chart AB-30. Once past *Aunt Pat's Creek*, and with the conspicuous three story house bearing approximately 50°, put the house on your stern and steer approximately 230°. As you follow your 230° course you'll soon find the waters getting quite shallow, 4' or less in places at MLW. You'll approach the shoreline of Lubbers Quarters quite closely and when the western shore of Tavern Cay bears 205° you can turn and head directly for it until you're back in deeper water just past the southern tip of Lubbers Quarters. Please use extreme caution on this route, it gets very shallow, I don't like to use it, but you might. Trust your eyes and your depthsounder here.

A quiet anchorage can be found in a small bight northeast of Tavern Cay as shown on Chart AB-30. This spot is good in winds from northeast through east to southwest, but it is wide open to the northwest.

The Southern Abacos

Fuel: Cherokee Sound
Haul-Out: None
Diesel Repairs: None
Outboard Repairs: Cherokee Sound
Propane: Cherokee Sound
Provisions: Cherokee Sound
Important Lights:
    Little Harbour: Fl W ev 4 sec
    Duck Cay, Cherokee Sound: Fl R (unreliable)

Hole in the Wall Lighthouse: Fl W ev 10 sec
Rock Point (Sandy Point): Fl W ev 6 sec

Tilloo Pond

Tilloo Pond - ¼ nm W of entrance to pond:
26° 27.00' N, 77° 00.50' W

Tilloo Pond is a wonderful, well-protected little anchorage about halfway down the western shore of Tilloo Cay as shown on Chart AB-31. *Tilloo Pond* will accept boats with drafts of less than 6', vessels drawing more than 3½'-4' will have to wait for the tide to enter and leave. This anchorage is a good spot to ride out a front, especially if you can duck in far enough behind Shearpin Cay as shown on the blowup on Chart AB-32. A strong west wind will create a bit of a surge in here at times as it funnels in through the entrance and bounces around inside, nothing dangerous mind you, but you might find it a bit uncomfortable. The docks in the pond are all private so don't tie up your dinghy there.

Navigational Information

If approaching *Tilloo Pond* from the north, from the northern end of Tilloo Cay or Lubber's Quarters, you can parallel the shoreline of Tilloo Cay southward to a waypoint at 26° 27.00' N, 77° 00.50' W, as shown on Chart AB-32. This will place you approximately ¼ mile west of the entrance into the pond. The western shore of Tilloo Cay has several small coves that are good for anchoring in easterly winds. If you're approaching from Witch Point on Great Abaco, you can make a beeline for the waypoint given and be in good water all the way.

If approaching *Tilloo Pond* from the south, from *Middle Channel* at *Tilloo Bank*, once clear of *Tilloo Bank* you can head for the waypoint at the entrance to the anchorage. Be careful to avoid the northern edge of *Tilloo Bank*, it's easily seen and avoided. If you're approaching from Snake Cay, simply head straight for the waypoint at Tilloo Pond, almost due east in good water all the way.

From the waypoint, the entrance to *Tilloo Pond* is fairly straightforward. Heading east, the entrance lies between Shearpin Cay and the small rock north of the cay. At the time of this writing there was a green marker just south of the small rock and if that is there when you arrive, keep it to port. The entrance channel lies roughly halfway between the small rock and

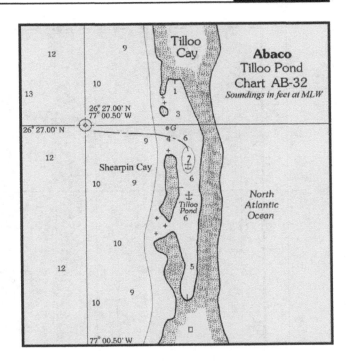

Shearpin Cay. Once over the bar turn to starboard to anchor behind Shearpin Cay, do not turn to port as the water shallows almost immediately there.

Snake Cay

Snake Cay - ¼ nm SE of:
26° 26.90' N, 77° 02.70' W

In the 1960's, Snake Cay was a hustling, bustling little port that was operated by the *Owens-Illinois Company* for their lumber operations. Today the equipment lies unused and the bottom is littered with pieces of concrete, steel, and who knows what else. Snake Cay's best attribute is that it is one of the best hurricane holes in the Abacos.

Navigational Information

If approaching from the north, from Witch Point or *Lubbers Quarters Channel*, you can head straight for a waypoint at 26° 26.90' N, 77° 02.70' W, which will place you approximately ¼ mile southeast of the southeastern tip of Snake Cay. If approaching from the south, from *Middle Channel* at *Tilloo Bank*, once clear of *Tilloo Bank* you can steer straight for this waypoint, Snake Cay will be clearly visible and bearing about 310°.

If the winds are southeast to southwest you can head north just a bit to anchor in the small bight formed

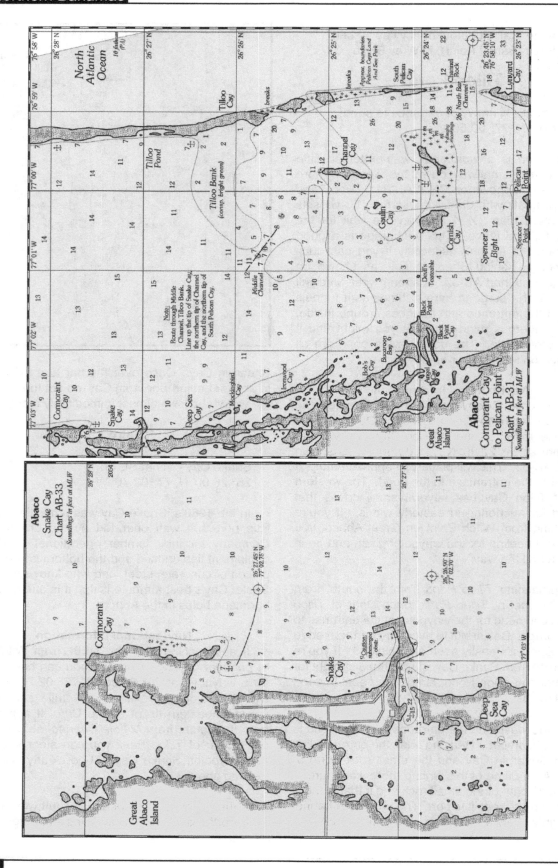

by the "foot" of Snake Cay, but be advised, there are several submerged obstructions here, especially the closer you get to shore and the old dock. Use caution when setting your hook here, there is a lot of junk on the bottom waiting to foul your anchor.

As I mentioned, Snake Cay is one of the best hurricane holes in the Abacos. There is a small, deep channel close in to the southern shore of Snake Cay that will take you back between Snake Cay and Deep Sea Cay and, if your draft allows, to a small deep pocket to the west of Deep Sea Creek. To access this area, follow close in along the southern shore of Snake Cay as shown on Chart AB-32. You'll pass between the shoal that lies northeast of Deep Sea Cay and the southern shore of Snake Cay in good water from 8'-20' in depth. There is a bit of current here so be prepared. You can anchor in the deep cut between Snake Cay and Deep Sea Cay or, if your draft allows, cross over the 3' bar (MLW) to head south/southwest to the conspicuous blue patch of water (7' at MLW) that lies west of Deep Sea Creek.

It's possible to anchor in the bight at the southern end of Cormorant Cay (Chart AB-33) in winds from west to almost north when this small anchorage will be calm. The flats to the west of Cormorant Cay and Snake Cay, like most in Abaco, offer excellent bonefishing. A waypoint at 26° 27.45' N, 77° 02.75' W will place you roughly a quarter-mile east/southeast of this small bight.

Well south of Snake Cay lies Bucaroon Bay as shown on Chart AB-31. In winds from southwest to northwest you can anchor in the lee of these cays and take the opportunity to do some flats exploring. This harbor is not good in a blow; the bottom is a mixture of hard sand and rocks.

As of this writing, developers were intent on reviving Snake Cay as a commercial development so keep your eyes open if you're in the area.

Negotiating Tilloo Bank

Tilloo Bank, Middle Channel - N waypoint:
26° 25.90' N, 77° 01.10' W

Tilloo Bank, Middle Channel - S waypoint:
26° 25.38' N, 77° 00.20' W

Navigational Information

Vessels heading southward to North Bar Channel or Little Harbour, who are not wishing to go outside into the deeper waters of the North Atlantic Ocean must instead negotiate the very shallow and conspicuous Tilloo Bank. Tilloo Bank presents no real difficulties for the average skipper; it can be rounded by following its very visible edge or bisected by using Middle Channel as shown on Chart AB-31.

If you're heading south in the Sea of Abaco from Lubber's Quarters, Witch Point, or Snake Cay, steer for a Waypoint at 26° 25.90' N, 77° 01.10' W. This position will lie approximately ¼ mile northwest of Middle Channel and roughly in line to pass across the Tilloo Bank in 6'-7' at MLW. From the waypoint you can take up a course of approximately 130° or follow a very easy and visible range. The courseline through here is not as important as staying between the two shallow areas of the Tilloo Bank and staying on the range. When heading south the range consists of putting Snake Cay on your stern and lining up the northern tip of Channel Cay and the northern tip of South Pelican Cay on your bow. Once past the highly visible Tilloo Bank you can round Channel Cay to starboard and proceed southward to anchor off Sandy Cay and enjoy the Pelican Cays Land and Sea Park or head further south to Lynyard Cay or Little Harbour.

If you're heading north from Little Harbour or perhaps North Bar Channel, pass between Sandy Cay and South Pelican Cay, and then take Channel Cay to port. Once clear of the northern tip of Channel Cay, turn to port to head to a waypoint at 26° 25.38' N, 77° 00.20' W. This will place you approximately ½ mile southeast of Middle Channel. From this waypoint you can take up a course of approximately 310° on Snake Cay to pass safely through Middle Channel. It's best to use the range here also. Line up the northern tip of Channel Cay and the northern tip of South Pelican Cay on your stern and put Snake Cay on your bow… this should bring you safely across in 6'-7'.

A lot of cruisers opt to avoid Middle Channel altogether and simply round the end of Tilloo Bank and this is fine; the bank is very visible and easy to follow. If heading south, from the northern waypoint of Middle Channel simply keep the visible bar to port and follow it around. You'll pass between Tilloo Bank and a smaller sandbar that lies northwest of Channel Cay. Round Channel Cay to starboard and you're on your way to Little Harbour. Northbound boats run this course in reverse.

What You Will Find Ashore

Cruisers should not miss stopping at the *Pelican Cays Land And Sea Park*. As shown on Chart AB-31, you can anchor in the lee of Sandy Cay in *Pelican Harbour* and dinghy around to the eastern shore of Sandy Cay where you can tie your dinghy up to the moorings there. The anchorage to the west of Sandy Cay can often get a bit rolly as the seas from the ocean find their way around the northern end of Sandy Cay. The chart shows the boundaries of the *PCLSP* and no marine or plant life, and no coral or shells may be taken from the confines of the Park. Take nothing but photographs, leave nothing but footprints.

North Bar Channel

North Bar Channel - ½ nm WNW of:
26° 23.60' N, 76° 59.00' W

North Bar Channel - ½ nm ESE of:
26° 23.45' N, 76° 58.10' W

Navigational Information

North Bar Channel is an excellent route to or from the *North Atlantic Ocean*. When *Little Harbour Bar* is too rough to cross *North Bar Channel* is often passable. If approaching from the ocean-side, head to a waypoint 26° 23.45' N, 76° 58.10' W as shown on Chart AB-31. This waypoint places you approximately ½ mile east/southeast of *North Bar Channel*. From this waypoint head just north of west passing between tiny North Channel Rock and the submerged reef that lies north of Lynyard Cay. Once again let me repeat, the course in degrees is not as important as passing safely between North Channel Rock and Lynyard Cay. A good range here is to line up your bow with the southern tip of Sandy Cay and the northern tip of Cornish Cay and head in on that range, approximately 295°. I never use the range, the cut is wide and all you really need do is stay in the middle keeping an eye out for the reef off Lynyard Cay.

Vessels wishing to head out into the ocean via *North Bar Channel* can head to a waypoint at 26° 23.60' N, 76° 59.00' W, approximately ½ mile west/ northwest of *North Bar Channel*. From the waypoint ocean-bound vessels can head out *North Bar Channel* following the above directions in reverse.

Lynyard Cay

Lynyard Cay is a very popular anchorage in prevailing northeast through southeast winds. My favorite anchorage is just south of the westward lying sandbar that lies off the northern end of Lynyard Cay southeast of Pelican Point on Great Abaco (as shown on Chart AB-34). There are no facilities ashore here, but if you're waiting for the tide to get into Little Harbour, or if you've just arrived from Eleuthera and want to rest for the night, Lynyard Cay is the spot.

Navigational Information

If you're approaching from the north, from the *North Bar Channel* area, head south favoring the Great Abaco shoreline south of Pelican Point to avoid the not-so-conspicuous sandbar off Lynyard Cay. Once clear of the shoal, head east and tuck up into the anchorage shown on the chart lying southwest of the house in the small cove. Actually, anywhere along the western shore of Lynyard Cay is a fine lee anchorage, but that small cove, and two more closer to the southern end of Lynyard are the best.

If you're approaching from the south, from Little Harbour, head north/northeast after leaving Little Harbour and pass well to the east of Bridges Cay. Watch out for the shallows on the eastern shore of Bridges Cay and also avoid the shallow area that lies northwest of Goole Cay as shown on Chart AB-34. You can actually pass between this shoal and Goole Cay in 7'-9' of water to head northward along the Lynyard Cay shore.

If you've just entered via *Little Harbour Bar* and you want to anchor for the night, you can parallel the reef on your starboard side and pass between Goole Cay and the above-mentioned shoal. If this is not to your liking you can keep on your heading (345°) towards Bridges Cay and turn northward to clear the shoal lying west of Goole Cay as shown on Chart AB-34.

When heading north or south along here, keep an eye out for the shallow bar that works out from the southern tip of Bridges Cay northward to about 26° 22' N along the Great Abaco shoreline.

Just east of Goole Cay lies an old *VW* van in about 12' of water. It once knew life as *Taxi 18* in Marsh Harbour.

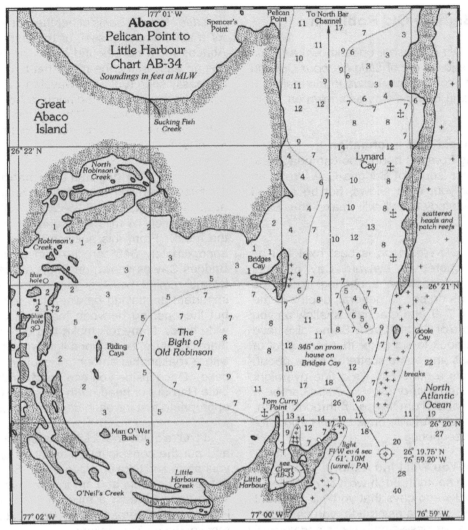

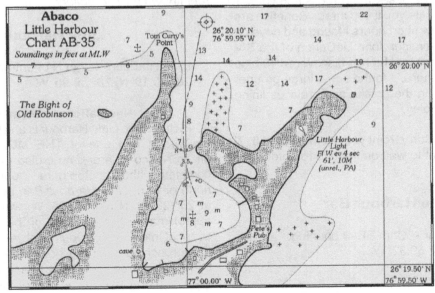

The Bight of Old Robinson

The *Bight of Old Robinson*, once known as *Little Harbour Bay*, lies just west of *Little Harbour Cut* and the entrance to Little Harbour, between the mainland of Great Abaco and Bridges Cay as shown on Chart AB-34.

Navigational Information

If approaching from the north, you can head west just after you pass south of Bridges Cay. You can anchor wherever your draft allows, but be advised that a strong easterly swell will make the *Bight* uncomfortable.

The *Bight of Old Robinson* is best explored by dinghy while anchored at Lynyard Cay or Little Harbour but if you insist on anchoring inside the bight, by all means do so. In general, depths in the center range from 7'-9' and gradually shallow as you approach the shore of Great Abaco. Some folks have trouble getting a hook to set here; there are a lot of large grass clumps and some scattered rocks about. If your anchor gets a good bite it's a fine overnight anchorage, and the *Bight of Old Robinson* can be a bit of a haven in winds from the south through north, though I would much prefer to be in Little Harbour for a blow of any consequence.

What You Will Find Ashore

In a curve from south through west to north lies a string of small rocks and cays that you will not want to miss exploring. Using a rising tide, you can enter the mouths of some of these small creeks and you will delight in the marine life you'll find there. Bonefish are everywhere! In a few short hours I found and dove on two blue holes and cruiser John DeCarion of the S/V *Packadreams* tells me that he has discovered 10 blue holes tucked up in there. I found some large grouper and lobster inhabiting the cracks and crevices lining the sides of these holes.

Just inside Tom Curry Point you can anchor in 5'-7' at MLW, a good spot to wait on the tide to enter Little Harbour.

Little Harbour Bar

Little Harbour Bar - ½ nm SE of opening:
26° 19.30' N, 76° 59.32' W

Little Harbour Bar is either the last exit to the ocean for a southbound vessel, or the first entrance to the Abacos for a northbound boat. In most conditions it is an easy entry, the reefs that border it break and are easily seen (but not always!), but in heavy seas it would be prudent to head north to *North Bar Channel* or even *North Man-O-War Channel*, which is the safest in most conditions. Never try to cross *the Little Harbour Bar* at night!

Navigational Information

If you're arriving from offshore, head to a waypoint at 26° 20.10' N, 76° 59.95' W, which will place you approximately ¼ mile southeast of the cut between the reefs. From this position take up a heading of approximately 345° on the conspicuous house on Bridges Cay as shown on Chart AB-34. Once again let me remind you that the course here is not as important as staying between the reefs (obviously!), but the opening between the reefs is actually very wide here. Many folk make this cut out to be worse than it really is, but in good light, moderate seas, and with a reasonable amount of caution it is a piece of cake. Once inside you can head for the waypoint to Little Harbour or head north to Lynyard Cay. See the appropriate text for each destination for more details.

If you're outbound at Little Harbour Bar, head south and put the conspicuous house on Bridges Cay on your stern and take up a course of 165° until you pass between the reefs and are in deep water. If heading south keep at least a mile off shore between Little Harbour and *Cherokee Sound* to avoid the dangerous reef known as *The Boilers*.

Little Harbour

Little Harbour - ½ nm N of entrance channel:
26° 20.10' N, 76° 59.95' W

Navigational Information

Picturesque Little Harbour is an almost land-locked anchorage and one of THE MOST popular stops on an Abaco itinerary; no cruise to Abaco would be complete without a stop here. Approaching from the north or from *Little Harbour Bar*, head to a waypoint at 26° 20.10' N, 76° 59.95' W, which will place you approximately ¼ mile north of the marked entrance channel into Little Harbour as shown on Chart AB-35. If approaching from the north make sure you clear the shallow areas off Great Abaco and Bridges Cay as shown on Chart AB-34. If approaching from *Little*

Harbour Bar make sure that you don't drift south, keeping clear of the reef that lies north of the eastern entrance point to Little Harbour.

From the waypoint, head generally south/southwest past Tom Curry's Point as shown on Chart AB-35. Here you'll be in deep water that gradually shoals to about 3½' in the marked channel just before you enter the deeper water of Little Harbour. This passage will require a rising tide for most boats and if you need to wait for the tide to come up, a good spot is inside Tom Curry's Point in the Bight of Old Robinson as shown on the chart.

The entrance channel into Little Harbour is marked (at the time of this writing) by four pairs of red and green markers (red, right, returning here!) and is easy to follow. Once inside Little Harbour anchor wherever you desire, but it's so much easier to pick up one of Pete's moorings ($10 per night as of this writing). If you do anchor please make sure that when you swing you'll not collide with the moored boats.

What You Will Find Ashore

I'm sure that by now most people are aware that the recent history of Little Harbour and the family of internationally acclaimed sculptor Randolph Johnston are entwined...if you're not, then let me try to fill you in. The history of this remarkable family could fill a book, and does. *Artist on his Island, A Study in Self-Reliance* by Randolph W. Johnston sells in several places in Marsh Harbour as well as Little Harbour. The book is basically an autobiography, and chronicles the Johnston family's exodus to a better life and their eventual choice of Little Harbour as their own little bit of Heaven on earth. The book has been primarily compiled from Johnston's diary, which he called "The Escapist's Notebook" or "The Good Life for Those Who Can Take It."

In 1950, Randolph Johnston was an assistant professor at *Smith College* in Massachusetts. He was also a sculptor who wanted to spend his time sculpting. Little Harbour was completely deserted save for the lighthouse keeper and his family. On New Year's Day of 1951, at the age of 46, Randolph Johnston and his family left behind what he described as the "Megamachine" and arrived at Man-O-War Cay in the Abacos 16 days later. They immediately set up housekeeping and began a life on this quiet boat-building cay.

Seven months after their arrival at Man-O-War, Randolph Johnston purchased a 47' schooner that was used to convey crawfish to market. The family hastily moved aboard *Langosta* and spent the next six months converting the commercial boat into the family home. Then in February of 1952, their shakedown cruise took them to Nassau. The plan was to putt about the Caribbean and then perhaps on to the South Pacific, sounds like any normal family of cruisers today doesn't it? Shortly they set off for the Exumas and began to realize that The Bahamas offered much of what they sought. When they sailed into Little Harbour on Abaco it was like love at first sight, Randolph's quest for a bit of Eden was fulfilled. These few paragraphs do no justice to the tales that Randolph Johnston weaves in his autobiography. You'll marvel at how the family lived in the huge cave at the southwest end of the harbour and the hardships they endured in transforming Little Harbour into a home and foundry for sculptor Randolph and son Pete.

Today, Randolph has passed away and Pete has taken over the foundry. His remarkable castings are exciting pieces and much sought after. His *Pete's Pub* is actually fashioned from the deckhouse of the schooner *Langosta* and is probably one of the most popular watering holes in the entire Abacos. When you're here you must visit the very laid-back *Pete's Pub* (now open 7 days a week) for food and drinks, and visit the *Gallery* to view some of the Johnston's works. The gallery is open from 1000-1600 daily except Sundays, more or less.

Cherokee Sound

Cherokee Sound - ¾ nm S of entrance channel: 26° 15.50' N, 77° 04.20' W

Navigational Information

If approaching Abaco from the south/southeast, from Eleuthera or perhaps Nassau via the *North Atlantic Ocean*, the first possible anchorage is at *Cherokee Sound*, about six miles south of Little Harbour. Cherokee boasts one very nice lee anchorage and another anchorage that, although harder to access and almost a mile from town, offers great protection and is fine if you need to ride out a frontal passage. Never attempt to enter either of these two anchorages if there is a heavy sea running, better to continue north and try *Little Harbour Bar* or *North Bar Channel*.

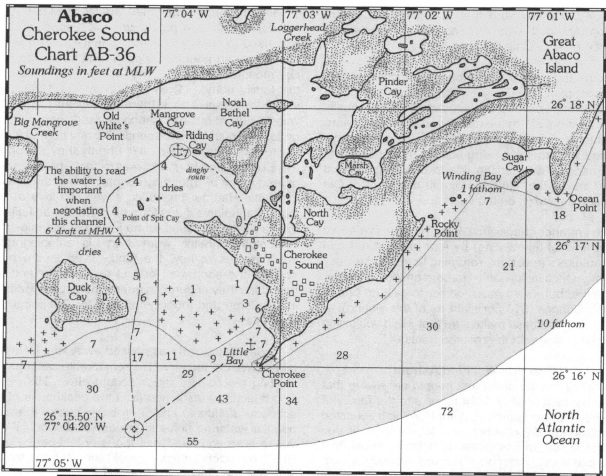

**Abaco
Cherokee Sound
Chart AB-36**
Soundings in feet at MLW

77° 04' W   77° 03' W   77° 02' W   77° 01' W

Loggerhead
Creek

Pinder
Cay

Great
Abaco
Island

Noah
Bethel
Cay

26° 18' N

Mangrove
Cay

Big Mangrove
Creek

Old
White's
Point

Riding
Cay

Sugar
Cay

Marsh
Cay

Winding Bay
1 fathom

The ability to read
the water is
important
when
negotiating
this channel
6' draft at MHW

dinghy
route

dries

4

Point of Spit Cay

North
Cay

Rocky
Point

7

Ocean
Point

18

dries

4

3

5

6

Duck
Cay

Cherokee
Sound

26° 17' N

21

1

1

1

3

6

30

10 fathom

7

7

7

7

17

11

9

Little
Bay

7

7

28

Cherokee
Point

26° 16' N

30

29

43

34

72

North
Atlantic
Ocean

26° 15.50' N
77° 04.20' W

55

77° 05' W

Cherokee
Sound

Little Bay

Cherokee
Point

Cherokee Sound

Photo Courtesy of Paul Harding, Safari Seaplanes

If you're approaching Cherokee from the north, say from *Little Harbour Bar*, keep at least a mile or more off Great Abaco to avoid the treacherous reefs system known as *The Boilers* that lies close in between Little Harbour and *Cherokee Sound*.

The anchorage in *Little Bay* is good for winds from northeast through east and is easily entered by rounding Cherokee Point and rounding up to anchor in the lee of Cherokee Point as shown on Chart AB-36. You will pass between the conspicuous reef that lies between Duck Cay and the mainland as well as the reef that runs WNW from Cherokee Point. Tuck in to the beach as close as your draft allows and enjoy your stay.

Cherokee has no marina but they do have their famous "long dock," probably the longest dock in The Bahamas. It is possible for shallow draft vessels to access the dock via *Little Bay*, but you must first sound the route in your dinghy or better still, call for a pilot (call *Cherokee Radio* on VHF ch. 16). The water near the dock is only about 1'-2' deep at MLW and the dock itself was almost cut in half by *Hurricane Floyd*. Today the dock is home to the *Sand Bar Restaurant*, the only restaurant in the town of Cherokee. Usually open on weekends, the *Sand Bar*, which serves beer and wine, will open more frequently during the season as needed.

Cruisers wishing to access the better protection offered by the anchorage at Riding Cay must approach the entrance channel east of Duck Cay from the waypoint at 26° 15.50' N, 77° 04.20' W as shown on Chart AB-36. This waypoint places you approximately ¾ mile south of Duck Cay and about a mile southwest of *Little Bay*. From the waypoint take up an approximate course of 007° towards the light on Duck Cay. The actual courseline is not that important, what is important is to line up the light on Duck Cay with the western tip of Point of Spit Cay and follow that range until about 150 yards south of Duck Cay avoiding the reef south of Duck Cay. At this point turn to starboard a bit and pass between Duck Cay and the conspicuous reef east of Duck Cay taking the reef to starboard and Duck Cay to port. You'll pass fairly close to Duck Cay, less than fifty yards, and continue north/northeastward. As you come to the conspicuous grassy patch north of Duck Cay you will turn to port on a heading that will bring you to clear Point of Spit Cay well to starboard. At the grassy patch, the shallowest on the route at 3' MLW, you should be able to pick up the dredged

channel that will wind around Point of Spit Cay and into the Riding Cay anchorage. The route past Duck Cay can only be done with excellent visibility and is good for less than 6' at high tide so watch the tide carefully when entering and leaving. If you have any doubts about using the channel leading into Riding Cay anchorage call *Cherokee Radio* on VHF ch. 16 and ask for someone to show you in. The Riding Cay anchorage is surrounded by shallow sandbanks on three sides and offers excellent protection even in southwest and westerly winds.

What You Will Find Ashore

Some folks will tell you that tiny, isolated Cherokee is "The Place! A little piece of heaven down below." No one quite knows for sure how "the place" got its name, but one theory has it that it was named after a local wild cherry tree and according to some very old English sailing charts was shown as "Cherry Cay." Another story details how the first settler was an old Cherokee Indian woman who arrived from North Carolina during the American Revolution. All records of marriages, births, deaths, crop yields and annual rainfall have been forwarded to Nassau since the early 1800's and no journals or diaries have survived to tell us the real history about Cherokee.

Before the Government of The Bahamas installed navigational lights to aid sailing ships, salvaging/wrecking was a very lucrative occupation for many Bahamians and the folks in Cherokee were no different. Then around the turn of the twentieth century boat-building, fishing and sponging soon took over as this little community swelled to over 400 persons (today there are less than a hundred families), making it the largest settlement in Abaco at that time. The residents also made rope from the sisal plant and collected shells which were sent away to be made into buttons as the Depression swept through The Bahamas. Although farming is still carried on in the surrounding fields, and many residents have jobs in Marsh Harbour, the majority of the 100 or so families of Cherokee still make a living from the sea, either by fishing, crawfishing, or as bonefishing guides.

Today you'll find a monument in Cherokee honoring her fishermen and their "Cherokee smacks," most of which were built right here in Cherokee. The old timers in Cherokee can tell you some truly interesting tales of the Cherokee fisherman. A Cherokee fishing smack was a unique vessel that stood out from other island fishing boats; they carried five sails instead of the usual seven. A smack and her crew of nine had none of the modern amenities that cruisers today take for granted. The crews would be gone for up to six weeks at a time earning their pay. The 1950's saw most of these smacks converted into power vessels and gone forever was the hail "Sail ho!" when the returning boats were sighted. The older folks however can still remember when all the smacks were anchored in Riding Cay Channel, a sight the rest of us can only imagine.

If you visit Cherokee by car you will have to park and walk through the town. In town you'll find a two-room schoolhouse, a Post Office and Library, a Laundromat, a gas station (you can dinghy in and get gas and diesel at the small dock in town), *Rainbow Delight* (a wonderful ice cream parlor that looks like a dollhouse and serves delicious ice cream and milk shakes), a *Batelco (BTC)* office, and the *Food Fair* grocery store. If you need propane see Rick Sawyer for same day service.

Some of the ladies of Cherokee make truly beautiful quilts that are traditional bride's gifts and a real find if you can pick one up. Some of the more enterprising ladies of Cherokee have gathered together a collection of old-time recipes and have preserved them in a locally published volume entitled *Abaco Cooks*.

Cherokee has some of the best bonefishing grounds in the Abacos as well as being on the edge of the *North Atlantic Ocean*. In the early 1950's, a fishing camp was built on the hill overlooking the sound and Cherokee has since been somewhat of a secret known only to the real fishing enthusiasts. The fishing camp did not survive, but many of its patrons return year after year to enjoy the waters of Cherokee Sound.

Schooner Bay Marina to Hole in the Wall

Schooner Bay Mar. - ¾ nm E of marked entrance:
26° 10.50'   77° 09.75'

Hole in the Wall - 1½ nm SE of:
25° 50.50' N, 77° 09.50' W

Roughly halfway between *Cherokee Sound* and Hole in the Wall, *Schooner Bay Marina* is part of the larger *Schooner Bay* complex being built southwest

of Cherokee Sound. The development offers a green version of an older Bahamian seaport. The marina is open and offers a nice stopover for vessels heading to or from Eleuthera. Full amenities should be available by the time this guide is printed. Vessels requiring a slip should hail the marina by VHF ch. 16, or email them at james@lindroth.cc at least a week in advance to secure a slip. Please bear in mind that the marina is not a wise stop during periods of northerly winds and seas.

Navigational Information

A waypoint at 26° 10.50' N, 77° 09.75' W, will place you approximately ¾ nm east of the marked entrance channel leading into the marina as shown on Chart AB-36A. From the waypoint, head west passing between the two outer markers and the very conspisuous reef. Never try to enter with strong seas running. Once you pass the second green marker turn to the south and head for the entrance to the marina on a southerly heading. Give a wide berth to the reef system lying northeast of the entrance channel.

Hole in the Wall

At the southern end of Great Abaco Island lies a long thin arm of rock that reaches southeastward into the mouth of the *Northeast Providence Channel* where it meets the *Atlantic Ocean*. This point is called Hole in the Wall after the large arch near the southern end of the point and it is one of the least visited sites in Abaco. At one time there were at least three "holes in the wall" as evidenced by their rocky remains on these 80' bluffs. Visitors can actually climb down into the "hole" on a calm day.

Navigational Information

A waypoint at 25° 50.50' N, 77° 09.50' W, will place you approximately 1½ nautical miles southeast of Hole in the Wall. From here you can take up a course for *Little Harbour Bar*, Nassau, Eleuthera, or you can forge westward around Southwest Point to work your way along the southern shore of Great Abaco Island to Sandy Point. Vessels can find temporary shelter on the western shore of Hole in the Wall. Round the southern tip and parallel the shoreline northward and you'll find shelter in the bight below the lighthouse in winds from northwest to east.

What You Will Find Ashore

Located on higher ground just north of the rugged spit is the *Hole in the Wall Lighthouse*. Today the light is automated (Fl W ev 10 sec, 168', 19nm) which is a bit of a loss in a sense. It was always an interesting and educational outing to rent a car in Marsh Harbour and travel the 55 or so miles south to the Lighthouse to visit the keepers and their families.

The lighthouse is now the home of the *Bahamas Marine Mammal Survey* and we shall discuss that group in a moment. You can still get there by car, but you'll need a high-clearance vehicle.

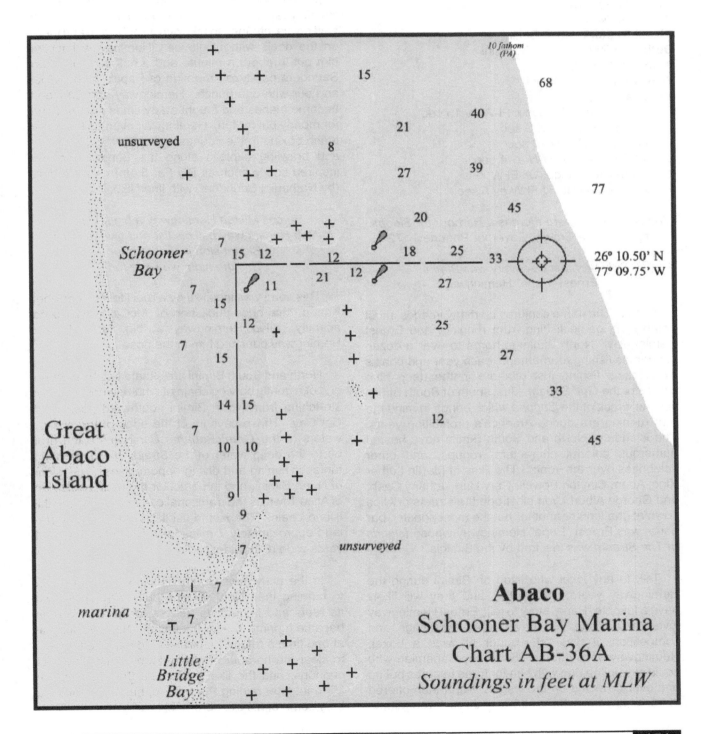

Abaco
Schooner Bay Marina
Chart AB-36A
Soundings in feet at MLW

The Biminis

Ports of Entry:
 North Bimini: Alice Town (any marina)
 South Bimini: *Bimini Sands Marina*
 Cat Cay: *Cat Cay Marina*
Fuel: North Bimini, South Bimini, Cat Cay
Haul-Out: None
Diesel Repairs: North Bimini
Outboard Repairs: North Bimini
Propane: North Bimini
Provisions: North Bimini
Important Lights:
 Great Isaac Lighthouse: Fl W ev 15 sec
 North Rock: Fl W ev 3 sec
 Gun Cay: Fl W ev 10 sec
 Cat Cay Marina: Fl W ev 4 sec
 Ocean Cay Range: Qk Fl W
 South Riding Rock: Fl W ev 5 sec

The Biminees, where there is a Harbour for Sloops.
Report to The Crown, Governor Phenney, 1721

"My greatest discovery was Bimini."
Ernest "Papa" Hemingway

Bimini. The name conjures up many images, most notably big game fishing, rum running, and Ernest Hemingway. North Bimini is home to over a dozen big games fishing tournaments each year and boasts world class fishing just offshore in the deep blue waters of the *Gulf Stream*. Just south of South Bimini lies the wreck of the *Sapona* which brings to mind the rum running era during America's prohibition years. The islands of North and South Bimini have hosted numerous colorful characters, rogues, and other celebrities over the years. The likes of Martin Luther King, Adam Clayton Powell, Gary Hart, Johnny Cash, and George Albert Lyon all strode the streets of Alice Town at one time or another but the most popular, bar none, was Ernest "Papa" Hemingway whose *Islands In The Stream* was inspired by the Biminis.

Talk to any local who lived on Bimini during the Hemingway years, 1935-1937, and they will likely have a favorite "Papa" story to tell. Ernest Hemingway loved hard living, he thrived upon challenge and competition, it was no wonder he was a boxer. Hemingway once offered $50 to any Bahamian who could stay in the ring with him for three minutes but no one ever collected on the wager. Papa then offered $250 to anyone who could last three three-minute

rounds with him using 6 oz. gloves. Now $250 was a lot of money in those days and Papa finally got a taker. His name was Willard Saunders, a muscular, 170 pound, bull-necked fisherman who is said to have been able to carry a piano balanced atop his unusually large skull. He approached Hemingway one day as Papa returned from fishing aboard his 38' *Pilar* and Hemingway offered to go get the gloves. Saunders said no, he intended to take him on right then and there, on the dock, without gloves. Hemingway knocked him out in about a minute and a half but not before Saunders paralyzed the side of Papa's face for half an hour with one punch. Hemingway and Saunders became friends and fought many times after that, not for money but for fun. Hemingway even built a ring to teach boxing to the youngsters of Bimini. His boxing and brawling exploits along the Bimini waterfront inspired songs such as *Big Fat Slob In The Harbour* (by Nathaniel Saunders) with lines like:

He call Mistah Hemingway a big fat slob.
Mistah Hemingway ball his fist and give him a nob.
Big fat slob in the harbour.
This the night we have fun.

This song was inspired by a real life incident when Knapp, the once-publisher of *McCall's* magazine, actually called Hemingway a "big, fat slob" and Hemingway punched him in the nose.

North and South Bimini are situated at the northern end of a gently curving chain of small islands and cays stretching from North Bimini southward past South Cat Cay. These cays lie at the edge of the shallow waters of the *Great Bahama Bank* where the drop off to the deep water of the *Straits of Florida* offers fantastic fishing and diving opportunities. The island of North Bimini, and in particular the main settlement of Alice Town, is the traditional center of activity in this island chain. The island itself is a long thin strip of land approximately 7 miles long and only about 700 yards wide at its widest point.

In the early days South Bimini was better suited to farming than North Bimini, but North Bimini with its reefs and immediate access to the *Gulf Stream* became a prime site for habitation. North Bimini was at one time a refuge for pirates and early settlers had to clear the harbour of pirate debris, hulls, muskets, cannons, and the like. It is said that Capt. Henry Morgan, after raiding Porto Bello, hurried to Bimini to bury some of his treasure.

The waters of the Biminis were so rich in wrecks that wreckers from Grand Bahama moved to Bimini to take advantage of the sea's bounty. Bimini's five founding families settled the area in 1835 and were licensed to engage in wrecking. In later years Biminites lived off the sea in one form or another, either harvesting shells, conch, and fish, or using Bimini's prime location off the eastern coast of the United States to run blockades during the Civil War and once again during the American Prohibition years. It has been said that the prohibition years actually "built" Bimini. "Pappy" Chalk set up a seaplane service to Bimini in 1919 and planes still operate today in and out of Bimini. Visitors must take care not to anchor in the "runway" that begins just off the seaplane ramp in the harbour and stretches northeast towards the anchorage off *Bimini Big Game*.

If you are interested in the history of Bimini, you should pick up a copy of Ashley B. Saunders *History of Bimini*, available in Bimini. This is a wealth of information and some amazing old photos.

Approaches to the Biminis

Hillsboro Inlet:
26° 15.19' N, 80° 04.55' W

Ft. Lauderdale/Port Everglades:
26° 05.57' N, 80° 05.40' W

Miami - Government Cut:
25° 45.70' N, 80° 05.80' W

Cape Florida:
25° 38.74' N, 80° 07.70' W

Angelfish Creek:
25° 19.35' N, 80° 12.60' W

Mackie Shoal Light - 200 yards N of:
25° 42.00' N, 78° 39.00' W

Russell Beacon - ½ nm N of buoy:
25° 29.00' N, 78° 25.54' W

NW Channel Light - 250 yards N of:
25° 28.40' N, 78° 09.80' W

The routes across the *Gulf Stream* to the Biminis from South Florida are magnetic and should not be used without applying corrections for the strength of the *Gulf Stream* as described in the section *Crossing The Gulf Stream*. With the exception of the courses across the *Great Bahama Bank* from the Berry Islands and the courses across the *Gulf Stream* from Angelfish Creek, you will find that you must steer quite a bit higher than the bearings given from Hillsboro Inlet to Cape Florida to allow for the set and drift of the *Gulf Stream*.

From *Hillsboro Inlet*, the waypoint off North Bimini bears 133° at a distance of 53 nautical miles while Gun Cay lies on a bearing of 139° at 58.3 nautical miles. From the sea buoy at Port Everglades, North Bimini bears 124° at a distance of 48.3 nautical miles while Gun Cay bears 131° at a distance of 52.7 nautical miles. From the sea buoy at *Government Cut* in Miami, North Bimini bears 93° at a distance of 42.8 nautical miles while Gun Cay bears 109° at a distance of 44.5 nautical miles. From the seaward entrance to the channel at Cape Florida on the southern end of Key Biscayne, North Bimini bears 90° at a distance of 44.5 nautical miles while Gun Cay bears 100° at a distance of 45 nautical miles. From the eastern entrance to Angelfish Creek at Key Largo, North Bimini bears 69° at a distance of 53.9 nautical miles while Gun Cay bears 77° at a distance of 51.6 nautical miles. From Great Stirrup Cay at the northern tip of the Berry Islands, North Rock bears 274° at a distance of 71 nautical miles. From *R2*, the first tripod marker leading to Bullock's Harbour and *Great Harbour Cay Marina*, North Rock bears 277° at a distance of 71.2 nautical miles while Gun Cay bears 266° at 74.6 nautical miles. From *Northwest Channel light*, Gun Cay bears 281° at 62.1 nautical miles. From a position two miles east of North Rock at 25° 48.06, 79° 13.50' W, *Mackie Shoal Light* bears 106° at 31.7 nautical miles, and from there *Northwest Channel Light* bears 123° at 29.7 nautical miles.

Great Isaac

Navigational Information
Standing sentinel at the northwest corner of the *Great Bahama Bank*, some 55 miles east of Ft. Lauderdale and about 20 miles north of North Bimini, at the convergence of *Straits of Florida* and the *Northwest Providence Channel*, is the white lighthouse of *Great Isaac Light* (FL ev 15 sec, 152 ft, 23m) on Great Isaac Island as shown on Chart BI-1. This chart is included as a reference to those mariners wishing to pass safely within sight of Great Isaac on their way to or from Grand Bahama, the Berry Islands,

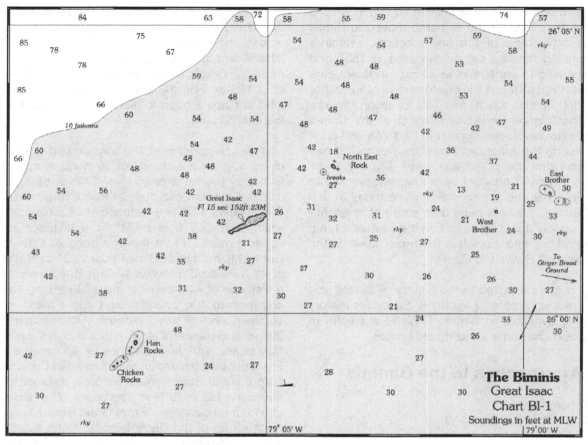

The Biminis
Great Isaac
Chart BI-1
Soundings in feet at MLW

or Nassau. It is possible to anchor in the lee of Great Isaac in an emergency, but it is not recommended as an overnight stop as the area is very rolly. The waters shoal to the southwest and east of Great Isaac and mariners heading for the Berry Islands and Nassau should give the waters here a wide berth. Especially to be avoided is the area shown on *DMA* charts and known as *The Gingerbread Ground*. The area is home to scattered reefs and rocks with numerous wrecks about, a diver's delight.

What You Will Find Ashore

Great Isaac Light, the 152' tall structure, once known as *Victoria Light* in honor of the former Queen of England, has quite a unique history. The light's structure was once a landmark in London. The *Great Exposition of London* was held in Hyde Park in 1851, and the centerpiece of the exposition was a 152' tall iron structure that was to become *Great Isaac Light*. The structure remained for several years after the exposition closed until it was finally removed, coded piece by coded piece, and packed away on three ships to be reassembled on Great Isaac Island in 1859. A powerful light was placed atop the structure

and red and white stripes were painted around the new lighthouse (today the lighthouse is white, no stripes).

The reconstruction, mostly done by the same workers who disassembled the structure, was plagued with accidents, deaths, and sightings of the ghost of the *Gray Lady*. It seems that several years before the reconstruction began a British square-rigger was dashed to pieces on Great Isaac and the only survivor was a tiny infant who had been washed ashore and found a few days later by salvers. The baby was sent to Bimini for medical care and eventually reunited with relatives in England. But the story did not end there; before each full moon the ghost of the baby's mother is said to walk the length of the ¾ mile long cay weeping and searching for her baby. A number of lightkeepers resigned their positions after only a month on the job after seeing *The Gray Lady of Great Isaac's Light*. The ghostly visits went on until after the turn of the century when a headstrong lightkeeper, who was also a layman in his church, performed a religious rite to convince the *Gray Lady* that her child was safe and had survived. The story goes that she never returned although some say that she can still be heard wailing on Great Isaac Island just before a full moon. In another eerie occurrence, two lighthouse keepers, Ivan Major and B. Mollings, disappeared on August 4, 1969, never to be seen again.

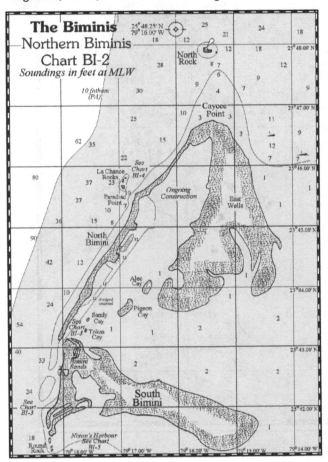

North Bimini

North Rock - ½ nm W:
25° 48.25' N, 79° 16.00' W

North Rock - 2 nm E:
25° 48.25' N, 79° 13.50' W

Bimini Roads Dive Site:
25° 45.99' N, 79° 16.69' W

North Bimini harbor new entrance:
 25° 42.60', 79° 18.50' W

North Bimini harbor old entrance:
25° 42.07', 79° 18.56' W

Navigational Information

Before we begin our discussion on entering the harbor at North Bimini, keep an eye out for a new, dredged and marked channel into North Bimini. This channel, due in 2008, is being built to make access to the new marina much easier.

When approaching from Florida, North and South Bimini tend to blend together when visual contact is first made. Try to look for the long stand of casuarinas with a few smaller patches just to their north. This will be North Bimini.

The good news for mariners is that there is a new and well-marked entrance channel into the harbor at North Bimini. For clarification purposes I will call this the new entrance, while the traditional entrance off South Bimini I will call the old entrance.

As shown on Chart BI-3, a waypoint at 25° 42.60', 79° 18.50' W, will place you approximately ¼ nm west of the entrance to the new marked channel. From the waypoint, head approximately E passing between the two outer markers following the channel as it bends NNE through a second set of markers. Keep the red marker off the northern tip of South Bimini to starboard and proceed into the harbor off Alice Town. The controlling depth for this channel is over 9', but there's a good chance that some of the buoys may be missing (having been struck by vessels entering the channel) so use caution. Henry Bank has been shifting over the last few years so be aware that the depths of the new and old entrance channels might be affected by this in the future.

As shown on Chart BI-3, a waypoint at 25° 42.07' N, 79° 18.56' W, will place you approximately ½ mile west of the old harbor entrance between North and South Bimini in about 16' of water. Never attempt this entrance in strong onshore winds and seas or at night unless you are very, very familiar with the area. If you are caught in strong onshore conditions anchor behind South Bimini in Nixon's Harbour and await better conditions. Finding the entrance range off South Bimini for the old channel is easy in good light. As you make out South Bimini you will see that it has a rather long beach on its western shore. Towards the center of the beach is a very conspicuous group of salmon colored condos that make up the *Bimini Sands Resort and Marina* development. Approximately 2/3 of the way south from the condos to the southern end of the beach you'll find a range consisting of two poles

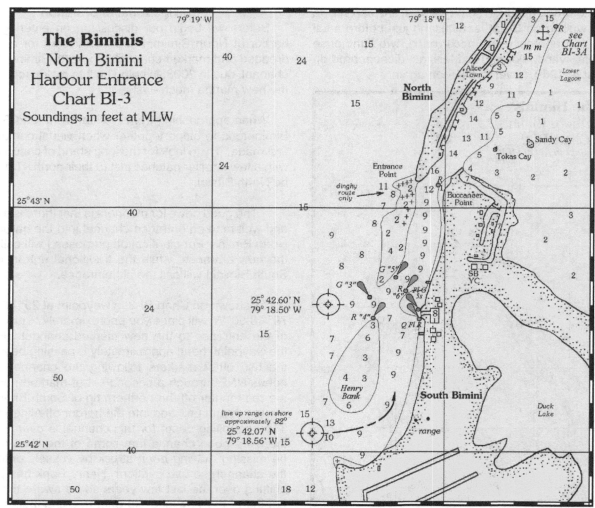

The Biminis
North Bimini
Harbour Entrance
Chart BI-3
Soundings in feet at MLW

Chalk's Seaplane at North Bimini

Photo by author

topped with orange/white range markers and flashing yellow lights (just to be on the safe side consider these lights to be unreliable). Line up the range markers and follow the course in between the two sandbars on an approximate heading of 82°. Here the heading is not as important as following the range so keep the poles lined up by paying more attention to the range than your compass. Once inside the clearly visible sandbar, turn to the north (to port) and pass between the sandbar and South Bimini in 6'-9' of water at MLW. When heading northward from the range, parallel the beach staying at least 50 yards off. As you approach the jetties on South Bimini swing to the west just a bit as you pass them and then swing back to the east just a bit as you proceed northward into the harbour off Alice Town following the new marked entrance channel. As you approach North Bimini favor the North Bimini side of the channel at Entrance Point to avoid a shoal that works westward from the northwestern tip of South Bimini. Pass the marinas and the town dock and you'll find the anchorage is north of the *Bimini Big Game Fishing Club*, the last marina to port. Do not anchor off the other marinas as this is the runway for *Pan Am* airlines.

The anchorage area narrows down to a channel heading northeastward paralleling the shore of North Bimini towards *Bimini Bay Resort and Marina* (www. biminibayresort.com) as shown on Chart BI-3A. The *Bimini Bay Resort and Marina* offers several gated communities with luxury condos and homes boasting their own private slips (slips must be purchased, simply owning a condo does not entitle you to a slip, but it does permit you to purchase one, only homeowners can own a slip), a huge 230-slip marina (for vessels from 40' to 205' in length) with a dredged entrance channel (14' deep by 120' wide), a marina complex called *Bimini Town* with a marine supply store, Wifi, a fishing tackle outlet, a dive shop, a fish and fresh produce market, several bars and restaurants, a beachside pool, a spa for a much needed massage, the elegant *Casa Lyon* restaurant, and *Customs* and *Immigration* offices on site. There's also to be a huge hotel and a 20,000 square foot casino, a Robert Trent Jones Jr. designed golf course called *The Devil's Triangle*, and all sorts of water-related activities including fishing, snorkeling, and SCUBA diving for guests and residents. The golf course will take up most of the northern tip of North Bimini and residences and the hotel/casino will occupy the spot where the old Rockwell House once stood at Paradise Point, this landmark will soon cease to exist except

in our memories. One good thing, perhaps the only good thing some might say, about this complex is that it will require the dredging of a deep entrance channel into Bimini to accommodate the fast ferries and cruise ship tenders that are poised to bring people in and out of the complex.

There is plenty of room in the designated anchorage area, but it is best to set two anchors in a *Bahamian Moor*, one anchor up current and one anchor down current. The current flow parallels the shoreline here and it is quite strong so make sure your anchors are set properly, not only must you worry about the current, in some places there are rocks and other debris scattered about, make sure your anchor is set well before retiring. It is a pleasant enough anchorage as long as you don't mind the local skippers flying past you in small fast boats (remember your anchor light) and a noisy power plant on shore. You can dinghy in to the dock across the street from the government complex or ask one of the marinas if you can use their facilities. Since the onslaught of new construction at the new *Bimini Bay* complex at the northern end of Bimini and the dredged (14' at MLW) channel leading to the site, those who choose to anchor in the area should be advised to anchor so as not to obstruct the channel. Large freighters enter here to drop off construction equipment and supplies and they have little enough room to maneuver without having to dodge anchored vessels.

Just off Entrance Point is a dinghy channel lying south of a set of rocks that are awash at low water. Fifty years ago this was the dredged entrance channel into Bimini Harbour but now it is only used for dinghies and small boat traffic.

What You Will Find Ashore
Skippers wishing to clear in must tie up at one of the marinas along the waterfront, *Brown's*, *Weech's*, *Sea Crest*, *Bimini Blue Water*, and *Bimini Big Game Club*, most of whom monitor VHF ch. 16 or 68, except *Weech's*, they monitor VHF ch. 18. The dockmaster at each marina will provide you with the proper *Customs* and *Immigration* forms. The skipper, after filling out the forms must then walk to the large pink *Customs* building to clear in and then to *Immigration* which is right next door, by the straw market. If nobody is in the *Immigration* office you may proceed northward past *Bimini Big Game* to the pink government office complex where the police station is located. Here you'll find the main *Immigration* office for Bimini.

The main harbour at North Bimini sits along the shore of Alice Town and is what most visitors simply refer to as "Bimini". To the west of town lies a seemingly endless curving, and in some places rocky, beach, excellent for a day of, swimming, fun and games, or just catching rays. Most amenities on North Bimini can be found along the King's Highway in Alice Town. Bars, restaurants, marinas, and gift shops line the road between the Chalk's terminal and the government office complex just north of the harbour. I highly recommend renting a golf cart to see the island, its a comfortable and efficient way to travel, and you can find a golf cart rentals all over town at such places as the Compleat Angler or Sun Crest Marina, and further north on either side of the road past Bimini Big Game.

Starting at the southern terminus of the Queen's Highway you'll find a small cemetery. Just west of the cemetery you can explore the wreckage of an old Belizean freighter, the Gallant Lady. Just north of the cemetery is the Chalk's Airline Terminal, and heading northward you'll find the Fisherman's Paradise Bar and Grill serving breakfast, lunch and dinner. Next is the famous, or infamous, End Of The World Bar, a must stop for party-goers, but with a warning. The tradition is to leave your underwear hanging on the wall or ceiling, try to pick out the celebrity underwear.

The first marina you will come to is Weech's Bimini Dock, which also houses the Bimini General Store and Marine Supplies, a small but well-stocked stocked marine supply and hardware store that also sells fishing tackle. Weech's has 6 rooms for rent, ask at the marina for more information or give them a shout on the VHF, Weech's monitors VHF ch. 18. Across the street from Weech's is Bill and Nowdla Keefe's Bimini Undersea Adventures, a well-run dive shop where SCUBA enthusiasts can get all the latest info on dive sites. If you need to refill your spirit locker walk across the street from Weech's and visit the Beverage Depot. Just up the road is the Perfume Shoppe and CJ's Deli serving delicious breakfast, lunch, dinner, ice cream and pastries.

Proceeding northward you'll come to the pink Customs building with the Immigration office located right next door, northward, between Customs and the small straw market. Across the street from the Customs building is the Bimini Museum, a wonderful place to visit and learn about the history of this unique little island, while next door is a small public library.

The next marinas you come to north of the Customs building are the Seacrest Hotel and Marina and then the Bimini Bluewater Resort Ltd. The Seacrest Hotel is the large three story yellow building with an excellent view from each room. Bimini Bluewater Resort has a guest house, cottages, and two bedroom suites for rent. Across the street from Bimini Bluewater is the late Ossie Brown's Compleat Angler Hotel and Bar, probably the most popular stop for tourists in Bimini. The Compleat Angler was one of the first fishing clubs in Bimini and dates back to the 1930's. Here you can get a drink, see or be seen, or watch satellite TV to while away the time. The deep dark wood of its interior creates an ambiance of its own, this was Hemingway's favorite place and you can feel it as you enter. You can almost picture him there, sipping a drink and carousing with his friends after a long day of fishing on his beloved Pilar. There is a special room in his honor just off the entrance to the bar replete with photographs of Hemingway and some samples of his writing. The photos document many of Papa's greatest catches and show him boxing with some local fighters.

Next to the Compleat Angler and just across the street from Sea Crest Marina, you will find The Royal Bank Of Canada, Butler and Sands Liquors, and Capt. Bob's Restaurant (breakfast, lunch, and dinner). Capt. Bob's is the "in" place for breakfast. Capt. Bob is a native Biminite and has fished the waters of his home for over 50 years. Just north of The Compleat Angler is the newly reopened All My Children Hotel named after the owner's children and not the TV soap opera. The hotel has 50 rooms and two penthouses for rent as well as two bars. The last marina to the north is The Bimini Big Game Fishing Club And Anchorage Inn situated along the narrow streets in the northernmost section of Alice Town. The inn itself sits atop the hill in the center of the island with views of both the harbour and the ocean, a fantastic spot for dining. Here you will find two penthouses, 35 rooms, and 12 cottages for rent. The marina boasts the elegant Gulf Stream Restaurant and for lunch there is the Big Game Sports Bar upstairs. There is also a swimming pool and small gift shop on the premises. Just north of the gate to the marina is the Bimini Breeze where you'll meet the owner, Yama Bahama, the internationally known Middleweight Boxing Champion of The Bahamas. It seems only fitting that the Champ should come from Bimini. About ½ mile north of the Big Game Club is Brown's Supply Store where you can get your propane tanks refilled.

Here in town you will also find the *Red Lion Pub* (closed on Mondays) serving drinks and delicious lunch and dinners (their *Shrimp Delight* has been recommended by *Esquire Magazine*), *Watson Super Market, Pinder's Food Store, Ena's Take Out, La La's Restaurant, Sue and Joy's Variety Store*, and *Bonefish Bill's Bait and Tackle*. At the corner of *Sherman Street* and *King's Highway* you will find *The Burger Queen* and *Opal's* which sits just up *Sherman Street* and serves excellent Bahamian and American dishes. Just north of *Bimini Breeze* is the government office complex which houses the police station and a post office. The complex was once the *Lerner Marine Laboratory*. Just north of the complex is a coin laundry between the police station and *Roberts Foodstore* which is located just before the road takes a turn south of the large power plant.

As the road passes northward to Bayley Town, where most Biminites live, you will pass numerous small stores and shops, some appearing to do business out of the owner's living room. Heading north you'll pass the large *Batelco* complex (look for the big satellite dish) and The *Bahamas Electricity Corp.* (the noisy building). Along this stretch of the *King's Highway* you'll find places such as *Tootsie's Groceries, B&F Video World, Dun's Florists, E L K Pub & Sports Bar, Cheryl's Variety Store, Davis Variety and Snack Store*, and *Scoe's Takeout* (its a take-out because it only has one table). Further north you'll find the *Seaside Café* located right on the water, *Chiquita's One-Stop, Rolle's Supermarket and Variety, Sandra's Restaurant and Sports Bar* (monitors VHF ch. 68) and *King Brown's Food and General Supplies*, a very well-stocked supermarket and hardware store. The local dentist, Dr. Larry Bain's office is just south of *Brown's*. Further north is *Porgy Bay* and the *Tiger's Den* for takeout food, and the *Jones Porgy Bay Variety Store*. If you head just a bit more north you'll find the *Bimini Community Clinic*.

Just past *Porgy Bay* the pavement ends and turns left to the beach (westward) and here you will find one of the most beautiful spots on the island lying just past the cemetery known as *Spook Hill*. As you top the rise the long curving beach and vivid watercolors are a perfect backdrop for the shaded picnic tables under the casuarinas atop the beach. Local residents have a picnic here each day of Easter week.

To the east of North Bimini lies a mangrove island named East Wells. East Wells is very reminiscent of Shroud Cay in the Exumas. It is a maze of mangrove lined tidal creeks leading into a large lake in the

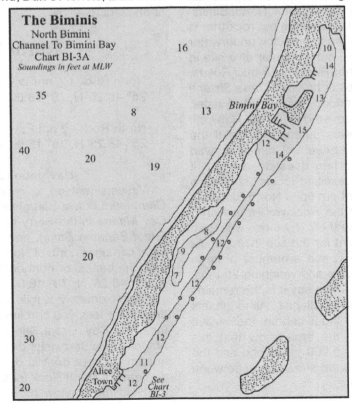

The Biminis
North Bimini
Channel To Bimini Bay
Chart BI-3A
Soundings in feet at MLW

center. If you approach the island from Bimini Harbour and wind your way up the creeks you may be lucky enough to find the *Healing Hole*, a spring that is said to have curative powers. Any bonefishing guide can take you here as well as the creek where Dr. Martin Luther King Jr. wrote his *Nobel Prize* acceptance speech. The waters of the lagoon between North Bimini, East Wells, and South Bimini is an excellent marine nursery and bonefishing location.

Fishermen hoping to test the Bimini waters will find themselves in some of the most productive fishing grounds of the world boasting numerous world record catches. These waters are home to marlin, sailfish, dolphin, wahoo, mackerel, shark, grouper, and snapper. Conch and bonefish can be found on the flats surrounding North Bimini, East Wells, and South Bimini. Lobster are normally found outside the harbour around the reefs, rocks, and drop-offs. Deep sea, reef fishing, and bonefishing guides are so plentiful in Bimini that we cannot list them all, it is best to inquire at any of the marinas. If you wish to rent a boat call Charlie Weech at 242-347-3290.

There are some super dive sites off of North Bimini that can pique the interest of anyone, diver or not. A good place to start is at La Chance Rocks, the offlying rocks just to the west of North Bimini. There is a cave in the southeasternmost rock that is 10' deep and excellent for those pursuing underwater photography. Probably the most popular dive site in this area is known as *Atlantis Rocks*, or *Bimini Roads*, lying approximately ¼ mile northeast of *Three Sister's Rocks*, also called *La Chance Rocks* in 15' of water. The site was allegedly discovered by Dimitri Rebikoff, the inventor of the *Pegasus* submarine, but if the truth be known dive legend Skeet LaChance showed him where the site was when questioned about it by Rebikoff. To find this exciting locale (shown on Chart BI-4) line up the northern tip of North Bimini on a heading of 60° and put the *Rockwell House* on a bearing of 164° and you are there (for those who wish to cheat there is a waypoint for the site in *Appendix A*). On the bottom you will see a number of large rocks, some up to 16' square and weighing 25 tons, that resemble a road and some say it is the remains of the ancient lost continent of Atlantis. Although this is purely speculation one thing is certain: radioactive dating of fossils found in the area show that this structure was above water 5,000 years ago and the rock formations themselves are shown to be between 5,000 and 10,000 years old.

The *English Wreck* lies 1¼ miles northwest of *North Rock Light* and is found when the light bears 155° and *Rockwell House* bears 190°. The ribs of this wreck can be found in 17' of water at the edge of the *Moselle Bank*. There is little left these days but pottery and other debris have been found in the general area.

Moray Alley can be found to the west of *La Chance Rocks* when *Rockwell House* bears 80°. The reef system is composed of numerous coral heads 10'-15' tall in an area about 150 yards wide and extending for ½ mile. Here you'll find a lot of canyons, passages, crevices, gorgonians, sea fans, and large fish including a few sharks. As you can see, the *Rockwell House* is often used as a navigational landmark here, what will we do when it is gone?

Hawksbill Reef lies on a slope to the west of *Moray Alley* on the edge of the *Gulf Stream*. The sloping bottom is covered with scattered coral heads and barrel sponges and descends to about 50' where it levels off to a sand bottom with more scattered heads.

There are quite a few sunken planes off the eastern and southern shores of North and South Bimini for snorkelers to enjoy.

North Rock

North Rock - ½ nm W:
25° 48.25' N, 79° 16.00' W

North Rock - 2 nm E:
25° 48.25' N, 79° 13.50' W

Navigational Information
Vessels wishing to cross the banks to the *Bell Channel* in Lucaya, Slaughter Harbour or *Great Harbour Cay Marina* in the Berry Islands (see: *Crossing The Great Bahama Bank*), and even *Northwest Channel Light* can pass north of North Rock and then turn east onto the banks, or northeast for Lucaya. A waypoint at 25° 48.25' N, 79° 16.00' W (Chart BI-2) will place you approximately ½ mile west of North Rock. If you draw 6' or less you can immediately lay your course for Chub Cay, Great Stirrup, or *Great Harbour Cay Marina* in the Berry Islands once you pass North Rock abeam. If your draft is over 6' you should continue due east of North Rock for approximately three miles to avoid the shallow (6' at low water) sandbank to

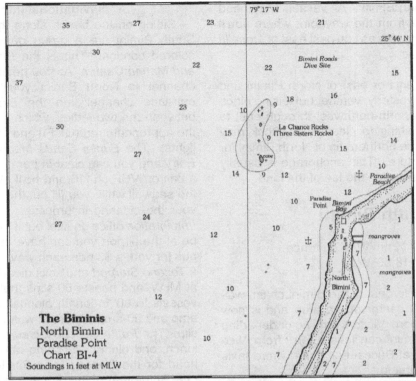

The Biminis
North Bimini
Paradise Point
Chart BI-4
Soundings in feet at MLW

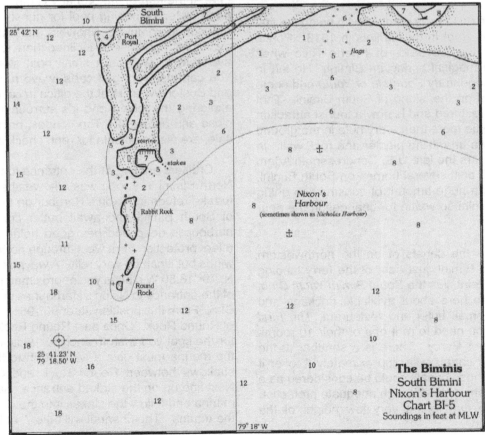

The Biminis
South Bimini
Nixon's Harbour
Chart BI-5
Soundings in feet at MLW

the northeast of North Bimini. All vessels may head northeast to Lucaya from the waypoint where you'll find good water all the way as you past east of *Moselle Bank* and Great Isaac.

It is possible to anchor east of North Bimini and East Wells to avoid westerly weather but it is no place to be in winds from north-northwest through east to south. Mariners wishing to clear North Rock may anchor just west of the northern tip of North Bimini for a quick, early departure. This anchorage is usually rolly even though you are in the lee of the land.

South Bimini

Nixon's Harbour - ¼ nm W of entrance:
25° 41.23' N, 79° 18.50' W

South Bimini, the largest of the Bimini chain, was once the agricultural center of the area and is now home to the only airport. Visitors arriving or departing by air from South Bimini can take a ferry from Alice Town to the landing at Buccaneer Point where taxis will take you to the airstrip.

Juan Ponce de Leon is credited with being the first European to set foot in the Biminis in 1513. Ponce de Leon was the Governor of Puerto Rico when he heard of a magical spring on Bimini. He left in search of the legendary *Fountain of Youth* and some say he found it on the island of South Bimini. That site has been restored and is now a tourist attraction although it is little more than a dry hole in the ground surrounded by a crumbling plaster and rock wall. In more recent years the late U.S. Congressman Adam Clayton Powell built several homes on South Bimini. Today there is a huge amount of construction going on at South Bimini so watch for changes in the near future.

Deep inside the canals of on the northwestern shore of South Bimini, just east of the ferry landing at Buccaneer Point, lies the *South Bimini Yacht Club*. You can inquire here about available dockage and check on the small hotel and restaurant, *The First Floor Bar*. If you need to rent one of their 10 rooms see the manager Percy. There is a sandbar at the entrance to the canals with approximately 4' over it at low water. These canals could be considered as a possible hurricane hole although adequate protection is questionable due to the very low height of the surrounding land.

Navigational Information

Sitting on the beach along the western shore of South Bimini are a group of conspicuous salmon colored condos. This is the *Bimini Sands Condos and Marina Center*. As you head down the entrance channel to North Bimini you'll see the dredged entrance channel into the *Bimini Sands Marina* between the two jetties, which are also marked with the appropriate red (Qk Fl) and green (Fl G ev 5 sec) lights. The *Bimini Sands Marina* is now a *Port of Entry* and you can clear in here; give the dockmaster a call on VHF ch. 16 and he'll allow you to tie up to the seawall while you fill out the forms and complete your the clearing in process. There is a *Customs/ Immigration* office on site, but if the officers happen to be at the airport you can have the dockmaster call a bus for you, a $3 ride each way. The marina itself is a *Texaco Starport* and sells diesel and gas, carries 8' at MLW, and boasts 60 slips that can accommodate vessels to 80' in length alongside. Electricity is 30-amp and 50-amp and fresh water is available at each slip. The *Petite Conch Restaurant* serves breakfast, lunch, and dinner beginning at 0700. For libations, head for the *Healing Hole Bar* to enjoy a tall, cool one. At the rear of the property is the *Tiki Bar* and the fresh water swimming pool for guests of the marina and condo complex. Showers and laundry are also available. For those so inclined there is a tennis court available as well as a small boat storage building. You can also rent golf carts, wave runners, kayaks, and Boston Whalers at the office in case you feel like exploring the island and it's surrounding waters up close and personal. The condos, besides being for sale, are also available for rent, check at the office.

Cruisers arriving at the entrance to the harbour at North Bimini in strong westerly weather are advised to take refuge in Nixon's Harbour on the south shore of South Bimini and await better conditions. The harbour is deep and has good holding in sand. It offers protection from west through north to northeast winds but it can be very rolly. A waypoint at 25° 41.23 N, 79° 18.50 W places you approximately ¼ mile west of the entrance to Nixon's Harbour as shown on Chart BI-5. From this position steer 90°-95° and pass south of Round Rock. Once past Round Rock simply head for the spot you wish to anchor. Vessels heading for the marina must give a wide berth to the rocks and shallows between Round Rock and South Bimini. Next line up on the staked entrance channel into the marina and follow the stakes into the deeper water of the marina. The channel will take 7' at high water. A

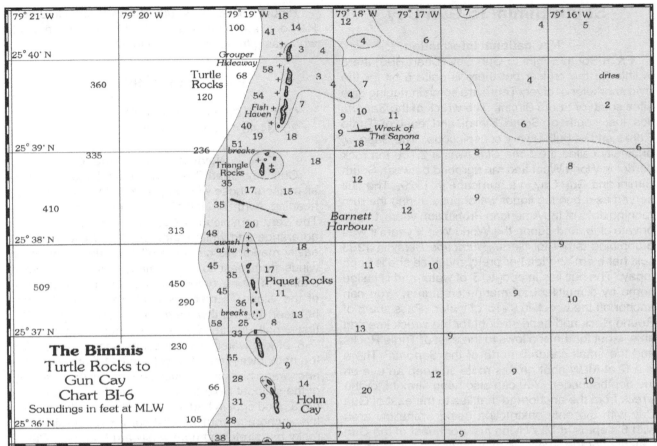

The Biminis
Turtle Rocks to
Gun Cay
Chart BI-6
Soundings in feet at MLW

note about Round Rock, this is a nice shallow water snorkeling site amid rocks and corals.

What You Will Find Ashore

The southwestern tip of South Bimini is the site of the *Beach Club Marina* (*Bimini Reef*) with its restaurant, 50-slip marina, and 40 room hotel. Emil, the manager, invites all boaters to give him a call on VHF 68 for reservations and entrance details. The marina has no repair facilities or fuel but can accommodate vessels up to 50' with a 7' draft, though Emil boasts 8' to 10' of draft can make it into the marina with the right tide, call the marina on VHF for information on their depths before you try to enter. The marina complex is also the home of *SCUBA Bimini*. Just north of the marina is a small "F" shaped canal whose only entrance is along the western shore of South Bimini. The canal system is known as Port Royal, is dotted with homes, mostly owned by Americans who fly in on weekends and holidays. A draft of 5' can make it over the bar at the entrance and into the 7'-9' water inside in the event of bad weather. Here you can tie to the mangroves or anchor in a stretch between houses.

The finest hurricane hole in the Biminis is up the creek along the northern shore of *Nixon's Harbour*. One skipper I know of took his 67' sailboat drawing 7'4" into the creek on the high tide and had plenty of water where he tied to the mangroves although he did bump a few times on the way in. The channel is easy to see with its flagged markers on each side, follow the flags in and anchor in any of the three pockets. The creek to the east is the deepest and longest with the best protection while the creek to the left leads to the *Shark Lab*, otherwise known as the *Bimini Biological Field Station*. This is where Dr. Samuel Gruber, from the *University of Miami*, and his staff carry on lemon shark research. The shallow waters between North Bimini and South Bimini is a lemon shark nursery with adults mating every April and May. Juvenile lemons live in the lagoon for years until they are old enough to leave. Dr. Gruber and his staff capture specimens in the lagoon to tag and release. Some specimens are fitted with transponders, which allow the researchers to follow the shark on its travels through the waters in the vicinity of the lagoon for years until they are old enough to leave.

South Bimini to Gun Cay

Navigational Information

From South Bimini to Gun Cay (Chart BI-6) there is little for the cruiser but there is quite a bit for the avid snorkeler or diver. There are some intriguing dive sites south of South Bimini. The wreck of the *Sapona* lies just south of South Bimini and east of Turtle Rocks and its bulk is very conspicuous. The *Sapona*, originally called the *Lone Star*, was a 2,700 ton rock carrier in World War I and ran aground between South Bimini and Gun Cay in a hurricane in 1929. The hull served as a bootleg liquor warehouse during the rum running days of the American Prohibition years, then a private club, and during the World War II years it was a bombing target for fliers. *Hurricane Betsy* in 1965 split her stern and left her pretty much as she is seen today. The hull lies in about 15' of water and is called home by a multitude of marine creatures. You can anchor off the wreck in 9'-15' of water. Pass south of Round Rock and head straight for the wreck keeping an eye out for the shallows to the east of Turtle Rocks and the small sandbar north of the *Sapona*. There is a 5' at MLW spot on this route so keep an eye on the depthsounder. You can also head straight for the wreck from the anchorage that lies to the east of Gun Cay with the only obstruction being a shallow area with 6' depths at MLW lying just northeast of the Gun Cay anchorage. Vessels may enter Barnett Harbour and head straight for the wreck.

What You Will Find Ashore

North and South Turtle Rocks lie just south of South Bimini and boast some interesting dive sites. The northernmost cay is known as *Grouper Hideaway*. This reef begins at 25' with some low profile coral and rock ledges while a set of engines from a wreck lies off its northern tip. A site called *Fish Haven* is the best diving in the area. It lies between the third and fourth cays. This reef slopes down to about 40' with a canyon leading southward.

Vessels heading along the western shores of these cays between Bimini and Gun Cay will have deep water all the way but take care that the strong rising tide does not push you onto the rocks themselves. The shallowest areas are just to the east and northeast of Gun Cay and the sandbars just to the west of Turtle Rocks in the area of the *Sapona*. Do not head too far east as you can run up on some very shallow water very quickly along this route.

Piquet Rocks, just south of the entrance to Barnett Harbour, are named after Captain Piquet, a pirate who was a frequent visitor to these waters.

Gun Cay

Gun Cay Channel - ¼ nm NW:
25° 34.48' N, 79° 18.15' W

Navigational Information

Gun Cay, Chart BI-7, is a popular jump off spot for all cruisers, those with only a week to spare, or those heading north or south to or from distant islands. The very conspicuous *Gun Cay Light* (it resembles an orange and white lighthouse-FL W every 10 sec) easily marks this cay from offshore day or night. In winds from east to south many vessels choose to anchor in Honeymoon Harbour on the northern tip of the island. Enter this anchorage from the west between the northwestern tip of Gun Cay and the first small unnamed cay to its northwest in about 7'-8' at low water. Find a sandy spot inside to drop the hook away from the rocks in 6'-12' of water. The anchorage boasts a beautiful beach but the wreckage of the sailboat *Nola* on shore reminds one that this is not a good spot in bad weather. It is possible to enter this anchorage from the east but you must skirt a long rocky bar stretching northwestward from Gun Cay all the way to the first set of rocks to the north.

Another popular anchoring spot is along the western shore of Gun Cay just south of the northern tip of the island. There is good holding here in sand but a swell usually runs through the anchorage and a second anchor or bridle is advised to keep your boat pointed into the swell unless you like rolling all night. In westerly or very light east to south winds, most vessels anchor on the eastern shore in 7'-10' of water. To anchor on the eastern shore, or to continue on to Chub Cay in the Berry Islands you must negotiate *Gun Cay Pass* between Gun Cay and Cat Cay.

A waypoint at 25° 34.48' N, 79° 18.15' W, will place you approximately ¼ mile northwest of *Gun Cay Pass* in about 20'-25' of water. Head generally southeastward around the southern tip of Gun Cay being sure to favor the Gun Cay shore. There is a large rocky bar working out from Cat Cay and you must pass between Gun Cay and this bar. Simply round the southern tip of Gun Cay staying about 50 yards off and you will have 15' all the way in. Once inside you may head northward toward the anchorage

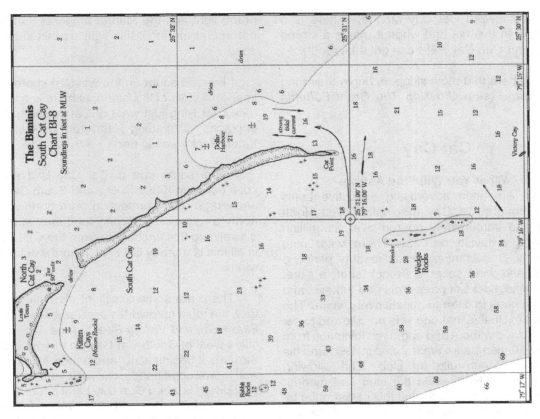

The Biminis
South Cat Cay
Chart BI-8
Soundings in feet at MLW

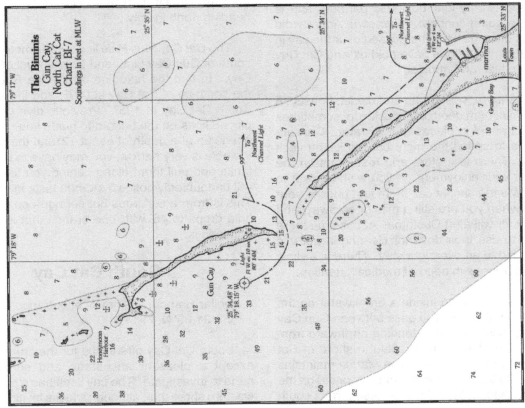

The Biminis
Gun Cay,
North Cat Cat
Chart BI-7
Soundings in feet at MLW

or southward toward *Cat Cay Marina*. There is a lot of current in this cut and when it meets a strong opposing wind *Gun Cay Pass* can get a bit rough.

It is from here that most skippers begin their long banks passage (see: *Crossing The Great Bahama Bank*).

Cat Cay

What You Will Find Ashore

In 1931, American advertising executive Louis R. Wasey bought Cat Cay (originally called North Cat Cay) and immediately poured over $1 million into creating a lavish retreat. There were nine tennis courts, a swimming pool, a beauty parlor, a masseuse, and wine cellar, a French chef, a skeet shoot, a casino, flocks of pheasants and turkeys, and over 250 servants to cater to guests every whim. The club was so exclusive that one was not allowed to set foot on the island without and engraved invitation from one of the 100 members. Wasey died in 1961 and his heirs declined to subsidize the club. The following year Hurricane Betsy leveled the club and marina. The club was purchased following this catastrophe by Willard F. Rockwell, Jr., chairman of *North American Rockwell* and twenty-four business partners and is once again a going concern. *Hurricane Andrew* did quite a lot of damage when he passed over the cay in 1992 but rebuilding efforts have paid off and Cat Cay is once again lush and tropical.

Cat Cay Marina, selling gas and diesel, boasts 75 slips with a minimum depth of 8' dockside, sometimes less in the channel in places at low water. Cruisers are welcome to spend the night but the island itself is off-limits. There is a store and restaurant on the premises for your enjoyment. If you wish to clear in at *Cat Cay Marina* simply call them just prior to your arrival, say when you are still a mile or so away, and the dockmaster will alert Customs. At this time there is a charge to use their dock for clearing in but this may be applied to an overnight stay. There is a clinic on Cat Cay for those in need of medical attention.

The marina is located inside a breakwater on the east side of Cat Cay. As you pass between Gun Cay and Cat Cay, give the bar extending northward from Cat Cay a wide berth then parallel the shore of Cat Cay southward to the *Marina*. The *Marina* maintains a flashing white light (once every four seconds) on the eastern breakwater. The Cat Cay airstrip runs south of the light and the Marina requests that boaters do not anchor north of this light as this is an air traffic zone.

If headed south on the western shore of Cat Cay keep well west of the island as there is a long shallow rocky bar lying just west of Cat cay with 4'-6' over it in places. If heading south from here steer to keep Kitten Rocks well to port.

At the south end of Cat Cay is a shallow little cove between Kitten Rocks and South Cat Cay. This anchorage offers protection from northwest through north to east winds. Strong southeast winds will bring a swell into this anchorage from the Gulf Stream. All in all this is a pretty fair spot in northwest to northeast winds.

There are some excellent dive sites around Cat Cay, the most noteworthy are *Tuna Alley*, the *Cat Cay Blue Hole*, and *Victory Reef*. *Tuna Alley* lies some 2 miles west of South Cat Cay on the edge of the Gulf Stream. It begins at 40' and bottoms out at 90' and is wall to wall coral heads, canyons, and passages. The best diving is when Gun Cay Light bears 010° and the south tip of Cat Cay is at 60°. The reef gets its name from the bluefin tuna that migrate through the area heading north in July.

The *Cat Cay Blue Hole* lies approximately 3½ miles south of Gun Cay Light and ¼ mile west of South Cat Cay. To find the hole line up Wedge Rock at 150°, the south tip of Cat Cay at 007°, and the south tip of South Cat Cay at 105°. Previous dive groups have placed lines on the bottom to guide you. The bottom opens up at a depth of about 12' and the entrance to the hole is very narrow, you may have to take off your tanks and pull them along behind you to enter. You will undoubtedly notice a strange taste in your mouth. This is from a sulfurous hot spring deep below. The hole drops to 45' with one branch that is said to be bottomless.

South Cat Cay

Dollar Harbour - ½ nm W of entrance:
25° 31.00' N, 79° 16.00' W

South Cat Cay offers little for the cruising skipper except a pleasant anchorage and some offshore reefs to investigate. The cay itself has a beach on the western shore that, although it looks inviting, is littered

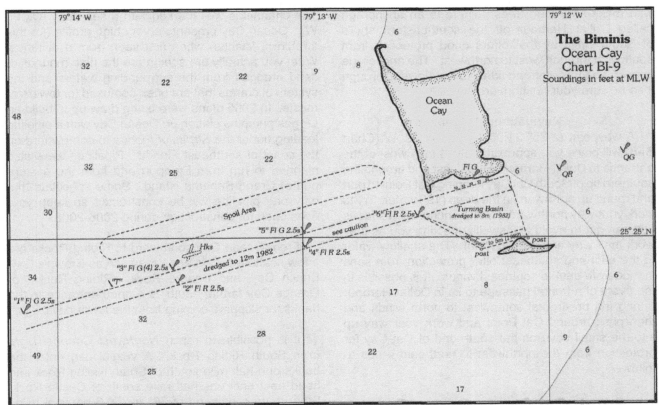

The Biminis
Ocean Cay
Chart BI-9
Soundings in feet at MLW

79° 14' W

79° 13' W

79° 12' W

Ocean
Cay

Fl G

QG

QR

32

22

22

9

8

48

32

25

22

6

30

22

6

Spoil Area

"6" Fl R 2.5s

Turning Basin
dredged to 8m (1982)

25° 25' N

"5" Fl G 2.5s

see caution

dredged to 5m (1982)

post

Hks

post

34

"3" Fl G (4) 2.5s

dredged to 12m 1982

"4" Fl R 2.5s

6

"T"

"2" Fl R 2.5s

8

17

"1" Fl G 2.5s

32

9

28

49

22

6

25

17

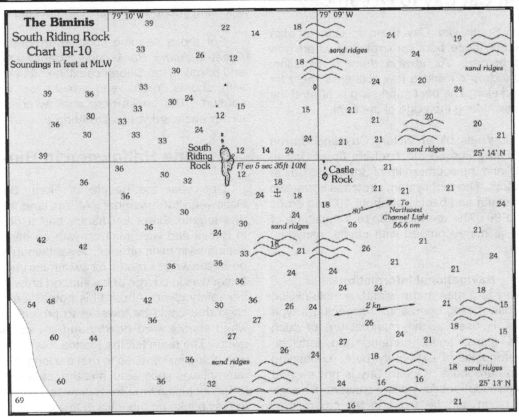

The Biminis
South Riding Rock
Chart BI-10
Soundings in feet at MLW

79° 10' W

79° 09' W

39

22

14

18

24

19

33

26

12

18

sand ridges

24

sand ridges

30

24

20

24

39

36

33

0

24

20

24

36

30

30

24

15

15

21

21

20

30

33

24

21

21

21

39

33

South
Riding
Rock

12

14

24

24

21

21

sand ridges

25° 14' N

36

30

12

Fl ev 5 sec 35ft 10M

Castle
Rock

21

36

32

18

21

21

21

36

9

24

18

To
Northwest
Channel Light
56.6 nm

24

30

18

80°

26

21

42

36

30

24

sand ridges

26

21

24

42

36

24

24

21

36

24

24

24

21

18

47

36

2 kn

21

15

54

48

42

30

36

26

24

26

18

15

36

27

21

60

44

27

27

24

21

18 sand ridges

36

sand ridges

26

24

18

60

36

32

24

16

16

25° 13' N

69

16

21

with rocks and dead trees. There is an anchorage called Dollar Harbour off the southeastern shore of South Cat Cay that offers good protection from southwest through west to northwest. The anchorage is deep and has a strong tidal current flowing through it so be sure your anchors are set well.

Navigational Information

A waypoint at 25° 31.00' N, 79° 16.00' W (Chart BI-8) will place you approximately ½ mile west of the entrance to Dollar Harbour. Head east and around the southern tip of South Cat Cay keeping Cat Point to port and round up northward in the deep (19') water. Try to work your way northward into the anchorage as far as you can get to avoid any swells affecting you as they work their way around Cat Point. The shallow water to the east and southeast offer protection from seas in moderate east to southeast winds. It is possible in the event of a frontal passage to lie in Dollar Harbour during the pre-frontal southwest to north winds and then pass around Cat Point and work your way up into the small cove on the south end of Cat Cay for protection from the northwest to northeast winds to follow.

South Cat Cay to Ocean Cay

South of South Cat Cay there is little to offer cruisers except those bent on exploring where few have gone before. As always there is excellent fishing at the drop off and a few scattered reefs for the avid snorkeler. The best snorkeling is around the scattered rocks along the edge of the bank.

Victory Reef lies off of Victory Cay and Barren Rocks. To find it line up the northern tip of Barren Rocks at 60° and the southern tip of South Cat Cay at Cat Point at 25°. The reef system stretches some two miles to the south and begins at about 40' and drops off to around 90'. The reef is home to a multitude of fish life and is honeycombed with caves, canyons, and grottoes.

Navigational Information

Ocean Cay is a man made island, a multi-million dollar aragonite mining operation. Aragonite, a type of limestone, is used in the manufacture of such products as glass, soda, cement, and fertilizer. Bahamian aragonite is extremely pure, containing 97% calcium carbonate. Ocean Cay is private and has no accommodations for visiting cruisers although the turning basin can be used in an emergency.

The channel is well marked with a sea buoy (Qk FL W). Ocean Cay presents a very high profile (for this stretch of islands) when first seen from a distance. What you actually are seeing are the high mounds of sand dredged from the surrounding waters and the system of cranes that are often confused for towers or masts. In 2005 plans were being draw up to build an LP gas pumping station on Ocean Cay with a pipeline leading under the *Straits of Florida* to somewhere on the coast of southeast Florida. Pipelines were also planned to run from Freeport and from the eastern end of Grand Bahama Island. Some speculate that only one pipeline will be constructed so keep your eyes open for construction during 2006-2008.

From Ocean Cay southward to Riding Rocks are a few scattered reefs and cays such as Brown's Cay, Beach Cay, and Square Rock. Riding Rocks, or Orange Cay farther south, is a good entrance to the banks for skippers coming from the lower cays.

It is possible to reach *Northwest Channel Light* from South Riding Rock. A vessel can enter the banks one-half mile south of South Riding Rock and head east until one-half mile south of Castle Rock. From there a heading of 80° for 56.6 nautical miles will bring you to Northwest Channel Light.

For those heading south from Orange Cay, the *Great Bahama Bank* curves gently southeastward and parallels the Cuban coastline. Its edge is littered with shoals, reefs, and wrecks so use extreme caution. The banks here shallow considerably the closer eastward you get to Andros.

One Halloween in Bimini

One year the people of North Bimini had a Halloween to remember. At this time the Bahamian dive-legend Skeet LaChance had a dive operation in Bimini and was involved with an offshore record-setting swimming attempt. A gentleman was trying to break the world's record for swimming underwater and Skeet was in charge of his support crew and acted as his safety diver. Aboard his boat Skeet had a large cage that could be lowered to protect the swimmer when sharks were nearby and yet still allow him to swim. The team left the Florida Keys and everything was going just fine, so to make a long story short, the attempt was successful and the team was heading in to Bimini just in time for Halloween and they decided to play a joke on the folks in town.

Skeet radioed ahead and informed the folks in Alice Town that he had caught some sort of strange sea creature and was bringing it in alive. What strange sea creature you ask? Well, the gentleman that set the swimming record is the same man who played the original *Creature* in the old movie, *The Creature From The Black Lagoon*, and he just happened to have one of his old costumes with him, after all he figured, Halloween was just around the corner. Skeet set the shark cage upright on deck and Skeet's friend donned his *Creature* suit and climbed into the cage, the crew wet him down with salt water and hung some Sargasso weed on him for effect.

When Skeet got to the dock the whole town was there to see what "Mr. Skeets caught." At this time there were about 2,300 people living in Bimini, most of whom were standing shoulder to shoulder on the town dock to see Skeet's creature. There were grown men laughing, gesturing and talking loudly and even louder children running around being loud children. There were chatty women nursing little babies, giggling schoolgirls not knowing what to expect, and old timers who had seen more than their share of strange fish and wanted to see one more. As Skeet tied up to the dock the crew removed the tarp from the cage and the locals fell silent. As the tarp was drawn back the *Creature* rose from its haunches and emitted a tremendous roar, and then shrieking and shaking the bars until it seemed it was on the verge of ripping apart its prison, the *Creature's* outstretched arms flailed about in an attempt to reach for the people on the dock. For about 20 seconds the Creature put on his show and the crowd was so silent that you could hear a pin drop. Finally the roaring, screeching Creature managed to fling open the door to the cage and the entire crowd of people turned and fled as one entity, all running at the same speed and with nobody being trampled. Within 30 seconds the waterfront of Alice Town was deserted, the only noise being the sound of slamming doors from blocks away. Nobody in Bimini went out *Trick or Treating* that night, not until Mr. Skeets left with his *Creature*.

Crossing the Great Bahama Bank

Fuel: Biminis (Cat Cay) Berry Islands (Chub Cay, Great Harbour Cay)

Haul-Out: None

Diesel Repairs: Berry Islands (Great Harbour Cay)

Outboard Repairs: Berry Islands (Great Harbour Cay)

Propane: Berry Islands (Great Harbour Cay)

Provisions: Berry Islands (Chub Cay)

Important Lights:

Russell Beacon: Fl W ev 4 sec
Mackie Beacon: Fl W ev 2 sec
Sylvia Beacon: Fl W ev 4 sec
Northwest Shoal Buoy: Fl W ev 2 sec
NW Channel Light: Fl W ev 3 sec

> *Note: Navigators should be cautious, while crossing the Bahama Bank, never to follow vessels, if they alter course often, as the New Providence Wreckers have frequently decoyed them for the purpose of plunder; a crime which the most barbarous nation would punish with the greatest severity. This is not published to give offense to anyone, but it applies to some of the Providence Navigators, and it is our duty to point out danger to Mariners, from which the Editor will never deviate, or hide from investigation.*
>
> from *Blunt's*
> **THE AMERICAN COAST PILOT**, 1812

Things have changed quite a bit on the *Great Bahama Bank* since that pilot was published over 190 years ago. About he only dangers lurking about nowadays are *Mackie Shoal* and the remains of the *Northwest Channel Light*, which only lies a foot or so above sea level at low tide.

Your passage across the *Great Bahama Bank* from Bimini or Gun Cay to Great Stirrup Cay, Bullock's Harbour, or Chub Cay will likely be the longest, and sometimes most boring leg that you will face in your Bahamas cruise. Vessels venturing east from North Rock will find the water getting progressively deeper (20'-200' in places) as you approach Little Stirrup Cay in the northern Berry Islands. Those ves-sels heading from North Rock to *Northwest Channel Light* will generally be in shallower water, usually 20' or less until they round *Northwest Channel Light* and cross over the drop off into the deeper water lying just southeast of the light. There are scattered reefs and small heads all over the banks but except for the shallows southeast of North Rock, the shallows east of Gun Cay, the *Mackie Shoal* area, and *Northwest Shoal*, there is nothing shallow enough to create a danger for a vessel drawing less than 7'.

When departing the Biminis bound for the northern Berrys or Chub Cay, weather plays a huge factor in determining when you leave. Your crossing of the *Gulf Stream* behind, you now must face the shallow waters of the *Great Bahama Bank*. Here you won't face the larger seas of the *Gulf Stream,* but you may have to deal with a strong wind-blown chop. Consistent winds of 15-25 knots from the east or southeast for a short length of time will often create waves on the banks up to 5', close together, and steep. For sailors this can make your passage a very uncomfortable beat in choppy conditions, and trawlers won't like these conditions as well. Unlike the *Gulf Stream* it is fine to cross the banks in moderate northerly winds. Sailors will love those conditions. Also bear in mind that when transiting this body of water that you will be affected by tidal currents that normally flow in a northeast/southwest direction. These currents are affected by the wind strength, and their direction and rate of flow vary as you approach the Biminis, the northern Berry Islands, and the tip of the *Tongue of the Ocean* at *Northwest Channel Light*.

Almost ten years ago, five new lights were installed on the *Great Bahama Bank* by the *US Coast Guard, Sylvia Beacon Light, Mackie Shoal Light, Russell Beacon Light, Northwest Shoal Light*, and *Northwest Channel Light*. All lights are reported to be flashing white atop 18" diameter steel pipes 20' high. The problem now arises that since the *USCG* graciously installed the working lights, who will be in charge of the upkeep and maintenance on these aids to navigation? The answer is the Bahamian government. Let's face it folks, with the government's track record of maintaining lights, let's consider that these lights may not be working when you need them, like the rest of the lights in The Bahamas you should consider them "unreliable." The characteristics and positions for the lights (as per *USCG Notice to Mariners* July 11, 2000) are as follows:

Sylvia Beacon Light (LL 11928), FL W 4s
25° 27' 26.697" N, 079° 01' 34.971" W.

Mackie Shoal Light (LL 11933), FL W, 2s
25° 40' 54.720" N, 078° 39' 27.105" W.

Russell Beacon Light (LL11964), FL W 4s
25° 28' 30.080" N, 078° 25' 30.032" W.

Northwest Shoal Light (LL none), FL W
2s, 25° 29' 53.976" N, 078° 13' 53.990" W.

Northwest Channel Light (LL 11960), FL W 3s
25° 28' 05.705" N, 078° 09' 37.984" W.

From North Rock

Vessels proceeding from North Bimini may pass north of North Rock and enter the banks to begin their crossing. North Rock is equipped with a light (*FL W ev 3 sec, 40', 8M*) but, as with most lights in The Bahamas, consider it unreliable at best as it may or may not be working when you pass it. North Rock is so small and low that it is virtually impossible to see at night until you are almost on top of it, radar helps but not all vessels are so equipped. A waypoint at 25° 48.25' N, 79° 16.00' W will place you approximately ½ nautical mile west of the light. From this position steer 90° onto the banks keeping North Rock to starboard. Stay at least 150-100 yards north of the light to avoid the rocks close in and to the east of it. Head east for at least two miles to a waypoint at 25° 48.25' N, 79° 13.50' W. From this position Skippers wishing to head to Chub Cay can take up a course of 106° for 31.7 nautical miles to a waypoint at 25° 42.00' N, 78° 39.00' W. This position lies just north of the *Mackie Shoal Light* and well north of *Mackie Shoal*. From here take up a course of 123° for 29.7 nautical miles to bring you to a waypoint at 25° 28.40 N, 78° 09.80' W, or just north of *Northwest Channel Light*.

Just two miles northwest of *Northwest Channel Light* on this route you will see the *Northwest Shoal Light* (*FL W ev 2 sec*), which marks a reef strewn shoal area with depths less than 6' over some of the heads. Make sure you pass to the south and west of this light. From this position you can probably see *Northwest Channel Light*. Pass the *Northwest Channel Light* on its north side and you may then take up your course for Chub Cay (115° for 14.1 nautical miles) or Nassau (124° for 49.5 nautical miles)

From the waypoint two miles east of North Rock, skippers wishing to head to Great Stirrup Cay can take up a course of 94° for a distance of 70.3 nautical miles. Those mariners wishing to head to *Great Harbour Cay Marina* at Bullock's Harbour can steer 97° for 69.4 nautical miles to pick up the tripod marker R2 at 25° 46.11' N, 77° 56.59' W.

From Gun Cay

Vessels departing from the eastern shore of Gun Cay and bound for the northern Berry Islands should be advised that the first 4-5 miles of their passage will be over some shallow sandbanks that in places barely carry 5' at MLW. If you attempt this route do it on a mid-tide or better and make sure the tide is rising. From the eastern shore of Gun Cay a course of 86° for 74.6 nautical miles will bring you to *R2*, the tripod marker marking the entrance to the channel to Bullock's Harbour. Vessels wishing to make Great Stirrup Cay should proceed northward from this position and then eastward around the northern shore of Little Harbour Cay. Skippers wishing to make *Northwest Channel Light* can take up a course of 101° for 62.1 nautical miles (this will bring you north of *Russell Beacon*). A waypoint at 25° 28.40 N, 78° 09.80' W, will place you north of the new *Northwest Channel Light*.

Skippers leaving the *Cat Cay Marina* must clear the very visible shallow sandbank lying north and east of the marina. Once past this take up a course of 101° for 62.1 nautical miles and you will find yourself at *Northwest Channel Light*.

From Lucaya

From the seaward entrance to *Bell Channel* at Lucaya it is possible for boaters to cross the *Northwest Providence Channel* and then the *Great Bahama Bank* to arrive at *Northwest Channel Light*. From Lucaya take up a course of 165° for 64.5 nautical miles. This will place you to the west of *Northwest Shoal Light*. Round the buoy to the south and take up a course of 123° for the final two miles or so to *Northwest Channel Light*.

From South Riding Rock

Entering the banks south of South Riding Rocks skippers can take up a course for *Northwest Channel Light* after passing Castle Rock on the port beam.

From this position take up a course of 80° for 56.6 nautical miles to bring you to *Northwest Channel Light*. As you approach the light be sure to keep the light on your starboard side as you round it. This route takes you across the southeastern extremity of the Elbow Bank, lying about 10-20 miles along the course line from South Riding Rock. Here you will encounter some depths in the 6'-10' range at low water.

There is an old route from Orange Cay to *Russell Beacon* (53° for 51.2 nautical miles) and thence to *Northwest Channel Light*. I do not recommend this route as the waters in the area have shoaled considerably and can barely take 6' at low water in places. Scattered heads and small patch reefs are frequent the closer you get to *Russell Beacon* on this course.

A Final Note of Caution

It has been reported that a downed airplane is lying in 10'-15' of water approximately 9-10 miles WNW of *Northwest Channel Light*. The approximate position is 25° 33.815' N, 078° 18.720' W. I have not seen the wreck but I am told that it is not visible at high water but that part of it does rise above the surface at low water. Use caution when transiting the area!

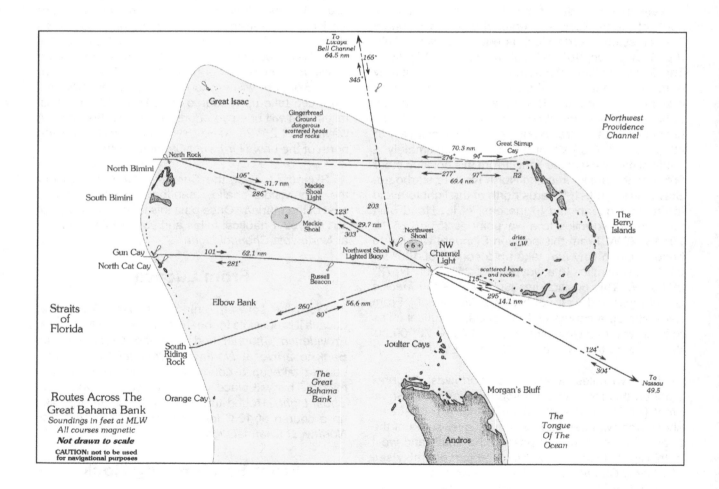

The Berry Islands

Ports of Entry: Chub Cay, Great Harbour Cay
Fuel: Chub Cay, Great Harbour Cay
Haul-Out: None
Diesel Repairs: Chub Cay, Great Harbour Cay
Outboard Repairs: Chub Cay, Great Harbour Cay
Propane: *Great Harbour Cay Marina*
Provisions: Chub Cay, Great Harbour Cay
Important Lights:
    Great Stirrup Cay Lighthouse: Gp Fl W (2) ev 20s
    Bullock's Harbour: Fl W ev 6 sec
    Little Harbour Cay: Fl W ev 2 sec
    Chub Point: Fl W&R ev 10 sec

East of the Biminis and approximately two-thirds of the distance to Nassau lie the Berry Islands. The Berrys form a crescent along the northeastern edge of the *Great Bahama Bank* near where it drops off into the deep waters of the *Northwest Providence Channel*. Along the eastern shore of the Berry Islands the drop off into the deeper waters lies a mile or more offshore in some places while in other locations, such as at Chub Cay, the drop off lies just a few hundred feet off Chub Point. The entire bight on the western side of the crescent is very shallow with many sand bores and areas that dry at low water. Here a draft of less than 5' can feel it's way along the western shores of the Berrys in good visibility and on a rising almost high tide from Bonds Cay northward to the Market Fish Cays.

A great many cruisers hurry through the Berry Islands on their way to Nassau, the Exumas, and beyond, and this is sad; if you do this you'll miss so much. Some skippers don't care for the protection (or lack of it) offered by the cays. Although there are just a few true all weather harbors amongst the 30 some-odd cays which make up the Berry Islands quite a few lee anchorages can be found from almost any wind direction, and two fine hurricane holes can be accessed at Little Harbour Cay and in Bullocks Harbour at *Great Harbour Cay Marina*. Most of the lee side anchorages offer good protection from seas, but some swell seems to work its way in at times. The deep waters of the *Northwest Providence Channel* and the *Tongue of the Ocean* offer fantastic fishing opportunities and make the Berrys an ideal staging area for the fishing tournaments out of Chub Cay. The shallow grassy banks are teeming with conch while the rocks and reefs along the cays are home to lobster, grouper, and snapper just waiting to hop into your frying pan. These shallow waters are tailor made for shallow draft monohulls, multihulls, and small outboard powered boats, offering many opportunities to explore where few others can go.

Approaches to the Berry Islands

Mackie Shoal Light - 200 yards N of:
25° 42.00' N, 78° 39.00' W

Russell Beacon - ½ nm N of buoy:
25° 29.00' N, 78° 25.54' W

NW Channel Light - 250 yards N of:
25° 28.40' N, 78° 09.80' W

From North Rock in the Biminis a course of 94° for 71 nautical miles will bring you to the northwestern tip of the Berry Islands where a waypoint at 25° 49.64' N, 77° 57.41' W marks the beginning of the channel to *Great Harbour Marina* while a waypoint at 25° 49.60' N, 77° 55.66' W, opens up the entrance to Slaughter Harbour just southwest of Great Stirrup Cay. Just past Great Stirrup Cay a waypoint at 25° 49.40' N, 77° 53.30' W, will open up the anchorage at Great Harbour including Panton Cove and Goat Cay. Those mariners wishing to head directly for *Great Harbour Cay Marina* at Bullock's Harbour from North Rock can steer 97° for 71.2 nautical miles to arrive at the first tripod on the route to Bullock's Harbour at 25° 46.11' N, 77° 56.59' W.

From Freeport, a course of 137° for 61.2 nautical miles will bring you to the Great Stirrup Cay/Slaughter Harbour waypoint while from Lucaya the course is 143° for 55 nautical miles. From the seaward entrance to *Bell Channel* at Lucaya it is possible for boaters to cross the *Northwest Providence Channel* and then the *Great Bahama Bank* to arrive at *Northwest Channel Light*. From Lucaya take up a course of 165° for 64.5 nautical miles. This will place you to the west of *Northwest Shoal Light*. Pass the buoy to the south and take up a course of 123° for the final two miles or so to *Northwest Channel Light* (see the previous chapter *Crossing The Great Bahama Bank*).

From the western entrance of Nassau Harbour a course of 308° for 35.7 nautical miles will bring you to the Chub Cay waypoint. A course of 321° for 30.4 nautical miles from Nassau brings you to a point just ¼ mile east of the entrance to the anchorage at Little Whale Cay, while a course of 333° for 34.4

nautical miles will bring you to the waypoint off the Frozen-Alder/Little Harbour Cay anchorage. Just a little further north lies the Devil's Hoffman anchorage where a course of 334° for 37 nautical miles from Nassau Harbour will place you approximately ¼ nautical mile off the entrance to the anchorage.

Little Stirrup Cay and Great Stirrup Cay

Slaughter Harbour entrance - ½ nm N of:
25° 49.60' N, 77° 55.66' W

Panton Cove entrance - ½ nm NE of:
25° 49.40' N, 77° 53.30' W

The Stirrups (Chart BR-1) lie at the northern corner of the Berry Islands where the *Northwest Providence Channel* bends to the west towards Florida. Their unique location has kept these waters quite busy over the years. A wrecker named Captain Cameron once practiced his art in these waters using Little Stirrup

Cay as his home while notorious pirates such as the infamous Blackbeard often passed here on their way from Nassau to the eastern shores of America. The reign of William IV saw the settlement of Williams Town laid out on Great Stirrup Cay and a *Customs* house built, but with the death of William IV, so went the town. During the American Civil War, Federal gunboats regularly patrolled the waters surrounding Little and Great Stirrup Cay to catch gunrunners rounding the corner from Nassau bound for the southern U. S. Coast. Over half a century later, Federal agents again patrolled this area looking for rum-runners during the American Prohibition years, and again for drug-runners in more recent times. This is definitely a popular spot.

The 92-acre Little Stirrup Cay was named after a former owner named Sterrup. Both Little Stirrup and Great Stirrup Cay are private; a cruise line has leased the cays and built facilities ashore for its guests. The cruise ships anchor just north of Little Stirrup Cay and ferry passengers ashore to enjoy a sample of the "Bahamian Out-Island Lifestyle". In fact, the cruise

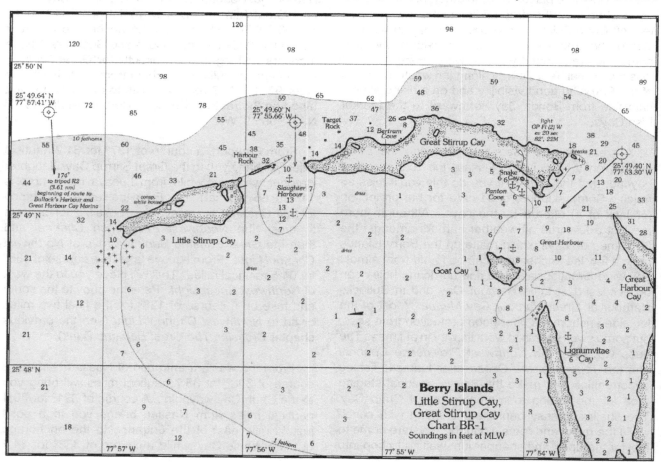

Berry Islands
Little Stirrup Cay,
Great Stirrup Cay
Chart BR-1
Soundings in feet at MLW

ships call this locale *Coco Cay*, I guess that sounds more tropical and out-islandy than Little Stirrup Cay. The manager of Little Stirrup Cay told me that they don't mind if visiting yachtsmen wish to come ashore and look around as long as there are no guests ashore (this means no cruise ships anchored offshore) and that visitors contact Little Stirrup Cay on VHF ch. 16 first to ask permission. Cruisers in Panton Cove are welcome to come ashore on the western end of Great Stirrup Cay to explore the lighthouse (built in 1863, GP Fl W ev 20 sec, 82' 22M), or the remains of the U.S. missile tracking station. In years past cruisers anchored in Slaughter Harbour or Panton Cove dinghied ashore on Great Stirrup Cay and crossed the island on foot to mingle with cruise ship guests and help themselves to the free buffet. It didn't take long for the cruise ship crews to get wise and realize that the cruisers were very tanned compared to the comparatively pale liners guests. So much for the free buffets.

Bertram's Cove, where the cruise ship passengers used to alight, is named after Commander Manuel Bertram of H.M.S. *Tweed,* who died and was buried here by his crew on July 20, 1834. There is a plaque commemorating Commander Bertram that was left by the crew of the *Tweed*. Commander Bertram's survey work is the foundation of some of the charts of The Bahamas now being used.

Navigational Information

Approaching the northern Berry Islands from Bimini or Grand Bahama your first sign of the Berry's will probably be the very conspicuous white house on Little Stirrup Cay (see Chart BR-1). There is a fair anchorage between Little Stirrup Cay and Great Stirrup Cay called Slaughter Harbour which has 8'-10' inside and is good for the winds of east through southeast, but is not to be considered in a strong frontal passage as it is wide open to the southwest and the north.

A waypoint at 25° 49.60' N, 77° 55.66' W will place you approximately ½ mile north of the entrance. When entering favor the eastern side of the channel, the Great Stirrup Cay side, as there is a rocky shoal that works out from the northeastern tip of Little Stirrup Cay that is home to a rock that is awash at high water. There is a line of red buoys that begin outside the harbor between Little Stirrup Cay and the rock off its northeastern shore that follows the shoreline inside past the dock and beach. These red floats

are not navigational buoys, they mark a swimming and snorkeling area. Once inside Slaughter Harbour don't travel too far south as the water shoals quickly. Holding is fair to good in grass and sand, make sure your anchor is set and don't try to stay in Slaughter Harbour in strong northerly winds.

Just east of Great Stirrup Cay lies the entrance to Great Harbour, a much better anchorage than Slaughter Harbour with good protection from the westerly winds that are found in the prelude to a fontal passage.

A waypoint at 25° 49.40' N, 77° 53.30' W, places you approximately ½ mile northeast of the entrance to Great Harbour. Head in between the rocks just off the eastern point of Great Stirrup Cay and the northern tip of Great Harbour Cay in 7'-13' of water, the shallower water will be close in to the Great Stirrup shore. Vessels seeking refuge from west winds can go straight over to Goat Cay and anchor in the lee along its eastern shore, but better protection can be found along the eastern shore of Lignumvitae Cay where you can find protection from the south through the northwest almost to north. Here you'll find a large sandy spot with great holding just below the conspicuous house atop the cay.

The most frequented anchorage is at Panton Cove, just inside the southeastern tip of Great Stirrup Cay as shown on Chart BR-1, where you can anchor in 6'-8' (MLW) close in to Snake Cay and shallower draft vessels can anchor in 5-6' (MLW) just to the west and northwest of Snake Cay. You'll find good protection here in winds from the northwest through north to east, but in strong east-southeast winds the swells come right in the entrance to Great Harbour making for an uncomfortable surge.

So, let's review, what do you do if a front threatens while at Great Stirrup Cay? First you find shelter from south through northwest winds along the eastern shore of Lignumvitae Cay, and then when the winds goes into the north/northwest through the northeast, you can raise your anchor and move to Panton Cove for shelter from the north/northwest through the southeast. Yes, it is a bit of moving, but it's worth it for good protection.

From Great Harbour dinghies can follow the channel between Great Harbour Cay and Cistern Cay all the way to the entrance to *Great Harbour Cay Marina*.

Great Harbour Cay,
Bullock's Harbour,
Great Harbour Cay Marina

Great Harbour Marina - entrance - nm NNW of:
25º 49.64' N, 77º 57.41' W

Great Harbour Route - R daymark below range:
25º 44.81' N, 77º 52.10' W

Great Harbour Cay - eastern anchorage:
25º 46.03' N, 77º 49.41' W

Great Harbour Cay (see Charts BR-2 and BR-3) is the largest cay in the Berry Islands being over 7 miles long and ¾ mile wide in spots. The southernmost portion was once called *Merryman* and the northern portion *Tiger Bay*. This northernmost section was even later subdivided into areas known as Grape Tree and Sistare. Some 500 people live in the Berry Islands and most of them reside here at Great Harbour Cay. Many are wealthy foreigners with splendid villas or condos overlooking the eastern shore of Great Harbour Cay with its beautiful, long, curving *Queen's Beach*.

Navigational Information

The route to the entrance to *Great Harbour Cay Marina* and Bullock's Harbour (see Chart BR-2) begins at the western tip of Little Stirrup Cay and bends its way southeastward across the banks in 9'-12' of water until you arrive at the entrance to Bullock's Harbour and *Great Harbour Cay Marina*. From a waypoint northwest of Little Stirrup Cay (see Chart BR-1) at 25º 49.64'N, 77º 57.41' W take up a course of 174º for the tripod marker that sits on the horizon about 3.61 miles south of you. Once you clear the shallows along the southwestern tip of Little Stirrup Cay you will have deep water on both sides of your course all the way to the marker; if you find yourself in water that is shallowing you are probably too far east, the deeper water lies to the west of you, in fact, to the west the deep water extends all the way to Bimini.

A waypoint at 25º 46.11' N, 77º 56.59' W places you approximately 200 yards east of the tripod marker and you may pass it to either side. Once abeam of the tripod marker take up a course of 111º (for reference see section *Approaches To The Berry Islands*). This will put the conspicuous *Batelco* tower at Bullock's Harbour just off your port bow. The rest of the markers are single poles and can be taken on either side and you will have no less than 9' to the final marker. Simply steering approximately 110º and looking for the markers is usually the best way to enter. From *R10*, look just off your port bow ashore and you will see a house on the ridge with a 110º range. The range is designed to bring you in to the last red marker, a red diamond, where you will turn to port and line up on the entrance cut to Bullock's Harbour. There will be a green marker *G12* just outside the cut to lead you in. At this point you will travel through a narrow cut blasted through the rolling hills to a lake inside and *Great Harbour Cay Marina*. The cut is approximately 80' wide and has 8' at low water. Once inside follow the marked channel as it winds around to the marina or, if you need fuel, pull up to the *Shell* fuel dock just to starboard inside the entrance. You will have at least 7' here at low water. The marina is tucked into the eastern corner and is surrounded by a nice condo development. It looks almost as if it belongs in south Florida instead of The Bahamas.

What You Will Find Ashore

Bullock's Harbour is the hub of the Berry Islands in that it is the largest settlement and the only one with a government administration office, a post office, and a clinic. *Great Harbour Cay Marina* offers all amenities and is the perfect place to ride out the fiercest frontal passage or even a hurricane. It is entirely landlocked and is situated in a tight "L" shape and well protected. The marina's dockmaster monitors VHF ch. 16, 68, and 14, and is happy to welcome you to the Berry Islands and take care of all your needs while you enjoy your stay here. The marina boasts 86 slips which will accommodate boats up to 150' long with drafts of 9'. It is possible to arrange for a mechanic or even someone to clean and wax your vessel here but there is no propane available.

Great Harbour Cay is a *Port of Entry* and if you inform the dockmaster upon your arrival he will arrange for *Customs* and *Immigration* to visit your vessel. The marina offers showers, laundry facilities, ice, a dive shop, and is home to a small store that carries a limited selection of marine supplies and handles scooter and bicycle rentals. Ivan Bridgewater's *Marina Store* is a good spot to pick up some groceries, fresh milk and produce, and frozen meats. The best grocery store on the island is *Whitewater*. You can contact *Circle-Circle,* the local bus/taxi, on VHF ch. 16, for a ride to *Whitewater*.

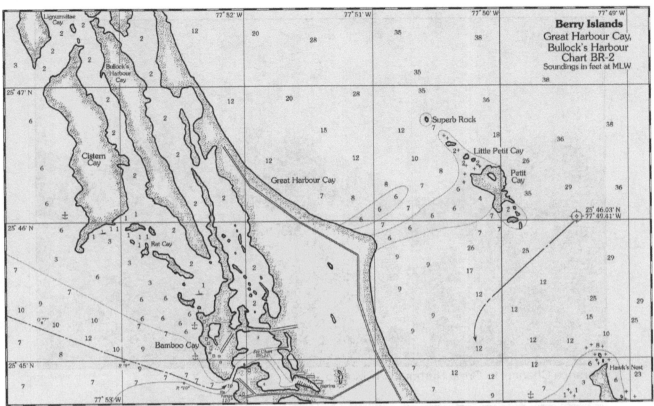

Berry Islands
Great Harbour Cay,
Bullock's Harbour
Chart BR-2
Soundings in feet at MLW

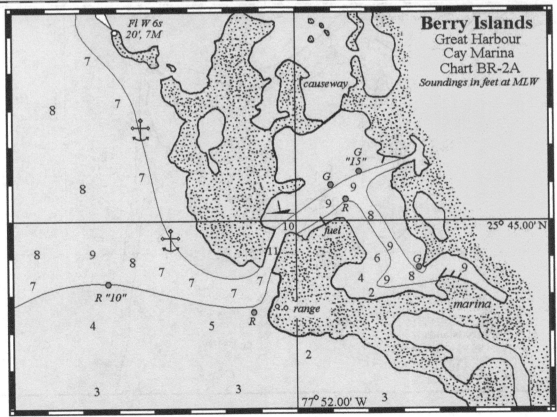

Berry Islands
Great Harbour
Cay Marina
Chart BR-2A
Soundings in feet at MLW

Entrance Channel to Great Harbour Cay Marina

Photo by Author

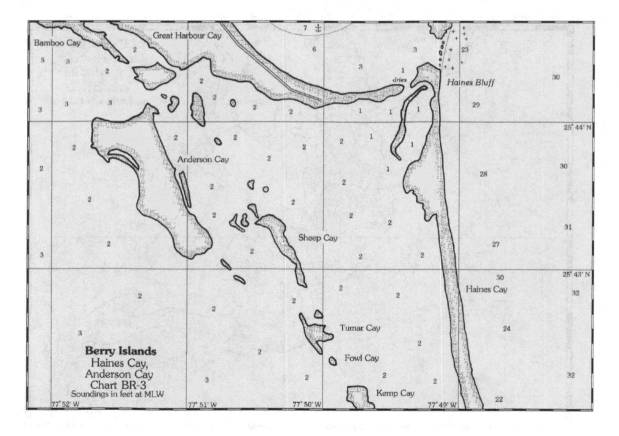

There are a dozen restaurants and bars in the vicinity including *The Wharf* situated right next to the marina property. *The Wharf* monitors VHF ch.16 and is open Wednesday through Saturday for dinner by reservation only. There's also the *Backside Inn* with cold beverages and cocktails, *Coolie Mae's Take Away* serving Bahamian dishes for lunch Monday through Saturday, *The Graveyard Inn*, open all day and night with outstanding Bahamian food and near the beach you'll find *Mama and Papa T's Beach Club* serving breakfast and lunch every day except Sunday. Also worth investigating is *The Pool Bar* at the marina, the *Watergate Chicken Shack* which is open daily serving light snacks of chicken and fish, and *D & L Snacks*.

Navigational Information
There is a little known, and little used route from Great Harbour Cay to *Northwest Channel Light*, but it requires good visibility, the ability to read the water's depth, a good weather forecast, and the help of the tide. From *RG4* a vessel of 7' draft, can take up an approximate heading of 240° and work her way around the western edge of the shallow banks that lie to the west of the Berry Islands. You should make *Northwest Shoal Light*, which lies about 3-4 miles northwest of *Northwest Channel Light*, your waypoint for this route. You will skirt the edge of shallow banks that lie west of the Berry Islands and which are strewn with shallow sandbores. You can anchor in the lee of these sandbores in prevailing winds if needed. Once past these sandbores you will once again be in deeper water. If you wish to avoid these sandbores, steer more westerly from Great Harbour Cay before turning southwards to *Northwest Shoal Light*.

When approaching *Northwest Shoal Light* try not to run up on *Northwest Shoal*. Pass to the west of the shoal and light.

The eastern shore of Great Harbour Cay offers an excellent lee in winds from southeast to almost northwest. The anchorage is beautiful and the holding is good. To enter (see Charts BR-2 and BR-3) from the east you must pass well north of Hawk's Nest which lies at the northern tip of Haines Cay and Petit Cay which lies approximately midway along the eastern shore of Great Harbour Cay.

A waypoint at 25° 46.03' N, 77° 49.41' W, is an excellent place from which to enter. Steer roughly southwest passing well south of Petit Cay and well north of Hawk's Nest in 25' of water and work your way inside along the shore to the southern most end of the small bay where you can anchor in 8'-10'. Keep well clear of the shallows between Petit Cay and Great Harbour Cay and the shallows lying southwest of Hawk's Nest and the southern tip of the bay.

What You Will Find Ashore
Bamboo Cay (Chart BR-3), lying just west of Great Harbour Cay, was once thought to be the most politically and commercially important cay in the Berry Islands. The sandy patches on the north side were once a burial ground but the soil is so shallow that the coffins often floated on the salt water. The cay once had a few fruit trees along its shores and when asked why the island had such few trees, the residents of the Bullocks Harbour area said that "*They did not plan for posterity and what they themselves may not live to reap-posterity must look out for itself.*" The residents at that time (1920's) were primarily involved with sponging and boat building. Just north of Bamboo Cay is a small unnamed cay ¼ mile long and 200' wide. It has a creek with a mouth about 50' wide known as the *waterfall*, the strong tidal flow through here overturned and caused the sinking of several unskillfully handled small boats.

Anderson Cay (Chart BR-3), lying approximately ½ mile west of the southern end of Great Harbour Cay is very high with a cliff dropping right down to the water's edge while the northern end is swampy with an old coconut orchard on the northwestern tip. There is an old well on the western side that is very brackish and filthy, but was of some use when cattle were raised on the cay in the late 1800's to early 1900's. Anderson Cay can only be explored by dinghy as the waters surrounding it are very shallow.

Hawksnest Cay at the northern tip of Haines Cay was named after ospreys that nested among the bluffs on its eastern shore. Under one of the bluffs is an interesting formation. About 100' inland and surrounded on the northern, eastern and southern sides by rock is a small pool with a beach along its western shore. This pool is connected to the sea by a "hole in the wall" which lies under the bluff. At high water the archway is 18" high with 4' of water under it. On the western shore of Haines Cay are some interesting boulder formations.

The cays south of Great Harbour Cay (see Chart BR-4), Money Cay to Ambergris Cay, are excellent for beachcombing and exploring by dinghy. The bight

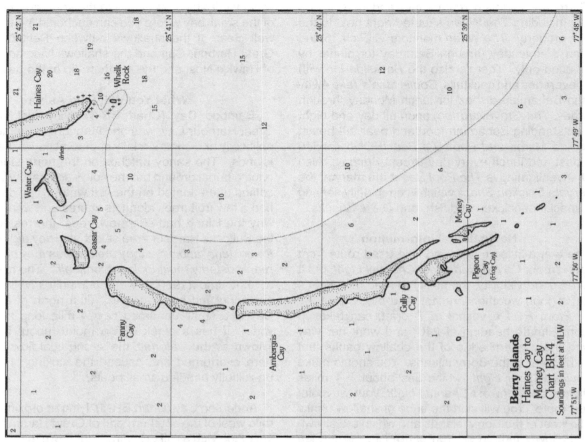

Berry Islands
Haines Cay to
Money Cay
Chart BR-4
Soundings in feet at MLW

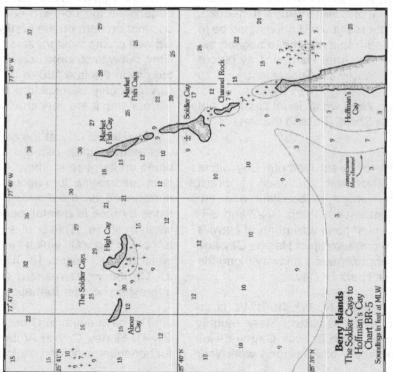

Berry Islands
The Soldier Cays to
Hoffman's Cay
Chart BR-5
Soundings in feet at MLW

between the southern tip of Haines Cay to the Market Fish Cays is deep, 9'-18' and vessels can anchor off the cays in settled or westerly weather. The western shores of these cays are very, very shallow with mangroves everywhere. To the east lie the Market Fish Cays (Chart BR-5) where just off the southwest point of Soldier Cay divers might find remnants of the wreck of the schooner "*Beatrice*" dating back to the 1800's.

A nice anchorage in prevailing (east-southeast) winds can be found in the lee of Soldier Cay just off a low lying but very beautiful beach. Enter from the north of the Market Fish Cays and proceed southward in their lee until just off the beach where you can anchor in 8'. Vessels drawing less than 5' can, with the help of the tides, work their way southward to the anchorages at Devil's-Hoffman by following the distinct blue water that curves westward around Hoffman Cay. By playing the tides you can make it as far as the anchorage at Devil's-Hoffman.

Hoffman's Cay, Devil's Cay

Devil's-Hoffman Anchorage - ¼ nm E of:
25° 36.55' N, 77° 43.50' W

With the exception of Bullock's Harbour, the inner harbor at Little Harbour Cay, and the anchorages in Great Harbour, one of the finest anchorages in the Berry's, if you are looking for all around protection from a frontal passage, is the anchorage between Hoffman's Cay and Devil's Cay, usually just called Devil's-Hoffman (see Chart BR-6). Though it may get a bit rolly or surgy at times, it offers a lee from nearly all wind directions. A few small seas may work their way in from the banks in winds from west to northwest but nothing to fear if you are anchored properly. I must warn you that there is a fair bit of current here and the holding can be iffy at times as the bottom is scoured in places, and when the wind moves east of north it will be time to move onto the banks in the

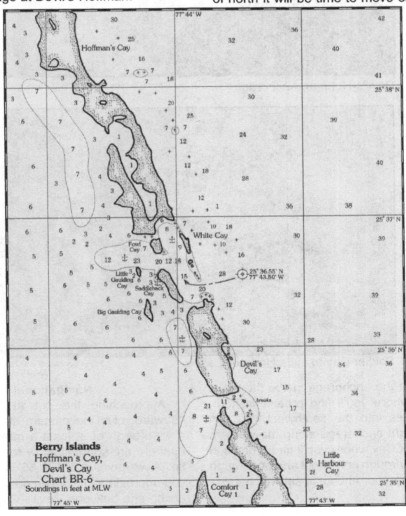

Berry Islands
Hoffman's Cay,
Devil's Cay
Chart BR-6
Soundings in feet at MLW

Devil's-Hoffman Anchorage

Photo Courtesy of Paul Harding, Safari Seaplanes

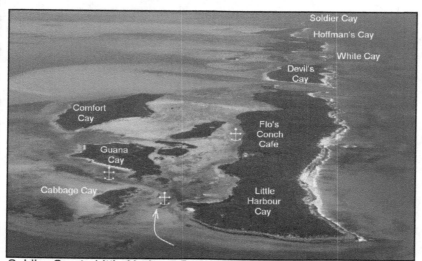

Soldier Cay to Little Harbour Cay

Photo Courtesy of Paul Harding,
Safari Seaplanes

lee of the cays. But the anchorage inside the cut is not the only spot where you'll find protection here. When the wind goes into the southwest you can find shelter in the tight anchorage along the western shore of Saddleback Cay where you'll find protection from the southwest through northwest and on through northeast. Make sure your anchor is set well here.

Navigational Information

Approaching the cut at Devil's-Hoffman from seaward, give the eastern shore of Hoffman's Cay a wide berth of at least a mile to a mile and a half as there are some shallow reefs well off its northern tip. A waypoint at 25° 36.55' N, 77° 43.50' W, places you approximately ¼ mile east of the entrance to the anchorage between Devil's Cay and Hoffman's Cay.

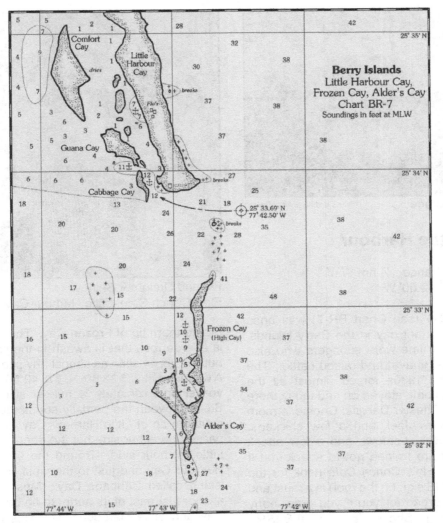

Berry Islands
Little Harbour Cay,
Frozen Cay, Alder's Cay
Chart BR-7
Soundings in feet at MLW

Steer for the middle of the cut between Devil's Cay to the south and the small rock to the north. Reefs line both sides of the cut but if you stay in the center you will have 20' at low water.

Once inside round up to starboard and tuck up to anchor just off the small beach on White Cay. In easterly weather I will anchor well out onto the banks west of the Devil's-Hoffman anchorage (which will be far too rough in winds from the northeast through the southeast) in 12'-15' northwest of Little Gaulding Cay.

There is current here but no surge. There are also several deeper pockets of water along the western shore of Hoffman's Cay, Devil's Cay, and west of the northern tip of Little Harbour Cay that are good lee anchorages in prevailing winds.

Navigational Information

Devil's Cay was once called Bird Cay and has two hilly ranges to about 40'. Along the southern and eastern shore of the cay are several nice beaches separated by cliffs. Vessels drawing less than 4½' can work their way south on the inside from here to the cut between Little Harbour Cay and Frozen Cay but the ability to read water, good visibility, a high tide, and nerves of steel are a necessity. Hoffman's Cay has a great blue hole awaiting your exploration. Surrounded by rock you can jump right in and explore the small cave at the bottom. From the anchorage at Saddleback Cay or in the lee of Fowl Cay (see Chart BR-6) dinghy northward along the western shore of Hoffman's Cay to the second beach where you'll find a well kept trail that leads to the blue hole. Big Gaulding Cay has a nice little beach on its eastern shore with a small cave hole and a table set up for visitors.

Little Harbour Anchorage

Photo Courtesy of Alicia Bonnet

Little Harbour

Little Harbour entrance - ½ nm W of:
25° 33.69' N, 77° 42.50' W

Little Harbour Cay (see Chart BR-7) was once called the most important cay in the Berry Islands. Its inhabitants at this time were spongers who also grew sisal, coconuts, guava, and raised cattle. The sponge blight in the 1930s forced almost all the settlers to move but some stayed on and today there is only the family of Chester Darville, Chester's mom Flo, Chester's nephew Joel, and a few chickens, goats, potcakes, ducks, peafowl, and a few attack trained geese (they are trained not to attack you if you're intoxicated). Flo's *Conch Café* (look for the huge YOU WELCOME sign on the roof) is a must and Flo will bake some bread for you if you order early enough in the morning. Chester is the local *BASRA* rep and quite the host. If you've been to the Berry Islands and haven't stopped in at *Flo's*, you haven't been to the Berry Islands.

Next to Bullock's Harbour, the inner harbor at Little Harbour Cay is the best hurricane hole in the Berry Islands. The entrance channel can take vessels with a 5½' draft inside to anchor in a pocket of water a little over 6' deep at low water, or along the mangroves just north of *Flo's Conch Café* in 7'-11' of water. Getting in the anchorage is tricky as the channel is not well defined, but a 5' draft can just make it in just before high tide.

Navigational Information

Little Harbour Cay is fairly easy to spot from offshore as it is high, bold, and has a distinctive spread of palm trees along its central ridge. To gain the anchorages at Little Harbour Cay you must enter from seaward between the southern tip of Little Harbour Cay and

Flo and Daughter Shirley,
Flo's Conch Cafe, Little Harbour Cay

Photo Courtesy of
Alicia Bonnet

the northern tip of Frozen Cay. The only obstruction is a large rock that is awash in the center of the cut but it is very visible as almost any sea breaks upon it. A waypoint at 25° 33.69' N, 77° 42.50' W, will put your vessel approximately ½ mile east of the entrance. Steer between the partially submerged rock and the southern tip of Little Harbour Cay. The rock can be passed on either side but the deeper water is on the Little Harbour side. Round the south end of Little Harbour Cay and just to the west lies a small rocky island called Cabbage Cay. Most vessels tend to anchor just east of its northern tip between Cabbage Cay and Little Harbour Cay. This is a very good anchorage but it can get quite rough when a strong wind is blowing in through the cut from the southeast. When that happens it is best to go around the north end of Cabbage Cay and anchor in its lee just south of Guana Cay but be sure to double check your holding here; west winds can make this anchorage rough. Vessels with less than a 6' draft who wish to enter the inner harbor below *Flo's Café* should only do so on a rising, almost high tide with good visibility. The ability to read the water is a necessity here if you wish to keep from going aground. The entrance channel begins just north of Cabbage Cay to the east of the small, unnamed rock off Guana Cay and proceeds in towards the dock below *Flo's*. It takes a small dogleg left and then right just before the deeper water opens up near the dock and flows northward for a ways along the western shore of Little Harbour Cay. Use two anchors here, bow and stern if possible, as there is no swinging room. The Darville's have a few moorings here, and if you have trouble finding the entrance channel call Chester or his nephew Joel on VHF ch. 68 (hail *Little Harbour* or *Flo's Conch Café*).

If you would like to charter a vessel in The Bahamas, and in particular in the Berry Islands and Little Harbour area, contact Conchy Jeffrey at conchyjeff@pocketmail.com or saltydogsailing@hotmail.com. For more info on Flo's visit www.greatharbourproductions.com/flos.

Frozen Cay, Alder Cay

Skippers wishing to anchor in the lee of Frozen Cay, sometimes shown as High Cay on some charts, or farther south at Alder's Cay should turn to port once they enter the cut between Little Harbour Cay and the partially submerged rock as shown on Chart BR-7. Vessels can anchor in the lee of Frozen Cay almost anywhere along its length but in strong east and southeast winds a strong surge works its way in and along the shore. The rolliest night I ever spent in The Bahamas was spent behind Frozen Cay. At the southern tip of Frozen Cay is a private bonefish camp and its distinctive green roofs are visible from well out to sea.

A good anchorage lies in the bight between Frozen Cay and Alder Cay in 7'-9' over a grassy bottom with a reputation for being poor holding. It is well sheltered from all directions except north with a reef protecting you from the swells coming in from seaward. The entrance lies close to the Alder Cay shore. Approach the anchorage heading south from the cut and keep west a little until you can line up the entrance channel on a northwest/southeast line. There is 5' in the entrance at low water.

Both Frozen and Alder Cays are private and visits ashore must be by invitation only. Vessels drawing less than 7' can go around Alder Cay to the west to make the northern tip of Bond's Cay.

Bond's Cay to Bird Cay

Little Whale Cay - ¼ nm E of entrance:
25° 26.77' N, 77° 45.13' W

Bonds Cay is a long slender cay lying just south of Alder Cay. The cay is steep-to on the eastern shore with a few small beaches on the western side. Coconut orchards, sisal, and guava trees once flourished here and previous settlers raised some cattle here in the late 1800s. In the center of the cay is an old salt pond and the ruins of pasture walls. This cay was once covered in "honeysuckle" weed, a plant that cattle often ate and which would fatten them for 6-9 months and then rapidly kill them. Today Bond's Cay is uninhabited and may stay that way for a while. A couple of years ago a cruise line attempted to buy the cay to develop a resort similar to the one on Little and Great Stirrup Cays in the northern Berry Islands but the deal fell through.

Navigational Information
If approaching Bond's Cay (see Chart BR-8) from the *Northwest Providence Channel* give the cay a

Frozen-Alder Cay Anchorage   Photo Courtesy of Paul Harding, Safari Seaplanes

wide berth of at least 1½ miles to avoid the shallow reefs lying off its eastern shore. Vessels drawing less than 5' can anchor along the western shore of Bond's Cay if approaching from the south. The inside passage from the north has shoaled and is tricky unless you are very good at reading the water or have a local pilot. If you wish to anchor behind Bond's Cay enter through the cut between Sisters Rocks and the southern tip of Bond's Cay favoring the Bond's Cay shore and avoiding the shallow reefs between the Sisters Rocks and Bond's Cay. Then simply steer northward staying close in to shore and anchor as far north as your draft will allow.

Just south of Bond's Cay lies Little Whale Cay (see Chart BR-9) with its very conspicuous light atop a stone tower that resembles a small lighthouse from offshore. Vessels may anchor along its northwestern shore but the area is shallow, rocky, surgy, and the entrance around the northern tip of Little Whale Cay is riddled with shallow reefs. The better anchorage is between Little Whale Cay and Whale Cay but the entrance can be rough when a strong northeast to southeast wind opposes the outgoing tide. A waypoint at 25° 26.77' N, 77° 45.13' W, will place you approximately ¼ mile east of the cut. To enter the anchorage you must pass north of a small reef that lies just off the northern tip of Whale Cay so favor the Little Whale Cay shore as you enter. From the area of your waypoint line up the northern tip of Frazer's-Hog Cay (on the horizon about 3 miles west) on your bow and steer in on a heading of 270° favoring the Little Whale Cay side of the cut. If the 270° course does not look right ignore it and favor the Little Whale Cay shore using your eyes to tell you if you can clear the reef. Anchor anywhere inside in 7'-20' of water. Favor the Whale Cay side for southeast winds and the Little Whale Cay side for northeast winds. There is a lot of current here so use two anchors.

What You Will Find Ashore

Little Whale Cay is one of the prettiest and best managed private cays in The Bahamas. On first glance you will notice the excellent stone work in the seawall the surrounds most of the island. Just off the anchorage lies the man-made marina (private) and stone church that was built over 50 years ago. At that time it was a parish of the *Church of England* and was named *Our Lady Star of the Sea*. At that time the cay was owned by a Stamford, Connecticut yankee named Wallace Groves who is also known as the founder of Freeport on Grand Bahama. Little Whale

Cay was developed as a winter home for the Groves with many terraced gardens and a huge aviary and duck pond. The inland lake of just less than 5-acres is one of the few fresh water lakes in The Bahamas and is home to over 200 teal ducks. Mr. Groves raised all sorts of livestock on the island, cows, donkeys, mules, and monkeys, as well as numerous species of birdlife such as chickens, pheasants, peacocks, flamingos, parrots, ducks, turkeys, and geese. Much of the birdlife was grown for personal consumption, but today, under the new British owner, the birds are strictly for watching, not for the pot. Today Little Whale Cay remains private and visits ashore must be by invitation only. The huge boulders that replace the broken seawall on the northwest side of the cay were brought from Freeport and placed there after Hurricane Andrew's destruction.

Whale Cay (Chart BR-9) has a unique history. It was once a coconut and sisal plantation and the private domain of Miss Marion B. Carstairs, an English woman well known in powerboat racing and aviation circles. She lived in the huge mansion on the cay and often threw very elegant, some say absolutely decadent, parties with many famous celebrities such as Betty Davis and Rock Hudson in attendance. The island had many fine roads built on it and Miss Carstairs and her guests often raced cars and motorcycles up and down the island at all hours of the day and night. Miss Carstairs actually owned the entire Berry Island chain at one time. She had purchased the entire group of islands and immediately sold all save Bird Cay Whale Cay, and Little Whale Cay. For more information about Marian Carstairs and Whale Cay see the section at the end of this chapter entitled *Marian Carstairs and Whale Cay*.

If passing Whale Cay to seaward give the island a wide berth of at least 1½ miles to seaward to avoid the extensive shallow reefs lying off its eastern shore. *Whale Cay Light* on the southeast side of the island was destroyed in Andrew and may not be rebuilt any time soon so consider it not functioning at the present time. There is a fair lee anchorage under the lighthouse at the southwestern end of the cay good in north to east winds although some surge works its way in around the point here. To gain the anchorage pass between Bird Cay and Whale Point and anchor just off the little beach wherever your draft allows. There is the hull of a wrecked sailboat on the pretty little beach and a submerged barge near the center of the cove. Watch out for snakes if you check out

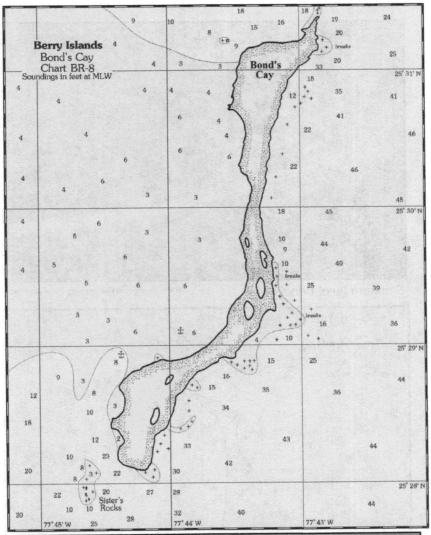

Bond's Cay to Little Whale Cay   Photo Courtesy of Paul Harding, Safari Seaplanes

Southern tip of Bond's Cay

Photo Courtesy of Paul Harding, Safari Seaplanes

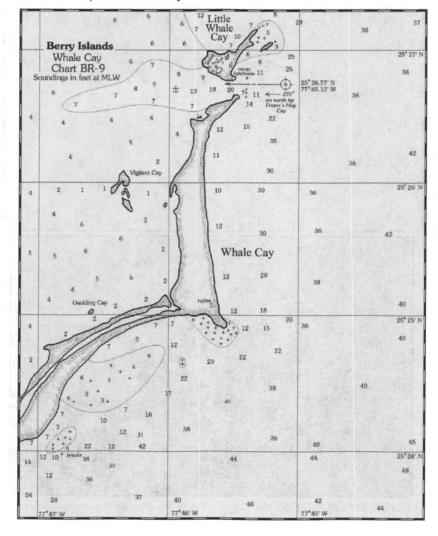

the lighthouse, but remember, there are no poisonous snakes in The Bahamas. Whale Cay is private and visits ashore are by invitation only.

Divers will want to check out *Whale Point Reef* lying just a quarter of a mile off Whale Point. Here scattered heads begin sloping off to a sandy bottom with huge coral heads in 60' of water. Some of the heads are 15' high and the structure is home to an abundance of sea life. A little further out a drop off to 300' supports just a few solitary heads. Start your dive with *Whale Point Light* bearing 300° and the conspicuous white house bearing 50°.

Navigational Information

Bird Cay (Chart BR-12), the most southern of the Berry Islands, is often mistakenly called Frazer's-Hog Cay which is actually the eastern half of the cay now more commonly called just Chub Cay (see next section *Chub Cay, Frazer's Hog Cay*). Bird Cay is approximately 130 acres and has several small ponds and groves of citrus and coconut. In the 1920's spongers lived here and also grew sisal on the island. Today the island is private with many elegant homes scattered about the cay. There is a lee side anchorage just off the southwestern tip of the cay but it gets very rolly in there when the surge works its way around the southern tip in east to southeast winds. The anchorage is just off the very conspicuous stone quarry near the tip of the cay.

To enter the anchorage a waypoint at 25° 23.45' N, 77° 51.05' W, will place you just southwest of the southwestern tip of Bird Cay. Head up into the lee of the cay along its western shore and anchor where your draft will allow. The anchorage shallows quickly the further north you head along the cay's lee shore. Bird Cay light was destroyed in *Hurricane Andrew* and may not be rebuilt for some time so don't expect it to be there when you are.

Chub Cay, Frazer's Hog Cay

Frazier - Hogg/Bird Cay:
25° 23.45' N, 77° 51.05' W

Chub Cay - 1 nm S of and on the 35° range:
25° 23.90' N, 77° 55.08' W

Chub Cay (see Chart BR-13) is the most visited island in the Berry chain, due to its prime location on the route from Nassau to Bimini across the *Great Bahama Banks*. Lying approximately 35 nautical miles from Nassau, Chub Cay is the popular stopping place for cruisers seeking to unwind after the long banks run or, if heading north, to prepare for the stretch to Bimini or Gun Cay.

Devastated by *Hurricane Andrew*, *The Chub Cay Marina and Hotel*, now simply known as the *Chub Cay Club*, has now been rebuilt for the better. Chub Cay is a *Port of Entry* and skippers can clear *Customs* and *Immigration* at the *Chub Cay Club* dock. There is a fee for using the marina dock to clear *Customs* but if you stay overnight the fee is applied to your dockage (you'll also have to pay this fee if you plan to tie up just to pick up some groceries at the store).

Navigational Information

To find your way into the marina and anchorage a waypoint at 25° 23.90' N 77° 55.08' W will place you approximately one nautical mile south of the entrance to the marina and anchorage and on the 35° range. The range consists of two small daymarks that are lit red at night. If approaching at night look for the bright lights of the power station ashore lying well to the west of the *Batelco* tower with its flashing red light. The range is just a little west of the brightly-lit power station showing one red light over the other. *Chub Point Light* should show white when you're on station to take up the range. Take up an approximate course of 35° on the range and remember that the deeper water will be to your starboard. If you must stray, by all means, stray east as the principal danger, and one that must definitely be reckoned with, is *Mama Rhoda Reef* lying east and southeast of Mama Rhoda Rock. You can keep *Chub Point Light* close to starboard as there is deep water within 50 yards of the light. The light is sectored showing red in the dangerous sectors. Of course, this light is like all lights in The Bahamas, which is to say it is unreliable at best and subject to change.

If you are approaching Chub Cay from the east it is best to stay outside (south of) Diamond Rocks as there are some shallow reefs closer into the Chub Cay shore.

The Chub Cay anchorage, lying northwest and west of the light on Chub Point offers good protection from north through east but it can get rolly in anything from east to southeast, even in light winds a swell seems to work around Chub Point. Cruisers often complain of a scoured bottom and poor holding here.

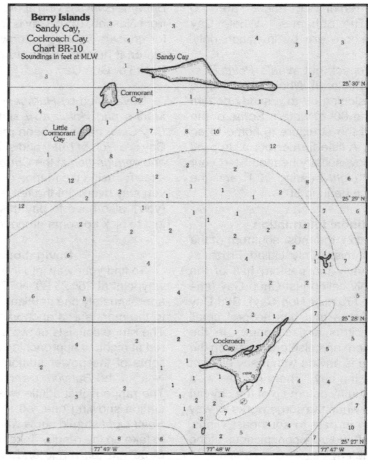

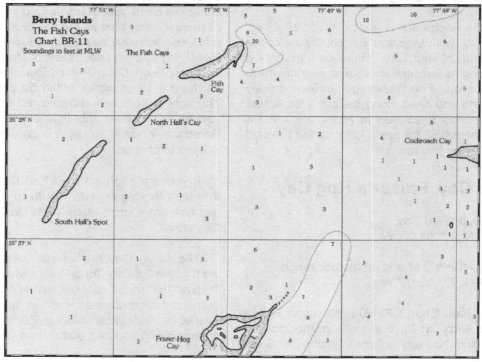

A good anchorage for boats drawing 4' or less lies between Crab Cay and Chub Cay as shown on Chart BR-13. This is where the fishing boats go to ride out fronts as the shallow bar (1' at low water) to the north of it breaks all northerly seas. There is a lot of current in here so use two anchors in a Bahamian moor. In northerly winds you can move east of Chub Point (but WATCH OUT for the shallow reefs as shown on Chart BR-13) just off the beach for a beautiful, calm anchorage, but be prepared to move back when the winds begin to come out of the east. Another nice spot is inside Texaco Point (as shown on Chart BR-12), but sometimes a surge works it's way around the point and makes for a rolly stay.

Another anchorage is along the eastern shore of Frazer's-Hog Cay, the easternmost of the two islands that are usually referred to as Chub Cay, it's best to use two anchors here as there is a lot of current. From the waypoint at 25° 23.45' N, 77° 51.05' W, work your way northward along the eastern shore in the deeper channel that parallels the shoreline, staying at least 100 yards off the land as you keep a lookout for the very visible shallow bar to the east between Frazer's-Hog Cay and Bird Cay. Here you'll find 7'-12' until you approach the area south of the large dock that was once the *Berry Islands Club* where you'll find up to 20' in places. The bottom is scoured in places and holding is iffy at best so take the proper precautions when setting your anchor. The area immediately off the dock and just a bit north and south of the dock is littered with rocks and old moorings, including and old trailer and dragline so use caution here and don't get your anchors fouled. This area is not the best spot to anchor in strong northeast-east winds even though most of the seas created by these winds are broken by the shallow bar between Frazer's-Hog Cay and Bird Cay to the east. The problem here is that you wind up beam-to the strong northeasterly winds as your vessel lies with the tidal current making for an uncomfortable ride twice a day.

The best spots to anchor are north or south of the dock at the *Berry Islands Club* and a bit northward towards the point at the northeast tip of Frazer's Hog Cay. At the northeast point of Frazer's Hog Cay is a shallow sand bank that is often occupied by a colony of large rays who like to settle in the sand with only their eyes showing. Be careful if you're walking through here, don't step on one, although they show no fear of humans they are not the least bit aggressive.

What You Will Find Ashore

I'm happy to relate that the *Berry Islands Club*, formerly the *Frazer's Cay Club*, is once again fully operational. The marina offers 15 slips, electricity, R/O water, fuel, showers, Wifi, a great restaurant, a beach grill, a bar, and a gift shop. The marina also offers gas and diesel and can arrange transportation to *Customs* for you. For more info call Howard at 242-357-5617 or Harry at 242-466-9364 or 504-655-8464.

The building housing the *Berry Islands Club* was the first house ever built on Chub Cay over 50 years ago and the marina predated the later *Chub Cay Marina*, which was built in 1962. In its prime the site was also known as the *Berry Island Club* and was originally built by the *Stamford, Conn. Yacht Club*.

The club has a lot of history. The *Berry Islands Club* was once host to the likes of Ernest Hemmingway and other avid fishermen of the day who frequented these waters when this was the only fuel stop between Nassau and Bimini.

On the other side of the island, the *Chub Cay Marina and Resort* has 80 slips with a least depth of 7'-9'. Three new computer-controlled generators work hard to insure you of uninterrupted 115v-30-amp to 220v-3 phase-100 amp power available at daily or metered rates. The marina, which monitors VHF ch. 68, is a *Texaco Starport* selling diesel and gas as well as R/O water that is available at each slip. Laundry and shower facilities are also located on shore next to Patricia White's well-stocked *Island Store* (food as well as spirits, but no meat or fish). There are five telephones located on the island (you must use a *Batelco* card, you can pick these up at the *Island Store*) with three at the marina itself, copy and fax service is available and cable TV is now at each slip. You can rent a golf cart and ride around the island where access to the hotel's swimming pool, beach, and tennis courts is now available for guests of the marina. The marina has transparent kayaks for rent if you wish to check out *Mama Rhoda Reef*, as well as cell phones, but you'll have to rent the phone plus purchase the card. *The Harbour House Restaurant and Lounge* serves breakfast, lunch, and dinner in a relaxed and informal atmosphere (open from 0700-0900 for breakfast, from 1200-1400 for lunch, and from 1900-2100 for dinner). If you just need to tie up at the dock to pick up a few groceries be forewarned that the marina charges $25 for this

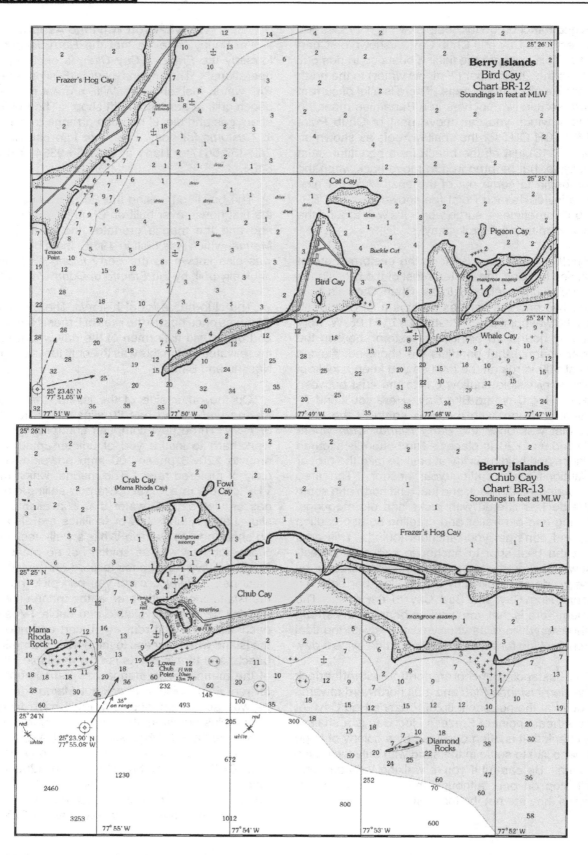

Berry Islands
Bird Cay
Chart BR-12
Soundings in feet at MLW

Berry Islands
Chub Cay
Chart BR-13
Soundings in feet at MLW

luxury. The marina also charges a fee of $100 to tie up for *Customs* clearance, but the fee is waived if you stay overnight.

Those not arriving by boat to Chub Cay can fly in on the nearby 5,000' runway. Fishermen will want to charter with Capt. George to sample the local piscatorial action. You can also try Joe Louis as a fishing guide, just ask at the marina office. There is an island bus that charges $3 per person and monitors VHF ch. 71. Also on the marina grounds you will find the *Bahama Islands Adventures Dive Charters* where you can arrange a custom dive charter for you or your group in the surrounding waters diving the steep wall drop off at Rum Cay or the reefs off Bird Cay. For information in the U.S., call 1-800-329-1337. If you need outboard repairs, ask Jared or Terence, the dockmasters at *Chub Club*, to contact Anthony Martin, the local wrench. Basil Sands can be contacted for diesel repairs when he's not working at the local power plant. Mr. Oliver, the chief of maintenance at the marina may be able to help you with any wiring, plumbing, or refrigeration problems on your boat.

A great dive or snorkel is *Mama Rhoda Reef* lying just south of Mama Rhoda Rock. The reef begins in about 10' of water with scattered heads forming a huge reef structure of coral mounds and crevices down to a depth of almost 80'. Parallel walls rise some 10' high and span 30' wide to a depth of about 75'. The reef gives way to a sandy shelf followed by a deep-water drop off with just a few scattered heads. Best diving begins about ½ mile south of Mama Rhoda Rock with the Chub Cay water tower bearing 355º and Chub Point Light bearing about 75º. For those interested in the names of places such as this, Mama Rhoda Cay was named after Rhoda Morris who lived on what is now known as Crab Cay (then Mama Rhoda Cay) in the late 1800's. She lived off the generosity of the local spongers but died a pauper in an asylum on New Providence.

Shellers should ask about *Sanddollar Hill*, a spit of sand that is only an island at low water and lies to the west of Chub Cay along the edge of the banks. Here shelling is great after a blow. Cockroach Cay, lying approximately 2½ miles northeast of Frazer's-Hog Cay has a large duck pond in the center that was once a good hunting spot.

The mangrove creeks along in the interior of Chub Cay/Frazer's-Hog Cay are ideal for exploration.

The entrance is north of Diamond Rocks along the Frazer's-Hog shore. There are some shallow reefs lining the entrance channel into the tidal creeks so be careful in your dinghy.

Marian Carstairs and Whale Cay

Whale Cay forms the southeastern corner of the Berry Islands chain, a crescent shaped string of thirty some cays lying along the eastern edge of the *Great Bahama Bank*. The pale green waters to their west are so shallow that some areas dry at anything below a half tide and fishermen can still find conch in knee deep water. To the east lie the cobalt blue waters of the deep *Northwest Providence Channel* where the offshore fishing is nothing short of impressive. South of Whale Cay, wavelets from the northern tip of the much deeper *Tongue of the Ocean* tickle the beautiful little beach at Buckle Cut.

Today Whale Cay, sometimes called Big Whale Cay, is a quiet, well-kept private cay. Its roads, gardens, and houses are immaculately kept by local caretakers who reside on the island in their own small houses. The old mansion on the western shore looks as if it was built last year. It wasn't. It was built in 1936. From 1934, when the cay sold for $440,000, until 1975 when the cay sold for $1 million, Whale Cay was the private domain of Marian Carstairs of powerboat racing fame. Ms. Carstairs was the sole ruler of Whale Cay, and none dared deny her authority, not even the government in Nassau.

Marian Carstairs was born in 1900 and inherited a fortune derived primarily from her grandfather's partnership with John D. Rockefeller in the early years of the *Standard Oil Company*. Even early on, as well as in her later years, she enjoyed dressing as a man. Marian Carstairs preferred to be called simply, Joe, and Joe Carstairs touted her lesbian nature with grace and poise in a period when it was not as socially acceptable as it is today. In spite of her obvious sexual bent, it has been speculated that Joe Carstairs married a man briefly to secure her inheritance after her mother threatened to cut off her lesbian daughter.

Joe soon began driving British military officers around in Ireland between 1916 and 1919 when she headed for France to help out with the war effort. It was during these years that Joe took to wearing close cropped hair and men's boots. After the war

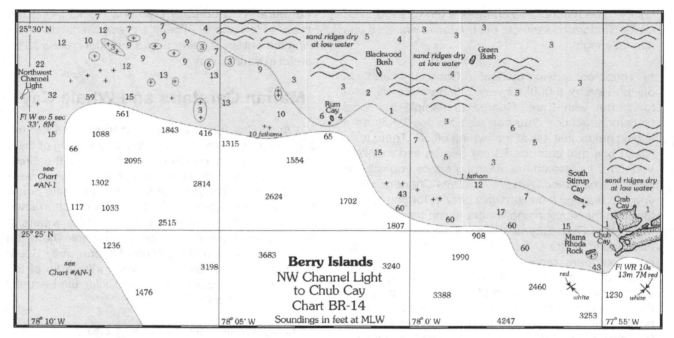

Joe moved back to London where she would drive a motorcycle to work. To say that Joe Carstairs had a lust for living life to the fullest would probably be an understatement. During these years her love of speed matured as she would often race her cars and motorcycles against all comers. Then, in 1925, Joe Carstairs purchased her first powerboat, *Gwen* (later renamed *Newg* after capsizing) and for the next five years immersed herself in powerboat racing where she became the premier British powerboat racer and the "fastest woman on the water." Also in 1925, Joe became involved with Lord Tod Wadley who was to become her lifelong companion. Lord Tod Wadley was extremely short, only about 13" tall, and made of leather. He was a small male doll that had been manufactured in Germany and given to Joe Carstairs as a present from a girlfriend. Joe dressed up Lord Tod Wadley in the finest clothes and took him everywhere, even putting his name on the plaque at her front door.

Of course, being rich, famous, and wild, Joe Carstairs learned how to throw a party early on and how to successfully hobnob with the best of them. During this period Joe Carstairs' name was associated with Alice B. Toklas, Gertrude Stein, Beatrice Lilly, Dolly Wilde (Oscar Wilde's niece), Greta Garbo, Tallulah Bankhead, and Marlene Dietrich with whom she had a brief affair (so infatuated with Dietrich was Carstairs that she later offered her Whale Cay), Dietrich declined but Carstairs deeded her a beach

on the island instead). Of course publicity follows a lifestyle such as hers and in the early 1930's, Joe Carstairs sought escape. She saw an ad for an island in The Bahamas and suddenly she was on her way.

When Joe Carstairs went shopping for an island and settled upon Whale Cay, she found that she had to purchase the entire Berry Island chain or nothing at all. Reluctantly agreeing to the purchase, she immediately sold all the islands save Bird Cay, Whale Cay, Little Whale Cay, and Bonds Cay. Ms. Carstairs was the half-sister of Sir Francis Francis who later purchased nearby Bird Cay and Bond's Cay just to the north. Sir Francis Francis' previous four ancestors were also named Francis Francis. Sir Francis passed away several years ago but Lady Francis still lives on Bird Cay and maintains her British traditions with elegance, style, and taste; tea promptly at four, dinner promptly at eight, formal dress required. I have never met Lady Francis, but I feel that she will not appreciate what I have to say about Whale Cay. I find the recent history of Whale Cay most intriguing. Not just because of the lifestyle enjoyed there, but in light of the range of guests who enjoyed it. People like Bette Davis, Rock Hudson, and numerous other celebrities from the worlds of politics, entertainment, and sports who at one time or another relished in the pleasures available on Whale Cay.

Joe Carstairs turned the scrub-covered island into her own version of paradise though she constantly fought poisonwood, dust, the subtropical heat, rain, poor living conditions (tents), mosquitoes, sandflies, and workers who didn't want to work in spite of Joe Carstairs' admonitions (they called her 'the boss'). Soon Joe had 200 people working on the island and her micropolis was taking shape. She soon had built the *Great House* with its *Whale Cay Museum*, it was actually the library of the *Great House* which housed trophies, weapons, stuffed fish and wild animals, and various other curios pertaining to Joe Carstairs' life including the stuffed island dog, John. She also built a huge cistern, several roads, rebuilt the lighthouse, and thoroughly landscaped the majority of the island. With the infrastructure in place Joe began bringing all manner of boats to the cay. She soon designed and helped build an 85' schooner in a shed on the island.

But life on Whale Cay was not all fun and games. Joe Carstairs actually ruled the island and was the only figure of authority to her burgeoning population of workers and staff. She had several workers whom she armed and used as her own island police force and she often had to act as judge, jury, and executioner to handle acts of violence, theft, and other petty offenses. At one time Joe received notice from the government in Nassau after they had reviewed a complaint by a former employee of Whale Cay. Nassau informed Joe by letter that her legal ministrations were illegal and Joe Carstairs simply tore up the letter and added it to the trash pile. By her own admonition Joe Carstairs ruled a country and nobody else could tell her how to run it. Whale Cay had its own police force, church, and economy, complete with its own bank and store that was said to have been the largest in The Bahamas in 1940 when Whale Cay's population swelled to over 500 souls. But Joe Carstairs was more than despot, tyrant, ruler, and Queen; she was often mother-confessor for her workers and frequently helped them out with their personal problems. While she detested lazy workers, she fired those that worked her people too hard. Children born on the island were taken to her for naming she was so loved. She educated her workers, instituted a health-care program for them, and even paid for their funerals.

Joe Carstairs loved to party, she was constantly throwing parties on Whale Cay. Guests would call the parties elegant affairs hosted by a lovely lady. The locals called them decadent orgies directed by a wild lesbian (at one party it is said that everyone was nude. except for Joe who only wore a hunting knife strapped to her thigh).

Residents of neighboring islands began noticing the sounds of fast cars and motorcycles at all hours of the day and night. Whale Cay has an excellent network of small, narrow roads built out of crushed native limestone. It seems that Joe Carstairs and her guests would race her fleet of cars and motorcycles up and down the roads whenever it suited them. There were no cops, no red lights, no speed limit; the waters edge the only real obstacle.

The water's edge is also a favorite spot for guests to relax, sun bathe, and swim. The residents of the nearby cays soon learned to accept the fact that nobody on Whale Cay's beaches wore clothes. They also soon learned to accept the fact that if they looked too hard, they might spot a couple in the middle of lovemaking. Not too bad really, even by Bahamian standards. It happens on all the islands. But soon neighbors were eyeing something new to their conservative moral beliefs. Men and women in the throws of passion…with other men and women, homosexuality being almost unknown at that time in The Bahamas.

During World War II, with the need for an Army of some sort to defend The Bahamas, Joe Carstairs rose to the occasion. Joe already had her own army of sorts, her *Boy Scouts* as she called them, the *87th Bahamas Boy Scout Troop* that was actually a group of 100 men. Joe Carstairs supplied them with weapons, and imported combat veterans to train the young men. She soon had her own army and though they never saw any action, they were instrumental in a rescue. In 1942 the American ship *Potlach* was torpedoed off Bird Rock and Crooked Island. Joe Carstairs was asked to take her own boat and mount a rescue mission through waters that were well known to German U-boat skippers. She eventually found and rescued 47 sailors and transported them to Nassau.

Other than that one event, Joe's "army" did little in the way of defense, rather they were used for show. When the Duke of Windsor arrived in Nassau as Governor in 1940, the *Boy Scout* troop, all decked out in their finest regalia, lined the streets and Joe Carstairs even supplied a 25-man band from Whale Cay. The Duke visited Whale Cay in 1941 and was astounded at the quality of the roads verbally wishing that every out-island had roads built of such high standards.

After World War II, a neighbor complained to a magistrate in Nassau concerning the activities on Whale Cay and stirred up a hornet's nest of interest in some circles. The magistrate took it upon himself to visit Whale Cay and put and end to the mischief once and for all. Upon landing at Whale Cay the magistrate was surrounded by Queen Carstairs' armed *Boy Scouts*, her elite *Royal Guards*. Joe arrived shortly thereafter and informed the magistrate in no uncertain terms that Whale Cay was her island and that he was not welcome. The magistrate was to leave immediately and she did not give a damn about what he had to say about the law and this and that. This was her island BY GOD and nobody had any say-so here but her. Nassau, *His Majesty's Court*, and the magistrate himself could all go to hell as far as she was concerned. She ruled here and that was that. The magistrate had no choice but to return to Nassau, give his report, and Ms. Carstairs was never bothered by Nassau bureaucrats again.

A hurricane in 1949 devastated the cay, but the worst damage it did was to run off Joe Carstair's girlfriend. The following years showed a decline in the island population until by 1957 there were less than 100 people on Whale Cay. Joe Carstairs' health began declining as did her popularity with her own workers who now stood outside the *Great House* shouting abuse at her.

Carstairs began spending more time in Miami living on a houseboat with a new girlfriend and finally sold Whale Cay in 1975 for $1 million saying that increasing drug trafficking forced the sale before she was provoked into shooting someone. After the sale she spent the winters in Florida and the summers in Long Island like so many other snowbirds.

Marian Carstairs, the fastest woman on water, poet, Queen, patron, general, admiral, pilot, ship designer, car and motorcycle racer, died in December of 1993 just a few weeks short of her 94th birthday. An American newspaper carried the story with the headline "Ruler of Whale Cay Dies."

There is so much more to Joe Carstairs life. If anyone is interested in learning the details of Joe Carstairs' life and times, pick up a copy of her biography, *The Queen of Whale Cay* by Kate Summerscale, it's listed in the *References* section in the back of this book. There is so much more to the tale and it can be found in Ms. Summerscale's work.

Andros

Ports of Entry: Congo Town, Fresh Creek,
Mangrove Cay, Morgan's Bluff
Fuel: Fresh Creek, *Kamalame Cove Marina*
Haul-Out: None
Diesel Repairs: Fresh Creek
Outboard Repairs: Fresh Creek
Propane: Morgan's Bluff, Nicoll's Town, Fresh Creek
Provisions: Morgan's Bluff, Nicoll's Town, Fresh
Creek, Mangrove Cay
Important Lights:
Morgan's Bluff channel: Fl R & G
Bethel Channel Range: Fl W ev 5 sec (two lights)
AUTEC G. Murphy Buoy: Fl W
Fresh Creek entrance channel: Fl G
AUTEC Site #1 sea buoy: Fl W ev 4 sec
High Cay: FLW ev 4 sec
Autec Site #2 Sea Buoy: Fl W
AUTEC #3 sea buoy: Fl W ev 4 sec
Little Golding Cay: Fl W ev 5 sec
South Bight Sirius Rock: Fl W ev 3 sec
Duncan Rock: Fl W ev 3.3 sec
Tinker Rock: Fl W ev 4 sec
Green Cay: Fl W ev 3 sec

Andros is the largest of all Bahamian Islands with over 2300 square miles of land area lying about 20 miles from New Providence at its closest point. The approximately 105-mile long by 40-mile wide island resembles a huge jigsaw puzzle separated by hundreds of creeks creating a massive swampy interior, a home to numerous birds and ducks that is best explored by small boat or dinghy. There are three "rivers" which divide the pine-forested island into three distinct sections at North, Middle, and South Bight, while Mangrove Cay serves to separate the northern from the southern part of Andros. Andros is widely known for its vast mangrove creeks, which offer some of the finest, if not the best, bonefishing in the world. Offshore the island is home to the world's third largest barrier reef along its eastern shore at the Tongue of the Ocean. There is spectacular diving anywhere along its 145-mile length where it drops some 6,000' to the canyon-like bottom of the Tongue of the Ocean.

The island was originally shown as *Espirtu Santo* by the early Spaniards on early charts around 1550. There are quite a few stories as to how the island received its name. Although there is an Andros Island in the Aegean Sea with little, save a temple dedicated to *Bacchus*, to set it apart from any other island in the Aegean, a popular theory is that the island was named after Sir Edmund Andros, Commander of the Forces in Barbados from 1672-1674. From 1674 onward Andros was successively Governor of New York, Massachusetts, Virginia, and Maryland, a very busy man indeed. In a map of 1872 the island is called *San Andreas,* and in 1806 is once again called *Andreas Island.* The island most likely received its name in 1787, when Andros was selected as a haven by over 150 beleaguered residents of *St. Andro* on the Mosquito Coast of Nicaragua. The islanders requested to be moved to Andros after an 1873 treaty with Spain led to their evacuation. The Bahamas provided transportation and deeded several parcels of land to some 70 men of British descent.

After the Siboneys and Lucayans left the island the first permanent settlers are believed to be Seminole Indians who sailed their canoes across the *Straits of Florida.* Bahamian wreckers told the Seminoles that there was a free land to the east. Fleeing what they thought was to be a life of slavery at the hands of southern plantation owners, some 40-50 Seminoles and a party of escaped black slaves paddled their canoes across the *Gulf Stream* and settled on the deserted western shore of Andros between 1821 and 1840. The settlement was called Red Bays after the color of the sands in the area. The government of The Bahamas didn't even know about them until the hurricane of 1866 wiped out the settlement. The Seminoles contacted the government representative and told him of their plight, offering to buy land to become citizens. In 1879, the government resettled the Seminoles 10 miles farther south at Lewis Coppice and renamed it Red Bays. Today if you visit Red Bays you will find that the residents create some of the most delightful basketry to be found in The Bahamas. Quite a few of the people you meet in Red Bays are direct descendants of these same Seminole warriors. I'd like to add that those in search of excellent straw work should make an effort to visit this small community. The ladies here create some first class work that is usually sold in Nassau for much more than you can purchase it for in Red Bays. You will find some great deals on straw work here; some people sell their work out of their homes, or you can check with the small variety store on the road into the settlement.

The legend of the *Chickcharnie*, sometimes written as Chick Charnie or Chickcharnee, the red-eyed creature who lives in pine trees, is said to have a basis in a Seminole Indian story. The *Chickcharnie*, as the legend says, is an elf-like creature resembling a bird with red eyes, three fingers, and three toes. In some versions they have a tail which they use to hang from trees. The *Chickcharnie* builds its nest between the heads of three pine trees, which it binds together in the form of a tripod and is generally peaceful when left unmolested. The legend states that the Chickcharnies adopted and trained Billy Bowleg, the great Seminole medicine man who was able to cure any disease. Taking young Billy at the age of 14, the *Chickcharnies* kept him for five years and when he returned to his people his reputation as a healer spread throughout The Bahamas.

One source of the story of the "little red men" originated with Hilton Albury, a successful sponge merchant and sportsman who lived on Andros at the beginning of the 20th century. He spent a lot of his time hunting birds in the interior of Andros, which had an incredible number of ducks in the winter. To keep his fertile hunting ground secret it is said that he began the tale of a band of pygmies who lived in the interior of the island and shot intruders with poisoned arrows. His tale and the *Chickcharnie* legend were somehow merged and corrupted in the retelling.

Many people felt the wrath of the *Chickcharnies* when they began to destroy their beloved forest. A story is told of a preacher who cut down all the trees on his land because he believed they were occupied by *Chickcharnies*. It is said that if you see a *Chickcharnie* that you will have good luck for the rest of your life, but if you are harboring any bad thoughts about the *Chickcharnie*, or if you try to harm it, then your life will be filled with bad luck, the *Chickcharnie* may even turn your head around backwards. A perfect example of being struck with bad luck by a *Chickcharnie* may be Neville Chamberlain, the former Prime Minister of England who grew up on Andros managing his father's sisal plantation. Against the advice of his foreman he cut down one of the *Chickcharnie's* favorite trees. The *Chickcharnies* worked their hoodoo on Chamberlain which stayed with him to Munich and may have changed the course of history.

Today researchers believe that the residents of Andros actually mistook the *Giant Barn Owl*, which once inhabited the island but is now extinct, for the legendary *Chickcharnie*. If you happen across a *Chickcharnie* remember not to laugh or turn your head. The island is also said to have a Loch Ness-type monster, a sea dragon called the *Lusca*. Other mythological Androsian creatures are the *Bosee Anansee*, and the *Yahoo*.

A very real creature that you may spy is the rare great lizard cuckoo. Barely able to fly, this docile creature will allow you to come within a few feet of it before it hops or waddles away. Up until World War II there were flocks of pink flamingos on the island. Bored pilots on training missions out of Nassau would often fly over the vast flocks of pink birds to stir them up and set them in flight. After a few years of these types of disturbances the flamingos fled for quieter waters. Although there are quite a few cays throughout The Bahamas that have colonies of small iguanas growing up to 3', there have been reports of iguanas on Andros growing to 6'. One creature that you will find in great numbers here are buzzards. Yes, that's right. Buzzards! You won't find them on other Bahamian islands but on Andros they are everywhere. Some people jokingly refer to them as the *Bahamian Air Force*.

The western shore of Andros is undeveloped and the settlement of Red Bays on the northwestern tip of the island is the only inhabited area on the entire western shore. The very shallow waters off the western shore of Andros are known as *The Mud*, a fantastic, rich, 20-mile wide sponging ground running from South Bight to the northern tip of Andros. Over the last few decades the western shore of Andros has gained notoriety for the drug smuggling activity in the area. For the better part of the late 1970's through the mid to late 1980's, Andros was a very popular spot with those who sought fortune by running cocaine and marijuana to the United States (Please note that this is **not** the case today). Most of the local areas had their own "groups" of young people who were often involved with illegal activities, some would now call them gangs. Each group had their own "turfs," for example, there might be a group called, say, the *Mastic Point Boys*, or the *Nicoll's Town Boys*, or the *Lowe Point Boys* (all fictitious names mind you!). They even had a bar where they partied and that each group treated as neutral territory.

At about this time pilots were warned not to fly low over Andros. It seems that planes that were flying low over Andros were considered drug runners and certain, roguish characters would shoot at the wings or wing tanks hoping that they would blow up and the

Western shore of Andros showing creeks and blue holes

Photo Courtesy of Paul Harding, Safari Seaplanes

plane would crash and not burn up on landing saving the precious cargo for the shooters. A modern version of the old Bahamian art of wrecking. I have heard of tales of two pilots who were found deep within the pine barrens of Andros hanging from a tree with their throats cut. One person I know of lived on Andros during this time and decided to visit Red Bays one day. On the road to Red Bays he was met by two locals on motorcycles with automatic weapons who suggested that my friend did not wish to visit Red Bays that particular day. Of course my friend agreed and went elsewhere, thankful for the sound advice.

Mariners during those years were advised by the *U.S. Coast Guard* to avoid the waters to the west of Andros. Many stories of boats being hijacked surfaced during this era, as well as lots of rumors. Most of the boats hijacked were fishing boats that plied the local waters. It is said that the "pirates" would come out in small boats at night to sneak aboard their intended victim and kill those aboard. An American boat with Bahamian owners was said to have been hijacked in just this way. In defense of the good people of Andros who are probably irritated by this account, you must understand that hijackings were also occurring in the Biminis and in the Freeport area at this time also.

The eastern shore of Andros is home to the third largest barrier reef in the world and has few entrances for vessels of any draft, all of which are impassable in a rage. The *Tongue of the Ocean* just offshore is a huge canyon in the sea with soundings up to one thousand fathoms. The *AUTEC* base at Fresh Creek has a small club on base called the *One Thousand Fathom Club*.

Andros is the only Bahamian island where fresh water meets seawater. There are several fresh water ponds and creeks stemming from springs in the interior of the island. The inland waterways of Andros offer a spectacular opportunity for dinghy exploration and fishing. Just pick a creek and head upstream, you'll find something along the way to pique your interest, but bring plenty of bug spray.

Andros is virtually honeycombed with blue holes, over 400 are scattered throughout the island and its surrounding waters. While these blue holes extend vertically to great depths in some places, most extend horizontally also. These blue holes are said to have formed over 15,000 years ago when the sea level was approximately 300' less than it is today. Some of these blue holes are home to a centipede-like crustacean, *Remepedia*, which is found nowhere else and whose closest relatives are fossils over 450 million years old.

In the 1960's, a Toronto research chemist by the name of George Benjamin began exploring the blue holes in and around Andros. Benjamin believed that these blue holes were actually part of a system of underwater caves that had once been above water. In

South Bight he found a cave, now called *Benjamin's Blue Hole*, that is one of the world's greatest underwater caves. In 1970, George Benjamin, and his son Peter, proved that these caves had actually at one time been above sea level. They discovered a spectacular cave absolutely bristling with stalactites and stalagmites. For those of you unfamiliar with spelunking, stalactites and stalagmites are deposits formed from dripping water and water cannot drip in a submerged cave. Jacques Cousteau later visited Andros and with Benjamin's help filmed the cave and renamed it *The Grotto*. *The National Geographic Magazine* published a story about George Benjamin's exploits in 1970.

In September of 1996, deep in an inland blue hole called *Stargate*, divers excavated an ancient Lucayan canoe. The 6' long canoe, which may be as much as 500-800 years old and carved from a single log, was discovered by Rob Palmer about 60' down in the 300' deep blue hole. Palmer, who first dove *Stargate* in 1985 when he filmed it for the *National Geographic Society*, had actually been working in the deeper levels of the hole when he made his discovery. Palmer, who has been diving on blue holes for 15 years, had previously discovered 16 Lucayan skeletons in another nearby blue hole on Andros.

Why the canoe was placed on a ledge in the blue hole remains a mystery. Speculation has it that the canoe was actually too small to have been used at sea and that it may have been placed in the cave as part of a burial custom. Lucayan myths of creation centered around an underground world. They believed that their race, as well as the sun and the moon, arose from the center of the earth. As a burial custom it may have meaning as a spiritual return to the place of their origin. The canoe is slated to become an exhibit at The *Bahamas National Museum* in Nassau.

Approaches to Andros

Andros lies "down to leeward" from Nassau making it easy to get to for sailors but hard to return from against the prevailing winds. From the western entrance of Nassau Harbour, the waypoint off Morgan's Bluff bears 295° at a distance of 36.3 nautical miles. From the waypoint off Chubb Cay, Morgan's Bluff bears 208° at a distance of 13.6 nautical miles.

The entrance to Fresh Creek bears 214° from Golding Cay at the western end of New Providence at a distance of 20.2 miles. From Chub Cay, Fresh Creek bears 174° at a distance of 40.4 miles. From the northern Exumas, Fresh Creek is a straight shot in hazard free waters. From Warderick Wells, Fresh Creek bears approximately 298° at a distance of 62.1 nautical miles. From Gun Cay in the Biminis, the waypoint at the northern tip of the Joulters bears 105° at 62.5 miles.

The barrier reef that stretches along the eastern shore of Andros has only a few navigable breaks. The narrow waterway between the reef and Andros is very shallow and strewn with numerous shallow heads and patch reefs. The inside route from Morgan's Bluff to Fresh Creek should only be attempted by vessels drawing 6' or less with good visibility and a rising, almost high tide in some places. The inside route from Fresh Creek southward to South Bight should only be attempted by vessels drawing less than 5'.

AUTEC, the *Atlantic Undersea Testing and Evaluation Center,* has several buoys placed in strategic positions in the *Tongue of the Ocean* east of Andros. They are listed in *Appendix D* and their positions noted. Use caution when approaching these buoys as *AUTEC* and the *U.S. Navy* may be conducting tests and may ask you to keep a distance of at least 3 nautical miles from their position. Bear in mind that the position of these buoys may change with the needs of *AUTEC*.

The Joulters Cays

North Joulters:
25° 24.25' N, 78° 09.45' W

Joulters East:
25° 22.30' N, 78° 07.35' W

Joulters Cay anchorage - ¼ nm E of bar:
25° 18.52' N, 78° 07.00' W

Off the northern tip of Andros, stretching from just north of Morgan's Bluff to just south of Northwest Channel Light, lie the Joulters Cays. To the north and west of the Joulters lies an enormous shallow bank, some of which is high and dry at low tide while other areas are overgrown with mangroves. Coming from Gun Cay, there is a route that passes north and then east of the Joulters bringing you to Morgan's Bluff by a passage inside the reef. This route will bring you around and through several shallow areas with quite

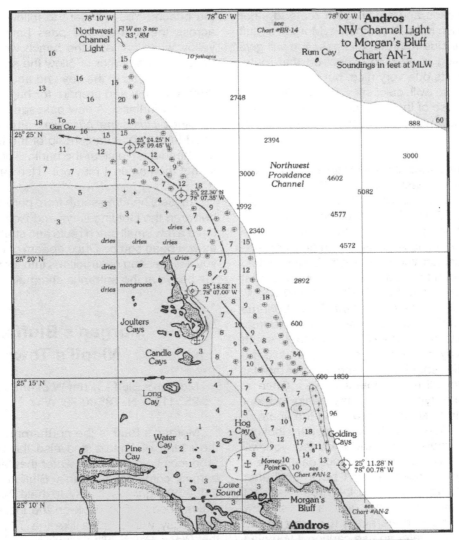

Andros
NW Channel Light
to Morgan's Bluff
Chart AN-1
Soundings in feet at MLW

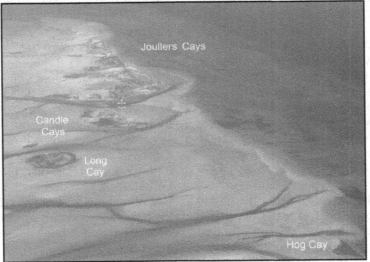

The Joulters Cays

Photo Courtesy of Paul Harding, Safari Seaplanes

a few shallow heads and small patch reefs to steer around. If you wish to head south from Morgan's Bluff to Fresh Creek inside the reef, this passage will give you a small inkling of what to expect on that route. The Joulters boasts one very nice, but tricky to enter anchorage that we will discuss. The Joulters are noteworthy because of their unique sand, one of only three places in the world where this type of sand is found.

Navigational Information

Vessels heading east from Gun Cay can steer approximately 105° for 62.5 miles to a waypoint at 25° 24.25' N, 78° 09.45' W. This will place you in about 15' of water well north of the bank that surrounds the Joulters to the north and west as shown on Chart AN-1. From this position you must really begin piloting by eye as you begin to head in a generally southeast direction to a waypoint at 25° 22.30' N, 78° 07.35' W, which places you near the edge of the *Great Bahama Bank*, well east of the worst shallows and sandbores. Vessels with drafts of less than 5' can turn more south and work their way through this maze and avoid the small detour to the east but the detour is not that far out of the way for all the trouble it saves. Once at this easternmost waypoint, you may begin to steer a little more south to southwest to close the shore of the Joulters about ½-1 mile off. Keep a sharp lookout for shallows and reefs, there are still a few you will have to pilot your way around. To your east there is no barrier reef yet, it really doesn't begin until after Morgan's Bluff though there is a long reef just east of the Golding Cays. There are quite a few shallow heads and small patch reefs along the edge of the bank and the deeper water so use caution if you plan to proceed to the east into deeper water.

As you approach the long white beach on the eastern shore of the cays to your starboard side, you may wish to enter the lovely anchorage that lies of its southern point. Vessels with drafts of 5' or less can enter on a high tide. There is a shallow bar with almost 3' over it at low water that you must cross before you get into the deeper channel which has 6'-7' along the beach. The anchorage area at the southern tip has 8' at low tide. A waypoint at 25° 18.52' N, 78° 07.00' W, will place you approximately ¼ mile east of the shallow bar. From this waypoint follow the darker water in towards the rocky bluff with the old house that is partly hidden by casuarinas. Well off your port bow, just east of the long white beach, you will see a very obvious yellow/white shallow bar that parallels the beach. You will want to follow the darker water across the 3' area and pass between the obvious yellow/white bar and the beach where you will pick up the deeper water. Follow the shoreline around to the southern tip of the cay and anchor wherever your draft will allow and prepare for bugs if the weather is hot and windless. A new passage may have opened up since *Hurricane Michelle*. From the anchorage head to the southeastern tip of the island where you can head east to clear the bank. This may have filled in, but then again it may not. Use caution.

Vessels heading south from here can steer to pass between the Golding Cays and Hog Cay, but you will have a few small patch reefs and shallow bars to avoid as you head south. Once abeam of the Golding Cays you will have no obstructions into Morgan's Bluff save the buoys at the entrance channel.

Morgan's Bluff and Nicoll's Town

Morgan's Bluff - ¼ nm W of entrance channel: 25° 11.28' N, 78° 00.78' W

Morgan's Bluff is the northernmost settlement on the island of Andros and also the busiest. Andros produces so much fresh water that tankers and water barges come to Morgan's Bluff to take on some 6,000,000 gallons a day to help Nassau meet her water needs. The dock on the inside of the jetty is kept busy with tankers like the *Titas* or barges like the *Black Point*. The small inner harbour and the large concrete dock just inside the jetty at Pleasant Bay are used by the smaller freighters and mailboats. For many years there has been some concern about yachtsmen using the inner harbour in bad weather. Many people said that you cannot use the harbour, that it was prohibited, that the locals would tell you to leave. It may have been that way at one time, but today cruisers are welcome. The inner harbour is now open to cruising boats if needed, but I recommend it only in case of an emergency. This is a dredged harbour and the holding is fair to good inside but you'll be better off with one anchor down and another line tied off ashore to a bollard, but please do not block the docks. Visitors are welcome to tie off to the freight boats if needed during bad weather, they usually don't mind, but ask first.

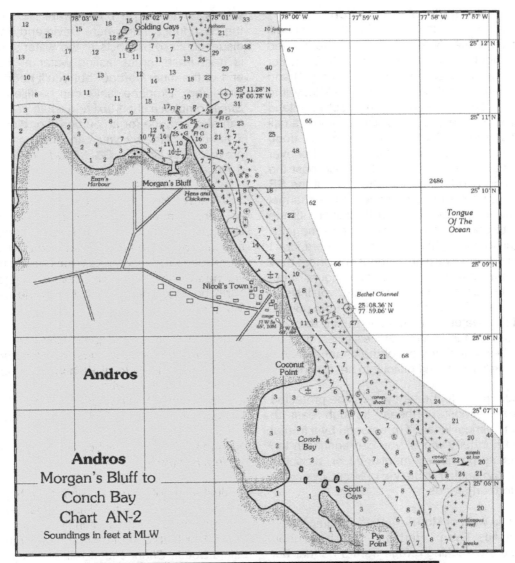

Andros

Andros
Morgan's Bluff to
Conch Bay
Chart AN-2
Soundings in feet at MLW

Morgan's Bluff   Photo Courtesy of Paul Harding, Safari Seaplanes

Navigational Information

A waypoint at 25° 11.28' N, 78° 00.78' W will place you approximately ¼ mile west of the buoyed entrance channel as shown on Chart AN-2. Enter the well-marked channel (easy to enter at night) and follow the channel westward past the rock jetty into Pleasant Bay. There is a large range set up inland but it is really only necessary for larger ships, small boats will have no problem in this wide, 25' deep channel (watch out for large ship traffic whenever entering or leaving by this channel). Once past the jetty turn to port and tuck up into the cove at the SE end of the bay, be sure not to anchor in the channel leading to the inner harbour or in the vicinity of the large concrete dock on the western side of the jetty. Always run an anchor light when anchored here, don't even think of staying overnight without one, there may be large vessels moving in and out at all hours of the day and night so practice safe anchoring, you'll sleep better. Holding in the anchorage ranges from poor to good in 7'-11' of water, you just have to find the right spot. Pick one of the lighter patches of sand close in to shore. Don't anchor west of the channel as the bottom is very rocky and difficult to set an anchor.

If you tuck up inside the bay you will be protected in winds from almost northeast through east to southwest and almost west. If threatened by a frontal passage and northerly winds, you can anchor in the inner harbour as previously mentioned or, as some suggest, you can anchor in the lee of Hog Cay in 6'-7' of water in northerly winds.

About a mile west of Morgan's Bluff and just inside Money Point lies Evans Harbour. This is a good harbour if you are seeking refuge from a norther but only if you draw less than 3'. Another possibility is to anchor inside Lowe Sound. Here the entrance carries just under 3' at low water with 4' and more inside in places and you will have to eyeball your way in here, never attempt it at night or in poor visibility. Deeper draft vessels can anchor in as far as their draft allows and you'll gain some protection from the shallow banks and small cays to your west, northwest, and north.

What You Will Find Ashore

On the southwest side of the inner harbor at Morgan's Bluff is *Willie's Water Lounge* where you can get lunch, dinner, cold beverages, conversation, local knowledge, and even arrange a car rental through owner Wilmore Lewis. Willy also has a pool table

and is developing a book swap. Next to *Willie's* is the *Esso* fuel center where David and Patrick Romer dispense *Esso* products at the water's edge. There is free, fresh, great tasting water at the southeast end of the inner harbour but you'll need a hose and jerry jugs. Propane tanks can be filled at the huge *Shell* complex a short taxi ride south of *Willie's*. Willie can also arrange for an outboard or diesel mechanic if needed. Nearby you can pick up a few limited provisions at *Curry's*, *G&H Food Store*, and *Roberts & Rose Market*.

Nearby *Henry Morgan's Cave* is a system of subterranean limestone caves complete with stalagmites and stalactites. They are said to hold the treasure of the infamous pirate and Morgan's Bluff namesake Sir Henry Morgan but nobody has reported finding treasure here. The cave is on the main road north between the jetty dock and the settlement of Morgan's Bluff.

In late October Morgan's Bluff plays host to the *All Andros and Berry Islands Regatta*. On the beach at the southeast side of Pleasant Bay is the site of the *Regatta Village* where a plaque commemorates the *All Andros Regatta* and Morgan's Bluff. *Regatta Village* was built in 1994 and includes a viewing tower, numerous stalls, and a grandstand. At the end of June a mini-regatta is held to raise funds for the *All Andros Regatta*.

Just south of Morgan's Bluff is the highest section of Andros and here you will find the largest settlement (600 people) on Andros, Nicoll's Town. The hills are about 100' high and there is a break in the reef here called *Bethel Channel* that will take approximately 7' at low water. The town is very spread out with some of the houses and facilities right on the beach while most of the business on the main road that stretches towards Morgan's Bluff. A taxi or rental car is needed to explore this area. In fact, a rental car is the best way to see the areas from Morgan's Bluff south to Behring Point (be forewarned, you will be dodging some potholes and the occasional land crab).

Cruisers wishing to head south from Morgan's Bluff to Nicoll's Town or Fresh Creek inside the reef should read the next section, *Morgan's Bluff to Fresh Creek, The Inside Route*, for navigational information concerning that passage. In that section you will learn how to arrive at Nicoll's Town by sea and where to anchor.

If you elect to explore Nicoll's Town by car, and you drive down the main road leading from Morgan's Bluff to Nicoll's Town, you will first come across *Zelda's Restaurant*, *CIBC Bank*, an *Androsia* outlet store, a *Batelco* office, the government clinic with its resident doctor, and then the huge, pink *Government Building*, a beautiful Georgian-styled structure resembling *Government House* in Nassau. Nicoll's Town also has a small *International Square*, dedicated to the spirit of international friendship and cooperation. Behind the bank is *Lori's Cornucopia Deli* with its pool table and a little further down the road, as you approach the beach area, is the *Pineville Grocery*, a gas station, a branch of *Scotiabank*, and the noteworthy *Rumours Restaurant and Disco* with live music on weekends. A little further on is the *Pinewood Cafeteria*, the *Green Windows Inn and Restaurant* with a *Texaco* station (propane refills here) and convenience store next door.

As you approach the beach area you will find *Welle's Grocery*, *Rolle's Takeaway*, the *Dayshell Restaurant*, *Hunter's Restaurant and Bar*, and the *Donna Lee Motel and Restaurant* where you can also arrange for diving or fishing charters and even rent a car. The *Andros Beach Hotel* is a delightful place to stay. The restaurant can seat about 50 people and its red brick and wooden beam decor seems almost out of place in an out island getaway. Another good stop is *Angie's Poop Deck*, and if you need some medications visit *First Choice Prescription Pharmacy* near *Angie's*. Just north of town on the beach is a lovely little resort, The *Bahamas Coconut Farm Guest Lodge*.

On the main highway headed south from Nicoll's Town you will pass a *NAPA* store and then you'll see a small dirt track to the east the leads to *Uncle Charlie's Blue Hole*, you can't miss the huge sign. A little further south you'll come to the road to Red Bays that leads off to the west, and then, if you stay on the main road heading south, you'll arrive at the *Big Pine Yard Shopping Center* with a grocery, liquor, and variety store.

Heading south still you'll come to *Barbie's Restaurant* just before the airport. Barbie's serves everything from cracked conch to pizza and is a very popular spot. South of the airport, you might be surprised to find a *Mennonite* farm community along the main highway. A group of *Mennonites* from Pennsylvania established this community in 1983 and their neat orchards full of rich, green, fruit trees are a startling sight after driving past mile after mile of pine woods and scrub brush. Almost as startling is the sight of the *Mennonite* families in their traditional dress, quite the difference from the average islanders attire. The thirty or so *Mennonites* in this community are a true success story. They produce almost as much as the rest of the island's farmers and their garage keeps many local cars in top running condition. Most of the local resorts serve their fruits and vegetables with all their meals.

Morgan's Bluff to Fresh Creek
The Inside Route

Bethel Channel - ½ nm ENE of break in reef: 25° 08.36' N, 77° 59.06' W

Staniard Rock Passage - 1 nm ENE of reef: 24° 52.40' N, 77° 51.00' W

Navigational Information

Vessels drawing over 5' that are headed to Fresh Creek from Morgan's Bluff should head outside into the *Tongue of the Ocean*. Once outside keep at least a mile east of the barrier reef, roughly 3 miles or more offshore. If you draw between 5'-6', you can still take part of the inside route, but you'll have to go outside at Staniard Rock to arrive at the entrance to Fresh Creek. Bear in mind that a hurricane may change this route at any time, so use extreme caution.

Skippers whose vessels draw 5' or less can, with the help of the tide, excellent visibility, nerves of steel, and confidence in their ability to read the water, make a successful passage inside the reef from Morgan's Bluff to Fresh Creek. This trip is roughly 30 miles and a boat averaging 5-6 knots will take almost a full tide for the passage. When planning your departure remember that the shallowest spots are at the south end at Fresh Creek with a few spots off Staniard Creek, and one rocky spot about a mile or two south of Morgan's Bluff. I usually leave Morgan's Bluff anywhere from just past low tide to mid-tide with my 5' draft. I have left Morgan's Bluff at high tide and arrived at Fresh Creek at the end of the ebb tide and bounced quite a few times before getting over the bar between Fresh Creek and Long Cay and into the entrance channel. Study the charts, allow for your speed and the local conditions (wind and wave), and hen set out with good light. Never head south too

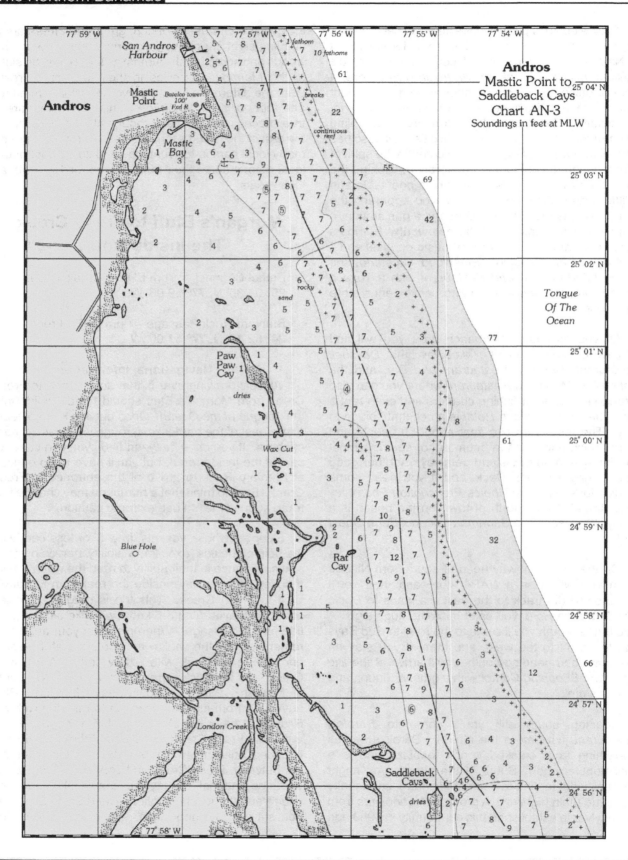

Andros
Mastic Point to
Saddleback Cays
Chart AN-3
Soundings in feet at MLW

early in the morning as the sun is right in your eyes and you may never see the rocky patch known as the *Hens and Chickens* just south of Morgan's Bluff which is sometimes difficult to discern even in good light.

The venerable *Yachtsmen's Guide to The Bahamas*, the "Bible" of cruisers for so many years, shows much more water inside the reef than is really there in many places. This is not an indictment of that excellent publication, rather only an indication of how things change in the islands. Depths mentioned in this section, as throughout this entire guide, are in feet at *mean low water*, which means it is possible to have a lower tide than what is shown on the chart.

I do not recommend that first timers to The Bahamas attempt the inside route along the eastern shore of Andros, it can make even the most experienced Bahamas veteran a little nervous. If you have any doubts about your ability to safely traverse this area, by all means, head outside into the deeper, safer, water. I almost deleted the course lines on the Charts for the passages inside the Andros barrier reef. For some reason skippers seem to want to follow those lines religiously and often forget to use their eyes. This route cannot to be treated like that. This can be a dangerous route in some circumstances. There are places you must pilot your way between sandy shoals and rocky patches that dry at low water. If a squall were to come through at that moment and reduce your visibility to almost nothing you could find yourself in one a heck of a fix. There are no waypoints to get you through this one. Your eyes are your only means of piloting through here. Take your time, keep your eyes open, and pay constant attention to the surrounding waters. If something were to divert your attention at the wrong time you could find yourself high and dry for the next 6-12 hours or worse. Use the course lines given only as a guideline. If you are familiar with the short passage through the reef at Samana into the Propeller Cay anchorage (see the chapter *Samana*), you will understand why this route has been called "30 miles of Samana." It's really not that bad, but it is definitely to be respected. Don't worry about not having course lines. Keep this text handy and I will talk you through this route section by section and you'll have a real test of your piloting skills. OK, ready to go?

Vessels heading south from Morgan's Bluff to Nicoll's Town inside the reef should round the jetty in the entrance channel heading east. Once past the jetty, turn to starboard and parallel the shore southward towards Nicoll's Town as shown on Chart AN-2. The water is still fairly deep here and the barrier reef does not reappear until about 1¼ miles south of the entrance channel to Morgan's Bluff. You can head in as close as 50-100 yards from shore here. On the first hill south of the jetty you will see the settlement of Morgan's Bluff. South of that hill, just east of the second hill and the small coconut palm trees, is a shallow rocky patch known as the *Hens and Chickens*, sometimes shown on some charts as the *Devil's Backbone*. There are two ways to pass this reef. Some publications suggest that you pass 50 yards off the rocky shoreline between the shoal and the shore in 9' of water. This would be fine if there really was that much water there. The truth is that there is 6' through here in places at low water over a rocky bottom. I prefer to head out into the slightly deeper water to the east of the rocky bar and pass it to the east, between the rocky bar and the outer barrier reef, angling back in towards shore at the north end of the long white beach that leads to Nicoll's Town. Here you will pass between the *Hens and Chickens* off your starboard beam, some small patch reefs off the north end of the beach, and a dark line of rocky ledges and heads that you should keep to port. Pass between the dark line and the small patch reefs off the beach in 7'-9' of water at low tide. It would help to have someone on the bow through here.

Paralleling the beach southeastward the water will get progressively deeper the further south you go towards Nicoll's Town, anywhere from 9'-13' at low water. Follow the shore staying a hundred yards or so off and you will come to the small point at Nicoll's Town with a dock at the *Andros Beach Hotel*. You can anchor here in settled weather or light easterly winds. This spot is also good for winds from south to west. The small anchorage shoals quickly in towards shore.

Heading south from Nicoll's Town give the point of land and its offlying shallow bar a fair berth and you will be in about 13' of water. On the hill to your starboard side you will soon see the lighted range (247°) for the *Bethel Channel*. The *Bethel Channel* is narrow and carries about 7' at low tide. A waypoint at 25° 08.36' N, 77° 59.06' W, will place you approximately ½ mile east/northeast of the eastern entrance of the *Bethel Channel*. Line up on the range and strictly follow it in. The range sits on the side of a hill without any trees

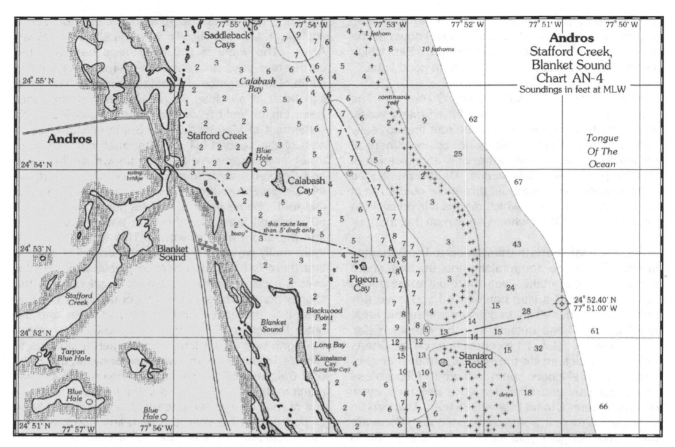

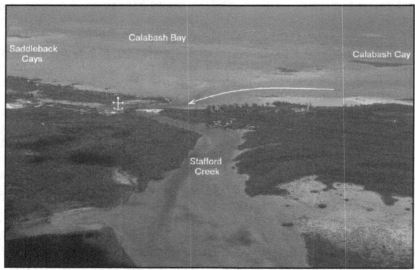

Stafford Creek

Photo courtesy of Paul Harding, Safari Seaplanes

on it. As you approach the shore do not turn north or south until less than 150 yards east of the shore. This is to avoid the shallow reefs, which line both sides of the channel, especially the northern side.

Once past *Bethel Channel* you must give Coconut Point a wide berth as shown on Chart AN-2. There is a shallow rocky bar that juts out eastward from the point and even as you head around it in water from 7'-10' deep you will be passing over scattered rocks.

You can anchor just south of Coconut Point about 200-250 yards off shore in winds from northwest to north. You can also anchor in Conch Bay about ¼ mile off the beach, shallow draft vessels can work much farther in for better anchoring.

Heading southeast from Coconut Point you will see a very conspicuous, bright green sandbar. Keep this sandbar to your port side as you head for Mastic Point, the easternmost point of land on the horizon. From Coconut Point you will be steering approximately 150°-155° for Mastic Point. You will have 6'-7' at low water through here, in some places as much as 8' or 9'. As you approach Pye Point as shown on Chart AN-2, you will see what appears to be a pair of small pilings to port. Give these a wide berth, they are actually the masts of a sunken freighter that lies in a large break in the reef. About 100 yards east of these masts is the sunken wreck of another, smaller vessel whose mast is awash at high water. The wrecks make for good diving but they are definitely hazards to navigation. You can actually take a 6' draft through the break in the reef or around the bright green sandbar mentioned above, but you will be threading through some shallows and then some heads in the vicinity of the wrecks themselves.

South of Pye Point watch out for some shallow reefs, stay at least 150 yards or more offshore. Between Pye Point and Mastic Point, as shown on Chart AN-3, is San Andros Harbour, once home to the *Mastic Point Field Station*. The field station has closed and the harbour is unused except by small local craft. Give the conspicuous jetties that mark this harbour a wide berth in at least 7' at low water. There is a submerged barge just off the entrance that is awash at high water, and several shallow patch reefs in the same general vicinity.

Tiny San Andros Harbour is not a good refuge unless absolutely necessary. The shoreline is littered with wrecks and the holding is iffy at best. The settlement south of the harbour is called New Town and no facilities are available. Mastic Point, Chart AN-3, and the New Town area were once home to a 20,000-acre sisal plantation owned by Neville Chamberlain's father. The plantation was a failure since sisal does not grow well in the Andros pine barrens, or perhaps it was the work of a *Chickcharnie*. It is possible to anchor south of Mastic Point as shown on Chart AN-4 but you really can't get in too close to shore unless you draw less than 3'. There is a small

store, *Adderly's Convenience Store*, located in the community of Mastic Point.

Heading southeast from Mastic Point as shown on Chart AN-3, keep Paw Paw Cay well to starboard and you will have 7' most of the way with an occasional 5' or 6' spot at low water. You will see a small casuarina covered cay to starboard, this is one of the small cays just north of Paw Paw Cay. Keep it also well to starboard, about ¼-½ mile. The coves and bays between Paw Paw Cay and the mainland of Andros are a delight to explore by dinghy, but they are too shallow for most boats unless you draw less than 3'. From Mastic Point southeastward you will still be maintaining an approximate course of 150°. You are now aiming for the eastern end of a conspicuous flat island on the horizon with a slightly higher hump on its eastern end. This is Rat Cay. Don't plan on steering a straight course on Rat Cay though, you'll find some shoals and other obstructions to steer around, but the water will get deeper as you approach Rat Cay, in places 10'-12' at low tide. As I mentioned before, head for the eastern end of Rat Cay keeping Paw Paw Cay a good ¼-½ mile to starboard to avoid the green sandbank that lies just to the east of Paw Paw Cay. Off Paw Paw Cay you will see several dark grassy areas that, though they may look deeper, may not actually be deeper than the green areas you are going across. Watch out for the 3'-4' rocky bar southeast of Paw Paw Cay and east of Wax Cut. Keep Rat Cay to starboard heading south and you can pass within ¼ mile of the eastern end of Rat Cay.

From Rat Cay you can begin steering to pass east of the Saddleback Cays as shown on Chart AN-3. On the horizon you will see a point of land with a small beach. To the east of it is a fair sized cay with two smaller cays to its east. This fair sized cay and the two smaller ones are the Saddleback Cays. You will actually be steering a curving course towards them, first heading for the larger of the cays and then steering to pass east of the two smaller cays. As you get close to the Saddleback Cays you will notice a large green sandbank closing in on your port side towards the larger of the Saddleback Cays. This sandbank has some 4' spots at low tide with two 6' channels (at low tide also) through it. The first is just off the larger of the Saddleback Cays, and the other channel lies about ¼ mile off in the darker strip that splits the sandbank. When you get close you will see the two channels if you have good visibility.

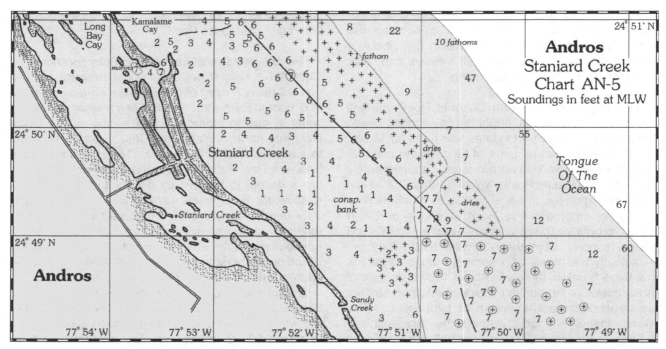

Kamalame Cay Resort and Marina
at Staniard Creek

Photo Courtesy of Paul Harding,
Safari Seaplanes

Once past the Saddleback Cays you can begin to steer for the next island on the horizon, Pigeon Cay, as shown on Chart AN-4. As you head for Pigeon Cay, northeast of Calabash Cay you will have to steer around some 4'-5' sandy spots in only 6' at low water.

Are you having fun yet? Stay about ½ mile east of Calabash Cay as you head towards Pigeon Cay keeping the large green sandbank to port and you will once again find yourself in 7' at low water. You can anchor just north of Pigeon Cay in 5'-6' at low water. There is a green sandbank just off Pigeon Cay that, although it looks shallow, actually has 7'-10' over it in places at low water. Vessels drawing less than 5' can anchor south of Calabash Cay.

From Pigeon Cay, vessels drawing 4' or less can head northwest to Stafford Creek, but only with a good high tide and excellent visibility. Pass north of Pigeon Cay and head in on the conspicuous white schoolhouse that is obscured by casuarinas just west of the small beach at the northern end of the Blanket Sound settlement. Head in on this schoolhouse on a course of 287° until you see the small orange buoy in the water just offshore. At one time this buoy was a stake, now it is a buoy that moves around with each blow. If you get confused and can't find your way in, call the *Forfar Field Station* on VHF ch. 16 and they can talk you in, they'll be happy to help. If the buoy is there, keep it to port and proceed northward paralleling the shore and staying between the shallows off the shore and the shallow bank north of the buoy and south of the conspicuous wreck. Round the last of the small cays to port between it and the very obvious sandbank to their north and head into Stafford Creek. The creek has a lot of current and anchoring is tricky at best. A good spot in bad weather, even a minimal hurricane, is tucked up into the small pocket north of the bridge but you must watch out for the current on the south side of the creek by the bridge. Located just off the southeastern end of the bridge is a small blue hole that creates a whirlpool effect at times that can slam a small boat into the bridge or shore before you realize it. At slack tide the hole is a good dive but only during the 20-minute slack period. Use caution if diving the hole because as soon as the current begins to flow again, it does so with a vengeance.

Stafford Creek has no facilities and the only site of real interest is the *Forfar Field Station*, an educational and research center for high school and college students and educators located on *Forfar Drive*. The station is owned by *International Field Studies* of Columbus, Ohio, a non-profit educational organization. The station has two sailboats that they use to teach a combined sailing, marine biology, and botanical program. For more information about their educational opportunities can call (in the U.S.) 800-962-3805 or write to *International Field Studies*, 709 College Ave., Columbus, Ohio. The *Forfar Field Station*, once known as the *Andros Reef Inn*, was constructed by Archie Forfar and I'll discuss its unique history in the last section in this chapter entitled *A Dive Too Deep-The Story of Archie Forfar*.

In the mid 1900s, oil companies explored the Stafford Creek area and drilled deep into the earth but could not remove the drills and had to abandon their entire rig. The old swing bridge once opened for boaters seeking refuge during hurricanes but hasn't

opened in years and probably never will again. If you dinghy up the creek about 11 miles upstream you will come to the old *Owens-Illinois* docks. When this lumberyard was in full swing some 40 years ago, Stafford Creek was kept dredged. Today the creek hasn't seen a dredge in almost 3 decades and it, and the waters around the settlement of Stafford Creek and Staniard Creek are silting in again. Just north of the bridge over Stafford Creek is *Love at First Sight*, a restaurant with some cabanas for rent.

Heading south from Pigeon Cay and Stafford Creek, you will notice Staniard Rock on your port side. Steer approximately 170°, about halfway between Staniard Rock and the conspicuous white roof on shore keeping Staniard Rock well to port as there are shallow rocky bars both north and south of it. Staniard Rock lies south of a well-used but not well-marked channel. Vessels wishing to enter from seaward are advised to eyeball their way through here. A waypoint at 24° 52.40' N, 77° 51.00' W, will place you approximately ¼ mile east of the cut in the reef. From this position take up a course of approximately 230°-250° to steer between the reefs. This course is not that important, what is important is staying between the reefs (easily seen in good light) and then avoiding the shallow bar on the inside. The cut lies approximately 300-400 yards north of Staniard Rock. The light on the Staniard Rock has been destroyed and no plans are in the works for its replacement. The barrier reef comes in very close on your port side between Pigeon Cay and Staniard Rock, you'll see it breaking. Vessels with drafts of over 5' wishing to make their way to Fresh Creek should head outside the reef utilizing the channel north of Staniard Rock, the shallows just north of Fresh Creek will not allow you to complete the inside route.

In the last few years, a new marina has opened up just north of Staniard Creek as shown on Chart AN-5. At the southwest tip of Kamalame Cay (Long Bay Cay), a gentleman has built a resort called *Kamalame Cove* aimed at attracting a very wealthy clientele. The *Kamalame Cay Marina* is now open for business charging upwards of $3 a foot. The marina carries diesel and gas, has a restaurant and some limited provisions, and is intended to be primarily for the folks who've bought a home on the island. Unfortunately the channel has not been dredged yet so the marina is restricted to drafts of about 4' with a good high tide. You can anchor just inside the point in the basin west of the northern tip of Staniard Cay. From a position southwest of Staniard Rock (see Chart AN-4 and then AN-5), steer approximately west/southwest for the point of land at the end of the long white beach. This is the northern end of Staniard Creek as shown on Chart AN-5. You will have to eyeball your way in as you round the point, 5' can make it inside on a high tide. South of *Kamalame Cay* is the settlement of Staniard Creek with its *Central Andros Inn and Restaurant*, *J&J Foodland*, the *Staniard Creek Grocery*, and a small beach resort called the *Colors Beach Club*.

As I mentioned before, vessels heading south from Pigeon Cay should steer approximately 170°, heading roughly about halfway between Staniard Rock and the conspicuous white roof on shore keeping Staniard Rock well to port. Once past the area of Kamalame Cay you may begin to parallel the shoreline again. This next stretch of the passage is possibly the trickiest part of the entire route. This can be a nerve-wracking stretch of water, not for the faint of heart or the deep of draft. The water gets very shallow here, anywhere from 5'-6' at low water in places with a few 4' spots thrown in just to keep you on your toes (as if you weren't already on the edge of your seat, right?). Very soon, off to starboard, you will begin to see a large curving and very shallow, white sandbank stretching southeastward from the shore. There is a small dark channel between the northwestern tip of the sandbank and the eastern shore of Andros that may look inviting from offshore but don't attempt to pass between the sandbank and the shore. The water between them is very rocky and shallow though it looks deeper from a mile away. As shown on Chart AN-5, you can head southeastward past the shallow bar along its eastern edge but you will have to negotiate an area of numerous shallow, breaking, awash at high water reefs between the sandbank and the offshore barrier reef. These reefs and ledges are easily seen and avoided and the good news is that the water begins to get back to 7' depths at low tide. Once past the shallow bank you can angle back in towards shore somewhat as shown on Charts AN-5 and AN-6 where you will have fewer reefs and shoals to avoid in depths of 7'-9' at low water. Closer in to shore you'll be dodging shallow green sandbars instead of the brown reefs that lie further offshore. You'll notice that you're still about ½ mile offshore through here.

Your next obstacle is the conspicuous and easily avoided *Lightborn Bank* just off the beaches to your starboard side as shown on Chart AN-6. You will have plenty of deep water to pass it to the east, 7'-11' in places at low water. Watch out for a couple of shallow bars off Love Hill. You'll be steering approximately 140° through here towards the point of land off your starboard bow that is the entrance to Fresh Creek. You will see a large green sandbank in front of you that will lead you to believe that *Lightborn Bank* extends far out to the east, almost to the reef. Don't panic, this green bank is fairly deep. Put your bow on the point of land at the entrance to Fresh Creek and steer approximately 140° and you will find 7'-8' across the bank the whole way.

Well, now you've got the *AUTEC* towers and the entrance to Fresh Creek in sight. However, the shallowest part of this route lies just ahead, just before you enter the Fresh Creek channel. If you left Morgan's Bluff within an hour of high tide, averaging 5-6 knots, and you draw over 4½', you might as well anchor for awhile and let the tide come up, you ain't getting through here. If you draw 4½' or less you might try to sneak through on a low tide but you'll likely bump.

There are two routes from offshore Small Hope Bay to the entrance channel at Fresh Creek as shown on Chart AN-7. The eastern route, along the shore of Goat Cay and Long Cay, will just carry 5' on a good high tide. The western route that parallels the Andros shoreline is good for nearly 5½' on the same good high tide. At low tide only the western route, along the Andros shoreline is good for 4'-4½', and like I said, you'll bump, maybe even run aground if you can't steer around some shallow sandy spots. Keep an eye out for stray heads through here.

First we'll look at the eastern route that lies along the western shore of Goat Cay and Long Cay. When abeam of the dock at the *Small Hope Bay Lodge* (Chart AN-7), head towards Goat Cay. At high tide you can pass to the west of Goat Cay and Long Cay, passing close in to the southern end of Long Cay. You'll have to steer between Long Cay and the large shallow bank to its west. Once past Long Cay keep the *AUTEC* tower and the shallow bank to starboard to enter the Fresh Creek entrance channel. This route has a controlling depth of 3' at low water just off the southern third of Long Cay, nearly 5' can make it through here on a good high tide. The western route from Small Hope Bay to Fresh Creek parallels the shoreline of Andros much closer in as shown on

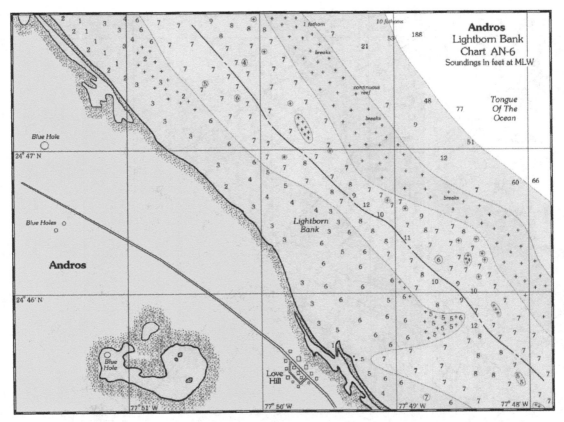

Chart AN-7. When abeam of Goat Cay in 7' at low water, take up a course for the point at the northern end of the entrance to Fresh Creek. You will have 4' through here at mean low water, in some places slightly more but you will probably have to weave your way through some shallow patches and bump your way across the bar that runs parallel to the northern side of the entrance channel to Fresh Creek. Once in the channel keep to the northern side until just inside and then head towards the docks at the *Lighthouse Marina* off your port bow as shown in greater detail on Chart AN-7A.

Now you can take a deep breath, relax your white-knuckle death-grip on your wheel or tiller, and prepare to unwind in Fresh Creek. You've earned it!

Fresh Creek

Fresh Creek - ¼ nm ENE of entrance channel:
24° 44.25' N, 77° 45.65' W

AUTEC Buoy (George Murphy Buoy):
24° 43.25' N, 77° 44.97' W

Fresh Creek is probably the most frequented harbour by cruising boats visiting Andros. Fresh Creek gets its name from the fresh water creek that runs back into the wilderness of Andros for some forty miles (although today it is for the most part brackish), there joining up with some small fresh water lakes. I've heard some of the locals say that if you head upstream far enough that you can drink the water surrounding your boat. At one time a hurricane raised the level of the creek over 10' and some vessels that were tied off in the creeks for protection were swept inland as much as 5 miles where some still sit today.

Navigational Information

Though the area is called Fresh Creek, the creek actually separates two towns. On the north shore is the much larger Coakely Town while on the south side of the creek sits Andros Town. A waypoint at 24° 44.25' N, 77° 45.65' W, will place you approximately ¼ mile east/northeast of the well-marked entrance channel into Fresh Creek as shown on Chart AN-7 (at night, the loom of the lights of the *AUTEC* base and Coakely town, coupled with the flashing amber lights of the *AUTEC* towers will give you a good idea of whether you're in the right vicinity or not) and in

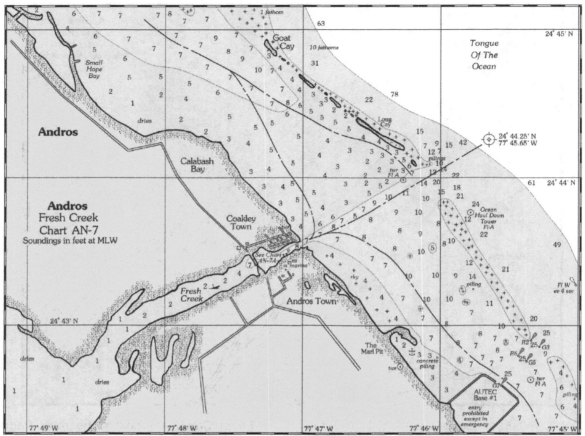

Fresh Creek

Photo Courtesy of Paul Harding, Safari Seaplanes

greater detail on Chart AN-7A. Another good landmark is a wreck on the barrier reef lying a couple of miles north of Goat Cay, and the hulk of the *Lady Gloria*, which lies on the southern side of the entrance to Fresh Creek. The *Lady Gloria* was tied to the government dock for years and when somebody tried to move her out of Fresh Creek, she wound up where she now rests, her bow almost on the beach.

At the seaward end of the entrance channel, you will see two steel pilings just southeast of the small rock lying south of Long Cay. Keep these pilings to starboard. Next you will see an amber-lighted *AUTEC* tower, keep it also to starboard passing south of it. Head straight in to the entrance channel from here avoiding the shallow sandbank to starboard between the *AUTEC* tower and shore. You'll see the Lady Gloria on the southern side of the channel at the edge of the land, and just past her, also on the southern side of the channel just inside the mouth of Fresh Creek is a new light that flashes green. You might wish to steer around the darker patches you see as you work your way down the entrance channel. I found two shallow bars at the entrance to Fresh Creek that carry around 6' at low water. One lies approximately 200 yards east of the entrance and the *Lady Gloria*, and the second lies only about 100 yards east of the entrance. When approaching the entrance keep halfway between the center and the northern shore of the entrance, this is where the deeper water is and keeps you off the rocky shoal north of the southern jetty.

Once inside, favor the southern side of mid-channel, only the southern side of the entrance channel was dredged, the northern side is shallow. On the southern side of the channel are the docks of *Lighthouse Marina*, and once past the docks you can anchor between the marina and the bridge, but watch out for the shoal at the southwestern end of the small cove just west of the marina. Do not anchor near the marina or the large triple piling just west of the marina, the fast ferry from Nassau comes into Fresh Creek 4 times a week and ties a line to that piling to pivot and back up to the dock west of the marina. The deepest water and the best holding is in the northwestern side of the harbour towards the bridge, but the entire anchorage area is littered with old engine blocks and other debris so use caution when setting your anchors. Two anchors are recommended here as there is little swinging room if it's crowded and there's a lot of current here.

What You Will Find Ashore

On the south side of the harbour is the *Lighthouse Hotel and Marina*, an excellent place to stop. They have a fine restaurant and bar, copy and fax service, and the front desk or the dockmaster can arrange a car rental for you. The hotel itself is a great place to unwind even if you don't rent a room. You can dine on the verandah or just pull up a chair and relax, or perhaps you'd like to take a swim in their fresh water pool. Whatever suits your mood, they aim to please. This is a great place to meet other cruisers and some of the people who live aboard here and work at the

nearby *AUTEC* base. The marina has expanded their dockage and can accommodate boats of 100' LOA and 9' draft. There is ample fresh water at the dock with 50-amp and 15-amp electrical service, and washers and dryers are available. Fresh Creek is a *Port of Entry* and vessels wishing to clear *Customs* and *Immigration* should contact *Lighthouse Marina* on VHF ch. 16. The dockmaster will supply you with the proper forms and call the officials for you. The marina boasts a new fuel dock, the old one was destroyed by the fast ferry. If you need a bonefish guide, call *Bonefish Bradley* at 357-2242. For a taxi give Linwood Johnson a call at 368-2579, or 464-3141. If you require Internet access, visit Troy at *Digital Sounds* about 4 miles north of Fresh Creek on the *Queen's Highway*. Just a few yards from the commercial dock is a *Shell* gas station.

Just a hundred yards up from the dockmaster's office is a branch of the *Royal Bank of Canada* and the office of the *Minister of Tourism*, Peter Douglas, who used to manage the *Small Hope Bay Lodge*. Stop in and have a chat with Peter, he's a delight to converse with. Peter is a native Androsian who is extremely proud of his island and his heritage. The Bahamas needs more government officials as concerned about their country as Peter.

Outside the entrance to the marina, a short five-minute walk away, is the *Androsia Boutique*. You've probably seen the batik *Androsia* for sale throughout The Bahamas. It is manufactured and sold here on Andros and this boutique, a sort of factory outlet store, has some great deals waiting for you, they take all major credit cards. Nearby is the *Androsia Factory*, check in the outlet store for a self-guided tour of the factory. If you're stuck in Fresh Creek waiting on weather, you might want to take advantage of the batik classes offered by the *Androsia Factory*. The price of the class is $10 and that covers a piece of cloth that you will design and prepare. The factory staff then dyes the material and you get to take it home with you. Check at the *Androsia Boutique*, that's where they post information on the classes, a great opportunity to take home something special.

Across the harbour from the *Lighthouse Marina* is Coakely Town. You can walk across the bridge or dinghy over to the landing at the commercial dock or you can tie up to the concrete dock at *Chickcharnies Hotel*, the large, yellow, two story hotel that dominates the waterfront on the northern shore. The dock itself

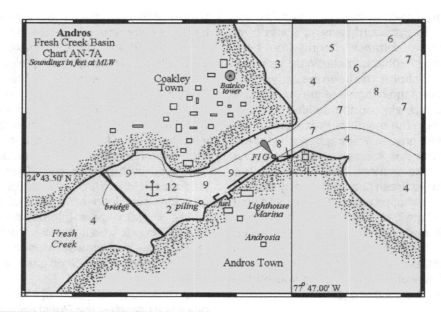

Androsia Factory, Fresh Creek

Photo by Author

Marina, Fresh Creek   Photo Courtesy of Paul Harding, Safari Seaplanes

is a rough concrete wall with barely 5' at low water, you'll need plenty of good, fat, fenders if you try to tie up here. The hotel has a very nice restaurant serving breakfast, lunch, and dinner, a bar, a well-stocked grocery store, and the hotel can also arrange for car rentals.

In town along the eastern shore, you'll find *Skinny's Landmark Restaurant And Lodge* with *Donny's Sweet Sugar Lounge* and the *Beverage Depot* also on the premises. Across the street are the government offices, a *Batelco* office, police station, and a post office. On the side streets north of the *Chickcharnies Hotel* you fill find *Adderly's Grocery*, a well-stocked grocery store with a Laundromat next door, the *Andros Market*, and the *Fashion Time Clothing Store*. At the corner is the *Square Deal Restaurant And Bar*, and nearby is *Gaitor's Variety Store*, and *Treats*, a small bar with a pool table. On the road heading north of Coakely Town is the *Oasis* restaurant.

But the most popular spot in town is definitely *Hank's Place*. Hank Roberts used to be the dockmaster at the *Lighthouse Marina* and left to focus on his own restaurant, and it's a good one. Hank has a large dock with a covered outside pavilion and he serves up some very, very good food. Hank's future plans call for some dredging and the addition of some new docks to turn *Hank's Place* into a marina, so keep your eyes posted for this.

A mile north of Coakely Town is the small hillside community of Calabash Bay where you will find a small gift shop, the *Sunshine Cafe* serving Bahamian and American dishes, and right on the beach you'll find the bright red *Samicka's Fish Fry* serving great seafood from 1300 daily. A mile or so north of Calabash Bay is the small community of Love Hill. Here is an *Esso* station, liquor store, and the *Quick Wash Laundromat*. Still further to the north is Small Hope Bay with its extremely laid back *Small Hope Bay Lodge*. Small Hope Bay is said to have been named by the legendary pirate Sir Henry Morgan who decided that there was "small hope" that anyone could find his buried treasure here. He might have been right as no reports of treasure finds have surfaced in the area.

Calling *Small Hope Bay Lodge* "laid back" is not just an advertiser's tool, this place is just that. Founded by Canadian Dick Birch in 1960, the Birch family has created and maintained a true out island getaway that I cannot help but recommend. There are no phones, no TV's, and no keys for the rooms. The only rule seems to be that you must enjoy yourself and have fun. The lodge specializes in SCUBA and snorkeling trips to the nearby reefs and blue holes and they also cater to bonefishing or sportfishing enthusiasts. The lodge offers 20 cottages built of coral and Andros pine set among a beautiful shoreline of casuarinas and palm trees. On its beach is a bar that is famous for its conch fritters and its rum-laced sundowners. The restaurant offers excellent breakfasts, lunches, and dinners with reservations. Children under 12 can dine in a separate dining room with a chaperone to allow their parents a little "adult time." There is a lovely beach and the lodge gives free snorkeling lessons. They have a huge library and book trade, a game room for checkers and chess enthusiasts, and a very nice gift shop. On the main highway at the entrance to the lodge is a small grocery store and *Rolle's Variety Store*. Just north of Small Hope is the *T&T Snack Food and Variety Store*.

If you dinghy up Fresh Creek past the bridge you will come to an area of very nice homes on the southern shore of the creek. The wreck of an old ferryboat lies mid-stream about ½ mile west of the bridge. The ferry, I'm told it was a very old *Staten Island Ferry*, was brought to Andros many years ago, before the bridge was built. The ferry carried the materials for building the bridge over Fresh Creek and some of the laborers on the bridge lived on the ferry during construction. While the ferry was intended to make regular Nassau/Fresh Creek runs, its only usage was during the building of the bridge and she lies today where she lay then. Further up the creek are two blue holes, one appears as if it is filled with sand, but if you put your hand or a spear in it and wiggle it, the "sand" moves about like Jell-O.

At the southern point of the entrance channel to Fresh Creek you will see the remains of a lighthouse that dates back over a century (1892). The cannon you see mounted there are said to have come off the wreck of a British Man of War that sank in the channel just off the point.

Just south of the entrance channel to Fresh Creek is the main *AUTEC* (*Atlantic Undersea Testing and Evaluation Center*) base (#1) on Andros. There are three other smaller bases up and down the island's eastern shore at Salvador Point (#2) just north of Cargill Creek, the southern end of Big Wood Cay (#3), and at Golding Cay (#4) at South Bight. It's not unusual to see a *U.S. Navy* warship or submarine in these waters, the *U.S. Navy* conducts test on submarine and anti-submarine weapons in the 6000' deep *Tongue of the Ocean*. Farther south in the *Tongue of the Ocean* the *U.S. Navy* also conducts preparedness tests of surface ships. The *AUTEC* base is run by a private contractor with a minimum of Naval personnel on hand. If you happen to be in the area during testing you won't even know it. You will not be warned by radio, the Navy will simply wait for you to pass before resuming testing (unless of course they are in the very visible process of testing a surface ship). *AUTEC* wants all boaters to understand that all *AUTEC* bases are *U.S. Navy* Installations and entrance is prohibited except in real emergencies. A summer squall, running out of gas, or just stopping for lunch are not real emergencies. If you have any questions *AUTEC Base #1*, Fresh Creek, monitors VHF ch. 16 and answers to *Snapper Base*. South of Fresh Creek, *AUTEC* maintains several towers and buoys, all flash amber at night. Some of the smaller buoys are hard to see even at night. Use caution when transiting this area at night.

If you take the road a few miles south of Fresh Creek you will come to a "T" intersection. The road to the left leads you to the entrance to the *AUTEC* base and the road to the right continues south to Behring Point. Just a couple of miles south of this intersection is Bowen Sound whose only facilities are the *Mackie Shopping Plaza*, which is really just a small convenience and sundry store, *Kell's Grocery & Takeaway Snacks*, and the small *R&G Grocery*.

Fresh Creek to North Bight The Inside Route

Leaving Fresh Creek and heading south you will have another test of nerves. Feel like playing again? If not, head outside, it's much safer and easier on the blood pressure. This next section, from Fresh Creek south to North Bight on the inside is shallower and strewn with more heads than the inside route from Morgan's Bluff to Fresh Creek and you remember how much fun that was. I recommend that vessels drawing more than 4½' go outside at Fresh Creek if headed south to Cargill Creek or South Bight. The inside route is long, winding, and shallow, there are many 4' spots at low water that must be avoided. There are no real anchorages between Fresh Creek and North Bight (with the exception of lying in the lee of High Cay, Long Rock, or Green Cay) and entire trip takes at least one full tide for vessels maintaining a speed of 5-6 knots, which only adds to the problem. Once again, unless you are adamant about using this route, I suggest going outside. Piloting by eye is the only way you're going to get through here, don't leave too early in the morning as the sun will be right in your eyes.

Navigational Information

If you are headed outside (Chart AN-7) you must give a wide berth to the amber lighted *AUTEC* tower that sits outside the reef about ¼ mile south of the entrance channel, *AUTEC* suggests two miles to the east. There is a 1½" cable that heads down from the tower at about a 30°-45° angle, it's called the *Ocean Haul Down Cable*, and is used to haul equipment, targets, shapes, anything the *U.S. Navy* needs, down to the floor of the *Tongue of the Ocean* where there is a huge base and sheave. Besides the cable being a danger there is the possibility that you may hit what it is being hauled up or down. If you pass this way at night and you see a lot of lights about, keep clear.

If you are headed south from Fresh Creek inside the reef, head out the entrance channel and when at least 200 yards east of the southern jetty (to avoid the shallows that lie along the eastern shore of Andros between Fresh Creek and the Marl Pit), turn to starboard and take up a course for roughly the middle of the northern breakwater of the *AUTEC* base as shown on Chart AN-7. This is to avoid the shallow reefs just west of the piling that lies inside the reef and about halfway between the Fresh Creek entrance channel and the *AUTEC* base. On the eastern shore of Andros is a small hook of land that juts out and creates a basin that is locally called the *Marl Pit*. At one time it was an excellent anchorage and refuge from frontal passages. Today it has filled in to the point that only vessels with drafts of less than 3' can avail themselves of its protection. You will notice a concrete piling inshore just south of the *Marl Pit*, ignore it, it sits in less than 6' of water at low tide. As you pass that conspicuous steel piling to port you may begin to work your way to pass just outside the eastern breakwaters of the *AUTEC* base. Parallel the eastern breakwater crossing the entrance channel until abeam of the southern breakwater.

Once past the entrance to the *AUTEC* base as shown on Chart AN-8, set your bow generally pointing to High Cay on the horizon. Follow the curve of 7' deep water staying closer to the reef than to the shore. Soon you will be in water less than 6' deep at low water. Get used to it. You will be in water less than one fathom deep at low tide for the next 10-12 miles. Keep the Plum Cays to starboard as you approach High Cay as shown on Chart AN-9. Just west of High Cay is a small pocket of water 7' deep at low tide. Boaters often anchor in the lee of High Cay, but the holding is poor here, the bottom is scoured except for a small area off the northwestern tip of the island where you can still find some good sand where you can drop your hook. Off High Cay is a deep reef that comes up from the depths of the *Tongue of the Ocean* called the *Dallas Reef*. The reef was named after the *U.S. Navy* submarine *Dallas* after she ran aground and stayed there three days. Passing south of High Cay is much like turning the corner, the waters south of High Cay are often much rougher than those north of High Cay. In prevailing winds you can anchor in the lee of Long Rock in approximately 7'-8' at low water.

Heading south from Long Rock pass well off the eastern shore of Andros in 4'-6' at low water as shown

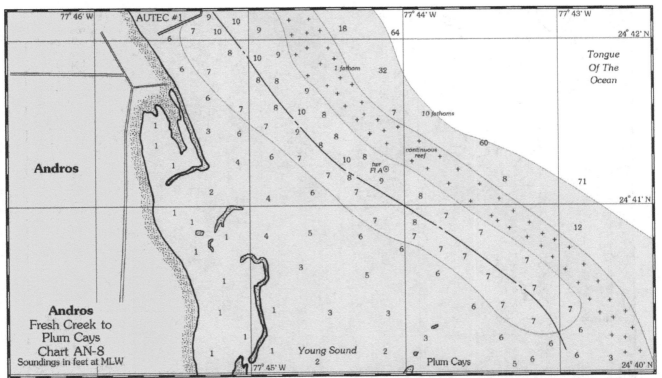

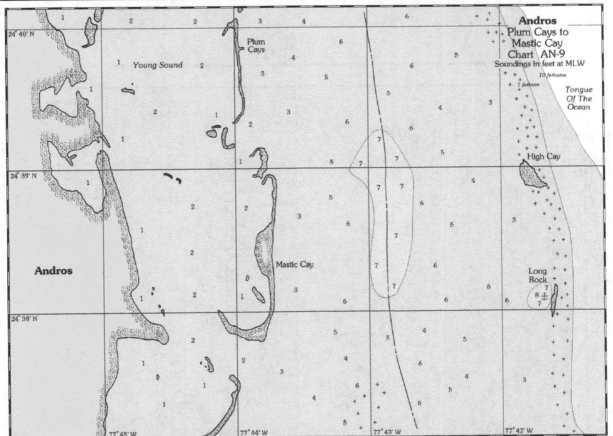

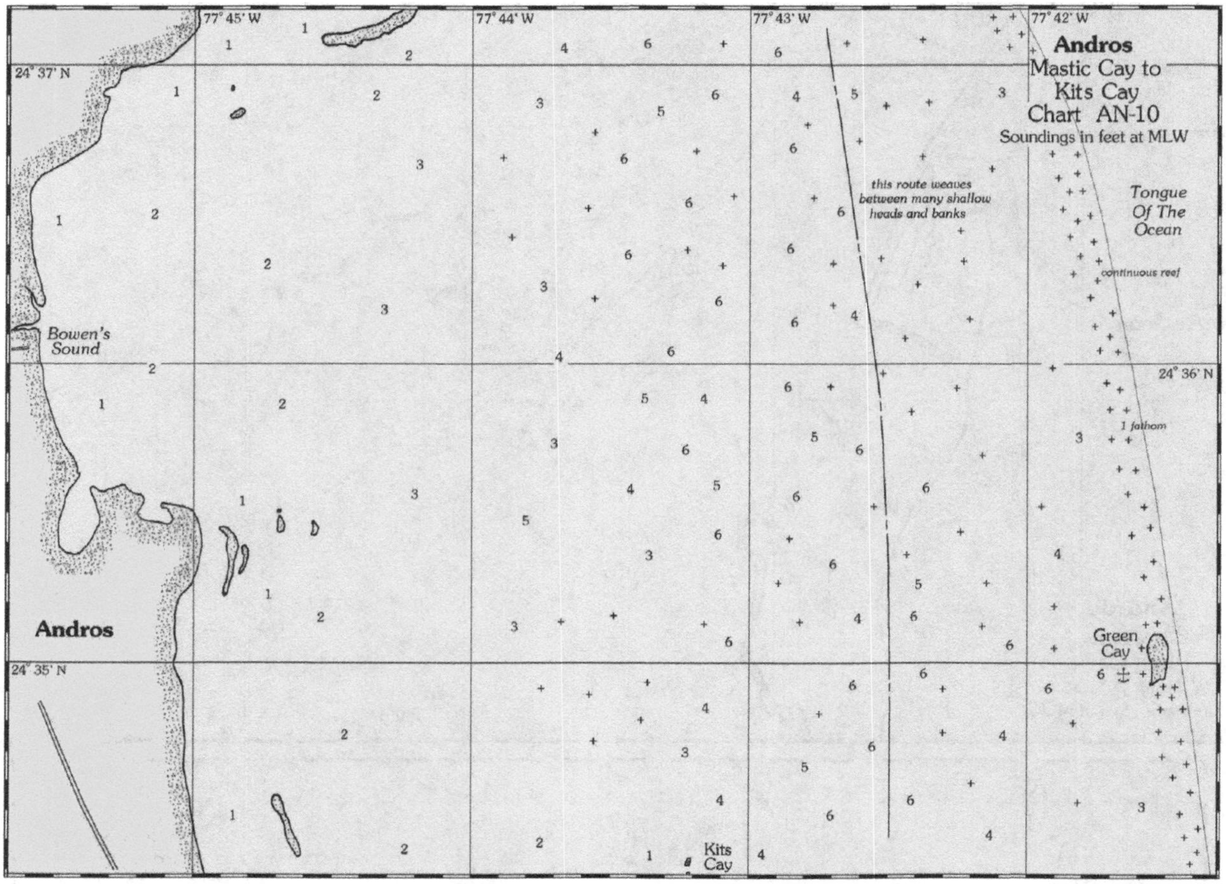

Andros
Mastic Cay to
Kits Cay
Chart AN-10
Soundings in feet at MLW

77° 45' W 77° 44' W 77° 43' W 77° 42' W

24° 37' N

this route weaves between many shallow heads and banks

Tongue
Of The
Ocean

continuous reef

Bowen's
Sound

24° 36' N

1 fathom

Andros

24° 35' N

Green
Cay

Kits
Cay

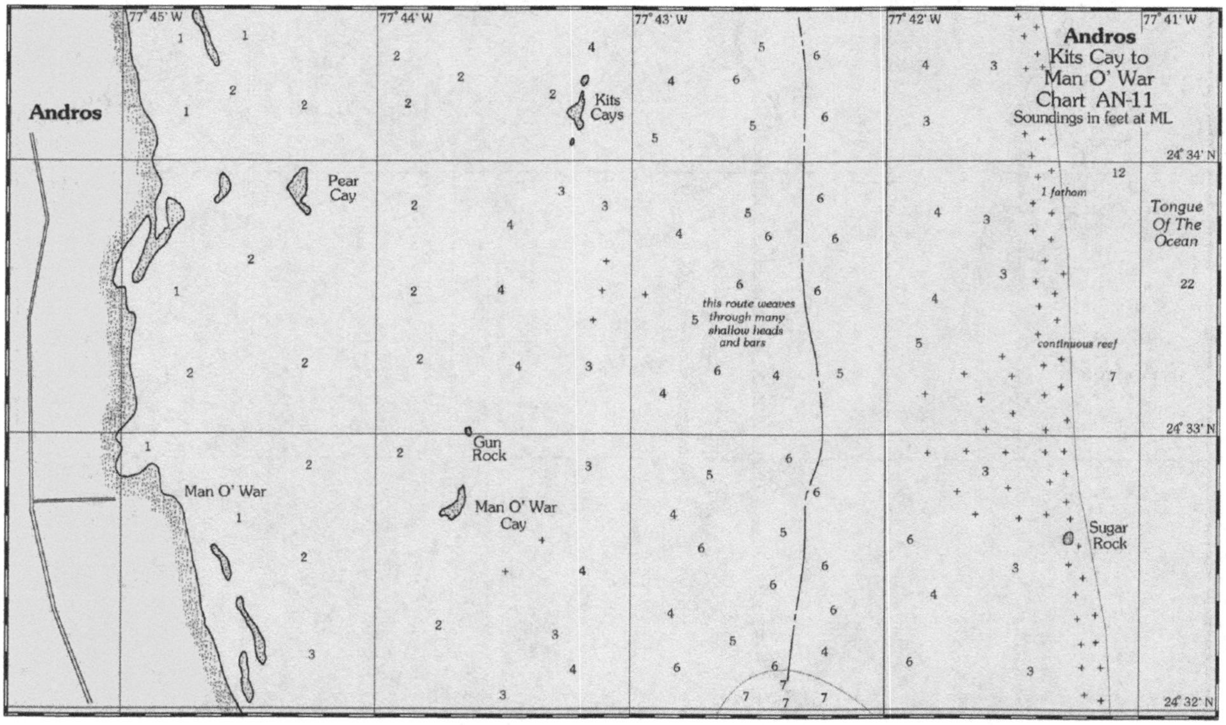

Andros
Kits Cay to
Man O' War
Chart AN-11
Soundings in feet at ML

77° 45' W 77° 44' W 77° 43' W 77° 42' W 77° 41' W

Andros

Kits
Cays

24° 34' N

1 fathom

Tongue
Of The
Ocean

Pear
Cay

this route weaves through many shallow heads and bars

continuous reef

24° 33' N

Gun
Rock

Man O' War

Man O' War
Cay

Sugar
Rock

24° 32' N

on Chart AN-10 and AN-11. Through here you will be weaving your way through numerous reefs and shallow bars especially in the area north of Green Cay. In prevailing conditions you can anchor in the lee of Green Cay in 5'-6' at low water. Heading south from Green Cay as shown on Chart AN-11, stay between the visible barrier reef and the eastern shore of Andros leaving Kits Cays and Man of War Cay well to starboard. Once again, you will have to eyeball your way through here, between many shallow bars and heads. Are you wishing that you were outside yet?

North Bight

Salvador Point - ½ nm E of sea buoy:
24° 29.95' N, 77° 41.40' W

AUTEC Site 1 & 2 Buoy:
24° 36.32' N, 77° 38.35' W

Navigational Information

As you approach Salvador Point, Cargill Creek, and North Bight as shown on Chart AN-12, you will find yourself temporarily free of the many heads and shoals that plagued you over the last few miles. Heading south, pass about halfway between Andros and Bristol Galley Island in 7'-9' of water. Directly ahead of you lies AUTEC Base 2 at Salvador Point. You will likely notice its large tower, jetty, buildings, and marked entrance channel. Cross the channel and continue heading southward to Behring Point.

If you are outside the reef and wish to enter the waters west of the reef via the AUTEC channel, a waypoint at 24° 29.95' N, 77° 41.40' W, will place you approximately ½ mile east of the sea buoy that marks the 9' deep channel. AUTEC does not mind if cruisers use their channel as long as you do not block any of their vessels or attempt to enter their bases. There is a large, unmistakable range ashore that leads you in on a heading of approximately 269°. Follow the channel markers until well inside the reef and then turn north or south as you wish.

Heading south, on your starboard side is the settlement of Cargill Creek. Continue on past Behring Point and the settlement of Behring Point keeping and keep an eye out for the rocky bar that you will want to keep to port as you head south. Round up inside Pye's Harbour and you can anchor in 4'-7' at low tide if you pick your spot right. You will be open

to prevailing winds here but if it's not blowing to bad, you'll be comfortable enough.

What You Will Find Ashore

If you take the dinghy north to Cargill Creek, just north of the bridge, you'll find a Batelco office, Gateway Liquors, an excellent restaurant Dig Dig's Bahamian-American Cuisine (dinner by reservation please - 368-5097), Carter's Convenience Store, and two very nice bonefishing lodges. The Andros Island Bonefish Club and the Cargill Creek Fishing Lodge both have bars and restaurants and are right next to each other just north of the bridge. Both provide dinner with reservations but only Cargill Creek Fishing Lodge monitors VHF ch. 16. Here too you'll find the Mt. Pleasant Fishing Lodge, Capt. Neymour's Restaurant & Bar, the Big Yard Restaurant, a small bonefishing tackle store, and Neymour's Service Station. Just south of the bridge at Cargill Creek is a small food store, an even smaller hardware store, and the Sea View Restaurant and Bar serving breakfast, lunch, and dinner.

Continuing on the road south past Cargill Creek you'll come to a "T" intersection. If you go straight you'll come to the jetty at Independence Park, but if you take a left (eastward) the road leads you to Behring Point, and if you take a right (westward) you'll immediately come to the Tranquility Hill Fishing Lodge with 10 rooms, satellite TV, and a fine restaurant. Staying west on this road you'll parallel lovely North Bight and come to the end of the road in Coakely Bight, home to Bonefish Charlie's Restaurant and Bar.

Middle Bight and Mangrove Cay

Middle Bight - ¼ nm E of sea buoy:
24° 20.10' N, 77° 39.45' W

AUTEC Site 3 & 4 Buoy:
24° 19.34' N, 77° 36.07' W

Navigational Information

The route from North Bight to Middle Bight will not be discussed in great detail and not charted in this edition of this guide (if there is enough interest it may be included in a later edition). The route is very shallow and literally strewn with shallow heads and patch reefs. So difficult is this route that all boats, even locals frequently, must pass outside the reef at the AUTEC tower that sits north of Middle Bight. If you are headed to Middle Bight from North Bight, I

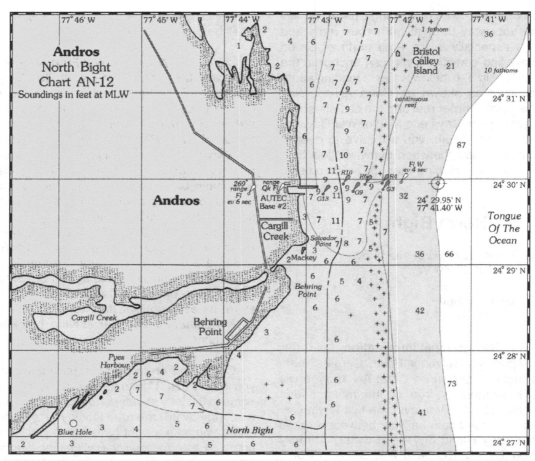

Andros
North Bight
Chart AN-12
Soundings in feet at MLW

Andros

Cargill Creek

Cargill Creek

Behring Point

Pyes Harbour

Blue Hole

North Bight

Salvador Point

Mackey

Behring Point

Bristol Galley Island

continuous reef

Tongue Of The Ocean

AUTEC Base #2

269° range Fl ev 6 sec

range Qk Fl

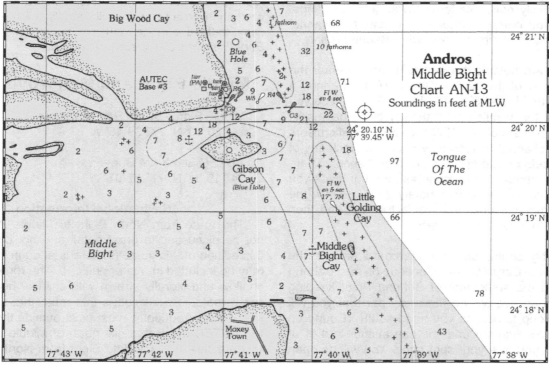

Big Wood Cay

Blue Hole

AUTEC Base #3

Gibson Cay
(Blue Hole)

Middle Bight

Moxey Town

Andros
Middle Bight
Chart AN-13
Soundings in feet at MLW

Tongue Of The Ocean

Little Golding Cay

Middle Bight Cay

suggest heading out the *AUTEC* channel at Salvador Point, turning south well outside the reef, and heading inside at the *AUTEC* channel at Middle Bight. *AUTEC* has so generously marked these channels for us, it's a shame that we don't use them. The passage from North Bight to South Bight and further is extremely difficult for vessels with drafts over 4'. A draft of 5' could make it through with a good high tide, but the route is strictly piloting by eye. Your attention on this route will be so concentrated on piloting by eye that you will have little room for error. Use extreme caution if you decide to pilot your way through here.

If you would like the help of a pilot, contact Hank Roberts, the owner of *Hank's Place* in Coakely Town. There is a good anchorage to the northwest of the northern tip of Big Wood Cay, but you have to head west around a shallow bar to access Big Wood Cay.

When entering Middle Bight from the *Tongue of the Ocean*, it is best to take advantage of the marked *AUTEC* channel for *Base #3* at the southeastern tip of Big Wood Cay as shown on Chart AN-13. A waypoint at 24° 20.10' N, 77° 39.45' W, will place you approximately ¼ mile east of the sea buoy. Simply follow the markers in keeping the reef to starboard and Gibson Cay off to port. Farther south, Little Golding Cay has a light that flashes white every 5 seconds, stands 17' above the water, and is visible for 7 nautical miles.

One of the most popular anchorages in Andros lies west of Gibson Cay. Pass between Gibson Cay and the *AUTEC* base on the southeast tip of Big Wood Cay, giving the rocky shoal south of the base a wide berth, and follow the deep blue water westward to anchor west of Gibson Cay. There is a lot of current here so use caution. You'll see some white buoys on your way through the channel, these are *AUTEC* buoys, not channel markers.

On the west side of Gibson Cay are several more white buoys, these are the hurricane moorings for the *AUTEC* boats. If you choose to anchor here be sure to set two anchors so you can ride to the strong current properly. There is deep water even further west of Gibson Cay with several areas to anchor, all exposed more or less to the prevailing winds. Keep an eye out for several small patch reefs through here.

There is an oceanic blue hole in the center of Gibson Cay that is connected to the sea by subterranean tunnels teeming with ocean fish. In the mid-1900s, the 222' *Vagabondia* was a frequent visitor to Middle Bight. She drew 12' and her owner, William Mellon, even put a mooring in Middle Bight to which he could lay to when in Andros.

Vessels wishing to head to South Bight should once again go outside at Middle Bight and enter South Bight via the unmarked but wide, deep entrance channel. The inside route from Middle Bight to South Bight, though easier than the route from North Bight to Middle Bight, still has areas where the water is 4' at low tide and there are plenty of coral heads and shallow patch reefs to avoid. I know that a few of you will say that the mailboats use this route so why shouldn't I. You can use the route, but I, in all honesty, cannot recommend this route for a 6' draft vessel. Yes, the mailboats do use this route, and they draw 6'. What one must understand is that the mailboat Captains know these waters, they use the tides, and they accept the fact that they must frequently pay the price for error by replacing props, an expensive proposition. Many carry extra props with them. Do you?

South of Middle Bight lies Mangrove Cay, an island to itself in some manners, some residents deny being from Andros…they want it to be made clear that they are from Mangrove Cay! Mangrove Cay is a picturesque settlement of nodding coconut palms. In a cave near Mangrove Cay an ancient Lucayan canoe and paddles were found. Mangrove Cay is said to be the bonefishing center of Andros. The adult bonefish mate in North Bight and South Bight and their young mature in the calm waters of the interior of Andros, which has led to the construction of many fish camps in the interior.

The eastern shore of Mangrove Cay has a number of small communities that are rarely visited. The northernmost settlement is Moxey Town, just across the Middle Bight from *AUTEC Base #3*. Moxey Town is sometimes called Little Harbour and is the site of the three day *August Monday Regatta*. In town there is a *Shell* service station and fuel can be delivered to the town dock but you will have to dinghy it out to the big boat. For fuel call Hubert King at 369-0478 or ask in town. In town you will find a Laundromat, a small hardware store, and the *Travelers Rest Restaurant* for lunch and dinner with reservation. Moxey Town also offers *Lundies Restaurant* and *Terry's Apartments*. Nearby is the 60' high Crow Hill where on the top are

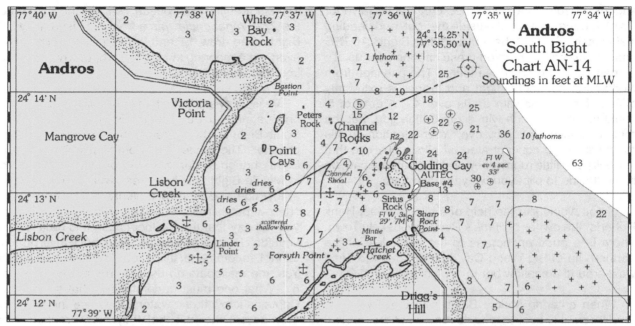

Lisbon Creek, South Bight

Photo Courtesy of Paul Harding, Safari Seaplanes

many caves where crows have constructed unique multi-tiered communities to hatch their young.

South of Moxey Town, small villages like Swains, Dorsetts, Grants, Burnt Rock, and Pinders line the shoreline amid groves of coconut palms facing the *Tongue of the Ocean*. In Dorsett you'll find Nelson Thompson's *Swain's Wholesale and Retail Bar* which probably should be in Swain's judging by the name.

The *Mangrove Cay Inn* at Pinder's lies about a two-minute walk away from the beach.

South Bight

South Bight - 1 nm NE of entrance:
24° 14.25' N, 77° 35.50' W

The creek system that makes up South Bight is very extensive and quite deep is some places. I've heard that with the help of a high tide it is possible to take a 4' draft through South Bight from the *Tongue of the Ocean* to the vast flats that lie on the western shore of Andros. I've also heard this about Middle Bight, but have yet to work my way through these two areas as I draw 5'. The entrance to South Bight is wide and deep, no need to use an *AUTEC* channel here.

Navigational Information

A waypoint at 24° 14.25' N, 77° 35.50' W, will place you approximately 1 mile northeast of the entrance channel to South Bight. From this position take up an approximate course of 248° on the southernmost of the two Channel Rocks. Eyeball your way through and as you approach Channel Rocks swing to port to avoid them.

Once inside, between Channel Rocks and Golding Cay, where the *AUTEC* base is, watch out for the shallow *Channel Shoal* about mid-channel south of Channel Rocks.

What You Will Find Ashore

At the southern end of Mangrove Cay, Chart AN-14, lies the small settlement of Victoria Point, sometimes called Bastion Point. The settlement is rich in fresh water, there are wells almost everywhere.

A mile inland from Victoria Point lies the settlement of Lisbon Creek. Lisbon Creek was, and still is, the center of boat building activities on the island of Andros with a few *Family Island Regatta* winners constructed here. You can work your way into the mouth of the creek with 6' at low water. About 300 yards east of the creek a dredged channel is very visible in all but the late afternoon sun. The creek was dredged about a few years ago and will now take a 6' draft a considerable distance inside where you can get excellent protection even in strong easterly winds.

It has been suggested that boaters can anchor in Drigg's Hill Harbour to await the tide to go up the creek. I do not recommend it. The local *AUTEC* people often moor their boats in the harbour and they have reported numerous instances of theft and vandalism to their vessels. Bear in mind what the *AUTEC* people have to say about this harbour and use your own judgment, I believe you're better off

anchoring behind Golding Cay or off Forsyth Point. If you draw less than 5' you can also anchor south of Linder Point working your way in with a high tide.

In Lisbon Creek, Sylvia Bannister has a unique guesthouse appropriately named *Bannister's House*. Sylvia and her husband Henry have collected pet turtles for over 25 years and their restaurant, the *Aquamarine Club*, has a turtle pen, which connects to the sea right from the dining room. When I was last there Sylvia had nine hawksbill turtles that she would feed lettuce daily. The Bannisters do not eat or serve turtle on their menu. Henry is an excellent guide to this area and knows of several blue holes in the immediate area.

Accommodations can also be found at the *Longley Guest House*. Leroy Bannister is a guide for diving and fishing and has lived hereabouts fishing, farming, and racing sailboats all his life. His bar, *Leroy's Harbour Bay* is the most popular spot in town and Leroy can arrange to have diesel and gas delivered to the dock for boaters. Leroy is one of the premier boat builders in this area, but Ralph Moxey in Moxey town will tell you that Leroy has never beat him. *Elliott and Pat's Inn* will pick you up for dinner in their taxi as groceries and restaurants are all but out of walking range for even the hardiest trekkers.

Driggs Hill lies at the northern tip of south Andros on the southern side of South Bight. They have a new dredged harbour that was at one time said to be a future home to cruise ships, but this has never come about. Just south of Sirius Cay is a pile marking the northern side of the harbour. The green piling is halfway in. A day range is inside but hard to see from outside the channel. You can tie to the tires along the eastern wall but use caution as it is no place to be in a strong easterly wind. There is a free government ferry that plies the waters between Driggs Hill and Lisbon Creek twice a day.

About two miles south of Driggs Hill is the *Emerald Palms By-The-Sea* resort. Not far from the airport at Congo Town, this seaside resort has it all, palm trees, a swimming pool, 20 air-conditioned rooms with ceiling fans, TV, VCR, refrigerators, and, last but not least, romantic four poster double or king size beds. Dinners are by reservation and the *Emerald Palms* will provide transportation. The resort can also arrange diving and fishing charters for you.

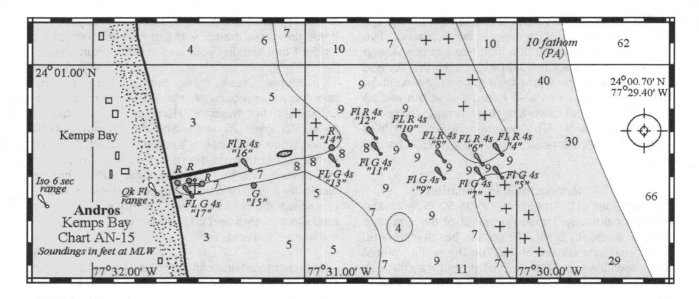

Drigg's Hill, Middle Bight

Photo Courtesy of Paul Harding, Safari Seaplanes

Congo Town is a *Port of Entry* for The Bahamas and a main waypoint for incoming flights to clear in. It has a 5,000' airstrip between High Rock and Congo Town itself. Although spread over a few square miles, the actual center of Congo Town is a place known as *The Jungle*. *The Jungle Club* run by Babar Paul and her mother is an excellent restaurant situated right on the beach. *The Congo Beach Hotel Restaurant and Bar* even offers satellite TV. The manager, Jerry Davis, also has a grocery store with very good prices. Two miles north on the water at the border of Congo

Town and Long Bay is the *Las Palmas Beach Hotel*. It is the only truly modern resort in South Andros with a large swimming pool, tennis court, and offering world class deep sea and bonefishing charters.

Kemps Bay

Kemps Bay - ½ nm ENE of entrance channel:
24° 00.70' N, 77° 29.40' W

Kemps Bay is a popular spot for visitors to Andros and the entrance is shown on Chart AN-15. Here you'll find Norward Rahming whose diversified holdings include a grocery store, a resort, a shipping company, a lumberyard, and a school bus system. One of his newest enterprises is the *Royal Palm Beach Lodge* in town by the beach. Here you can purchase groceries, diesel, gas, kerosene, or rent a car for an island excursion. In town you'll find a branch of the *Bank of The Bahamas*. Just north of town is the *Kemp's Bay Club*, a wonderful little tropical paradise for tourists seeking a private getaway. The *Kemp's Bay Club* can organize bonefishing trips for interested parties.

There is an old *AUTEC* base in Kemp's Bay that was returned to the Bahamian government and I understand that Norward Rahming is planning to build a marina there. The entrance channel, the only way in to Kemp's Bay, is a narrow but marked dogleg channel. The markers may or may not be there as they are no longer maintained.

Navigational Information
As shown on Chart AN-15, a GPS waypoint at 24° 00.70' N, 77° 29.40' W, will place you approximately ½ mile east/northeast of the marked entrance channel. Use caution and follow the markers in towards the small basin south of the breakwater as shown on the chart where there is room for two boats, just don't block the dock as the mailboat and other commercial vessels come in and out of here regularly.

What You Will Find Ashore
You can get fuel, water, groceries, some hardware items, and ice at *Rahming's General Store* where you can also get your laundry done. For dining try *Kemps Restaurant* at High Rock, the *Royal Palms Restaurant* in Kemps Bay, and *David's Takeaway* in Smith Hill. If you need refrigeration repairs contact Bert Ammons at the *Kemps Bay Club*, and if you would like to rent a car, contact *Nascov* in Deep Creek at 369-5001. *Johnson's Electronics* in Smith's Hill also has a few hardware items.

From Kemp's Bay to The Bluff are many deserted beaches, numerous coconut groves, one after another, and some very shallow water. The Bluff is home to the local government complex which includes a government clinic, a fishing co-op processing plant, and the main *Bahamas Electricity Corporation* (*BEC*) station for Andros.

About three miles south of Deep Creek is the small settlement of Little Creek where you will *find M & S Takeaway*. South of Little Creek and just north of High Point is Pleasant Bay. A good landmark to the area is the plane stranded along the shore. High Point is home to an *AUTEC* Base, the smallest one on Andros.

Mars Bay is the southernmost settlement on Andros. Small boats only can enter at high tide and anchor in its harbor, which is nothing more than a blue hole. It is a shame that only small boats can get in here as this is one of the prettiest harbors in The Bahamas with palm trees growing along the shaded beach. The settlement of Mars Bay lies a few hundred yards inland with a few very clean, if not modern, homes. In town you will find Mrs. Wilbur Smith who has given birth to 24 children. It is interesting to note that many people in Mars Bay hail from the Exumas, the Staniel Cay area in particular.

South from Mars Bay, around the southern tip of Andros the fishing and diving is fantastic but the piloting is murderous, shoals and shallow reefs abound. You will certainly have to work your way in to find any sort of shelter and then if a blow built up overnight, you would not be able to leave until daylight.

Green Cay

Green Cay - ¼ nm W of western tip:
24° 02.60' N, 77° 11.70' W

Green Cay, Chart AN-16, lies on the western side of the *Tongue of the Ocean* at the western edge of the *Great Bahama Bank*, which stretches eastward towards the Exumas. Green Cay and its surrounding waters are a popular spot for fishermen from Exuma as well as Andros and I've decided to include it in both *The Exuma Guide* and this publication (technically it is closer to the island of Andros).

Navigational Information
As shown on Chart AN-16, a waypoint at 24° 02.60' N, 77° 11.70' W, will place you approximately ¼ mile west of the western tip of Green Cay. In prevailing winds the best anchorages lie along the northern shore of Green Cay, though any spot that you choose that is nearer the *Tongue of the Ocean* will be certainly open to the surge that originates from that body of water. A couple of anchorages on the southern side of Green Cay offer a lee in northerly winds, but here

again, the closer you get to the *Tongue of the Ocean*, the more surge you will have to endure.

Green Cay has a bit of a history in the annals of piracy in The Bahamas. Some of the pirates of three centuries ago were known for their barbarous acts of cruelty, which were not reserved solely for their enemies. Pirates often served their own brand of justice by marooning their fellow pirates, as well as captives, on deserted islands. In 1718, Green Cay played host to a marooning that may have given the island its name. Most maroonings led to death for those marooned, but the lucky band that was banished to Green Cay survived, probably due to the indecisiveness of the very men that marooned them.

Refusing to join his mutinous crew to go *a-pyrating*, Captain William Greenaway and seven others were set ashore on Green Cay to await their deaths. Just as the new pirates sailed away from Green Cay, they suddenly had a slight change of heart. They returned to Green Cay and collected Greenaway and his men, and brought them out to a captured sloop. They left them aboard the sloop, but before leaving they fouled the main sheet, cut the huge foresail to the size of a small jib, and then continued to slash the sails and rigging to pieces until the sloop was virtually useless.

Greenaway and company were now worse off than before. They were without food and water, anchored a mile offshore, and only Greenaway could swim. Greenaway found a small broken hatchet on board and went ashore with the blade tied around his neck. He built rafts from trees and he and his men ferried fruits, berries, and cabbages out to the sloop from the small cay as they went about rebuilding their vessel.

A week later the small band had the sloop fit enough to set sail, but to their horror they saw the pirates returning. They jumped onto their rafts and fled to the safety of Green Cay where they watched the pirates sink their vessel in deep water. For eight days the group lived in the bush, eating berries and fish and hiding whenever the pirates came ashore and called out to them. Promising them safe passage off the cay Greenaway and his men came out of the bush to find that they had been tricked. The mutineers forced Greenaway and two of his men to join their crew and marooned the other five men back on Green Cay.

The five survived for weeks on what little they could eke out of the bush and nearby waters. One day they looked to seaward and saw the pirates returning once more. This time, possibly thanks to Greenaway, the pirates left behind a cask of flour, a bushel of salt,

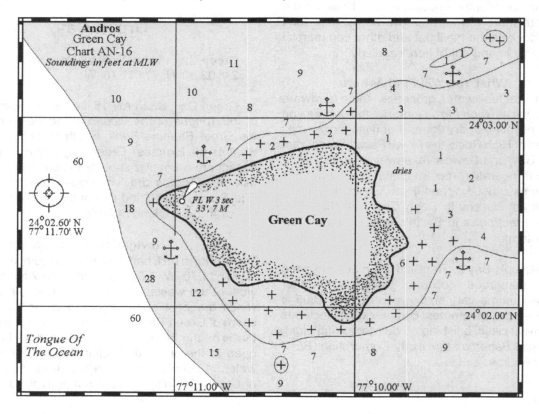

two muskets, two bottles of gunpowder, a container of musket shot, an axe, a dozen knives, and several pots and pans along with three good hunting dogs. With the aid of the dogs the group was able to catch some of the hogs on the cay and dine on roast pork. Before long the small band built a hut and began to wait comfortably for a passing ship. When the happy group finally spotted a sail it turned out to be the pirates again. This time the pirates burned down their hut and ate all their roast pork. They left behind a bottle of rum with a promise never to return.

The mutineers never did return to Green Cay. Soon after leaving Green Cay they were captured by a Spanish ship who, after hearing Greenaway's story, sent Bahamian John Sims to rescue those marooned on Green Cay.

A Dive Too Deep
The Story of Archie Forfar

On December 22, 1959, the *Able Lady*, a 40' schooner, left Miami bound for Nassau. On board were the captain, Archie Forfar, his wife Toni, and three friends on their way to spend the holidays with more friends in Nassau. On Christmas Eve the good ship and crew were caught in a storm while passing to the north of the island of Andros. In the poor visibility and rough seas the vessel went off course and fetched up on the barrier reef that fringes the eastern shore of Andros, a graveyard for many a vessel. Despite being the third largest barrier reef in the world it was reputedly not marked on the ship's chart. There was no time for the captain and crew to use the new radio that they had just installed in Miami prior to their departure. The storm tossed crew clung to the wreckage for 15 hours until they were blown up on nearby Rat Cay.

They spent Christmas Day on the island thankful to be alive though stranded, bruised, and very, very weary. On Boxing Day, Archie and Toni swam and walked across the shallow waters between Rat Cay and the mainland of Andros. Nearing exhaustion, the couple were finally found by the Rev. Wellington Hannah who happened to be out conching in his boat. The crew was picked up and everyone was taken to the nearby settlement of Mastic Point for some hot food before being flown to Nassau and then back home to their native Canada. Despite the circumstances, sometime during that shore visit Archie Forfar made

the decision to return to Andros where he would live until his untimely death in 1971.

Archie quickly returned to Andros and initially, using the skills acquired as a construction worker in Canada, became the handyman for the dive resort at Small Hope Bay which was owned by fellow Canadians Dick and Rosie Burch. But Archie was not satisfied here. He had dreams to fulfill and he nurtured the idea of having his own place. Archie applied for a permit from the Bahamian government and as soon as it arrived he began work on an overgrown area at the mouth of Stafford Creek.

Living out of a small tent at first, working with shovels and a machete, Archie set about transforming the property. Rather than build somewhere to live, Archie had a workshop as his top priority. The lodge and cabins soon followed, all built from local limestone and termite resistant pine. The cabins were designed with one corner oriented towards the prevailing wind so as to funnel the air and also reduce storm damage. Archie also incorporated a unique system of wooden slats to control ventilation. Archie then built an electrical generator and wired all of the buildings. Next he drilled wells and installed all the plumbing. Two large tanks were erected on a tower for a water supply. Archie used solar power to heat the water for the kitchen and then constructed a sewage system using heavy bars chipping into the limestone to house three 1,000-gallon septic tanks. These achievements may not seem significant until you come to know the island's resources, almost everything has to be imported.

Archie struck up lasting friendships with the native community. Emily Johnson, a Bahamian who lived nearby, would often bring food to Archie's tent, taking care of him when he neglected to. The local folks loved Archie and he loved them.

Toni Forfar soon joined her husband but found the island very lonely and she experienced difficulty in adjusting to the rather unique lifestyle. Toni was a qualified mid-wife, but there is some speculation that Archie may have been unable to provide her with the children that she so desperately longed for. Toni occupied her days as Archie's business manager, successfully organizing the finances, making the purchases, setting up the contracts for the lodge, and running the bar.

Archie's *Andros Reef Inn* was now up and running. Archie continued to build his dreams into the resort. A qualified pilot, Archie was able to fly in supplies on his own plane or by taking his boat, *Cochine*, to Nassau or the U.S. As Archie's place thrived the local people benefited. The locals will tell you that Archie "lifted us up"; as building supplies and other materials became available for Archie, they also became available for the local folks. Groceries and gas were sold at the inn and there was a bar, pool table, jukebox, and a large fireplace around which everyone was welcome. The Androsians were made as welcome as any of the visiting divers. Archie's guests came from all classes of people with all sizes of wallets and varied diving backgrounds. On any given week you might look around and find a batch of novices wanting to learn the basics of diving in the shallow waters near the beach, thrilled to be diving on the protected patch reefs near shore, while a glance to seaward might reveal several internationally respected "name" divers who were more concerned with researching the murky depths of a blue hole or pushing their endurance to the limit by descending to incredible depths to explore the face of "the wall." "The wall" being the eastern edge of the Andros barrier reef where it drops almost vertical to the bottom of the Tongue of the Ocean some 6,000 feet. It was at this time that Archie met George Benjamin, a Toronto research chemist and dive aficionado. Together Archie and George explored more than 54 of the over 400 blue holes that dot Andros. The results were published in an article in *National Geographic Magazine* in 1970. Along with a gentleman from Florida, Archie plotted a treasure course of 27 wrecks and Archie's fame and reputation were growing as fast as his resort was becoming a success.

But as Archie emptied and refilled air tanks, Toni emptied and refilled glasses. Toni and Archie just weren't getting along. Toni's dependence on alcohol increased until she became ill and had to leave for Canada. She eventually did return but their old troubles surfaced and she could only bear to stay a short time. Eventually, in early 1971, she was forced to give up the island and Archie remained. Archie and Toni are the only ones who truly know what came between them. All anyone else knew is that they had sadly drifted apart.

Later that year a 22-year-old diving instructor named Anne Gunderson visited the *Andros Reef Inn*. She immediately lifted the gloom that had surrounded the 39 year-old Archie since Toni's departure. They dived together and thoroughly enjoyed each other's company. Archie and Anne practically lived together even after Toni returned to run the resort again.

Around that same time, several divers had been diving very deep in the Tongue of the Ocean and there was an apparent preoccupation with breaking records for depth. Dick Burch, with the help of a Canadian chemist, succeeded in one deep dive already. Archie Forfar, though almost 40, was still one of the best divers around and he had achieved many accomplishments which other people discounted as impossible. And even though Anne was a very, very ambitious person, no one who knew them was quite sure why they decided to attempt a record-breaking dive to 450'.

Their training took place over a six-month period during which time they completed many committing dives of up to six hours. Their anticipated descent would take only four or five minutes, but long decompression stops were necessary on the way back up at various points due to the great depths involved. Soon the couple felt thoroughly prepared, physically and psychologically. Even so Tom Mount, the founder of *IANTD*-the *International Association of Nitrox and Technical Divers*, a close friend of Archie's and a dive instructor himself, advised against it. Tom recounts, "We debated it. He was convinced that it was foolish and he shouldn't do it, but Anne was going to do it anyway...and that's really what it amounted to, he was looking out for her." Many others who were involved on the periphery of the challenge say Archie was pushed into it by an arrogant promoter from Miami who wanted to oversee the event and bring great publicity to the feat (and perhaps coins to his pocket).

As the boat motored out to the dive site on the morning of December 11, 1971, Archie and Anne applied ice packs to their faces in readiness for the cold waters they would encounter at depth. Next they made their customary final checks as they had done so many times before, they had already had three undocumented dives to this depth. With them on the voyage out to the dive site were Dick Burch, two island Commissioners, and several representatives from the press to witness the attempt.

A descending line, an old greasy steel cable buoyed at the surface, was weighted to the bottom in a little over 500' of water at the wall. A clamp carried by the divers would be attached to the line at depth to verify the record and other pins were to be unattached on their way back up for further proof. Archie and Anne left the surface accompanied by four safety back-up divers, three of which were positioned strategically up the shot line, a fourth, Jim Lockwood, would accompany Archie and Anne to 300'.

The first indication of trouble came thirty minutes later from a diver off a second boat who reported that he'd been down to 150' and could only see four divers on the line. He went down again, this time carrying a slate to determine which two divers were missing. A written message from one of the backups confirmed that it was Archie and Anne. It seems that their safety line had snagged and they had released it. Then, for some reason, opted to continue the descent negatively buoyant by dropping the weights that were slid onto their feet and deflating the buoyancy vests they wore. News was slow reaching the surface because the divers had to decompress during their ascent. When Jim Lockwood surfaced, he informed onlookers that he had accompanied Archie and Anne to 400', but had then fell faint and had to begin his ascent. Jim had actually blacked out and relied on his fellow safety divers up the descending line to halt his progress and give him time to straighten out before letting him continue his ascent. Realizing that there could be a problem, two of the backup divers went down to investigate. At somewhere below 400' one of the pair was affected by the sensation of tunnel vision (sometimes experienced during deep dives when breathing compressed air, you can hear and feel things but lose the sense of sight) and had to find his way back up. The second diver managed to reach even lower from where he could see Archie and Anne another 30' below him. Their fins were moving and he could see bubbles rising. Anne was laying on her back on a ledge in the wall, ten feet away from Archie who was leaning over the weight which anchored the shot line, he appeared to be working on it. The second diver was then briefly affected by tunnel vision. When his sight cleared there was no movement from the two below him, no bubbles were rising. Feeling unable to reach Archie and Anne at his present depth any longer, he too began his ascent. Another diver reported seeing Archie trying to swim to the surface with Anne in his arms, a near impossible and fatal feat at that depth.

Bob Black, the near-legendary head diver of the

nearby *AUTEC* base, was called to the scene and asked how long they had been down. When told they had been down an hour and a half he sadly shook his head and said they wouldn't be coming back up. He asked Toni if she wanted him to contact some military personnel who could bring the bodies up and she declined. She said that Archie wanted to be with his girlfriend and he now could have her down there. Bob cut the descending cable where it still lies today. Bob Black is of the opinion that Anne was in a state of nitrogen narcosis and that Archie had gone down to help her. She might have been disoriented at depth trying to unhook from the line and remember all she had to do for her ascent.

In a state of shock witnesses made statements to the police in Fresh Creek. No one was prepared to guess what went wrong. The only information was from the divers who had been acting under extreme stress. Divers know that oxygen in compressed air becomes toxic and critical at 220' while nitrogen, at only 100', can become a narcotic. Divers can get what is called nitrogen narcosis, a pleasant high and anesthetic that can inhibit rational thinking and coordinated movement. Archie and Anne, and perhaps Jim Lockwood, had been experienced with coping with such difficulties. Many people close to the attempt say that the choice of Jim Lockwood as a backup was curious. Apparently it was common knowledge that in the recent past he had acted as a safety on a dive when several fatalities had occurred.

All concerned returned to the inn, each alone with their thoughts. The parents of Archie Forfar and Anne Gunderson came to Andros looking for an explanation they never received. All they found was hearsay and rumors and this is where so many questions were aroused. It has been mentioned that Archie had been in for a medical checkup in Canada six weeks prior to the dive and it was rumored that he was suffering from a lung complaint. If that is so, how could he continue diving, especially at that depth? The Gunderson's heard that Anne was pregnant by her boyfriend back in Canada while others claimed the father was Archie. One of the more nagging questions was why Archie transferred 1½ acres of his land the night before the dive to Irma Johnson and another acre to a gentleman from the *AUTEC* base? Why did he offer his new stone cottage to Bob Black, the head diver on the *AUTEC* base at Fresh Creek who warned him not to attempt the dive, as did Dick

Burch? These could be attributed to premonition say those involved. But what about the $16,000 in cash that was missing from Archie's safe the day after the accident? Who had the combination besides Archie? What about Archie's rare and expensive collection of shells, where did it disappear to the day after the dive? The last two could have been written off to theft say those involved. But when the executor of the Archie's estate went to check on a bank account in Nassau that Archie had owned he found some startling information. The bank reported that a few days after the accident a person signed a withdrawal slip in Archie's handwriting withdrawing the entire balance of some $15,000.

One thing is for certain, Archie was a professional. He was very experienced and often counted on himself to do the "impossible." It has been speculated that the dive might have been a stunt concocted by Archie and Anne to get away from it all and start over in Latin America where a little money can go a long way (it was mentioned that Archie could have surveyed the area of the dive site during any of the hundred of dives he made in that area, including some in Jacque Cousteau's submersible in the weeks just prior to the dive). It would have been very easy for Archie to stash some tanks in the area in order to surface somewhere else far away though professional divers don't agree with this opinion saying he would have been seen coming ashore on Andros. Maybe not though if everyone was looking at a cable leading to a 500' depth along the barrier reef.

The *Andros Reef Inn* was left in the hands of one of the stockholders who was unable to maintain it. He was prone to fits of rage and began selling everything off. When Toni returned a year later, Archie Forfar's dream lay in ruin. All her work and suffering had been in vain. Toni returned to Canada where she underwent surgery for cirrhosis of the liver and died on the operating table a few months later.

During the last years of his life Archie had taken a special interest in the operations and goals of a non-profit organization called *International Field Studies* (*IFS*) who were operating out of an abandoned schoolhouse that Archie was helping to renovate on a nearby beach. All the equipment and resources Archie had at his disposal were made available to the students visiting the island. The schoolhouse renovation was nearing completion in December of 1971 when Archie had planned his final dive.

In the following years, the *Andros Reef Inn* was made available to *IFS* for leasing and then purchase, becoming what is now called the *Forfar Field Station*. A great deal of restoration was necessary and some changes too. Archie no longer serves up inspiration in the bar and the diving is a little more conservative perhaps, but Archie has left his mark. The old water tower was only made redundant in February of 1989 and the old generators still powered the buildings until they were retired in favor of mains electricity in November of 1990. Archie's cabins survived *Hurricane David* intact in 1979. The exhibits in the classroom are still in the original case and the old fireplace still cranks up on cold winter evenings. And some people still wonder about Archie Forfar. As a final note, it's said that Archie is still regularly seen around *Forfar Field Station*, it's not unusual to hear one of the residents of the station remark that he saw Archie walking around the previous night...

New Providence

Ports of Entry: Nassau, Lyford Cay
Fuel: Nassau. Lyford Cay
Haul-Out: Nassau
Diesel Repairs: Nassau, Lyford Cay
Outboard Repairs: Nassau, Lyford Cay
Propane: Nassau, Lyford Cay
Provisions: Nassau, Lyford Cay
Important Lights:
    Goulding Cay W end: Fl W ev 2 sec
    Fort Fincastle: Fl W ev 5 sec
    Paradise Island: Fl W or R ev 5 sec
    The Narrows: Fl R ev 5 sec
    Porgee Rock: Fl W ev 3 sec
    Chub Rock: Fl W ev 5 sec
    Lyford Cay: Fl W ev 2 sec
    Coral Harbour: Fl W ev 2 sec
    East Point: Fl W ev 6 sec

The island of New Providence lies on a corner of the *Great Bahama Bank* and is bounded to the west by the deep water of the *Tongue of the Ocean* and along its northern and northeastern shores by the *Northwest* and *Northeast Providence Channels*. The southern shore is relatively shallow and one must pass a fair distance offshore to pass south of New Providence if bound for the Exumas. The 147 square miles of New Providence is home to over half the population of The Bahamas owing that distinction to the fact that its major city, Nassau, the capital of The Bahamas, lies along its northeastern shore. New Providence was once known as *Nequa* in Lucayan times.

Approaches to New Providence

New Providence can be reached by a variety of shallow and deep-water routes. From the Caribbean skippers can travel northward up Exuma Sound to cross the banks from Exuma. From the east vessels can approach the island from Eleuthera via the banks or in the deeper water of the *Northeast Providence Channel* along with vessels heading south from Abaco. From the U.S. coast most skippers take either the traditional Bimini-Chubb-Nassau route or they may pass north of Great Isaac and round the northern Berry Islands to make landfall at Nassau. This same route can be utilized by boats heading south from Grand Bahama. From Andros it is but a short hop across the *Tongue of the Ocean* to the western edge of New Providence.

Nassau

Nassau Harbour - W entrance:
25° 05.33' N, 77° 21.35' W

Porgee Rocks - ¼ nm S of:
25° 03.50' N, 77° 14.55' W

Nassau is the Capitol of The Bahamas and has a very long and active history in the New World. The city was originally a haven for Pirates such as Henry Morgan, Edward Teach (AKA Blackbeard), Charles Vane, and Calico Jack Rackham. Originally called Charles Town, Nassau was burned and looted by the Spanish and captured by the Americans in its day. Nassau has also served as home to blockade runners during the American Civil War years, rum runners during the American Prohibition years, and was quite often a stopover for drug runners from the more recent drug running years. Nassau is now touted world wide as a prime vacation destination with its beautiful beaches, near perfect weather, casinos, and nightlife.

Nassau Harbour lies between the northeastern shore of the mainland of New Providence and the extremely touristy Paradise Island, once known as Hog Island, the place where Bahamians would picnic on the northern beach on weekends half a century ago. At one time Edward Lynch, later of *Merril-Lynch*, owned a winter home called *Shangri-La* on the western end of the island. In the late 1930s, the home was purchased by Swedish industrialist Axel Wenner-Gren for $15,000 (today the home has become the *Ocean Club* on *Cabbage Beach*). Wenner-Gren took to refurbishing the mansion and dredged a foul inland lake named *Burnside's Pond* cutting two canals, one leading into Nassau harbour, the other leading north to the sea. Wenner-Gren built two bridges over the canals and the entire lake was renamed Paradise Lake. Later a boathouse was built near the lake and the cove that was to become *Hurricane Hole Marina* was constructed. Wenner-Gren had close ties with Nazi Germany and in the years prior to and during World War II, it was suspected that his construction on Hog Island would somehow be used to further the German war effort, so much so that Wenner-Gren was declared a *persona non grata* in The Bahamas, which angered him to no end. Wenner-Gren was famous for his parties at *Shangri-La*, and was close to David, the Duke of Windsor, who was the Governor of The Bahamas at this time. Over the years following

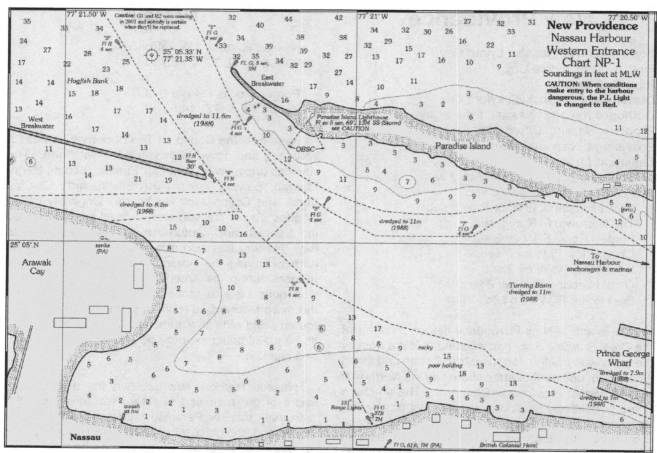

Nassau, Western Harbour
and Paradise Island

Photo Courtesy of Paul Harding, Safari Seaplanes

World War II, Wenner-Gren spent more and more time living in Mexico although he still purchased lots on Hog Island and continued to visit the island hosting his lavish parties. At one of his parties in 1959 he met the wealthy American playboy Huntington Hartford, whose grandfather had found the *Great Atlantic and Pacific Tea Company* which evolved into the huge chain of *A&P Grocery Stores*. On the back of a dinner menu, the two men drew up an agreement of the sale of Hog Island for $20 million. Complaints from Hartford's lawyers that the "menu agreement" as it was called, was not valid and the price far too high, brought about a more proper sale whereby Harford bought the island for $9.5 million in 1961.

Hartford knew the name had to be changed and applied to the government to change it, so on May 23, 1962, Hog Island officially became Paradise Island. In a few short years the island was transformed from a quiet Bahamian cay into one of the world's prime tourist destinations complete with major hotels, restaurants, an airport, a golf course, marinas, and the new huge *Atlantis* resort with its walk-through aquarium. An 11th century cloister was transported to the island and rebuilt as the *Versailles Gardens*. The cloister was originally from a 14th century French monastery and was brought to the United States by William Randolph Hearst. Hartford acquired the cloister and brought it to Paradise Island in the 1960's. In 1966, Hartford sold 75% of his holdings to the *Mary Carter Paint Company* who constructed the 500-room *Loew's Paradise Island Hotel*. In 1968, the ownership evolved into what is today known as *Resort's International*. Celebrities who have at one time or another sought refuge on Paradise Island include Howard Hughes and the Shah of Iran.

Navigational Information

There are only two entrances to *Nassau Harbour*, a deep-water entrance from the west and a shallower entrance from the *Great Bahama Bank* lying to the east. Most first time visitors to Nassau will usually enter the harbour from the west (be sure to keep a good lookout for large ship traffic, Nassau is a busy port). There are two things to remember when entering *Nassau Harbour*. First, all boats must call *Nassau Harbour Control* on VHF ch. 16 to request permission to enter the harbour from either the western or the eastern entrance. The controller will ask you to switch to VHF ch. 9 and proceed to inquire as to your destination, last port of call, documentation number, and destination within the harbour, whether you plan to anchor or tie up at one of Nassau's many fine marinas. Second, you must also call *Harbour Control* when leaving the harbour, *Nassau Harbour Control* is very proud of the records they maintain concerning ship traffic so don't blow off calling them in the mistaken assumption that they won't miss you. The records *Nassau Harbour Control* keeps are primarily aimed at commercial vessels and for private vessels it is a courtesy for you to call and check in so don't forget to do so.

Approaching Nassau at night from the north, either the Abacos or the Berrys, your first sight will probably be the flashing white light atop the water tower at *Fort Fincastle*. This revolving light flashes white approximately once every 5 seconds. A waypoint at 25° 05.33' N, 77° 21.35' W, will place you approximately ½ nautical mile north/northwest of the harbour's western entrance. The entrance to the harbour is very straightforward and wide, lying between two rocky breakwaters. On the shore of the eastern breakwater lies the *Paradise Island Lighthouse* with its flashing light. At night you can of course use the red and green lights on the buoys or the range lights ashore to come in on a heading of 151°. Remember that The Bahamas use the *IALA* (*International Association of Lighthouse Authorities*) *Maritime Buoyage System* more commonly known as the three *R's, Red, Right, Returning*. It is absolutely imperative that when approaching the western entrance to Nassau Harbour, you do not mistake the small arched bridge leading to the *Coral World* attraction on Silver Cay (1 mile east of the actual harbour entrance) for the *Paradise Island Bridge*. A few years ago a 45' catamaran did just that and in attempting to enter what the fatigued skipper thought to be Nassau Harbour ran aground, holed his boat, and lost her on a reef. This one incident was not the first and will most likely not be the last. The skipper who takes this for the entrance has no idea until it is too late that he is actually coming in over a reef. It is not unusual for the outer buoys at the western entrance of Nassau Harbour to be missing, winter storms and huge seas frequently destroy them so keep your eyes open as you approach and don't be surprised if you don't find the marks identical to what is shown on the charts.

The entrance to Nassau harbour during winter frontal passages can be absolutely impassable. With large northerly swells a rage will build up across the entrance closing the entrance. When this occurs the light on Paradise Island will change to red. If in doubt call *Nassau Harbour Control*.

Entering *Nassau Harbour* from the east, usually for vessels arriving from Exuma or Eleuthera, is also easy. A waypoint at 25° 03.50' N, 77° 14.55' W, will place you approximately 500 yards south of Porgee Rocks as shown on Chart NP-4. From this position you should parallel the southern shore of Athol Island and Paradise Island working your way towards *The Narrows*. Keep south of *The Narrows*, that's where the deeper water lies, and then parallel the southern shore of Paradise Island and either head east under the bridge or south between Potter's Cay and the light which marks the rocky bar just to the east of Potters

Cay. Vessels may also head for the marinas along the northern shore of New Providence east of the bridge by steering straight towards the *Nassau Harbour Club* as soon as they come abeam of the eastern point by the *Nassau Yacht Club* (see Chart NP-3).

The easternmost of the two Paradise Island bridges is shown on Government charts as having a vertical clearance of 21 meters or 69'. Locals boat operators and marina operators tell me that the actual height is somewhere between 65' and 68' at low water. This seems to be a bit of a gray area so use caution if your mast height is over 65'. Even *BASRA* seems unsure of the actual height of the bridge. The westernmost bridge, the new bridge, has a vertical clearance of 70' at low water.

After entering the harbour some folks (very, very few anymore) anchor directly off the beach at the *Hilton Hotel*, formerly the *British Colonial Hotel,* the large pink building that sits directly east of the cruise ship docks, older cruising guides say to anchor here, but I don't recommend it. The holding is poor, only a little sand over coral, its better to anchor inside the harbour proper just past *Prince George Wharf* (the cruise ship docks). But if you happen to get down this way by car or bus, you'll find the *Nassau Pirate Museum* and bar just one block up from the Hilton. Next door is *ITS, International Telecomm Services* where you can access the Internet and buy international phone cards. Across the street from the *Hilton* is Conch Fritters, a great restaurant that's always busy, a *McDonald's*, the *U.S. Embassy*, a very nice antique shop, and west of the hotel is more Internet access at *Internet Works*.

So if you don't want to anchor off the *Hilton*, after entering bear to port to pass *Prince George Wharf* and its cruise ships to starboard and head towards the conspicuous Paradise Island bridges. Keep an eye out for the large mooring buoy (for ships) lying just east of the eastern end of *Prince George Wharf*. Most vessels will anchor south of the center of the harbour between Potter's Cay and *Marine Diesel*, just off *BASRA* and *Friday's*. Due to the increased ship traffic in Nassau Harbour over the last couple of years, vessels anchoring west of *Marine Diesel* towards the remains of the old *Sugar Reef Restaurant* may be asked to move. Large ships come in and out of the harbour 24-hours a day to load and unload their cargo along the docks east of *Sugar Reef* and small boats anchored in this area are definitely in danger. If

you are anchored in an unsafe place *Nassau Harbour Patrol* or the *Defense Force* will definitely remind you to move. Vessels drawing over 5' should be aware of the shallow bar in the center of the harbour lying east/west; it's shallower towards its western end.

Vessels anchoring near the western edge of Potter's Cay should be advised that large vessels are now using the western tip of Potter's Cay for loading and unloading supplies. If you are attempting to head to *East Bay Marina*, which lies at the southwestern foot of the easternmost *Paradise Island Bridge*, let me advise you that the marina has all but closed. The docks are in a complete state of disrepair, the worst I've ever seen them, and the only boats in there are some local fishing boats.

Off the southwestern tip of Potter's cay is a shallow spot (4') that usually grounds a boat every week during the season. The entrance into the old *East Bay Marina* through the westernmost *Paradise Island Bridge* carries approximately 54' at low water along the Potter's Cay side of the channel. I'm told that you can get 55' through there, but the official word is that the bridge has a clearance of 54'.

The large pink building on the southern shore of Paradise Island just east of the *Prince George Wharf* is now *Club Med.* You can anchor off its shore in 8'-12', as long as you don't mind *Karaoke* nights and live entertainment most evenings. The building was once known as the *Porcupine Club*, a very exclusive retreat for millionaires, membership was limited to 125 and you had to be worth a minimum of one million dollars. It was built in 1912 on seven acres on Paradise Island by a group of American millionaires who belonged to a club in Philadelphia by the same name.

Once past the *Paradise Island Bridge* some skippers seek to anchor along the southern shore of Paradise Island. Watch out for traffic here and stay out of the channel. Some vessels pass between Potter's Cay and the light which marks a shoal area just 100 yards to the east of the cay. This shoal area continues some ways east in the center of the harbour. After you pass between the light and Potter's Cay steer to starboard and pass the rows of marinas where you may find anchorage between the last marina on your right, the *Nassau Harbour Club*, and the at the extreme eastern end of the harbour. The only traffic you will encounter here is a few high-speed boats, some party boats, and some small boat traffic. At the eastern end

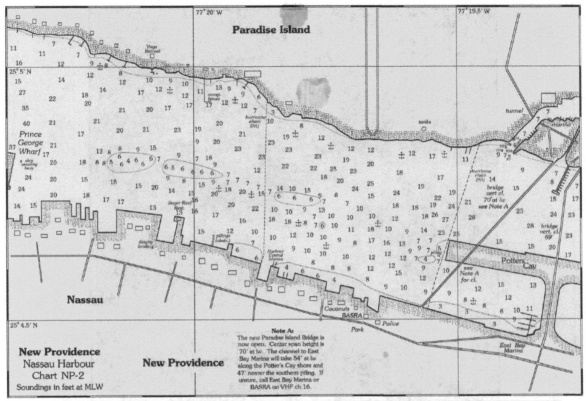

New Providence
Nassau Harbour
Chart NP-2
Soundings in feet at MLW

New Providence

Note A:
The new Paradise Island Bridge is now open. Center span height is 70' at lw. The channel to East Bay Marina will take 54' at lw along the Potter's Cay shore and 47' nearer the southern piling. If unsure, call East Bay Marina or BASRA on VHF ch. 16.

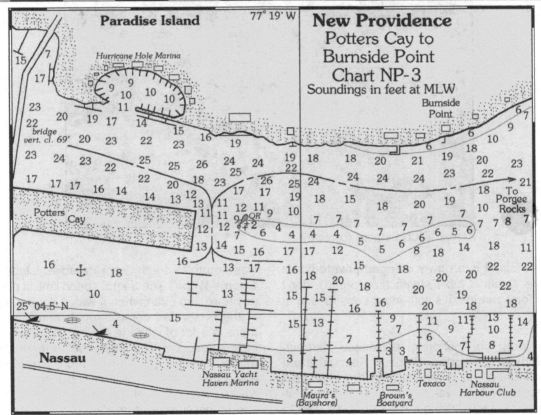

New Providence
Potters Cay to
Burnside Point
Chart NP-3
Soundings in feet at MLW

The Atlantis Resort, Paradise Island Photo Courtesy of Paul Harding, Safari Seaplanes

Ocean Club Estates (private) Photo Courtesy of Paul Harding, Safari Seaplanes

of Paradise Island is a newly dredged private home project, the *Ocean Club Estates* (see photo), don't mistake it for a marina, it's still under construction in places.

A final word on anchoring in Nassau Harbour. Nassau Harbour is a working harbour. Although there is a 5-knot speed limit in the harbour do not expect the harbour to be a no wake zone. Large and small vessels are constantly plying the waters from east to west, north to south, from Paradise Island to *Prince George Wharf*. The 5-knot speed limit is not enforced anymore and even when it was it did not deter many of the boats that come through here, consequently there is a lot of wake in the harbor. Some skippers may choose to anchor along the northern shore of the harbour, but you are a little more exposed to wake along there. There really is no place in the harbor where you are free of the wake of passing water taxis and tourist hauling drink/dive party boats. If you do

Paradise Harbour Club & Marina

Photo Courtesy of
Paul Harding,
Safari Seaplanes

of construction debris, a few anchors, and who knows what else. If you have problems bringing your anchor aboard you've probably hooked something or other. Good luck!

If you need a dinghy dock you can use the dock at *Harbour Central Marina*, just west of *BASRA*. *Friday's*, formerly *Crocodile's*, will allow you to use their dinghy dock if you wish to dine at their restaurant or during the hours of 0900-1030 and 1500-1600, but you are not allowed to bring garbage ashore here or jerry jug fuel back to your dinghy,

What You Will Find Ashore

Nassau hosts quite a few marinas along its shores. On the Paradise Island side of the harbour, east of the bridges, is the upscale *Hurricane Hole Marina*, catering primarily to mega-yachts on the outside and smaller vessels inside its protected cove, and the new *Paradise Harbour Club*. *Hurricane Hole* has 64 slips and can accommodate vessels of 7' draft inside and 11½' draft on the outside. Propane refills are available if you leave the dockmaster your tank and *WIFI* is available. *Hurricane Hole* also hosts

not feel comfortable where you are anchored, or if the large ships are just a little too close, you should move; the sooner the better. If the tug and barge is turning down the channel west of Potter's Cay and she is just off your bow, then it is time to move your vessel. Even if you are damaged you will be hard pressed to gain compensation. There is virtually no such thing as a lawsuit in The Bahamas. By the way, the bottom of *Nassau Harbour* is littered with all kinds of junk such as car frames, refrigerators, steel cables, all manner

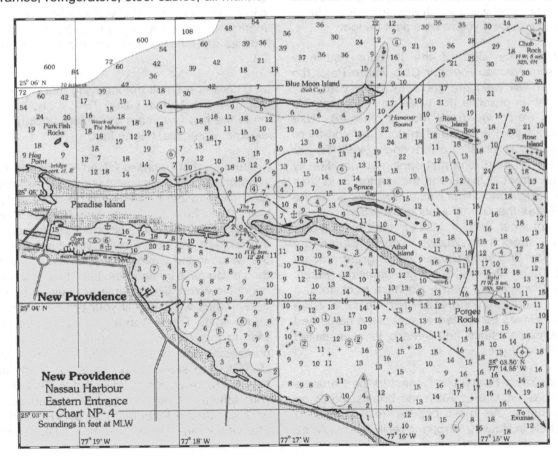

New Providence
Nassau Harbour
Eastern Entrance
Chart NP- 4
Soundings in feet at MLW

the annual *Charter Boat Show*, attracting luxury yachts from around the world. The *Hurricane Hole Fuel Dock* is situated just on the western side of Paradise Island Bridge along the southern shore of Paradise Island and they offer diesel, gas, and some dockage. If you need Internet access visit the News Café at the marina. Farther east lies the *Paradise Island Harbour Club*. What may seem to be a private marina is actually open to the public though they have no fuel sales. They do have a hot tub, the *Columbus Tavern*, and plans are in the works for a saltwater pool and swim-up bar.

The most elegant place in town is the extremely upscale *Atlantis Marina* at the huge *Atlantis* resort. What a place! Though quite a bit pricey by some standards, the service is unbeatable, and access to the resort has got to be considered as a day pass to walk around is $30 for visitors, unless you're staying at the marina of course. *Atlantis Marina* is a full service marina with diesel and gas and all the amenities including *WIFI*. The aquarium and shark tank at the resort are not to be missed. Casino action will keep you up all hours of the night and the quality of the food served in the hotel will quench any appetite. This is not the place to be if you're on a tight budget.

On the other side of the harbour you may choose from *Nassau Harbour Club* where Peter the dockmaster will welcome you and make your stay as pleasant as possible (for more on Peter, see the section *St. Peter, the Turtle Man of Nassau*). Use of the hotel's pool is included in dockage and there is also a laundry on site, a fuel dock, *WIFI* ($5 per hour or $12 all day), and a shopping center directly across the street. Upstairs at the marina is *Ichiban Japanese Sushi and Steak Restaurant*, owned by the same folks as the nearby *Montagu Gardens*. If you need to rent a car, see Mr. Moss in the hotel's lobby. Across the street from *Nassau Harbour Club* is the *Harbour Bay Shopping Center* with a great grocery store, a *Dairy Queen, Subway, Domino's Pizza, Church's Chicken and Game Room*, a bookstore, a pharmacy, a hardware store, a *Radio Shack*, a video store, *Mail Boxes Etc.* (Internet access), a bank, and a nice computer sales and service location called *Lignum Technologies*.

Nassau Yacht Haven lies closest to the *Paradise Island Bridge* on *Marina Row* and boasts the *Poop Deck*, arguably the most popular restaurant and watering hole in Nassau. Propane refills are available

daily here and vessels can have their mail forwarded to *Yacht Haven* and have it await their arrival. Send your mail to you on your boat at *Nassau Yacht Haven Marina*, East Bay Street, P.O. Box SS 5693, Nassau, New Providence, Bahamas. There is also a dive shop, laundry, and *WIFI* service. Across the street is a pharmacy, a liquor store, *Harbourside Marine*, an *Outback Steakhouse*, while closer to the bridge is the *Asia* all-you-can-eat Chinese buffet.

Between *Nassau Harbour Club* and *Nassau Yacht Haven* lie *Brown's Boat Basin* (where you can get hauled out), *Bayshore Marina*, who can haul out vessels to 40', and the *Texaco* fuel dock (with its dinghy dock, telephone, and small store). At *Texaco* you can leave your garbage as well as your used motor oil and even fill up your jerry jugs with water.

Just west of the *Paradise Island Bridges*, west of BASRA and *Friday's* is a new marina, *Harbour Central Marina* offering 38 slips with full electric and water, ice, showers, diesel and gasoline, a Laundromat, and some provisions nearby at the *Texaco* mini-mart on *East Bay Street* just in front of the marina. The marina can accommodate a 100' vessel with an 8' draft. The marina also offers a dinghy dock for cruiser's use, as well as dry storage and haul out for powerboats to 28'.

There is a small marina lying just to the west of *Yacht Haven Marina* called *TPA*; it has just opened up in the last few years and offers dockage with full electric, water, ice, but no fuel.

Just west of *Paradise Island Bridge* is the BASRA (*Bahamas Air Sea Rescue Association*) headquarters. BASRA no longer has a dinghy dock available. Here you'll find Chris Lloyd is on duty from 0900 to 1700, five days a week and welcomes all visitors to come in and look around. Even if you can't stop, look in the window and wave, he'll appreciate it a lot more than if you pass by and treat him like a stranger. This is not New York City, people are quite a bit friendlier here. Chris will even fill your propane tanks for $3 above cost. Those with a more generous bent may wish to join BASRA or support the organization by purchasing one their hats or just making a donation. BASRA also sells some charts for those in need. You can have your mail delivered to BASRA to await your arrival but be sure to include you boat name on it so Chris will contact you by VHF and tell you when it has arrived (but you must listen to the VHF).

Nassau, Eastern Harbour

Photo Courtesy of Paul Harding, Safari Seaplanes

Hurricane Hole Marina

Potter's Cay

Hurricane Hole Marina

Photo Courtesy of Paul Harding, Safari Seaplanes

Marina at the Atlantis Resort

Photo Courtesy of Paul Harding, Safari Seaplanes

Bridges and Potter's Cay

Photo Courtesy of Paul Harding, Safari Seaplanes

Potter's Cay

Fruit Stand, Potter's Cay

Photo Courtesy of Anne DuPont

Jitney on Bay Street

Photo Courtesy of Alicia Bonnet

Selling Conch Shells on Potter's Cay

Photo Courtesy of Anne DuPont

The address is *BASRA*, P.O. Box SS6247, Nassau, Bahamas. For *UPS* or *Fed-X* packages address it to *BASRA*, East Bay Street, Nassau, Bahamas, and add your cruising permit number to the package label. Besides monitoring VHF ch. 16, *BASRA* also monitors 2182 and 4125 on single sideband. Most of the Bahamian fishing fleet uses 4125 and that is why *BASRA* monitors that frequency. *BASRA* also has a book trade for cruisers needing new reading material. Those wanting water should cross the street at *BASRA* and walk 60 yards west to the small spigot and concrete tub. Just to the east of *BASRA*, on the property that used to be a police station, the *Defence Force* is building a small base.

Cruisers can also have mail sent to either *Luden's Liquors*, or *Harbour Bay Liquors* and they will gladly hold it for your arrival. *Luden's Liquors* is quite a unique place and a must stop. Owner Dennis Knowles not only has the lowest liquor prices in town but an amazing collection of knickknacks, old artifacts, tools, bottles, and an amazing collection of mounted insects along with some live birds and bees. He also has a barn owl as a security guard in his warehouse. *Luden's* is on Dowdeswell St. just one block up from Bay St. If you want your mail waiting on your arrival have it sent to *Luden's Ltd.*, Dowdeswell St., P.O. Box 5649, Nassau, Bahamas. There is also a Laundromat on premises. *Harbour Bay Liquors* sits directly across the street from the *Nassau Harbour Club*. They will hold mail for your arrival, deliver your order of liquor to your boat, and accept faxes for you. Their address is *Harbour Bay Liquors*, P.O. Box SS 6218, Nassau, Bahamas. Their fax number is 242-394-0632.

One of my favorite stops lies just west of *BASRA*, *Friday's Restaurant*, formerly known as *Crocodile's*. *Friday's* has a wonderful laid-back atmosphere where you can dine on open air tables right on the edge of the harbour with a wonderful view of your anchored boat. Their daily happy hour specials are worth investigating and on Thursdays during the boating season *Friday's* hosts the weekly *Yachtspeople's Lunch* along with Carolyn (C6AGG) and Nick Wardle (*BASRA*, Coral Harbour). Do not miss one of these events. You can tie up to the dinghy docks along the wall, but not to the outer dock as it's private.

Everybody has probably heard the tales of theft in Nassau Harbour. They are true; there was quite a bit of theft in the past which lead to an increased police presence in the late 1990s. This has brought about a noticeable decline in theft in Nassau Harbour, but you should still lock up your dinghy. Also watch out for hustlers ashore, especially in the area of the roundabout at the intersection of *Mackey Street* and *East Bay Street* at the foot of the *Paradise Island Bridge* at Potters Cay. If you take your bicycles ashore, lock them up, even if you leave them for only a minute or two. It doesn't take long at all for someone to hop aboard one and pedal off.

Nassau offers those in need whatever they want, if it's not available locally it can be shipped in. You will find diesel and outboard mechanics, car rentals, *UPS* and *Fed-X*, sail and canvas repairs, a haulout yard, electronic repair, dive shops, shopping centers, and chandlers just as you would in any major metropolitan area. See *Appendix C* for the services available. Briefly, *Marine Diesel* lies along the southern shore of the harbour and can handle all manner of diesel repairs. North of the bridges you'll find *Lightbourne Marine* and *Maura's Marine*, both of whom supply marine gear, fishing tackle, and outboard sales and service, *Lighbourne's* is a *Mercury* dealer while *Maura's* is an *OMC* dealer. *Phillip's Sails* can handle all your sail repairs.

One could write a book itself strictly on Nassau, what to do, what to see. The best thing to do is pick up one of the tourist guides in any of the local marinas or shoreside shops for the latest scoop on land life and night life in Nassau. Most cruisers take advantage of the excellent bus system on New Providence that covers most of the island and Paradise Island as well. And speaking of bus rides, or jitney's as they are sometimes called, you must experience them. Take a ride downtown from the marinas on any of the buses heading west on *Bay Street*. Each bus is different according to the driver's preference. One bus might have loud reggae blasting out of its speakers while roaring down the road pell-mell to who knows where while the next bus may have gospel or opera on its sound system and its driver more laid back in his approach to driving. Almost all buses have some sort of music to entertain the riders. It is actually quite pleasant to see a Bahamian wish everyone a "Good afternoon!" as they climb aboard.

Downtown is a shoppers delight with all sorts of small shops offering the usual tourists goodies plus fine gems, quality cameras, tapes and CD's, and all sorts of electronic equipment. When the cruise ships are in, downtown can be a madhouse with tourists everywhere and Bahamians trying to sell them something or braid their hair. Young people will still try to sell you drugs on the street corners but this is changing due to the increased police presence.

If you've ever been here before you've probably stopped in at the *Straw Lady*, and I'm sorry to say report they have closed. For Internet access downtown, visit the *APG Business Centre* at the *East Bay Shopping Plaza*, the *IBM* building at *Bay Street* and *Church Street*, and the *Internet Café* on *Bay Street* and *East Street*. If you are into *Harley-Davidson's*, and who isn't these days, on Charlotte Street right by the cruise ship docks is the *Harley Davidson Motorclothes & Apparel* shop where you can pick up a Bahamas *Harley-Davidson* T-shirt and more (they even offer free delivery to your hotel).

Nassau is a city steeped in history, from the historic over-the-hill-section with its small shops and neighborhood atmosphere, to the three forts built to protect Nassau from all sorts of rampaging rogues, Fort Montague to the east, Fort Charlotte to the west, and Fort Fincastle above the city. An interesting stop is the *Queen's Staircase*, a 102' staircase built to celebrate the 65-year reign of Queen Victoria. The 65-steps are said to have been carved out of stone by slaves in the late 1700's, to provide an escape from Ft. Fincastle to town without exposing the troops to fire from ships in the harbour.

There's *Blackbeard's Tower*, the *Government House*, *Parliament*, and the *Straw Market* on *Bay Street*. *Bay Street* is nothing less than vibrant during *Junkanoo* with costumed dancers and musicians vying in heated competition (see *The Basics: Junkanoo*). You might want to check out the *Junkanoo Museum* with its large display of intricate *Junkanoo* masks and costumes. There's even some handicrafts for sale.

There's Potter's Cay with its mailboats and fishermen selling the fish, conch, and other goodies. The yellow *Produce House* is a good spot to pick up a deal on veggies in season. East of the harbour *Coral World's* 100' tower and *the Coral Island Observatory* is an excellent place to visit to see reef life in its natural habitat without getting wet. One of my personal favorites is the tour given by *Bacardi*. You may tour their plant, located on the southern side of the island, and check out samples of rum Monday-Thursday from 0900-1600 and Fridays from 0930-1530.

The *Ardastra Gardens*, a lush tropical park, is home to 300 birds, mammals, and reptiles including a marching band of pink flamingos. It boasts 18 acres of botanical gardens with 600 species of flowering shrubs and trees and an equally impressive cactus garden. Equally beautiful is *The Retreat*, the home of *The Bahamas National Trust* (*BNT*). Here the *BNT* has preserved 11 acres of tropical gardens with tours available.

West of downtown Nassau and the *Ardastra Gardens* lies *Cable Beach*, named after the first cable transmission that was received in The Bahamas. *Cable Beach* offers fine hotels, casino gambling, and the party animal hangout in the area named *The Zoo*, just a short bus ride from town Southeast of Nassau is the *St. Augustine Monastery*. Designed in Romanesque style by Father Jerome of Cat Island and Long Island fame, the monastery was originally built in 1945 as a boy's school.

The waters surrounding New Providence are teeming with dives sites many of which were featured in films such as *Thunderball*, *Never Say Never*, *Dr. No*, *Wet Gold*, *Splash*, *Cocoon*, *Day Of The Dolphin*, and the TV series *Flipper*. Divers wanting a guided tour or simply diving information should *contact Diver's Haven* (242-393-3285), *Bahamas Divers* (242-323-2644), *Sun Divers* (242-322-3301), *Underwater Tours* (242-322-3285), or *Coral Harbour Divers* (242-326-4171). *Coral Harbour Divers* leans toward longer, deeper reef dives for more experienced divers. *Stuart Cove's* and the *Nassau SCUBA Center* offer an exciting shark dive, which gives divers the chance to swim up close and personal with sharks in complete safety.

North of Paradise Island and Porkfish Rocks lies the wreck of the *Mahoney*. The *Mahoney* was a beautiful 212' steel-hulled, steam-powered yacht that was once known as *Candance*, *Firequeen*, *Firebird*, and the *Bahamian*, but was never actually called the *Mahoney*. I could find no one who actually knew how it came to be called the *Mahoney*. Some say she broke in two and went down in the hurricane of 1929 while others have said that she broke her tow line on the way to being scuttled and chose her own resting spot for eternity. Either way the hull was dynamited to prevent it from being a navigational hazard. The boiler is still intact though encrusted with fire coral. The *Mahoney* lies approximately one mile west of Salt Cay when the East Breakwater light bears 255°

and the *Holiday Inn* on Paradise Island bears 210°. This is a slack water dive due to the amount of tidal action.

Just north of the *Club Med* beach on Paradise Island and in about 45' of water lies the *Trinity Caves*. This site consists of three caves with two smaller ones a few hundred feet to the west of the main group. The reef consists mostly of soft corals with one stand of pillar coral. *Trinity Caves* is a protected area, no fishing is allowed at this site. This entire area along the northern shore of Paradise Island, from the tip of the eastern breakwater to north of the *Club Med* beach offers exciting diving with many deep reefs, holes, and crevices. One of the favorite dive sites around Nassau is the *Nassau Blue Hole* lying just east of New Providence. A waypoint at 25° 01.70' N, 77° 08.50' W will place you virtually on top of it. Be careful anchoring and enjoy the dive.

One last word on Nassau. You may see some security officials or Police on duty with dogs or even armed with submachine guns outside many business establishments. In fact many businesses must buzz you in before you can open the door to enter. This is just part of life in Nassau, don't feel threatened, you'll get used to it. Walking downtown around the straw market you will often be accosted by Bahamians who want to braid your hair, hustle up a cab for you, give you directions for a dollar, sell you drugs, or even sing you a song for a dollar. Everyone must survive on the tourist dollars. If you are not interested simply tell them no and keep walking, they usually get the message.

Nassau to Lyford Cay and Coral Harbour

Golding Cay - 1¼ nm NW of:
25° 02.15' N, 77° 35.35' W

Lyford Cay - ¼ nm N of entrance:
25° 04.00' N, 77° 30.94' W

Navigational Information

Arawak Cay, lying just south of the western entrance to Nassau Harbour (Chart NP-1 and NP-3), houses some old buildings that were once used as a *Customs* office and bonded warehouses. Today Arawak Cay is a prime commercial dock with many of the Nassau water barges that ply the waters between

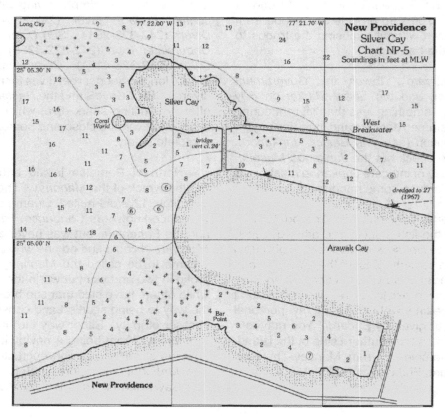

Morgan's Bluff, Andros and New Providence docking here. You will likely see a colorful Haitian sailboat anchored off the eastern tip of Arawak Cay awaiting cargo to carry back to Haiti. These stout wooden vessels pass out the eastern entrance to Nassau Harbour and work their way south through the Exumas via the mailboat route and out into *Crooked Island Passage* and beyond. Onshore at Arawak Cay you'll find the enticing *Arawak Village*. Here you'll find row upon row of colorful little restaurants and snack shacks offering the freshest seafood in a comfortable atmosphere. The village was constructed to revitalize Arawak Cay and it seems to be working.

On some older charts, specifically *DMA* Chart 26309, New Providence and Nassau Harbour, a channel is shown around the southern shore of Arawak Cay with a small bridge. This channel is no longer there, it has been filled in from the bridge eastward almost to the tip of Arawak Cay.

To the west of the bridge a deep channel is sometimes shown along the southern shore of Arawak Cay. If this was ever there it must have been a long time ago. The only vessels that can transit this area now are small outboard powered boats as there are numerous rocky patches along the southern shore; see Chart NP-5.

What You Will Find Ashore

Silver Cay, accessible from the arched footbridge leading from Arawak Cay, is home to one of Nassau's most popular attractions, *Coral World*. Here visitors can descend into the submarine world of the reef environment while staying entirely dry. Through *Coral World's* glass viewing windows one can get up close and personal with all sorts of marine creatures that inhabit the reef lying 15' below the surface along the western shore of Silver Cay. If approaching by dinghy don't expect to get close to the *Coral World* tower, about 100 yards out from the tower is an encircling rope and buoy network.

Long Cay lies just west of Silver Cay and is private. A few years ago some plans were in the works in to open a nightclub/restaurant with room rentals, but the owners are said to have changed direction and the island is likely to remain private for some time to come.

Balmoral Island, sometimes called Discovery Island and shown on some navigational charts as

North Cay, and which is now shown as Sandal's Cay, is a private island lying just west of Long Cay and north of Cable Beach at the mouth of Goodman's Bay. The island is the private property of the *Sandals* resort on the mainland of New Providence and is used as a nude beach for its guests. Cable Beach is the home to several resorts, casinos, fine restaurants, and numerous smaller hotels.

Silver Cay, Long Cay, and Sandal's Island make up a line of barrier islands that run along the outer reef just north of New Providence. The best snorkeling is along the reef in 10' on the northern shore of the island so choose a day with settled weather for your exploring. The reef is very shallow, 1'-2' in many places and there are only a few breaks. A cruising vessel should stay well offshore and not venture inside the reef as there is very little inside that is of interest to a cruising boat unless one wishes to run aground on any of the many small, shallow heads and patch reefs strewn hereabouts. Dinghy trips should be considered instead with the mother vessel anchored in Nassau or in Old Fort Bay.

Navigational Information

Just east of Delaport Point is the entrance channel leading into the *Sandyport Development*, see Chart NP-6, a private time-share and condo community. The entrance channel takes only 1½' at low water and is often blocked by a chain. The security guard in the small shack just under the bridge (14' vert. cl.) is your contact if you wish to enter though there is nothing of interest inside unless you wish to check out the time-shares for sale. West of here is a lot of development, a lot of condo projects from here to Cave Point and Love Beach.

A little further west lies Gambier Village which one might mistake for an out-island town, similar in looks to Cat Island. Just offshore lies *Gambier Reef*, about one mile off the beach when *Delaport Radio Mast* bears 90° and *Gambier Cut*, a conspicuous ravine, bears 190°. The drop-off begins at about 80' with much star coral and other scattered heads before thinning out after 100'.

Just around the point lies Old Fort Bay where dolphins and mantas frolic in its harbour. Old Fort Bay is sometimes shown on charts as *Charlottesville Bay* and is a very pretty beach lined cove, excellent in easterly winds. Although Old Fort Bay offers excellent natural protection in prevailing winds, it is seldom

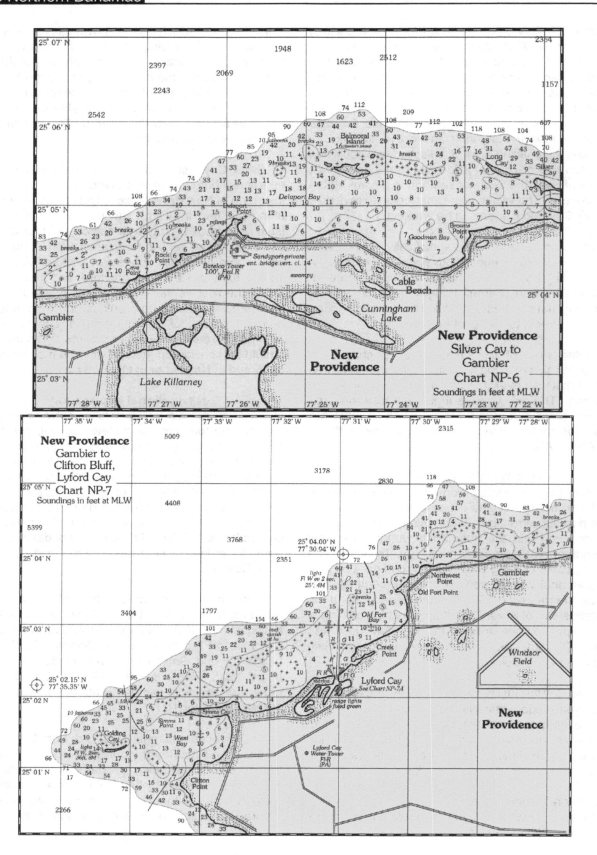

used by the cruising skipper. It's a shame, most yachts carry on to Nassau and bypass this wonderful place. The entrance can be rather tricky and should only be attempted in good light, never at night. One must pass between the shallows off Old Fort Point and the shallows lying just east of the well-marked Lyford Cay channel.

Just a little further west lies Lyford Cay, one of the most exclusive and wealthiest residential areas in the world. *Lyford Cay Marina* is private but yachtsmen are invited to refuel (diesel and gas) and pick up whatever they may need from the nearby *City Market's Grocery Store*, hardware store, liquor store and bank. Some minor repairs are available and you can contact the Asst. Harbourmaster, Gino Rahming, who is standing by on VHF ch. 16 to assist you in any way possible. During the winter season the marina is open only to members and their guests, however during the less crowded summer months it may be possible to acquire a transient slip. Inquire as to availability on VHF.

The well-marked entrance channel to *Lyford Cay Marina* (see Chart NP-7 and in greater detail on Chart NP-7A) will allow vessels of 9½' draft to enter the marina. Vessels with drafts of 11' may tie up inside solely at their own risk. A waypoint at 25° 04.00' N, 77° 30.94' W, will place you approximately ¼ mile north of the light (Fl W) that marks the entrance channel to *Lyford Cay Marina*. Start steering south staying west of the light. Be sure to stay a little west of the light (if entering the marina channel keep the light to port) to avoid the shallows and breaking reefs to the east. There is a range ashore consisting of twin green lights at the marina, and a higher set of twin green lights on the hill above the marina. These lights stay on day and night. As you begin your passage south down the channel you will notice that there are three pairs of red and green daymarks, keep between these and finally you will come to the entrance jetties which have red and green lights on their respective sides. Just inside, before the marina, white floodlights shine across the opening. The fuel dock is to port immediately inside.

Divers will enjoy *Lyford Cay Reef*, a gorgeous blue-toned wall dive starting at about 80' and dropping straight down to the bottom of the *Tongue of the Ocean*. The cliff begins at about 115' when the eastern tip of Goulding Cay bears 225° and the Lyford Cay Water Tower bears 150°. This area can be very

rough due to the current so try to time your dive on an incoming tide. It is suggested by the pros to start your dive at the deepest depth and work your way up. You will see coral and caves with a very distinct bluish tone with a lot of sponges, sea fans, and soft corals.

Another popular dive site in the area is *Lambton Wall*. *Lambton Wall* lies about 2 miles west-northwest of Lyford Cay when the Lyford Cay water tower bears 125° and Simms Point bears 190°. Here a sandy

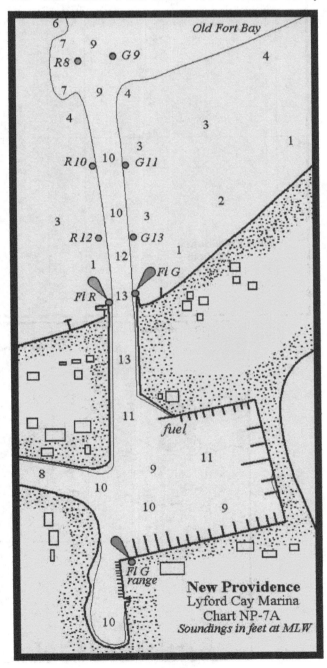

New Providence
Lyford Cay Marina
Chart NP-7A
Soundings in feet at MLW

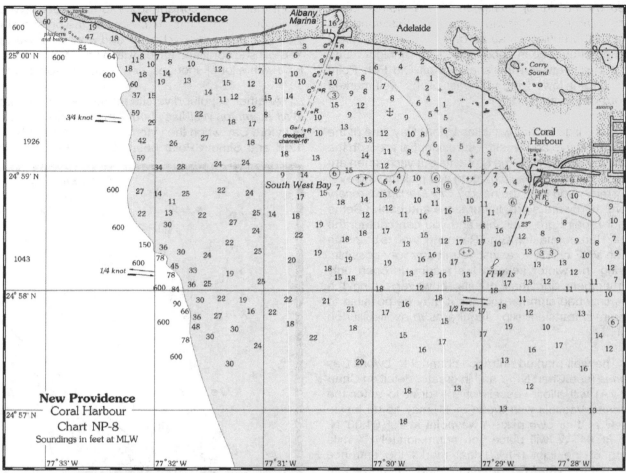

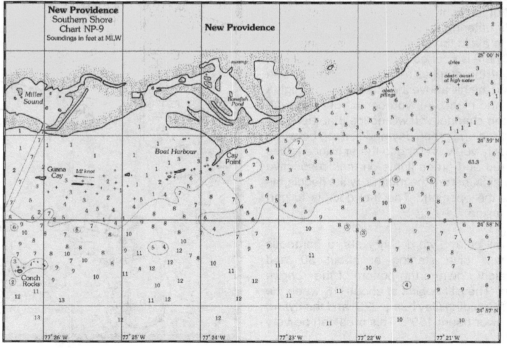

slope begins at about 30' of water with scattered coral heads at a 70° angle to about 40'. At around 50' there is a nearly vertical drop which joins another sandy slope at 115' creating an underwater range of small mountains and valleys.

Leaving Lyford Cay and heading south cruising vessels should stay well outside the fringing reef as shown on Chart NP-7. A nice anchorage is shown in West Bay and is accessible from two directions, neither of which should be attempted at night or in poor visibility. Small shallow heads and patch reefs abound. It is possible to pass between Goulding Cay and the reefs off Simms Point in 8'-10' of water, however, I prefer to pass south of Goulding Cay and enter from the south, between Clifton Point and the small shallow reef strewn area to its west. This route usually gives better visibility but you are limited to 7' at low water. Never remain anchored here overnight if bad weather threatens. First, the holding is fair at best in shallow sand over a rock base. Second, if you had to leave at night you would not be able to see your way out and you would stand a better than good chance of going up on a reef or rock.

Marking the western extremity of New Providence is Goulding Cay, sometimes shown on charts as Golding Cay. Goulding Cay is a bird sanctuary and nesting area and is protected by The *Bahamas National Trust*. Divers will want to check out *Goulding Cay Reef* lying just north of Goulding Cay when Clifton Point bears 130° and Goulding Cay Light bears 230°. The elkhorn coral reef begins in about 25'-30' of water about 500' north of Goulding Cay. Some of the coral comes to within 6'-7' of the surface. The reef is about 600' long in a northeast-southwest direction and vanishes into the abyss of the *Tongue of the Ocean*. The reef strewn waters around Goulding Cay were once used by wreckers to lure ships to their end. A waypoint at 25° 02.15' N, 77 ° 35.35' W, will place you 1¼ miles northwest of Golding Cay in deep water as shown on Chart NP-7. From this waypoint you can head to Fresh Creek or southern Andros, or if approaching from Andros, alter your heading to parallel the northern shore of New Providence on your way to the western entrance to Nassau Harbour. Caution: Do not attempt to steer directly for the waypoint off the western entrance to Nassau Harbour from the waypoint northwest of Golding Cay, you will run hard aground. Instead, follow the charts and stay well offshore avoiding the fringing reefs west of Nassau.

From Goulding Cay around to Coral Harbour the western shore begins to take on a rocky, barren, bluff sided appearance until you round the point past Clifton Pier. The caves in the bluffs were once shelter for Lucayan Indians and later on, pirates. Just off Clifton Point you will see two large platforms and numerous large buoys, see Chart NP-8. These are for the large fuel ships to tie to when they offload their cargoes to the New Providence fuel companies. Give this area a wide berth.

Once past the fuel platforms you will make out the point at Coral Harbour, Chart NP-8. It will look like a very large, square sided bluff. In reality it is a low jetty with a large abandoned concrete high rise just south of it that from a few miles off resembles a large cliff. Ashore between Clifton Point and Coral Harbour lies the town of Adelaide. Adelaide has the distinction of being one of the first black settlements established in New Providence after the abolition of slavery. *South West Bay* can be used as a sheltered anchorage in strong north-northeast winds.

Located in *South West Bay* (as shown on Chart NP-8) is the marked, dredged entrance channel (16') to the upscale *Albany Marina*. The marina boasts a 15-acre basin that can accommodate 71 mega-yachts to 250' LOA with a draft of 16'. Each of the side-tie slips has full electric, a pump-out, RO water, along with telephone, Internet, and cable TV connections. The fuel dock has a high-speed diesel pump for rapid fueling. On site amenities include a spa, salon with massage therapists, a fitness center with a 25 meter pool, a boxing ring, family water park, a water sports pavilion, an adult clubhouse with 5-Star dining and a lounge, adult pool and bar, tennis center, a children's clubhouse with covered playground, a golf course, conference room, and an equestrian center. Albany Marina monitors VHF ch. 16 and 74. You can also reach them by phone at 242-676-6020, or email droderick@albanybahamas.com.

As you approach the entrance to Coral Harbour you will notice the large light tower lying about a mile offshore. This is shown on current *DMA* charts as being abandoned. It is far from abandoned. It flashes white approximately every 20 seconds to direct the *Royal Bahamas Defence Force* vessels to their base inside Coral Harbour. The best approach into Coral Harbour is to steer toward the light to avoid the shallows just offshore between Clifton Point and Coral Harbour as shown on Chart NP-8. Pass on either side of the light and take up a course of approximately 23° for the entrance. The entrance channel is very conspicuous, lying between two rock jetties just north of the abandoned concrete high rise. The easternmost jetty has a red flashing light, remember red, right, returning. Once inside you will notice the large *Defence Force* base just to starboard, which was once an elegant marina before it folded in 1972. As you work your way past the base you will come to the canals that make up the small, palm-clad community of Coral Harbour.

Vessels transiting the area south and west of Coral Harbour must be aware of the *Defence Force* firing range that stretches approximately 9 miles west and 8½ miles south of the entrance to Coral Harbour. When the *Defence Force* is using the area for gunnery practice they will make an announcement on VHF ch. 16 to all concerned mariners. Vessels engaged in gunnery practice will display a red flag by day and red fixed or red flashing lights by night.

The Southern Shore of New Providence

There is really not much to say about the southern shore of New Providence (Charts NP-9 and NP-10). The shore is generally low-lying and fringed with many stands of casuarinas. There are absolutely no facilities hereabouts. The only thing the southern shore has to offer is some good bonefishing in places like *Malcolm Creek* and the *Bonefish Pond* inside Cay Point. The waters inshore dry at low water in many places as far as ¼ mile or more out from shore. There are many scattered heads, patch reefs, shallow bars, and the wreckage of a few old boats to maneuver around. Ashore you will see a few scattered houses and one small community.

Vessels wishing to pass south of New Providence, say perhaps from Andros to Exuma, should give the southern shore of New Providence a wide berth. At a very minimum I would suggest passing 2½ nautical miles south of any land masses. If leaving Coral Harbour pass well south of the offlying rocks just south of Coral Harbour as well as Conch Rocks (Chart NP-9).

The Eastern Shore of New Providence

Port of New Providence entrance:
25° 00.14' N, 77° 15.68' W

The eastern shore of New Providence (Chart's NP-4 and NP-10) is shallow close to shore while the deeper waters are strewn with reefs, some with less than 6' over them at low water. The only place of interest is the *Port of New Providence*, a very nice canal community, but no anchorages or marine facilities are available.

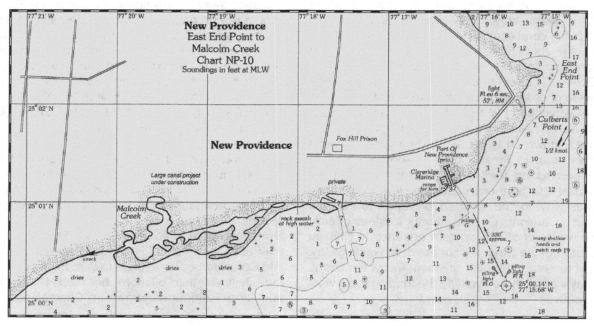

Some folks say that navigating from the eastern entrance to Nassau Harbour around the eastern tip to the *Port of New Providence* is akin to stumbling through a minefield, in fact some call the area "the minefield." There are definitely some shallow heads on this route, even lining the edges of the entrance channel itself, but with good visibility it should be no problem. Do not attempt this at night unless you are extremely familiar with these waters, even then I cannot recommend transiting this area.

A waypoint at 25° 00.14' N, 77° 15.68' W, will place you approximately ¼ mile southeast of the first set of markers that define the entrance channel as shown on Chart NP-10. The markers here flash red and green at night. Line up between the first set of markers and steer towards the entrance to the complex on a course of 330°. Ashore you will see some large light pink condos that look white from offshore. The entrance is just to the west of these buildings. A little further down the channel you will come to a pair of daymarks, stay between these and you will soon be upon the jettied entrance channel to the *Port of New Providence*. The route into the *Port of New Providence* can handle 6' at low water.

St. Peter
The Turtle Man of Nassau

I was sailing along on the *Great Bahama Banks* one fall day when I saw what I thought was a man in the water, his head bobbing along just above the surface, miles from anywhere. On approaching I discovered it was a huge loggerhead sea turtle the size of a car hood. Nothing out of the ordinary until you realize that these magnificent animals are getting scarce and harder to find. When Columbus first sailed in these waters he noticed some areas where there were scores and scores of turtles which the great explorer mistook for rocks in the water.

Throughout The Bahamas, Bahamians have been catching and raising turtles for centuries. Deep holes along the shores of some of these rocky cays were used as turtle kraals (pens) and owners built up walls around their lips while other kraals were carved out of the native limestone to farm the animals. Then, as today, the turtles were highly prized for their tasty meat and for the beauty of their shell, which is used for making jewelry and other items. Sailing ships once kept turtles aboard as a source of fresh meat.

The turtles would be kept on their backs so their weight would not crush their lungs and they were kept constantly wet. Turtles could last indefinitely like this as long as they were fed and kept wet.

Today's ships stock huge freezers to the brim before departure guaranteeing the crew and passengers a steady supply of meat for their voyage. Only a few islanders, mostly in the more remote areas still eat sea turtles and that will always be, it's a matter of survival. Unfortunately some trendy restaurants throughout the cays still have turtle on their menu, turtle steaks and turtle soup. Tasty? Absolutely! Pricey? You bet! Politically correct? That depends on public opinion which, like the weather, is subject to change. Apparently enough tourists shell out the bucks to experience this unique gastronomic delight to keep turtle on the menu. When they return home, will they go to their local supermarket and buy a few turtle steaks? No. Will they put it on their weekly menu? No. Will they petition their schools to put it on the lunch menu? Of course not. It's only an island t'ing mon!

Have you ever gotten close to one of these large pelagic turtles? Have you ever swam with one? Have you ever touched one, looked in their gentle, doe-like eyes? They are quite graceful in their movements and inspiring to watch. By now some readers are probably comparing me to a child who has named a pet pig and refuses to allow it to become an entree. Get real! I love bacon but turtles were not raised for slaughter, they are majestic ocean roamers who suffer enough from eating all the plastic that we humans throw overboard to clog up their digestive systems. I am told that some of the larger turtles can be over 200 years old. So old that they may have witnessed the coming of the Loyalists in 1783.

Now they are fast going the way of the whales, all for a positive cash flow in some dingy tourist dive with sticky salt and pepper shakers, dirty tablecloths, surly help, and a 15% gratuity added to the check (Gratuity? For What?).

Nassau is the capitol of The Bahamas, both politically and culturally, and like all major metropolitan areas Nassau has always had, and still has, more than its share of shysters and heisters, shucksters and hucksters, con-men and thieves, and all sorts of other rogues whose only intention is making a buck and damn all the rules. Amidst all this survives a saint with a heart as big as all The Bahamas, Saint Peter, the turtle man of Nassau.

Peter Attaloglou was born in Athens, Greece, and shortly after his marriage to a Bahamian woman of Greek descent he moved to Nassau where he is now the dockmaster of the *Nassau Harbour Club*. One day in Nassau, Peter witnessed the slaughtering of a large Hawksbill turtle, a protected sea turtle highly valued for its meat and shell. If you have ever witnessed the butchering of a large sea turtle you may understand, if you haven't then I will spare you the gory details. The needless butchering of this peaceful, gentle animal set Peter on a course that has been spiritually rewarding yet financially draining. Peter now goes far out of his way to save the large sea turtles that fishermen often bring in to the dock.

In Nassau the local fishermen can sell turtle meat for $5 a pound to the restaurants that still keep it on their menu. Somewhere else they can then scrounge another $50 or more for the shell and maybe a little extra change for the head. For a 175 pound turtle a fisherman can reap $400-$500 selling it this way. Peter on the other hand cannot afford to compete with the prices the restaurants pay. He can only afford at most, $1 a pound, but that way fishermen get quick, easy money and don't have to bother with cleaning up the mess of butchering the creature. In 1994, Peter spent over $1,000 of his own money just on purchasing turtles, not to mention spending $50 or more a week per turtle for food.

Peter's turtles are well cared for. Peter keeps them in a 60' x 20' x 4' deep pen at the *Nassau Harbour Club*. Peter has a marine biologist friend who takes blood samples of each one to find out where they are from and then tags the turtles. When his charges grow strong enough Peter turns them over to the warden at the *Exuma Cays Land And Sea Park*, who releases them within the protected confines of the park. Until Peter and the Park joined forces Peter would release his turtles in the waters surrounding New Providence.

Most turtles come to Peter in fairly good shape, but thoroughly exhausted and very scared. Fishermen, after spotting the turtle, will swim with it, chasing it sometimes for hours until the creature tires and can be wrestled into the boat. After a week or so in its new surroundings the turtle will begin to settle down and eat again. Once Peter bought a large Hawksbill

turtle that had been speared through the neck. Peter tended to his wounds as best he could, but the turtle was unable to dive to eat, it could only eat what was on the surface. So Peter, who usually feeds a turtle 50 pounds of conch a week, packed conch meat inside lettuce so that it would float. This Hawksbill turtle is now a resident of Exuma Park. Peter soon picked up another large Hawksbill that had a huge chunk bitten out of its side by a shark. Local turtle experts were "too busy" to help so Peter took it upon himself to find some antibiotics and treat the turtle himself. He would slice open conch meat and place the antibiotics inside. The wound healed and the turtle is free once more roaming the waters of the Exumas. Peter cannot save every turtle that is brought into Nassau Harbour but what he does is certainly a start. Peter sadly admits that the larger turtles are getting fewer and fewer. He cannot even remember the last time he saw a leatherback.

Peter has done all this of his own accord and asks nothing in return. His satisfaction comes on the day of their release, that's Peter's payoff. Personally I believe there should be a fund to ease Peter's self-sacrifice but Peter does not see it that way, the burden is his and his alone, he asks for no help. So if you're sailing through the New Providence area or the northern Exumas, and you should have the opportunity to see a large sea turtle in the wild you can thank the saints above, primarily St. Peter over in Nassau.

New Providence to Eleuthera

Fuel: None
Haul-Out: None
Diesel Repairs: None
Outboard Repairs: None
Propane: None
Provisions: None
Important Lights:
  Porgee Rock: Fl W ev 3 sec
  The Narrows: Fl W ev 5 sec
  Chub Rock: Fl W ev 5 sec
  Fleeming Channel west: Fl R ev 4 sec
  Fleeming Channel east: Fl G ev 4 sec

The cays stretching from New Providence to the northern tip of Eleuthera offer good diving and although there is no true all-weather anchorage, there are several lee-side anchorages available. In northerly winds it is possible to traverse the waters to Eleuthera on the southern side of the cays while in southerly winds you can pass to the north of the cays for a slightly calmer ride.

Nassau to Rose Island

Chub Rock - ¼ nm N of:
25° 06.85' N, 77° 14.60' W
Porgee Rocks - ¼ nm S of:
25° 03.50' N, 77° 14.55' W

Navigational Information

Athol Island lies just east of Paradise Island and was once, and still is, used as a quarantine island. In fact some of the older charts show the quarantine buildings. The last time Athol Island was used in this capacity was during the Haitian influx to The Bahamas in the early 1990's. Many refugees were quarantined on Athol Island and some lost their lives trying to swim *The Narrows* to freedom. *The Narrows* will accommodate a vessel with less than 7' draft at mean low water, but I wouldn't take 6' through there

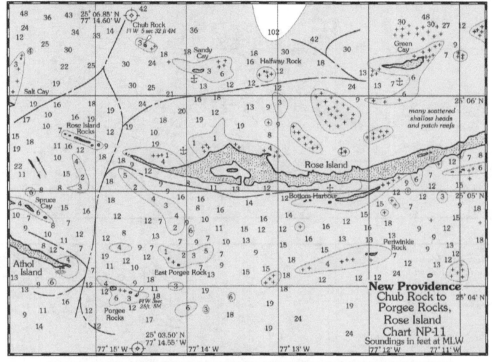

Bottom Harbour, Rose Island   Photo Courtesy of Paul Harding, Safari Seaplanes

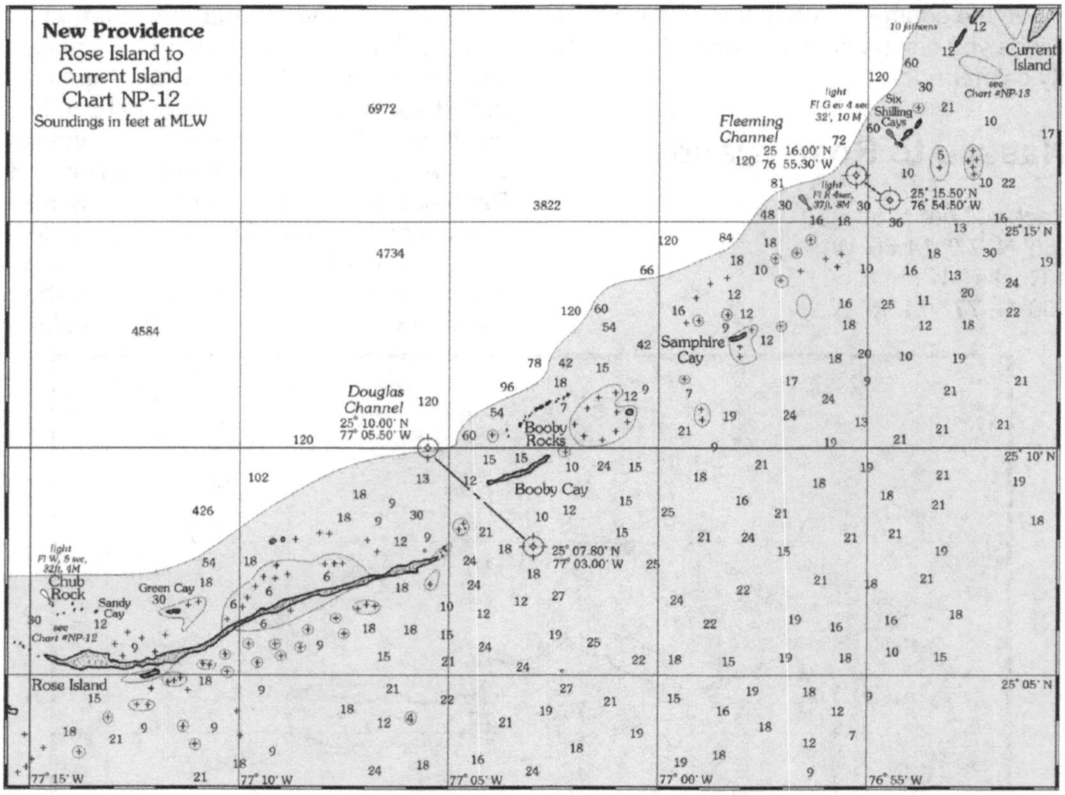

New Providence
Rose Island to
Current Island
Chart NP-12
Soundings in feet at MLW

Fleeming
Channel

Six
Shilling
Cays

light
Fl G ev 4 sec
32', 10 M

25° 16.00' N
76° 55.30' W

light
Fl R 4sec,
37ft, 8M

25° 15.50' N
76° 54.50' W

Current
Island

see
Chart #NP-13

Samphire
Cay

Douglas
Channel
25° 10.00' N
77° 05.50' W

Booby
Rocks

Booby Cay

25° 07.80' N
77° 03.00' W

light
Fl W, 5 sec,
32ft, 4M

Chub
Rock

Sandy
Cay

Green Cay

see
Chart #NP-12

Rose Island

10 fathoms

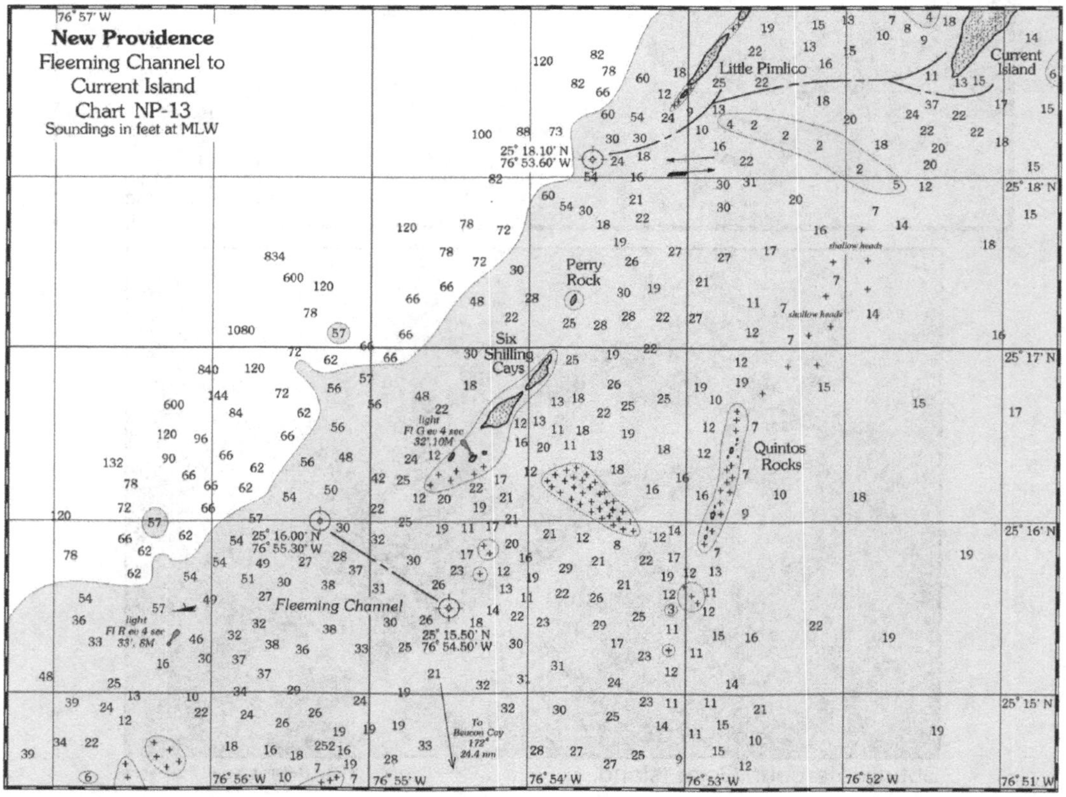

New Providence
Fleeming Channel to
Current Island
Chart NP-13
Soundings in feet at MLW

Little Pimlico

Current
Island

25° 18.10' N
76° 53.60' W

Perry
Rock

shallow heads

shallow heads

Six
Shilling
Cays

light
Fl G ev 4 sec
32', 10M

Quintos
Rocks

25° 16.00' N
76° 55.30' W

Fleeming Channel

25° 15.50' N
76° 54.50' W

light
Fl R ev 4 sec
33', 8M

To
Beacon Cay
172°
26.4 nm

except on a rising tide as there are several shallow bars south of *The Narrows Light*, none of which are visible.

Navigational Information

The channel through *The Narrows* lies along the Athol Island shore between *The Narrows Light* and Athol Island and is situated in a southeast-northwest direction as shown on Chart NP-4. Do not attempt to pass west of the light unless you have a very shallow draft; all you will find is rocks. This can be a tricky area; there is a lot of current here. If heading north through *The Narrows* (see Chart NP-4) head east past *The Narrows Light* and then turn and head back to the west/northwest staying halfway between the light and Athol Island. Watch out for the shallows south and southeast of the light and then once through *The Narrows* you can take up a course to a settled weather anchorage that lies off the northern shore of Athol Island just off the small beach. Holding is fair at best so make sure your anchor is set well here. Just northeast of this anchorage lies the new Spruce Cay complex which you can't miss. Its landmark lighthouse resembles the real thing. Just off the western tip of Spruce Cay are some isolated reefs that snorkelers will enjoy. Vessels can transit either north or south of Spruce Cay, there is deep water off both shores.

Salt Cay, now usually called Blue Lagoon Island, lies north/northwest of Athol Island and is an enormous tourist draw in the Nassau area. It is home to 12 beaches as well as a huge entertainment center that seats 1,000 people. Other popular tourist stops on Salt Cay are *Sting Ray City* where you can dive with numerous manta rays, *Blue Lagoon*, and the *Dolphin Encounter* where you can swim with their playful dolphins. The island is for rent when there are no cruise ships due in the harbour and the owners discourage any visits by dinghy, they request that you take one of their boats over from Nassau.

Chub Rock, as shown on Charts NP-4 and NP-11, is an important little piece of real estate in the New Providence area. Smaller than a large truck, the only redeeming quality of this low, flat, rock is its light that marks the heavily traveled passage between the banks and the *Northeast Providence Channel*. Boats leaving the banks usually pass between Salt Cay and Chub Rock keeping Chub Rock to starboard to head northward out into the deeper water. From here you can take up your course to Abaco, the Berry Islands, Grand Bahama, Royal Island, or Spanish Wells. To leave by Chub Rock from Nassau you must first pass

through *The Narrows* between Paradise Island and Athol Island. Once through *The Narrows*, head to a position halfway between Salt Cay and Rose Island Rocks. Watch out for the shallow rocky areas shown on Chart NP-4 and NP-11 on this route. Once past Salt Cay and Rose Island Rocks head for a position northwest of Chub Rock giving Chub Rock a wide berth to avoid the reef just off its western end.

From Nassau harbor or if approaching from a point southeast of Athol Island, one can also head to Porgee Rocks and then take up a northerly course to pass between the western tip of Rose Island and Rose Island Rocks. From this position you can then steer approximately northwest to round Chub Rock well off. If you are approaching from offshore a waypoint at 25° 06.85' N, 77° 14.60' W, will place you approximately 200 yards north of Chub Rock.

What You'll Find Ashore

Athol Island has some nice diving just off its shores. At the southeastern end of Athol Island is the *LCT Wreck* that is visited on a regular basis by dive boats from Nassau. It is the wreckage of a World War II vintage landing craft that was used to ferry freight to Exuma after the war years. She was purposely ran aground at her present location by her crew who could wanted to salvage her cargo as she left Nassau and began taking on water. The wreck was used as the scene for an underwater fight in the James Bond thriller *Thunderball*. The bow sits in 5' of water while the stern lies in 13'. To find the *LCT Wreck* line up *Porgee Rock Light* on a bearing of 110° and the eastern tip of Athol Island at 30°. Along the northern shore are some isolated reefs that some of the local dive boats frequent near the anchorage shown on Chart NP-4.

Rose Island to Current Island

Little Pimlico Island - ½ nm SW of:
25° 18.10' N, 76° 53.60' W

Fleeming Channel - ¼ nm N of entrance:
25° 16.00' N, 76° 55.30' W

Fleeming Channel - ¼ nm S of entrance:
25° 15.50' N, 76° 54.50' W

Douglas Channel - 1 nm NW of:
25° 10.00' N, 77° 05.50' W

Douglas Channel - 1 nm SE of:
25° 07.80' N, 77° 03.00' W

Navigational Information

Rose Island is a popular anchorage for both visiting cruisers and local boaters. The most popular anchorage is on the south side of Rose Island at Bottom Harbour as shown on Chart NP-11. Vessels heading to this anchorage from Nassau should head east to Porgee Rock and head northward between Athol Island and Porgee Rock towards the western tip of Rose Island. Once you arrive at the western tip of Rose Island follow the shoreline eastward to anchor in Bottom Harbour.

Another fine anchorage is just off the nice beach on the northern side of Rose Island just east of its western tip. From Nassau you can head for a position between Salt Cay and Rose Island Rocks. Pass between them and head east to work you way in to the Rose Island shore as shown on Chart NP-12. You can also use the route from Porgee Rocks to the western end of Rose Island. Once at the western tip of Rose Island, pass between Rose Island and Rose Island Rocks and turn to starboard to work your way into the anchorage as shown on Chart NP-11. Watch out for the reefs at the western tip of Rose Island.

North of Rose Island lies Sandy Cay, sometimes called Gilligan's Island. Truth be known, Sandy Cay had nothing to do with the popular TV show, it seems the story was told and grew with the retelling. All the better for Sandy Cay perhaps. There is a nice anchorage off the southern shore of Sandy Cay that is good in north to northeast winds or settled weather.

North or Rose Island and east of Sandy Cay lies Green Cay and *Green Cay Reef*. There is an excellent anchorage on the southern shore of Green Cay. There are two routes to access this anchorage from Nassau. The first is to go outside at Chub Rock and steer east until you can enter the anchorage at Green Cay as shown on Chart NP-12. A shorter route is to head east from Sandy Cay passing just south of Halfway Rock avoiding its reefs and the large reef south of it. Never try to head east from Green Cay along the shoreline of Rose Island; the area is foul with scattered shallow heads and reefs. Small outboard powered boats even have trouble here at times. Green Cay itself has a nice reef a bit off its northern shore with huge coral heads in 35'-50' of water. The heads themselves rise up some 25'-30' off the bottom. *Green Cay Reef*, a beautiful pillar coral reef lies southwest of Green Cay when the southern edge of Green Cay bears 80° and the western tip of Green Cay bears 45°.

The cays from Rose Island to Current Island have little to offer to cruising boats though some offer a lee anchorage in settled weather. Fishing and diving on the numerous reefs is superb. There are two deep water channels, *Douglas Channel* and *Fleeming Channel*, from the *Northeast Providence Channel* and the banks south of the cays. *Douglas Channel* lies between the eastern end of Rose Island and Booby Cay as shown on Chart NP-12. A waypoint at 25° 10.00' N, 77° 05.50' W, will place you approximately 1 mile northwest of the channel while a waypoint at 25° 07.80' N, 77° 03.00' W, will place you approximately 1 mile southeast of the channel. Pass between Rose Island and Booby Cay giving the reefs off the eastern end of Rose Island a wide berth. *Fleeming Channel* is often used by cruising boats wishing to traverse the waters between the Abacos and the Exumas, or between northern Eleuthera and the northern Exumas. A waypoint at 25° 16.00' N, 76° 55.30' W, will place you ¼ mile north the entrance to *Fleeming Channel* while a waypoint at 25° 15.50' N, 76° 54.50' W, will place you approximately ¼ mile south of the channel entrance as shown on Chart NP-12 and in greater detail on Chart NP-13. *Fleeming Channel* is wide, deep, obstruction free, and marked by lights on both sides.

Further northward, near Current Island, a waypoint at 25° 18.10' N, 76° 53.60' W, will place you approximately ½ mile southwest of Little Pimlico Island as shown on Chart NP-13. This waypoint will allow you to pass south of Little Pimlico Island to access the southern tip of Current Island or to parallel the eastern shore of Little Pimlico and Pimlico Island or the western shore of Current Island to head to Current Cut. For more information on this route see the chapter *Eleuthera: The Current and Current Cut*.

The Pirates of Nassau

"What right do you have to infest the seas?"
Question from Alexander the Great
to a captured pirate

*"The same that thou hast to infest the universe;
but because I do this in a small ship,
I am called a robber;
and because thou actest the same part
with a great fleet,
thou art entitled a conqueror."*
Response of the captured pirate

*"Damn ye, you are a sneaking puppy,
and so are all those who will submit to be governed
by laws which rich men have made for their own
security, for the cowardly whelps have not the
courage otherwise to defend what they get by their
knavery. But damn ye altogether.
Damn them for a pack of crafty rascals, and
you, who sire them for a parcel of hen-hearted
numbskulls. They vilify us, the scoundrels do; then
there is only this difference, they rob the poor under
cover of the law, forsooth,
and we plunder the rich under the protection of
our own courage; had ye not better make one of
us, than sneak after the arses of those villains for
employment?*
Pirate Captain Charles Bellamy,
to a captured merchant captain
who refused to join him.

Stories about the Bahamas and Pirates go hand in hand, and have for over three hundred years. If I was a reincarnationist I could easily convince myself that I sailed these waters three centuries ago searching for prey to rob and plunder at my whim. Jimmy Buffet's not the only one.

Piracy, the act of robbery or forcible depredation upon the high seas, *animo furundi*, is often called the third oldest profession. The Bible refers to pirates as "Princes of the Sea," although the *sweet trade,* as it is sometimes called, could hardly be termed a royal occupation.

One of the earliest reports concerns certain Mediterranean sea-rogues that captured a youth named Julius Caesar and held him for ransom for six weeks. Forced to watch while his shipmates were bound back to back and tossed overboard, young Caesar eventually caught and crucified his captors. Plutarch writes of a prosperous pirate trade in ancient Rome that flourished during times of civil strife. These pirates became so powerful that they set up a pirate nation in Cilicia, now a part of Turkey. It required Pompey the Great and hundreds of ships to finally cleanse Rome of its scourge of piratical activity.

The late 700's saw the Vikings begin their reign of terror on land and sea reaching as far as Spain by 912. The Arabs were masters of piracy in the Red Sea for centuries while the Barbary Corsairs of Tunis and Algiers ransacked the Mediterranean for several generations and by the 16th century had established a pirate nation of their own, the Barbary States in northern Africa. Here they reigned until France captured Algeria in 1830.

While all this was going on in the western world, the Chinese and Malay pirates were holding their own in the Far East up until the 17th century in Formosa, now Taiwan.

Although acts of piracy have been recorded since the times of the ancient Phoenicians, the *Golden Age of Piracy*, complete with its dashing buccaneers and Jolly Rogers spanned a very short period as time is measured. Roughly from the mid-1600's until the early 1700's although acts of piracy were still recorded well into the 18th and early 19th centuries and are still occurring today in a few isolated sea-lanes.

After Columbus' discovery of the New World, Spanish slavers began to decimate the local Lucayan population in the Bahamas, making slaves of those they captured for their mines in Cuba and Hispaniola and as divers for their pearl beds off Venezuela. Soon, Spanish vessels were transporting the wealth of the New World back across the Atlantic to Spain. The first recorded acts of piracy in the West Indies occurred in 1513 and later in 1520 when a French privateer captured a Spanish vessel enroute from Mexico to Spain. As Spanish shipping activity increased in the New World in the 1500's, the era of privateering in the Bahamas began. Spanish ships laden with the riches of the New World would pass near or through the Bahamas on their way back to Spain making wrecking very profitable in the surrounding waters. It was said that if a crewman were lucky enough to survive the wreck, it was uncertain as to whether he would survive the wreckers. If the Spanish knew of the location of their wrecks they would send crews to salvage the valuables but Bahamian wreckers were very successful at driving off the intruders and looting at their pleasure. As the Spanish captains became wise to the ways of the wreckers, wrecks became fewer and fewer, until the privateers had to find other uses for their talents. This was not difficult for the era of the buccaneers was in full swing.

The original buccaneers (*boucaniers*), the forerunners of the pirates, were based in northern Hispaniola. From 1629 to 1641, English buccaneers were organized as a company using the island of Providence (Providencia) off the Nicaraguan coast as a base and these years proved to be very prosperous for the Providence-based buccaneers. However, their prosperity ended abruptly in 1641 when the Spanish invaded the island and massacred every settler they could find. The few who escaped shifted their base of operations to Tortuga, a small, rocky island off the northern coast of Hispaniola and a freebooter stronghold.

The English were the first to consider planting a settlement on Tortuga in the 1630's, but soon thought better of it. Around 1640 the French sent a military engineer to fortify the island, which aroused the Spanish who attacked, killing most of the French. Control of Tortuga see-sawed for the next two decades, until the French finally prevailed.

The religious wars of the 16th century caused many French Protestants to try to elude the long arm of Rome by establishing settlements in the New World. The Portuguese destroyed their 1555 colony in Brazil and their 1564 colony at St. Augustine, Florida, was efficiently annihilated by the Spanish. A few survivors of these communities found their way to Hispaniola, which had been abandoned by the Spanish who were off chasing dreams of greater riches in Mexico, Colombia, and Peru.

They were a wild group of men from France who joined forces with others from Holland, and England, indentured servants, seafarers, and adventurers. Living in primitive conditions, they wore colorful, picturesque garb and hunted the semi-wild cattle and pigs on the island, descendants of escapees from Spanish farms. They roasted the meat over fires called *boucans*, a grill-like contraption of slender branches placed high enough above the fire to allow the drying and smoking of meat without roasting. These *boucaniers* would sell their smoked meat product, along with hides and tallow, to passing ships. Hispaniola soon became the location of a huge meat and hides trade. The *boucaniers* quickly learned to live less off hunting and to rely more on their commerce with Spanish ships, first in canoes, then "acquiring" ships, and finally in small flotillas. In essence, a boucanier in English dress was a buccaneer while a *boucanier* in French dress was known as a *flibustier*, or *freebooter*.

In the 1665, a freebooter from Normandy who called himself Pierre Le Grand (and who is often granted the honor of being the father of piracy in the West Indies), boldly captured a Spanish Galleon in the passage between Tortuga and the *Caicos Bank* while most of her crew slept. Le Grand and his 28 men approached the galleon in an old dilapidated raft, not far from sinking. The captain of the galleon spied their craft and laughed at the condition of their vessel and its ragtag crew, the Captain said he would not fear them even if they were the size of his own galleon. Le Grand had bored holes in the bottom of his boat to insure that his men were properly motivated, that either they would take the galleon or the sea would take them. Le Grand and his men pulled alongside the galleon and wedged the big ship's rudder and climbed aboard just as their own little boat sank beneath the waves. Le Grand and his men took the ship without a shot and Le Grand himself burst into the officer's cabin in the midst of a quiet card game. Le Grand took the ship to France after allowing those of the galleon's crew who would not join his ranks to depart on the island of Hispaniola.

Le Grand and his men, were part of an elite group of pirates to have ever taken a Galleon, in fact they may be the only pirates to capture such a prize. Le Grand and his men divided their spoils, sailed away wealthy men, and retired from the sea. Twenty-three of Le Grand's twenty-eight men retired to a life of ease in France, while the other five settled in the paradise of the Caribbean. Le Grand himself was said to have lived happily to a ripe old age and his success inspired countless men with dreams of easy wealth for the taking, and launched a half-century of piracy that has inspired thousands of stories, novels, and movies and brought us an equal number of colorful, treacherous characters.

There was one French freebooter that was quite civilized in comparison to his peers. The Chevalier de Gramont was a gentleman pirate who maintained a base on Île aux Vaches off Haiti's Tiburon Peninsula. His compound was graced with all the amenities that civilization had to offer at that time and de Gramont himself was deeply involved with French politics, rendering the French Governor at Gonaves financial, diplomatic, defense, and intelligence services.

Soon, recruits from every European trading nation began to pour into Tortuga. This loose gathering of adventurers were accustomed to extreme hardship and soon formed armed bands. The practical French, endeavoring to bring about a more orderly life in Tortuga, imported a shipload of 50 *filles de joie* from France, reasoning that some female companionship would have a stabilizing effect on their lonely outpost (unfortunately, in that sort of environment, jealousy raised its ugly head and many men and women met their ends prematurely). The Tortugans drew up strong codes of honor that they chose to live by and were extremely well led. For over 75 years these buccaneers were the scourge of the Spanish fleet and called themselves the *Brethren of the Coast.*

Most prominent of the buccaneers were Edward Mansfield and the legendary Sir Henry Morgan who used to recite Biblical verses to his crew substituting the Devil for any references to God. In 1664, Mansfield conceived of a permanent settlement upon a small Bahamian island, New Providence, and Henry Morgan agreed. The proprietary government in Charles Town, renamed Nassau in 1695, was favorable to the buccaneers and Charles Town became quite the haven for these *Brethren of the Coast.* The waters in the harbor were perfect for pirate vessels. Too shallow for the deep draft British Man-of-War but deep enough for the smaller, more nimble shallow draft vessels that the pirates preferred. The hills provided an excellent view of the surrounding waters, the reefs supplied all the fish and shellfish the pirates could eat, and the interior offered fresh water springs, wild pigs, pigeons, ducks, and fruits.

Mansfield's early and untimely death created confusion in the leadership of the buccaneers and Morgan set them off on a course of plunder and profit. Perhaps the greatest feat of piracy ever recorded may have been Sir Henry Morgan's sacking of Panama in 1671 when the legendary swashbuckler sailed away with over $100 million worth of gold, silver and precious gems. The years between 1671 and 1686 were a time of buccaneer ascendancy as the buccaneers gained major European finance against the Spanish Empire. After the capture of Jamaica in 1655, Port Royal, just outside of Kingston, became the headquarters for English buccaneers and remained so for 20 years. Under Sir Thomas Modyford and Sir Henry Morgan their achievements reached a climax. The *Treaty of Madrid* with Spain in 1670, the death of Sir Henry Morgan in 1688, and finally the destruction by earthquake of Port Royal in 1692 dispersed these Jamaican based buccaneers.

There is no fine line as to when the buccaneers became pirates. *Webster's Dictionary* offers little difference between the two. History suggests that the code of honor of the early buccaneers was forgotten and the bands degenerated into piracy. The buccaneers had articles called *chasseparties* that allocated duties, rewards, and compensations. In all things, their brotherhood was expected to observe a rigid code of honor called *la coutume de la côte*, which roughly translated means *the custom of the coast.* Despite their code and the *chasseparties*, the English and French buccaneers were always quarreling. The number of English buccaneers at Tortuga having to rely on French protection increased year by year. The Jamaican and Carolina legislatures passed severe acts against them and the buccaneers became less and less particular about their prey. By 1685, their own people were even calling them pirates. Whatever unity there was between the British and French buccaneers dissolved when their two countries went to war after William of Orange ascended the English Throne in 1689. This struggle was to last 126 years with only one long break. Loyal English were no longer welcome in Hispaniola and when the Anglo-French fighting reached the Caribbean in 1691, the last of the English pirates left the safety of Tortuga and settled in areas of the Bahamas.

The English pirates began to take on bigger game. Bermudan and colonial American ships trading between the Turks, Inagua, and the Colonies became fair game. One captain referring to the pirates hiding places in the Bahamas said, "*As surely as spiders abound where there are nooks and crannies, so have pirates sprung up whenever there is a nest of islands offering creeks and shallows, headlands, rocks, and reefs-facilities, in short, for lurking, for surprise, for attack, for escape.*" The pirates felt safe in the Bahamas because of their knowledge of the waters and because of the ineffectual, if not sympathetic government in Nassau.

Nassau in the 1690's had become, in the words of then Proprietary Governor Nicholas Webb, "... a common retreat for pirates and illegal traders" and a "...receptacle for all rogues." Harsh words for a man who was not far removed from the ranks of the pirates himself. Of course there is always the possibility that he was bragging. Nassau had become a lawless tent city of brigands, the "Flying Gang" as they called themselves, the only permanent buildings being taverns where pirates spent their hard won booty on rum, gambling, and prostitutes. Here pirates could find buyers for their plunder, careen and repair their vessel, and laze all day in hammocks if they so desired. Three of their favorite drinks during this period were *bumboo*, a mixture of rum, sugar, water and nutmeg, *rumfustian*, a blend of raw eggs, sugar, sherry, gin, and beer that was drunk hot, and Blackbeard's own mixture of rum and gunpowder. So much fun did these freebooters have in Nassau that a saying sprang up that when a pirate slept he did not dream of going to heaven, he dreamt of returning to New Providence.

Nassau had as leaders during the latter 1600's through the early 1700's a succession of men who were little better than the pirates themselves, *pirate-brokers* as they were described. In 1684 Robert Clarke was appointed by the Crown to govern the island colony. This one action angered the Spanish to no end. Clarke was as corrupt as any pirate, "pirate proven" it was said about him. The outraged Spanish soon raided Nassau and roasted Clarke on a spit. In 1690, Cadwallader Jones became Governor and selected an executive council made up of some of Nassau's most infamous pirates. His council soon accused him of high treason and selected one of their own to govern in his stead.

The government in Nassau was just about as corrupt as it could get. Hog Island, now Paradise Island on the northern shore of Nassau Harbour, was granted to a former governor, the unscrupulous Nicholas Trott for £50. When the notorious pirate Henry Every asked for permission for he and his crew to land at Nassau and take on water, Trott asked for and received 20 *Pieces of Eight* for each pirate who landed in Nassau, 40 pieces for their Captain, and £1,000 in plunder, the total amount paid being over £7,000. When one of the pirates broke a glass while dining in Trott's home, he charged the man £3.16s, a sum that would have kept a man in England in the finest beef for a year. When Every received reports

that the French had taken Exuma with three ships and 320 men, Trott gave the pirates permission to stay. Every's crew soon broke up as did his vessel *Fancy*, which he gave to Trott who immediately salvaged her guns and placed them in an earthen fort to repel Spanish attack. Trott's cousin, also named Nicholas, was a judge in Charleston, South Carolina who hated pirates and all types of outlaws. He was best known for trying and sentencing to death the *Gentleman Pirate*, Stede Bonnet in 1718.

In 1701 a merchant named Captain Elias Haskett came to Nassau to fill the vacant governorship. He found "disaffection and insecurity" was the rule in Nassau. When he attempted to imprison the pirate Read Elding he only succeeded in stirring up a mini-rebellion. A pistol butt broke the governor's skull and Haskett was expelled to New York aboard a small ketch. To be fair, it must be noted that Haskett was no saint himself, having arrived in Nassau to avoid creditors in England. His brief rule as governor was described as tyrannical.

The Spanish, realizing the worth of Nassau and the Bahamas against their fleet, attacked Nassau in October of 1703. They plundered the town, spiked the guns, killed many of the men, and left with eighty prisoners including then Acting-Governor Ellis Lightwood. The Spanish returned again in 1707 to finish the job. The population of the Bahamas in 1707 was between 400 and 500 families, mainly scattered over New Providence, Eleuthera, Cat Island, and Exuma. Pirates had free roam of the waters for the next ten years and by 1713 there were an estimated 1,000 active pirates operating in Bahamian waters.

Thomas Walker, a former judge in the Vice-Admiralty Court arrived in Nassau in 1715 determined to rid New Providence of its pirate population. He was humiliated, chased off the island, and fled to settle in a more hospitable South Carolina. Two pirate captains, Benjamin Hornigold and Thomas Barrow, immediately proclaimed a pirate republic with themselves as governors.

Some of the most notorious pirates to be found in the pages of history have been reported as lurking in Bahamian waters during these years. Mary Read and Anne Bonny, the "lady" pirates who sailed with Calico Jack Rackham, Stede Bonnet the Gentleman Pirate, Benjamin Hornigold, Charles Vane, and Edward Teach, better known as Blackbeard.

If any one pirate could embody the spirit of the era and of piracy itself, none would be better suited for it than Blackbeard. Although his independent pirate career only spanned two short years, he became the model for all sorts of pirate tales and adventures. His courage, his terrifying appearance, his larger than life feats, and his fourteen wives all helped create the mystique that made him a legend in his own time.

A restless Bristol seaman, Teach served aboard privateers during Queen Anne's War. He later drifted to Nassau where he learned the finer elements of the *sweet trade* from Captain Benjamin Hornigold. Hornigold, the dean of the West Indies pirates, was one of the fiercest and ablest of the New Providence pirates and was held in the highest esteem by his peers. Teach joined his crew in 1716 and Hornigold immediately recognized young Teach's courage, fighting ability, and thirst for blood and made him his protégé. Within a few months Hornigold put Teach in charge of his own sloop, one Teach himself captured after a furious battle. Teach named her *Queen Anne's Revenge* and immediately equipped her with six cannons and seventy handpicked men. Teach and Hornigold continued to cruise together and based themselves in Nassau. It was here that the legend of Blackbeard, the swashbuckling pirate began.

Beards were not common at the time and Teach discovered that he could grow an immense coal-black beard that covered most of his face, as wide as his ears and almost up to his eyes. He let it grow long and bound it in pigtails with colorful ribbons. Blackbeard was tall, wide, and muscular, a great bear of a man with large bushy eyebrows. He cultivated his fearsome appearance by the clothes he chose to wear. He would dress for the occasion, sometimes all in black with a huge, broad hat and knee boots, other times with a brightly colored silk or velvet coat with the sleeves turned back to the elbows, gaudy breeches, and low shoes with large brass buckles. A firm believer in first impressions, Teach sought to emphasize his evil nature. In battle he was a walking armory with as many as six pistols tucked into bandoliers across his chest and all manner of knives, daggers, and cutlasses in his belt. To heighten the effect Blackbeard would tuck slow burning fuses into his hair and beard and light them creating an even more terrifying image. Teach's appearance and well-known ferocity in battle caused many of the ships he preyed upon to surrender without a fight.

Many superstitious sailors believed Blackbeard to be the Devil incarnate. There are many tales of the "pranks" he pulled to show his superiority to his crew and anybody else who doubted him. The most popular account has Blackbeard and several of his men descending into a hold below decks to ". . . make a hell of our own, and try how long we can bear it." Closing up all the hatches he filled several pots with brimstone and other flammable materials and set them on fire. With his men almost suffocating Teach ordered the hatches opened after his crewmen pleaded for air, quite impressed that he had held out the longest. Blackbeard once suggested playing a game of gallows, the object being to see who could swing the longest without perishing. There is no account of anyone playing this game with their beloved Captain.

One night Blackbeard was sitting at the table in his cabin drinking with his mate, Israel Hands, and one other crewman. Blackbeard pulled out two pistols under the table and cocked them. The crewman, seeing what might happen next, excused himself and returned to the deck. After he left Blackbeard blew out the candle, crossed his arms, and fired both pistols shooting Hands in the knee and crippling him for life. When later asked for an explanation by his crew he replied that if he did not now and then kill one of them they might forget who he was. Is it any wonder that Israel Hands later turned King's evidence against Blackbeard? Hands received a pardon and died a street beggar in London.

For all his gruff exterior, Blackbeard was quite the ladies man. When he entered a tavern, he soon attracted an admiring group of the fairer sex. He would not allow a woman to serve him a drink, he preferred to serve them. His female entourage would soon be doing all they could to attract his attention, sitting on his lap, dancing for him clothed and nude, and sooner or later Blackbeard would focus his attention on one woman and she would be his for the duration of his stay. Blackbeard had a weakness for these women, falling in love quickly and deeply. Consequently he would find himself back on the *Queen Anne's Revenge* standing in front of the mate taking marriage vows. Not once. Not twice. But fourteen times. To his crew it was a running joke, to Blackbeard it was a source of embarrassment, and to the women, they usually took it as a lark though to be said to be Blackbeard's wife certainly gave them some prestige among the *brethren of the coast* and other seafarers.

While Blackbeard certainly spent a lot of time in the bars of Nassau, he preferred to be off on an adventure. On a hill just east of town he constructed a watchtower whose ruins still survive today. He favored staying in his tower instead of wasting away his life in the taverns of New Providence. His crew set up tents on the path outside the tower and Blackbeard would frequently descend and hold court under a huge tree, trading loot, interviewing future crew, planning his next cruise, and drinking rum. Teach had a high tolerance for alcoholic beverages and there are many tales of his unmatched drinking ability. Teach, ever the showman, once mixed gunpowder in his rum, set it on fire, and drank the concoction impressing all present.

Teach and Hornigold set out in 1717, probably the last time Blackbeard saw Nassau. The pair soon shook hands and went their separate ways with Hornigold returning to Nassau. At one point in his career Blackbeard took under his wing Major Stede Bonnet, the *Gentleman Pirate*. Bonnet was a retired officer of the King's Guards and owned a substantial sugar plantation near Bridgetown on the island of Barbados. Bonnet came from a good family and was very well educated and refined compared to most *Brethren of the Coast*. Bonnet was held in high esteem by his Barbadian neighbors and it was quite a shock to them when he turned to the *Sweet Trade* in 1717. Some of his friends suggested that he did it simply to get away from the nagging of his shrewish wife.

Bonnet purchased a sloop with his own funds even though it was customary for pirates to steal their vessels. He outfitted her with ten guns and named her *Revenge*. Bonnet then set out to recruit a crew of seventy men, some experienced, some not, and set sail one night without even so much as a goodbye for Mrs. Bonnet.

Bonnet's skills as a Captain were lacking, his crew had little confidence in his abilities. There was even talk aboard the *Revenge* of replacing the good Major. He did not have a truly illustrious career as piratical careers go, the term *bungling* is often used as an adjective for Bonnet's misadventures. Every time he turned around it seemed that he was being taken advantage of and having doubts concerning taking up the profession in the first place. Perhaps it was his experience as an officer and a gentleman that caused him to become such an easy mark for his peers.

Bonnet somehow managed to capture a few prizes before the dandy, English gentleman pirate met up with the savage, larger than life Blackbeard. It is said that opposites attract and the two got along so well that they decided to go *a-pyrating* together.

It did not take long for Blackbeard to recognize that Bonnet was an amateur at his chosen profession. Blackbeard put his second-in-command, Lieutenant Richards, in charge of Bonnet's ship and while this pleased Bonnet's crew it humiliated the good Major. Blackbeard explained that he did this so Bonnet would not have to concern himself with the rigors of command and so that the Major could live a more leisurely lifestyle. Bonnet in effect became Blackbeard's prisoner. Bonnet settled in on Blackbeard's ship, the *Queen Anne's Revenge*, and began having second thoughts about taking up his current lifestyle. He toyed with the idea of moving to a Spanish or Portuguese colony saying that he could not return to Barbados and look another Englishman in the eye after the deeds he had done.

After capturing several ships Blackbeard sailed to Topsail Inlet in North Carolina where he returned command of the *Revenge* to Bonnet. At then end of the summer of 1718, Teach told Bonnet of his plans to avail himself of a pardon and suggested that Bonnet do the same. Bonnet went to Bath to seek a pardon from then Governor Eden who suggested he sail to St. Thomas for a commission as a privateer for the upcoming war with Spain. When Bonnet returned to the *Revenge*, he found that Blackbeard had stripped her clean and marooned 25 of her crew on a desolate sand spit before sailing away with her plunder and the rest of her crew.

Bonnet repaired his vessel and went off in search of the treacherous Blackbeard. Having gained experience under Blackbeard's tutelage, he succeeded in taking several ships including one particularly rich prize that he landed at the Cape Fear River in September of 1718. Here he was captured and taken to Charleston where he succeeded in bribing his way out of jail. Bonnet was recaptured in November and eventually went to trial with 33 of his former crew. Bonnet hoped that his former standing as a gentleman would bend the judge's disposition his way but this was not to be. Bonnet was executed in November of 1718 despite an impassioned plea for mercy that Daniel Defoe tells us impressed ". . .the People of the Province, particularly the women," with his "piteous Behaviour under sentence." Bonnet had promised that if released, he would gladly cut off all his limbs save his tongue which he would use to only call upon God. Bonnet may have set two firsts for pirates. He was the first pirate to buy a ship, and, after reading too many tales of piracy on the high seas, actually may have made someone walk the plank. While someone, somewhere actually had to walk a plank for the stories of this particular punishment to have a basis, this cruel treatment did not take place as commonly as some tales would have us believe.

Shortly after Blackbeard tricked Bonnet, Blackbeard himself sought and received a pardon. For a time Blackbeard settled in Bath, took a wife, and was a model husband and businessman. The notorious ex-pirate accommodated his lavish tastes by spending his pirate loot and when that ran out off he went to sea again.

Blackbeard finally met his end on November 22, 1718 at Okracoke Island in North Carolina. He was defeated after furious close in fighting with Lt. Robert Maynard and several of his men who were hesitant to move in close until Blackbeard had already been wounded several times. Maynard reported that Blackbeard had suffered five pistol shots and twenty cutlass wounds before falling. Lt. Maynard hung Blackbeard's head from his bowsprit and dumped his headless corpse overboard. Legend has it that Blackbeard's corpse then swam around Maynard's sloop several times before sinking.

Across the Atlantic Ocean in London constant argument and complaint was beginning to stir officials to action. The Crown received letters of complaint from citizens, captains, and governors of every maritime colony. Finally the Crown took action. In 1717, a Royal Proclamation was read in Nassau to the gathered pirates offering pardon for those who surrendered immediately. The offer of pardon was laughed at, only five pirates, one of which was the notorious Captain William Jennings, took advantage of the offer and went to Bermuda. The Crown realized that the Bahamas needed a strong governor who was backed by force and began a search for the right man. Stepping forth was Woodes Rogers.

Rogers was born in Dorset in 1679 and like Blackbeard, was a Bristol seaman and an ex-privateer. He had already earned a portion of fame for his around the world privateering voyage of 1708-

1711 during the War of the Spanish Succession. Woodes Rogers returned having captured 20 ships and over £800,000 of Spanish plunder. It was on this voyage that Rogers rescued Alexander Selkirk from the island of Juan Fernandez. Rogers' account of this event gave Daniel Defoe the inspiration for his novel *Robinson Crusoe*. Oddly enough, William Dampier, one of Rogers' pilots on this expedition, was the man who was in charge of the privateering expedition that Selkirk was engaged in when the future castaway began his self-imposed exile after arguing with the captain of the vessel he was aboard.

In 1717, Rogers was proclaimed "Captain-General and Governor-in-Chief," the first Royal Governor of the Bahamas. Woodes Rogers, as a privateer, had previous dealings with the likes of the notorious pirates Vane, Rackham, and Hornigold in places as diverse as Madagascar and Providence. He knew them and their ways well. In April of 1718, armed with the Amnesty Declaration, Rogers set sail for Nassau aboard the 460-ton *Delicia* and in the company of four British warships, the frigates *Milford* and *Rose*, and the sloops *Buck* and *Shark*. Arriving off Eleuthera on July 20, 1718, residents of Harbour Island came out to warn Rogers that there were over 1,000 pirates in Nassau and that although most would probably agree to the pardon, Vane had no intention of surrendering and that Blackbeard had long since moved on to other waters. Delighted at this news, Rogers sailed for Nassau.

On July 24, Rogers and his fleet lay off Nassau. Vane sent Rogers a letter with the terms under which he would surrender. Vane did not receive a speedy reply to his letter and when the *Rose* and the *Shark* proceeded into the harbor to reconnoiter, they received a startling welcome from Vane. Vane had loaded a captured French vessel with explosives, set her afire, and cut her loose to drift up against the *Rose*. The *Rose* and the *Shark* were forced to flee the harbor for the safety of the open sea. At dawn, Vane hoisted the skull and crossbones form his mizzen and the flag of St. George from his mainmast and, as his crew was raising sail, fired a gun in contempt at Rogers. Vane, with his quartermaster Calico Jack Rackham, then set full sail out the shallow eastern entrance of the harbor, his ship loaded with plunder. Rogers, with his deeper draft vessels could not follow Vane across the banks. Within three days Vane had captured two vessels bound for Nassau and landed on a small island, some say in the Abacos others claim the

Exumas, to divide their loot. Vane, who for several years was the scourge of the Turks and Caicos Salt Rakers, was never seen in the Bahamas again and was eventually executed in Jamaica in 1720.

After Vane's departure, Rogers landed and walked ashore between two lines of about 300 filthy, drunken pirates who fired their guns into the air while cheering for "good King George." Woodes Rogers announced the King's Pardon and the ex-pirate Captain William Jennings tuned to the crowd and shouted "All right you bastards! Line up!" The Proclamation, valid until September 5, 1718, pardoned all pirates of their crimes if they would take an oath not to return to their former trade. Rogers immediately set about proclaiming martial law and securing the town and all vessels within the harbor. Taking advantage of the pardon, pirate Captains Thomas Burgess and Benjamin Hornigold, Blackbeard's former mentor, were shrewdly appointed "privateer commanders" by Rogers.

Captain John Augur, who also accepted the King's Pardon, so impressed Woodes Rogers that he was given command of two vessels to go trading amongst the islands for supplies for Rogers colony on New Providence. A few days out Augur met with two sloops and, old ways being hard to break, entered back into the *sweet trade*. Heading to the West Indies a hurricane forced him back to the Bahamas, just the place he did not want to be, and Augur wound up shipwrecked in the Exumas. When Woodes Rogers learned of these events he sent an armed sloop under Captain Benjamin Hornigold to capture Auger and return him to Nassau to stand trial. After a bloody fight, Auger and thirteen others were captured and brought back to Nassau in chains, three of Auger's men dying of their wounds along the way. Tried by a council of their former fellow pirates, Auger and his crew were sentenced to death. On the gallows Augur and his men pleaded with their onetime comrades to rescue them. The crowd, pardoned pirates all, responded by saying that it was time for them to repent. Augur, who had been entrusted with a ship by Rogers and was the first to be hanged, sipped a glass of wine "...with wishes for the good success of the Bahama Islands and the Governor."

Some of Augur's men did not wish to go out with such kind words on their lips. One of them, Dennis McCarthy, sometimes shown as being spelled MaCarty, a 28-year-old ex-prizefighter turned pirate, soon found himself on the way to the gallows after Augur. As his fellow pirates watched, he slowly climbed the thirteen steps to the gallows on what is now the British Colonial Hotel's west beach. McCarthy, bedecked with colorful ribbons in his hair as became a boxer in those days, stood proud on the gallows, certain in his knowledge that he at least, still held fast to his principles. He surveyed the throng, once his mates and fellow conspirators, and said his final words. "Some friends of mine have often said I will die in my shoes, but I would rather make them liars." Dennis McCarthy then kicked off his shoes and was promptly hanged.

Another young man, 22 year old Thomas Morris, also decked out in ribbons, shouted from the gallows: "I do heartily repent: I repent that I have not done more mischief, and that we did not cut the throats of them that took us, and I am extremely sorry that you ain't all hang'd as well as we." Thirty-four-year-old William Lewis, another ex-boxer, wanted to die drunk and loudly demanded wine before his comrades stretched his neck. He was allowed to go to the afterlife with a head full of wine.

In another incident, Captain Thomas Anstis and five other men commandeered a sloop called the *Buck* in Nassau in order to go *a-pyrating*. They cruised in and about the islands of the Caribbean and Bahamas and eventually came under the command of Captain Bartholomew "Black Bart" Roberts, arguably the greatest pirate of the Golden Age of Piracy. There are tales tell of them being a very rough bunch, rougher than most. Tiring of the game, they left Roberts and sought pardon from the Crown in 1722. They waited for nine months on a small island off the Cuban coast for a response and, when no answer was received, Anstis and his crew set sail in two vessels and went back on *the grand account*. British warships immediately set them upon and one of their vessels was sunk but the tricky Captain Anstis escaped to Tobago. There a man of war, the *Winchester*, came upon the captain and crew who set their own ship afire and fled into the jungle. Captain Anstis had now lost all authority of his ragtag, discontented crew and was later shot while asleep in his hammock.

While Pirates were being hung in Nassau and marooned at Green Cay, several notable scoundrels were still at large such as Charles Vane's former quartermaster Calico Jack Rackham. Rackham came by his command when Vane was ousted as skipper of their ship. Shortly after fleeing from Woodes Rogers, Vane the crew maintained, showed cowardice when he failed to attack a French vessel. The crew voted Vane out and Rackham in. Calico Jack had Vane and those who voted for him cast off in a small sloop and Rackham and his crew began a new voyage of plunder and looting. In May of 1719 Rackham put into Nassau and sought pardon from Woodes Rogers. Since England was once again at war with Spain, Rogers offered Rackham pardon and Calico Jack settled in Nassau.

A stranger piratical trio than Calico Jack Rackham, Anne Bonny, and Mary Read would be hard to find. Anne Bonny had a pleasant enough childhood, growing up in a wealthy family, she had everything she could want. When of age she married young James Bonny, a penniless sailor and known rogue. The young couple moved to Nassau where James sought employment as an informer when Rogers offered amnesty. Anne, having somewhat higher moral standards than her husband, grew disgusted with him and was soon swept off her feet by the dashing and recently pardoned Calico Jack Rackham.

Calico Jack, named after the striped pants he so loved to wear, courted Anne Bonny lavishly with expensive gifts, even offering to buy her a divorce which was a common if not entirely legal practice at the time. James Bonny complained to Woodes Rogers who threatened to have Anne Bonny stripped and flogged if she did not return to her husband. Instead of returning to a man she loathed she eloped with Rackham. Desiring to return to the pirate's way of life, Rackham, Anne Bonny, and Rackham's crew stole a vessel in Nassau and headed back to sea, with Bonny dressing in men's clothes. Rackham later put Anne Bonny ashore with friends in Jamaica when she became pregnant until such time as she gave birth and could rejoin him. She later accompanied Rackham on all his later exploits.

Calico Jack Rackham was not the most successful of pirates. On one two-year cruise through the Caribbean, though he captured over 20 ships, most of his prizes were small schooners and fishing smacks. He once captured eight fishing boats at Harbour Island, Eleuthera and made off with only their nets and tackle. Off one schooner he is reported to have only removed ". . . 50 rolls of Tobacco and nine bags of Piemento."

Mary Read, once dressed as a boy by her mother hoping to deceive relatives for an inheritance, kept up the ruse in later years. She was apprenticed as a footboy to a French Lady but, seeking more out of life, entered the King's service as a cabin boy aboard a Man Of War and later joined an army unit as a cadet and fought bravely. She fell in love and eventually married another soldier who at first did not realize that she was a woman. Mary and her husband opened a tavern in Holland and after her husband died from fever, she again dressed up as a man and went on board a vessel bound for the West Indies. She soon joined up with a band of privateers under Woodes Rogers on the island of Providence. Mary Read claimed she detested the life of the pirate, however, when some of the crew mutinied and returned to their former lifestyle, with them went Mary Read. When she voyaged aboard a Dutch ship that was taken by Rackham, she jumped at the chance to sign the pirate articles and join the crew. No one had guessed she was a woman. And then along came Anne Bonny.

Bonny thought Read was a rather handsome young fellow and became enamored of her, forcing her to reveal her secret. A jealous Calico Jack, noticing the partiality Bonny was showing to Read, threatened to shoot both Anne and Mary. Once again her secret was revealed. Mary Read later fell in love with another crewmember and revealed herself to him. When her lover fell into a disagreement with another crewmember and the two were to duel ashore in two hours, Read found out and engaged the crewmember in an argument and promptly killed him. Rackham once asked Read why she had chosen the pirate lifestyle and did she fear hanging. She replied that as to hanging, that it was no great hardship, "...for if it were not for that, every cowardly fellow would turn pirate and so infest the seas, and men of courage would starve."

In 1719, Calico Jack was finally captured and was removed from his ship in Jamaica. During the battle Anne Bonny, Mary Read, and one other crewmember were the last fighters on deck, the rest of the crew fleeing below. Mary Read tried in vain to rouse the crew, firing down into the hold, finally killing one and wounding another before the lady buccaneers were captured. Rackham, who was at this point estranged from his beloved, had taken to abusing a bush hallucinogen and was removed from his below decks hiding spot in a stupor. In court, when the magistrate asked if the "lady pirates" had anything to say, they promptly announced: "My Lord, we plead our bellies!" Both women were pregnant and English law at the time forbade hanging a mother-to-be no matter how serious her crime. Mary Read later became ill and died in prison while Anne Bonny, through the intercession of some notable Jamaican planters, and perhaps her wealthy father, escaped the noose and was never executed. Calico Jack, while awaiting execution, was allowed a brief visit from Anne Bonny. Instead of consoling Rackham, she only told him that she was sorry to see him here and that if he had fought like a man he would not have to die like a dog. Anne Bonny wound up in Virginia, married with children. South of Warderick Wells are a series of rocks named Teach Rock, Bonny Rock, and Read Rock.

Even after the surrender of Rackham, there were still an estimated 2,000 pirates at large throughout the waters of the Bahamas and the Caribbean. The Spanish attempted to attack Nassau again in February of 1720 only to be repelled by two warships and furious musket fire. In failing health, Woodes Rogers left Nassau in March of 1721 for England. After spending his personal fortune on rebuilding Nassau, he received no help from the Crown and spent some time in prison for debt. The savior of Nassau in a debtor's prison, this was his reward.

Rogers was succeeded by George Penny as Governor of the Bahamas. Penny's one illustrious feat is that he managed to capture the infamous Spanish pirate Augustino Blanco. Blanco had utterly ravaged Cat Island, driving the inhabitants from their homes and taking whatever he chose and leaving little of any worth. Blanco and four of his crew were tried and executed in Nassau in October of 1722.

But Woodes Rogers was to make a comeback. He returned to Nassau on August 25, 1729 for his second term as Governor with the benefit of a salary of £400. He died in Nassau on July 15, 1732. He had succeeded in ridding Nassau of pirates and the former buccaneer capitol had a bright new future. Woodes Rogers gave the Bahamas their first motto: *Expulsis Piratus-Restuta Commercia* or *Pirates Expelled-Commerce Restored*.

A few years after Rogers' death, the only reported find of buried treasure occurred on New Providence. An earthen jar containing 1,000 pieces of eight was discovered buried under an orange tree. A pirate named Benjamin Sims claimed the booty saying he had given it to his brother several years ago for safekeeping. The governor allowed Sims to keep the money with the proviso that one-half the money be left to the Church in his will.

Eleuthera

Ports of Entry: Governor's Harbour, Harbour Island, Rock Sound, Spanish Wells, Powell Point

Fuel: Davis Harbour, Governor's Harbour, Harbour Island, Rock Sound, Runaway Bay, Spanish Wells

Haul-Out: Spanish Wells

Diesel Repairs: Harbour Island, Spanish Wells

Outboard Repairs: Deep Creek, Governor's Harbour, Harbour Island, Spanish Wells

Propane: Governor's Harbour, Harbour Island, Rock Sound, Spanish Wells

Provisions: Governor's Harbour, Harbour Island, Rock Sound, Spanish Wells

Important Lights:

Egg Island: Fl W ev 3 sec
Royal Island: Fl W ev 5 sec
Spanish Wells: Fl G ev 2 sec
Man Island: Gp. Fl W (3) ev 15 sec
Hatchett Bay: Fl W (2 4 sec) ev 15 sec
Governor's Harbour: Fl W ev 4 sec
Poison Point: Fl W ev 15 sec
East End Point: Fl W ev 4½ sec

Eleuthera is an island of firsts. It was the first republic in the New World with the first constitution and the first Parliament. Eleuthera was originally shown on charts as *Cigateo* although it had many variations such as *Ziguateo*, *Ciguateo*, *Guateo*, *Sygateo*, *Segatoo*, and *Sigatoo*. Early maps and charts show the island as *Ilathera* and *Islathera*, thought to be corruption's of the Spanish *Isla de Tierra*, and in one instance it is called *Alabaster Island*. The 70 settlers of William Sayle's *Eleutheran Adventurers*, who you shall learn of in the next paragraph, named her *Eleutheria* for the Greek word for freedom, *eleuthros*. Today the name has dropped the "i" and is simply known as Eleuthera.

The first inhabitants of Eleuthera of which there is proof were the peaceful Lucayan Indians who were enslaved by the marauding Spaniards in the early 1500's. The Spaniards put the Lucayans to work in their mines in Cuba and Hispaniola and sold them as divers for the rich pearl beds off Venezuela. But the first attempt at actual colonization of the island was in 1649, when former governor of Bermuda, William Sayles, along with several merchants in London formed a company called the *Company of Eleutherian Adventures* with the object of settling this and adjacent islands. An *Act of Parliament* was passed

in response to their petition and they were granted the whole area to be known as Eleuthera and off they sailed. Each *Adventurer* was required to pay into the public fund £100 and in return was guaranteed 300 acres to begin with and later 2,000 acres. The waters of The Bahamas at that time were teeming with seals and Sayles was enthusiastic about the commercial possibilities, he was intent on establishing a seal oil trade with Barbados. Whether he did this or not is unknown although he and the seals are both now long gone.

Sayles and his *Adventurers* wrecked their two vessels somewhere along the northern shore of Eleuthera and took shelter in a huge cave known today as *Preacher's Cave* along the northern shore between Spanish Wells and Harbour Island. Although they only lost one crewman, the group lost all their provisions. They had a hard struggle to survive even with a relief ship sent from Boston. The colonists spread out throughout Eleuthera with some building homes at Governor's Harbour. Many early settlers returned to Bermuda while others were driven from Eleuthera by the Spanish in 1680 and emigrated to Boston and in particular North Yarmouth near Portland.

This island has a little bit of everything that The Bahamas has to offer. Sunny beaches, deep water, shallow banks, grassy rolling hills, rocky cliffs, and a healthy agricultural, fisheries, and tourism oriented economical base.

Tides along the eastern and northern shores of Eleuthera including Harbour Island, Spanish Wells, Royal Island, and the waters north of *Current Cut* are the same time as Nassau. Tides in the *Bight of Eleuthera* along the western shore of the island and including *Davis Channel*, Powell Point, Rock Sound, Governor's Harbour, and Hatchet Bay are approximately 2:17 later than Nassau tides and are generally .2' less.

Approaches to Eleuthera

Egg Island Cut - 1½ nm WNW of Cut:
25° 29.60' N, 76° 54.75' W

Most boats headed to north Eleuthera arrive from Abaco, leaving *Little Harbour Bar* and making landfall somewhere in the vicinity of Royal Island or Spanish Wells. From *Little Harbour Bar* in Abaco (waypoint at

26° 19.30' N, 76° 59.32' W) it is approximately 49.2 nautical miles on a course of 179° to the waypoint (25° 29.60' N, 76° 54.75' W) lying 1½ nautical mile west/northwest of the cut between Egg Island and Little Egg Island where you can pilot your way in by eye to the anchorage at Royal Island. If leaving Little Harbour and bound for Spanish Wells via *Ridley Head Channel* the pilot pickup waypoint lies 46.7 nautical miles away on a course of 170°

From Nassau to Royal Island there are a few different routes to take. If you leave the eastern entrance to Nassau Harbour bound for Royal Island you can pass between Paradise Island and Athol Island passing south of Blue Lagoon Island (Salt Cay) and enter the *Northeast Providence Channel* at *Chub Rock Light* (see the previous chapter, *New Providence to Eleuthera*). The waypoint southwest of the wreck of the *Arimora* (25° 27.87' N, 76° 53.75' W) is approximately 28.3 nautical miles on a course of 49° on this route. Once in sight of the wreck pass around its remains on the south side and take up a course of 55° for the final 3.4 nautical miles to the entrance to the anchorage at Royal Island (using a waypoint at 25° 30.60' N, 76° 51.73'W). If you wish you can pass north of the wreck, between Egg Island and Little Egg and parallel the shore of Royal Island until you arrive at the mouth of the anchorage. If taking this route give the reef at the southern end of Little Egg a wide berth. Vessels leaving Nassau may also opt for the route lying south of Athol Island and Rose Island.

There are virtually no dangers from the eastern end of *Davis Channel* all the way to *Current Cut* close in along the eastern shore of Eleuthera. You can coast along the shore all the way northward past Gregory Town, almost to the Glass Window. The entire eastern shore of Eleuthera is basically a lee shore in the prevailing winds and is seldom cruised except in passing. Don't try to head from the western end of *Davis Channel* directly to the waypoint west of *Current Cut*. There are a few shoal spots of less than 6' that must be avoided. It's best to head northward along the western shore until you get to the area around Tarpum Bay and then take up your course for *Current Cut*.

Vessels heading to or from the Exumas have several different routes. The most northerly route begins at a waypoint at 24° 52.82' N, 76° 49.50' W, which lies approximately 500 yards northwest of

Beacon Cay. From the waypoint you can steer 003° for approximately 25.6 nautical miles to a waypoint at 25° 18.45' N, 76° 51.29' W, which lies approximately ½ nautical mile southwest of the southwestern tip of Current Island. From this waypoint you can parallel the eastern shore of Current Island headed to the settlement of The Current, or, pass along the western shore of Current Island and head to either Royal Island or Spanish Wells. Also beginning at Beacon Cay it is possible to steer 352° and pass into the *Northwest Providence Channel* via *Fleeming Channel*. Here a waypoint at 25° 16.00' N, 76° 55.30' W will place you approximately ¼ nautical mile north of the mouth of the *Fleeming Channel*. This is a good jumping off spot for Hole in the Wall or Sandy Point, Abaco, Nassau, and even Royal Island.

Cruisers leaving Beacon Cay may also pass north of Finley Cay to head towards Hatchet Bay, Governor's Harbour, or Rock Sound. All skippers leaving Beacon Cay for any of these routes should only do so in daylight and with good visibility. Just north of Beacon Cay you will begin to encounter large coral heads and reefs. Few at first, but quite thick about 6½ to 10 nautical miles north of Beacon Cay. Some are very shallow, less that 6', but there is plenty of deep water from 7'-22' between them so steering around them is not a problem.

From Warderick Wells, Powell Point bears 36° at a distance of 36.0 nautical miles. From Highborne Cay you can steer 76° for 26.5 miles to arrive at Powell Point.

Although many cruisers visiting Eleuthera do so as part of their journey from Abaco to points south, and a few head over from Nassau, the vast majority of cruising boats travel Eleuthera from south to north. For these vessels Eleuthera is usually part of a Cat Island, Little San Salvador, Abaco route that is popular with boats returning from George Town to the U.S., and often for those who are returning from the Caribbean northwards and wishing to sample something other than deep water passages. For these reasons we will visit Eleuthera from the south to the north.

The Southern Coast of Eleuthera

Davis Harbour - ¾ nm W of entrance buoy:
24° 43.80' N, 76° 15.75' W

East End Point - 1 nm SW of:
24° 35.90' N, 76° 09.25' W

The southwestern shore of Eleuthera, from Powell Point to East End Point at the southern tip of Eleuthera, has only one facility but it is a good one, *Davis Harbour Marina*. The shoreline has few lee anchorages and no settlements on the shore itself, all are inland.

Navigational Information

If approaching from Half Moon Cay (Little San Salvador), steer approximately 285° for 9.8 miles to a waypoint at 24° 35.90' N, 76° 09.25' W, which places you about 1 mile southwest of the rocks lying south of East End Point as shown on Chart EL-1. Give the point a wide berth if coming from the north as the shoals extended offshore to the east and northeast of the point for over 2 miles. There is a light at East End Point that flashes white every 4½ seconds, stands 65' above the water, and can be seen from 6 nautical miles away.

There is a nice lee anchorage at coconut palm framed Lighthouse Bay that is good in winds from north to east but not southeast as some seem to think. The bottom is sand and rock but it's not hard to find a sandy spot to drop your anchor. Just north of Lighthouse Bay near Black Rock Point is an old graveyard just under the line of casuarinas at the top of the beach. These graves are very old, most of the dates on the rocks used as headstones are weathered to nothing. This area can also be reached by road from Bannerman Town. Bannerman Town is little more than a few houses these days, most people have moved away. On the road north of the cemetery are the ruins of a very old church. Bannerman Town was named after the former Governor of The Bahamas, Sir Alexander Bannerman. The few settlements at the southern end of Eleuthera are best visited by road. South of Bannerman Town, at the end of the dirt track that is used as a road, lie the wind swept cliffs at the southern tip of Eleuthera. Here you can gaze out to sea and view the outline of Little San Salvador 10 miles away, and on a clear day, maybe, just maybe...Cat Island.

Vessels heading northwards along the southwestern shore of Eleuthera towards Davis Harbour or Powell Point should give the shoreline a berth of at least a mile. Although it is possible to follow the shoreline closer in, dodging the shallows banks and reefs, some of the shoals stretch westward almost a mile while in other places the 10 fathom line lies very close to shore.

Along the coast north of Black Rock Point and Bannerman Town you will see the bright red roofs of the Princess Cay area at Wemyss Bay. This facility and beach is manmade and was constructed by the *Princess Cruise Line* for their passengers to use when the ships pass through this area in the fall and winter. Last year over 110 cruise ships and some 255,000 visitors called here, but during late spring and summer the place is nearly deserted as the liners go elsewhere.

North of Princess Cay you will come to Wemyss Bight and the entrance to *Davis Harbour Marina* as shown on Chart EL-2. The marina lies about 2 miles south of the very conspicuous wreck of a rusty freighter by a tall stand of casuarinas. A waypoint at 24° 43.80' N, 76° 15.75' W, will place you approximately ¾ mile west of the red buoy (sometimes it's difficult to see) that marks the entrance channel to *Davis Harbour Marina*. Take the red buoy to starboard when entering the marina and head in on a bearing of 70° on the range consisting of a very visible white cross in the rear and a much less visible short white pole in the foreground. A good landmark is the cross and the *Shell* sign. Take up an approximate course of 70° on the white cross and you will soon make out the three pairs of channel markers in front of you. Take the red ones on the right and head in making a dogleg to port to enter the marina proper after the last pair of poles. The controlling depth for this channel is 5' at low tide. If you are in doubt as to the state of the tide call the dockmaster on VHF ch. 16.

Until *Cape Eleuthera Marina* opened, *Davis Harbour Marina* had a lock on the boating facilities in southern Eleuthera. Nowadays it remains busy primarily catering to sportfishing vessels trying their luck in the very productive surrounding waters. *Davis Harbour Marina* can accommodate 8 boats with drafts up to 7½'. This very protected marina sells diesel, gas, and RO water, has laundry facilities, and takes major credit cards. The marina is no longer associated with the elegant *Cotton Bay Club* on southern Eleuthera as the club has, for now anyway, closed down.

The nearby town of Wemyss's Bight was named after the early Scottish proprietor who deeded this land to his heirs. In town you will find a government

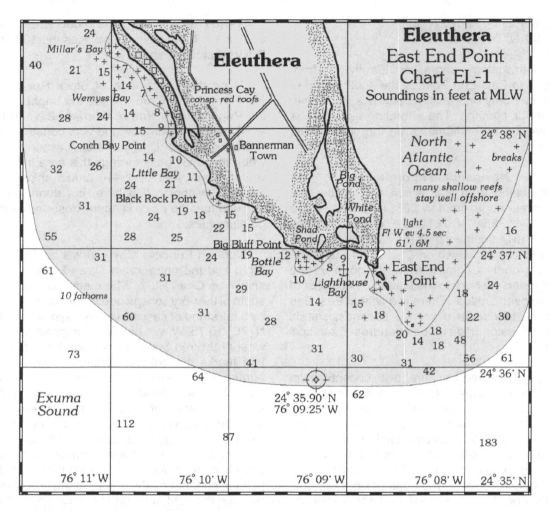

Eleuthera
East End Point
Chart EL-1
Soundings in feet at MLW

Millar's Bay

Wemyss Bay

Princess Cay
consp. red roofs

Conch Bay Point

Little Bay

Black Rock Point

Big Bluff Point

Bottle Bay

Lighthouse Bay

Bannerman Town

Big Pond

White Pond

Shad Pond

North Atlantic Ocean

breaks

many shallow reefs stay well offshore

light
Fl W ev 4.5 sec
61', 6M

East End Point

24° 38' N

24° 37' N

24° 36' N

24° 35' N

Exuma Sound

24° 35.90' N
76° 09.25' W

10 fathoms

76° 11' W   76° 10' W   76° 09' W   76° 08' W

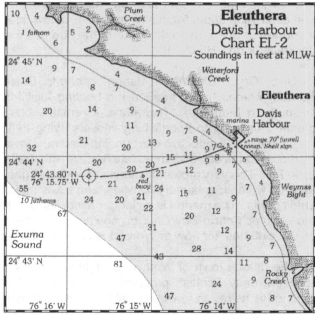

Eleuthera
Davis Harbour
Chart EL-2
Soundings in feet at MLW

Plum Creek

Waterford Creek

Eleuthera

Davis Harbour

marina

range 70° (unrel)
consp. Shell sign

Weymss Bight

Rocky Creek

1 fathom

24° 45' N

24° 44' N

24° 43.80' N
76° 15.75' W

10 fathoms

Exuma Sound

24° 43' N

red buoy

76° 16' W   76° 15' W   76° 14' W

Davis Harbour Marina

Photo Courtesy of Paul Harding,
Safari Seaplanes

clinic, *Kell's Take Away*, which also sells *Shell* gas and has a Laundromat on site. You're also near the *R&W Restaurant and Bar*, and *Mary's Restaurant*, and *Tropicana's*.

Powell Point

Powell Point - ¼ nm W of entrance to marina: 24° 50.23' N, 76° 21.09' W

Powell Point is a popular jumping off spot for cruisers bound for the Exumas and points south or those bound from Exuma northward along the shore of Eleuthera to Abaco. *Cape Eleuthera Marina* is an excellent and inexpensive place to hang out and wait for weather and is a *Port of Entry* for The Bahamas, ask for the forms when you arrive.

Navigational Information

A waypoint at 24° 50.23' N, 76° 21.09' W, places you approximately ¼ mile west of the entrance to *Cape Eleuthera Marina* which sits almost ¼ mile south of Powell Point as shown on Chart EL-3. The entrance is straightforward, simple, and deep, a draft of 12' can enter here at low water (there is a hole at the entrance that I have sounded to a depth of 49' that it is full of big fish awaiting the chance to offer themselves up to your dinner plate; there are some similar holes just off the beach lying south of the marina entrance). To enter the marina pass between the entrance jetties and follow the water around to the south where the marina opens up. There is an unlit range at the entrance on a bearing of approximately 90° but the entrance is so easy as to make the range unnecessary. The fuel dock sits at the southeastern end of the harbour by the small bridge. *Cape Eleuthera Marina* sells diesel, gas, and water and takes major credit cards.

In late 1970, work began at Powell Point on the $35 million development that came to be called *Cape Eleuthera*. Originally seen as a 20-year project it was originally owned by *Avon Harbour Ltd*. and included 5,000 half-acre residential lots, a hotel and marina complex, beach club, and a golf course. Today a few condos and houses are privately owned, some on a time-share basis, and the rest of the facilities lie dormant. More recently, construction began to make this marina the bustling place it was designed to be. Now you'll find *Barracuda's Beach Bar* and the *Bahama Coffee Company* ashore while new power boxes and showers are found on all the docks. The

marina can handle 55 of the largest vessels with drafts to 12' and offers a deli, baker, provisioner, market, spirits, ice, propane, and a business center with internet access. This modern marina is a far cry from the days when Cape E was little more than a ghost town. Well done!

Just south of the entrance to the marina is No Name Harbour as shown on Chart EL-3. To enter take Chub Rock well to port and steer generally eastward staying in the deeper water between the shallow rocky bars to your port and starboard. The entrance is not easily made out from Chub Rock, you'll probably have to pick it out with the binoculars. Once inside you can anchor well up any of the fingers, some of which have 13'-25' in them with only 6'-7' between the deeper parts. No Name Harbour was dredged out by the owners of the Cape Eleuthera project and the harbor is in essence owned by them. This means that they can charge to anchor here, the same rate as at the marina. No Name Harbour offers excellent protection and could even be considered as a possible hurricane hole. The only problem with the harbor is the fact that it is dredged out. This creates some sheer rock walls and less than ideal holding. The best spot in a hurricane would be in the upper northeastern finger. Skippers will have to tie to trees and probably set an anchor or two ashore on the land to be secure in here and even then a major storm surge could decimate the place. Bugs are definitely a problem here as at *Cape Eleuthera Marina* and *Davis Harbour Marina*. Look for a lot of home construction here in the near future.

On the northeastern shore of the Cape Eleuthera property, east of Powell Point (Chart EL-3), are some dredged harbours that face north and east. These have 7'-9' of water inside but the entrance is guarded by shallows that restrict entry to vessels of less than 6' and only at high tide. I do not recommend anchoring in here and only mention them as alternatives. I believe No Name Harbour and *Cape Eleuthera Marina* offer better protection, however, if there's a place to hide from a storm, you need to know about it.

What You Will Find Ashore

Just inland from Powell Point is the community of Deep Creek. Deep Creek sits on the edge of Deep Creek, which is definitely not that deep. Initially hurt by the closing of the Cape Eleuthera resort, Deep Creekers now have a stable economy again. If you want to visit Deep Creek, or any place in Eleuthera

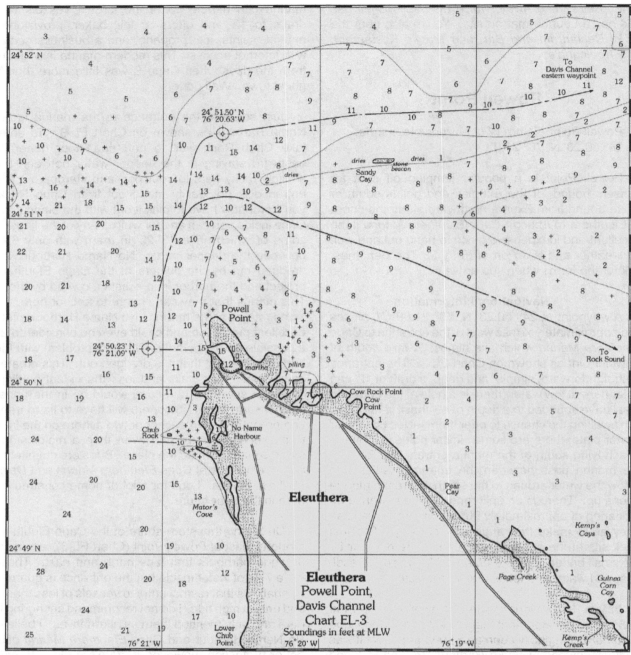

Eleuthera
Powell Point,
Davis Channel
Chart EL-3
Soundings in feet at MLW

for that matter, you can call *Friendly Bob* on VHF ch. !6 (Bob rents cars and has a taxi service as well as a liquor store in Deep Creek). At the top of the hill as you come into town from Powell Point is *Pinder's Marine*, a *Yamaha* dealer. Here owner Trevor Pinder repairs outboard engines and has a nice supply of marine supplies and necessities and will deliver to *Cape Eleuthera Marina* and *Davis Harbour Marina*. Next to Pinder's is *Hilltop Liquors*. At the bottom of the hill on the right is *Shiril's Restaurant* with some of

the best cracked conch you will find in The Bahamas. Across the street from *Shiril's*, in the concrete building with no sign, is *Friendly Bob's Liquor Store, Car Rental, and Taxi*. If you need a rental car, call Friendly Bob. One of the hottest spots in town is *Arthur's* (with satellite TV) at the top of the hill just off the main road.

Between Deep Creek and Rock Sound lies Green Castle, the largest and oldest of the communities on

Powell Point, No Name Harbour
and Cape Eleuthera Marina

Photo Courtesy of Paul Harding,
Safari Seaplanes

Cape Eleuthera Marina

Photo Courtesy of Paul Harding,
Safari Seaplanes

Davis Channel

Davis Channel - E end:
24° 52.25 N, 76° 16.30' W

Davis Channel - W end:
24° 51.50' N, 76° 20.63' W

The *Davis Channel* is the passage from Powell Point northeastward to the western shore of Eleuthera. The channel passes between the shoals that lie southeast and east of the Schooner Cays and a long shallow sandbar that parallels the shoreline of

Eleuthera east of Powell Point. There's good water inside the channel, once you find it.

Navigational Information

From Powell Point as shown on Chart EL-3, work your way northward to the waypoint at 24° 51.50' N, 76° 20.63' W which marks the western end of the *Davis Channel*. To starboard you will clearly see the long sandbar that is marked by the 22' tall stone beacon on Sandy Cay. To port you will see what looks like deep water for a great distance. It will shallow quickly. From this position you will make your way to a waypoint at 24° 52.25' N, 76° 16.30' W, which lies at the eastern end of the *Davis Channel*. Do not just set a course and put the boat on autopilot, keep a sharp lookout as the channel narrows in a couple of places. The general idea is to parallel the very obvious sandbank on the southern side of the *Davis Channel* until past its eastern end if heading northward or to Rock Sound. Shallow water has been encroaching on the channel more and more over the years and you might find you'll have to adjust your course to port or starboard on occasion to avoid the shallows that are more prevalent near the western end of *Davis Channel*.

Vessels heading northward from *Davis Channel* to Governor's Harbour or Hatchet Bay can take up their course for those destinations after reaching the eastern waypoint for *Davis Channel* at 24° 52.50' N,

76° 16.30' W. Vessels wishing to enter Rock Sound without having to dodge coral heads can head straight east for the mainland of Eleuthera from the eastern waypoint of *Davis Channel* and then turn south to parallel the shoreline ½ mile off until at the waypoint for Rock Sound.

Boats heading to Rock Sound and drawing less than 6' or less can bypass *Davis Channel* and head directly to Rock Sound at low tide (that's right, I said 6' or less-I know that "other" publications say only 5' but there is actually more water here than what is shown in the "other" publications). From the waypoint at the western end of *Davis Channel* pass south of the conspicuous sandbar that is marked by the beacon on Sandy Cay and head generally southeast past the second large sandbank that lies south of the one marked by the beacon as shown on Chart EL-3. Once clear of this second sandbank you can head east for the waypoint at the entrance to Rock Sound at 24° 50.30' N, 76° 11.70' W. As shown on Chart EL-3 and EL-4 you will have good water all the way. Further east you will begin to pick up some scattered shallow heads and small patch reefs but these are easily seen and avoided.. Never attempt this route in the early morning when the sun is in your eyes.

Vessels can also bypass *Davis Channel* from Rock Sound to Powell Point by following the above directions in reverse. From the waypoint at the entrance to Rock Sound head directly west (270º) for the northern tip of land on the horizon. That tip of land is Powell Point. As shown on Chart EL-3 and EL-4, you will have deep water all the way with only a few heads to dodge and the two sandbars. The heads and sandbars are easily seen in good visibility. Don't attempt to head to Powell Point on this route in the late afternoon when the sun is in your eyes.

What You Will Find Ashore
Northwest of Powell Point and the *Davis Channel* lie the Schooner Cays, a very popular place for local fishermen. The *Wild Bird Act* has declared the Schooner Cays, and the more northerly Finley Cay, a protected area and off limits for bird hunting. Wood Cay is home to a large population of White Crowned Pigeons who were once hunted for their eggs. Fishermen from Eleuthera once inhabited Wood Cay for periods of time and evidence of their tenure is the fresh water well they built. The Schooner Cays lie along the northern edge of Exuma Sound. The area is very shallow and sand bores abound. Some

of the deep blue channels leading in between the sandbores from Exuma Sound run through to deeper water in the Bight of Eleuthera but most of them are dead ends. The locals number the channels and can tell you which number will take you through. This area has not been surveyed and if you attempt to investigate the surrounding waters you must have good visibility. The ability to read water, as you would guess, is necessary here.

Rock Sound

Rock Sound - ½ nm W of entrance:
24° 50.30' N, 76° 11.70' W

Rock Sound is the largest settlement on Eleuthera as well as the commercial center. In old documents Rock Sound is shown as Wreck Sound owing to the major source of income for its inhabitants. A changing of the nature of the economy led to a changing of the name over the years. The anchorage in Rock Sound has good holding and can be a refuge from a frontal passage in winter. When winds come out of the southwest and west, boats will tuck up under the lee at the northwestern end of Rock Sound. When the wind goes northeast its time to head back over to the eastern side of the sound.

Navigational Information
A waypoint at 24° 50.30' N, 76° 11.70' W, will place you approximately ½ mile west of the entrance to Rock Sound as shown on Chart EL-4. Give Sound Point a wide berth as you head east and once clear of the shallows off the point you can steer towards the large white church to the northeast. Anchor anywhere you like off the town, the holding is excellent here. If a frontal passage threatens the best place to avoid southwest through northwest to northerly winds is in the northwestern corner of Rock Sound tucked in as close as you can get. For shelter from southeast to southwest winds the southern shore of Rock Sound is excellent. A 6' draft can enter tuck in very well at the entrance to *Starve Creek* at the south end of Rock Sound east of Poison Point. The light on Poison Point flashes white every 15 seconds, stands 24' above the water, and is visible for 7 miles. A good shelter in southeast to south/southwest winds lies just west of Poison Point with a nice little beach to cavort on while awaiting better weather. The bluffs on the southern shore of Rock Sound offer some nice overhangs and small cave holes for exploring. There is a remarkable cave under Poison Point that is well worth exploring.

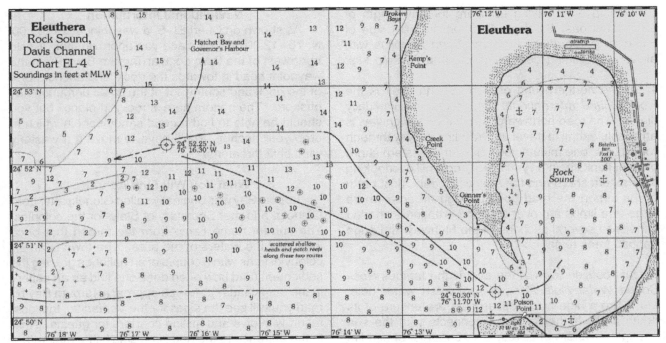

What You Will Find Ashore

Rock Sound is a *Port of Entry* for The Bahamas and skippers seeking clearance should anchor off the concrete dock by the large pink building that houses the *Customs* and *Immigration* offices. Don't block this dock unless *Customs* instructs you to as the mailboat lands here. A faucet on the western wall of the *Customs* building delivers good water at no charge but be sure to bring a short length of hose with your jerry jugs. Inshore from the *Customs* building is the *CC Super Wash*, the local Laundromat, *Gem's*, *Ron's Marine and Auto Parts*, *PK's Auto Rentals*, and *Eleuthera Office Supply* with its copy/fax service and internet access.

South of *Customs*, north of the white church, is the long town dock where most cruisers like to anchor. In the vicinity of the main road are a couple of clothing boutiques, a tailor shop, and an *Esso* gas station. To the north of the town dock, across from the *Esso* station, in a large pink building is the government clinic and nearby, a couple of gift shops. At the base of the *Batelco* tower is the local *Batelco* office where phone calls can be made and phone cards purchased. Across the *Queen's Highway* from the *Batelco* office is a small grocery store, and up the side streets you will find *Sammy's Place*, the local hangout serving breakfast, lunch, and dinner. Proprietors Sammy and Kathleen Culmer also have rooms for rent with satellite TV. Nearby are *Lita's Blue Diamond Restaurant*, *Sawyer's Food Store*, *Haven Bakery*, *Dingle's Convenience Store*, *D & N's Down Home Pizza*, and the *Apple Hole Farm Meat Market and Deli*, a bit of a walk but well worth it.

North of the *Customs* building on the main road is *Discount Liquors*, and across the street *Cairey's Garage and Service Station*. On the left just past *Cairey's* is the *Marketplace Shopping Center* that will likely be the center of your shopping activity while in Rock Sound. Here you will find *Rock Sound Hardware* with its huge selection of tools and supplies. You can get your propane bottles filled here also. Right next door is the best stocked grocery store on the island, the *Rock Sound Grocery*, which also runs the gas pumps outside and can deliver your groceries to the dock for you. Next to the grocery is a small liquor store and a *NAPA* auto parts store. Across the side street from *NAPA* is a branch of *Barclay's Bank* open five days a week till 5 p.m. The rear of the mall can be accessed by dinghy.

A little over ¼ mile north of the Customs dock you will see the silver/white roof of a long building, this is the *Marketplace Shopping Center*. You will have to drop someone off here as the shoreline is rocky close in and it is not a place to leave an inflatable. There is a small beach a few hundred yards north of the mall where you might land but the houses around it are private so you might want to ask permission before tying up there for any length of time. Just past *Barclay's Bank* on the east side of the road is *Eleuthera Fish and Farm Supplies* with all sorts of fishing gear, anchors, and first aid kits.

At the northern end of Rock Sound itself is the *Rock Sound International Airport* with regular daily flights. The road northward, the *Queen's Highway*, is an absolute thrill to travel on. Winding its way through rolling hills, one minute you'll have the western shore on your flank, the next you'll be up on a hill overlooking the eastern shore and the Atlantic Ocean. Just north of the airport the road goes through an area where large tree limbs arc over the road creating a shaded canopy to several sections of the highway and huge baobab trees reign.

Just outside town to the east is the famous *Rock Sound Water Hole Park*, a semi-fresh water hole. Much like a blue hole, researchers are unsure of its depth and whether or not it connects with the sea through a system of caves. There is a lot of sea life in the 360' diameter hole but some locals say they are placed there by local fisherman who often donate a couple of groupers or snappers from their catch. One time a gentleman decided to play a trick on his neighbors and he put a small shark in the hole. Well, being a small town, the culprit was soon discovered and taken to court. His was sentenced to staying by the hole until he caught the shark and removed it. Three days later he was found the right bait and removed the shark from the hole and the local inhabitants could once again go for a swim in the hole. The walls of the hole drop down about 15' and from there they fall away sharply.

You'll find Wifi in the harbour at Rock Sound thanks to *Dingle Motors*.

Tarpum Bay

Tarpum Bay - ¾ nm NW of town dock:
24° 59.00' N, 76° 12.00' W

Vessels heading north from Rock Sound can parallel the shoreline staying at ½ mile off to avoid the shallows and a few scattered heads. North of Rock Sound lies Tarpum Bay, a small settlement stretching for over a mile just along the western shore. The only approach is by dinghy as the water is very shallow up to ½ mile offshore by the conspicuous rocky bar. The holding here is fair in sand but only in calm weather.

Navigational Information

As shown on Chart EL-5, a waypoint at 24° 59.00' N, 76° 12.00' W, will place you approximately 1 mile northwest of the town dock at Tarpum Bay. From the waypoint head in towards the dock and anchor north of the dock and southwest of the small unnamed cay offshore. The bottom here is rocky in places but you should be able to find a good sandy spot in which to drop your anchor. You'll have to move if a westerly wind shift threatens.

What You Will Find Ashore

Tarpum Bay was originally called Glenelg after Lord Glenelg, a former Secretary of State for the colonies. The current name came from the tarpon that once inhabited the waters of the area. The town is an art colony of sorts with a couple of art galleries gracing the settlement (and how often does one find an art gallery in the out-islands?). As you approach Tarpum Bay by road you will see the signs for the *Ventaclub*, the local resort with dive and sailing charters for guests. Next to the entrance to the hotel is a small strip mall with a building supply center, hardware store, a meat shop and a *Shell*.

As you enter Tarpum Bay you will find *Pop's Welding*, *DD's Variety*, *Barbies Food Store*, *Bert's For The Best Food Store*, *Kinky's Korner*, *Shell Service Station and Auto Parts*, and *Audrey's Boutique* while on the waterfront you'll find *Shines Famous Seafood*. Next door you'll find *Ethyl's Cottages and Car Rentals*, *Bayside Liquors*, *Bayshore Snacks and Cold Drinks*, *Barbie's Snacks*, and *Carey's Buywise Hardware and Grocery*.

Just to the north you'll find the *Hilltop Haven Restaurant And Bar* and *Ingraham's Beach Inn and Restaurant*. There is a government clinic in Tarpum Bay and several trash bins located around town that you may use to dump your sealed garbage bags. The newest addition to Tarpum Bay is *Bertha's Go-Go Ribs* that has moved to Tarpum Bay from Deep Creek, a sister store to the well-known *Bertha's* in Nassau.

North of Tarpum Bay is a road that will take you to the eastern shore of Eleuthera and across a tiny bridge to ritzy Windemere Island, a favorite spot of the British Royal Family.

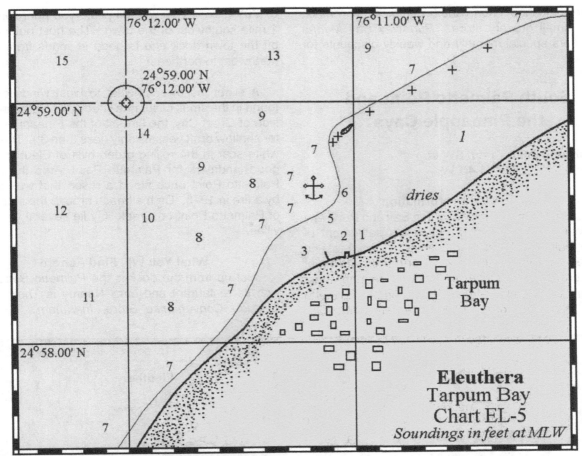

Eleuthera
Tarpum Bay
Chart EL-5
Soundings in feet at MLW

Eleuthera
Ten Bay to
Creek Bay
Chart EL-6
Soundings in feet at MLW

Ten Bay and
Runaway Bay Marina

Ten Bay - 1 nm W of anchorage:
25° 07.30' N, 76° 10.40' W

Navigational Information

Northeast of Tarpum Bay along the western shore of Eleuthera you'll find a good anchorage in prevailing winds in Ten Bay as shown on Chart EL-6 where a waypoint at 25 07.30' N, 76 10.40'W, places you approximately 1 mile west of the anchorage. The bottom here is thick grass and sand and offers protection in wind from north/northeast through southeast.

Just a bit over a mile to the northwest of Ten Bay is Creek Bay where you can anchor just outside the entrance to *Runaway Bay Marina*. The marina boasts 21 slips (expected to be 40+ by the time this guide is published) with full electric and water, a restaurant, laundry, bait shop, phone and fax service, car rentals, and a small grocery store. *Runaway Bay Marina* also offers special monthly and weekly discounts for cruisers.

South Palmetto Point and the Pineapple Cays

Palmetto Point - 1 nm SW of:
25° 07.70' N, 76° 11.40' W

Navigational Information

Just a bit to the northwest of Ten Bay and Runaway Bay Marina lies the small beachside settlement of South Palmetto Point where a large concrete and wooden dock marks the town. North Palmetto Point lies north of the Queen's Highway though most cruisers call South Palmetto Point simply Palmetto Point. As shown on Chart EL-7, A waypoint at 25°

07.70' N, 76° 11.40' W, will place you approximately 1 mile southwest of the town. The best holding lies off the town dock and is good in winds from north/northwest to northeast.

A slight lee in southwest to west winds can be found in the small casuarina lined cove on the eastern side of Great Cay, the largest of the Pineapple Cays, for shallow draft vessels only (less than 3'). The great white scar in the rolling green hills of Eleuthera is a good landmark for Palmetto Point. Atop the cliff at Palmetto Point once stood a resort that was gutted by a fire in 1975. On the beach area to the southeast of Palmetto Point on Creek Bay lie several very nice villas.

What You Will Find Ashore

Just up from the dock is the *Palmetto Beach Inn* with its restaurant and bar. Nearby is *Thompson's Seaside Convenience Store*, *Ingraham's Grocery*,

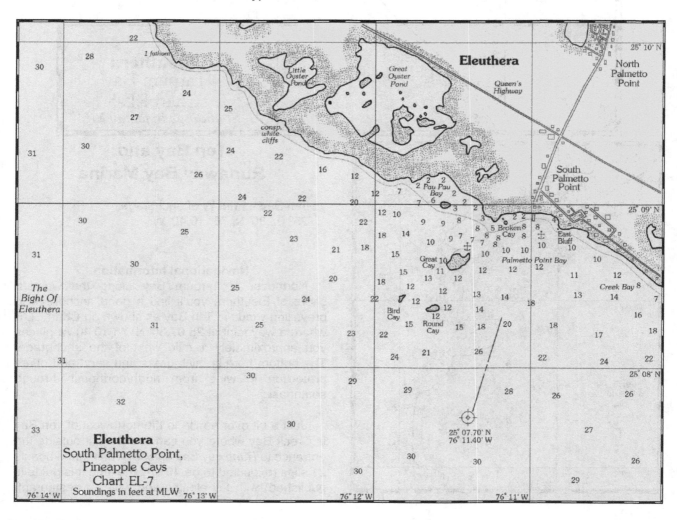

and *Millard's Variety Store*. The principal hangout is *Mate and Jenny's Pizza*, a do-not-miss stop sitting just up the road from the dock toward the *Queen's Highway*. Visit Palmetto Point if for not other reason than to visit Mate and Jenny's. Just inland from *Mate and Jenny's* is the *Queen's Highway* where you'll find *Pinder's Meats and Fruits*, a *Shell* station, a Laundromat, *Unique Hardware and Building Supplies*, the *Eleuthera Dental Centre*, and on the *Queen's Highway* is *Sand's Enterprises* who has it all, food, clothes, auto accessories, hardware, and gifts.

Governor's Harbour

Governor's Harbour - 1 nm W of:
25° 11.75' N, 76° 16.25' W

Located about midway up (or down depending on which way you're headed) the island of Eleuthera, the town of Governor's Harbour a lovely oasis along what is so often a rocky shoreline. Here you'll find an anchorage that is protected in all but westerly winds with most facilities within walking distance, all set against a lovely backdrop of colorful houses and buildings spread on the hillsides overlooking the harbor. In the past, some cruisers were put off by the *Club Med* water sports center located in Governor's Harbour, but since *Club Med* closed, the anchorage is far more peaceful.

Navigational Information
Just north of Palmetto Point and around the corner lies the entrance to Governor's Harbour. A waypoint at 25° 11.75' N, 76° 16.25' W, will place you approximately 1 mile west of the entrance to Governor's Harbour as shown on Chart EL-8. From this position head eastward taking the northern tip of Cupid's Cay to starboard. Anchor wherever your draft will allow. The anchorage is good only in moderate prevailing winds or settled weather as there is notoriously poor holding here (grassy with a lot of old moorings and debris scattered about). Governor's Harbour is wide open to the westerly prelude to a frontal passage although it does give some shelter from a southwest wind. Never attempt to pick up any mooring you see in the vicinity of Governor's Harbour. All the moorings that were once in the harbour and south of Cupid's Cay earned a bad reputation for neglect. Practice safe anchoring instead.

Just south of Cupid's Cay is a small anchorage that offers good protection in strong northwest through north to east winds if you can get your anchor to set in the grassy, rocky bottom in the lee of Laughing Bird Cay, usually just called and shown as Bird Cay on most charts. When entering this anchorage you can pass either side of Bird Cay. This anchorage is usually taken over by local boats and is very rough in anything from a southeast to southwest wind. Balara Bay to the north offers fair protection in the lee of Levi Island but this entire area is no place to be in a frontal passage, it would be much safer to head to Pelican Cay, Hatchet Bay, or Rock Sound. Besides, many locals are hip to putting their boats in *Balara Bay* for protection and they'll likely get there before you. The best holding is in the sand close to shore. *French Leave Marina* has slips for two boats to 100' LOA.

What You Will Find Ashore
You can land your dinghy on the beach by the seawall and once ashore, at the curve in the road in the center of the town frontage, you'll find the center of Governor's Harbour commercial district. Here is *Eleuthera Supply Limited*, the local grocery, hardware store, and gas station. *Eleuthera Supply* almost always has fresh produce and they can also fill your propane tanks on Mondays, Tuesdays, and Fridays. Nearby you will find the *Clear Water Dive Shop*, a *Barclay's Bank*, *Rolle's Ice Cream Parlour*, *Tasty Treats Ice Cream, Daiquiris, and Deli*, the *Governor's Harbour Bakery*, *Sands Laundry and Dry Cleaning*, and several gift and T-shirt shops. To the north lie the *LeClair Food Centre*, and the *Buccaneer Club Restaurant and Bar*. There is now Wifi access in the harbour thanks to the Library.

On the *Queen's Highway* just south of the main part of town but an easy walk up from the water's edge, is Eleuthera's only movie house, the *Globe Princess Theater*, with movies every evening at 2015. Next door is *Rolle's Auto Parts* and a *Royal Bank of Canada*. If you need a car call *Griffin's Car Rentals* at 332-2077/9 located at the *Griffin's Auto Repair and Esso Service Station* just south of the theater. Here too you'll find *Sawyer's Food Store* and *Pammy's Restaurant and Bar*. For car rentals you can also call *Nixon-Pinder Car Rentals* at 332-2568. Also in town is a government clinic with a doctor and nurses in attendance.

Cupid's Cay, that small plot of land that sits at the outer edge of Governor's Harbour, houses the *Customs* office and the government dock. The cay received its name when someone said that the

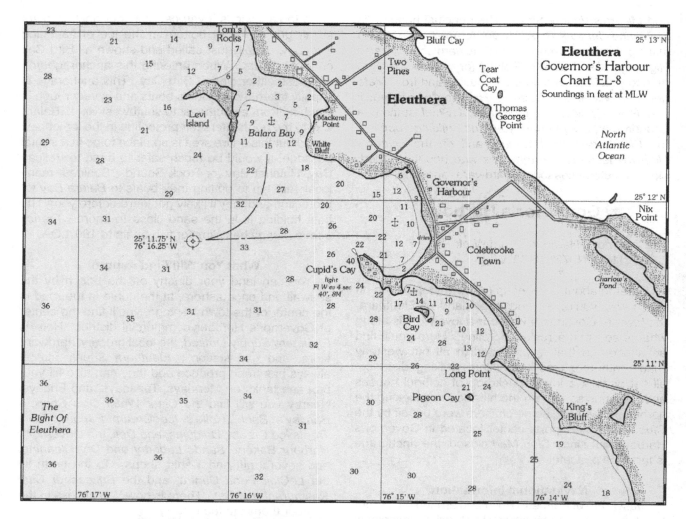

Cupids Bay to Governor's Harbour

Photo Courtesy of Paul Harding,
Safari Seaplanes

curving piece of land resembled the bow of Cupid. The first inhabitants could only walk across to the cay at low tide carrying whatever supplies they could handle. Over the years a wooden bridge was built that was later destroyed in the hurricane of 1929. Finally, when the current causeway was built, people flocked to Cupid's Cay, now home to over a hundred souls. Most of the quaint, pastel-colored buildings on Cupid's Cay are very old and all are very close together, the roads being very narrow. The main stop on Cupid's Cay is the magnificent century-old *Haynes Library*, the largest library outside of Nassau. For a cold drink visit *Dockside Daiquiris* on Cupid's Cay, and if you're hungry stop in at *Ronnie's Hi-D-Way* restaurant.

Pelican Cay and Holmes Bay

Pelican Cay - ½ nm SW of:
25° 16.30' N, 76° 20.50' W

Holmes Bay - ½ nm SW of:
25° 14.40' N, 76° 18.90' W

Navigational Information
North of Governor's Harbour the water is deep very close to shore with no obstructions save a few offlying rocks, which we shall now discuss. A few miles north of Governor's Harbour are several nice anchorages in the vicinity of *Governor's Harbour International Airport*. As shown on Chart EL-9, A waypoint at 25° 14.40' N, 76° 18.90' W, will place you approximately ½ mile southwest of the entrance to the anchorage in beautiful Holmes Bay. This is an excellent anchorage in winds from northwest to east.

From the waypoint steer south of the southernmost rock called Flapper Rock. Once past Flapper Rock head northward to anchor off the beach, once the site of the *Tranquillity Bay Club*. You can also enter the anchorage by passing between Billing Bay Point and the first rock to its south but there is a large rock south of the point that is awash at high water. The deeper water lies south of the rock that is awash and the northernmost of the two offlying cays.

Just north of Holmes Bay is Billing Bay. This anchorage is fine in north to east winds but there is no beach and the bay is mainly used by fuel tankers supplying fuel to the airport, you will be happier anchored at Holmes Bay.

North of Billing Bay lies Pelican Cay which offers excellent protection in winds from the northwest to the northeast. As shown on Chart EL-9, A waypoint at 25° 16.30' N, 76° 20.50' W, will place you approximately ½ mile southwest of Pelican Cay. From the waypoint head south of Pelican Cay to anchor off its western shore. When the wind starts heading back into the east you will probably want to move over and tuck in against the western shore of Eleuthera. In winds from east to southeast you can anchor north of Pelican Cay in the lee of the very shallow bank that stretches between Pelican Cay and the mainland of Eleuthera.

James Cistern

James Cistern- ¼ nm SE of town dock:
25° 19.20' N, 76° 22.30' W

North of Pelican Cay sits the village of James Cistern along the western shore of Eleuthera and you'll find that you can't get in closer than ¼ mile from shore and you will have to anchor out a little to gain access to the settlement via their new town dock. The spectacular view from the top of the hill at James Cistern offers the Atlantic Ocean to the east and the Bight of Eleuthera to the west.

Navigational Information
As shown on Chart EI-10, a waypoint at 25° 19.20' N, 76° 22.30' W, will place you approximately ¼ mile southeast of the newly constructed town dock where you can tie up your dinghy while exploring the town. Anchor as close to shore as your draft allows and you'll be fine in northeasterly winds, although it may get a bit rolly in southeasterly breezes. James Cistern is no place to be anchored in winds out of any westerly direction.

What You Will Find Ashore
James Cistern was named after a former governor of The Bahamas, Sir James, while he was serving at Governor's Harbour. It seems that Sir James left on horseback in search of water and discovered a natural water hole in the area where the town is now. The cistern was built up and people began to drift in and settle nearby. The best way to visit this community is by car. When approaching from the south you will find several eating establishments such as *Savory Snacks*, *Mom's Snack Shop*, and *Kell D's Restaurant and Bar*. There is a small gas station with a phone booth in town, along with the *Halfway Laundromat*, and *Marty's Electronics*.

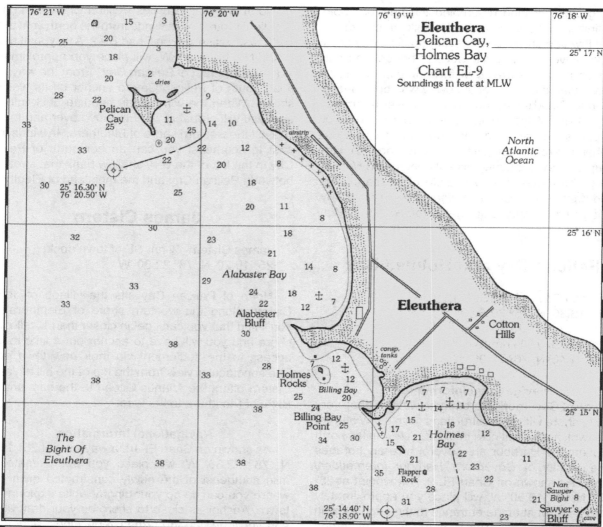

Eleuthera
Pelican Cay,
Holmes Bay
Chart EL-9
Soundings in feet at MLW

North
Atlantic
Ocean

Pelican
Cay

Alabaster Bay

Alabaster
Bluff

Eleuthera

Cotton
Hills

consp.
tanks

Holmes
Rocks

Billing Bay

Billing Bay
Point

Holmes
Bay

The
Bight Of
Eleuthera

Flapper
Rock

Nan
Sawyer
Bight

Sawyer's
Bluff

cave

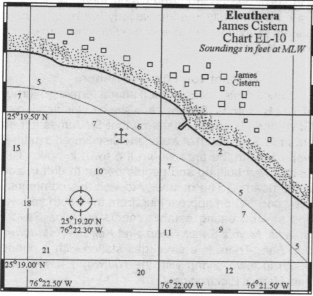

Eleuthera
James Cistern
Chart EL-10
Soundings in feet at MLW

James
Cistern

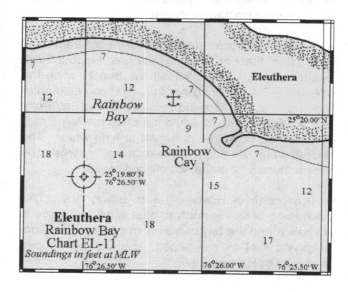

Eleuthera

Rainbow
Bay

Rainbow
Cay

Eleuthera
Rainbow Bay
Chart EL-11
Soundings in feet at MLW

On the highway north of James Cistern is the very well stocked *Big Rock General Store* with its gas pumps, hardware, appliance, building supply outlet and car rentals. *Big Rock* offers delivery for yachtsmen to James Cistern or Hatchet Bay with a minimum purchase.

Rainbow Bay

Rainbow Bay - ¼ nm SW of anchorage:
25° 19.80' N, 76° 26.50' W

North of *Big Rock*, and about 2½ miles south of Hatchet Bay, is the *Rainbow Inn and Restaurant*. The restaurant and bar has a good view of the Bight of Eleuthera as well as good dining and live music and cottages to rent. This is a great place to have dinner and watch the sunset. Ask about transportation from Hatchet Bay.

Navigational Information

As shown on Chart El-11, you can anchor in Rainbow Bay just west of Rainbow Cay. A waypoint at 25° 19.80' N, 76° 26.50' W, will place you approximately ¼ mile southeast of the anchorage in the lee of Rainbow Cay. Anchor as close to shore as your draft allows and you'll find good protection in winds from north through east and southeast.

Hatchet Bay

Hatchet Bay - ¼ nm S of entrance:
25° 20.50' N, 76° 29.70' W

Navigational Information

As shown on Chart EL-12, *Hatchet Bay* is actually a small bay southeast of the small inland cove that most call *Hatchet Bay*, but which is really named *Hatchet Bay Pond*. For our purposes in this section whenever we refer to *Hatchet Bay* we will be talking about *Hatchet Bay Pond* as shown in detail on Chart EL-13. The entrance to Hatchet Bay (Chart EL-12 and EL-13) is sometimes difficult to distinguish from offshore. It is a narrow, 90' wide pass called *Harbour Cut* that was blasted through sheer rock with two small jetties stretching inwards from the *Bight of Eleuthera*. The light atop the bluff on the western side of the entrance flashes white twice in four seconds and repeats that characteristic every 10 seconds. The light is 57' above the water and is visible for 8 miles. The easiest landmarks for this area are the large white silos, once part of a large plantation, standing like silent sentinels up and down this stretch of coast, and the 265' Batelco tower with its flashing red light. A waypoint at 25° 20.50' N, 76° 29.70' W, will place you approximately ¼ mile south of the pass into *Hatchet Bay*. From this position had straight in and anchor wherever you choose.

The holding in *Hatchet Bay* is good in some places, worse in others, although it may be a fine spot to ride out a norther it is definitely no place to be in a hurricane as many found out in Hurricane Andrew (you will still see the wrecks along the shore from that catastrophe). The anchorage on the west side of the bay is grassy with a few rocks while the anchorage in front of the marina is mud. By no means anchor off the dock at Alice Town on the eastern side of the harbour as mailboats and propane tankers come in here with regularity. Moorings are available, call Bandit on VHF ch. 16.

What You Will Find Ashore

If you haven't been here in a while you might be saddened to learn that *Marine Services of Eleuthera* has closed down, nothing remains but the concrete floor. You can still tie to the western end of the seawall, but there are no facilities and no electricity or water.

Across the street from the town dock is *Marilyn's Take-Out* serving good local cuisine and on the southern shore of Hatchett Bay is the settlement of Alice Town where you can jerry jug gas for your dinghy. In town you will find the *Sea Side Club* serving cold beverages, *Assories Ice Cream and Drinks*, the *Forget-Me-Not Club*, *Triple T's Groceries*, *Pinder's Store*, *CJ's Variety*, *Dee Mart Variety*, and the *Red Dirt Laundromat, Snack Shack And Game Room*.

If you need a taxi driver you might find one hanging out at the *Sea Side Club* although the easiest way to reach a taxi is to hail one on VHF ch. 16. You can also get a car rental or taxi by calling *Larry Dean's Taxi Service and Car Rentals* at 335-0059 or 332-2568.

Across the street from the town dock and about two hundred yards north along the *Queen's Highway*, is the well stocked *Sawyer's Grocery Store* with fresh fruits, vegetables, and meats. Next door is a small gift shop and a liquor store.

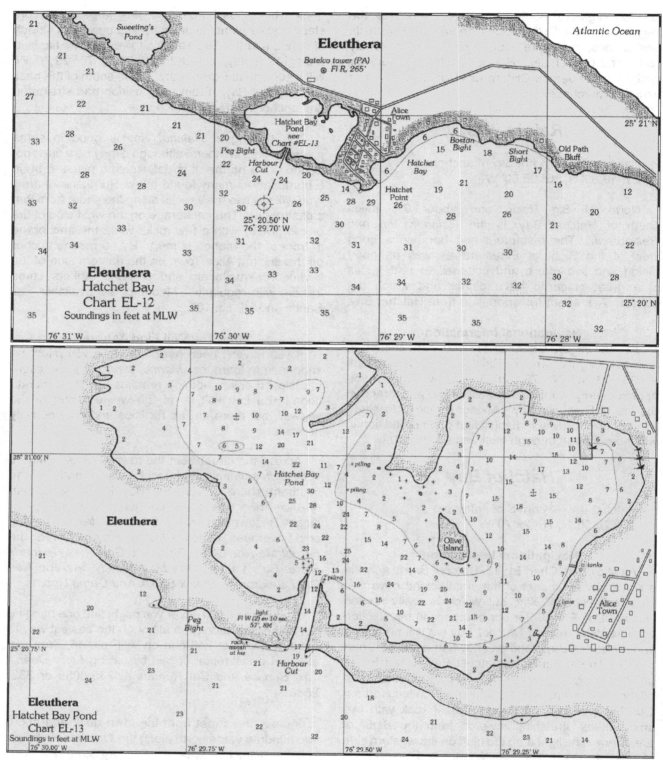

North of *Hatchet Bay*, on the western side of the *Queen's Highway*, is a large inland pond, larger than *Hatchet Bay* itself, called *Sweeting's Pond*. A small dirt road leads to the pond which is said to be haunted and allegedly has a Loch Ness type creature living within its waters. Just north of this pond is the entrance to the huge *Hatchet Bay Cave*. Turn left on the dirt road by the silos and just over the rise you will see a clearing with the cave's entrance on your right. Watch out for the bats, but more important, beware of the bat guano.

Three miles north of town, on the eastern side of the *Queen's Highway*, you will come to a sign and a dirt road leading across the hills towards the *Atlantic Ocean* and *Surfer's Beach*. This beach is famous among surfing aficionados the world over who have been coming here since the 1960's, some even moving here permanently. With a good swell running some awesome waves come barreling in daring only the best to ride them.

North of the beach along the eastern side of the *Queen's Highway* at *Eleuthera Shores* is a nightclub called *Cush's Place* with live music sometimes supplied by the owner, the well-known Calypso artist, *Dr. Seabreeze*.

Gregory Town

Gregory Town - ¼ nm SW of:
25° 23.15' N, 76° 33.75' W

Navigational Information

About five miles north of Hatchet Bay you will come to the small settlement of Gregory Town as shown on Chart EL-14. The water between Hatchet Bay and Gregory Town is deep close in to shore with no offlying dangers. This picturesque little settlement of pastel painted houses is nestled among several hillsides overlooking the Bight of Eleuthera and Pittman's Cove, just an opening in between two steep cliffs which leads to the town dock where you can land your dinghy. The cove should not be considered as an anchorage, it's really too small and is usually used by small local boats. It is advisable to visit Gregory Town by car. Only in settled weather should you attempt to anchor off and dinghy in between the cliffs to the town dock due to the surge bouncing back and forth off the cliffs. There is a small cove less than ½ mile north of town that would be an adequate anchorage for a visit to town in settled weather. A waypoint at 25° 23.15' N, 76° 33.75' W, will place you approximately ¼ mile southwest of the entrance to the cove at Gregory Town as shown on Chart EL-14. The best places to anchor are in the small coves northwest of Gregory Town, Annie Bight or Sookie Bight, but only in settled weather. Another good spot to anchor is about 3 miles northwest of Gregory Town in Hall's Bight, just below Mutton Fish Point.

What You Will Find Ashore

The scenery here will remind one of someplace other than The Bahamas. Perhaps New England, Spain, or maybe Scotland. The town was originally called Pittman's Cove but was renamed after James Gregory who was appointed Governor of The Bahamas in 1849. Gregory Town's biggest claim to fame is its pineapples industry and the pineapple wine and rum produced on the *Thompson Brothers* plantation just north of town. The first weekend of June Gregory Town becomes a small city when thousands of visitors pack its streets for the annual *Gregory Town Pineapple Festival*.

If you choose to visit Gregory Town the time spent will be well worth it. At the heart of town is *Thompson Brothers Super Market* with fresh fruits and vegetables as well as excellent prices on fresh and frozen meats. You can also purchase gas here and you will find film, batteries, and a few other sundry items inside. The market is set to close down and may be by the time you get there. In the immediate are of the super market are several small gift shops. Across the street is *Jay's Laundromat* and just up the hill is *Thompson's Bakery*, known far and wide for their delicious treats and baked goods (they also serve hamburgers). For meals try the *Driftwood Café* and *Elvina's Restaurant* (excellent) which boasts a pool table, satellite TV, and also rents cars and bicycles.

Gregory Town is THE place for pineapples in Eleuthera. Check with Joe Darville who lives just up the hill from the store, you'll see the sign that says "Darville Residence". If anyone in town has pineapples, Joe will. *Thompson Brothers* once distilled an excellent pineapple rum in Gregory Town but everywhere I turn people tell me that it's not made anymore, and that is a loss my friends.

The biggest event to ever happen to Gregory Town never even happened. It was the *International World Peace Festival*, a proposed 1970 rock concert scheduled to take place in Gregory Town which was canceled by the Bahamian government. The festival's promoter told the world in an interview on *ZNS* radio that The Bahamas "...grows the best grade of marijuana in the world." A *ZNS* broadcaster took up the issue on her radio program and even visited Gregory Town in her attempt to thwart promoters. The festival never came off and today the closest Gregory Town gets to mainline rock music is the home owned by rock star Lenny Kravitz.

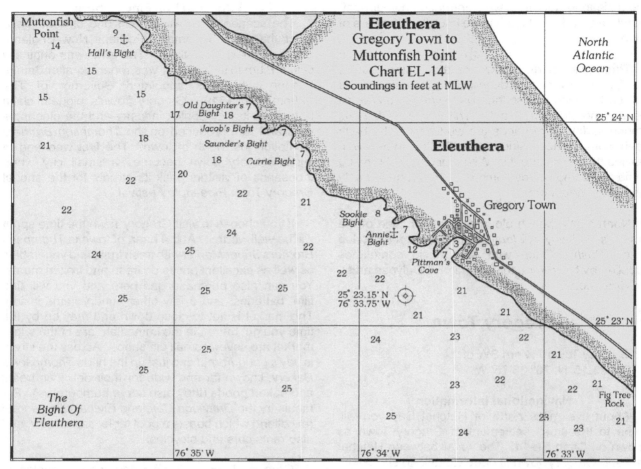

Eleuthera
Gregory Town to
Muttonfish Point
Chart EL-14
Soundings in feet at MLW

North Atlantic Ocean

25° 24' N

Eleuthera

Muttonfish Point
14
9 ⚓
Hall's Bight
15
15   15
17   *Old Daughter's* 7
         Bight 18
21   18   *Jacob's Bight*   7
         Saunder's Bight
22   18   *Currie Bight*   7
22   20
24   25   21
                    Sookie Bight   8
24   25   22   *Annie* ⚓ 7
                    Bight
25   25   25   12
                    22   *Pittman's Cove*   3
                                              7
25° 23.15' N   22   22
76° 33.75' W ⊕   21
25   21
25   24   21
                    23   22
The Bight Of Eleuthera   25
                    23   22   21
25   25   23   22   21
                                                    Fig Tree Rock
                    25   23   23   21
                    24

Gregory Town

25° 23' N

76° 35' W   76° 34' W   76° 33' W

Town Dock, Gregory Town

Photo by author

The Glass Window

The Glass Window - ¼ nm W of anchorage:
25° 25.70' N, 76° 36.30' W

Navigational Information

From Gregory Town northward to the Glass Window, the western shore of Eleuthera has some scattered cliffs which drop right down to the water and a few small coves good for settled weather anchoring only. The water is deep close in to shore except in the vicinity of the Glass Window. As shown on Chart EL-15, in prevailing winds you can anchor just north of Muttonfish Point and northward in the lee of Goulding Cay Point where a waypoint at 25° 25.70' N, 76° 36.30' W places you approximately ¼ mile west of the anchorage and a little over ½ mile south of the Glass Window.

What You Will Find Ashore

Between Upper and Lower Bogue and Gregory Town along the Queen's Highway sits a remarkable sight, The Glass Window. The Glass Window, once the subject of a painting by the American artist Winslow Homer, is a beautiful rock formation where the *Bight of Eleuthera* and the *Atlantic Ocean* almost meet. It was originally a natural rock bridge 85' above sea level, which was washed away in a hurricane in 1926 and replaced by a bridge in 1960.

The site was originally called the *Narrow Passage* and in 1872 an enormous wave rose without warning and washed over the arch and island carrying away several young couples who were picnicking there. To the east lies the cobalt blue water of the open Atlantic Ocean while to the west lies the *Bight of Eleuthera* in its myriad shades of emerald and turquoise. The *Queen's Highway* crosses the span via a large concrete and steel bridge. A rage on Halloween Day of 1991 spawned a rogue wave that picked up the bridge and moved the northern end of it 7' westward. When you are atop the bridge and look down at the Atlantic Ocean your mind will reel as you realize the forces involved in moving such a structure.

It is most likely a short time, geologically speaking, before the rock underneath the bridge is eroded and the *Atlantic Ocean* and the *Bight of Eleuthera* meet forever effectively cutting Eleuthera in two. In March, 1996, the huge seas of a severe northeasterly blow hit the bridge and washed away two people, one of whom survived. You can anchor your boat well west of the bridge and dinghy in but only in settled weather.

Rotten Bay, The Bogues

Rotten Bay, Lower Bogue - ½ nm S of:
25° 26.20' N, 76° 42.00' W

Navigational Information

Along the northwestern shoreline of Eleuthera north of the Glass Window are the two communities of Upper Bogue and Lower Bogue. Access to these towns is best accomplished by road as the shoreline offers little lee except in northwest to northeast conditions. In these conditions you can anchor off the jetty south of Lower Bogue in Rotten Bay. As shown on Chart EL-16, a waypoint at 25° 26.20' N, 76° 42.00' W, which places you approximately ½ mile south/southeast of the old jetty where you can follow the road a quarter of a mile or so to Lower Bogue.

What You Will Find Ashore

Nearly all visitors ask what is the difference between Upper and Lower Bogue. Well, Upper Bogue sits on the upper road while Lower Bogue sits on the lower road. Simple, isn't it? The Bogues were once called *Bog* due to the characteristics of the surrounding land. The low marshes actually filled with fish during a hurricane in 1965 and some are still there in small ponds well inland.

Lower Bogue seems to be the commercial center of the Bogues with a *Batelco* office, the *Reliable Laundromat*, the *C & R Convenience Store*, *Juggie's Videos*, the *Seven Seas Restaurant and Bar*, *Johnson's Grocery*, *Eleuthera Meats and Convenience Store*, *Agnes Bakery*, *Brendee's Groceries*, *Kelly's Convenience & Snacks*, the *Purplemae Restaurant*, *Gullies Calypso Café*, *A&R Snack and Ice Cream Parlour*, the *Auto Parts Store,* and last but certainly not least, *Lady B's Lifesaver Restaurant and Takeaway*. There is also a government packing house in Lower Bogue and a Post Office in Upper Bogue.

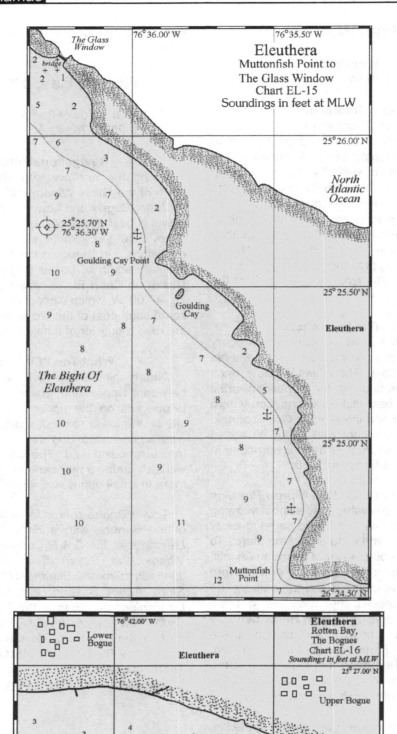

Eleuthera
Muttonfish Point to
The Glass Window
Chart EL-15
Soundings in feet at MLW

The Glass Window

bridge

North Atlantic Ocean

25° 26.00' N

25° 25.70' N
76° 36.30' W

Goulding Cay Point

Goulding Cay

25° 25.50' N

Eleuthera

The Bight Of Eleuthera

25° 25.00' N

Muttonfish Point

26° 24.50' N

76° 36.00' W   76° 35.50' W

Eleuthera
Rotten Bay,
The Bogues
Chart EL-16
Soundings in feet at MLW

Lower Bogue

Eleuthera

Upper Bogue

25° 27.00' N

Rotten Bay

25° 26.20' W
76° 42.00' W

76° 42.00' W   76° 41.00' W

The Current and Current Cut

Current Rock - ½ nm NW of:
25° 24.50' N, 76° 51.42' W

Current Cut - ½ nm NW of W entrance:
25° 24.40' N, 76° 48.00' W

Current Cut - 1 nm SSE of E entrance:
25° 22.94' N, 76° 46.61' W

Meek's Patch - ¼ nm NW of N tip of:
25° 31.60' N, 76° 47.30' W

At the northwestern tip of Eleuthera sits *Current Cut* and the small settlement of The Current. The Current is primarily a fishing town; the men stay gone for weeks at a time while the women raise their families and crank out some excellent straw work. The original settlers here came from Scotland and, like the *Eleutheran Adventurers*, they were shipwrecked on the *Devil's Backbone*. Some of The Current's 200-year-old wooden clapboard houses were all but destroyed by *Hurricane Andrew* but after a few years of rebuilding the half-mile long town is as charming and picturesque as ever.

Navigational Information

Approaching Current Cut from the Hatchett Bay or Governor's Harbour, A waypoint at 25° 22.94' N, 76° 46.61' W will place you approximately 1 mile south/southeast of the eastern entrance to Current Cut as shown on Chart EL-17. From this position head approximately 270°-280° until you can turn to starboard and parallel the shoreline of Current Island northward to *Current Cut* (which is shown in greater detail on Chart EL-18). There is a small cove west/southwest of the waypoint that offers good protection in winds from the west and northwest. In calm prevailing conditions you can anchor here to await the change of tide at Current Cut. Heading northward stay close to shore, about 50-150 yards off, and follow the coastline northward until you can round the last offlying rock to port giving it a wide berth. Then head straight through the cut to the other side. Try to time your passage at slack tide or when the tide is ebbing. Going east to west against a flood tide is very difficult as the current flows at speeds of over 5 knots at times. Once through you can take up your course to Royal Island or Meek's Patch and Spanish Wells as you choose.

Vessels wishing to pass through *Current Cut* from the west to the east should head for a waypoint at 25° 24.40' N, 76° 48.00' W, which will put you about ½ mile northwest of the western entrance to the cut. In prevailing conditions you can anchor anywhere in the lee of Eleuthera or Current Island to await the tide. Try not to head east against an ebbing tide in *Current Cut*. I have motored against the tides in *Current Cut* many times and although it is safe in a boat with a good auxiliary, the prudent navigator will await a favorable tide. Quite often people run aground at *Current Cut* and it is usually after they pass through the cut from west to east. Their mistake is almost always not turning southward quick enough to parallel the shoreline and avoid the shallows east of *Current Cut*. These grassy bars are sometimes hard to see and often skippers are unaware that they are so shallow. Once past the offlying rock at the eastern end of *Current Cut* (be sure to give it a wide berth as you round it to the north), turn sharply to starboard and parallel the shoreline southward staying about 50-150 yards off until you come to the cove I mentioned in the last paragraph that lies almost 1 mile south/southwest of *Current Cut*. When abeam of the point at the north end of this cove you can turn to the west and take up your course for Hatchett Bay or Governor's Harbour.

What You Will Find Ashore

On the northern bank of *Current Cut* is a dock where the mailboat *Current Pride* loads and unloads her cargo of people and supplies. On the south side of *Current Cut*, at the northern end of Current Island, is a small dock that is used by people from Little Bay and The Current as a landing for Current Island. On the northern shore of Current Cut, at the western end of the cut is a small concrete lined canal that would make a good refuge but only for shallow draft boats, all the local boats head there at the first sign of threatening weather.

Vessels can pass along the shore of Current Island either north or south or pass to the east of Pimlico Island and Little Pimlico Island along the shore of those two islands. The eastern shore of Current Island is deep with few obstructions from *Current Cut* southward. The only other danger is a shallow sandbank east of the southern tip of Current Island as shown on Charts EL-17 and EL-18.

Vessels can also coast along the western shore of Current Island from *Current Cut* southward but the

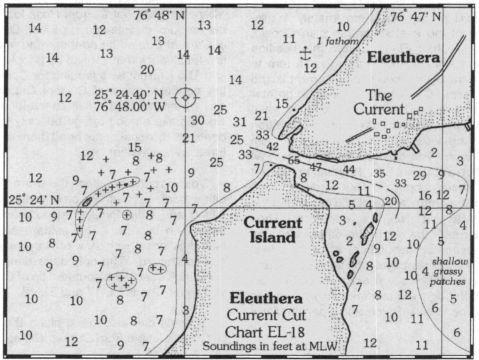

Eleuthera
Current Island
Chart EL-17
Soundings in feet at MLW

Eleuthera
Current Cut
Chart EL-18
Soundings in feet at MLW

channel gets narrow and shallow, 7' at low water, the further south you go. Just southwest of *Current Cut* are two small offlying cays with shallow reefs around them and east of them. Give these a berth of ¼ mile. I cannot recommend passing between these rocks and Current Island unless you have good visibility and you can read the water well. There are a few rocky bars here that are hard to see. The mailboat does come through here though and you might follow him if you draw less than 6' and the tide is low. Watch out for the shallow bar in the center of Bar Bay.

The southern tip of Current Island has a fierce current (2-3 knots and more at times) just off the point; be careful here. There is a nice anchorage off the beach on the southwestern shore of Current Island. You will need two anchors here due to the strong current. From *Current Cut* you may also head southwest along the eastern shores of Pimlico and Little Pimlico Islands as shown on Chart EL-17. This route is much deeper and wider than the one along the western shore of Current Island though it too is affected by strong currents.

Along the western shore of Current Island is the small village of *Little Bay*. Here you will find about 100 residents. Most of the men are fishermen who are gone for weeks at a time in search of lobster, conch, and scalefish. The chief point of interest in Little Bay is the cemetery. Sitting in an open field, there are several large limestone rocks that were carved out and used for tombs.

Navigational Information

Vessels heading to Spanish Wells or *Current Cut* from Nassau have another route to choose from. A waypoint at 25° 24.50' N, 76° 51.42' W, will place you approximately ½ mile northwest of Current Rock as shown on Chart EL-17. The light that once stood on Current Rock was destroyed and no body seems to know when or if it will be rebuilt. If heading north to Spanish Wells or over to Current Cut, keep Current Rock and its surrounding reefs to starboard. If heading to *Current Cut*, give the north end of Current Rock a berth of at least ½ mile. Keep an eye out for Southwest Reef which lies north/northwest of Current Rock.

What You Will Find Ashore

If you choose to anchor off The Current and wish to dinghy in to town you will find the well-stocked *Durham's Grocery*, *Griffin's Snack Bar*, a Texaco

gas station, a *Batelco* office, and *L&M's Bakery and Takeaway*. Near the dock you'll find *Monica's Curio Shop* for those in need of cards or gifts.

Divers will want to take advantage of the unusual drift dive that *Current Cut* has to offer. The western end of the cut is 65' deep in places with sheer canyon-like walls rising vertically on both sides. Drifting by the scoured walls at 5 knots or more can be a thrilling experience for the avid SCUBA enthusiast wanting something just a little bit different. SCUBA divers can often drift through four times without exhausting a tank of air. The drift dive has been described as the closest thing to flying for the SCUBA diver.

There is a little known cave along the northern shore above The Current in which the suspected remains of a Lucayan Indian was found. He had apparently been murdered, shot in the head by the invading Spanish.

Three miles west of *Current Cut* on a heading for Egg Island lies *Mystery Reef* in the middle of a large sandy area in 25' of water. Six colorful, large, and imposing coral heads crop up 10'-20' with schools of fish darting in and out in abundance. This is an excellent spot for underwater photography.

On Current Island is the small, outlying community of Little Bay with its nearly 100 inhabitants. Rarely attracting visitors, the town's small store carries only the barest necessities. Most of the residents here are fishermen.

North of The Current, almost as far as the landing for Spanish Wells, is the settlement of The Bluff lying about 5 miles south of Spanish Wells as shown on Chart EL-19. The Bluff was originally a settlement of liberated slaves. The settlement contained many fine orange orchards at that time and shipped much of its product to the U.S.

Here on the water's edge just above the dock you will find the huge, elegant *Miss Annie Hotel*. By Bahamian out-island standards, the impressive yellow building reminds one of the grand hotels of a former era, but by American standards, it is about the size of your ordinary mansion. Here you'll find a government clinic with a nurse on duty and a town water faucet located on the dock. Around the corner you'll find *Sawyer's Food Store*, *Anderson's Groceries* (the pink store-they usually have fresh produce), and *Onassa's*

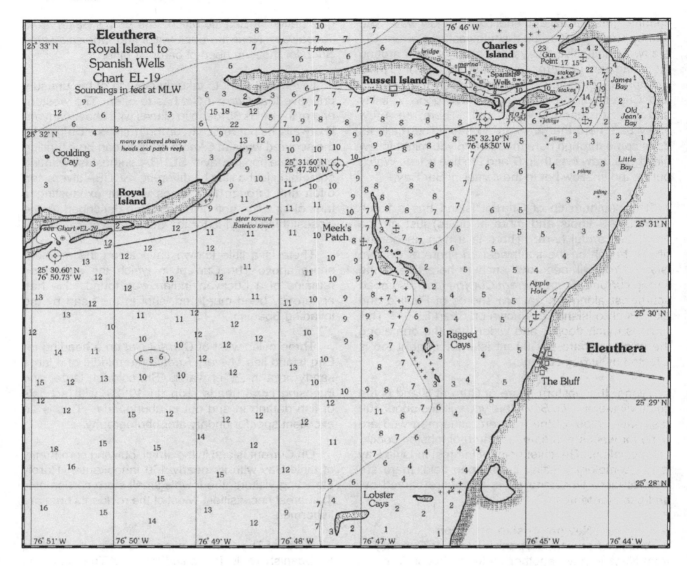

Eleuthera
Royal Island to
Spanish Wells
Chart EL-19
Soundings in feet at MLW

Snacks. *Arlie's Restaurant* is nearby but their hours are sporadic, they're not always open, but that's okay, their food is worth the wait.

As shown on Chart EL-19, a vessel of 6' draft can anchor just north of the town dock at The Bluff in a patch of deep water called the *Apple Hole* just off the shoreline. From the western entrance to Spanish Wells head straight for The Bluff leaving Meeks Patch to starboard. You will have 5'-6' at low water on this route. The anchorage should only be considered in the prevailing east to southeast winds, winds from any other direction makes this anchorage untenable. Even if you don't anchor near The Bluff, the town is only a long dinghy trip from Spanish Wells.

Egg Island Cut

Egg Island Cut - 1½ nm WNW of Cut:
25° 29.60' N, 76° 54.75' W

Wreck of the *Arimora* - ¼ nm SW:
25° 27.87' N, 76° 53.75' W

Just to the southwest of Royal Island lies Egg Island and *Egg Island Cut* as shown on Chart EL-21. Most boaters headed south from Abaco usually pass through *Egg Island Cut* to anchor at Royal Island or head towards Current Cut or Spanish Wells. Boaters headed north pass through the cut to take up their course towards Little Harbour at Great Abaco.

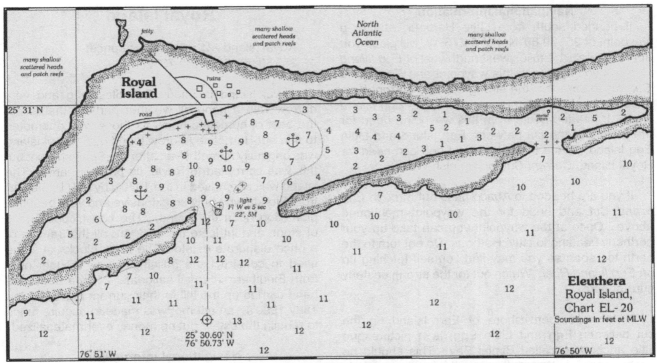

Eleuthera
Royal Island,
Chart EL-20
Soundings in feet at MLW

25° 30.60' N
76° 50.73' W

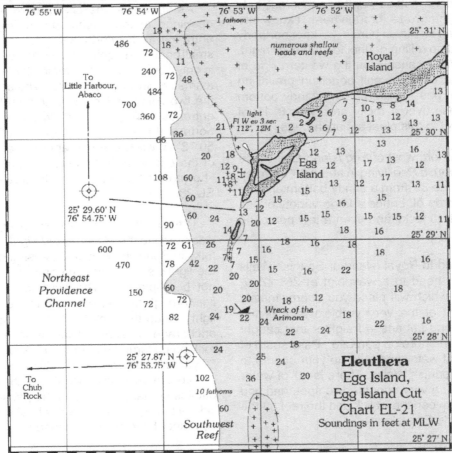

Eleuthera
Egg Island,
Egg Island Cut
Chart EL-21
Soundings in feet at MLW

Navigational Information

If headed south from Little Harbour, Abaco, a waypoint at 25° 29.60' N, 76° 54.75' W, will place you approximately 1½ miles west/northwest of *Egg Island Cut*. As you approach this waypoint and *Egg Island Cut*, make sure that the strong easterly current here does not push you to the east and up on *Egg Island Reef*. If headed south from this waypoint, head for the middle of the cut between Egg Island and Little Egg Island. Once through the cut you can head for Royal Island, *Current Cut*, or Spanish Wells.

If you are headed to Abaco pass out through *Egg Island Cut* and head for the waypoint mentioned above. Once at the waypoint you can take up your northerly heading to Little Harbour. Do not turn to the north too soon as you may find yourself fetching up on *Egg Island Reef*. Watch out for the strong easterly current here.

On the southern shore of Egg Island, in the cut between Egg and Little Egg, is a picturesque little anchorage called Bimini Bay. This should be considered a daytime, settled weather anchorage only due to the surge that works through here. I knew one skipper that sought shelter in here in 25-knot northerly winds and wound up rolling gunnel to gunnel all night. Some skippers like to anchor on the western side of Great Egg Island off the small beach in prevailing winds. This spot has a good holding sandy bottom but you must pass over a rocky area with 8'-11' of water over it to get to this pleasant anchorage.

Due west and northwest of *Egg Island Light* is the *Egg Island Lighthouse Reef* lying in about 60' of water. Heads rise up some 35' from a sandy bottom and the proximity to the drop off brings a large variety of fish from large jewfish to jacks and even a few pompano to the reef.

Vessels headed to Royal Island or Spanish Wells from Nassau can head to a waypoint at 25° 27.87' N, 76° 53.75' W, which will place you approximately ¼ mile southwest of the very visible wreck of the *Arimora*, a 250' long Lebanese freighter that caught fire and ran aground here on purpose. Pass south of the wreck in 20' of water and take up your course to Royal Island or Spanish Wells. There is 20' of water around this wreck, a very popular dive spot, and you can even pass between the wreck and the reef off the southern tip of Little Egg Island.

Royal Island

Royal Island - ¼ mile S of entrance:
25° 30.60' N, 76° 50.73' W

Royal Island is about 3½ miles long and very narrow with a good all weather harbour that is not the best of hurricane holes as those who attempted to ride out Hurricane Andrew found out. Royal Island was originally named *Ryal*, after the Spanish coin, but this was corrupted to Royal, its present name. The island was purchased in the 1930's by a W.P. Stewart from Florida who built an extensive and very beautiful plantation upon the island. The conspicuous ruins of stone and intricate tile work are all that remain of a once elaborate estate. The huge blocks of stone used to construct the buildings were brought over from Eleuthera in small sailboats, 21 to a boat, and hand carried up the hill to their current place. In the early 1990's, an attempt was made to acquire funds to rebuild the estate but no money ever materialized.

Navigational Information

As shown on the chart, there are actually three openings to the anchorage at Royal Island. The entrance to the northeast is navigable only by very small boats or dinghies. Even then use caution as there is only about a foot of water in places compounded by a small rocky bar just inside. The best landmarks are the two hills, the highest points on Royal Island, the entrance to *Royal Island Harbour* lies about ½ mile north of these hills. A waypoint at 25° 30.60' N, 76° 50.73' W will place you approximately ¼ mile south of the entrance to the anchorage at Royal Island as shown on Chart EL-19 and in greater detail in Chart EL-20.

In the middle of this pass sits a large rock that once was home to the *Royal Island Light*. I'm told by some folks in Spanish Wells that passing cruisers removed the light's solar panel and batteries and the light will not be replaced. The entrance to the anchorage lies through the narrower cut to the southwest of the light. Keep the rock to starboard upon entering the anchorage. The cut that lies just to the northeast of the rock has a large submerged rock lying approximately 50 yards inside and just barely under the surface. It is possible to pass on either side of the submerged rock but it is so hard to see and the passage on the other side of the light is so easy it is best to ignore this route no matter how inviting it appears.

Egg Island to Royal Island

Photo Courtesy of Paul Harding,
Safari Seaplanes

Royal Island Resort Construction

Photo Courtesy of
Paul Harding,
Safari Seaplanes

The holding is great here so don't be afraid to anchor in the white mud/sand/grass bottom. I once rode out a frontal passage here with my two *CQR's* buried, the wind blowing a sustained 50+ knot for six hours with gusts to 70, and if I did move, it was not enough to notice. The skippers and crews of the boats that rode out Hurricane Andrew here would probably tell you a different story though.

What You Will Find Ashore

Ashore you will find plenty of ruins that testify to the once grand estate that flourished here over half a century ago. Be sure to check out the beautiful tile work in the buildings, some of which is painted over, and the intricate concrete finishing on the road that leads up the hill from the dock. Use caution as you approach the dock. There are some shallow heads just to the southwest of the dock. A huge section of the outer end of the dock is submerged due to hurricane damage and there are a few pieces of re-bar rising up to spear the errant dinghy. The western section of this submerged dock is above water at low tide.

Royal Island is becoming the home for a huge resort development under construction by *Cypress Equities* and the *Staubach Company* (CEO former *NFL* quarterback Roger Staubach). At this time there is a new RORO harbor just outside the entrance to the anchorage at Royal Island with a no-anchoring zone near the landing (see photo). The entrance to the main harbor is marked by red and green flashing lights (privately maintained) at each side of the entrance channel. The resort will feature a private clubhouse, 80 luxury hotel suites, fine dining and casual restaurants, and a marina able to accommodate yachts to 300' in length; they even boast a high-speed fueling operation) and a Customs office (so you can envision Royal Island becoming a *Port of Entry* when this happens). Also on tap for construction is a Jack Nicklaus designed 18-hole golf course.

Spanish Wells

Spanish Wells Harbour - E entrance:
25° 32.60' N, 76° 44.35' W

Spanish Wells Harbour - W entrance:
25° 32.10' N, 76° 45.40' W

Meek's Patch - ¼ nm NW of N tip of:
25° 31.60' N, 76° 47.30' W

Spanish Wells was once called *Sigatoo* when the area was occupied by Lucayan Indians in pre-Columbian times. The Spanish slavers named the area Spanish Wells for the abundance of good water found thereabouts from which they could fill their casks. Some of today's inhabitants are descendants of the Loyalists who fled from the American Revolution while others are descended from William Sayles *Eleutheran Adventurers*, English Puritans who arrived in 1648 just off the northern tip of Eleuthera seeking freedom to work and worship their God as they saw fit. One hundred and fifty seven *Eleutheran Adventurers* came ashore after piling up their ship on the *Devil's*

Backbone. They lived in caves on the northern tip of Eleuthera for almost two years before 57 went to Spanish Wells and 100 left for Harbour Island. They held religious services in these early years in what is now known as *Preacher's Cave* on the northern shore of Eleuthera just inland from the *Devil's Backbone*. During the War of 1812 Spanish Wells was plundered and partially burnt by an American vessel.

Although in most of the settlements in The Bahamas the principal religion is Anglican, Spanish Wells is Methodist, the only Methodist island in The Bahamas. This is because John and Charles Wesley, the founders of Methodism, landed in the area for several months on their way to Georgia in the New World. Spanish Wells was once known as a dry island due to the Methodist influence but today that has changed and you can now buy a drink in any of several bars on the island.

Today's Spanish Wellsians have an unusual accent, not quite British, Bahamian, or American yet somewhere in between standing quite on its own in The Bahamas. Spanish Wells has a thriving seafood industry with a strong industrial base and does not rely on tourism for its economy. Agriculture plays a minor role in the economy of Spanish Wells. The hills of Russell Island contribute oranges and tangerines while local gardens boast tomatoes, lemons, cucumbers, and even pineapple. The town itself is crime-free, you can walk anywhere at anytime of the day or night without fear, but bring a flashlight as they shut down the city streetlights at 9:00 p.m. The attractive houses, some dating back 150 years, are well kept and almost all are nicely landscaped. Every Christmas season the homeowners in Spanish Wells join in a Christmas lighting competition. The highly decorated houses vie for prizes and the entire island puts on a very festive air.

Spanish Wellsians are very independent and quite proud of it. I will probably have a few of my Spanish Wells friends mad at me for including their lovely island in the same chapter with Eleuthera. They make it very clear that they are not from Eleuthera.... they are from Spanish Wells!

Navigational Information

Vessels heading to Spanish Wells from either Royal Island or Current Cut should head for a waypoint just off Meek's Patch at 25° 31.60' N, 76° 47.30' W, as shown on Chart EL-19 (if you don't have a GPS, you can steer for the Batelco tower at Spanish Wells until you can make out the entrance channel). From this waypoint head to a waypoint at 25° 32.10' N, 76° 45.50' W, which will place you just south of the pilings that mark the western entrance to the harbour. Here you will see two large steel I beams about 8'-10' out of the water. The westernmost one is slightly leaning, probably due to a boat collision. Pass between the two and keep the inner I beam to starboard and you will enter the channel to the harbour. The channel is also marked by a green light at the entrance that flashes green, every 2 seconds, stands 12' high, and is visible for 2 nautical miles. South of these entrance pilings are some scattered pilings painted orange that lead towards the mainland of Eleuthera. Ignore them, they mark a channel where a cable is buried.

Just a few hundred yards up the channel at the end of the jetty on your port side, another channel branches off to the west (to port) leading to *Spanish Wells Yacht Haven Marina*. The passage lies between the tip of the shoal bank to port and the piling that you must keep to starboard. Keep the shoal bank to port as you approach the marina and look for the large boat shed, you can't miss it. Between the spot where you turned to port from the main channel and the marina, almost where the stake marks the small boat channel to starboard, there is a 5' spot at low water, this is the controlling depth for this channel to the marina. If you need assistance call the marina on VHF ch. 16.

To venture into Spanish Wells Harbour proper simply continue up the main channel as it bears away to the east away from the marina entrance channel keeping the conspicuous piling to port, never venture north of that piling. There is a small anchorage and mooring area at the far eastern end of the harbour on the south side of the channel just before you enter the eastern entrance channel.

For a mooring call Bradley Newbold, *Cinnarbar*, on VHF ch. 16. Bradley has moorings in town along the waterfront though you will be rocked regularly from passing boats (he can also arrange to bring you some freshly baked bread or you can visit *Kathy's Bakery* in town). This is a commercial area, there is no speed limit and you will not see a "No Wake" sign. Wake is a part of life for boats tying up along the dock at Spanish Wells so be prepared.

Spanish Wells

Photo Courtesy of Paul Harding,
Safari Seaplanes

Spanish Wells waterfront

Photo Courtesy of Anne DuPont

Seafood Market, Spanish Wells

Photo Courtesy of
Anne DuPont

Preacher's Cave, Eleuthera

Photo by Author

The eastern entrance channel is easily seen in good visibility and well marked. There is a line of pilings that you need to keep to your port side as you head east. Vessels coming into Spanish Wells from *Ridley Head Channel* or Harbour Island should proceed to a waypoint at 25° 32.13' N, 76° 44.35' W, which will place you just east of the mouth of the eastern entrance. Keep the poles to starboard and follow the channel into the harbour and you will have 10' all the way in at low water. The poles have red reflectors on them to aid a nighttime approach.

If approaching from Meek's Patch, it is possible to pass south of Spanish Wells from the western entrance to the eastern entrance in the channel that rounds George's Cay. From the pilings south of the western entrance to the harbor, head east keeping just south of the offlying rocks. There is a small orange tipped piling between the channel pilings and the first small cay to port. Keep that piling to port as you head eastward. To starboard you will see a pair of these orange tipped markers and then a few more stretched out towards Eleuthera. Ignore them, they mark a cable channel that is too shallow for navigation. The shallowest part of this route is in the area of the orange tipped piling and the first rock that lies south of George's Cay. Here you will find 5'-6' at low water. Once you get past the first small rock the water begins to get progressively deeper from 7' to 15'. Keep the small offlying rocks close to port staying about 50 yards off and once past them you will begin to pick up three pilings. Keep these very conspicuous pilings to port as you head eastward. Some of these pilings are painted green but ignore the paint atop them. If using the red-right-returning maxim these should be painted red and I have no idea how these came to be painted incorrectly. Personally, I don't know why someone would want to take this route to get to the eastern side of the harbour near Gun Point. By taking the channel through Spanish Wells Harbour you avoid the shallows, get to see a bit of the town, and only lengthen your trip by a few minutes, less than ½ mile.

If heading from the eastern entrance south to the western entrance, follow the above route in reverse. Keep the green painted pilings to starboard, then follow close in to the offlying rocks on your starboard side. As you approach the pilings at the western entrance to the harbour you will cross the shallowest part of this route, 5'-6' at low water. Once you arrive at the pilings the water gets progressively deeper from 7'-9'

and more as you continue to head west. Keep the northernmost orange tipped piling to starboard and ignore the orange pilings that lie south of the western entrance, these mark a buried cable that leads to the mainland of Eleuthera.

There are some excellent settled weather anchorages just east of Spanish Wells off the eastern edge of the channel in some deep water pockets surrounded by steeply rising grassy topped sandbanks as shown on Chart EL-19. There is 10'-20' in these pockets and holding is excellent although not a place to ride out a frontal passage. Another excellent anchorage east of Spanish Wells is in the bight just off the beach south of Gun Point on the mainland of Eleuthera. If a front is approaching it would be wise to head back into Spanish Wells or over to Royal Island.

What You Will Find Ashore

There are three places in Spanish Wells to obtain diesel and gas. From the east along the shore the first business you come to is *Ronald's Marine and Service Center*, an *Evinrude* and *Johnson* dealer as well as a chandlery, they also have a fuel dock for diesel and gas. Next as you head west you will come across the *Anchor Snack Bar* which serves some of the best food in town, reservations are suggested for dinner on the weekends as the locals tend to keep them quite busy Fridays and Saturdays. Next door is the purple building that used to be *Langousta's Restaurant And Bar*. Next along the road is *Marguerita's Dry Goods* and then *Pinder's Supermarket* where you can get fuel and water right at the dock. Next door is the *R & B Boat Yard* where you can get your boat hauled out and the hull repaired or painted. *R&B* can haul boats up to 100 tons on their railway and their new lift can haul a boat to 45' LOA with a 29' beam.

Next is *Spanish Wells Marine and Hardware Ltd.* with a complete selection of marine goods, diesel and gas at their *Texaco Starport* fuel dock, *Mercury* repairs (some say they have the best *Merc* mechanic anywhere), some hull and electrical repair, and ice. Further west is the old building that once housed the *Sea View Restaurant* and which is now *Jack's Outback*. Jack serves excellent food but no alcohol although he doesn't mind if his customers bring their own. If you need a diesel mechanic, welding, or refrigeration repairs you can call *On Site Marine and Auto* at 333-4389. If you walk up the hill past *Pinder's Supermarket* you will come to a gift shop and a hardware store. If you take a left here and head towards the water tower you will come to the *Captain's Diner* with its Laundromat in the back of the building. *Magic Photo*, next to the *CW Grocery* (with a laundry on site), offers one-hour developing and is located on the main road and 10th Street.

If you need propane take your tanks to *Pinder's Tune-Up* for a refill. And if you need medical attention there is a clinic near the *Spanish Wells Food Fair* with a doctor, dentist, and nurse on call. Food Fair also has a pharmacy if you need your scripts refilled.

There are several nice gift shops in town such as *Nadene's Straw Works*, *The Islander Shop*, the *Ponderosa Shell Shop*, *The Quilt Shop*, *Oliver's Straw Hut* (on *Main Street*, they sell T-shirts as well as art), *Three Sisters Variety*, and Vernicia's *Patchwork Center*. Specialty shops include *Pet Supplies* and *Spanish Wells Florist*. Next door to the *Islander* is the *Spanish Wells Museum*, and if you need canvas or sail repairs, contact *Spanish Wells Canvas* on Ch. 16.

Heading westward down the creek west of town lies *Spanish Wells Yacht Haven Marina* with 10 slips that can accommodate a vessel of 110' LOA. There is satellite service to each slip, a Laundromat, restaurant, and a cocktail bar. The marina also offers water, ice, showers, telephones, bike rentals, and a book swap. Accommodations are available nearby. Dockside power is 220 and 110 volt.

West of *Yacht Haven* is *Adventurers Paradise Hotel* where you'll also find *Uncle Mike's Lil Grocery Store*. Over the hill from *Yacht Haven Marina* and slightly to the west lies the large *Food Fair* supermarket and pharmacy with the best provisioning in the area, quite comparable to Nassau prices.

If you find yourself with nothing to do and want to catch the latest releases check out *Crazy Frank's Videos* which lies just up the road to the east. Although there is not a local dentist, one visits weekly from the mainland of Eleuthera on Thursdays and Fridays if your teeth are giving you problems while in the area. Dr. Pfeifer, formerly of Abaco, now has a small practice in Spanish Wells.

Meek's Patch, as shown on Chart EL-19, is a nice spot to anchor in some conditions. In easterly winds you can anchor off the small beach on the western side, when the winds go southwest to west, you can anchor off the even nicer beach on the eastern side of the cay. This cay is a popular picnic and swimming spot for local boaters and on holidays and weekends it may get crowded.

For excellent guide service to this area, including fishing, diving, or navigating *Ridley Head Channel* or the route to Harbour Island (along *The Devil's Backbone*), try Broadshad Pinder (333-4427, VHF ch.16-*A1 Broadshad*), Bradley Newbold (333-4079, VHF ch. 16-*Cinnabar*), Little Woody, Dave Roberts, John Roberts, or Preston Sands.

Ridley Head and The Devil's Backbone

Pilot pickup point N of Ridley Head Channel:
25° 34.50' N, 76° 44.30' W

Bridge Point - N waypoint:
25° 34.32' N, 76° 43.03' W

Bridge Point - S waypoint, just off Bridge Point:
25° 33.90' N, 76° 43.18' W

Ridley Head Channel - S waypoint:
25° 33.54' N, 76° 44.33' W

Hawk's Point - just N of Devil's Backbone route:
25° 33.53' N, 76° 40.85' W

Current Point - just N of Devil's Backbone route:
25° 33.05' N, 76° 39.88' W

Turning point on Devil's Backbone route:
25° 32.26' N, 76° 39.17' W

Harbour Island is one of the most popular vacation destinations for visitors to The Bahamas and getting to Harbour Island may well be one of your greatest feats of piloting. I suggest that first timers, those new to cruising these waters, hire a pilot from Spanish Wells to show you the way along the *Devil's Backbone*. If you refuse to hire a pilot you should rethink your situation. This is not an easy run unless you are an experienced Bahamas hand and are confident in your ability to read the water. This can truly be a dangerous route, but there are many others equally as deadly in The Bahamas. Personally, I think the entrance into the Propeller Cay anchorage at Samana is harder

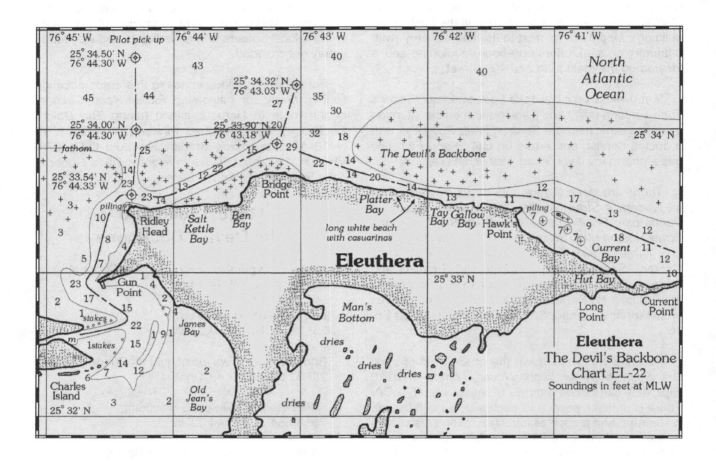

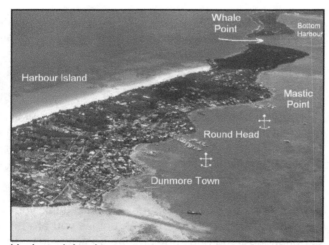

Harbour Island

Photo Courtesy of Paul Harding,
Safari Seaplanes

Government Dock,
Valentine's Marina,
Harbour Island

Photo Courtesy of Paul Harding,
Safari Seaplanes

to see and almost as dangerous if you stray. The controlling depth for the *Devil's Backbone* route is 6' at low water. If you're not inclined to try the *Devil's Backbone*, there is a new fast ferry from Nassau to Spanish Wells (two trips daily) to Harbour Island and back. The fare is $90 round trip and takes about an hour and a half.

The *Devil's Backbone* should only be run on a fairly calm day (as in no large ocean swells) and with good visibility. Any large swells or strong winds out of any northerly quadrant make this an extremely risky route. I have run this route in 6'-8' leftover northeasterly swells from a low-pressure system that was hundreds of miles to the northeast and the passage was highly uncomfortable to say the least. To arrange for a pilot see the last paragraph in the previous section on Spanish Wells.

Vessels returning from Harbour Island to Spanish Wells should follow these directions in reverse. If you hired a pilot when headed to Harbour Island, you may feel confident enough to try the route by yourself on the return trip.

CAUTION: I am going to give you some waypoints that lie along this route. These waypoints are for reference only or for entering or leaving by *Ridley Head Channel* or *Bridge Point Channel*. Never attempt to run waypoint to waypoint on this route. Eyeball navigation is the only way through here unless you hire a pilot. If you insist on using waypoints, I urge you to change your mind and hire a pilot.

Navigational Information

When leaving Spanish Wells for the *Devil's Backbone* one must first negotiate the channel past Ridley Head as shown on Chart EL-16. Leaving the eastern entrance channel to Spanish Wells turn to port and take Gun Point to starboard to take up your course for Ridley head as shown on Chart EL-22. Once you round Gun Point you will see Ridley Head towards the northeast and the huge steel I-beam that sits a little to seaward of it. Take up a course to a position north of that I-beam.

Just past Gun Point on this route you will find some shallows with 7' over them at low tide. Do not attempt to pass between the I-beam and Ridley Head as this area is foul with shallow rocks and heads. Watch out for the scattered reefs on your port side as you approach Ridley Head. A waypoint at 25°

33.54' N, 76° 44.33' W, will place you just north of Ridley Head and is the southern waypoint for vessels entering *Ridley Head Channel* from seaward. Let us pause here and discuss *Ridley Head Channel*. If you are heading east along the *Devil's Backbone* you can skip the next paragraph.

Ridley Head Channel is a good but narrow passage from the Spanish Wells area to the North Atlantic Ocean. Many boats bound to or from Abaco use it as it gives a better angle on the prevailing wind and a slightly shorter distance than the course from *Egg Island Cut*.

If you are not experienced at eyeball navigation and are approaching this area from offshore wishing to use *Ridley Head Channel* to enter the Spanish Wells area, I suggest calling for a pilot as mentioned in the last paragraph in the section on Spanish Wells. A waypoint at 25° 34.50' N, 76° 44.30' W is a good spot to await a pilot.

If you wish to negotiate *Ridley Head Channel* without the assistance of a pilot head to the northern waypoint for the *Ridley Head Channel* route at 25° 34.00' N, 76° 44.30' W. This position is approximately ½ mile north of Ridley Head and the southern waypoint at 25° 33.54' N, 76° 44.33' W. The course from the northern waypoint to the southern waypoint is almost due south. Head for the southern waypoint but don't just steer that course until arrival. You must watch out for the reefs on both sides of the channel. Particularly dangerous is the very visible reef that will come up off your port bow just as you approach the southern waypoint. This was once marked by a steel I-beam which has since been knocked down to just under the surface of the water. It is almost awash at low water. The I-beam sits at the eastern edge of the reef so give it a wide berth.

Once at the southern waypoint you can head around Gun Point to Spanish Wells or continue eastward to Harbour Island along the Devil's Backbone route.

Vessels continuing eastward from Ridley Head along the *Devil's Backbone* route should proceed eastward from Ridley Head taking care to stay south of the reefs lying just east of *Ridley Head Channel*. Head generally east until abeam of the last palm trees in the grove on the shore on your starboard side. Once past these palm trees head for a point north of the next point of land which is called Bridge Point.

Here you will be heading slightly more to seaward, passing between the offshore reefs on your port side, and the reefs that lie southwest of Bridge Point just off the shore of Eleuthera at *Ben Bay*. A waypoint at 25° 33.90' N, 76° 43.18' W, will place you in good water north of the reefs that lie just off Bridge Point. This waypoint is also the southern waypoint for the *Bridge Point Channel* route. Let us once again pause while we discuss Bridge Point Channel. Vessels continuing along the *Devil's Backbone* eastward can skip the next paragraph.

An open water entrance to the *Devil's Backbone* lies just off Bridge Point with deep water all the way in from the ocean. It is an excellent entrance for boats bound for Harbour Island, or even for boats bound for Spanish Wells that do not want to negotiate *Ridley Head Channel* which is considerably narrower and quite a bit riskier. *Bridge Point Channel* is a deep, wide, obstruction free channel that is sometimes called the *Wide Opening*. Vessels entering from seaward should head to a waypoint at 25° 34.32' N, 76° 43.03' W, which lies about ½ mile north of the southern waypoint at Bridge Point. The passage from the northern waypoint to the southern waypoint at 25° 33.90' N, 76° 43.18' W, is wide, deep, and obstruction free. The closest reef lies a few hundred yards to the west and over ¼ mile or more to the east. Once at the southern waypoint you can turn and head to Ridley Head and Spanish Wells or continue east along the *Devil's Backbone*.

Okay, now back to the *Devil's Backbone* route. Once past Bridge Point you will enter the trickiest part of the entire route, the narrow passage between *Devil's Backbone Reef* and the shoreline of Eleuthera. Once past Bridge Point you will begin heading in closer to the shoreline. Ahead of you is a long beach with an equally long stand of casuarinas behind it. Head in for this beach where you will pass between *Devil's Backbone Reef* and the beach staying about 30-50 yards off the beach. Continue close in past the beach until you reach Hawk's Point. A waypoint at 25° 33.53' N, 76° 40.85' W lies just north of Hawk's Point. Continue east and once past Hawk's Point the channel gets a little wider. You can now breathe a sigh of relief. You have passed through the trickiest part.

Just east of Hawk's Point is a rocky bar marked by a piling. Keep this bar and piling to starboard. Pass between the piling and the reefs to its north. The shoreline of Eleuthera can take 7' close in here but there are some shallow heads and bars between the piling and Eleuthera in Current Bay.

Continuing eastward past the piling head for the next point of land which is called Current Point. As shown on Chart EL-23 the waters on your port side will open up as you come abeam of Pierre Island. In olden days large sailing boats would anchor here because they could not get closer to Dunmore Town. As you pass Current Point you will see another steel I-beam to the east. Pass to the south of this piling within 50 yards or so. This is the shallowest part of the *Devil's Backbone* route and you will find 6' of water here at low tide. As you head southeast past this piling you will be steering approximately 140° and you will have to eyeball your way past the shallow bar to your starboard side.

A waypoint at 25° 32.26' N, 76° 39.17' W, is clear of the sandbar and a good reference for your southward turn. From this position head southward staying clear of the sandbars west of Harbour Island as you make your way south to the anchorage or marinas at Dunmore Town. Vessels heading to Spanish Wells along the *Devil's Backbone* from Harbour Island should head to this waypoint and then begin steering approximately 320° to pass south of the steel piling. Then follow the directions for the *Devil's Backbone* route in reverse.

What You Will Find Ashore
For snorkelers and SCUBA divers alike there are some excellent dive opportunities in the waters surrounding the *Devil's Backbone*. Along the *Devil's Backbone* lies the *Train Wreck*, a wooden barge bearing a train that sank in 15' of water in 1865. It is said that it was a Union train captured by the Confederacy and sold to a Cuban sugar plantation owner to raise money for the war effort. Now overgrown with elkhorn and brain coral, the wreck consists of three sets of wheel trucks believed to be part of a locomotive and pieces of wooden beams lying half buried in the sandy sea floor.

A few hundred yards away from the *Train Wreck* lies the wreck of the *Cienfuegos* in 10'-35' of water. The *Cienfuegos*, a *Ward Line* passenger liner, sank in 1895 but not before saving all her passengers and even salvaging her cargo of rice. All that remains of the wreck is a twisted section of her 200' hull, two huge heat exchangers, a boiler, and the main shaft.

Also aground on the *Devil's Backbone*, just a few feet from the wreck of the *Cienfuegos*, lie the remains of the grain and passenger ship *Vanaheim*, an 86' coaster that hit the reef during a winter storm in 1969 and was pushed over the reef where she broke up in 15' of water. She was carrying a load of potatoes and onions and is now known as the *Potato and Onion Wreck*. Other wrecks along this treacherous reef system include the *Carnarvon*, a 186' steel freighter that sank in 30' of water in 1916 (I've also heard she sank in 1918) and a 76' shrimper that went down in 20' of water in 1969. For those wishing to visit these sites, check with *Valentines Yacht Club Dive Shop* on Harbour Island or with one of the guides listed above at Spanish Wells.

For those few who wish to see Harbour Island without the risk of running the *Devil's Backbone* you can catch a ferry from the mainland of Eleuthera. First take the ferry from Spanish Wells to the mainland and then just ask any taxi driver about it. You can also catch the mailboat from Spanish Wells, or the fast ferry from either Spanish Wells or Nassau.

Harbour Island

Whale Point - ½ nm ENE of:
25° 28.70' N, 76° 37.30' W

S entrance, outer waypoint of N route:
25° 28.50' N, 76° 37.81' W

S entrance, outer waypoint of S route:
25° 28.43' N, 76° 37.78' W

S entrance, inner waypoint of N route:
25° 28.42' N, 76° 38.90' W

S entrance, inner waypoint of S route:
25° 28.11' N, 76° 37.94' W

Well, we've discussed how hard it is to get there, now let's see what you're missing if you don't try. Harbour Island is one of the oldest settled islands in The Bahamas. It is occasionally called *Briland* (and its inhabitants *Brilanders*), which is a slurred corruption of Harbour Island. The 3-mile long island's only settlement, Dunmore Town, is named after the Earl Of Dunmore who was once the Governor of Virginia. The Earl later acquired a summer residence on Harbour Island when he was Governor of The Bahamas from 1786-1797. Prior to that Dunmore

Town was primarily a military post with *Barracks Hill* and a few old guns being the only reminders of that age. Dunmore Town was a settlement before the United States was a nation and, until recently, the second city of The Bahamas next to Nassau.

From the 1700s until the World War II, Dunmore Town was known as a shipbuilding center and the largest ship ever constructed in The Bahamas, the four-masted *Marie J. Thompson*, was built here in 1922. The famous pirate Calico Jack Rackham is said to have once raided Harbour Island and burnt a few fishing boats. Harbour Island was also once a sugar refinement center and the *Brilander's* skill in the refinement process gave them an important second industry, the distillation of rum. With the advent of prohibition Harbour Island became quite a popular spot. Today the island is tourism oriented, the guests focusing on the three mile long pink sand beach. Reflective of the tourist industry here, prices are a little higher for most goods.

Navigational Information
When skippers reach the last waypoint on the *Devil's Backbone* route, the one that places you well southeast of the last piling and east of the large sandbank at 25° 32.26' N, 76° 39.17' W, you can take up a route southward to the anchorage off Dunmore Town proper as shown on Chart EL-23. Most boaters anchor off Dunmore Town simply because it offers easy access to shore. For those not so inclined there are other nice anchorages throughout the area.

A good anchorage in northeast to southeast conditions lies at the southern end of Man Island as shown on the chart. In westerly weather you can head over to the mainland of Eleuthera at the ferry landing as shown on Chart EL-23. Here you will find shelter in winds from southwest to northwest. For shelter from southeast to southwest winds you can head all the way to the southern end of the bay. Leave the sandbank off Dunmore Town to port and head towards Cistern Rock. Pass between Cistern Rock and the shallow bank to its east and you can anchor off the beach at the southern end of the bay in 7'-8' of water at low tide.

If you do intend to anchor off Dunmore Town proceed south from the waypoint and give the sandbank northwest of Dunmore Town a wide berth. After passing the sandbank head in to shore and anchor wherever you choose. If you prefer a less

76° 40' W 76° 39' W 76° 38' W 76° 37' W 76° 36' W

Pierre Island

+ 1 fathom

46

54

10 fathoms

Eleuthera
Harbour Island
Chart EL-23
Soundings in feet at MLW

72

25° 33' N

12 40 15 ⚓ 7
10 18
8 7 ○ piling 5

Current Point

5 6 6 7

6

Man Island

9

18

46

97

North Atlantic Ocean

4
3

4

6

8
7

8 8 548 10 12

11 ⚓
7

25° 32.26' N
76° 39.17' W

7 7
3

6

8 8

10

6 7 8 9 10
11
8 9 10 11
7 8 9
3
9 10
3
7
9

7

10

7 7

8 7

Iron Sound Rock

Jacob's Island

The Narrows

24

192

25° 32' N

Little Pigeon Island

Pigeon Island

Centipede Cay 3 Eastmost Rock

Old Jean's Bay

9 9 7

7 7 7 +

+

25° 31' N

Westmost Rock

Nurse Creek

Pear Rock

3
3

7

7 8 9
4
4
11 15
9 12 15
3 12
10

7 9
2 1 2
4
Girls Bank
2 1
1 1
1

14
12 10
14 17 jetty
Dunmore Town

Harbour Island

+
+
+

25° 31' N

8
8
11
10 11 12 12 14

⚓ 8
11 13
11 12 13
8

Three Islands

14 15 15

14 10
13 10 ⚓
8
8

Round Head

Pond Rock

22

60

87

25° 30' N

Maho Creek

7
7
7 9
11
7 9 10

Mastic Point

+

+

+

+

9 10
9 10

6 3
+

47

25° 29' N

7 7
7
7

7 6
5 6
3
3 3 2
2
4 4
2

3
6
5 3 3 2
2
26
20 22
20
12
2 9
6 2 2

25° 28.70' N
76° 37.30' W

Whale Point

Eleuthera

Cistern Rock

2 8 9

9

2 Cistern Bay

6

Bottom Harbour

2 21
1
2

53

25° 28' N

small cove about ½ mile south of the marina. You can tie up to the beach around the town dock, the large concrete wharf with the yellow building on it, north of the marinas (you'll find *Customs* here). Often the marinas will let you tie up for a few hours if you ask first or you can land your dinghy at Harbour Island Marina or on the beach near the government dock.

What You Will Find Ashore

There are three marinas on Harbour Island. South of the town dock is *Valentines Yacht Club*. *Valentines* is the largest marina (42 slips) in the area and has complete amenities including a dive shop on premises. The dockmaster will make you feel right at home and can accommodate vessels to 165' with a 9' draft.

Here you'll find *The Reach Restaurant and Bar* right on the water's edge while across the street is *Valentines Yacht Club Inn* and its dining room (reservation required for dinner). The marina can arrange a laundry take out service for you. About a mile south of Valentines is the *Harbour Island Club and Marina* nestled among beautiful shade trees on a grass covered hillside. The marina sells diesel and gas 7 days a week, can accommodate vessels with a beam of 23' and a draft of 9', and is home to the *Devil's Backbone Bar and Restaurant*. Guests have access to a fresh water pool at the clubhouse, showers, and cable TV. The marina can also arrange laundry service and golf cart rental (you can also do your own laundry at the *Seaside Laundromat*).

Between the two marinas lies the swank *Romora Bay Club and Marina* boasting one of the best views on the island. On site are *Sloppy Joe's Bar* and *Ludo's Restaurant*. One of the most peculiar (and popular) places in town is the *House of Assembly*. Just a block up and inland from Valentines is a large shady tree with all kinds of lights draped on its lower branches. But what catches your eye is the number of knickknacks and hand painted signs placed there by Brilanders and visitors. Clichés, jokes, Psalms, words to live by, you'll find them all here and perhaps a few local Brilanders in the chairs and hammocks around the place.

Navigational Information

Harbour Island is big with sportfishermen who use the southern entrance for speedy access to the deep waters off the shores of Eleuthera. There are two entrance channels south of Harbour Island, one I call the northern route and one I call the southern route, both are shallow and tricky. These routes are a little trickier than the Devil's Backbone, it's harder to read the depths here, but they are less dangerous in general. The northern route will take a 5' draft at high tide. Vessels with drafts over 3½' should wait for high tide to attempt the northern route. The southern route can take a 5' draft at low tide but there is a narrow spot where you must thread between two shallow banks that are less than 100'-150' apart.

To exit via the northern channel, head south from the anchorage at Dunmore Town and round the first highly visible sandbar that stretches westward from the southwestern end of Harbour Island as shown on Chart EL-23. From the western shore of Harbour Island head for a waypoint at 25° 28.42' N, 76° 38.90' W (the inner waypoint on the N route), where you can take up a course of 80° which will bring you to the southwestern tip of Harbour Island. This will bring you over the deepest water to a waypoint at the southern tip of Harbour Island at 25° 28.50' N, 76° 37.81' W (the outer waypoint on the northern route). A draft of 5' can go through here with no problem at high tide but be careful not to steer too far north or south of your course or you will find yourself in shallower water. A 6' draft could work its way through here with a good high tide but the first two hundred yards closest to the first waypoint are the shallowest and you will have to zigzag and feel your way through here.

To head out the southern channel, head south from Dunmore Town and pass to the west of the highly visible sandbar, passing between it and Cistern Rock. Follow the curve of the sandbank around to the inner waypoint. You will have to eyeball this route. The curve of the route basically follows the curve of the bay. Steer between the two shallow banks staying over the green spot (the brown and dark areas are shallow grassy bars) that is marked by small white floats (one on either side) at the time of this writing, and head towards the outer waypoint and then out into the North Atlantic Ocean.

Vessels wishing to use the above mentioned entrances south of Harbour Island from the *North Atlantic Ocean* should head to a waypoint at 25° 28.70' N, 76° 37.30' W, which will place you approximately ½ mile to the east/northeast of Whale Point as shown on Chart EL-23. Enter the cut, then, slightly favoring the Harbour Island shore being careful to avoid the shallows stretching northward from Whale Point. Once inside head to the outer waypoint for either the northern or southern route, whichever one you plan to use.

When running the above routes in reverse, for the northern routes, head approximately 260° from the outer waypoint towards the inner waypoint. When within a boat length or two of the piling round the piling to starboard and take up your course to clear the sandbar south of the Harbour Island anchorage.

If running the southern route, take up a position at the outer waypoint and head for the inner waypoint. The inner waypoint lies between two shallow banks about 100'-150' apart. The ability to read the water is necessary here. From the inner waypoint follow the deeper water around to pass between Cistern Rock and the shallow bank to your starboard side. Once clear of Cistern Rock head for the anchorage of your choice.

House of Assembly, Harbour Island

Photo by Author

Cat Island

Ports of Entry: Smith's Bay, New Bight, Airport
Fuel: *Hawk's Nest Resort*
Haul-Out: None
Diesel Repairs: Ask at *Hawk's Nest Resort*
Outboard Repairs: Arthur's Town
Propane: Check at *Hawk's Nest Resort*
Provisions: Arthur's Town, New Bight, Old Bight,
   Orange Creek
Important Lights:
   Bennett's Harbour: Fl W ev 4 sec
   Smith's Bay: Fl W ev 4 sec
   Devil Point: Fl W ev 5 sec

The original Lucayan name for Cat Island was *Guanima,* but after the time of the Spanish explorers the island was called *San Salvador*. Some of the older families still retain land titles referring to the island by that name. Some of these same older residents insist that Columbus' first landfall was at Cat Island instead of the more widely accepted San Salvador. Cat Island acquired its current name in the 18th century, some say the island was named after William Catt, a little known pirate or British sea captain, depending on whose side you take. Another opinion is that the island was named after the hordes of feral cats that the English discovered on the island in the 1600's, descendants of tame cats orphaned by the Spanish in their quest for gold. In the 1700 and 1800's the island was home to many fairly successful Loyalist cotton plantations.

Cat Island, one of the finest agricultural producers in The Bahamas, is approximately 45 miles long, from Orange Creek in the north to Port Howe in the south, and the island averages about 4 miles in width. Cat Island is akin to Eleuthera in that it is bordered by the North Atlantic Ocean along its windward eastern shore, while the leeward western shore sits on a large shallow bank with many possibilities for lee anchorages.

The culture of Cat Island is very traditional, some residents still cook in outside ovens. Cat Islanders are warm, friendly, and very proud of their island. Tradition dictates that when the last of a generation dies his house is left for the spirit to reside in and the remaining family members gather stones from the site to construct a new dwelling. Elsewhere, particularly in the northern end of the island, homeowners place spindles atop their houses to keep harm from befalling anyone who resides there, a lightning rod for evil spirits of sorts. Many believe that the spirits of the dead still walk Cat Island. Obeah, a form of magic, is still practiced on Cat Island though most residents won't talk about it except in covert whispers and only if they know you. Many Cat Islanders are hesitant to enter the inland blue holes, possibly due to the stories of monsters lurking within or perhaps because things floating in the hole one week are found in the Atlantic the next week. Bush medicine is widely practiced and the people of Cat Island are known for their longevity, less so today than two centuries ago when a certain Daddy Sundown died in 1810 at the young age of 120.

One of the traditional types of music of Cat Island (as well as most of the islands of The Bahamas) that you will likely hear on Cat Island is the well known *Rake n' Scrape*. The instruments may consist of, but are not limited to, a bass, similar to an American washtub bass and made of a length of wood, an old tin tub, and a piece of fishing line, a rhythm section containing a conch shell horn, a harmonica which is just a paper covered comb, a concertina, and a carpenter's saw scraped with a piece of metal. Setting the beat is the smoking drum made out of goatskin with a flame inside to heat it up.

Although far from remote, Cat Island is seldom visited mainly due to its lack of all weather harbors and protection from fierce northers. The only true protection being at Bennett's Harbour, Smith's Bay, and in Hawk's Nest Creek although smaller, shoal draft vessels may find shelter in some of the extensive creek systems along Cat Island's western shore. In prevailing winds, cruising Cat Island's western shore is truly pleasurable. Even if the wind is blowing 20 knots or more, you can sail right in the lee of the land ½ mile or less offshore in most places and sometimes within 50 yards of the shoreline in 9' of water. There are only three large sandbars to avoid, one at Hawk's Nest Point, another at Bonefish Point, and the largest at Alligator Point.

There are no propane filling facilities on Cat Island, all tanks must be shipped to Nassau by mailboat for filling.

Approaches to Cat Island

From Calabash Bay, Long Island, Hawk's Nest Point bears 007° at a distance of 31.1 nautical miles.

From Conch Cay Cut at George Town, Exuma, Hawk's Nest Point bears 34° at a distance of 38.8 miles. If approaching Hawk's Nest Point from Conception Island, beware of the reefs off the southern shore of Cat Island that lie some two miles off the land.

Vessels heading north along the western shore of Cat Island should be aware that the drop off to the deeper water of Exuma Sound lies just off Hawk's Nest Point in the south and follows the contour of Cat Island northward staying between 8 and 9 miles to the west of Cat Island. This area is unsurveyed and although deep reefs exist all along the drop off, there may be some shallow heads or reefs also. Likewise, there may be any number of shallow heads or reefs inshore of the drop off between the 10-fathom line and Cat Island's western shoreline. Caution is advised when traversing this area.

The vast majority of cruisers visiting Cat Island do so from south to north as Spring approaches and the chance of a frontal passage is lessened. We too shall visit Cat Island in that direction.

The Southern Coast

The southern tip of the "foot" of Cat Island was a lair for pirates and wreckers. Stretching from Columbus Point at the "heel" to Devil's Reef at the "toe," the southern coast was treacherous to shipping. Between Columbus Point and Devil's Point is the deceptively named Port Howe. It is not a port as the name implies, it is really no more than a mass of jagged coral where wreckers once lit fires to lure passing shipping into contributing to their economy. It is said that the buccaneer Arthur Catt used these same wreckers for his piratical schemes. Port Howe was named after Admiral James Howe, the first English Commander during the Revolutionary War. Today Port Howe has an airstrip and it is more noted for its coconut palms and lush pineapple fields. An interesting stop is the ruins of the *Andrew Deveaux Plantation*. Col. Andrew Deveaux earned fame for driving the Spanish from Nassau in 1783, and for this feat was rewarded with 1,000 acres on the southern end of Cat Island. Still intact is the mansion with its hand-pegged kitchen.

Columbus Point is believed to be where Columbus landed on Cat Island. At the roundabout, a landmark on the road that stretches the width of the foot of Cat Island, is a conch shell monument utilizing some 570 conch shells that has been erected here to commemorate that event. West of the roundabout lie McQueens, *Hawk's Nest Creek*, and Devil's Point. East of the roundabout lies Port Howe and Bain's Town, home of Cat Island's *Masonic Lodge* and *The Galleon Bar*. The reef offshore along the 12 mile front is very popular with SCUBA divers. Wall diving begins at 50' and drops to the bottom between 2,000 and 6,000' with a myriad of coral canyons, caves, and tunnels. Nearby *Cutlass Bay* is an adult's only resort with a nude beach.

In Greenwood, nine miles north of Port Howe, the *Greenwood Beach Resort* sits a hundred feet above the Atlantic Ocean and boasts an 8-mile long stretch of pink beach and their restaurant offers fine dining. *The Cat Island Dive Center* is also on premises and offers a full service dive shop facility for those wishing to explore the reefs of Cat Island. They conduct shore dives, night dives, and also provide boats for wall diving off the eastern shore and Port Howe. They accommodate all divers and certification is available with dive gear and accessories for rent.

North of the roundabout is Armbrister Creek where at one time a small railroad came from the other side of Cat Island bringing sisal to be shipped to Nassau. Little remains of it today, almost all the rail was sent to England during World War II for armament manufacture although a few lengths can be found supporting cauldrons in backyard kitchens. The nearby *Pilot Harbour Restaurant* offers Cat Island seafood and boasts a beautiful sunset view from its waterfront location. Dean's Wood, just east of the road, contains what is left of a government forestation project from the 1930's. Madeira (mahogany) trees were planted to make furniture and some still remain in the wild.

Standing upon a crest above the *Atlantic* Ocean near the roundabout, about 500' off the road, are the remains of an octagonal fortress divided by a double-faced chimney. This was used as a lookout to signal islanders when pirates were approaching so they could run to nearby caves and hide. It is also said that it was used by pirates scanning the waters for passing prey. There are tales of pirate gold buried here.

South of Cat Island in the mouth of *Exuma Sound* lies the *Tartar Bank*. The *Tartar Bank* is a huge underwater mountain, which rises to within 7 fathoms of the surface from the surrounding depths. The top of the bank is only a few hundred yards in diameter and the walls slope away from it like a cone. This creates some excellent diving opportunities for the SCUBA enthusiast, but you must be wary of the currents. The tidal action in the mouth of *Exuma Sound* creates strong currents that swirl around and over the bank and even the most experienced divers should exercise the utmost caution when diving in this area. Skippers too should be alert as to dangerous sea conditions on the bank when wind and tide oppose. Needless to say the fishing in this area is superb.

Hawk's Nest Creek

Hawks Nest Point-1 nm W of point:
24° 08.55' N, 75° 32.45' W

Navigational Information
At the very toe of the "foot" of Cat Island, is Hawk's Nest Point and Hawk's Nest Creek. The creek will take 6' over the bar at low water, but it shallows quickly once past the marina. As you approach McQueen's the water even gets too shallow for most dinghies. Hawk's Nest is one of the oldest British settlements on Cat Island, being originally settled in the 1600's but later destroyed by Pirates in 1717.

Hawk's Nest Creek may well be an important stop on your Cat Island cruise. The creek and marina offer excellent protection from frontal passages and almost anything short of a hurricane, but the holding in the creek is questionable. If really strong winds threaten, I would rather get a slip in the marina than try to anchor in the creek.

A waypoint at 24° 08.55' N, 75° 32.45' W, will place you approximately ¾ mile west of the entrance to Hawk's Nest Creek as shown on Chart CT-1. Contact the marina on VHF ch. 16 if you have any questions about entering their channel. The outer edge of the channel lies just north of the offlying rock and is marked by a red and a green floating buoy. Pass between the two, remember *red, right, returning*, and head up the creek keeping the conspicuous jetty to port. There is a shallow spot at the mouth of the entrance channel with 6' at low water and another spot about 150 yards further in with the same depth. Once past the end of the jetty the marina's fuel dock will be immediately to port. Just past this dock the marina basin opens up to port with 10 slips accommodating drafts up to 7½'.

If you wish to anchor in the creek, head upstream past the marina and anchor wherever your draft will allow. A 5' draft can work up stream a good way and shallow draft vessels even further. I must caution you about anchoring in Hawk's Nest Creek. The bottom is very, very rocky, and it's hard to get an anchor to set in the thin sand. As if that was not enough, the strong current threatens to drag you along with it; there are countless stories of skippers who have dragged their anchors in this creek. The further up stream you go, the better the holding, but not much better. Make sure your anchor is well set, dive on it if you can before you turn in for the night. And don't forget the bug juice, this anchorage is notorious for those vile, biting insects we all love so much.

What You Will Find Ashore
The Hawk's Nest Club and Marina offers 10 slips, 2 moorings, diesel and gas, water, ice, showers, and full electric hookups. There is a washer and dryer at the resort, but if you don't feel like doing your own laundry the staff can handle it for you for a small fee. Bicycles and golf carts are complimentary for marina or resort guests and the resort also rents cars and scooters. The office at the resort has a phone and fax for those who need to keep in touch. If you would like some fresh baked goodies ask at the marina office. The marina store has a few basic marine supplies, a book swap, and a video lending library. Propane tank refills can be arranged by the marina, but the tanks must be sent to Nassau for filling on the weekly mailboat from Smith's Bay and this can take some time. The dining room at the resort has a beautiful waterfront view and serves up some extraordinary cuisine. Folks come from all over the island, even from the other resorts to sample the dining at the *Hawk's Nest Resort*. The resort has 10 rooms and one 2 bedroom house for rent, all equipped with satellite TV. For more information call them on VHF ch. 16 or by phone at 242-357-7257. The resort has a fully equipped dive facility on site with a compressor and dive gear for rent. They also have a 26' boat (with captain) available for dive or fishing charters. If you would like a fishing guide contact the marina office and ask for Nathaniel Gilbert or one of their other excellent guides. The resort can also handle your request for bait fish. Bonefishermen will love the upper reaches of Hawk's Nest Creek.

At the entrance to Hawk's Nest Creek are two small houses on the northern shore. The old, gray, ramshackle, three story house is said to have

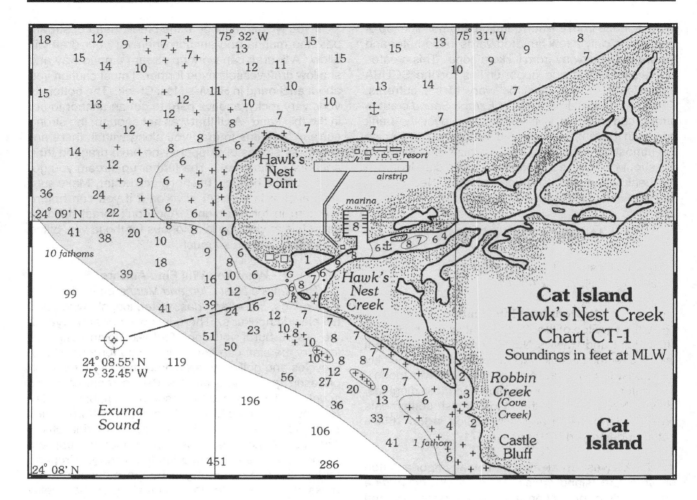

Cat Island
Hawk's Nest Creek
Chart CT-1
Soundings in feet at MLW

Entrance to Hawk's Nest Creek and marina

Photo Courtesy of Paul Harding,
Safari Seaplanes

hosted the ex-Panamanian dictator and convicted drug smuggler Manuel Noriega during the years when this part of Cat Island, due to its secluded airstrip, was heavily into a positive cash flow. The structure today is unsafe to enter but if you look inside you may see the false floors that were torn up by drug agents when they closed down this hive of activity over a decade ago.

The Bight

Bonefish Point-¾ nm SW of western tip of shoal:
24° 16.50' N, 75° 28.90' W

New Bight-¾ nm SW of Batelco Tower:
24° 16.75' N, 75° 25.75' W

Old Bight-¾ nm NW of anchorage:
24° 13.40' N, 75° 25.20' W

Navigational Information
Heading north and east from Hawk's Nest Creek, you must clear the small sand bar off the northwestern tip of Hawk's Nest Point (Chart CT-1 and CT-2) to continue east. Once past the bar you can head directly for New Bight, Fernandez Bay, on continue along the coast to Old Bight staying ¼ mile offshore.

About 5 miles northeast of Hawk's Nest Point, situated on a hillside overlooking the long beach at the southern end of The Bight, is McQueen's as shown on Chart CT-2. The homes are very traditional, stone and thatched roofs, and the inhabitants are primarily Rolles from Exuma. Pre-Columbian Lucayan cooking areas were found in the vicinity of McQueen's. You can tuck in close to anchor off the beach at McQueen's, but watch out for the small patch reefs and shallow heads just offshore. They are easily seen and avoided. Never try to come in close to this shore at night.

At the south end of The Bight, in the crook of the "foot" of Cat Island, is the community of Old Bight. As shown on Chart CT-3, a waypoint at 24° 13.40' N, 75° 25.20' W, will place you approximately ¾ mile northwest of the anchorage area off Old Bight as shown on Chart CT-3. Head in to the beach in prevailing winds as far as you can and drop the hook in excellent holding sand. Many cruisers heading northbound from George Town make this their first stop. Never anchor here in strong winds from southwest to northeast.

What You Will Find Ashore
Old Bight is home to the old *St. Francis of Assisi Catholic Church*, which was also built by Father Jerome who also built *The Hermitage* at New Bight (read a little further in this section for more information on Father Jerome). The church's Gothic facade, frescoes, and detailed interior sculptures are quite

Cat Island
Hawk's Nest Creek
to Whale Creek
Chart CT-2
Soundings in feet at MLW

impressive. Old Bight is also home to a high school and a government clinic. For those wishing to spend money, Old Bight has a number of shops including *Winniefred Dry Goods and Straw Mart, Jade's Unisex Beauty Parlour*, and *The Corner Drugstore*. For groceries you can pay a visit to *Southern Food Fair* and *Dawkin's Food Store*. For dining out try the *Peter Hill Restaurant, Pilot's Harbour, Beaches Delight*, the *Pass me Not Restaurant and Pool Parlour*, and *C.A.*

Rolle's Bar. The largest goat farm in The Bahamas, the *Mango Hill Ranch*, is located here in Old Bight. One mile south of the road to Greenwood, look up the *Straw Lady of Cat Island* for excellent straw work. Access to Old Bight is via Old Bight Landing.

Navigational Information
New Bight is the capitol of Cat Island and sits at the northern end of The Bight. Most cruisers stay

Cat Island
Whale Creek to
Fernandez Bay
Chart CT-3
Soundings in feet at MLW

north of the town at Fernandez Bay, but some anchor off the town, where you'll find a good lee anchorage in winds from northeast to southeast as shown on Chart CT-3. Vessels heading northward from Hawk's Nest Point can head straight to New Bight once they clear the sandbar lying northwest of Hawk's Nest Point. Another alternative is to cruise the western coastline of Cat Island staying about ¼ mile offshore. A waypoint at 24° 16.75' N, 75° 25.75' W will place you in The Bight approximately ¾ mile west/southwest of the *Batelco* tower. Anchor wherever you choose off the town. There is no longer an active navigational light at The Bight, the *Batelco* tower more than makes up for its loss though, it is a great landmark, day or night.

What You Will Find Ashore

At the head of the dock, under the *Batelco* tower, is the *Government Administration Building* and the *Batelco* office. Just south of the dock is the *Bluebird Restaurant and Bar*. Across the street are the ruins of the old *Armbrister Plantation*, easily seen from the waterfront. These are the ruins of the great house of Henry Hawkins Armbrister, which was burned by slaves during a revolt during those heady days prior to emancipation. The house was actually pre-Loyalist period, it was built in the 1760's.

The local hotel, *The Bridge Inn,* offers 12 rooms at reasonable rates and has a restaurant on premises. You can access town by using the town dock located by the *Batelco* tower. In town you will find the *Commissioner's Office* and police station in the *Government Building* and nearby, a *Shell* gas station.

You can land your dinghy at the government jetty or on the long white beach off town. In town you can find plenty of places to spend your money such as the *New Bight Food Store* (the best grocery on the southern side of Cat Island), the *Honourable Harry Bethel's Wholesale Bar*, *Idelle Dorsete's Convenience Store* (fresh bread here), *Virie McKinney's Convenience Store*, the *Sweet Things Confectionery*, and *Romer's Mini Mart*. Most of these places are on the main road north of the *Batelco* tower.

One of the most interesting places in The Bahamas, *The Hermitage*, is probably the most noted tourist attraction on Cat Island. *The Hermitage* is situated just outside of New Bight atop 206' high *Mt. Alverna* (sometimes called *Mt. Comer*) the highest point of

land in The Bahamas. *The Hermitage* is a monument to the faith of one man, John Hawes, known as Father Jerome. Father Jerome, born in 1876, spent five years studying at the *Royal Institute of British Architecture* before entering *Lincoln Theological College* to become an Anglican Minister. In 1911, Father Jerome went to Rome to study three years for the Catholic Priesthood. He built both St. Paul's and St. Peter's Churches in Clarence Town, Long Island (see the chapter *Long Island, Clarence Town*). He later went to Australia to pursue the callings of his faith as a bush priest, but when it came time to retire he chose Cat Island. Father Jerome received permission from the Catholic Bishop in Nassau to retire on Cat Island as a hermit and in 1939 he arrived and surveyed *Mt. ALverna*. In 1940 he began construction of *The Hermitage*, a miniature replica of a European Franciscan Monastery. Father Jerome built the entire structure by himself out of native rock including the *Stations Of The Cross*. He chose a place where he could look to the east and see the cobalt blue of the Atlantic Ocean and to the west where he could gaze upon the emerald and turquoise waters of the banks. Father Jerome lived here until his death at age 80. He is buried beneath *The Hermitage* that he so lovingly built with his own hands. *The Hermitage* is only a 20 minute-walk from town; after you pass the portal inscribed "*Mount Alverna*" take the path that bears off to the right and winds straight up the hill past the *Stations Of The Cross*. You must signal your approach by striking a stone on a piece of scrap metal left hanging there for that purpose at the turnoff.

Just north of New Bight is Freetown, basically a suburb of New Bight (along with Pigeon Bay and Doud's), and where car rentals are available at the *New Bight Service Station*, the *Shell* station next to *Lorry's Fashion Store*. You can call them on VHF ch. 16 (*New Bight Service*), and inquire about a mechanic here if you need one. Just north of Freetown is a straw market in the little blue wood store next to the *Last Chance Bar*. *The Bridge Inn*, famous for its Bahamian fare and Saturday night dances, has 12 rooms with private baths and television. The interior of the inn is decorated with handsome murals of fish and marine life and one panel depicts some of Cat Island's history. Freetown was settled by freed slaves, actually they were put on ships to be sold into slavery but were rescued enroute and settled on Cat Island, never really being sold into slavery. Just north of Freetown lies the *Cat Island International Airport*. In Doud's you can dine at the *Two Corners Inn*.

Navigational Information

Vessels headed north must detour around Bonefish Point and its shallow bar that stretches about a mile southwest of the point. This bar actually starts well to the east at the north end of The Bight as shown on Chart CT-3. A waypoint at 24° 16.50' N, 75° 28.90' W, will place you approximately ¾ mile southwest of the southwestern tip of the bar. From here you can head straight to Fernandez Bay, Smith's Bay, or points north as you wish.

Fernandez Bay

Fernandez Bay-¾ nm W of:
24° 19.10' N, 75° 29.55' W

Fernandez Bay is home to the *Fernandez Bay Village Resort* and has one of the most beautiful beaches on Cat Island. Fernandez Bay has been in the Armbrister family, one of the oldest families on Cat Island, since the 1780's, although the resort has only been open a little over 40 years. Jacqueline Onassis once stayed aboard her yacht just offshore here. The resort is a well-laid out series of villas, each with a kitchen and maid service, and guests can take their choice of activities such as snorkeling, windsurfing, skiing, or sailing. A divemaster on premises leads SCUBA divers and snorkelers to deep-water reefs some 7 miles west of Fernandez Bay. Among the features are coral heads 100' in diameter and wall diving in water from 70'-100' deep. Certifications and dive gear rentals are also available for guests of the resort. The restaurant offers fine dining serving breakfast, lunch, and dinner (with reservations by noon), an open-air beach tiki-bar is simple to use, it works on the honor system, make your drink, sign your name, and pay later. The resort also has a book-swap that you are welcome to use.

Navigational Information

The anchorage off the horseshoe shaped beach at the *Fernandez Bay Village* resort is easy to enter and offers good holding in 8' over a sandy bottom. As shown on Chart CT-4, a waypoint at 24° 19.10' N, 75° 29.55' W, will place you approximately ¾ mile west of the entrance to Fernandez Bay. Steer eastward between the northern tip of the bay and the small, unnamed rock in the middle of the entrance, slightly favoring the north side of the channel. The best holding is in the northern end of the bay and if you head too far to the east the bottom gets rocky and the holding is poor. If your draft is not too deep, less

than 6', you can tuck in close to the northern shore if west and northwest winds threaten. Although you can anchor in the southern part of Fernandez Bay to escape southerly winds, the bay is not a pleasant place to be in the prelude to a frontal passage. If the wind is forecast to be strong out of the south to west, a better place to be would be north about a mile at Smith's Bay (see the next section: *Smith's Bay*). If you have a draft of less than 3', and bad weather threatens, you might be able to work your way in over the bar at high tide into Armbrister Creek where some local fishing boats are moored. There are a couple of spots inside the creek where the depths are 3' at low water but the entrance is about 1' at low water. Sound the entrance carefully before attempting to enter.

What You Will Find Ashore

Fernandez Bay Village Resort has gotten a bad reputation from cruisers over the years. If you've cruised these waters at all you've probably heard tales that the resort is unfriendly towards cruisers and that the management does not want cruisers to stop here. Actually they don't mind cruisers stopping here and taking advantage of the common area, restaurant, and bar, as long as the skippers and crews don't abuse what they use. The problem concerning their bad rap relates to those cruisers who have misused the facilities at Fernandez Bay, been rude to the staff, and been anything but honorable at the honor bar. Over the years this would tend to make anyone less than a Saint wince whenever a boat enters the

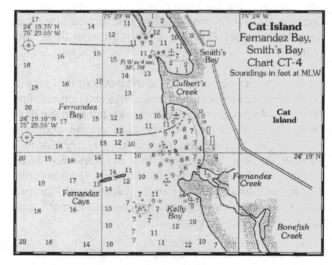

anchorage. Perhaps that is why some members of the staff, a few of whom are former cruisers, are not exactly enthusiastic when greeting incoming boaters. I would like to take a moment to look at both sides of this sad state of affairs. The cruisers and the Resort need to take a few steps in each others sandals and perhaps all will walk away happier. I am not trying to repair the damage, let's just say I'm trying to make each side aware of the other's point of view. Let's start with the boaters. Okay boaters, let's pretend that you are the resort managers and look at this from their viewpoint. If you're not interested, skip the next two paragraphs.

When I first started cruising I was quite naive. I thought all cruisers lived in a sort of symbiosis with Mother Nature. To me it seemed like the logical way to live. Man, was I wrong! Many cruisers haven't a clue about living in sync with their surroundings. That seems to be one of the problems here at Fernandez Bay. The bay is small and really doesn't get a lot of flushing action. The resort asks that cruisers use their holding tanks when anchored in the bay as the waste washes up on shore if discharged overboard. Right on the resort's front yard so to speak. Some boaters throw all sorts of trash overboard such as eggshells or organic debris from meals, all of which washes up on the resort's beach. On the other hand don't walk up to the resort and dump your garbage into a bin, the resort will not dispose of boater's garbage. Once a cruiser asked to rinse off at the outside shower, which is used by guests to rinse off after swimming off the beach. The manager graciously said yes, but later, when she looked down to the waterfront, the cruiser was soaping up and taking a full-fledged shower. This is a resort, they have guests, and guests do not want to see this. The resort is not here for the boaters, their guests are their livelihood.

Some cruisers tend to treat all people who work with the public as servants. More than a few times boaters have entered the office with no hellos, no good mornings, no introductions, and said that they needed to use the phone or fax, that it was important, and that it needed to be done now! The resort is a small, family-run operation. "A little manners goes a long way!" as the staff says. The honor bar, it's a wonderful thing. yet some cruisers have sat there for hours, getting happier by the minute, and when it comes to pay the bill they claim that they only had a couple of beers. The resort has a common area under the casuarinas where all the deck chairs are and boater are welcome to use this area and relax. The hammocks are to be saved for guests and the guest areas off to either side of the common area are for guests only. Many boaters simply make themselves at home and wander aimlessly around the grounds. What must the resort do? Hire a security guard?

I hope the resort staff can see fit to place themselves in the topsiders of the visiting yachtsmen for a moment. Not all cruisers have bad manners. Not all cruisers have evil intentions. No matter how much you have been abused, the resort must not indict all cruisers for the actions of a few. The innocent must be accorded the benefit of a doubt. Some of us would like to walk up to your establishment, hoping to make use of your bar and restaurant, and receive a genuine welcome. I am not suggesting any answers. The problem exists and it is up to both the cruisers and the resort to work at it to satisfy each other, the resort is not going away and cruisers will always be stopping here.

If Fernandez Bay is not where you wish to stop, there is an excellent anchorage just south of Fernandez Bay called Kelly Bay. Here you'll have good protection from winds from the north/northeast to the east/southeast. The sandy bottom is excellent holding and the pretty beach is deserted, no one from the resort comes here. The Fernandez Cays are home to a colony of white-crowned pigeons, please don't disturb their fragile nesting sites.

Smith's Bay

Smith's Bay--¾ nm W of:
24° 19.75' N, 75° 29.55' W

This area of Cat Island is heavily agricultural and Smith's Bay is most noted for its government packing house. Prior to its construction in 1971, growers had to ship their produce to Nassau, a headache for all involved necessitating a middleman or family member in Nassau. Now growers receive a check from the packing house, which handles everything involved with its shipment and sale. Smith's Bay residents make their living farming and fishing as do most of the people you will meet along this shoreline. Smith's Bay was once a much larger settlement, which will be obvious when you notice the layout of the buildings. In town there is a tree called the *Passion Tree* because it is said to bleed a red liquid at Easter. Smith's Bay is a *Port of Entry* and there is a *Customs* and *Immigration* office here.

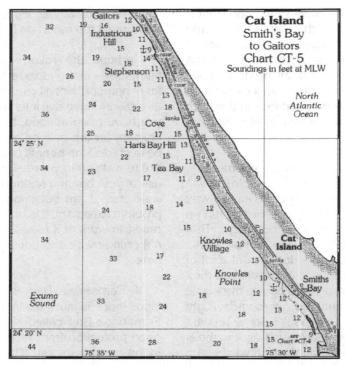

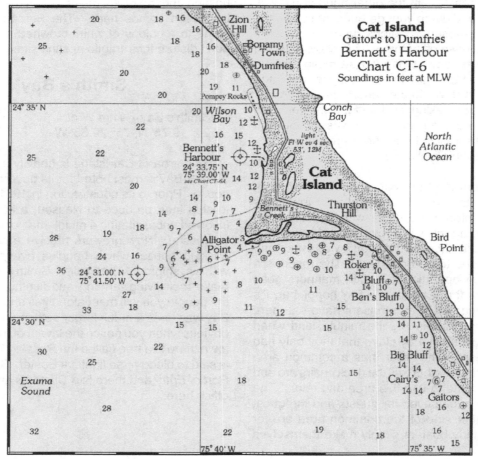

Navigational Information

A waypoint at 24° 19.75' N, 75° 29.55' W, will place you approximately ¾ mile west of the entrance to the harbour at Smith's Bay in Culbert's Creek as shown on Chart CT-4. Head generally eastward to pass between the opening between Cat Island and the small, unnamed cay to the north. There is a lighted range (Fl R) to lead you in. The front range is a white pole topped with an orange daymark and a red light, and the rear range is an inverted triangle as a daymark. You'll have 9' at the entrance and it deepens inside to 11' just off the long concrete dock. If approaching from Fernandez Bay you can stay ¼ mile offshore and you'll be there before you have hardly a chance to warm up the engine or trim the sails.

The only place deep enough to anchor in Smith's Bay is between the dock and the entrance. Smith's Bay offers good protection in a frontal passage but a good size sea can work its way in with westerly winds. If you intend to anchor here to get out of bad weather don't block access to the dock as the mailboat calls in here on a weekly basis, usually on Wednesdays, and other freight boats are in and out at other times. If you need fuel you can make arrangements with the service station in New Bight to deliver to the dock in Smith's Bay.

What You Will Find Ashore

In town, well north of the town dock, you can have a cold one at *Hazel's Hideaway Bar*, sometimes called the *Sea Side Bar,* and other times simply called *Hazel Brown's Bar,* with its distinctive bright green exterior. Owner Hazel Brown offers cold drinks, the coldest beer in The Bahamas she claims, and pleasant company. Four miles to the east along the path is a surfer's beach on the Atlantic shoreline. There is a clinic in Smith's Bay with a resident doctor who resides in town. Shoppers can visit *The Heritage Convenience Store* or perhaps have another cold one at *The Haulover Restaurant and Bar* or the *Wayside Restaurant*. If you wish to stay in town, the *Little Bay Inn* has 6 rooms with private baths and shared kitchens.

Navigational Information

Vessels heading north from Smith's Bay have no dangers if they stay at least ¼ mile offshore. This part of the coast is basically one long lee anchorage. Just tuck in close to shore in prevailing winds and drop the hook wherever you like. Just north of Smith's Bay are a small string of rocks lying about 200 yards or so offshore. They all sit on the edge of the one fathom line with the exception of a small break north of Smith's Bay. Here cruisers can head in towards the southern end of the first beach lying about ½ mile north of the entrance to Smith's Bay. Pass south of the large rock lying off the beach, you must eyeball your way in, good visibility is important. The area between the rocks has 7' at low water and there is up to 9' inside.

What You Will Find Ashore

North of Smith's Bay lies friendly Tea Bay and Knowles Village, with its colorful primary school sitting just a few paces from the water's edge (see Chart CT-5). Tea Bay got its name from the plantation owners who would meet here daily in the shade of a large tree for tea. In Tea Bay you will find *Linnette's Convenience Store*, *The Liquor Store*, and the *Snack Counter and Vegetable Stand*. In Knowles Village you will find the *Bachelor's Restaurant and Bar* serving excellent Bahamian cuisine, *Moncur and Sons Grocery*, and the *Up and Down Bar*. A little further north, The Cove sits approximately midway down the western shore of Cat Island, the halfway point. The town was originally called Jesse Cove and was first inhabited by a Loyalist. Off The Cove on the Atlantic shore are the wrecks of the *Whisky* dating back to the last century and the *S.S. Modegard*, which sank on the reef in 1910. On the western shore, partially hidden by the casuarinas, are some fuel tanks that feed the large power station just inland, a small antenna tower marks the power station.

Further north are the settlements of Stephenson, Industrious Hill, Cairey's, and Gaitor's. Stephenson has an area known as Poitier Village where the few residents claim kinship to their native son, the famous actor, Sydney Poiter. Inland of Stephenson two caves that are home to a healthy population of bats. There is a small cave at the point just above Stephenson on the western shoreline. I have not investigated this cave so I can tell you nothing about it. Perhaps you might check it out and tell me. Any takers? Industrious Hill is not so industrious, it is more agricultural than anything and it's the home of the multi-chambered *Bat Cave*, another dark hole in the ground spelunkers will want to climb into and explore. Cairey's was founded by Eleuthera pineapple farmers in the late 1800's when Cat Island and Eleuthera were the major pineapple growers in The Bahamas.

North of Gaitor's at Ben's Bluff, Chart CT-6, is a small cave mouth on the western shore of Cat Island just above the water's edge. The cave consists of a main tunnel with a large chamber off to the left and an even larger one at the rear of the cave. The entire cave is only 50'-60' long, the largest chamber is about 20' x 40' x 15' high and is home to a large number of bats. You must check this one out, even if you're not a spelunker.

Another worthwhile stop is at the nearby village of The Bluff where you'll find Anita *Wilson's Triple X Restaurant and Bar, Mack's Restaurant*, and the *Island General Shopping Center*, a well-stocked grocery store. *The Pigeon Cay Club* on the beach has 5 rooms and 8 cottages for rent.

Just to the east of Alligator Point, around Roker's, is an excellent anchorage in winds from the north to northeast as shown on Chart CT-6. Here a long white beach (easily seen from far away due to the white sand ridge behind it) stretches east from Alligator Point to Roker's where it follows the curve of Cat Island as it turns southeastward. In northerly winds anchor just south of the long beach, but watch our for the shallow stray heads and small patch reefs that this area is strewn with. Never attempt this at night. In easterly winds you can anchor in the lee of Roker's.

Bennett's Harbour

Alligator Point-½ nm SW of southwestern tip:
24° 31.00' N, 75° 41.50' W

Bennett's Harbour-½ nm W of entrance:
24° 33.75' N, 75° 39.00' W

Navigational Information
Bennett's Harbour, Chart CT-6 and in greater detail on Chart CT-6A, was originally settled by freed slaves and this community of some 400 is spread around a small harbour that is alleged to have hidden pirates in days of old. Today the only regular visitor is the Nassau mailboat, *The North Cat Island Special*, which calls weekly for the fresh produce that can be found in season at the produce exchange. *The Ocean Spray Guest House* offers fine accommodations to the weary traveler. On the water's edge you will find the *Beverage Restaurant and Disco*. Also in town you might wish to stop at the *Remanda Inn Restaurant and Bar*, the *Wayside Convenience Store*.

Vessels heading north for Bennett's Harbour must first round Alligator Point with its long, shallow, rocky bar. A waypoint at 24° 31.00' N, 75° 41.50' W, will place you approximately ½ mile southwest of the shoal's southwest tip. From here you can head generally northeast towards Bennett's Harbour. At Alligator Point, *Bennett's Creek* (also shown as *Pigeon Creek*) is alive with sea life (good bonefishing) and worth the time to explore by dinghy. The mouth of the creek is blocked by a bar with less than 2' at low water. Shallow draft vessels can find a good anchorage inside the creek in 5' of water a bit over ¼ mile from the mouth of the creek at the spot that *Bennett's Creek* winds northward and *Pigeon Creek* continues eastward.

A waypoint at 24° 33.75' N, 75° 39.00' W, will place you approximately ½ mile west of the entrance to Bennett's Harbour. From this position steer generally east and round the spit of land and its offlying shoal and turn to starboard to anchor in the small harbour near the dock as shown on Chart CT-6A. This is a very small anchorage and there is no such thing as swinging room here if there is more than one boat present. Don't block the dock as the mailboat and other freight boats call here regularly. This is a good spot to ride out a front although it gets a little choppy inside when strong winds from the northwest to north push in the seas. There's also a lot of current here, two anchors are a must. Bennett's Harbour has room for two to three vessels of moderate draft, no more than 6' or so. On the eastern shore of the small harbour you will see some shallow ponds, the remnants of the days when the creek system was expanded during World War II to create salt pans. If the weather is settled or out of the northeast to southeast, you'll find a fine anchorage at the northern end of the little cove north of the dock at Bennett's Harbour and south of Pompey Rocks (see Charts CT-6 and CT-6A)..

What You Will Find Ashore
North of Bennett's Harbour is Dumfries. Originally settled by Loyalists and once named Ways Green, Dumfries is home to the dramatic *Great Crown Cave*, said to stretch for over three miles and which should only be visited with the help of an experienced guide from Dumfries or Arthur's Town, ask for Mr. Gaitor in Dumfries. This vast labyrinth and its chambers is a spelunkers delight and you can ask for directions at *C&S Farm Supply* (they also carry hardware, plumbing supplies, and occasionally fresh produce). The path north of the *Gossip Bar* leads to this cave passing

Bennett's Harbour

Photo Courtesy of Paul Harding, Safari Seaplanes

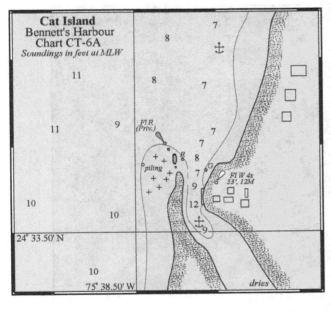

Cat Island
Bennett's Harbour
Chart CT-6A
Soundings in feet at MLW

the occasional *Rake and Scrape* band and their mutton souse is excellent. Here you'll also find the *Stubbs Grocery Store*, and *The Gossip Bar and Restaurant*, which frequently has live music.

Arthur's Town and Orange Creek

Arthur's Town-½ nm SW of:
24° 36.80' N, 75° 41.20' W

North of Bennett's Harbour is Arthur's Town, the commercial center of Cat Island with an 8,000' long airstrip. Arthur's Town was raided by the Spanish in the 1700's and later in that century was settled by Loyalists from America. It is said that Sydney Poitier lived here for a time as a child.

Navigational Information

Boats heading to Arthur's Town from Alligator Point or Bennett's Harbour have deep water all the way with few obstructions save a few shallow heads very

through a huge stretch of mangroves growing to upwards of 40'. After you visit to the earth's innards, you might enjoy stopping at *The Turning Point Club* where the sign warns "Eat Before Drinking." Sage advice that I can testify to. The *Turning Point* features

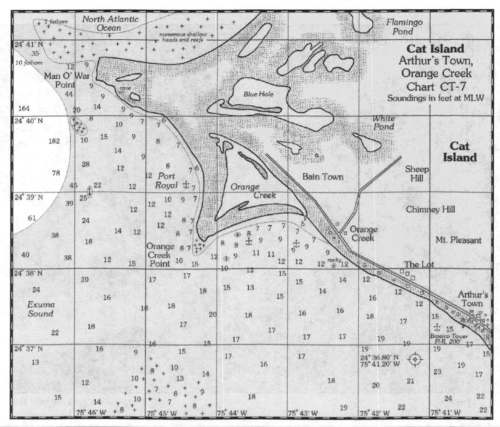

Chart content:

North Atlantic Ocean

Flamingo Pond

Cat Island
Arthur's Town,
Orange Creek
Chart CT-7
Soundings in feet at MLW

Man O' War Point

Blue Hole

White Pond

Cat Island

Sheep Hill

Bain Town

Port Royal

Orange Creek

Chimney Hill

Orange Creek

Mt. Pleasant

Orange Creek Point

The Lot

Exuma Sound

Arthur's Town

Batelco Tower Fl.R. 200'

24° 36.80' N
75° 41.20' W

Arthur's Town

close inshore. The 200' *Batelco* tower makes and excellent landmark day or night. A waypoint at 24° 36.80' N, 75° 41.20' W, will place you approximately ½ mile southwest of Arthur's Town. Vessels can anchor anywhere, north or south of Arthur's Town as shown on Chart CT-7, the water is deep and the holding good. This is a lee anchorage, prevailing winds only.

What You Will Find Ashore

You can land your dinghy in the small basin near the large coconut grove by the *Batelco* tower, or you can tie to the town dock as long as it's not being used. At the head of the town dock is the *Commissioner's Office* and the Police station. These buildings sit right on the large grassy town square called *Christie Park*. Surrounding the square you will also find the post office, the *Batelco* office, the school, and a clinic. Nearby is the *Lover's Boulevard Disco and Satellite Lounge,* the *Hard Rock Cafe Restaurant and Bar*, *Boggy Pond Bar*, *Jabon Convenience Store and Car Rental*, *Campbell's Big Bull Food Store*, *Family Market*, *Gina's Takeaway*, *Nancy's Takeaway*, *E & K Takeaway*, *Dean's Inn*, and *In The Mud*. The pink building with concrete steps leading down to the waterfront just north of the town dock and the school is *Pat and Dell's Cookie Center Restaurant and Takeaway.* Here you can pick up some excellent baked goods and owner Patrick Rolle also rents scooters.

If you need a mechanic or if you just need something welded or fabricated, visit *Captain Black's Welding*. The first weekend in May finds Arthur's Town hosting the *Annual Heritage Festival,* an exhibit of historical artifacts while the first weekend in August you'll find the *annual Cat Island Regatta* in full swing.

The northernmost settlement on Cat Island is Orange Creek, which received its name from the color of the creek when certain light and bottom conditions exist. You can anchor just off the mouth of the creek in 8"-14' of water as shown on Chart CT-7. Some of this bottom is rocky so pick a good sandy spot to drop your hook. Just west of the mouth of Orange Creek is a beautiful long beach that makes for an excellent anchorage in northerly winds.

Orange Creek is important for cruisers because it has a gas station with one of the island's few mechanics. There are two new hotels in Orange Creek, the *Sea Spray Inn* and the *Orange Creek Inn*, both of whom sell groceries and ice while the *Orange Creek Inn* also offers a laundry. In town you'll also find a clinic, a post office, *Magnolia's Bar,* and *Seymore's Bayside Grocery*, and *CJ's Eatery*. The *Orange Creek Food Store* also has washers and dryers on site if you need to do your laundry while anchored here; they can also send and receive faxes for you.

Orange Creek itself has waters that are in some places up to 6' deep but the bar at the entrance restricts entry boats with drafts of less than 3' at high water. The creek has a few scattered wrecks along with some fishing boats anchored inside. As Orange Creek shallows, in return for the loss of depth one gains some excellent bonefishing grounds. Inland, Orange Creek boasts two blue holes whose levels rise and fall with the tide. Their most famous blue hole is known as the *Bad Blue Hole*. This blue hole, off Dickies Road behind Orange Creek, is said to be home to a ferocious monster who likes to eat horses. It has been said that a man and his dog out hunting near this blue hole disappeared thus adding fuel to the fire of the legend. Orange Creek is also home to the *Griffin Cave*, another spelunker's delight. Northward, after the road runs out, sits a lonesome two-story house at Man O' War Bluff. The structure looks as if it is haunted and it is said to be.

Vessels can round Orange Creek Point to anchor at Port Royal in 7'-10' of water with beautiful beaches and a good holding sand bottom as shown on Chart CT-7. This spot is excellent in northeast to east winds. At Man O" War Point is a large cave right at sea level, definitely worth a dinghy ride. North of Man O' War Point is one of Cat Island's most beautiful beaches. The beach is inaccessible by road but not by dinghy. About a mile from Man O" War Point you will see a coconut palm grove. Here you will find the *Drip Cave*, said to be a Lucayan cave.

At the extreme northwestern tip of Cat Island, north of Man O'War Point, is an extensive reef system that offers fantastic opportunities for fishing, snorkeling, and SCUBA diving. A word of warning, the locals say that there are a lot of sharks on the reef so use caution. I only dove on the reefs four times over the years and never saw any sharks, but that doesn't mean that they didn't see me.

Half Moon Cay
(Little San Salvador)

Fuel: None
Haul-Out: None
Diesel Repairs: None
Outboard Repairs: None
Propane: None
Provisions: None
Important Lights: South shore: Fl W ev 2½ sec

West Bay-1 nm W of anchorage:
24° 34.48' N, 75° 58.60' W

Little San Salvador-1 nm S of light:
24° 32.70' N, 75° 56.30' W

Half Moon Cay, lying between Eleuthera and Cat Island, is an excellent stopover in anything but strong westerly weather. If you wonder why the cay would once be called "Little" San Salvador, being as it is so far from the island of San Salvador, you must remember that Cat Island was known as San Salvador for a long period of time.

In early 1997, the island was purchased by the *Holland America Cruise Line* and developed Little San Salvador into what is now known as Half Moon Cay, an out island paradise strictly for guests of their cruise ships. The lovely anchorage at West Bay is no longer a cruiser's haven, in fact the powers-that-be on the island request that if you must anchor here, do so at the northwestern end of the harbour so as not to interfere with their guest's water sports activities. There are still rumors going around that managers of the operation plan to install moorings on the northwestern side of the harbour for visiting cruisers, but as of this writing none are in place. While you are permitted by Bahamian law to walk any beach on any Bahamian Island up to the high water line, the caretakers of Half Moon Cay frown on such activity while cruise ships are in the harbour. When the cruise ships are not present (they're usually in port 2-3 days a week) you can hail *Half Moon Cay* on VHF ch. 16 to request permission to come ashore.

Approaches to Half Moon Cay

From anywhere in the Exumas it is a straight shot across *Exuma Sound* to Half Moon Cay. From *Conch Cut* in Exuma Park, a bearing of 68° for 34.6 miles will bring you to the waypoint that lies approximately 1 mile west of the West Bay anchorage at 24° 34.48' N, 75° 58.60' W, as shown on Chart CA-8. A vessel leaving the north anchorage at Warderick Wells should steer 82° for 37.7 miles while those departing Staniel Cay at *Big Rock Cut* will run 34.3 miles at a heading of 55°. From *Joe Cay Cut* in Pipe Creek, West Bay lies 35.0 miles distant on a course of 62°.

From Bennett's Harbour, Cat Island, a course of 93° for 15.6 miles will place you at a waypoint at 24° 32.70' N, 75° 56.30' W, which lies approximately 1 mile south of the light as shown on Chart CA-8. Vessels heading to Half Moon Cay from Arthur's Town or Orange Creek should head to the area of Bennett's Harbour to take up the course for the waypoint south of Half Moon Cay. I have traveled west/southwest from Orange Creek and there are a lot of shallow patch reefs lying west of the Long Rocks, especially in the area of 24° 36.00' N, 75° 44.60' W. These reefs are easily seen and avoided in good light. All vessels heading to Half Moon Cay from Bennett's Harbour or points north must keep well south of the Long Rocks and Tea Cay. Between Tea Cay and the Long Rocks to its north and east are numerous shallow patch reefs and there are places where there are few if any passages between them. It's best to avoid this area unless you intend to dive on the reefs. Vessels heading to Half Moon Cay from Fernandez Bay should steer 306° for 27 miles to reach the waypoint south of the light. From the waypoint south of Half Moon Cay, boats can head generally northwest, parallel to the shoreline but not too close in to avoid the shallow patch reefs, and then make the turn into West Bay.

For those heading to Half Moon Cay from Eleuthera, simply parallel the southwest shoreline of Eleuthera from Cape Eleuthera southward and once clear of East End Point take up a course of 105° for 9.8 miles to the anchorage at West Bay.

West Bay

Navigational Information

A waypoint at 24° 34.48' N, 75° 58.60' W, will place you approximately 1 mile west of the anchorage area at West Bay as shown on Chart CT-8. From this waypoint simply head straight in and anchor wherever you choose in the northwestern part of West Bay, the holding is great throughout the entire anchorage area. West Bay is an excellent anchorage in even the strongest north to southeast winds but it is not the place to be in anything westerly.

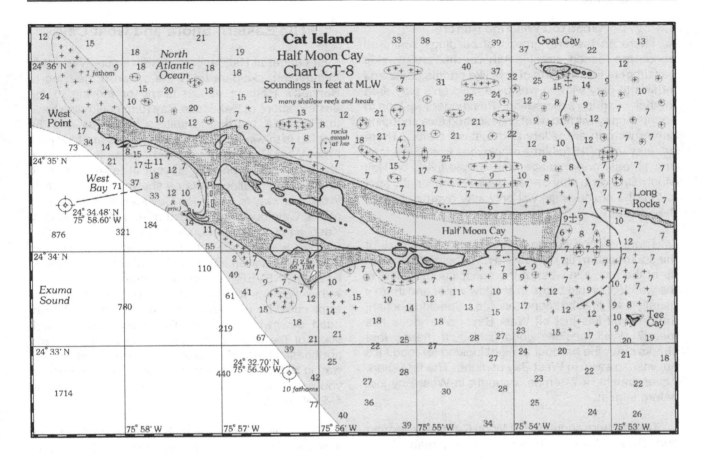

Half Moon Cay: West Bay to
Tee Cay and Long Rocks

Photo Courtesy of Paul Harding,
Safari Seaplanes

What You Will Find Ashore

There are several groups of buildings scattered about the beach area. Ashore the cruise ship passengers find all sorts of toys like paddle boats and jet skis to play with as well as a children's play area for their offspring's recreation. Passengers wishing to spend money will find what is described as a shopping center with an art gallery and "native" crafts. There are upwards of 15 full-time employees from Cat Island and at least one management couple living on Half Moon Cay on a day-to-day basis. One bright spot is that the cruise ships will only stay overnight when they do stop.

There is good fishing on the reefs off the rock at the southeastern tip of West Bay. At the northwestern tip of the bay, just west of the conspicuous rocks, is the wreck of an old barge in shallow water and there's usually a lot of fish around this site. Speaking of fish, the drop off lies just off West Bay. What does this mean? Well, besides good fishing, it means that sharks enter the harbour at night looking for food. It's not wise to swim in West Bay at night. The first shark I ever caught, a 7' lemon, I caught in West Bay just before sunset.

The northern shore of Half Moon Cay is a fisherman and diver's delight. There are many, many large and small reefs lying along the shoreline stretching eastward past Goat Cay and Long Rocks. There is a huge, shallow reef system that stretches northward for over a mile from West Point at the northwestern tip of Half Moon Cay and I have seen some very large lobsters come off these reefs. The long beach on the northern shore of Half Moon Cay is excellent for beachcombing, especially after a northerly blow.

Along the southern shore of Half Moon Cay are quite a few shallow reefs. The main draw on the southern shore is the shallow entrance to the extensive creek system in the interior. East of the creek is a small bay that looks inviting but really isn't, it is very shallow, 1'-2' at low water, and very rocky. Just a little southeast of this beach is the wreck of a large vessel. Part of the bow of this upside down wreck juts above the surface at low tide as shown on Chart CA-8.

The Eastern Shore and Goat Cay

If caught at Half Moon Cay with westerly weather threatening, skippers have the option of heading to Bennett's Harbour at Cat Island or moving to the eastern shore of Half Moon Cay (one could also head to Eleuthera, but that is quite a bit further and the first leg is to windward if westerly winds are blowing). From West Bay, head southward along the southern shore of Half Moon Cay staying at least ½ mile off to avoid the shallow reefs as shown on Chart CA-8. Work your way towards Tee Cay and then steer north of Tee Cay towards the western end of Long Rocks. Keep an eye out for the shallow reefs and bars that you will want to leave to port. You'll have no less than 7' of water on this route if you're careful. Never, I repeat, NEVER attempt this route at night, even with waypoints it would be too dangerous, a small error could be disastrous (if you must leave at night head downwind to Bennett's Harbour staying well south of Tee Cay and the rocks that lie to its east and northeast). Once clear of the reefs you can work your way in to the eastern shore of Half Moon Cay where you can tuck in between the reefs and the shore in 6'-9' of water.

From this area one can head over to Goat Cay which lies a little over a mile north of the eastern tip of Half Moon Cay. I think visiting Goat Cay by dinghy is the best idea, but you can take the big boat over and anchor off the cay in settled weather if you so desire. The anchorage is open to the prevailing east and southeast winds though, only giving a little lee in northerly winds. To head to Goat Cay, follow the directions to arrive along the eastern shore of Half Moon Cay. Passing between the reefs off the northeastern tip of Half Moon Cay and the western tip of the Long Rocks you will have 7' along this route at mean low water. Once between the reefs steer towards Goat Cay, the larger and westernmost of the cays to your north. The water will get progressively deeper as you approach Goat Cay and you will have to zigzag your way through a few shallow reefs that are easily seen and avoided in good visibility. Again, never attempt this at night. Goat Cay is encircled by shallow reefs and the best place to anchor is south of its western end. Dinghy in to the small beach and you can snorkel the nice reefs right off the beach. Goat Cay is home to a flock of white crowned pigeons.

References
And Suggested Reading

A Cruising Guide to the Caribbean and the Bahamas; Jerrems C. Hart and William T. Stone, Dodd, Mead and Company, New York, 1982

A Cruising Guide to the Exuma Cays Land and Sea Park; Stephen J. Pavlidis with Ray Darville, Night Flyer Enterprises, U.S.A. 1994

A History of The Bahamas; Michael Craton, Collins Press, London, 1969

A History of The Bahamas; Michael Craton, San Salvador Press, Ontario, Canada, 1986

American Practical Navigator; Nathaniel Bowditch, LL.D., DMA Hydrographic Center, 1977

Bahamas Handbook and Businessmen's Manual; Sir Etienne Dupuch, Jr., Etienne Dupuch Jr., Publications Ltd., Nassau, Bahamas

Coastal and Offshore Weather, The Essential Handbook; Chris Parker, Christopher Parker Jr., Green Cove Springs, FL. 2003.

Dictionary of Bahamian English; John A. Holm, Lexik House Pub., Cold Springs, NY, 1982

Great Inagua; Margery O. Erikson, Capriole Press, Garrison, NY, 1987

HF Radio E-Mail For Idi-Yachts, Captain Marti Brown, Cruising Companion Publications, Marathon, FL. 2003.

History of Bimini; Ashley B. Saunders, New World Press, Bimini, 2000

Island Expedition, The Central And Southern Bahamas; Nicolas and Dragan Popov, 1988, Graphic Media, Miami, FL.

Mystical Cat Island; Eris Moncur, Northstar Press, Miami, FL, 1996

On and Off the Beaten Path; Stephen J. Pavlidis, Seaworthy Publications, Cocoa Beach, FL, 1997

Out Island Doctor; Dr. Evans W. Cottman, Hodder and Stoughton, London, 1963

Reptiles and Amphibians of The Bahamas; Bahamas National Trust, 1993

Sailing Directions For The Caribbean Sea; Pub. #147, Defense Mapping Agency, #SDPUB147

Secrets of the Bahamas Family Islands 1989; Nicolas Popov, Dragan Popov, & Jane Sydenham; Southern Boating Magazine, May 1989

The American Coast Pilot; Blunt, 1812

The Aranha Report on the Berry Islands; Land and Surveys Dept., Nassau, New Providence, Bahamas 1925

The Bahamas Handbook: Mary Moseley, The Nassau Guardian, Nassau, Bahamas, 1926

The Bahamas Rediscovered; Nicolas and Dragon Popov, Macmillan Press, Ltd. London 1992

The Ephemeral Islands, A Natural History of the Bahamas; David G. Campbell, MacMillan Education, 1990

The Exuma Guide, A Cruising Guide to the Exuma Cays, 3rd Edition; Stephen J. Pavlidis, Seaworthy Pub., Cocoa Beach, FL 1995

The Gentleman's Guide to Passages South; Bruce Van Sant, Cruising Guide Publications, 1989 and 1996

The Ocean Almanac; Robert Hendrickson, Doubleday, NY, 1984

The Pirates Own Book; published by A. & C. B . Edwards, NY, and Thomas, Cowperthwait, & Co., Philadelphia, 1842

The Statute Law of The Bahamas; Revised Edition 1987, Chapter 355

Appendices

Appendix A: Navigational Lights

Navigational lights in The Bahamas should be considered unreliable at best. The actual characteristics of each light may differ from those published here and are subject to change without notice. It is not unusual for a light to be out of commission for long periods of time. Listing of lights reads from north to south.

LOCATION	LIGHT	COLOR	HT.	RANGE
Abacos				
Memory Rock	Fl ev 3 sec	W	37'	11 nm
Barracuda Shoal	Fl ev 4 sec	W		
Indian Cay Rock	Fl ev 6 sec	W	40'	8 nm
Little Sale Cay	Fl ev 3 sec	W	47'	9 nm
Carter's Cay	Fxd	R	200'	25 nm
Angelfish Point (Crab Cay)	Fl ev 5 sec	W	33'	8 nm
Whale Cay	Fl ev 5sec	W	40'	8 nm
Treasure Cay (marina entrance)	Fl	W		
Guana Cay	Fl	W	30'	5 nm
Man-O-War Cay	Fl	W	30'	5 nm
Marsh Harbour	Fl ev 4 sec	G		
Marsh Harbour	Fl	G		
North Parrot Cay	Fl	R		
White Sound	Fl	W		
Elbow Cay Lighthouse	Gp. Fl (5) ev 15s	W	120'	15 nm
Little Harbour	Fl ev 4 sec	W	61'	10 nm
Duck Cay (Cherokee Sound)	Fl	R	29'	6 nm
Hole in the Wall Lighthouse	Fl ev 10 sec	W	168'	19 nm
Rock Point	Fl ev 6 sec	W	35'	10 nm
Channel Cay (Mores Island)	Fl ev 2.5 sec	W	32'	6 nm
Grand Bahama				
Sweetings Cay	Fl ev 5 sec	W	23'	8 nm
GLWW Sea Buoy	Fl	W		
Bell Channel Sea Buoy	Fl ev 2 sec	W		7 nm
Freeport Lighthouse	Fl (3) ev 15 sec	WR	52'	12 nm
Freeport-E channel	Qk. Fl (2)	R		
Freeport-W chnnel	Fl ev 4 sec (2)	G		
Freeport-W jetty	Fl ev 4 sec	G	23'	2 nm
Freeport- W Jetty	Fl ev 4 sec	G	13'	2 nm
Freeport- E Jetty	Fl	R	19'	3 nm
Freeport-lower range	Fxd	G	26'	3 nm
Freeport-upper range	Fxd	G	46'	3 nm
Freeport-Borco Oil Terminal	Fl (3) ev 7 sec	W		5 nm
Freeport-Borco Oil Terminal	Qk. Fl	W		
Pinder Point Light	Gp. Fl (3) ev 5s	WR	64'	12 nm
Riding Point Tower	Fl	R	135'	6 nm
Settlement Point (West End)	Fl ev 4 sec	W	32'	6 nm
Indian Cay	Fl ev 6 sec	W	40'	8 nm
The Biminis				
Great Isaac Lighthouse	Fl ev 15 sec	W	137'	11 nm
North Rock	Fl ev 3 sec	W	40'	8 nm
Bimini Sands Jetty North	Fl ev 5 sec	G	15'	5 nm

LOCATION	LIGHT	COLOR	HT.	RANGE
Bimini Sands Jetty South	Qk Fl	R	15'	5 nm
Gun Cay	Fl ev 10 sec	W	80'	14 nm
Cat Cay Marina (privately mntd.)	Fl ev 4 sec.	W	12'	5 nm
Ocean Cay Range	Qk Fl	W	35'	7 nm
South Riding Rock	Fl ev 5 sec	W	35'	10 nm
The Great Bahama Bank				
Russell Beacon	Fl ev 4 sec	W	20'	8 nm
Mackie Beacon	Fl ev 2 sec	W	20'	8 nm
Sylvia Beacon	Fl ev 4 sec	W	20'	8 nm
Northwest Shoal Buoy	Fl ev 2 sec	W	12'	5 nm
NW Channel Light	Fl ev 3 sec	W	33'	8 nm
The Berry Islands				
Great Stirrup Cay Lighthouse	Gp Fl (2) ev 20s	W	82'	22 nm
Bullock's Harbour	Fl ev 6 sec	W	20'	7 nm
Little Harbour Cay	Fl ev 2 sec	W	75'	9 nm
Chub Point	Fl ev 10 sec	W & R	44'	7 nm
Andros				
Morgan's Bluff channel	Fl	R & G		
Bethel Channel Range	Fl ev 5s	W	60/65'	9 nm
AUTEC G. Murphy Buoy	Fl	W		
Fresh Creek entrance channel	Fl	G	25'	5 nm
AUTEC #1 sea buoy	Fl ev 4 sec	W		
AUTEC #1 channel	Fl ev 4 sec	G #3		
AUTEC #1 channel	Fl ev 4 sec	G #5		
AUTEC #1 channel	Fl ev 4 sec	R #6		
AUTEC #1 channel	FL ev 4 sec	G #7	16'	
High Cay	FL ev 4 sec	W	70'	5 nm
Site 1 & 2 Sea Buoy	Fl	W		
AUTEC #2 sea buoy	Fl ev 4 sec	R		
AUTEC #2 channel	Fl ev 4 sec	G #3	16'	
AUTEC #2 channel	Fl ev 4 sec	R #4	16'	
AUTEC #2 channel	Fl ev 4 sec	R #6	16'	
AUTEC #2 channel	Fl ev 4 sec	G #9	16'	
AUTEC #2 channel	Fl ev 4 sec	R #10	16'	
AUTEC #2 channel	Fl ev 4 sec	G #13	16'	
AUTEC #2 F. range	Qk Fl	W	22'	
AUTEC #2 R. range	Fl ev 6 sec	W	42'	
Site 3 & 4 Sea Buoy	Fl	W		
AUTEC #3 sea buoy	Fl ev 4 sec	W		
AUTEC #3 channel	Fl ev 4 sec	G #3	19'	
AUTEC #3 channel	Fl ev 4 sec	R #4	19'	
AUTEC #3 channel	Fl ev 4 sec	W	33'	
AUTEC #3 channel	Fl ev 4 sec	R #6	16'	
AUTEC #3 channel	Fl ev 4 sec	G #9	16'	
Little Golding Cay	Fl ev 5 sec	W	17'	7 nm
AUTEC #4 channel	Fl ev 4 sec	G #1	19'	
AUTEC #4 channel	Fl ev 4 sec	R #2	19'	
South Bight Sirius Rock	Fl ev 3 sec	W	29'	7 nm
Duncan Rock	Fl ev 3.3 sec	W	37'	6 nm
Tinker Rock	Fl ev 4 sec	W	8 nm	
Green Cay	Fl ev 3 sec	W	33'	7 nm

LOCATION	LIGHT	COLOR	HT.	RANGE
New Providence				
Goulding Cay W end	Fl ev 2 sec	W	36'	8 nm
Fort Fincastle	Fl ev 5 sec	W	216'	18 nm
Paradise Island	Fl ev 5 sec	W or R	68'	W-10 nm, R-5 nm
Nassau W entrance	Fl ev 4 sec	G #1		
Nassau W entrance	Fl ev 4 sec	R #2		
Nassau E breakwater	Fl ev 5 sec	G		9 nm
Nassau W breakwater	Fl ev 5 sec	R	30'	
Nassau W entrance	Fl ev 4 sec	G #3		
Nassau W entrance	Fl ev 4 sec	R #4		
Nassau W entrance	Fl ev 4 sec	G #5		
Nassau W entrance	Fl ev 4 sec	R #6		
Nassau W entrance	Fl ev 4 sec	G #7		
Range Light front	Fxd	G	37'	7 nm
Range Light rear	Fxd	G	61'	7 nm
The Narrows	Fl ev 5 sec	R	12'	2 nm
Porgee Rocks	Fl ev 3 sec	W	23'	5 nm
Chub Rock	Fl ev 5 sec	W	25'	4 nm
Lyford Cay	Fl ev 2 sec	W	25'	4 nm
Coral Harbour - entrance	Fl	R		
East Point	Fl ev 6 sec	W		8 nm
New Providence to Eleuthera				
Porgee Rocks	Fl ev 3 sec	W	23'	5 nm
The Narrows	Fl ev 5 sec	W	12'	2 nm
Chub Rock	Fl ev 5 sec	W	32'	4 nm
Fleeming Channel west	Fl ev 4 sec	R	37'	8 nm
Fleeming Channel east	Fl ev 4 sec	G	32'	10 nm
Eleuthera				
Egg Island	Fl ev 3 sec	W	112'	12 nm
Spanish Wells	Fl ev 2 sec	G	12'	2 nm
Royal Island	Fl ev 5 sec	W	22'	5 nm
Man Island	Gp. Fl (3) ev 15s	W	93'	12 nm
Hatchett Bay	Fl (2 4s) ev 15s	W	57'	8 nm
Governor's Harbour	Fl ev 4 sec	W	40'	8 nm
Poison Point	Fl ev 15 sec	W	38'	8 nm
East End Point	Fl ev 4½ sec	W	61'	6 nm
Half Moon Cay (Little San Salvador)				
South shore	Fl ev 2½ sec	W	69'	13 nm
Cat Island				
Bennett's Harbour	Fl ev 4 sec	W	53'	12 nm
Smith's Bay	Fl ev 4 sec	W	38'	7 nm
Devil Point	Fl ev 5 sec	W	143'	12 nm
Exumas				
Beacon Cay	Fl ev 3 sec.	W & R	58'	8 nm
Elbow Cay	Fl ev 6 sec.	W	46'	11 nm
Dotham Cut	Fl ev 5 sec.	W	36'	8 nm
Galliot Cut	Fl ev 4 sec.	W	50'	7 nm
Conch Cay	Fl ev 5 sec.	W	40'	8 nm
Jewfish Cut	Fl ev 2½ sec.	W	38'	8 nm
Hawksbill Rock	Fl ev 3.3 sec.	W	40'	6 nm

Appendix B: Marinas

Some of the marinas listed below may be untenable in certain winds and dockside depths listed may not reflect entrance channel depths at low water, check with the dockmaster prior to arrival. For cruisers seeking services "Nearby" may mean a walk or short taxi ride away.

MARINA	FUEL	GROCERY	DINING	E-MAIL or WEBSITE
Abacos				
Elbow Cay				
Hope Town Marina	D & G	Nearby	Yes	clubsoleil@oii.net
Hope Town Hideaways	None	Yes	Yes	info@hopetown.com
Lighthouse Marina	D & G	Nearby	Yes	lighthouse@oii.net
Sea Spray Resort	D & G	Nearby	Yes	seaspray@oii.net
Grand Cays				
Rosie's Place	D & G	Limited	Yes	
Green Turtle Cay				
Abaco Yacht Services	D & G	Nearby	Nearby	
Black Sound Marina	None	Nearby	Nearby	
Bluff House	D & G	Yes	Yes	bluffhouse@oii.net
Green Turtle Club	D & G	Nearby	Yes	info@greenturtleclub.com
Leeward YC & Marina	None	Nearby	Nearby	info@leewardyachtclub.com
Other Shore Club	D & G	Nearby	Nearby	relax@othershoreclub.com
Guana Cay				
Baker's Bay Marina	Scheduled to open in 2009			
Orchid Bay Marina	D & G	Nearby	Nearby	
Man O' War Cay				
Man O' War Marina	D & G	Nearby	Yes	mowmarina@hotmail.com
Marsh Harbour				
Boat Harbour Marina	D & G	Yes	Yes	info@abacoresort.com
Conch Inn Marina	D & G	Yes	Yes	themoorings@batelnet.bs
Harbour View Marina	D & G	Nearby	Yes	info@harbourviewmarina.com
Long's Landing	None	Nearby	Nearby	
Mangoe's Marina	D & G	Nearby	Yes	
Marsh Harbour Marina	D & G	Nearby	Yes	jibroom@hotmail.com
Schooner Bay	None	Nearby	Nearby	james@lindroth.cc
Spanish Cay				
Spanish Cay Marina	D & G	Limited	Yes	info@spanishcay.com
Treasure Cay				
Treasure Cay Marina	D & G	Yes	Yes	info@treasurecay.com
Walker's Cay				
Walker's Cay Club	Closed, For Sale, the future of this marina is uncertain			
Andros				
Kamalame Cove	D & G	Yes	Yes	Yeskamalame@batelnet.bs
Lighthouse Marina	D & G	Nearby	Yes	
Berry Islands				
Berry Islands Club	D & G	Nearby	Yes	
Chub Cay Marina	D & G	Yes	Yes	
Great Harbour Cay	D & G	Nearby	Yes	
Grand Bahama				
West End				
Old Bahama Bay Marina	D & G	Yes	Yes	info@oldbahamabay.com

MARINA	FUEL	GROCERY	DINING	E-MAIL or WEBSITE
Lucaya				
Bahama Bay	D & G	Nearby	Nearby	info@bahamiaservices.com
Flamingo Bay YC	None	Nearby	Nearby	info@flamingobayhotel.com
Grand Bahama YC	D & G	Nearby	Yes	info@grandbahamayc.com
Ocean Reef Yach Club	None	Nearby	Nearby	www.oryc.com
Sunrise Resort & Marina	None	Nearby	Nearby	www.sunriseresortandmarina.com
Port Lucaya	D & G	Nearby	Yes	info@portlucayamarina.com
Xanadu Beach	D & G	Nearby	Nearby	info@xanadubeachhotel.com
Deep Water Cay Marina	D & G	Nearby	Nearby	
The Biminis				
North Bimini				
Brown's	None	Nearby	Yes	
Bimini Big Game Club	D & G	Nearby	Nearby	
Bimini Blue Water Resort	D & G	Nearby	Nearby	
Seacrest Marina	None	Nearby	Nearby	
Weech's Bimini Dock	None	Nearby	Nearby	
South Bimini				
Bimini Reef	None	No	Nearby	
Bimini Sands	None	No	Yes	
Cat Cay				
Cat Cay Marina	D & G	Nearby	Nearby	
Cat Island				
Hawk's Nest Resort	D & G	Yes	Yes	info@hawks-nest.com
Eleuthera				
Cape Eleuthera	D & G	No	No	
Davis Harbour	D & G	No	No	
French Leave Marina	None	Nearby	Nearby	info@frenchleaveresort.com
Harbour Island Club	D & G	Nearby	Yes	
Romora Bay Marina	None	Nearby	Yes	
Runaway Bay Marina	None	Limited	Yes	
Spanish Wells Yt. Haven	D & G	Nearby	Nearby	
Valentine's	D & G	Nearby	Yes	
New Providence				
Albany Marina	D & G	Nearby	Yes	marina@albanybahamas.com
Atlantis Marina	D & G	Yes	Yes	www.atlantisresort.com
Bayshore Marina	D & G	Nearby	Nearby	
Brown's Boat Basin	D & G	Nearby	Nearby	
Harbour Central Marina	D & G	Nearby	Nearby	
Hurricane Hole Marina	D & G	Yes	Yes	info@hurricaneholemarina.com
Lyford Cay Marina	D & G	Yes	Yes	
Nassau Harbour Club	D	Nearby	Yes	
Nassau Yacht Haven	D & G	Nearby	Yes	info@nassauyachthaven.com
Paradise Harbour Club	None	Nearby	Yes	
Texaco Fuel Dock	D & G	Nearby	Nearby	

Appendix C: Service Facilities

The area code for all the islands of The Bahamas is 242.

FACILITY	LOCATION	TELEPHONE	VHF CALL OR E-Mail
Boat Towing			
Towboat US	Marsh Harbour, Abaco	367-4600	*www.towboatbahamas.com*
Towboat US	West End, Grand Bahama	543-3925	*www.towboatbahamas.com*

FACILITY	LOCATION	TELEPHONE	VHF CALL OR E-Mail
Car Rentals			
A & A Car Rentals	Marsh Harbour, Abaco	367-2148	
A & P Auto Rentals	Marsh Harbour, Abaco	367-2655	
Alison's Car Rentals	Treasure Cay, Abaco	365-8193	
Andros Beach Hotel	Nicholl's Town, Andros		*Andros Beach*
Avis-Airport	Nassau, New Providence	327-7121	
Avis-Paradise Island	Nassau, New Providence	363-2061	
Avis-West Bay St.	Nassau, New Providence	326-6380	
Big Daddy	South Palmetto Pt, Eleu.		*Big Daddy*
Big Rock General Store	James Cistern, Eleuthera	335-6355	
Bill's Car Rental's	Fresh Creek, Andros	557-5149	
Budget-Airport	Nassau, New Providence	327-7121	
Budget-Paradise Island	Nassau, New Providence	363-3095	
Chickcharnies Hotel	Fresh Creek, Andros	368-2025/6	
Cornish Car Rentals	Treasure Cay, Abaco	365-8623	
Covenant Car Rentals	Murphy Town, Great Abaco	367-4007	
D & E Rent A Car	Love Hill, Andros	368-2454	
D's Minivan Rentals	Marsh Harbour, Abaco	367-3980	
Dollar-Airport	Nassau, New Providence	377-7301	
Dollar-British Colonial	Nassau, New Providence	325-3716	
Dollar-Cable Beach	Nassau, New Providence	327-6000	
Donna Lee Motel & Rest.	Nicoll's Town, Andros	329-2194	
Driver Rent A Car	Nassau, New Providence	394-8551	
Ellis Whymms	Andros Town, Andros	368-6224	
Ethyl's Car Rental	Tarpum Bay, Eleuthera		*Ethyl's Cottages*
Flamingo Car Rentals	Marsh Harbour, Abaco	367-4787	
Friendly Bob's	Powell Pt., Eleuthera		*Friendly Bob*
Griffin's Car Rentals	Governor's Harbour, Eleu.	332-2077/9	
H & L Rentals	Marsh Harbour, Abaco	367-2840	
Hawks Nest Marina	Hawks Nest Pt., Cat Island	357-7257	*Hawks Nest*
Hertz-Airport	Nassau, New Providence	377-6321	
Hertz-Paradise Island	Nassau, New Providence	377-6866	
Jay's Auto Center	Fresh Creek, Andros	357-2764	
K&S Car Rentals	Marsh Harbour, Abaco	367-2655	
Larry Dean's Car Rentals	Hatchet Bay, Eleuthera	332-2568	
Lighthouse Marina	Fresh Creek, Andros		*Lighthouse Marina*
Marine Serv. of Eleu.	Hatchet Bay, Eleuthera	335-0186	*Marine Services*
McKenzie's Car Rental	Treasure Cay, Abaco	365-8849	
Moss Transportation	Nassau, New Providence	393-0771	
Nascov	Deep Creek, Andros	369-5001	
National	Nassau, New Providence	327-8300/1	
New Bight Shell Sta.	New Bight, Cat Island	342-3014	*New Bight Service*
Nixon-Pinder Car Rentals	Governor's Harbour, Eleuthera	332-2568	
PK's Auto Rentals	Rock Sound, Eleuthera	334-4236	
Poinciana Nassau,	New Providence	393-1720	
Rental Wheels	Marsh Harbour, Abaco	367-4643	
Royal Palm Beach Lodge	Kemp's Bay, Andros	329-4608	*Royal Palm*
Runaway Bay Marina	Palmetto Point, Eleuthera	332-1744	*Runaway Bay Marina*
Thrifty Car Rental	Nassau, New Providence	377-0355	
Wilmac Rent A Car	Airport, Great Abaco	367-4313	
Wallace's U Drive	Nassau, New Providence	393-0650	

FACILITY	LOCATION	TELEPHONE	VHF CALL OR E-Mail
Diesel Repair/Parts			
Anthony Martin	Chub Cay, Berry Islands		*Chub Cay Marina*
Asterix	Marsh Harbour, Abaco	367-3166	*Asterix*
Atlantic Equipment	Nassau, New Providence	323-5701	
Bahamas Diesel	Nassau, New Providence		
Bodie's Engine Repair	Marsh Harbour, Abaco	554-9241	
Bradford Yacht & Ship	Freeport, Grand Bahama	352-7711	*Bradford Yacht & Ship*
Captain Black's Welding	Arthur's Town, Cat Island		
Clifford Saunders	Alice Town, North Bimini		*ask at any marina*
Diesel Power	Nassau, New Providence	325-8319	*Diesel Power*
Gratitude Marine	Marsh Harbour, Abaco	367-2480	
Great Harbour Cay Mar.	Bullock's Harbour, Berry Islands		*Great Harbour Cay Marina*
Frank Harding	Nassau, New Providence	393-2181	*Harding Marine*
Hartwell Russell	Marsh Harbour, Abaco	367-2502	
Ingraham's Marine	Nassau, New Providence	323-5835	
Knowles Marine	Grand Bahama	351-2769	
Lightbourne Marine	Nassau, New Providence	393-5285	
Mal-Kemp Marine Co.	Nassau, New Providence	322-7131	
Marine & Land Industries	Freeport, Grand Bahama	352-2219	
Marine Diesel Ltd.	Nassau, New Providence	322-7135	*Marine Diesel*
Marine Garage	Nassau, New Providence	393-3177	
Marsh Hrbr Boat Yard	Marsh Harbour, Abaco	367-4011	
Maura's Marine	Nassau, New Providence	393-7873	
On Site Marine	Spanish Wells	333-4382	*On Site Marine*
Pinder's Marine	Marsh Harbour, Abaco	367-2274	
Pinder's Tune Up	Spanish Wells	333-4262	
Roberts Marine	Green Turtle Cay, Abaco	365-4249	*Roberts Marine*
Sea Services	Marsh Harbour, Abaco	367-6805	
Sunpower Marine, Ltd.	Nassau. New Providence	322-2144	
T & T Garage	Harbour Island, Eleuthera		
Tom Cat Enterprises	Elbow Cay, Abaco	366-0135	
Valentines Marina	Harbour Island, Eleuthera		
Electronics/Electrical			
Andrew's Marine Electric	Marsh Harbour, Abaco	367-2163	*Andrew's Electric*
Bahamas Elect. Lab. Co.	Freeport, Grand Bahama	352-2286	
Bradford Yacht & Ship	Freeport, Grand Bahama	352-7711	*Bradford Yacht & Ship*
Direct Enterprises	Harbour Island, Eleuthera		
Hi-Technology	Nassau. New Providence	322-6918	
Knowles Marine	Grand Bahama	351-2769	
Wellington Pinder	Hope Town, Abaco	366-0106	
Roberts Electrical	Man-O-War Cay, Abaco	365-6020	
Fabrication/Welding			
Abaco Marine Prop	Marsh Harbour, Abaco	367-4276.	
Captain Black's Welding	Arthur's Town, Cat Island		
CJ Welding (MHBY)	Marsh Harbour, Abaco	367-4011	
Curtis Weldin	Freeport, Grand Bahama	352-9840	
George Town Marina	George Town, Exuma	345-5116	*George Town Marina*
Hartwell Russell	Marsh Harbour, Abaco	367-2502	
Island Engineering Co.	Freeport, Grand Bahama	351-8718	*lottie2boys@hotmail.com*
Ken Crosdale Welding	Freeport, Grand Bahama	352-6457	

FACILITY	LOCATION	TELEPHONE	VHF CALL OR E-Mail
Knowles Marine	Grand Bahama	351-2769	
Pop's Welding	Tarpum Bay, Eleuthera		
Progress Welding	Freeport, Grand Bahama	352-5359	
QSL	Freeport, Grand Bahama	352-9198	
R & B Boat Yard	Spanish Wells	333-4462	R & B Boatyard
R.D. Mechanical	Freeport, Grand Bahama	352-7830	
T&I Iron Works	Freeport, Grand Bahama	352-9420	

Generator/Starters

Abaco Starters	Marsh Harbour, Abaco	367-4970	
Atlantic	Freeport, Grand Bahama	352-5981	aep@bahamas.net.bs
Freeport Starter & Gen.	Freeport, Grand Bahama	352-9051	

Haul Out

Abaco Yacht Services	Green Turtle Cay, Abaco	365-4033	Abaco Yacht Services
Bayshore Marina (to 40')	Nassau, New Providence	393-8232	Bayshore Marina
Bradford	Freeport, Grand Bahama	352-7711	
Brown's Boat Basin	Nassau, New Providence	393-3331	Brown's Boat Basin
Edwin's Boat Yard	Man-O-War Cay, Abaco	365-6007	Edwin's Boat Yard
George Town Marina	George Town, Exuma	345-5116	George Town Marina
Harbour Central Marina	Nassau, New Providence	321-3272	Harbour Central Marina
Knowles Marine	Grand Bahama	351-2769	
Marsh Harbour Boat Yd.	Marsh Harbour, Abaco	367-4011	
R & B Boat Yard	Spanish Wells	333-4462	R & B Boatyard

Hull Repair/Painting

Abaco Yacht Services	Green Turtle Cay, Abaco	365-4033	Abaco Yacht Services
Albury Brothers	Man-O-War Cay, Abaco	365-6086	
Bradford	Freeport, Grand Bahama	352-7711	
Brown's Boat Basin	Nassau, New Providence	393-3331	Brown's Boat Basin
Cooper's Marine	Nassau, New Providence	393-7475	
Edwin's Boat Yard	Man-O-War Cay, Abaco	365-6007	Edwin's Boat Yard
George Town Marina	George Town, Exuma	345-5116	George Town Marina
Knowles Marine	Grand Bahama	351-2769	
Marsh Harbour Boat Yd.	Marsh Harbour, Abaco	367-4011	
R & B Boat Yard	Spanish Wells	333-4462	R & B Boatyard
Spanish Wells Mar.	Spanish Wells	333-4035	Sp. Wells Hrdwr. & Mar
Winer Malone	Hope Town, Abaco		

Internet

Airport Business Centre	Nassau, New Providence		
APG Bus. Centre	Nassau, New Providence		
Atlantis Marina (WIFI)	Nassau, New Providence		
Coconut Telegraph	Marsh Harbour, Abaco	365-8836	
Cyber Café-Int'l. Bazaar	Freeport, Grand Bahama	351-7225	
Cyber Café- Port Lucaya	Lucaya, Grand Bahama	374-2839	
Cyber Café- Royal Oasis	Lucaya, Grand Bahama	350-7000	
Digital Sounds	Fresh Creek, Andros	464-3031	sirraldo@hotmail.com
Eleuthera Office Supply	Rock Sound, Eleuthera		seashell@batelnet.bs
Friday's	Nassau, New Providence	323-3341	
Hopetown Wedding	Elbow Cay, Abaco		
Hurricane Hole Marina	Nassau, New Providence		
Internet Café	Nassau, New Providence		
In Touch Data Systems	Freeport, Grand Bahama	351-3160	intouch@coralwave.com
Internet Works	Nassau, New Providence		

FACILITY	LOCATION	TELEPHONE	VHF CALL OR E-Mail
Island Services	Harbour Island, Eleuthera		harbourisland@hotmail.com
ITS	Nassau, New Providence		
Mail Boxes Etc.	Nassau, New Providence		
Man O' War Marina	Man-O-War Cay, Abaco		mowmarina@hotmail.com
Nassau Harbour Club	Nassau, New Providence		
News Café	Nassau, New Providence		
Nippers	Great Guana Cay, Abaco		www.nippersbar.com
Office General	Governor's Harbour, Eleu.	332-2894	dawniep@batelnet.bs
Old Bahama Bay Marina	West End, Grand Bahama	350-6500	info@oldbahamabay.com
Orchid Bay Marina	Great Guana Cay, Abaco	365-5175	www.orchidbay.net
Out Island Internet (OII)	Marsh Harbour, Abaco	367-3006	accounts@abacoinet.com
Port of Call Marina	Marsh Harbour, Abaco		poc@batelnet.bs
Public Library	Marsh Harbour, Abaco		
Public Library	Treasure Cay, Abaco		
Sid's Grocery	Green Turtle Cay, Abaco		
Tikal	Nassau, New Providence		
Westside Business	Freeport, Grand Bahama	348-5033	
Yacht Haven Marina	Nassau, New Providence		

Marine Supplies

FACILITY	LOCATION	TELEPHONE	VHF CALL OR E-Mail
Abaco Hardware	Marsh Harbour, Abaco	367-2827	
Abaco Yacht Services	Green Turtle Cay, Abaco	365-4033	Abaco Yacht Services
Adnil Marine Supplies	Freeport, Grand Bahama	352-1856	
B & D Marine Ltd.	Marsh Harbour, Abaco	367-2522	B & D
Bimini General Store	Alice Town, North Bimini		Bimini General Store
Boat Harbour Marine	Marsh Harbour, Abaco		Boat Harbour Marina
Bradford Yacht & Ship	Freeport, Grand Bahama	352-7711	Bradford Yacht & Ship
Brown's Boat Basin	Nassau, New Providence	393-3331	
Cash Marine Repair	Freeport, Grand Bahama	352-9154	www.cashmarine.com
Cooper's Marine	Nassau, New Providence	393-7475	
Dolphin Marine	Green Turtle Cay, Abaco	365-4262	Dolphin Marine
Edwin's Boat Yard	Man-O-War Cay, Abaco	365-6007	Edwin's Boat Yard
G B Marine Supplies	Freeport, Grand Bahama	351-3442	
Green Turtle Club	Green Turtle Cay, Abaco	365-4271	Green Turtle Club
Harbourside Marine	Nassau, New Providence	393-0262	
Ingraham's Marine	Nassau, New Providence	323-5835	
Lightbourne Marine	Nassau, New Providence	393-5285	Lightbourne Marine
Lighthouse Marina	Hope Town, Abaco	366-0154	
Man-O-War Hardware	Man-O-War Cay, Abaco	365-6011	
Man-O-War Marina	Man-O-War Cay, Abaco	365-6013	Man-O-War Marina
Marine & Land Industries	Freeport, Grand Bahama	352-2219	
Marsh Harbour Boat Yard	Marsh Harbour, Abaco	367-4011	
Marty's Electronics	Jame's Cistern, Eleuthera		
Maura's Marine	Nassau, New Providence	393-7873	Maura's Marine
Montagu Hts. Serv. Ctr.	Nassau, New Providence	393-1160	
National Marine	Marsh Harbour, Abaco	367-2326	
Nautical Marine, Ltd.	Nassau, New Providence	393-3894	
OBS Marine	Freeport, Grand Bahama	352-9246	www.freeportskill.com
Paradise Marine (Xanadu)	Freeport, Grand Bahama		
Pinder's Marine	Deep Creek, Eleuthera	334-8330	Pinder's Marine
R & B Boat Yard	Spanish Wells	333-4462	R & B Boatyard
Roberts Hardware	Green Turtle Cay, Abaco	365-4249	Roberts Marine

FACILITY	LOCATION	TELEPHONE	VHF CALL OR E-Mail
Ron's Marine	Rock Sound, Eleuthera		*Ron's Marine*
Ronald's Marine	Spanish Wells	333-4021	*Ronald's Marine*
Spanish Wells Hrdwr.	Spanish Wells	333-4035	*Sp. Wells Hrdwr. & Mar.*
Standard Hardware	Marsh Harbour, Abaco	367-2660	
Stella Maris Marina	Stella Maris, Long Island	338-2055	*Stella Maris Marina*
Sunpower Marine, Ltd.	Nassau, New Providence	325-2313	*Sunpower Marine*
Top II Bottom	George Town, Exuma		*Top To Bottom*

Outboard Repair

FACILITY	LOCATION	TELEPHONE	VHF CALL OR E-Mail
Abaco Outboard	Marsh Harbour, Abaco	367-2452	*Abaco Outboard*
Abaco Suzuki	Marsh Harbour, Abaco	367-3695	
Abaco Yacht Serv.	Green Turtle Cay, Abaco	365-4033	*Abaco Yacht Services*
Adnil Mar. Supplies	Freeport, Grand Bahama	352-1856	
Albury Brothers	Man-O-War Cay, Abaco	365-6086	
Anthony Martin	Chub Cay, Berry Islands		*Chub Cay Marina*
B & D Marine Ltd.	Marsh Harbour, Abaco	367-2522	*B & D*
Brown's Boat Basin	Nassau, New Providence	393-3331	
Captain Black's Welding	Arthur's Town, Cat Island		
Cash Marine Repair	Freeport, Grand Bahama	352-9154	*www.cashmarine.com*
Chris Saunders	Alice Town, North Bimini		*ask at any marina*
Dolphin Marine	Green Turtle Cay, Abaco	365-4262	*Dolphin Marine*
Great Harbour Cay Mar.	Bullock's Harbour, Berry Islands		*Great Harbour Cay Marina*
Harbourside Marine	Nassau, New Providence	393-0262	
Harding's Supply Centre	Salt Pond, Long Island		
Hartwell Russell	Marsh Harbour, Abaco	367-2502	
Hope Town Marina	Hope Town, Abaco	366-0003	*Hope Town Marina*
Island Marine	Parrot Cay, Abaco	366-0282	*Island Marine*
Johnson's Garage	Harbour Island, Eleuthera		
Knowles Marine	Grand Bahama	351-2769	
Lightbourne Marine	Nassau, New Providence	393-5285	*Lightbourne Marine*
Marine & Land Industries	Freeport, Grand Bahama	352-2219	
Marsh Harbour Boat Yard	Marsh Harbour, Abaco	367-4011	
Lighthouse Marina	Hope Town, Abaco	366-0154	*Lighthouse Marina*
Man-O-War Marina	Man-O-War Cay, Abaco	365-6013	*Man-O-War Marina*
Master Marine	Marsh Harbour, Abaco	367-4760	
Maura's Marine	Nassau, New Providence	393-7873	*Maura's Marine*
Nassau Bicycle Co.	Nassau, New Providence	322-8511/2	
National Marine	Marsh Harbour, Abaco	367-2326	
Nautical Marine Ltd.	Nassau, New Providence	393-3894	
Outboard Shop	Marsh Harbour, Abaco	367-2703	*Outboard Shop*
Pinder's Marine	Deep Creek, Eleuthera	334-8330	*Pinder's Marine*
R & B Boat Yard	Spanish Wells	333-4462	*R & B Boatyard*
Roberts Hrd. & Marine	Green Turtle Cay, Abaco	365-4249	*Roberts Marine*
Ronald's Marine	Spanish Wells	333-4021	*Ronald's Marine*
Sea Horse Marine	Hope Town, Abaco	366-0023	*Sea Horse Marine*
Sp. Wls M&H.	Spanish Wells	333-4035	*Sp. Wells Hrdwr. & Mar.*
Sunpower Mar.	Nassau, New Providence	325-2313	*Sunpower Marine*
Under The Sea Marine	Mangrove Bush, Long Island		
Valentines Marina	Harbour Island, Eleuthera		
Waterways	Man-O-War Cay, Abaco	365-6143	

Propane

FACILITY	LOCATION	TELEPHONE	VHF CALL OR E-Mail
Abaco Gas-Corner Value	Marsh Harbour, Abaco	367-2250	

FACILITY	LOCATION	TELEPHONE	VHF CALL OR E-Mail
BASRA	Nassau, New Providence		BASRA
Blue Flame	Freeport, Grand Bahama	351-1107	
Brown's Hardware	Alice Town, North Bimini		Brown's Hardware
Chacara's Hardware	Harbour Island, Eleuthera		Chacara Hardware
Curry's Food Store	Green Turtle Cay, Abaco	365-4171	
Eleuthera Supply	Governor's Harbour, Eleuthera		Eleuthera Supply
Focol	Freeport, Grand Bahama	352-6771	
Freeport Oil	Freeport, Grand Bahama		
Robert Grant	West End, Grand Bahama	346-6207	
Great Harbour Cay Mar.*	Great Harbour Cay, Berry I.		Great Harbour Cay Marina
Harbour Central Marina	Nassau, New Providence	321-3272	Harbour Central Marina
Harbour View Grocery	Hope Town, Abaco	366-0033	
Hawks Nest Marina**	Hawks Nest Creek, Cat Island		info@hawks-nest.com
Hurricane Hole Marina	Nassau, New Providence		
Lowe's Food Store	Green Turtle Cay, Abaco	365-4243	
Lucayan Marina Village	Freeport, Grand Bahama		lucayanmarinavillage.com
Man-O-War LP Gas	Man-O-War Cay, Abaco	365-6057	
Nassau Harbour Club	Nassau, New Providence	393-0771	Nassau Harbour Club
Nassau Yacht Haven	Nassau, New Providence		nassauyachthaven.com
New Plymouth Hardware	Green Turtle Cay, Abaco	635-4305	
Old Bahama Bay Marin	West End, Grand Bahama		www.oldbahamabay.com
Pinder's Tune Up	Spanish Wells		
Rock Sound Hardware	Rock Sound, Eleuthera		
Rick Sawyer	Cherokee Sound, Abaco		
Shell Gas	Freeport, Grand Bahama	352-6771	
Shell	Morgan's Bluff, Andros		Willie's Water Lounge
Shell Station	New Bight, Cat Island		
Sid's Food Store	Green Turtle Cay, Abaco	365-4055	
Texaco Station	Nicoll's Town, Andros		
Williard Bethel	Elbow Cay, Abaco	366-0033	
Propellors			
Abaco Marine Prop	Marsh Harbour, Abaco	367-4276	
Knowles Marine	Grand Bahama	351-2769	
Sail Repair			
Bill's Canvas	Treasure Cay, Abaco		
Edwin's Boat Yd.	Man-O-War Cay, Abaco	365-6171	Edwin's Boat Yard
Jay Manni	Dickie's Cay, Abaco	365-6171	
Phillip's Sails	Nassau, New Providence	393-4498	
Sammie's Canvas	Fresh Creek, Andros	464-3155	
Spanish Wells Sails	Spanish Wells	333-4575	Spanish Wells Canvas

* Propane tanks must be shipped to Nassau by mailboat, turn around time approximately 1 week
** Propane tanks must be shipped to Nassau by mailboat, turn around time approximately 2 week.

Appendix D: Waypoints

Caution: Waypoints are not to be used for navigational purposes. The following waypoints are intended to place you in the general area of the described position. All routes, cuts, and anchorages must be negotiated by eyeball navigation. The author and publisher take no responsibility for the misuse of the following waypoints. . Waypoints are listed from north to south.

Latitude is "**North**" and longitude is "**West**."

Datum used is WGS84.

WAYPOINT DESCRIPTION	LAT.	LON.
South Florida		
Hillsboro Inlet	26° 15.19'	80° 04.55'
Ft. Lauderdale/Port Everglades	26° 05.57'	80° 05.40'
Miami-Government Cut	25° 45.70'	80° 05.80'
Cape Florida	25° 38.74'	80° 07.70'
Angelfish Creek	25° 19.35'	80° 12.60'
The Abacos		
Walkers Cay – ½ nm N of entrance W of Seal Cay (Seal Cay Cut)	27° 16.20'	78° 21.55'
Walker's Cay – beginning of staked route over sandbar	27° 14.00'	78° 24.20'
Grand Cays – ¼ nm S of entrance channel to harbour	27° 12.60'	78° 18.80'
Strangers Cay Channel – N waypoint	27° 12.33'	78° 09.80'
Double Breasted Cays – ½ nm S of	27° 10.85'	78° 16.40'
Strangers Cay Channel – S waypoint	27° 10.50'	78° 10.50'
White Sand Ridge – ½ nm west of	27° 08.00'	79° 11.00'
Strangers Cay – ½ nm SSW of anchorage	27° 07.10'	78° 06.70'
Moraine Cay Channel – N waypoint	27° 05.00'	77° 14.00'
Carters Cay Bank, route across bank from east – ¼ nm E of start	27° 04.25'	77° 58.75'
Barracouta Rocks Channel West- 2 nm NW of Little Sale Cay	27° 04.00'	78° 12.50'
Carters Cays – 1 nm SSW of Gully Cay	27° 03.80'	78° 01.15'
Barracouta Rocks Channel East- 1 nm NE of Sale Cay Rocks	27° 03.00'	78° 05.00'
The Fish Cays – ½ nm SW of	27° 01.90'	77° 50.20'
Moraine Cay – ½ nm S of anchorage	27° 01.80'	77° 46.25'
Allan's-Pensacola Cay – ½ nm WSW of entrance to anchorage	26° 59.20'	77° 42.20'
Great Sale Cay – ¼ nm W of Northwest Harbour	26° 58.50'	78° 14.70'
North Spanish Cay Channel, outer waypoint	26° 58.40'	77° 31.90'
Great Sale Cay – 1 nm SE of Tom Johnson Harbour	26° 58.15'	78° 10.45'
North Spanish Cay Channel, inner waypoint	26° 57.90'	77° 32.70'
Fox Town – ½ nm NW of Hawksbill Cays	26° 57.00'	77° 48.80'
South Spanish Cay Channel, outer waypoint	26° 56.55'	77° 28.85'
Crab Cay – ¼ nm N of Angelfish Point	26° 56.10'	77° 36.40'
Spanish Cay – ½ nm WSW of marina	26° 56.10'	77° 32.10'
South Spanish Cay Channel, inner waypoint	26° 56.00'	77° 29.50'
Mangrove Cay – ½ nm NW of	26° 55.50'	78° 37.50'
Memory Rock – 2¼ nm S of	26° 54.75'	79° 05.75'
Powell Cay – ½ nm W of anchorage	26° 54.25'	77° 29.50'
Coopers Town – ½ nm NE of	26° 52.70'	77° 30.10'
Manjack Cay – ¾ nm SW of anchorages	26° 48.80'	77° 22.80'
Green Turtle Cay – ½ nm W of anchorage off New Plymouth	26° 45.70'	77° 20.35'
Treasure Cay – ¼ nm SE of entrance channel	26° 39.53'	77° 17.00'
Whale Cay Passage, outer N waypoint	26° 43.70'	77° 14.10'
Whale Cay Passage, outer S waypoint	26° 42.90'	77° 12.60'
Whale Cay Passage, inner N waypoint	26° 42.80'	77° 15.60'
Great Guana Cay Harbour- ¼ nm S of	26° 39.50'	77° 06.90'
North Man-O-War Channel – outer waypoint	26° 38.00'	77° 01.30'
North Man-O-War Channel – inner waypoint	26° 37.00'	77° 01.90'
Leisure Lee – ¼ nm NE of entrance	26° 37.90'	77° 15.20'
South Man-O-War Channel – outer waypoint	26° 36.10'	76° 58.65'
South Man-O-War Channel – inner waypoint	26° 35.60'	76° 59.10'
Man-O-War Cay – 200 yards S of entrance channel to harbour	26° 35.30'	77° 00.22'
Marsh Harbour – ¼ nm NW of Outer Point Cay	26° 33.60'	77° 04.40'
Hope Town Harbour – ¼ nm W of entrance channel	26° 32.65'	76° 58.10'

WAYPOINT DESCRIPTION	LAT.	LON.
Boat Harbour Marina – ¼ nm SE of entrance	26° 32.50'	77° 02.50'
Marsh Harbour Boatyard- ¼ nm E of entrance	26° 31.85'	77° 02.80'
White Sound, Elbow Cay – ¼ nm WNW of entrance channel	26° 31.10'	76° 59.00'
Tilloo Cut – ¼ nm W of	26° 29.80'	76° 58.55'
Cormorant Cay – ¼ nm SE of anchorage	26° 27.45'	77° 02.75'
Tilloo Pond – ¼ nm W of entrance to pond	26° 27.00'	77° 00.50'
Snake Cay – ¼ nm SE of	26° 26.90'	77° 02.70'
Tilloo Bank, Middle Channel – N waypoint	26° 25.90'	77° 01.10'
Tilloo Bank, Middle Channel – S waypoint	26° 25.38'	77° 00.20'
North Bar Channel – ½ nm WNW of	26° 23.60'	76° 59.00'
North Bar Channel – ½ nm ESE of	26° 23.45'	76° 58.10'
Little Harbour – ½ nm N of entrance channel	26° 20.10'	76° 59.95'
Little Harbour Bar – ½ nm SE of opening between reefs	26° 19.30'	76° 59.32'
Cherokee Sound – ¾ nm S of entrance channel to anchorage	26° 15.50'	77° 04.20'
Schooner Bay Marina – ¾ nm E of marked entrance	26° 10.50'	77° 09.75'
Hole in the Wall – 1½ nm SE of	25° 50.50'	77° 09.50'

The Bight of Abaco

WAYPOINT DESCRIPTION	LAT.	LON.
Northwest Passage – N waypoint	26° 53.90'	77° 58.15'
Northwest Passage – S waypoint	26° 52.83'	77° 58.15'
Randall's Cay – ¼ nm NW of	26° 51.60'	77° 32.90'
Cave Cay – ½ nm SE of, entrance to route to Spence Rock	26° 50.70'	77° 52.40'
Randall's Creek – ¼ nm W of mouth	26° 50.00'	77° 31.50'
Spence Rock – ½ nm SSW of, entrance to route to Crab Cay	26° 48.70'	77° 51.40'
Basin Harbour Cay – ¼ nm SW of entrance to harbor	26° 47.75'	77° 30.10'
Norman's Castle – ¾ nm W of	26° 43.25'	77° 27.75'
Big Joe Downer Cay – ¾ nm W of anchorage at Amos Bight	26° 36.90'	77° 26.90'
Woolendean Cay – ¾ nm W of	26° 34.00'	77° 25.00'
Mores Island – ½ nm NW of	26° 20.55'	77° 35.20'
Mores Island – ½ nm W of Hard Bargain anchorage	26° 19.10'	77° 35.50'
Channel Cay – 2 nm SW of channel to Mores Island	26° 14.00'	77° 40.00'
Castaway Cay (Gorda Cay) – ½ nm WSW of cruise ship harbour	26° 04.50'	77° 32.90'
Sarah Wood Bars – entrance to Bight of Abaco from Sandy Point	26° 04.10'	77° 27.60'
Sandy Point – ¼ nm W of anchorage off settlement	26° 01.10'	77° 24.70'
Rocky Point – 1½ nm W of Rocky Point and clear of shoals	25° 59.60'	77° 25.80'

Grand Bahama

WAYPOINT DESCRIPTION	LAT.	LON.
Indian Cay Channel – eastern entrance to channel	26° 46.37'	78° 57.15'
Indian Cay Channel, Barracuda Shoal – ¼ nm S of	26° 45.65'	78° 58.30'
Indian Cay Channel – missing piling #3, NW of	26° 44.75'	78° 59.20'
Indian Cay Channel – ¼ nm SW of western entrance to channel	26° 42.80'	79° 00.60'
West End – ½ nm W of entrance channel to marina	26° 42.23'	79° 00.15'
Dover Sound – 1½ nm NW of entrance channel to GLWW	26° 38.40'	78° 39.70'
Peterson Cay – ½ nm SE of	26° 32.60'	78° 30.65'
Grand Lucayan Waterway - ¾ nm SSE of jetties at southern entrance	26° 31.30'	78° 33.33'
Freeport Harbour – 1 nm SSW of entrance jetties	26° 30.10'	78° 47.05'
Bell Channel - 1 nm SE of entrance channel	26° 29.95'	78° 37.70'
Xanadu Channel – ½ nm SW of entrance channel	26° 29.00'	78° 42.40'
Madioca Point - ½ nm SE of entrance channel to *Running Mon Marina*	26° 29.00'	78° 41.31'
Silver Cove - ¾ nm SE of entrance channel	26° 29.00'	78° 39.35'

The Biminis

WAYPOINT DESCRIPTION	LAT.	LON.
North Rock-½ nm W	25° 48.25'	79° 16.00'
North Rock-2 nm E	25° 48.25'	79° 13.50'

WAYPOINT DESCRIPTION	LAT.	LON.
Bimini Roads Dive Site	25° 45.99'	79° 16.69'
North Bimini harbor new entrance-¼ nm W of	25° 42.60'	79° 18.50'
North Bimini harbor old entrance-½ nm W of and on range	25° 42.07'	79° 18.56'
South Bimini-¼ nm W of entrance to Nixon's Harbour	25° 41.23'	79° 18.50'
Gun Cay Channel-¼ nm NW	25° 34.48'	79° 18.15'
South Cat Cay-½ nm W of entrance to Dollar Harbour	25° 31.00'	79° 16.00'
Across The Great Bahama Bank		
Mackie Shoal Light-200 yards N	25° 42.00'	78° 39.00'
Russell Beacon-½ nm N of buoy	25° 29.00'	78° 25.54'
NW Channel Light-250 yards N	25° 28.40'	78° 09.80'
Andros		
North Joulters-beginning of route to E of Joulter's Cays	25° 24.25'	78° 09.45'
Joulters East-at E edge of bank clear of maze of sandbores	25° 22.30'	78° 07.35'
Joulters Cay anchorage-¼ nm E of bar	25° 18.52'	78° 07.00'
Morgan's Bluff-¼ nm W of entrance channel	25° 11.28'	78° 00.78'
Bethel Channel-½ nm ENE of break in reef	25° 08.36'	77° 59.06'
AUTEC Buoy (Charlie Buoy)	24° 53.80	77°48.90'
Staniard Rock Passage-1 nm ENE of break in reef	24° 52.40'	77° 51.00'
Fresh Creek-¼ nm ENE of entrance channel	24° 44.25'	77° 45.65'
AUTEC Buoy (George Murphy Buoy)	24° 43.25'	77° 44.97'
AUTEC Site 1 & 2 Buoy	24° 36.32'	77° 38.35'
Salvador Point, AUTEC Base #2 channel-½ nm E of sea buoy	24° 29.95'	77° 41.40'
Middle Bight, AUTEC Base #3 channel-¼ nm E of sea buoy	24° 20.10'	77° 39.45'
AUTEC Site 3 & 4 Buoy	24° 19.34'	77° 36.07'
South Bight-1 nm NE of entrance channel	24° 14.25'	77° 35.50'
Green Cay- ¼ nm W of western tip	24° 02.60'	77° 11.70'
Kemps Bay- ½ nm ENE of entrance channel	24° 00.70'	77° 29.40'
The Berry Islands		
Great Harbour Marina-entrance channel-1 nm NNW	25° 49.64'	77° 57.41'
Great Stirrup/Slaughter Harbour entrance-½ nm N of	25° 49.60'	77° 55.66'
Great Stirrup/Panton Cove entrance-½ nm NE	25° 49.40'	77° 53.30'
Great Harbour Route-R daymark below range-200 yards W of	25° 44.81'	77° 52.10'
Great Harbour Cay-entrance to eastern anchorage	25° 46.03'	77° 49.41'
Devil's Hoffman Anchorage-¼ nm E of	25° 36.55'	77° 43.50'
Little Harbour/Frozen Alder Anchorage entrance-½ nm W of	25° 33.69'	77° 42.50'
Little Whale Cay-¼ nm E of entrance to anchorage	25° 26.77'	77° 45.13'
Frazier-Hogg/Bird Cay	25° 23.45'	77° 51.05'
Chub Cay-1 nm S of and on the 35° range	25° 23.90'	77° 55.08'
New Providence		
Nassau Harbour-W entrance	25° 05.33'	77° 21.35'
Lyford Cay-¼ nm N of light that marks entrance channel	25° 04.00'	77° 30.94'
W tip of New Providence-1¼ nm NW of Golding Cay	25° 02.15'	77° 35.35'
Nassau Blue Hole	25° 01.70'	77° 08.50'
Port of New Providence entrance channel	25° 00.14'	77° 15.68'
New Providence to Eleuthera		
Little Pimlico Island-½ nm SW of	25° 18.10'	76° 53.60'
Fleeming Channel-¼ nm N of channel entrance	25° 16.00'	76° 55.30'
Fleeming Channel-¼ nm S of channel entrance	25° 15.50'	76° 54.50'
Douglas Channel-1 nm NW of	25° 10.00'	77° 05.50'
Douglas Channel-1 nm SE of	25° 07.80'	77° 03.00'
Chub Rock-¼ nm N of	25° 06.85'	77° 14.60'

WAYPOINT DESCRIPTION	LAT.	LON.
Porgee Rocks-¼ nm S of	25° 03.50'	77° 14.55'
Eleuthera		
Pilot pickup point N of Ridley Head Channel	25° 34.50'	76° 44.30'
Bridge Point-N waypoint	25° 34.32'	76° 43.03'
Ridley Head Channel-N waypoint	25° 34.00'	76° 44.30'
Bridge Point-S waypoint, just off Bridge Point	25° 33.90'	76° 43.18'
Ridley Head Channel-S waypoint, just off Ridley Head	25° 33.54'	76° 44.33'
Hawk's Point-just N of point on Devil's Backbone route	25° 33.53'	76° 40.85'
Current Point-just N of point on Devil's Backbone route	25° 33.05'	76° 39.88'
Spanish Wells Harbour-just E of pilings at eastern entrance	25° 32.60'	76° 44.35'
Turning point on Devil's Backbone route to Harbour Island	25° 32.26'	76° 39.17'
Spanish Wells Harbour-just S of pilings at western entrance	25° 32.10'	76° 45.40'
Meek's Patch-¼ nm NW of northern tip of	25° 31.60'	76° 47.30'
Royal Island-¼ nm S of entrance	25° 30.60'	76° 50.73'
Egg Island Cut-1½ nm WNW of Cut	25° 29.60'	76° 54.75'
Harbour Island-½ nm ENE of Whale Point	25° 28.70'	76° 37.30'
Harbour Island-S entrance, outer waypoint of N route	25° 28.50'	76° 37.81'
Harbour Island-S entrance, outer waypoint of S route	25° 28.43'	76° 37.78'
Harbour Island-S entrance, inner waypoint of N route	25° 28.42'	76° 38.90'
Harbour Island-S entrance, inner waypoint of S route	25° 28.11'	76° 37.94'
Wreck of the *Arimora*-¼ nm SW	25° 27.87'	76° 53.75'
Rotten Bay, Lower Bogue- ½ nm S of	25° 26.20'	76° 42.00'
The Glass Window- ¼ nm W of anchorage at Goulding Cay Point	25° 25.70'	76° 36.30'
Current Rock-½ nm NW of	25° 24.50'	76° 51.42'
Current Cut-½ nm NW of western entrance	25° 24.40'	76° 48.00'
Current Cut-1 nm SSE of eastern entrance	25° 22.94'	76° 46.61'
Rainbow Bay- ¼ nm SW of anchorage	25° 19.80'	76° 26.50'
James Cistern- ¼ nm SE of town dock	25° 19.20'	76° 22.30'
Current Island-½ nm SW of southwestern tip	25° 18.45'	76° 51.29'
Little Pimlico Island-½ nm SW of	25° 18.10'	76° 53.60'
Gregory Town-¼ nm SW of	25° 23.15'	76° 33.75'
Hatchet Bay-¼ nm S of entrance	25° 20.50'	76° 29.70'
Pelican Cay-½ nm SW of	25° 16.30'	76° 20.50'
Holmes Bay-½ nm SW of	25° 14.40'	76° 18.90'
Governor's Harbour-1 nm W of	25° 11.75'	76° 16.25'
Palmetto Point-1 nm SW of	25° 07.70'	76° 11.40'
Ten Bay- 1 nm W of anchorage	25° 07.30'	76° 10.40'
Tarpum Bay- ¾ nm NW of town dock	24° 59.00'	76° 12.00'
Davis Channel-E end	24° 52.25'	76° 16.30'
Davis Channel-W end	24° 51.50'	76° 20.63'
Rock Sound-½ nm W of entrance	24° 50.30'	76° 11.70'
Powell Point-¼ nm W of entrance to marina	24° 50.23'	76° 21.09'
Davis Harbour-¾ nm W of entrance buoy	24° 43.80'	76° 15.75'
East End Point-1 nm SW of	24° 35.90'	76° 09.25'
The Exumas		
Beacon Cay-¼ nm NW of	24° 53.18'	76° 49.50'
Ship Channel-2 nm SE of Beacon Cay in Exuma Sound	24° 51.73'	76° 47.81'
Highborne Cay Cut-¼ nm ESE	24° 42.20'	76° 48.60'
Norman's Cay Cut-¼ nm E	24° 35.76'	76° 47.48'
Warderick Wells Cut-½ nm N	24° 24.86'	76° 38.24'
Conch Cut-½ nm NE	24° 17.55'	76° 31.43'

WAYPOINT DESCRIPTION	LAT.	LON.
Sampson Cay Cut-¼ nm NE	24° 12.78'	76° 27.55'
Big Rock Cut-½ nm NE	24° 11.66'	76° 26.38'
Dotham Cut-¼ nm E	24° 07.14'	76° 23.85'
Farmer's Cay Cut-½ nm E	23° 57.95'	76° 18.32'
Galliot Cut-¼ nm E	23° 55.62'	76° 16.50'
Cave Cay Cut-¼ nm E	23° 54.00'	76° 15.20'
Rudder Cut-¼ nm NNE	23° 52.52'	76° 13.48'
Adderly Cut-¼ nm ENE	23° 47.45'	76° 06.33'
Children's Bay Cut-¼ nm N of	23° 44.60'	76° 03.03'
Rat Cay Cut-¼ nm N	23° 44.31'	76° 02.82'
Square Rock Cay Cut-¼ nm ENE	23° 43.56'	76° 00.90'
Glass Cay Cut-¼ nm N	23° 42.50'	75° 59.44'
Soldier Cay Cut-¼ nm NE	23° 41.10'	75° 57.40'
Conch Cay Cut-½ nm NNW	23° 34.30'	75° 48.50'
Eastern Channel, Elizabeth Harbour-¼ nm NE	23° 29.81'	75° 39.95'
Jewfish Cut-1 nm N	23° 27.85'	75° 57.56'
Jewfish Cut-1 nm S	23° 25.37'	75° 56.25'
Hawksbill Rock-200 yards W	23° 25.31'	76° 06.31'
Hog Cay Cut-¼ nm N	23° 24.75'	75° 30.82'
Sandy Cay- ½ nm N of NE tip of sandbank	23° 24.93'	75° 21.62'
Hog Cay Cut-¼ nm S	23° 23.50'	75° 30.92'
Half Moon Cay (Little San Salvador)		
West Bay-1 nm W of anchorage	24° 34.48'	75° 58.60'
Little San Salvador-1 nm S of light	24° 32.70'	75° 56.30'
Cat Island		
Arthur's Town-½ nm SW of	24° 36.80'	75° 41.20'
Bennett's Harbour-½ nm W of entrance	24° 33.75'	75° 39.00'
Alligator Point-½ nm SW of southwestern tip	24° 31.00'	75° 41.50'
Smith's Bay--¾ nm W of	24° 19.75'	75° 29.55'
Fernandez Bay-¾ nm W of	24° 19.10'	75° 29.55'
Bonefish Point-¾ nm SW of western tip of shoal	24° 16.50'	75° 28.90'
New Bight-¾ nm SW of Batelco Tower	24° 16.75'	75° 25.75'
Old Bight-¾ nm NW of anchorage	24° 13.40'	75° 25.20'
Hawks Nest Point-1 nm W of point	24° 08.55'	75° 32.45'

Appendix E: Tidal Differences in The Bahamas

All tides mentioned in this guide are based on Nassau tides. Times of tides in other locations throughout The Bahamas vary from a few minutes to a few hours before or after Nassau tides. Times and heights are affected by local conditions, the season, and the phase of the moon. The tidal differences in this table are to be used as a general guideline only. Actual times may vary from times shown in this table. Time is "B" for before Nassau, and "L" for later than Nassau

LOCATION	TIME HW	TIME LW
Abraham's Bay, Mayaguana	10 min. L	13 min. L
Allan's-Pensacola, Abacos	35 min L	45 min L
The Bight, Cat Island	35 min. B	35 min. B
Cat Cay, Biminis	23 min L	23 min L
Clarence Town, Long Island	49 min. L	54 min. L
Datum Bay, Acklins Island	15 min B	15 min B
Elbow Cay, Cay Sal Bank	1h 26 min. L	1h 31 min. L

LOCATION	TIME HW	TIME LW
Eleuthera, eastern shore	19 min. L	26 min. L
Eleuthera, western shore	2h 17 min. L	2h 36 min. L
Freeport, Grand Bahama	same	same
Fresh Creek, Andros	13 min. L	5 min. L
George Town, Exuma	20 min B	20 min B
Great Stirrup Cay, Berry Islands	25 min L	25 min L
Green Turtle Cay, Abacos	5 min L	5 min L
Guinchos Cay	14 min. L	19 min. L
Little Inagua	10 min L	10 min L
Mastic Point, Andros	5 min L	5 min L
Matthew Town, Great Inagua	15 min. L	15 min. L
Memory Rock, Abacos	24 min. L	29 min. L
North Bimini	13 min. L	25 min. L
North Cat Cay	30 min. L	35 min. L
Nurse Channel, Jumentos	15 min. L	10 min. L
Pelican Harbour, Abacos	26 min. L	31 min. L
Royal Island, Eleuthera	5 min L	5 min L
Salt Pond, Long Island	1.5 hour L	1.5 hour L
San Salvador	35 min. B	35 min. B
Ship Channel, Exuma	15 min B	15 min B
South Riding Rock, Biminis	40 min L	40 min L
Start Point, Mayaguana	25 min L	25 min L
Walker's Cay, Abaco	1h 25 min L	1h 25 min L

Appendix F: Depth Conversion Scale

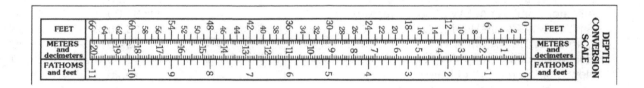

Appendix G: Metric Conversion Table

Visitors to The Bahamas will find the metric system in use and many grocery items and fuel measured in liters and kilograms. As a rule of thumb, a meter is just a little longer than a yard and a liter is very close to a quart. If in doubt use the following table.

1 centimeter (cm) = 0.4 inch	1 inch = 2.54 centimeters
1 meter (m) = 3.28 feet	1 foot = 30.48 centimeters
1 meter = 0.55 fathoms	1 fathom = 1.83 meters
1 kilometer (km) = 0.62 miles	1 yard = 0.93 meters
1 kilometer = 0.54 nautical miles	1 nautical mile = 1.852 kilometers
1 liter (l) = 0.26 gallons	1 gallon = 3.75 liters
1 gram (g) = 0.035 ounces	1 ounce = 28.4 grams
1 metric ton = 1.1 tons	1 pound = 454 grams

Index

About the Author

Photo Courtesy of Danielle Courteau

Stephen J. Pavlidis has been cruising and living aboard his 40' cutter-rigged sloop, *IV Play,* since the winter of 1989.

Starting in the Exuma Cays, 20 years ago, Steve began his writing career with guides to the many fascinating destinations he visited. Many of his books stand alone to this day as the quintessential guides to the areas he covers.

His books are different than most other cruising guides in some very significant ways. All of the charts in Steve's books were created using data personally collected while visiting each area using a computerized system that interfaces GPS and depth soundings.

You can find out more about this exceptional author by visiting his Web site, www.Seaworthy.com where there is current news and information about Steve's latest projects, as well as contact information.

Other books by Stephen J. Pavlidis:
Life at Sea Level, ISBN 978-1-892399-33-5
The Exuma Guide, 3rd Edition, ISBN 978-1-892399-31-1
A Cruising Guide to the Leeward Islands, 2nd Edition, ISBN 978-1-892399-36-6
The Northwest Caribbean Guide, ISBN 978-1-892399-24-3
The Puerto Rico Guide, 2nd Edition, ISBN 978-1-892399-32-8
The Southern Bahamas Guide, ISBN 978-1-892399-29-8
A Cruising Guide to the Virgin Islands, 2nd Edition, ISBN 978-1-892399-35-9
A Cruising Guide to the Windward Islands, ISBN 978-1-892399-18-2